The Kaiser Wilhelm Society under National Socialism

During the first part of the twentieth century, German science led the world. The most important scientific institution in Germany was the Kaiser Wilhelm Society, including institutes devoted to different fields of scientific research. Because these institutions were not connected to universities, researchers in them were not burdened by teaching obligations and enjoyed excellent financial and material support.

When the National Socialists came to power in Germany, all of German society, including science, was affected. The picture that previously dominated our understanding of science under National Socialism from the end of the Second World War to the recent past – a picture of leading Nazis ignorant and unappreciative of modern science and of scientists struggling to resist the Nazis – needs to be revised. This book surveys the history of Kaiser Wilhelm Institutes under Hitler, illustrating definitively the cooperation, if not collaboration, between scientists and National Socialists to further the goals of autarky, racial hygiene, war, and genocide.

The Kaiser Wilhelm Society under National Socialism

SUSANNE HEIM

Institute for Contemporary History, Munich/Berlin

CAROLA SACHSE

University of Vienna

MARK WALKER

Union College

CAMBRIDGE UNIVERSITY PRESS

CAMBRIDGE UNIVERSITY PRESS
Cambridge, New York, Melbourne, Madrid, Cape Town, Singapore,
São Paulo, Delhi, Dubai, Tokyo, Mexico City

Cambridge University Press
32 Avenue of the Americas, New York, NY 10013-2473, USA

www.cambridge.org
Information on this title: www.cambridge.org/9780521181549

First published 2009
First paperback edition 2010

A catalog record for this publication is available from the British Library

Library of Congress Cataloging in Publication data
Heim, Susanne, 1955–
The Kaiser Wilhelm society under national socialism/Susanne Heim.
p. cm.
Includes bibliographical references and index.
ISBN 978-0-521-87906-4 (hardback)
1. Kaiser Wilhelm-Gesellschaft zur fvrderung der Wissenschaften.   2. Science and
state – Germany – History.   3. National socialism and science – Germany.   1. Title.
Q49.K14174H45 2009
509.43´0904–dc22   2008054455

ISBN 978-0-521-87906-4 Hardback
ISBN 978-0-521-18154-9 Paperback

Thanks and Dedication

We would like to thank the Max Planck Society, which has generously supported both the original research program and the publication of this book; Reinhard Rürup and Wolfgang Schieder, who oversaw the research program; Birgit Kolboske, who helped organize this book and, together with Susan Richter and Charlotte Hughes-Kreutzmüller, translated the chapters; and of course the contributors themselves.

This book is dedicated to all the victims of National Socialism who suffered and sometimes died in the name of science, or through the actions of scientists, or both.

Contents

Tables

Illustrations

Editors

Susanne Heim is project coordinator of the documentation project "The Persecution and Extermination of the European Jews by Nazi Germany 1933–1945" at the Institute for Contemporary History in Munich and Berlin, and she has previously been the Charles Revson Fellow at the U.S. Holocaust Memorial Museum, Washington, D.C., and research director of the Max Planck Society's Research Program on the History of the Kaiser Wilhelm Society in the National Socialist Era. She is the author of *Plant Breeding and Agrarian Research in Kaiser-Wilhelm-Institutes 1933–1945: Calories, Caoutchouc, Careers* (2008) and (with Götz Aly) *Architects of Annihilation: Auschwitz and the Logic of Destruction* (2003) and editor of *Autarkie und Ostexpansion: Pflanzenzucht und Agrarforschung in Nationalsozialismus* (2002).

Carola Sachse is full professor of contemporary history at the University of Vienna and from 2000 to 2003 served as research director of the Max Planck Society's Research Program on the History of the Kaiser Wilhelm Society in the National Socialist Era. She is the editor (with Mark Walker) of *Politics and Science in Wartime: Comparative Perspectives on the Kaiser Wilhelm Institutes* (2005) and *Die Verbindung nach Auschwitz: Biowissenschaften und Menschenversuche an Kaiser-Wilhelm-Instituten* (2003) as well as author of *Der Hausarbeitstag: Gerechtigkeit und Gleichberechtigung in Ost und West 1939–1994* (2002), *Siemens, der Nationalsozialismus und die moderne Familie: Eine Untersuchung zur sozialen Rationalisierung in Deutschland im 20. Jahrhundert* (1990), and *Industrial Housewives: Women's Social Work in the Factories in Nazi Germany* (1987).

Mark Walker is John Bigelow Professor of History, Department of History, Union College, Schenectady, in New York and has received grants from the German Academic Exchange Service, the Social Science

Research Council, and the Humboldt Foundation. He is the author of *German National Socialism, and the Quest for Nuclear Power, 1939–1949* (1989) and *Nazi Science: Myth, Truth, and the German Atom Bomb* (1995); he has edited (with Monika Renneberg) *Science, Technology, and National Socialism* (1993), *Science and Ideology: A Comparative History* (2003), and (with Dieter Hoffmann) *Physiker zwischen Autonomie und Anpassung – Die DPG im Dritten Reich* (2007).

Contributors

Moritz Epple Historical Seminar, University of Frankfurt, Germany

Bernd Gausemeier Max Planck Institute for History of Science, Berlin, Germany

Rüdiger Hachtmann Center for Contemporary Historical Research (ZZF) in Potsdam and Institute for Philosophy and History of Science and Technology, Technical University of Berlin, Germany

Susanne Heim Documentation Project "Persecution of Jews 1933–1945," Institute for Contemporary History, Munich and Berlin, Germany

Günther Luxbacher Institute for Philosophy and History of Science and Technology, Technical University of Berlin, Germany

Helmut Maier Institute for History of Technology and the Environment, Ruhr-University of Bochum, Germany

Carola Sachse Institute for Contemporary History, University of Vienna, Austria

Helga Satzinger Wellcome Trust Centre for the History of Medicine, University College London, United Kingdom

Wolfgang Schieder (Emeritus) Historical Seminar, University of Cologne, Germany

Florian Schmaltz Historical Seminar, University of Frankfurt, Germany

Hans-Walter Schmuhl Faculty for History, Philosophy, and Theology, University of Bielefeld, Germany

Michael Schüring Department of History, University of California at Berkeley, United States

Bernhard Strebel Foundation for Memorials in Lower Saxony, Germany

Achim Trunk Historisches Seminar, University of Cologne, Germany

Jens-Christian Wagner Concentration Camp Memorial Mittelbau-Dora, Nordhausen, Germany

Mark Walker Department of History, Union College, Schenectady, New York, United States

Abbreviations

ADM	Archives of the German Museum, Munich (*Archiv des Deutschen Museums*)
AEL	Labor Education Camps (*Arbeitserziehungslager*)
APS	American Philosophical Society, Philadelphia
AVA	Aerodynamics Testing Institute (*Aerodynamische Versuchsanstalt*)
BArch	Federal German Archives (*Bundesarchiv*)
BIOS	British Intelligence Objectives Subcommittee
BLA	Main Brandenburg State Archives (*Brandenburgisches Landeshauptarchiv*)
CIOS	Combined Intelligence Objectives Subcommittee
DAF	German Labor Front (*Deutsche Arbeitsfront*)
DA-FB	Dean's Archive of the Department of Medicine, Frankfurt University (Frankfurt am Main), Human Genetics, Institute for Heredity (*Dekanatsarchiv des Fachbereichs Medizin der Universität Frankfurt am Main, Humangenetik, Institut für Vererbungswissenschaften*)
DFG	German Research Foundation (*Deutsche Forschungsgemeinschaft*)
DGM	German Society for Metal Science (*Deutsche Gesellschaft für Metallkunde*)
DMV	German Association of Mathematicians (*Deutsche Mathematiker-Vereinigung*)
DVA	SS German Experimental Institute for Nutrition and Alimentation (*Deutsche Versuchsanstalt für Ernährung und Verpflegung*)
DVL	German Experimental Station for Aviation (*Deutsche Versuchsanstalt für Luftfahrt*)
HAKrupp	Krupp Historical Archive, Essen (*Historisches Archiv Krupp*)
HWA	German Army Ordnance (*Heereswaffenamt*)

IDO	Institute for German Work in the East (*Institut für deutsche Ostarbeit*)
IWZ	Institute for Applied Army Research (*Institut für wehrwissenschaftliche Zweckforschung*)
KRA	Department for Raw Materials of War in the Armed Forces Ministry (*Kriegsrohstoff-Abteilung im Reichswehrministerium*)
KWI	Kaiser Wilhelm Institute
KWIA	KWI for Anthropology, Human Heredity and Eugenics (*KWI für Anthropologie, menschliche Erblehre und Eugenik*)
KWIB	KWI for Biology (*KWI für Biologie*)
KWIBC	KWI for Biochemistry (*KWI für Biochemie*)
KWIBF	KWI for Bast Fiber Research (*KWI für Bastfaserforschung*)
KWIBR	KWI for Breeding Research (*KWI für Züchtungsforschung*)
KWIC	KWI for Chemistry (*KWI für Chemie*)
KWIFD	KWI for Fluid Dynamics (*KWI für Strömungsforschung*)
KWIHF	KWI for Brain Research (*KWI für Hirnforschung*)
KWIMR	KWI for Medical Research (*KWI für medizinische Forschung*)
KWIMT	KWI for Metal Research (*KWI für Metallforschung*)
KWIP	KWI for Physics (*KWI für Physik*)
KWIPC	KWI for Physical Chemistry (*KWI für physikalische Chemie und Elektrochemie*)
KWS	Kaiser Wilhelm Society (*Kaiser-Wilhelm-Gesellschaft*)
MPG-Archiv	Archives of the Max Planck Society, Berlin (*Archiv zur Geschichte der Max-Planck-Gesellschaft*)
MPS	Max Planck Society (*Max-Planck-Gesellschaft*)
NA	National Archives, Washington, D.C.
NDW	Emergency Foundation for German Science (*Notgemeinschaft der deutschen Wissenschaften*)
NS	National Socialist (*nationalsozialistisch*)
NSBDT	National Socialist League of German Engineers (*NS-Bund Deutscher Technik*)
NSDAP	National Socialist German Workers Party (*Nationalsozialistische Deutsche Arbeiterpartei*)
OKH	German Army's High Command (*Oberkommando des Heeres*)
OKL	Supreme Command of the Air Force (*Oberkommando der Luftwaffe*)
OKM	Supreme Command of the Navy (*Oberkommando der Marine*)
OKW	Supreme Command of the Armed Forces (*Oberkommando der Wehrmacht*)
PAW	Prussian Academy of Sciences (*Preußische Akademie der Wissenschaften*)

PRO	Public Records Office, London
RDI	Reich Association of German Manufacturers (*Reichsverband Deutscher Industrieller*)
REM	Reich Ministry for Education and Science (*Reichserziehungsministerium*)
RFR	Reich Research Council (*Reichsforschungsrat*)
RLM	Reich Aviation Ministry (*Reichsluftfahrtministerium*)
RMEL	Reich Ministry for Food and Agriculture (*Reichsministerium für Ernährung und Landwirtschaft*)
RNS	Reich Food Estate (*Reichsnährstand*)
RSHA	SS Reich Security Main Office (*Reichssicherheitshauptamt*)
RuSHA	SS Main Race and Settlement Department (*Rasse- und Siedlungshauptamt*)
RVB	Reich Association of Bast Fibers (*Reichsvereinigung Bastfaser*)
RWA	Reich Office for Economic Expansion (*Reichsamt für Wirtschaftsausbau*)
RWM	Reich Ministry of Economics (*Reichswirtschaftsministerium*)
SGP	Samuel Goudsmit Papers, Niels Bohr Library, Center for the History of Physics, American Institute of Physics, College Park, Maryland
SN	Nuremberg State Archives (*Staatsarchiv Nürnberg*)
SS	Schutzstaffel
USHMM	United States Holocaust Memorial Museum, Washington, D.C.
VDI	Association of German Engineers (*Verein Deutscher Ingenieur*)
VOMI	Ethnic German agency (*Volksdeutsche Mittelstelle*)
WTF	Faculty of Defense Technology (*Wehrtechnische Fakultät*) at the Technical University of Berlin
WVHA	SS Office of Economic Administration (*Wirtschafts-Verwaltungshauptamt*)
ZFO	Head Office for Research into the East (*Zentrale für Ostforschung*)
ZSL	Central Office of the Justice Administration for Investigation of NS Crimes in Ludwigsburg (*Zentrale Stelle der Landesjustizverwaltungen zur Aufklärung von NS-Verbrechen in Ludwigsburg*)

Archives

American Philosophical Society, Philadelphia [http://www.amphilsoc.org/library/manuscri.htm]

Archives of the Berlin-Brandenburg Academy of Sciences (*Archiv der Berlin-Brandenburgischen Akademie der Wissenschaften*) [http://o2f.fh-potsdam.de/fotoarchive/Archive/Archiv_der_BB_Akademie_der_Wissenschaften/Archiv_der_BB_Akademie_der_Wissenschaften.htm]

Archives of the German Museum, Munich (*Archiv des Deutschen Museums*) [http://www.deutsches-museum.de/archiv]

Archives of the Humboldt University of Berlin (*Archiv der Humboldt-Universität zu Berlin*)

Archives of the Institute for History of Medicine of Heidelberg University, Kuhn Papers (*Archiv des Instituts für Geschichte der Medizin der Universität Heidelberg, NL Kühn*) [http://www.medgesch.uni-hd.de]

Archives of the Leopoldina, Halle (*Archiv der Leopoldina*) [http://www.leopoldina-halle.de/cms/de/akademie/archiv.html]

Archives of the Max Planck Society, Berlin (*Archiv zur Geschichte der Max-Planck-Gesellschaft*) [http://www.archiv-berlin.mpg.de/wiki/deutsch.php]

Archives of the Occupation of France by Germany and Austria (*Archives de l'occupation française en Allemagne et en Autriche*) [http://www.diplomatie.gouv.fr/fr/ministere_817/archives-patrimoine_3512/archives-diplomatiques_5142/lieux-conservation_12634/colmar_12637/bureau-archives-occupation-francaise-allemagne-autriche_26467.html]

Archives of the University of Arizona [http://www.library.arizona.edu]

Archives of the University of Göttingen (*Universitätsarchiv Göttingen*) [http://wwwuser.gwdg.de/~uniarch]

Archives of the University of Heidelberg (*Universitätsarchiv Heidelberg*) [http://www.rzuser.uni-heidelberg.de/~n31/index.htm]

Archives of the University of Münster (*Universitätsarchiv Münster*) [http://www.uni-muenster.de/Archiv]

Berlin State Archives (*Landesarchiv Berlin*) [http://www.landesarchiv-berlin.de/lab-neu/start.html]

Bodleian Library Oxford [http://www.ouls.ox.ac.uk/bodley]

Center for Research on Anti-Semitism, Berlin (*Zentrum für Antisemitismusforschung*) [http://zfa.kgw.tu-berlin.de/archiv.htm]

Central Office of the Justice Administration for Investigation of NS Crimes in Ludwigsburg (*Zentrale Stelle der Landesjustizverwaltungen zur Aufklärung von NS-Verbrechen in Ludwigsburg*) [http://www.zentrale-stelle.de]

Dean's Archive of the Department of Medicine, Frankfurt University (Frankfurt am Main), Human Genetics, Institute for Heredity (*Dekanatsarchiv des Fachbereichs Medizin der Universität Frankfurt am Main, Humangenetik, Institut für Vererbungswissenschaften*) [http://www.ub.uni-frankfurt.de]

Degussa Company Archives, Frankfurt am Main (*Unternehmensarchiv der Degussa*) [http://www.archive.nrw.de/Wirtschaftsarchive/DegussaAG_StandortMarl/index.html]

Federal German Archives, in Koblenz, Berlin, and Dahlwitz-Hoppegarten (*Bundesarchiv*) [http://www.bundesarchiv.de]

Heisenberg Papers, Max Planck Institut für Physik und Astrophysik, Munich

Imperial War Museum, London [http://collections.iwm.org.uk/?PHPSESSID= 1e62144fc0b046d726c40cef3136e123]

Institute for Contemporary History, Munich (*Institut für Zeitgeschichte*) [http://www.ifz-muenchen.de/archiv.html]

Krupp Historical Archive, Essen (*Historisches Archiv Krupp*) [http://www.thyssenkrupp.de/de/konzern/geschichte_archive.html]

Leo Baeck Institute, New York [http://www.lbi.org/archives.html]

Library of Congress, Washington, D.C. [http://www.loc.gov/index.html]

Main Brandenburg State Archives (*Brandenburgisches Landeshauptarchiv*) [http://www.landeshauptarchiv-brandenburg.de]

National Archives, Washington, D.C. [http://www.archives.gov]

Nuremberg State Archives (*Staatsarchiv Nürnberg*) [http://www.gda.bayern.de/archive/nuernberg/index.php]

Political Archives of the Foreign Office (*Politisches Archiv des Auswärtigen Amtes*) [http://www.auswaertiges-amt.de/diplo/de/AAmt/PolitischesArchiv/Uebersicht.html]

Prussian State Archives (*Geheimes Staatsarchiv preußischer Kulturbesitz*) [http://www.gsta.spk-berlin.de]

Public Records Office, London [http://www.nationalarchives.gov.uk/default.htm]

Rockefeller Archive Center, Sleepy Hollow, N.Y. [http://archive.rockefeller.edu]

Samuel Goudsmit Papers, Niels Bohr Library, Center for the History of Physics, American Institute of Physics, College Park, Maryland [http://www.aip.org/history/nbl]

United States Holocaust Memorial Museum, Washington, D.C. [http://www.ushmm.org/research/collections]

Kaiser Wilhelm Institutes Mentioned in this Book

German Entomological Institute (*Deutsches Entomologisches Institut*)

German Research Institute for Psychiatry (*Deutsche Forschungsanstalt für Psychiatrie*)

KWI for Anthropology, Human Heredity and Eugenics (*KWI für Anthropologie, menschliche Erblehre und Eugenik*)

KWI for Bast Fiber Research (*KWI für Bastfaserforschung*)

KWI for Biochemistry (*KWI für Biochemie*)

KWI for Biology (*KWI für Biologie*)

KWI for Biophysics (*KWI für Biophysik*)

KWI for Brain Research (*KWI für Hirnforschung*)

KWI for Breeding Research (*KWI für Züchtungsforschung*)

KWI for Cell Physiology (*KWI für Zellphysiologie*)

KWI for Cellulose Fiber Research (*KWI für* Zellwollforschung)

KWI for Chemistry (*KWI für Chemie*)

KWI for Coal Research (*KWI für Kohlenforschung*)

KWI for Comparative Public Law and International Law (*KWI für ausländisches öffentliches Recht und Völkerrecht*)

KWI for Cultivated Plants Research (*KWI für Kulturpflanzenforschung*)

KWI for Fluid Dynamics (*KWI für Strömungsforschung*)

KWI for Iron Research (*KWI für Eisenforschung*)

KWI for Labor Physiology (*KWI für Arbeitsphysiologie*)

KWI for Leather Research (*KWI für Lederforschung*)

KWI for Medical Research (*KWI für medizinische Forschung*)

KWI for Metal Research (*KWI für Metallforschung*)

KWI for Physical Chemistry (*KWI für physikalische Chemie und Elektrochemie*)

KWI for Physics (*KWI für Physik*)

KWI for Silicate Research (*KWI für Silikatforschung*)

KWI for Stockbreeding Research (*KWI für Tierzuchtforschung*)

KWI for Textile Fiber Research (*KWI für Faserstoffchemie*)

Research Unit for Virus Research (*Arbeitsstätte für Virusforschung*)

I

The Kaiser Wilhelm Society under National Socialism

Susanne Heim, Carola Sachse, and Mark Walker

THE KAISER WILHELM SOCIETY

The Kaiser Wilhelm Society (*Kaiser-Wilhelm-Gesellschaft*, KWS) was one of the most important scientific institutions in the twentieth century and for modern science.[1] In 1911, the German state, private industry, and science came together to establish an institution consisting of scientific institutes outside the university system with world-class facilities and researchers who had been liberated from teaching obligations. The first institutes were funded largely by private donations and were devoted to subjects of interest to German industry. The German or Prussian state also contributed, with the result that the KWS was a hybrid public–private institution.

The Kaiser Wilhelm Institutes (KWIs) quickly established a reputation for excellence in scientific research, boasted many Nobel laureates, and became the envy of other scientists inside and outside Germany. The KWS managed to thrive through the First World War, the postwar inflation, the new German experiment with democracy, and onset of the Great Depression. When Adolf Hitler was appointed German chancellor in 1933, the KWS was the most important institution in German science, and German science arguably led the world.

The relationship between science and society should be seen not only in terms of politics influencing science, or even science influencing politics, but more with the two serving as resources for each other, as Mitchell Ash has

[1] Monika Renneberg and Mark Walker (eds.), *Science, Technology, and National Socialism* (Cambridge: Cambridge University Press, 1993), 1–17; Jonathan Harwood, "German Science and Technology under National Socialism," in *Perspectives on Science*, 5, no. 1, (1997): 128–151; Margit Szöllösi-Janze, "National Socialism and the Sciences: Reflections, Conclusions and Historical Perspectives," in Margit Szöllösi-Janze (ed), *Science in the Third Reich* (Oxford: Berg, 2001), 1–35; for the history of the KWS, see Rudolf Vierhaus and Bernhard vom Brocke (eds.), *Forschung im Spannungsfeld von Politik und Gesellschaft. Geschichte und Struktur der Kaiser-Wilhelm-/Max-Planck-Gesellschaft aus Anlass ihres 75jährigen Bestehens* (Stuttgart: DVA, 1990).

argued.[2] National Socialism had a profound effect on German science, just as German scientists had a profound effect on the Third Reich. However, the National Socialist (NS) government was not fundamentally or consistently hostile to science. The so-called Aryan Science movements in physics, mathematics, and chemistry, as well as the related Aryan Technology movement, represented an attempt to create an "ideologically correct science"[3] but played only a minor if sometimes significant role in shaping National Socialist science policy.

The National Socialist regime did repress and restrict some research, but this was dwarfed by the generous support offered for other topics. Scientists who could contribute to racial hygiene, autarky, or rearmament could also find interested and influential patrons within the National Socialist state. The Third Reich purged Jewish and some leftist scientists from the civil service at the beginning of National Socialist rule,[4] but while many good and some great scientists were lost, they were replaced by many others who were also good, and considered racially and politically acceptable by the new regime. Some disciplines and institutions were affected more than others. For example, while Fritz Haber's KWI for Physical Chemistry had many "non-Aryans" on the staff and was hit very hard, the KWI for Breeding Research had not hired any Jewish scientists and therefore had none to purge.

In a 1990 article included in a collection of essays devoted to the history of the KWS and its post–World War II successor, the Max Planck Society (Max-Planck-Gesellschaft, MPS), Helmuth Albrecht and Armin Hermann noted:

The society attempted to avoid the pressure from National Socialism by first of all referring to its private character, and second adopting a strategy that its General Director Friedrich Glum described as "self-coordination." ... As already suggested,

---

[2] Mitchell Ash, "Wissenschaft und Politik als Ressourcen für einander," in Rüdiger vom Bruch and Brigitte Kaderas (eds.), *Wissenschaften und Wissenschaftspolitik: Bestandsaufnahmen zu Formationen, Brüchen und Kontinuitäten im Deutschland des 20. Jahrhunderts* (Stuttgart: Franz Steiner Verlag, 2002), 32–51.

[3] Michael Gordin, Walter Grunden, Mark Walker, and Zuoyue Wang, "'Ideologically Correct' Science," in Mark Walker (ed.), *Science and Ideology: A Comparative History* (London: Routledge, 2003), 35–65.

[4] See Richard Beyler, "'Reine' Wissenschaft und personelle 'Säuberungen.' Die Kaiser-Wilhelm/ Max-Planck-Gesellschaft 1933 und 1945," *Ergebnisse. Vorabdrucke aus dem Forschungsprogramm "Geschichte der Kaiser-Wilhelm-Gesellschaft im Nationalsozialismus,"* No. 16 (Berlin: Forschungsprogramm, 2004; further quoted as *Ergebnisse*, no., and year), Richard Beyler, Alexei Kojevnikov, and Jessica Wang, "Purges in Comparative Perspective: Rules for Exclusion and Inclusion in the Scientific Community under Political Pressure," in Carola Sachse and Mark Walker (eds.), *Politics and Science in Wartime: Comparative International Perspectives on the Kaiser Wilhelm Institutes, Osiris* 20 (Chicago: University of Chicago Press, 2005), 23–48, and Richard Beyler, "Maintaining Discipline in the Kaiser Wilhelm Society during the National Socialist Regime," *Minerva*, 44, no. 3 (2006), 251–266.

the strategy of the KWS leadership remained thoroughly ambivalent in this regard. Costly attempts to circumvent requirements as well as generous interpretatäten of the laws contrast with other cases whereby the regulations were obeyed precisely and with great care. KWS president Max Planck explained the KWS General Administration's tactics with the simile that one had to act "like a tree in the wind." Here he meant a certain accommodation where this was unavoidable, but on the other hand, as soon as the pressure fell, "standing back upright." In other words, when the immediate external pressure was gone, then the society should return to the principle of scientific freedom, which it had used up until 1933.[5]

Herbert Mehrtens has described such policies as "collaboration,"[6] a term that might imply that science and politics are on different sides or that the collaborating scientist was a "traitor" to science. Arguably "cooperation" is a better term for the multifarious connections between scientists and the National Socialist regime. "Cooperation" also fits well with two compatible concepts, the first proposed by Mehrtens, the "irresponsible purity" of science,[7] and the second by Mark Walker, the "apolitical ideology of science";[8] both argue that scientists engage in political behavior in their professional disciplines and within the greater society, but they define or characterize this as an "apolitical," "pure" search for truth.

Three years after Albrecht's and Hermann's essay, Kristie Macrakis published a book-length history of the KWS under National Socialism that was very generous both to the institution and its representatives. She concluded that

the Society responded to the measures of the National Socialist regime by accommodation and passive opposition. There were few, if any, public protests. ... The survival of basic biological research at the Society, and the fact that scientists who were barred from the university could find a niche there, are only several examples of the differences among the patterns of development at the Society and other institutions in National Socialist Germany. ... [T]he Society survived the nazification process more intact than the universities. ... During the mid-thirties, the Society took a step closer to the industrial power block and elected presidents from industry out of

[5] Helmuth Albrecht and Armin Hermann, "Die Kaiser-Wilhelm-Gesellschaft im Dritten Reich (1933–1945)," in Vierhaus and Brocke, 356–406, here 359, 371–372.
[6] Herbert Mehrtens, "Kollaborationsverhältnisse: Natur- und Technikwissenschaften im NS-Staat und ihre Histoire," in Christoph Meinel and Peter Voswinckel (eds.), *Medizin, Naturwissenschaft, Technik und Nationalsozialismus. Kontinuitäten und Diskontinuitäten*, (Stuttgart: GNT Verlag, 1994), 13–32.
[7] Herbert Mehrtens, "Irresponsible Purity: The Political and Moral Structure of Mathematical Sciences in the National Socialist State," in Monika Renneberg and Mark Walker (eds.), *Science, Technology, and National Socialism* (Cambridge: Cambridge University Press, 1993), 324–338, 411–413.
[8] Mark Walker, "Legends Surrounding the German Atomic Bomb," in Teresa Meade and Mark Walker (eds.), *Science, Medicine, and Cultural Imperialism* (New York: St. Martin's Press, 1991), 178–204.

expediency.... Ideology per se does not necessarily lead to the decline and destruction of science. During the war years ... there was some complicity with the National Socialist state as the Kaiser Wilhelm Society slowly integrated itself more completely into the societal structure.[9]

The scholars who contributed to the MPS research program on the history of the KWS during National Socialism (see below) collectively came to very different conclusions: (1) the KWS did defend its institutional autonomy, but this is something one might expect from any institution during the Third Reich and was certainly not "passive opposition"; (2) rather than "surviving" National Socialism, in relative terms the KWS was very successful in advancing its own agenda, achieving its own goals, and prospering under Hitler; (3) finally, the KWS was an integral part of the National Socialist system of domination that subjugated people inside and outside Germany and culminated in genocide and war.

THE POLITICS OF THE PAST

The history of the KWS under National Socialism is thus significant for several reasons and is an especially important chapter in the history of modern science. However, the MPS did not encourage, let alone facilitate, a thorough and critical history of the KWS from 1933 to 1945. It took nearly half a century for most German public and private institutions to begin dealing seriously with the legacy of National Socialism. The MPS was typical in this regard. For decades it resisted critical investigations of the conduct of the KWS during the Third Reich, in particular, any potential involvement in the crimes of the National Socialist regime.

As late as 1986, when the Free University of Berlin decided to place a memorial plaque on the building used by the KWI for Anthropology during the Third Reich, the MPS refused to share responsibility for this message:

The Kaiser Wilhelm Institute for Anthropology, Human Heredity, and Eugenics was in this building from 1927 to 1945. Together with their coworkers, the directors Eugen Fischer (1927–1942) and Otmar von Verschuer (1942–1945) provided a scientific foundation for the inhumane racial and population policies of the National Socialist state. By training SS-physicians and judges for the hereditary courts, and writing reports for investigations of ancestry and forces sterilizations, they made an active contribution to selection and murder.

The twin research of Verschuer's student and personal collaborator Josef Mengele in the Auschwitz concentration camp, which was approved by the Reich Research Council and financed by the German Research Foundation, was planned in this building and supported through investigations of organs from prisoners selected and murdered.

[9] Kristie Macrakis, *Surviving the Swastika: Scientific Research in Nazi Germany* (New York: Oxford University Press, 1993), 202–204.

These crimes remain unpunished. Von Verschuer was professor of genetics in Münster until 1965.
Scientists are responsible for the content and consequences of their scientific work.[10]

Although the reluctance of the MPS to confront a potentially incriminating and disturbing past is not surprising, in the end it only enhanced and intensified the stain on the institution's reputation.

During the 1980s, the biochemist Benno Müller-Hill researched and published a path-breaking book: *Murderous Science*.[11] Among other insightful and critical analysis of biomedical research under Hitler, Müller-Hill linked the KWI for Anthropology and its director Otmar von Verschuer, as well as the KWI for Biochemistry and its director Adolf Butenandt, to some of the inhuman experiments carried out by Josef Mengele in the concentration camp at Auschwitz.[12] Over the next two decades many historians and scientists scrutinized aspects of the KWS under National Socialism.

As a result, it gradually became very clear that the KWIs for Anthropology and Brain Research, as well as the German Research Institute for Psychiatry (which was also a part of the KWS) had been directly involved with sterilization, the so-called euthanasia campaigns that murdered children and adults who were classified as "life unworthy of life," human experimentation inside and outside of concentration camps, and the inhuman treatment of people in occupied territories.[13] Along with Müller-Hill, the science writer Ernst Klee was particularly vocal and influential in calling attention to what had happened during the Third Reich and to the insufficient response of the MPS to it.[14]

By the very end of the twentieth century, the climate in Germany had changed with regard to dealing with the National Socialist past. Several

---

[10] For a photograph of the plaque, see Carola Sachse, "Menschenversuche in Auschwitz überleben, erinnern, verantworten." in Carola Sachse (ed.), *Die Verbindung nach Auschwitz. Biowissenschaften und Menschenversuche am Kaiser-Wilhelm-Institute* (Göttingen: Wallstein, 2003), 7–34, here 19.

[11] Benno Müller-Hill, *Murderous Science: Elimination by Scientific Selection of Jews, Gypsies, and Others in Germany, 1933–1945* (New York: Oxford University Press, 1988).

[12] For Butenandt from the research program also see Robert N. Proctor, "Adolf Butenandt (1903–1995). Nobelpreisträger, Nationalsozialist und MPG-Präsident. Ein erster Blick in den Nachlass," *Ergebnisse*, no. 2 (2000), the chapters by Wolfgang Schieder and Achim Trunk in this book, and Wolfgang Schieder and Achim Trunk (eds.), *Adolf Butenandt und die Kaiser-Wilhelm-Gesellschaft. Wissenschaft, Industrie und Politik im "Dritten Reich"* (Göttingen: Wallstein, 2004), Jean-Paul Gaudillière and Bernd Gausemeier, "Molding National Research Systems: The Introduction of Penicillin to Germany and France," in Sachse and Walker, 180–202, and Achim Trunk, "Biochemistry in Wartime: The Life and Lessons of Adolf Butenandt," *Minerva*, 44, no. 3 (2006), 285–306.

[13] For the details, see Carola Sachse and Benoit Massin, "Biowissenschaftliche Forschung in Kaiser-Wilhelm-Instituten und die Verbrechen des NS-Regimes. Informationen über den gegenwärtigen Wissensstand," *Ergebnisse*, no. 3 (2000).

[14] See Carola Sachse, "Menschenversuche," 16–17.

German companies and banks stopped trying to stonewall or obstruct historical research and instead hired historians without restrictions or censorship to write the histories of their institutions during the Third Reich.[15] The MPS followed suit, and beginning in the middle of the 1990s, preparations began for a comprehensive reexamination of its history under National Socialism. By then, Butenandt and most of the other KWS scientists had passed away. Perhaps most important, the biologist Hubert Markl became president of the MPS and in 1997 established a presidential commission for research into the history of the KWS under National Socialism; he appointed two respected German historians, Reinhard Rürup and Wolfgang Schieder, for this task. Even so, the research program was controversial within the MPS and was seen by some as "fouling its own nest."[16] This commission then created a research program that was planned and organized by Doris Kaufmann and subsequently directed in turn by Kaufmann, Carola Sachse, Susanne Heim, and Rüdiger Hachtmann.[17]

Fifteen years after the initial publication of his book, Müller-Hill spoke at the inaugural conference of the MPS research program.

It is late, but not too late. Verschuer was the director of a KWS-institute and belongs to the history of the KWS/MPS. The documents ... clearly show that von Verschuer considered Mengele in Auschwitz to be his collaborator. It is irrelevant, that he [Verschuer] later claimed to have known nothing about the murders. The murders happened and are a part of the history of the KWS/MPS. The MPS should recognize that. Thus I suggest that the MPS does this, and that it invites the last surviving twins [from Mengele's experiments] to a conference. ... I suggest, that [at this conference] the MPS officially apologizes to the victims.[18]

Klee and articles in the respected and influential scientific journals *Nature* and *Science* subsequently echoed Müller-Hill's call for a conference.[19]

---

[15] For example, see Hans Mommsen, *Das Volkswagenwerk und seine Arbeiter im Dritten Reich* (Düsseldorf: Econ, 1996), and Gerald Feldman, *Allianz and the German Insurance Business, 1933–1945* (Cambridge: Cambridge University Press, 2001). From the MPS research program, see Gerald D. Feldman, "Historische Vergangenheitsbearbeitung. Wirtschaft und Wissenschaft im Vergleich," *Ergebnisse*, no. 13 (2003).

[16] For a description of how and why the presidential commission was founded, see Hubert Markl, "Die ehrlichste Art der Entschuldigung ist die Offenlegung der Schuld," in Sachse, *Verbindung*, 41–51, here 43–45.

[17] The research program has ended, and this collection of essays is one of the last publications produced by it.

[18] Benno Müller-Hill, "Das Blut von Auschwitz und das Schweigen der Gelehrten," in Doris Kaufmann (ed.), *Geschichte der Kaiser-Wilhelm-Gesellschaft im Nationalsozialismus. Bestandsaufnahme und Perspektiven der Forschung.* 2 vols. (Göttingen: Wallstein, 2000), vol. 1, 189–227, here 226–227

[19] See Sachse, "Menschenversuche," 20–21.

The research program held exactly such a conference in the summer of 2001. Markl took this opportunity to tell surviving victims of the twin experiments, scholars, and the public that

> since the Max Planck Society understands itself as the "descendent" of the Kaiser Wilhelm Society, it also has the obligation to accept responsibility for its guilt. The Kaiser Wilhelm Society tolerated or even supported research among its ranks that cannot be justified on any ethical or moral grounds. At least in a few areas, it thereby placed itself in the service of a criminal regime and as a result itself became morally culpable. ... Therefore I would like to apologize for the suffering of the victims of these crimes – the dead as well as the survivors – done in the name of science. ... In any case, when I apologize here personally and for the Max Planck Society representing the Kaiser Wilhelm Society, I mean the honestly felt expression of the deepest regret, compassion, and shame over the fact that scientists perpetrated, supported, and did not hinder such crimes.[20]

At the same conference, Wolfgang Schieder noted, "The surviving victims of these human experiments had and have to suffer the consequences for the rest of their lives. They have suffered extreme experiences that exceed the ability of historians, who usually depend on the evidence from written documents, to comprehend."[21]

THE RESEARCH PROGRAM

The research program has focused on four main areas: (1) the politics of the KWS General Administration and how the MPS dealt with the legacy of the KWS; (2) military research for both rearmament and the war economy; (3) agricultural and breeding research in the context of autarky policies; and, of course, (4) research oriented toward racial hygiene, racial policy, and heredity.

The story of science at the KWS during the Third Reich is neither the history of "good science" in the service of bad goals nor the tale of a bad regime ruining good science. The National Socialist regime and its policies did increasingly isolate German scientists from some of their international colleagues and, as noted above, expelled many talented researchers.[22] This certainly did not help German science, but neither was it a crippling blow. The KWS acted as a mediator between the professional interests of its

---

[20] Markl, 50–51.
[21] Wolfgang Schieder, "Die extreme Erfahrungen der Opfer übertreffen das Vorstellungsvermögen der Historiker," in Sachse, *Verbindung*, 37–38, here 38.
[22] For a comparative perspective on this, see Ronald Doel, Dieter Hoffmann, and Nikolai Krementsov, "National States and International Science: A Comparative History of International Science Congresses in Hitler's Germany, Stalin's Russia, and Cold War United States," in Sachse and Walker, 49–76.

scientific staff and the National Socialist regime's need for scientific expertise
to support its goals and policies. Up until the last weeks of the war, the KWS
was an effective and dependable partner of the National Socialist regime.
Indeed, only because of the effective mobilization or self-mobilization of
leading German scientists was the National Socialist regime able to fight for
six years against the most powerful economies in the world.

As Reinhard Rürup argued at the conference on bio-sciences and human
experimentation in Kaiser Wilhelm Institutes: "National Socialism did not
instrumentalize research, as often claimed after 1945, rather not a few
researchers attempted to instrumentalize the political system for their own
goals."[23] A comparative analysis of the KWIs in an international context
reveals that what was unique about the interaction of science and politics during the Third Reich was the freedoms the National Socialist regime allowed
its scientists, engineers, and physicians, not how it constrained them.[24] The
Third Reich set few boundaries for leading scientists who were able to make
their professional interests compatible with the political and military goals
of the National Socialist regime; if there were limits, these were usually due
to shortages of materials or money, not ethical, legal, or political restraints.
As the chapters in this book make clear, KWS scientists knew how to take
advantage of the specific and sometimes unique conditions the National
Socialist regime offered them to advance their own research agendas and
strive for the highest international scientific standards while simultaneously
catering to one or more National Socialist policies or goals.

Whereas scientific research was carried out in the individual KWIs, the
General Administration of the KWS was responsible for administering general personnel policy, tracking finance, and dealing with the various organs
of the German state.[25] During the Third Reich, this included (1) reacting
to the racial and ideological purge of the civil service and eventually all
institutions in Germany;[26] (2) participating in the mandatory rituals of first

[23] Reinhard Rürup, "Schlussbemerkungen," in Sachse, *Verbindung*, 319–324, here 323; also see
   Reinhard Rürup, *Schicksale und Karrieren. Gedenkbuch für die von den Nationalsozialisten
   aus der Kaiser-Wilhelm-Gesellschaft vertriebenen Forscherinnen und Forscher* (Göttingen:
   Wallstein, 2008).
[24] Sachse and Walker; also see Mitchell Ash, "Scientific Changes in Germany 1933, 1945, 1990:
   Towards a Comparison," *Minerva*, 37 (1999), 329–354.
[25] For the General Administration see Albrecht and Hermann, and Macrakis. From the
   research program, see Alexandra Przyrembel, "Friedrich Glum und Ernst Telschow. Die
   Generalsekretäre der Kaiser-Wilhelm-Gesellschaft: Handlungsfelder und Handlungsoptionen
   der 'Verwaltenden' von Wissen während des Nationalsozialismus," *Ergebnisse*, no. 20
   (2004) and Rüdiger Hachtmann's chapter in this book, as well as Rüdiger Hachtmann,
   *Wissenschaftsmanagement im Dritten Reich. Die Geschichte der Kaiser-Wilhelm-Gesellschaft
   1930/33 bis 1945/48* (Göttingen: Wallstein, 2008).
[26] For the history of scientific societies under National Socialism, see Dieter Hoffmann and
   Mark Walker (eds.), *Physiker zwischen Autonomie und Anpassung – Die DPG im Dritte*

the "national renewal," then National Socialism; (3) cultivating good relationships with influential leading National Socialists, often by incorporating them into the organization; and (4) forming part of the network to mobilize science for the policies of the National Socialist state, culminating in war and genocide. Many historians have argued that this "Faustian pact"[27] with the Third Reich had profound consequences for the scientists and science at the KWIs.

Racial science under Hitler was conceived from the very beginning as "applied research" and provided the connection between science, the political regime, and society.[28] Racial hygiene, which included both "positive" and

Reich (Weinheim: VCH, 2006), including the chapters by Ute Deichmann on chemistry and Volker Remmert on mathematics.

[27] For example, see Rüdiger Hachtmann's chapter in this book.

[28] The literature on racial hygiene and biomedical research under National Socialism is immense. As a start, see Gerhard Baader and Ulrich Schultz (eds.), *Medizin und Nationalsozialismus: Tabuisierte Vergangenheit – ungebrochene Tradition?* (Berlin [West]: Verlagsgesellschaft Gesundheit, 1980), Karl-Heinz Roth, "Schöner neuer Mensch. Der Paradigmenwechsel der klassischen Genetik und seine Auswirkungen auf die Bevölkerungsbiologie des 'Dritten Reiches,'" in Heidrun Kaupen-Haas (ed.), *Der Griff nach der Bevölkerung. Aktualität und Kontinuität nazistischer Bevölkerungspoltik* (Nördlingen: Greno, 1986), 11–63, Gisela Bock, *Zwangssterilisation im Nationalsozialismus. Studien zur Rassenpolitik und Frauenpolitik* (Opladen: Westdeutscher Verlag, 1986), Müller-Hill, *Murderous*; Robert Proctor, *Racial Hygiene: Medicine under the Nazis* (Cambridge, MA: Harvard University Press, 1988), Paul Weindling, *Health, Race, and German Politics between National Unification and Nazism, 1870–1945* (Cambridge: Cambridge University Press, 1989), Jonathan Harwood, *Styles of Scientific Thought: The German Genetics Community 1900–1933* (Chicago: University of Chicago Press, 1993), Stefan Kühl, *The Nazi Connection: Eugenics, American Racism, and German National Socialism* (New York: Oxford University Press, 1994), Ute Deichmann, *Biologists under Hitler* (Cambridge, MA: Harvard University Press, 1996), Stefan Kühl, *Die Internationale der Rassisten. Aufstieg und Niedergang der internationalen Bewegung für Eugenik und Rassenhygiene im 20. Jahrhundert* (Frankfurt am Main: Campus, 1997), Robert Proctor, *The Nazi War on Cancer* (Princeton: Princeton University Press, 1999), and Sheila F. Weiss, "German Eugenics, 1890–1933," in Dieter Kuntz and Susan Bachrach (eds.), *Deadly Medicine: Creating the Master Race* (Washington, DC: U.S. Holocaust Museum, 2004), 15–39 and 206–207. For a comprehensive review of the literature, see Sachse and Massin. The research program has also produced many publications on this topic: Hans-Walter Schmuhl (ed.), *Rassenforschung an Kaiser-Wilhelm-Instituten vor und nach 1933* (Göttingen: Wallstein, 2003), and Sheila F. Weiss, "Humangenetik und Politik als wechselseitige Ressourcen Das Kaiser-Wilhelm-Institut für Anthropologie, menschliche Erblehre und Eugenik im 'Dritten Reich,'" in *Ergebnisse*, no. 17 (2004), Ute Deichmann, "Proteinforschung an Kaiser-Wilhelm-Instituten von 1930 bis 1950 im internationalen Vergleich," in *Ergebnisse*, no. 21 (2004), Sheila F. Weiss, "'The Sword of Our Science' as a Foreign Policy Weapon. The Political Function of German Geneticists in the International Arena during the Third Reich," in *Ergebnisse*, no. 22 (2005), Susanne zur Nieden; "Erbbiologische Forschungen zur Homosexualität an der Deutschen Forschungsanstalt für Psychiatrie während der Jahre des Nationalsozialismus. Zur Geschichte von Theo Lang," *Ergebnisse*, no. 25 (2005), Mark Adams, Garland Allen, and Sheila F. Weiss, "Human Heredity and Politics: A Comparative International Study of the Eugenics Record Office at Cold Springs Harbor (United States),

"negative" eugenics, encouraged a broad spectrum of biomedical research ranging from attempts to find a scientific test for race to a plethora of research questions that in some way were relevant for the health of the "People's Community" (*Volksgemeinschaft*). A very large portion of the life sciences in Germany was intimately connected to National Socialist racial hygiene policies and goals. Scientists actively participated in the sterilization and so-called euthanasia programs, leading directly to genocide. The state in turn generously provided resources and research opportunities, especially because restrictions on human experimentation were lifted for certain populations.[29]

National Socialist science policy was not unique because it compelled scientists to carry out criminal experiments or research – for scientists were not forced to do so. Instead, the Third Reich distinguished itself from democratic states in particular because it loosened, suspended, or eliminated ethical rules and controls on an unprecedented scale and thereby either allowed or encouraged scientists, engineers, and physicians to take advantage of unprecedented, often unethical, and sometimes murderous research opportunities.[30]

The professional network that reached from the KWIs to the National Socialist concentration camps and "euthanasia" institutions created new opportunities for gaining access to involuntary subjects who could not resist the experiments. German biomedical researchers considered it legitimate to use someone who had been excluded from the "People's Community" or declared "the enemy" as an experimental subject in order to benefit

the Kaiser Wilhelm Institute for Anthropology, Human Heredity, and Eugenics (Germany), and the Maxim Gorky Medical Genetics Institute (USSR)," in Sachse and Walker, 232–262, Hans-Jakob Ritter and Volker Roelcke, "Psychiatric Genetics in Munich and Basel between 1925 and 1945: Program – Practices – Cooperative Arrangements," in Sachse and Walker, 263–288, Bernd Gausemeier, *Natürliche Ordnungen und politische Allianzen. Biologische und biochemische Forschung an Kaiser-Wilhelm-Instituten 1933–1945* (Göttingen: Wallstein, 2005), Hans-Walther Schmuhl, *The Kaiser Wilhelm Institute for Anthropology, Human Heredity and Eugenics, 1927–1945: Crossing Boundaries* (Heidelberg: Springer, 2008).

[29] For the human experimentation, see Alexander Mitscherlich and Fred Mielke, *The Death Doctors* (London: Elek, 1962) as well as Robert J. Lifton, *The Nazi Doctors: Medical Killing and the Psychology of Genocide* (New York: Basic, 1986), and Christoph Kopke (ed.), *Medizin und Verbrechen: Festschrift zum 60. Geburtstag von Walter Wuttke* (Ulm: Klemm und Oelschläger, 2001). The research program has produced many publications on this topic: Sachse and Massin, Sachse, *Verbindung*, Jürgen Peiffer, "Wissenschaftliches Erkenntnisstreben als Tötungsmotiv? Zur Kennzeichnung von Opfern auf deren Krankenakten und zur Organisation und Unterscheidung von Kinder- 'Euthanasie' und T4-Aktion," *Ergebnisse*, no. 23 (2005), Gerhard Baader, Susan Lederer, Morris Low, Florian Schmaltz, and Alexander von Schwerin, "Pathways to Human Experimentation, 1933–1945: Germany, Japan, and the United States," in Sachse and Walker, 205–231, Alexander von Schwerin, *Experimentalisierung des Menschen. Der Genetiker Hans Nachtsheim und die vergleichende Erbpathologie 1920–1945* (Göttingen: Wallstein, 2004).

[30] Rürup, "Schlussbemerkungen," 323.

Germany. This was not unique to Germany or National Socialism; it can also be seen in Japanese treatment of Allied prisoners of war and Chinese civilians, and had some similarities with the use of prisoners in the United States – although such experiments were neither as numerous nor as murderous in the United States as in Germany.[31]

The human experiments and unscrupulous use of human preparations (scientific samples taken either from people against their will or after they had been killed) for biomedical research were paradigmatic for the relationship between science and politics in the Third Reich. Arguably, the most significant examples of this are the extensive collaborations between the German state and the KWI for Brain Research and the German Research Institute for Psychiatry, respectively. Scientists benefited from access to this scientific material and thereby tainted themselves and their work with the blood of the victims.

Like racial hygiene, autarky was not a uniquely National Socialist policy; it was found in many countries as a consequence of the agricultural crisis of the 1920s and subsequent Great Depression.[32] However, the German experience in the First World War gave special emphasis to calls for national independence with regard to foodstuffs and other raw materials. The National Socialist policies of acquiring new "living space" (*Lebensraum*) and rearmament benefited animal and plant breeding research in the years before the war, and then profoundly expanded this field once the war began.

---

[31] See Baader, Lederer, Low, Schmaltz, and Schwerin.
[32] For autarky and National Socialism, see Karl Brandt, Otto Schiller, and Franz Ahlgrimm, *Management of Agriculture and Food in the German-Occupied and Other Areas of Fortress Europe: A Study in Military Government* (Stanford: Stanford University Press, 1953), Joachim Lehmann, "Faschistische Agrarpolitik im zweiten Weltkrieg: zur Konzeption von Herbert Backe," *Zeitschrift für Geschichtswissenschaft*, 28 (1980), 948–956, John Farquharson, *The Plough and the Swastika: The NSDAP and Agriculture in Germany 1928–45* (London: Sage, 1976), Martin Kutz, "Kriegserfahrung und Kriegsvorbereitung. Die agrarwirtschaftliche Vorbereitung des Zweiten Weltkrieges in Deutschland vor dem Hintergrund der Weltkrieg I-Erfahrung," *Zeitschrift für Agrargeschichte und Agrarsoziologie*, 32 (1984), 59–82, 135–164, Gustavo Corni and Horst Gies, *Butter-Brot-Kanonen: Die Ernährungswirtschaft in Deutschland unter der Diktatur Hitlers* (Berlin: Akademie Verlag, 1997). For the intellectual and scientific preparations for German expansion in the east and the "General Plan for the East," see Götz Aly and Susanne Heim, *Architects of Annihilation: Auschwitz and the Logic of Destruction* (Princeton: Princeton University Press, 2003), Mechtild Rössler and Sabine Schleiermacher (eds.), *Der "Generalplan Ost": Hauptlinien der nationalsozialistischen Planungs- und Vernichtungspolitik* (Berlin: Akademie Verlag, 1993). From the research program, see Susanne Heim (ed.), *Autarkie und Ostexpansion. Pflanzenzucht und Agrarforschung im Nationalsozialismus* (Göttingen: Wallstein, 2002), Susanne Heim, *Kalorien, Kautschuk, Karrieren. Pflanzenzüchtung und landwirtschaftliche Forschung in Kaiser-Wilhelm-Instituten 1933–1945* (Göttingen: Wallstein, 2003), Olga Elina, Susanne Heim, and Nils Roll-Hansen, "Plant Breeding on the Front: Imperialism, War, and Exploitation," in Sachse and Walker, 161–179, and Susanne Heim, "Expansion Policy and the Role of Agricultural Research in Nazi Germany," *Minerva*, 44, no. 3 (2006), 267–284.

Researchers working on animal and plant breeding became inextricably intertwined with the brutal German occupation of the East. New institutes were founded in countries occupied by or obedient to Germany, and research facilities, materials, and collections were seized in the name of science. This plunder advanced both the autarky policies of the regime and individual scientists' careers.

The militarization of scientific research during the Third Reich was also not uniquely connected to National Socialist ideology; its roots stretched back to the First World War, if not before.[33] However, the National Socialist

---

[33] The militarization of science under National Socialism also has a large literature. As a start, see Karl-Heinz Ludwig, *Technik und Ingenieure im Dritten Reich* (Düsseldorf: Droste Verlag, 1974), Herbert Mehrtens, "Angewandte Mathematik und Anwendungen der Mathematik im nationalsozialistischen Deutschland," *Geschichte und Gesellschaft*, 12 (1986), 317–347, Mark Walker, *German National Socialism and the Quest for Nuclear Power, 1939–1949* (Cambridge: Cambridge University Press, 1989), David Cassidy, *Uncertainty: The Life and Science of Werner Heisenberg* (New York: Freeman, 1991), Helmuth Trischler, *Luft- und Raumfahrtforschung in Deutschland 1900–1970. Politische Geschichte einer Wissenschaft* (Frankfurt am Main: Campus, 1992), Helmut Maier, *Erwin Marx (1893–1980), Ingenieurwissenschaftler in Braunschweig, und die Forschung und Entwicklung auf dem Gebiet der elektrischen Energieübertragung auf weite Entfernungen zwischen 1918 und 1950* (Stuttgart: GNT, 1993), Renneberg and Walker, Michael Neufeld, *The Rocket and the Reich: Peenemünde and the Coming of the Ballistic Missile* (New York: Free Press, 1995), Mark Walker, *Nazi Science: Myth, Truth, and the German Atom Bomb* (New York: Perseus, 1995), Herbert Mehrtens, "Mathematics and War: Germany 1900–1945," in Jose M. Sanchez-Ron and Paul Forman (eds.), *National Military Establishments and the Advancement of Science and Technology: Studies in Twentieth Century History* (Dordrecht: Kluwer Academic Publishers, 1996), 87–134, Ute Deichmann, "Kriegsbezogene biologische, biochemische und chemische Forschung an den Kaiser Wilhelm-Instituten für Züchtungsforschung, für Physikalische Chemie und Elektrochemie und für Medizinische Forschung," in Kaufmann, vol. 1, 231–257, Moritz Epple and Volker Remmert, "'Eine ungeahnte Synthese zwischen reiner und angewandter Mathematik.' Kriegsrelevante mathematische Forschung in Deutschland während des II. Weltkrieges," in Kaufmann, vol. 1, 258–295, Michael Eckert, "Theoretische Physiker in Kriegsprojekten. Zur Problematik einer internationalen vergleichenden Analyse," in Kaufmann, vol. 1, 296–308, Helmuth Trischler, "'Big Science' or 'Small Science'? Die Luftfahrtforschung im Nationalsozialismus," in Kaufmann, vol. 1, 328–362, Ute Deichmann, *Flüchten, Mitmachen, Vergessen. Chemiker und Biochemiker in der NS-Zeit* (Weinheim: VCH, 2001), Helmuth Trischler, "Wachstum – Systemnähe – Ausdifferenzierung. Grossforschung im Nationalsozialismus," in vom Bruch and Kaderas, 241–252. The research program has produced several publications on this topic: Helmut Maier, "'Unideologische Normalwissenschaft' oder Rüstungsforschung? Wandlungen naturwissenschaftlich-technologischer Forschung und Entwicklung im 'Dritten Reich,'" in vom Bruch and Kaderas, 253–262, Helmut Maier, "'Wehrhaftmachung' und 'Kriegswichtigkeit.' Zur rüstungstechnologischen Relevanz des Kaiser-Wilhelm-Instituts für Metallforschung in Stuttgart vor und nach 1945," *Ergebnisse*, no. 5 (2002), Helmut Maier (ed.), *Rüstungsforschung im Nationalsozialismus. Organisation, Mobilisierung und Entgrenzung der Technikwissenschaften* (Göttingen: Wallstein, 2002), Mark Walker, "Otto Hahn: Verantwortung und Verdrängung," *Ergebnisse*, no. 10 (2003), Walter Grunden, Yutaka Kawamura, Eduard Kolchinsky, Helmut Maier, and Masakatsu Yamazaki, "Laying the Foundation for Wartime Research: A Comparative Overview of Science Mobilization in

regime did generously provide resources and support for such research on an unprecedented scale. As Paul Forman has shown for physical research in postwar America, regimes can profoundly influence how scientists work – the questions they investigate, the methods they use, how they present their results – merely by offering to support particular research.[34]

The National Socialist generosity affected more fundamental research – for example, efforts at the KWI for Metal Research to find new metal alloys, and more applied research aimed at weapons research and development (R&D). This was one of the main areas of research at the KWI for Physical Chemistry from the beginning of the Third Reich, but once war began, several other institutes were mobilized for weapons R&D as well, including the KWIs for Chemistry,[35] Medical Research, and Physics.

The military research done at the KWS is relevant for solving an apparent paradox: the German war economy has long been assumed to have been chaotic and inefficient under National Socialist rule but was nevertheless able to produce a great deal, to increase this as time went on, and often to achieve very high quality. In part, this paradox is caused by the implicit use of the war economy and mobilization of science in the United States as the standard for Germany. When examined closely, however, it is clear that the German military-industrial-state-science complex often worked rather efficiently and functioned differently from the American example, using inter-

---

National Socialist Germany, Japan, and the Soviet Union," in Sachse and Walker, 79–106, Walter Grunden, Mark Walker, and Masakatsu Yamazaki, "Wartime Nuclear Weapons Research in Germany and Japan," in Sachse and Walker, 107–130, Moritz Epple, Andreas Karachalios, and Volker Remmert, "Aerodynamics and Mathematics in National Socialist Germany and Fascist Italy: A Comparison of Research Institutes," in Sachse and Walker, 131–158, Florian Schmaltz, *Kampfstoff-Forschung im Nationalsozialismus. Zur Kooperation von Kaiser Wilhelm Instituten, Militär und Industrie* (Göttingen: Wallstein, 2005), Helmut Maier, *Forschung als Waffe. Rüstungsforschung in der Kaiser-Wilhelm-Gesellschaft und das Kaiser-Wilhelm-Institut für Metallforschung 1900–1945/48*, two vols. (Göttingen: Wallstein, 2007), Helmut Maier (ed.), *Gemeinschaftsforschung, Bevollmächtigte und der Wissenstransfer. Die Rolle der Kaiser-Wilhelm-Gesellschaft im System kriegsrelevanter Forschung des Nationalsozialismus* (Göttingen: Wallstein, 2007).

[34] Paul Forman, "Behind Quantum Electronics: National Security as Basis for Physical Research in the United States, 1940–1960." *Historical Studies in the Physical and Biological Sciences*, 18 (1987), 149–229.

[35] See Mark Walker, "Otto Hahn: Responsibility and Repression," in *Physics in Perspective*, 8, no. 2 (2006), 116–163; this was originally published in German as part of the research program's preprint series, Walker, "Verantwortung." For a contrary perspective on Hahn published by the research program, see Otto Gerhard Oexle, "Hahn, Heisenberg und die anderen. Anmerkungen zu 'Kopenhagen,' 'Farm Hall' und 'Göttingen,'" *Ergebnisse*, no. 9 (2003). Also see the work of Ruth Lewin Sime, *Lise Meitner: A Life in Physics* (Berkeley: University of California Press, 1996), including two publications from the research program, "Otto Hahn und die Max-Planck-Gesellschaft. Zwischen Vergangenheit und Erinnerung," *Ergebnisse*, no. 14 (2004), and "From Exceptional Prominence to Prominent Exception. Lise Meitner at the Kaiser Wilhelm Institute for Chemistry," *Ergebnisse*, no. 24 (2005).

disciplinary committees spanning industry, the military, and the German state to coordinate research and production.[36]

Germany had a long tradition of a decentralized system of interinstitutional committees used to coordinate research, production, and resources to mobilize science and technology for (re)armament and war. This was continued during the National Socialist period and indeed fit into it well. Senior scientists, often representing different or multiple institutions, played a leading role in this mobilization of science and technology for particular aims. Many KWI directors took part in the various committees set up to organize research, especially after September 1939, for the war effort. It is clear that they pushed for a more active and ultimate participation in the war economy. Indeed, it appears that the polycratic nature of National Socialist rule and the war effort did not hinder science but instead facilitated and encouraged scientists' willingness and ability to make their research relevant for the practical needs of the National Socialist state.

THIS BOOK

This book includes a representative selection of the excellent work produced by the research program inaugurated by Hubert Markl, published for the first time in English. The first section of the book is devoted to research and personnel policies. Rüdiger Hachtmann examines the KWS General Administration – in particular its finance policies and how its highest officials networked within the National Socialist state. This was more of a "Faustian pact" than a "gilded cage" because the KWS mobilized itself for the Third Reich. Bernhard Strebel and Jens-Christian Wagner investigate how the KWS took advantage of the forced labor that pervaded the German economy for agriculture and construction as well as using foreign scientists and technicians against their will. Around one thousand people, including concentration camp inmates, labored for the KWS. Wolfgang Schieder places the biochemist Adolf Butenandt and his actions in the political context of the Weimar Republic and the Third Reich.

The second section deals with the most infamous science practiced during the Third Reich: racial research. Hans-Walter Schmuhl investigates the use of brains taken from victims of the so-called euthanasia campaign by the KWI for Brain Research. The institute was connected to this campaign in many diverse ways, and the remains of hundreds of victims were exploited. Achim Trunk takes a close look at the controversial suggestion from Benno Müller-Hill, that Adolf Butenandt was connected to human experimentation at Auschwitz. It is clear that Butenandt knew of Verschuer's research goal – to find a scientific basis for determining race – and he probably

---

[36] See Grunden, Kawamura, Kolchinsky, Maier, and Yamazaki, as well as Maier, *Forschung*.

knew that scientific samples were moving from the concentration camp to Verschuer's institute. However, this is arguably not the most important aspect of Butenandt's role in the Third Reich. Helga Satzinger uses gender to compare the scientific concepts of race and gene in the work of Richard Goldschmidt, who was forced to leave Germany, and Fritz Lenz, an enthusiastic race hygienist. Whereas Goldschmidt did not try to separate people along the lines of race and gender, this was precisely what lay at the foundation of Lenz's work.

The third section of the book deals with "eastern research," "living space," and breeding research. Susanne Heim examines the research program to use the Kog-sagyz plant as a source of rubber. This research, which also involved the SS, made sense and was only made possible by the autarky policies of the regime and the aggressive war and occupation in Eastern Europe. Günther Luxbacher studies textile research at the KWI for Bast Fiber Research, another research area facilitated by the efforts to achieve autarky. This case study also highlights the potential conflicts between KWIs and German industry when they collaborate on research of interest to the National Socialist state. Bernd Gausemeier investigates the botanical section of the KWI for Biology and the role it played in National Socialist science policy. This example reveals the problematic nature of what scientists asserted was "basic research" but actually was also relevant for the National Socialist efforts to encourage plant breeding.

The fourth set of essays investigates military research at the KWS. Helmut Maier studies the KWI for Metal Research and the ideology and policies surrounding the so-called German metals – metals available in Germany or alloys of them that were used to replace other metals in short supply. Thus this chapter also deals with the autarky policies of the regime. Moritz Epple examines one of the best examples of "big science" under National Socialism: aerodynamics research at the KWI for Fluid Dynamics. This scientific discipline is noteworthy because it remained at a world-class standard throughout the Third Reich and actually experienced an improvement in research opportunities under National Socialism. Florian Schmaltz surveys chemical weapons research at several KWIs. This research depended on a close collaboration with German industry and also included some involuntary experimentation on human subjects. Mark Walker uses recently discovered documents from Russian archives to examine nuclear weapons research at the KWIs. This new information demonstrates that at different times, these scientists were both more and less enthusiastic about making atomic bombs than previously known.

The final section of the book deals with the postwar period and how the MPS dealt with the legacy of the KWS under National Socialism. Carola Sachse analyzes the "whitewash culture" of postwar West Germany with special emphasis on the ambivalent rehabilitation of Verschuer. Michael

Schüring[37] examines the relationship between Butenandt and his predecessor Carl Neuberg. Butenandt took over the KWI for Biochemistry after
Neuberg was forced to leave Germany.

All of these essays are groundbreaking because they are based on research
in documents either recently discovered or recently made available to scholars. Taken together they provide a rich and subtle picture of the KWS under
National Socialism that sheds light on modern science, on how science
interacts with the modern Leviathan state, and on the history of National
Socialism and the Holocaust.

[37] Also see Michael Schüring, "Expulsion, Compensation, and the Legacy of the Kaiser
Wilhelm Society," *Minerva*, 44, no. 3 (2006), 307–324 and Michael Schüring, *Minervas
verstossene Kinder. Vertriebene Wissenschaftler und die Vergangenheitspolitik der Max-
Planck-Gesellschaft* (Göttingen: Wallstein, 2006)

SECTION I

RESEARCH AND PERSONNEL POLICIES

2

A Success Story? Highlighting the History of the Kaiser Wilhelm Society's General Administration in the Third Reich

Rüdiger Hachtmann

The recollections and "retrospectives" occasioned by the respective anniversaries of the Max Planck Society (*Max-Planck-Gesellschaft*, MPS) and Kaiser Wilhelm Society (*Kaiser-Wilhelm-Gesellschaft*, KWS) often give the impression that the years of the Third Reich had been an era of peril and courage for these organizations. For instance, in 1954 Otto Hahn, Nobel laureate and first president of the MPS, explained that only with the greatest of difficulties had it been possible "to maintain the Kaiser Wilhelm Society's independence, which at some point had been seriously at stake."[1] Following the collapse of the Nazi regime, others, like Nobel laureates Richard Kuhn and Adolf Butenandt, darkly spoke of the "grave and manifold difficulties ... during the increasingly deteriorating era of National Socialism" and "science treated as unworthy" with "disregard of its autonomy" during an era "we don't care to remember" and where "more than once everything had been at stake."[2]

A particularly impressive metaphor has been ascribed to Max Planck. According to Butenandt's interview with Kristie Macrakis in 1985, Planck described Nazi rule as "a thunder storm sweeping over us" that caused "some trees to come down." Yet "there was no point" in "shouting at a thunderstorm," he maintained. One had to wait until "the storm was

---

[1] Otto Hahn, "Ernst Telschow zum 65. Geburtstag," 2, manuscript in the Archives of the Max Planck Society (henceforth MPG-Archiv), Abt. II, Rep. 1A, Personalakte Ernst Telschow, Nr. 2; as an offprint from the *Mitteilungen der Max-Planck-Gesellschaft*, No. 4 (1954), 170–174, here 172, Archives of the Max Planck Society, Berlin (*Archiv zur Geschichte der Max-Planck-Gesellschaft*, MPG-Archiv), Abt. II, Rep. 1A, Personalakte Ernst Telschow, vol. 7.

[2] Richard Kuhn, "Zu Ernst Telschows 25jährigem Dienstjubiläum," offprint from the *Mitteilungen der Max-Planck-Gesellschaft* No. 5 (1955), 234/238, here 234 f., MPG-Archiv, Abt. II, Rep. 1A, Personalakte Ernst Telschow, Nr. 7; speech Butenandt gave during the commemoration for Ernst Telschow on October 31, 1988, in Munich, MPG-Archiv, Abt. II, Rep. 1A, Personalakte Ernst Telschow, Nr. 11.

over."[3] In reading those words, one almost sees those gentlemen opening their umbrellas, casting anxious glances to the sky to see if a branch was threatening to hit them on the head – huddled together, hoping that the bad weather would eventually move on.

Naturally, this was self-stylization with apologetic intentions. If the years of Nazi rule were mentioned at all, they were described as a struggle for survival.[4] However, that was only the case post-1945. Prior to 1945, neither the General Administration nor representatives of the majority of KWS institutes perceived the Third Reich as a devastating "thunderstorm." Well into the war, many believed that, thanks to the "national awakening" (*nationaler Aufbruch*) in 1933, the long-desired spring had finally come after a hard and icy winter. Some contemporaries may initially have noticed some "spring storms" in the form of isolated assaults by the SA [*Sturmabteilung* (Storm Troopers)] and the displacement of Jewish colleagues: sunshine interrupted by some downpours and occasional hailstorms. Yet soon bright summer weather prevailed, before once again increasingly bitter autumn storms replaced the friendly weather.

The weather metaphor introduced by Planck, or rather Butenandt, illustrates an important point of departure: for the KWS the years from 1933 until the onset of the massive air raids in 1942/43 were not the struggle for survival, as they claimed after 1945. In fact, the era of the Third Reich was considered a remarkable "success story" for the KWS and its general administration – as measured by the usual parameters of institutional self-portrayal. From the perspective of the contemporary actors, it remained a success far into the war for several reasons: since 1936 the Nazi regime and other sponsors had opened an unprecedented cash flow for the KWS. Numerous new institutes were founded under the KWS umbrella. During the war years alone, the number of Kaiser Wilhelm Institutes rose from 34 to 43; several more were in the planning stage. The traditional high standing in society that the KWS managed to maintain could be interpreted as another token of success. The society likewise held the new rulers in considerable esteem. The KWS was even allowed to maintain its rather antiquated name in the certainly not monarchic Third Reich.

The General Administration made considerable contributions to the KWS "success story"; it was the representative and mouthpiece of the institutes at

[3] Interview by Kristie Macrakis with Butenandt and Telschow (late May 1985), 1st version, 11 f., MPG-Archiv, Abt. II, Rep. 83 (Telschow papers), Nr. 10.
[4] This self-stylization prevailed until recently as well in studies about the KWS – for example, in the title of Kristie Macrakis, *Surviving the Swastika: Scientific Research in Nazi Germany* (New York: Oxford University Press, 1993). Also see Ulrike Kohl, *Die Präsidenten der Kaiser-Wilhelm-Gesellschaft im Nationalsozialismus. Max Planck, Carl Bosch und Albert Vögler zwischen Wissenschaft und Macht* (Stuttgart: Steiner, 2002), quotations on 227, 241, and 246.

large as well as the external link that dealt with the regime's diverse political entities. But this success had a price, and the political and moral price the General Administration had to pay was very high.

The following presentation focuses on the Society's General Administration, consisting at that time of about twenty people who were in charge of the day-to-day affairs of the KWS. Instead of covering the entire history of the General Administration for the years from 1933 to 1945,[5] some events will be highlighted. First, the KWS budget development will be outlined as an indicator for the material success of the General Administration's policy. Next is analyzed the position taken by the KWS and its General Administration with regard to the "seizure of power" (*"Machtergreifung"*) and "national awakening," which appears to begin with the establishment of Hitler's cabinet. The main part consists of how the policy of the General Administration noticeably changed beginning in 1933. This will include the continuities of the General Administration's policy, beginning with the Kaiser Wilhelm Society's foundation in 1911, which are discussed here under the heading "The KWS Negotiates with Itself." However, the main focus will be on the structural changes in the relationship of the KWS to the (Nazi) state after 1933 – in particular, how both the public relations of the General Administration and the communication structures and networks that tied it to the political structure were changed. The General Administration's structure was strictly hierarchical, and the "Harnack principle"[6] prevailing in the Kaiser Wilhelm Institutes applied in a way to the administration as well; therefore, attention will be turned to the director general (or as he has been called since 1937, the "secretary general"), who oversaw the General Administration.[7] This includes an examination of the political mentalities of Friedrich Glum (KWS director general from 1920 to 1937)[8] and Ernst Telschow (KWS Secretary General from 1937 to 1960).[9]

---

[5] Please see Rüdiger Hachtmann, *Wissenschaftsmanagement im Dritten Reich. Die Geschichte der Kaiser-Wilhelm-Gesellschaft 1930/33 bis 1945/48* (Göttingen: Wallstein, 2008).

[6] On the "Harnack-Principle," essentially taking an excellent scientist, giving him generous resources and support, and letting him determine the research direction of his institute, see especially Bernhard vom Brocke and Hubert Laitko (eds.), *Die Kaiser-Wilhelm-/Max-Planck-Gesellschaft und ihre Institute. Studien zu ihrer Geschichte: Das Harnack-Prinzip* (Berlin: de Gruyter, 1996).

[7] Here the General Administration in the narrower sense has to be distinguished from the "general administration" in the wider sense. The capitalized term refers to the central bodies of the KWS, in particular, the Senate and Executive Committee. In 1937 the latter was renamed the Presidential Advisory Board.

[8] From March 1918 until May 1920, Trendelenburg, the acting Secretary General, employed Glum as an unskilled worker (*"Hilfsarbeiter"*) in the then still small General Administration. Glum subsequently served as "Secretary General" from 1920 to 1927.

[9] Telschow (1889–1988) joined the General Administration in early March 1931 as an "administration assistant." On October 18, 1933, he became "Second Executive Director," in 1935 "Chief Executive Director," and on January 10, 1936, "Director" of the KWS before being

The history of the KWS in the Third Reich will be discussed in three periods. The first period, which can be called the "Max Planck/Friedrich Glum era," ends in 1936/37. The second one is circumscribed by the presidency of Carl Bosch and the "Telschow interregnum," the period from the death of Bosch on April 26, 1940, to Albert Vögler's assumption of the office on July 31, 1941, when the KWS remained for more than a year without president. Finally, the third period is marked by the presidency of Vögler and the end of the Nazi regime. This division into three periods corresponds with certain stages and important breaks in Nazi history in general: the years from 1933 to 1936 can be characterized as the years of system establishment or system stabilization. The introduction of the "Four-Year Plan" in September 1936 marks the beginning of a premature war economy during "peacetime." The "Four-Year Plan" was of crucial importance for the KWS and its institutes. Finally, the winter of 1941/42 marks the failure of the German blitzkrieg strategy (Battle of Moscow) and, in consequence, the conversion of the country into an intensified war economy.

BUDGET DEVELOPMENT OF THE KWS AND FINANCIAL POLICY OF THE GENERAL ADMINISTRATION

The only way to appropriately assess the success or failure of the financial policy of the General Administration is to draw comparisons with similar institutions. That is rather complex. The fact that the KWS was so unique, not only within the German Reich but also internationally, makes it difficult to find institutions suitable for comparison. To outline at least the dimensions of the Kaiser Wilhelm Society's fiscal success, the official KWS revenue is compared in Table 2.1 with revenues of the Prussian Academy of Sciences (*Preussische Akademie der Wissenschaften*, PAW) and the Emergency Foundation for German Science (*Notgemeinschaft der deutschen Wissenschaften*, NDW) and its successor the German Research Foundation (*Deutsche Forschungsgemeinschaft*, DFG).

Neither the Prussian Academy of Science nor the DFG is exactly comparable to the KWS. Moreover, there were extraordinary budgets and secret funds that were not included in the General Administration's total budget for the KWS. Nevertheless, the time series of the table gives interesting information. From 1933 to 1936 – that is, during the "Glum era" – the budget of the KWS rose only slowly. The amount of the 1931 budget was

appointed "Secretary General" and replacing Glum on July 15, 1937. From February 26, 1948, until May 18, 1960, Telschow was an "executive member" of the Executive Committee and at the same time "Director General" of the MPS General Administration; from 1960 until 1962 he retained considerable influence as the personal advisor of the new president Adolf Butenandt.

TABLE 2.1. *Revenues of the Kaiser Wilhelm Society, the Prussian Academy of Sciences, and the German Research Foundation from 1924 to 1944*

	Kaiser Wilhelm Society			Prussian Academy of Sciences			Emergency Foundation/ German Research Foundation		
	absolute (a)	index (b)	"state ratio" (c)	absolute (a)	index (b)	"state ratio" (c)	absolute (a)	index (b)	"state ratio" (c)
1924(d)	3289.0	61.9	34.4%	351.7	79.1	97.4%	3480.0	84.3	86.2%
1925	4632.0	87.2	53.2%	456.4	102.6	94.8%	6600.0	159.8	98.5%
1926	6199.9	116.8	51.6%	461.2	103.7	92.4%	6300.0	152.5	98.4%
1927	9962.1	187.6	62.5%	450.5	101.3	94.6%	8160.0	197.6	98.0%
1928	8243.4	155.2	52.5%	515.5	115.9	88.0%	8212.0	198.8	97.4%
1929	8859.3	166.8	59.4%	?	?	?	7272.0	176.1	96.3%
1930	7977.7	150.2	58.6%	595.6	133.9	92.8%	7420.0	179.7	94.3%
1931	5458.5	102.8	66.7%	575.4	129.4	87.1%	5702.0	138.1	89.3%
1932	5127.7	96.6	63.1%	520.4	117.0	88.2%	5010.0	121.3	87.8%
1933	5310.0	100.0	65.5%	444.8	100.0	88.9%	4130.0	100.0	96.9%
1934(e)	5618.8	105.8	60.1%	?	?	?	4666.0	113.0	93.7%
1935	5654.2	106.5	62.8%	?	?	?	4828.0	116.9	90.6%
1936	5726.8	107.8	84.5%	544.2	122.3	82.0%	2041.0	49.4	98.0%
1937	7452.6	140.4	88.4%	504.3	113.4	81.7%	7722.0	187.0	97.1%
1938	9649.1	181.7	70.9%	545.5	122.6	83.5%	8066.0	195.3	99.2%
1939(e)	10328.5	194.5	53.9%	694.6	156.2	82.1%	7239.0	175.3	98.1%

(continued)

23

TABLE 2.1. (*continued*)

	Kaiser Wilhelm Society			Prussian Academy of Sciences			Emergency Foundation/ German Research Foundation		
	absolute (a)	index (b)	"state ratio" (c)	absolute (a)	index (b)	"state ratio" (c)	absolute (a)	index (b)	"state ratio" (c)
1940	10842.1	204.2	54.9%	634.8	142.7	77.7%	6212.0	150.4	96.6%
1941	10394.3	195.7	?	680.0	152.9	77.7%	6053.0	146.8	99.1%
1942	14300.0	269.3	?	562.7	126.5	89.5%	9225.0	223.4	97.6%
1943	14700.6	276.8	63.7%	560.1	125.9	?	14079.0	340.9	99.4%
1944	14482.8	272.7	59.3%	552.0	124.1	?	?	?	?

(*a*) In 1000 Reichsmark (RM).

(*b*) Index 1933 = 100.0.

(*c*) Since state structures in a "classic" sense crumbled after the announcement of the Four-Year Plan, as Nazi organizations seized quasi-government powers, the governmental entities (Reich, Länder, etc.) described here in the "state ratio" (ratio of government expenditures to gross national product) from 1936 to 1944 can only be a coarse indicator and merely illustrate trends.Estimates of the data for 1924 to 1933 presume that during this time-frame, apart from the government subsidies and allowances on the part of the industry, an additional 12,522,000 RM of "miscellaneous receipts" were entered.

(*d*) Data of "miscellaneous receipts" of DFG estimated (average value of preceding and following year).

Source: Wolfram Fischer, Rainer Hohlfeld, and Peter Nötzoldt, "Die Berliner Akademie in Republik und Diktatur," in Wolfram Fischer (ed.), Die Preussische Akademie zu Berlin 1914–1945 (Berlin: Akademie Verlag, 2000), 533; AMPG, I. Abt., Rep.1a, vol. 406, 410, 412, 414, 416, 418.

not exceeded until 1936 – the year the Four-Year Plan was adopted and accelerated armament was introduced. Even before the Four-Year Plan was formally proclaimed in July 1936, Telschow acquired a key science policy position through his appointment as research coordinator within the Raw Materials and Foreign Currency Staff (*Rohstoff- und Devisenstab*), later renamed the Reich Office for Economic Expansion (*Reichsamt für Wirtschaftsausbau*). The table shows how much the KWS benefited from both the accelerated armament and Telschow's additional function as research coordinator: from 1936 to 1938 – that is, within two years – the budget of the KWS almost doubled. It took another leap from 1941 to 1942 when the war took a critical turn and the Reich once again significantly increased armament efforts.

The comparison with the Academy is also interesting: the total budget of the KWS tripled over the period from 1933 to 1942/44, while during the same time, the Academy's had increased by only about a quarter. Most notably, after 1937, the year Telschow officially took control of the General Administration, the budgets of the two institutions diverged. This trend was further enhanced by the critical turn of the war in fall 1941. This was caused by the deployment of resources to those branches of science from which the regime expected results critical for the war effort. Institutionally, these resources were much more concentrated in the KWS than in the Academy. Thus, the KWS was at the receiving end of an opulent flow of funds whereas the cash flow for the Prussian Academy of Sciences turned into a mere trickle.

Regarding the DFG in turn, comparison is especially revealing in two aspects; first, even in 1943 the total budget of the DFG or rather the Reich Research Council (*Reichsforschungsrat*, RFR) did not exceed the total budget of the KWS in spite of the RFR reorganization in early 1943 and its transformation into the crucial communications link as well as financial lubricant for many important war-critical research projects.[10] Second, the KWS total budget from 1933 to 1942 (apart from the "exceptional years"[11] 1936 and 1937) exceeded by 20 to 30 percent the funds that were available to the DFG. During the Weimar Republic, this advantage in budget size of the KWS compared to the DFG/NDW was noticeably lower. In 1926 and 1931 the NDW even registered slightly higher total revenues. Thus, the fact

---

[10] See Sören Flachowsky, *Von der Notgemeinschaft zum Reichsforschungsrat: Wissenschaftspolitik im Kontext von Autarkie, Aufrüstung und Krieg* (Stuttgart: Steiner, 2008).

[11] In mid-1936 the money supplies of the DFG were cut off, since the Reich Ministry for Education and Science (*Reichserziehungsministerium*, REM) wished to replace the willful and maverick president and "Aryan Physics" (*Deutsche Physik*) proponent Johannes Stark. In late December 1936 Rudolf Mentzel, head of the Science Office (*Amtes Wissenschaft*) in REM and one of the most influential science politicians in the Third Reich, was appointed new president of the DFG. From this point onward the DFG budget increased dramatically, similar to the budget of the KWS.

that the KWS succeeded in steadily extending its lead in funding after 1933 meant that the Nazi regime assigned great importance to the research being carried out within the KWS framework.

The development during the war as well as the general question of the validity of budgets after 1940 lies outside the scope of this survey. By 1942 at the latest, the *Reichsmark* no longer constituted the relevant "war currency." Instead, the institutes' "importance for the war" (*Kriegswichtigkeit*) classification, having the highest "priority levels" for research projects and "indispensable positions" (*Uk-Stellungen*) for researchers, was crucial because this was the only way to safeguard the required resources. It is clear, however, that the success story of the Kaiser Wilhelm Society continued well into the war. That was in no small part due to the General Administration and its productive efforts to mobilize these resources – especially under the guidance of Ernst Telschow and Albert Vögler. Vögler, in fact, was the founder and president of the board of the United Steelworks (*Vereinigte Stahlwerke*) in Germany and closely connected to Albert Speer; indeed, he succeeded in persuading Speer, who had been appointed the "economic dictator" in 1942, to give him essentially whatever he wanted.

THE EUPHORIA OF THE "NATIONAL AWAKENING" IN 1933

Black-and-white judgments like "success" or "failure" do not do justice to the political roles played by the Kaiser Wilhelm Society and the General Administration's leading representatives. At first this matter will be investigated for the early stages of the Nazi regime: How did the leading heads of the Society and General Administration position themselves with regard to the "seizure of power" (*Machtergreifung*) and "national awakening" that was set in motion with the establishment of Hitler's cabinet? This question can only be answered in the context of the general development briefly outlined here.

National Socialism was cultivated and raised in the womb of German society. A small clique surrounding Hindenburg did take the last step and help Hitler to come into power. But the handover of power to the National Socialists, who in July 1932 had received 37 percent, and in March 1933, 43 percent of the vote nationwide, was accompanied by a chorus of especially bourgeois and middle-class approval. The reasons for the often-euphoric approval of the transfer of power to the National Socialists were these:

Nationalism wounded by the defeat in World War I, linked to the desire for a revision of the humiliating "Treaty of Versailles," and a "Central European reorganization" under German hegemony

War memories, the glorification of the "Spirit of 1914," and the "front community" (*Frontgemeinschaft*) in World War I that many believed was recovered in the Nazi concept of the "people's community" (*Volksgemeinschaft*)

Antagonism toward the industrial proletariat as well as the social democrat and communist labor movements that was additionally fueled by
the "stab-in-the-back legend" (*Dolchstosslegende*)[12]

Anti-Republicanism, anti-Liberalism, anti-Parliamentarianism, anti-
Semitism

The 1933 myth of national renaissance worked particularly with academics, who had suffered since 1918 from the alleged intellectual and cultural crisis and longed for a unified authoritarian state. When scientific and
nonscientific employees of the KWS expressed often enthusiastic approval
of the "national awakening" in late January 1933, they were thus part of
the bourgeois mainstream. The frenzy of the "national awakening" pulled
them in.

"Everyone," Planck declared on May 23, 1933, during a General Meeting
of the KWS, "who truly loves our dear fatherland and who not only lives for
the moment but also thinks about the future, will immediately understand
that today everybody at all capable of work must stand ready for action,
that today there can only be *one* motto for all Germans, a motto that the
Reich Chancellor (*Reichskanzler*) [Hitler] himself has solemnly announced
in speeches all over Germany: The concentration of all available powers to
participate actively in the construction of our fatherland."[13]

Subsequent rejection of the Weimar democracy and a nostalgically
charged desire for an authoritarian state made people susceptible to the
"*Führer* [leader] myth," as, for instance, the case of Ludwig Prandtl,
director of the Kaiser Wilhelm Institute for Fluid Dynamics (*KWI für
Strömungsforschung*) and the KWS Aerodynamic Testing Station (located
at the University of Göttingen). On one hand, Prandtl supported the cause
of people unpopular with the regime on several occasions and at the highest levels of the regime; on the other hand, he was also fascinated by the
"Führer," describing him as a "man of tremendous mental power" because
Hitler had managed to get rid of "the last remnants of the Versailles Treaty."
True, Hitler had "made a bitter enemy of a million people in Germany,"
Prandtl explained admiringly in late 1938 to an English colleague, "but then
again turned 80 million people into the most loyal and ardent supporters."[14]

---

[12] The "Stab in the Back" legend refers to the claim that German soldiers had never been
defeated during World War I, rather had been "stabbed in the back" by socialists and Jews
on the home front.

[13] MPG-Archiv, Abt. I, Rep. 1A, Nr. 127/8.

[14] Prandtl to the British aerodynamic scientist G. I. Taylor (October 29, 1938) as well as to
Mrs. Taylor (August 5, 1939), reprinted in Cordula Tollmien, "Das Kaiser-Wilhelm-Institut
für Strömungsforschung verbunden mit der Aerodynamischen Versuchsanstalt," in Heinrich
Becker, Hans-Joachim Dahms, and Cornelia Wegeler (eds.), *Die Universität Göttingen unter
dem Nationalsozialismus*, 2. ed. (Munich: Saur, 1998) 684–708, here 696 f.

Such remarks illustrate how far enthusiasm for the "national awakening" and Hitler's "international victories" could go.

The Hitler administration was not only willing to break once and for all with the despised Weimar democracy. It also appeared to reconnect to imperial traditions disrupted in 1918 when it made "military (re-)preparedness" (*Wiederwehrhaftmachung*) and the "reorganization of Central Europe" its major goals. That was of particular importance for the Kaiser Wilhelm Society. Founded in 1911, before World War I, the society was conscious that, as Adolf von Harnack, first president of the KWS, put it in 1909, "military power and science [are] the two strong pillars of German greatness."[15] The name "Kaiser Wilhelm," and the obstinacy with which the Society and all its representatives held on to this name during the Weimar years,[16] were conspicuous signs for how deeply rooted these traditions were in the organization.

During the Weimar years, the Kaiser Wilhelm Society and its institutes preserved this tradition on their own. Beginning in 1926, the two KWIs for Coal Research in Breslau and Mühlheim, and the KWIs for Occupational Physiology, Iron Research, Bast Fiber Research, and Metal Research worked (as expressly sanctioned by Harnack)[17] for the German army (*Reichswehr*) on research projects. In 1929, the KWIs for Silicate Research and Fluid Dynamics joined them. Thus, the majority of the society's potential for research directly related to war was already actively involved in armament research during the years prior to the Nazi seizure of power. In fact, given "the rather modest means [of the Armed Forces] for such research work" and in spite of the KWS's financial straits, this work was done "in large part without payment," as the German Army Ordnance (*Heereswaffenamt*, HWA) noted appreciatively in late 1929.[18]

Thus, in late 1933, Planck could justifiably declare that the General Administration had "even during the period when the Treaty of Versailles imposed restrictions on science ... kept constantly and discreetly in touch with the Reich War Ministry (*Reichswehrministerium*) with

[15] Memorandum from Harnacks to Wilhelm II (November 21, 1909), in Generalverwaltung der Max-Planck-Gesellschaft (ed.), *50 Jahre Kaiser-Wilhelm-Gesellschaft und Max-Planck-Gesellschaft zur Förderung der Wissenschaften 1911/1961. Beiträge und Dokumente* (Göttingen: Max-Planck-Gesellschaft, 1961), 80–94, quotation on 89.

[16] For a comprehensive account, see Bernhard vom Brocke, "Die Kaiser-Wilhelm-Gesellschaft in der Weimarer Republik," in Rudolf Vierhaus and Bernhard vom Brocke (eds.), *Forschung im Spannungsfeld von Politik und Gesellschaft. Geschichte und Struktur der Kaiser-Wilhelm-/Max-Planck-Gesellschaft* (Stuttgart: DVA, 1990), 251–271, especially 210 f., 222–227.

[17] See Harnack to HWA (July 3, 1926), in Federal German Archives (*Bundesarchiv*, BArch), RH 8 I, Nr. 919.

[18] Draft of a letter from the HWA Economics Department to the Armed Forces' (*Reichswehr*) Ministerial Office (November 12, 1929), in BArch, RH 8 I, Nr. 919.

regard to working on subjects of military and political importance at various institutes."[19] Of course, this was something that the General Administration as well as the institute directors had to keep carefully hidden from both the allies and a critical Weimar public. Thus, "the money transferred for this kind of work" had been personally "delivered by a plainclothes officer to the General Administration's official in charge of military affairs."[20]

Against the backdrop of this tradition, it is no surprise that many of the KWS academic staff were only too willing to work with the by now openly conducted rearmament effort and later the war economy. During his presidency, Planck declared repeatedly on behalf of the KWS that "in the interest of the fatherland" the Society wanted to "expand and intensify the long-standing scientific connections to army, navy, and military medicine."[21] However, it was Ernst Telschow who in 1943 summed up these continuities with the laconic formula: "The saying coined in the early days of the Society about military power and science being the two strong pillars of the state has now attained its deepest meaning."[22]

"THE KWS NEGOTIATES WITH ITSELF"

Since its foundation, the KWS had attempted to bind to itself as many important policy makers and influential industry magnates as possible. Among other things this was achieved by voting these people into the senate or rather into the Executive Committee, the inner command circle of the KWS. This meant that right from the start, or indeed even prior to the foundation of the KWS in early 1911, the KWS could essentially "negotiate with itself" in crucial negotiations involving the Society's finances, the foundation or expansion of institutes, and other internal matters.

Two examples illustrate. In mid-December 1909, Adolf von Harnack, who two years later would become the first president of the KWS, met with "representatives of the Prussian Ministry of Education" to campaign for support for his idea to create a large-scale scientific institution independent of university teaching, and above all, to discuss the funding of a future Kaiser Wilhelm Society. Before long, these two "representatives of the

---

[19] Planck to Rust and Frick (December 13, 1933), MPG-Archiv, Abt. I., Rep. 1A, Nr. 188, Bl. 6–8 resp. MPG-Archiv, Abt. I., Rep. 1A, Nr. 189.

[20] Ministry of the Armed Forces (Army and Navy) KWS, appendix to KWS General Director to the Minister of the Armed Forces (December 21, 1933) MPG-Archiv, Abt. I., Rep. 1A, Nr. 188, Bl. 33/35. Also see Telschow's written record of a corresponding declaration by Glum during the KWI director's meeting on May 5, 1933, in the Berlin Palace, MPG-Archiv, Abt. I, Rep. 1A, Nr. 531/1, Bl. 35.

[21] Planck to Blomberg (December 15, 1933), MPG-Archiv, Abt. I, Rep. 1A, Nr. 188, Bl. 17 f.

[22] Telschow's preface to the 1942/43 KWS annual report, dated 5 November 1943, *Die Naturwissenschaften*, 31, No. 45/46 (1943), 524.

Prussian Ministry of Education," Friedrich Schmidt-Ott and Hugo Andres Krüss, became and remained for decades senators and vice-presidents of the KWS. Unsurprisingly, "both parties" came to terms and then attracted financial capital for the yet to-be-founded KWS.[23]

The "*Reich-Länder* (national government-German states) consultations" of June 22, 1922, where a permanently high government subsidy was established for the KWS, is another example of the phenomenon of "the KWS negotiating with itself." The physical chemist Fritz Haber, Harnack, Planck, and Schmidt-Ott attended for the KWS, the last now representing the interests of the KWS as its vice-president. The Prussian Ministry of Education and the Reich Ministry of the Interior (*Reichsinnenministerium*) were represented by the subsequent director of the Kaiser Wilhelm Institute for Comparative Public Law and International Law, Viktor Bruns; Karl Becker, who became the third vice-president of the KWS in 1930; and once again Hugo Krüss.[24] Moreover, Krüss, who was a member of the KWS Executive Council from 1925 onward, one of the three KWS vice-presidents from 1937 to 1945 and director general of the Prussian State Library, acted in the 1922 negotiations as official reporter for the Prussian and Reich governments. The outcome of the negotiations and the things Krüss committed to paper are perfectly clear.

In addition to Krüss and Schmidt-Ott, many names could be listed here. But one more will suffice: Friedrich Ernst Moritz Saemisch, who in 1921 had briefly been Prussian Finance Minister, and from October 1922 until 1938 was president of the Audit Court of the German Reich and the Prussian Superior Audit Office. From 1922 to 1934, he unified in his person the offices of head of the German Audit Court and Reich Savings Commissioner (*Reichssparkommissar*). Since the end of the 1920s, he had been a member without portfolio of the Reich Cabinet. He was more influential than the respective ministers of finance, who often came and went until 1933. He gained even more influence after 1933. Saemisch held his office beyond retirement age until mid-1938.

Saemisch, the "most important and influential president of the Reich Audit Court" in the twentieth century,[25] had hardly taken office when he was

[23] Susanne Pillokat, "Die Öffentlichkeitsarbeit der Kaiser-Wilhelm-Gesellschaft zur Förderung der Wissenschaften (KWG)," MA thesis, University of Mainz (1995), No. 2, Appendix B (Documents): B4 Rs.

[24] Peter-Christian Witt, "Wirtschaftsfinanzierung zwischen Inflation und Deflation: die Kaiser-Wilhelm-Gesellschaft 1918/19 bis 1934/35. Forschung im Spannungsfeld von Politik und Gesellschaft," in Vierhaus and vom Brocke, 579–656, here 594.

[25] See Franz Gilles, "Der Reichsrechnungshof zwischen obrigkeitsstaatlicher Tradition und geforderter Demokratisierung," in Theo Pirker (ed.), *Rechnungshöfe als Gegenstand zeitgeschichtlicher Forschung* (Berlin: Duncker and Humblot, 1987), 19–34, here 24 ff.; Rainer Weinert, "*Die Sauberkeit der Verwaltung im Kriege.*" Der Rechnungshof des Deutschen Reiches 1938–1946 (Opladen: Westdeutscher Verlag, 1993), 57.

appointed senator of the KWS in 1922 and thus rose to the highest echelons of the Society. There was a potential conflict of interest here, since his job was to scrutinize the national budgets and suggest cutbacks in his capacity as Reich Savings Commissioner and president of the Reich Audit Court. Yet, as a member of the leading KWS committees, he made sure instead that public funds kept flowing in abundance to the KWS even during the depression era and that the sometimes autocratic financial conduct of the KWS was not challenged. After his retirement in 1938, Saemisch changed roles again and became the personal legal advisor in financial affairs of the new Secretary General Telschow. In this capacity, Saemisch also made sure that after 1938 neither the audit court nor other state authorities kept too sharp an eye on the General Administration in financial matters.

This strategy of "the KWS negotiating with itself" – when its representatives formally faced state representatives in their negotiations for public funds – was continued after the National Socialist "seizure of power" by electing agents of the Hitler regime and top representatives of the Nazi movement into the Society's Senate and the Executive Committee or Presidential Advisory Board, respectively. But in order to turn the KWS into a key actor in the science political arena, it was not enough merely to cultivate political connections as before. The General Administration had to modify and expand its policy.

ATTRACTED BY NATIONAL SOCIALISM: TRANSFORMED SELF-CONCEPTION AND POLICY OF THE GENERAL ADMINISTRATION

The relations between the KWS and the Nazi Regime, including the armed forces (*Wehrmacht*), were not unilateral but rather an exchange. It was an alliance to their mutual benefit, in which each party sought what the other could offer, what Mitchell Ash has called "mutual resources."[26] Both sides had something to offer, both sides benefited mutually. The regime was aware that modern wars could be waged only with the support of modern science and that the KWS was not easily replaceable in this regard.

After the Hitler regime had been established and committed itself to accelerated armament – that is since mid-1934 or at least since the fall of 1936 – the KWS was handled with kid gloves. Despite the fact that the Third Reich was hardly monarchic, the Society was even permitted to maintain

---

[26] See Mitchell Ash, "Verordnete Umbrüche – Konstruierte Kontinuitäten: Zur Entnazifizierung von Wissenschaftlern und Wissenschaften nach 1945," *Zeitschrift für Geschichtswissenschaft*, 43 (1995) 903–925, here 904; Ash, "Wissenschaft und Politik als Ressourcen für einander," in Rüdiger vom Bruch and Brigitte Kaderas (eds.), *Wissenschaften und Wissenschaftspolitik. Bestandsaufnahmen zu Formationen, Brüchen und Kontinuitäten im Deutschland des 20. Jahrhunderts* (Wiesbaden: Steiner, 2002), 32–51, here 32 f.

the name it had defended successfully time and again against democratic challenges during the Weimar Republic. And it is no coincidence that the "Four-Year Plan Institutes" were organized according to the model of the Kaiser Wilhelm Institutes.[27]

Yet the regime did not automatically make its material resources available to the KWS. First, the General Administration had to mobilize the resources of public and quasi-public institutions in competition with other research institutions. The KWS proved very skillful at this, especially beginning in 1937. An adequate description of the changes in communication structures and networks made by the General Administration requires a fundamental knowledge of the structure of the Nazi system of control as well as the political activity of the KWS.

Making Politics Personal and Informal – Observations on Some Structural Characteristics of the Nazi System of Control

The Nazi regime not only had a polycratic structure and was molded by competition for power and influence. It also had a "personalized control organization" and thus was marked by a strong "personalization of politics." This means that individuals, in most cases old minions of Hitler like Göring, Rust, Darré, Backe, Todt, Rosenberg, Frick, Sauckel, and Ley, or paladins who ascended later like Speer and Brandt, personified ministries and the state as well as quasi-state institutions. Regarding internal structures, the "personalization of politics" meant that on the decision-making level, the usual divisions of labor and nonpersonal "chains of command" were no longer acknowledged. Bureaucratic codes of practice and the usual administrative control mechanisms became less important. Hence, a nonhierarchal and informal structure emerged as well as a high degree of external unpredictability and internal instability. However, the comparative instability of the resulting political structures did not necessarily hinder the efficiency to the regime and the science policy of the Third Reich – indeed, abandoning traditional chains of command sometimes facilitated and enhanced flexibility.

These aspects of the Nazi control system also influenced the KWS and the General Administration from 1933 onward. The policies of the General Administration were much more determined by individuals and personal relationships than was the case prior to the Nazi seizure of power. The fact that Telschow liked to talk about "the General Administration and thus

---

[27] Telschow to Kuhn (January 27, 1938), in MPG-Archiv, Abt. I, Rep. 1A, Nr. 2889/3. Eventually over forty Four-Year Plan Institutes were founded as scientific laboratories devoted to the war effort – independent from the KWS – within the course of the Four-Year Plan for accelerated armament.

myself"[28] is by no means a coincidence but instead mirrors those structural changes. The result of this "personalization of politics" was that since 1933 the classical state – that is, a strictly formalized "bureaucracy" with clear administrative practices and well-practiced administrative techniques – became less important and was replaced by a stronger "informalization" of politics. The long-standing and well-cultivated "channels" prevailing until 1933 now lost their meaning.

The General Administration now focused even more on networking – that is, connecting and cultivating old and new networks – than before 1933. The actors had to strive constantly to keep the positions they had acquired and possibly expand them. They could exploit new opportunities, which sometimes appeared out of the blue, for their own institution, in this case the KWS. The key role that informal communication was already playing during the first years of Nazi rule and the fact that the players involved were capable of pushing the right buttons can be illustrated by a quotation. Planck's laudatory speech for Vögler, who received the Harnack medal in 1936, acknowledged Vögler's merits in building relationships and networking in the interest of the KWS: "what he did backstage, the many unrecorded gatherings and conferences, that went unmentioned in the file memos." On "any such occasion," Vögler had smoothed "many awkward questions ... with his captivating eloquence," Planck continued, and paved the way for the interests of the KWS.[29]

For the Kaiser Wilhelm Society and its General Administration the new policy forms introduced step-by-step beginning in 1933 did not cause a rupture with the past. The institutes and administration of the KWS had already become experts at "informalized policy forms" because the KWS was a quasi-private institution, and even before 1933 it had "lived" with unsecured financial resources that had to be renegotiated time and again. On the other hand, new formal communication structures were developed during the Nazi era, and these were admittedly less permanent and altogether much more flexible. Perhaps even more important than the "quantitative" informalization of politics were the qualitative changes in both the informal and newly constructed formal relations. Communication rules, communication style, and the requirements for a successful image policy and public relations all changed. Hence, a new type of science manager was required. This can be outlined in more detail by scrutinizing (1) the political self-image of the two protagonists of the General Administration; (2) the different personnel networks the two built; (3) *how* they built those networks; and (4) the different forms of public relations, that is, image policy, that each practiced in the name of the Kaiser Wilhelm Society.

[28] Telschow to Jordens (December 14, 1953), MPG-Archiv, Abt. I, Rep. 1A, Nr. 2747.
[29] See Kohl, *Präsidenten*, 198.

Friedrich Glum – Biographical Facets

In contrast to Ernst Telschow, Friedrich Glum, a physician's son, had an educated middle-class background. Glum attended a classical secondary school and studied constitutional and administrative law. The subjects of his dissertation and other academic writing show that Glum had always been interested in politics on the grand scale: "Organization of the Megalopolis. The Constitutions of Paris, London, New York, Vienna, and Berlin" (1920) and his *Habilitation* (like a second Ph.D.) treatise, "Self-Administration of the Economy" (1925), followed among others by a comparative study, "The German and French Economy Council" (1929). Unlike his adversary and successor Telschow, Glum was an intellectual who positioned himself in the national conservative faction with political ambitions that went far beyond the bounds of the KWS. A rough sketch of Glum's political positions illuminates the structures of the networks he built and explains why the National Socialist disliked him and forced him to resign.

In his study "Secret Germany" (*Das geheime Deutschland*) published in 1930, he described "with amazed admiration ... the power of the fascist spirit. ... [Italian] fascism has given the nation ... new moral impulses." According to Glum, "the spiritual content of the fascist idea" was the opposite of the "material spirit," of the "bickering" and the "fights between political cliques in parliamentarianism." Though Glum opposed "party dictatorship," he emphasized: "If a Mussolini would appear here [in Germany] today, like him a statesman who recognized the current hardships, and established a plebiscitary dictatorship, we'd be certainly well advised to follow him. But ... I fear, the German people would not follow him."[30]

Glum tried to make up for the tactical error of having taken a position against a "party dictatorship" in a long article in the (haute) bourgeois newspaper *Berliner Börsenzeitung* on October 4, 1933. There he expressed excitement "that after Luther and the Wars of Liberation we are [at long last] experiencing a national revolution again. But the greatest thing about the national revolution of our days is that it tries to embrace and fulfill all the political, social and cultural desires of our people." This was followed

---

[30] Friedrich Glum, *Das geheime Deutschland* (Gräfenhainichen: Stilke, 1930), quotations on 9, 11 f., 70. For a detailed discussion, see Bernd Weisbrod, "Das 'Geheime Deutschland' und das 'Geistige Bad Harzburg': Friedrich Glum und das Dilemma des demokratischen Konservativismus am Ende der Weimarer Republik," in Christan Jansen, Lutz Niethammer, and Bernd Weisbrod (eds.), *Von der Aufgabe der Freiheit. Politische Verantwortung und bürgerliche Gesellschaft im 19. und 20. Jahrhundert. Festschrift für Hans Mommsen* (Berlin: Akademie Verlag, 1995), 285–308, especially 290 ff. On the positive reception of fascism in greater parts of the German bourgeoisie during the second half of the 1920s, where Glum's remarks should also be situated, see Wolfgang Schieder, "Das italienische Experiment. Der Faschismus als Vorbild in der Weimarer Republik," *Historische Zeitschrift*, 262 (1996), 73–125, especially 84 ff.

by a hymn in praise of Hitler: "Even as a former German nationalist one has to admit the brilliance with which he destroyed all the trade unions and parties, including his own allies, and erected the totalitarian state." "Hitler's world historical importance consists in having liberated Germany and thus doubtlessly Europe as well from the Asian bolshevism, which is alien to us." Then he concluded: "The present importance [of National Socialism] is how it breaks through the hostile world of un-German spirit to the awakening of the nation." Yet, in this article Glum also adopted a tone that had to alienate confirmed Nazis, when, for instance, he wrote in a patriarchal, bourgeois style in the *Börsen-Zeitung* that "there are also many people in the SA, SS and NSBO, who have not joined the movement out of idealism, but out of envy and anger."

Glum's "Old Boy" Network

Glum's political positioning during the Weimar years is also an indication of what kind of networking he would pursue in the same era. Glum, who as director general had established the General Administration in the first place, built his networks on basis of an haute bourgeois, National Liberal, or rather right-wing Conservative system of notables (the structure of which had hardly changed since the 1918/19 Revolution). A brief introduction of three of the numerous clubs and associations used by Glum as nodes for his network will illuminate the concrete meaning of this system.

A politically interesting association was the "Freiherr vom Stein League" (Freiherr vom Stein-Bund) Glum tried to establish in May 1932.[31] He gave the keynote address at the founding meeting of the Stein League, also known as the Cappenberger meeting on May 19 and 20, 1932, which was attended by high-ranking tycoons like Vögler, Springorum, and Blohm but also included Hans Rothfels and the editor of the Freiherr von Stein papers, Erich Botzenhart, among others. It was his intention, Glum elaborated, to use the Stein League to pave the way for a "spiritual Bad Harzburg." He was thus referring to the disintegration of the ample anti-Republican alliance of National Liberals, Conservatives, *Stahlhelm* (Steel Helmet, League of Frontline Soldiers), and NSDAP [*Nationalsozialistische Deutsche Arbeiterpartei* (National Socialist German Workers' Party)], which had been sealed during a big rally in this small town in the Harz mountains on October 11, 1931, and which had made the Hitler movement once and for all politically acceptable. Obviously, Glum thought that this right-wing alliance had only temporarily fallen apart. At any rate, in May 1932, in front of the influential audience that the members of the Freiherr vom Stein league

---

[31] Glum wanted to take advantage of a Freiherr vom Stein renaissance during the late Weimar years in the wake of the centenary of the (conservative) Prussian reformer's death in 1931.

represented, Glum expressed his hopes that possibly the right "was on the point of experiencing the ultimate victory under the banner of National Socialism."[32]

One of the many clubs Glum attended was the "German Men's Club" (*Deutsche Herrenklub*) founded in November 1924, which, as *Herrenklub*, had been the main source of support of Franz von Papen's presidential cabinet in 1932.[33] During the early 1930s, Glum's clubs also included the famous "National Club" (*Nationale Klub*)[34] as well as the "Club of Berlin" (*Club von Berlin*), founded in 1864. The latter club included among its members celebrities of late nineteenth- and early twentieth-century Prussia like Borsig, Siemens, Heinrich Mendelssohn, Bleichröder, Rathenau, Stresemann, Gropius, and Richard Strauss. The significance of this club cannot be exaggerated as a communication node for the business elite not only in Berlin but also in the whole German Reich.[35] The club co-opted new members based on the recommendation of two full members. Anyone, like Glum, who was a member of this club found himself at the core of German business elites and enjoyed great possibilities for making connections and forming alliances.

At the same time, the club established a network with important and high-ranking policy makers: apart from the "full" membership the club

---

[32] "*unter der Flagge des Nationalsozialismus unmittelbar vor dem Endsieg stehe*," in Weisbrod, 302.

[33] The "German Men's Club" was considerably influenced by the "Conservative Revolution" and served as a home to the old elites. Hindenburg acted as honorary chairman of the club. Glum definitely joined the "Mens' Club" in the early 1930s; his two deputies in the General Administration, Adolf Morsbach and Max Lucas v. Cranach, were members even before that. The Berlin club's register of 400 members listed at least fifty people who were also linked to the KWS as "Supporting Members."

[34] The "National Club" made it its main business to mediate between the conservative *haute bourgeoisie* and the Hitler movement. Glum joined in the late summer of 1932. From 1930 until 1936 Carl Eduard Herzog von Sachsen-Coburg-Gotha was chairman. This Saxon duke, a member of the inner executive circle of the KWS, also chaired the "Society for the Study of Fascism" (*Gesellschaft zum Studium des Faschismus*), which sympathized with the Mussolini regime. Albert Vögler, who subsequently became president of the KWS, sat on the advisory board of the "National Club."

[35] According to a collective-biographical analysis of the German business elites' network connections from the 1920s to the 1950s, the Club was the most influential node in the branching network of relations of German magnates and bankers from the mid-1920s until the late 1930s (at least) – outdoing by far the Reich Association of German Industry (*Reichsverband der Deutschen Industrie*), the Central Association of German Banks and the Banking Trade (*Centralverband des Deutschen Bank- und Bankiersgewerbes*), and other haute bourgeois communication links. See Martin Fiedler and Bernhard Lorentz, "Kontinuitäten in den Netzwerkbeziehungen der deutschen Wirtschaftselite zwischen Weltwirtschaftskrise und 1950. Eine quantitative und qualitative Analyse," in Volker R. Berghahn, Stefan Unger, and Dieter Ziegler (eds.), *Die deutsche Wirtschaftselite im 20. Jahrhundert. Kontinuität und Modernität* (Essen: Klartext-Verlag, 2003), 51–74, here 65, table 6.

also reserved an associate membership for "active members of the German Armed Forces or Navy [as well as] higher ranking officials of the Reich, governmental and local authorities." The political position of the Club of Berlin became apparent when it merged with the German Men's Club in 1937. Glum was a member of the Club of Berlin until he formally resigned from the KWS office in late 1937. Thus, the director general of the Kaiser Wilhelm Society resorted to an "old boy" network that ranged from National Liberals to the right-wing Conservative and German *völkisch* factions.

Glum hardly altered his attitude and politics after 1933. He kept on paying homage to the "corporative" concepts of Italian fascism. Thus, he gave a lecture on the "corporative construction in Italy" on March 17, 1934, in Danzig (Gdánsk).[36] In 1936, he had an audience of considerable length with Mussolini. It is also symptomatic that he organized a series of public events in the Harnack House, where his like-minded friends from the ranks of the "Conservative Revolution" gave the main lectures – for example, Hans Grimm (who coined the fatal slogan "a people without space" and who was a friend of Glum) and Carl Schmitt. None of these activities were well advised. The Italian fascism Glum raved about had become discredited with the Nazi regime in late 1933 (this changed in 1936/37). In turn, Spranger, Grimm, Schmitt, and others from the ranks of the "Conservative Revolution" were unable to provide Glum access to the movers and shakers of the Nazi regime, just as the Mens Club and other associations of the old elites failed to do so. The tight-knit network that he had established became rapidly devaluated with the "seizure of power" and under the new circumstances fell apart.

Vögler had already hinted at an early stage that the communication forms cultivated by Glum were no longer "opportune." The subsequent president of the Kaiser Wilhelm Society admonished that "the methods cultivated so far are no longer suited for our days and he [Vögler] could under no circumstances advocate them. Otherwise he feared great troubles for the Kaiser Wilhelm Society."[37] Glum was incapable of modifying the communication form in the way Vögler demanded. The new secretary general, Ernst Telschow, finally accomplished the change of course advocated by Vögler.

Ernst Telschow – More Up-to-Date

Telschow was different from Glum in many respects. His profession was not – at least not yet – law, but chemistry. In 1912, he was one of Otto Hahn's first two doctoral students and later for a short time was assistant

---

[36] See MPG-Archiv, Abt. I, Rep. 1A, Nr. 2822.
[37] Memo by Telschow (August 10, 1933), MPG-Archiv, Abt. I, Rep. 1A, Nr. 1168.

at the Chemistry Institute of the University of Berlin. From 1917 until December 1918, Lieutenant Telschow worked in the Ministry of War as Fritz Haber's liaison officer for industry, a position that allowed him to gain firsthand experience in science management and war science.

From the end of World War I until he joined the General Administration of the Kaiser Wilhelm Society in early 1931, Telschow managed his father's confectionery shop, which he expanded into one of Berlin's largest bakeries with many branches. As a confectioner's son, Telschow did not have the same educated middle-class background that Glum enjoyed. Telschow came from the lower middle class, and this obviously made it easier for him to gain access to leading Nazi officers, who often also came from the lower middle class or had even been socially marginal, until, much like Telschow, they had climbed the social ladder. It was easy for Telschow to assume the upright military posture called for during Nazi events but also to adopt the jovial tone characteristic of leading Nazis, which one employed to demonstrate that one "belonged."

Moreover, Telschow had no political ambitions comparable to those of Glum: it was not a coincidence that he had never exposed himself in public the way his predecessor did. Instead, he secretly joined the NSDAP on the May 1, 1933,[38] that is, immediately before the party temporarily stopped accepting new members due to the rush of men opportunistically trying to further their careers. In the subsequent period, he was able to present himself to Nazi officials as a party member, as a like-minded friend and a *par inter pares* – another significant difference from Glum. He was exactly the kind of person – not an ideological zealot like Gottfried Feder, Alfred Rosenberg, or Julius Streicher – that the Nazi regime needed to stabilize the power it had achieved since 1934 and to dare to reach for world domination.

First, Telschow opened new resources for the KWS by making formal political connections. Beginning in May 1935, he represented the KWS in the "Association of German Engineers" (Verband Deutscher Ingenieure, VDI). Thus, he succeeded in making early contact with the VDI president Fritz Todt, who subsequently became minister for Armament and Ammunition.[39] Even more important, three months before the Four-Year Plan was adopted and almost a year before Telschow was officially appointed KWS secretary general, Telschow assumed the office of research coordinator within the eminently important "Raw Materials and Foreign Exchange Staff" (*Rohstoff- und Devisenstab*) at the request of I.G. Farben and with the recommendation of KWI director Richard Kuhn.[40] Research coordinator was a key science policy position, in particular for the Kaiser Wilhelm Society, since the Raw

---

[38] Membership number 2,638,239. Telschow's "Parteistatistische Erhebung 1939" (July 3, 1939), BArch, Ahnenerbe, B 304.

[39] See Telschow to Todt (May 9, 1935), MPG-Archiv, Abt. I, Rep. 1A, Nr. 1014.

[40] See the correspondence in MPG-Archiv, Abt. II, Rep. 1A, Personalakte Telschow, Nr. 1.

Materials and Foreign Exchange Staff (subsequently called the *Reichsamt für Wirtschaftsausbau*) was crucial in acquiring research assignments and research funds. Taking this into account, it is no coincidence that the budget of the KWS in general soared after 1936/37 (see Table 2.1).

With his appointment as research coordinator, Telschow became a key figure within the General Administration and was made secretary general in July 1937. More and important functions followed, including, immediately after the start of war, the position of "Reich Defense Advisor and Military Intelligence Agent for all Kaiser Wilhelm Institutes" (*Reichsverteidigungsreferent und Abwehrbeauftragter für sämtliche Kaiser-Wilhelm-Institute*).[41] This post allowed Telschow to secure and expand the personnel and financial resources of the KWS even during the war and simultaneously required good connections to the SD (SS Security Service) and Gestapo.

Telschow took over the reins of the KWS under Carl Bosch, who in 1937 had replaced Max Planck as president of the Society but proved to be a weak president. Telschow remained the key player, not only under Bosch and during the ensuing "interregnum Telschow" 1940/41 but also during the administration of the second "industry president" Albert Vögler; Vögler held office after late July 1941 and – in spite of his many absences – was a strong president who reserved the right to make the ultimate decision in all crucial matters himself.[42]

Networks and Informal Connections: The Secret of Success of the General Administration under Telschow

The initially rather unimpressive Telschow systematically sought contact with National Socialist bigwigs. He was fully aware that after 1939 crucial connections were made at different communication points than before the "seizure of power." One very important new hot spot for the Kaiser Wilhelm Society was the "Aeronautics Club of Germany" (*Aero-Club von Deutschland*).

---

[41] See the Meeting of the KWS Advisory Board, (December 12, 1939), in MPG-Archiv, Abt. II, Rep. 1A, Personalakte Telschow, Nr. 1.

[42] See Kohl, *Präsidenten*, as well as Manfred Rasch, "Über Albert Vögler und sein Verhältnis zur Politik," *Mitteilungsblatt des Instituts für soziale Bewegungen*, 28 (2003), 127–156. Vögler had already been involved in right-wing conservative and semi-fascist activities during the 1920s; he developed closer contacts to the Hitler movement during the summer of 1931 at the latest. On November 30, 1932 – that is, a full three weeks *after* the November elections, in which the NSDAP lost a considerable number of votes– Vögler gave a thinly veiled endorsement of the Nazi movement on the main meeting of the "Vereins deutscher Eisenhüttenleute," an organization of large industrial firms, thus putting the crisis-ridden NSDAP back on the map for important industry circles.

The Aeronautics Club was founded in 1907. During the first years following the "seizure of power," Göring turned this club into an affiliated lobbyist
association of German aviation, where a mixture of new elite and power-
conscious members of the old elite socialized. According to its statutes, the
aim of the Aeronautics Club was "the advancement and cultivation of aviator
camaraderie in the National Socialist sense." It was, however, not possible
to simply join the Aeronautics Club. In fact, Hermann Göring himself in his
capacity as Reich Minister of Aviation invited "personalities who did great
services to aviation" to join the club.[43] Thus, being co-opted into the club was
a great political honor. As a result, the membership list reads like a who's who
of the political *crème de la crème* of those days: it included all ministers and
the most influential undersecretaries, the leading figures of the armed forces,
all high-ranking officers of the air force, about sixty prominent members of
the diplomatic corps, and about two thousand notables. Among the last group
were the top officials of almost all important National Socialist organizations,
leading representatives of the technical universities and aviation research
institutions, and powerful tycoons (including several senators of the Kaiser
Wilhelm Society, for instance, Bosch, Vögler, Krupp, Röchling, Siemens, Flick,
and Strauss). As the only representative of the KWS General Administration,
Telschow had been a member of this club since early April 1936.[44]

The Aeronautics Club possessed a splendidly equipped "House of the
Aviator" (*Haus der Flieger*) in the former Prussian *Landtag* (provincial
assembly) in the Prinz-Albrecht-Strasse (today the Berlin House of Deputies).
In 1936/37, Göring had it converted to serve his purposes. As a "place of
peace and recreation" where club members should meet "kindred spirits and
friends,"[45] the huge "House of Aviator" was equipped with a proper library,
a reading room, a state dining hall, where several hundred guests could be
seated, a bar, a tavern, a billiard room, a ping-pong room, a gym and a bath-
house, a dining room for ladies, plus several separate "boudoirs" where
members could talk in private.[46] Telschow did not neglect the opportunity
offered here to establish relations with influential personalities of the Nazi
regime; fortunately for him, the former Berlin Palace (*Berliner Stadtschloss*),
where the General Administration was housed, was in walking distance of
the Prinz-Albrecht-Strasse.

[43] Statute of the *Aero-Klub* (28 November 1935), MPG-Archiv, Abt. I, Rep. 1A, Bd. 910/1.
[44] See the membership list of the *Aero-Klubs von Deutschland* (1938), MPG-Archiv, Nr. 910/2.
[45] See the circular to all members (March 18, 1938), MPG-Archiv, Nr. 910/2.
[46] The services the *Aero-Klub* provided to its members were not confined to "club life" in the Prinz-Albrecht-Str. 5. Among other things, this club also offered its members study trips – for example, for four weeks to the United States, from April 10 to May 4, 1937, on the ocean steamer *Bremen* to New York, Chicago, Niagara Falls, and other cities. MPG-Archiv, Abt. I, Rep. 1A, Nr. 910/1, Bl. 18.

Since January 1937, Telschow had belonged to the Lilienthal Society, a similar communication node yet with a distinctly more scientific character. In 1941 he was even elected into the senate of this society.[47] But Telschow also cast his net internationally. Thus, on September 12, 1941, he was one of the founding members of the "German-Slovakian Association for a New Europe" (*Deutsch-slowakischen Vereinigung [für ein neues Europa]*), established by *SS-Obergruppenführer* Werner Lorenz for the "proclamation of the German Slovakian friendship"; this organization was presided over by Wilhelm Voss, director general of the *Reichswerke für Waffen- und Maschinenbau* "Hermann Göring" (Reich Factory for the Construction of Weapons and Machines) and later chairman of the board of directors of the *Skoda* works in Pilsen.[48]

Telschow was also a member of associations that directly served the goals of ideological indoctrination. For instance, from 1938 until 1945 he was a member of the "Academy for the Scientific Studies and Cultivation of Germanization." This so-called academy had been founded in 1934 by Karl Haushofer on behalf of Rudolf Hess[49] and became an important forum for National Socialist "Germanization" propaganda. The speakers who took the floor there included the NS *Gauleiter* (heads of Nazi districts) Jakob Sprenger, Fritz Sauckel (later the "General Plenipotentiary for the Employment of Labor" [*Generalbevollmächtigter für den Arbeitseinsatz*]), Hubert Klausner, Gustav Adolf Scheel (at that time chairman of the Reich Student Works [*Reichsstudentenführer*]), and Arthur Greiser (both *Gauleiter* and *Reichsstatthalter* [governor] of the so-called *Reichsgau Wartheland*), Roland Freisler, Leonardo Conti, and other prominent figures of those days. The Kaiser Wilhelm Society, for its part, was also able to contribute lecturers for scientific and ideological subjects: thus, for example, Otmar Freiherr von Verschuer gave a lecture titled "Population and Racial Issues in Europe" (*Bevölkerungs- und Rassenfragen in Europa*) in the Germanization Academy in late 1943.[50]

"Close Contact" with Leading Officials of the Regime

Beyond associations and semiofficial events, Telschow was keen on having close contacts to National Socialist bigwigs like the East Prussian *Gauleiter*

---

[47] See MPG-Archiv, Abt. I, Rep. 1A, Nr. 912 to 914.

[48] See MPG-Archiv, Abt. I, Rep. 1A, Nr. 916.

[49] Albert Vögler was a member of the "Small Council" (*Kleine Rat*) that chaired this academy. It was mainly funded by the "German Foundation" (*Deutsche Stiftung*); this foundation in turn had been created in 1920 to fund and coordinate in secret all "Germanization organizations" in the areas the German Reich had lost with the Versailles Treaty. See Reinhard Giersch, "Deutsche Stiftung (DStg), 1920–1940," in *Lexikon zur Parteiengeschichte. Die bürgerliche und kleinbürgerlichen Parteien und Verbände in Deutschland*, vol. II (Leipzig: Pahl-Rugenstein, 1984), 359–366.

[50] MPG-Archiv, Abt. I, Rep. 1A, Nr. 1008.

and later *Reichskommissar* in Ukraine Erich Koch,[51] the Mecklenburg *Gauleiter* Friedrich Hildebrandt,[52] and the Sudeten German *Gauleiter* and *Reichsstatthalter* Konrad Henlein.[53] At the turn of the year 1938/39, Telschow was even granted the honor of an audience with the *Reichsführer SS* and chief of German Police Heinrich Himmler.[54] The director of the Kaiser Wilhelm Society's institute for cultural studies in Rome, which was founded in early 1938 (and was more an institution for German cultural propaganda than for scholarly research), was Werner Hoppenstedt; a proud member of the National Socialist "old guard" and participant in the 1923 Munich Beer Hall Putsch,[55] Hoppenstedt was an important door-opener for Telschow – for example, with Julius Streicher.[56]

Telschow's relationship to Herbert Backe, the strong man in the agricultural sector of the Third Reich, was illustrative of the KWS Secretary General's profound adaptability. During the visit of then undersecretary Backe, Telschow noted in a memo dated August 16, 1933, that "In my view Backe is a representative of the extreme side of National Socialism."[57] This attitude underwent a drastic shift over the following years. In mid-1944, the relationship with Backe, by now Minister of Agriculture, had become so cordial that Telschow invited him to a private "supper at its simplest with my wife."[58] Telschow's association with Backe was not the only one that changed. Other originally quite reserved connections between Telschow and

[51] See press release (January 31, 1938), as well as Telschow to Koch (August 5, 1940), MPG-Archiv, Abt. I, Rep. 1A, Nr. 840/6 resp. Nr. 2858/7.

[52] See the 1940 correspondence, MPG-Archiv, Abt. I, Rep. 1A, Nr. 2858/4.

[53] In February 1939, more than a quarter of a year after the invasion of the Sudetenland by German troops, Telschow contacted NS-Gauleiter Konrad Henlein, who was appointed governor of the *Reichsgau* Sudeten a few weeks later, MPG-Archiv, Abt. I, Rep. 1A, Nr. 2200/1, Bl. 4–4a.

[54] See Telschow to Himmler (April 27, 1939), MPG-Archiv, Abt. I, Rep. 1A, Nr. 2034, Bl. 280a.

[55] On October 1, 1933, Hoppenstedt was appointed assistant director of the KWS affiliated "Bibliotheca Hertziana" in Rome. In February 1938 he was made director of the KWI for Cultural Science, the organization that emerged from the *Bibliotheca Hertziana*. On July 14, 1939, the "Führer" bestowed the title "professor" on the academically nondescript Hoppenstedt. After the war Hoppenstedt and Telschow maintained their amicable relations. For biographical data see MPG-Archiv, Abt. II, Rep. 1A, Personalia Hoppenstedt.

[56] Hoppenstedt to Telschow (June 7, 1938), MPG-Archiv, Abt. I, Rep. 1A, Nr. 1710.

[57] MPG-Archiv, Abt. I, Rep. 1A, Nr. 2603/4, Bl. 176.

[58] Telschow to Backe (*zu Hd. des persönlichen Adjutanten*) (June 5, 1944), MPG-Archiv, Abt. I, Rep. 1A, Nr. 894/2. Backe had also been "First Vice-president" of the KWS since July 1941. This was not the first time that small favors advanced amicable relations between the two men. For example, see Telschow to Backe (June 13, 1940), MPG-Archiv, Abt. I, Rep. 1A, Nr. 2833/1. On the relationship between Telschow and Backe, see Susanne Heim, *Kalorien, Kautschuk, Karrieren. Pflanzenzüchtung und landwirtschaftliche Forschung in Kaiser-Wilhelm-Instituten 1933–1945* (Göttingen: Wallstein, 2003).

leading figures in the Nazi regime often blossomed into close, sometimes confidential relationships, almost friendships.

Yet, unlike the close contacts the General Administration maintained with most of the ministries and institutions in the Hitler regime, connections to Goebbels's Ministry for Popular Enlightenment and Propaganda remained rather slim until 1940/41. In 1941, a serious plan evolved for founding a Kaiser Wilhelm Institute for Film Research with the expressively stated objective of establishing closer contacts with the Goebbels's ministry.[59] Though this plan was not realized because of the war, Telschow nevertheless managed to get a direct line to Goebbels's ministry. Beginning in the summer of 1944, Telschow received invitations on a regular basis to "confidential" lectures and discussions in the ministry of propaganda.[60]

Telschow recommended that others within the Kaiser Wilhelm Society follow his example. The directors of the Kaiser Wilhelm Institutes in particular were told not to be shy about making contact with high-ranking officials of the Nazi movement.[61] In time, this recommendation turned into "the strict order for the directors of the KWI constantly to maintain good and close relations with the local Party headquarters."[62]

On the Change of the General Administration's Public Relations and Image Policy after 1937

A series of substantial changes in public relations and image policy demonstrate how the politics of the KWS General Administration had changed since 1937. One example will be examined here. Before 1938, the KWS had not attached great importance to effective promotion and cultivation of its image. An annual report was written in factual terms and published in the journal *Die Naturwissenschaften* (The Natural Sciences). Individual Kaiser Wilhelm Institutes also issued similarly modest institute reports. But in 1938/39, the Kaiser Wilhelm Society abandoned this subdued and lofty tone. Thereafter, the General Administration published in the name of the KWS a substantial yearbook printed on the finest paper; it was not sold by bookstores but rather sent to specific patrons (as well as being distributed internally). Eight top high-ranking representatives of the Nazi regime – including Hitler, Göring, and Himmler – received a special deluxe edition bound in leather. Josef Goebbels and other Reich ministers, influential state

---

[59] See a four-page memo Forstmann wrote for Telschow on a meeting the two of them had with Dr. J. Grassmann, the head of department for film technology in the *Reichsfilmkammer* (June 28, 1940), MPG-Archiv, Abt. I, Rep. 1A, Nr. 969/4, Bl. 70–73.

[60] These lasted until March 1945. See MPG-Archiv, Abt. I, Rep. 1A, Nr. 886.

[61] For example, see the memo by Telschow (April 22, 1940) in MPG-Archiv, Abt. I, Rep. 1A, Nr. 2071/2.

[62] Note signed by Schattenfroh (December 5, 1944), MPG-Archiv, Abt. I, Rep. 1A, Nr. 2613/5.

secretaries, the commanders in chief of the *armed forces*, Gustav Gründgens, and fifty other recipients had to make do with cloth binding. Nevertheless, everybody showed polite appreciation for the beautiful present.[63] These individual gifts demonstrate how well the KWS General Administration under Telschow understood the necessity of paying homage to the Nazi personality cult if the organization was to tap the resources successfully.

FROM THE "MORALS OF EFFICIENCY" TO THE "FAUSTIAN PACT" WITH NATIONAL SOCIALISM

Beginning in 1937, and to some extent even earlier, the KWS General Administration demonstrated a willing and active affirmation of National Socialism. This adaptation process was initially carried by a "moral of efficiency" that pragmatically aimed to facilitate the best work and research conditions. Most members of the KWS (except for the few Liberal Democratic outsiders like Einstein, who emigrated) voluntarily and actively committed themselves to the regime despite partial conflicts with National Socialism.[64] Over the years, this commitment turned into a golden chain that could not be easily broken. However, the metaphor of "golden chain" is problematic because it obscures the readiness of the KWS to commitment itself. Despite friction with the National Socialist movement, the already mentioned strong identification of the actors with the "national awakening" and the "international successes" of the Hitler dictatorship as well as the traditional close ties of the KWS to the armed forces (Reichswehr, respectively Wehrmacht) had already politicized pragmatism and the "moral of efficiency."

But that was not enough. What might have been practically motivated in the beginning, and moreover was an expression of a widespread national

---

[63] See MPG-Archiv, Abt. I, Rep. 1A, Nr. 796–802. Even during the second half of the war, when many newspapers had to cease their publication due to the paper shortage, the KWS yearbook remained privileged. Even for the volume 1943/44 Telschow was able to "organize" the necessary amount of precious paper. See Telschow to the head of the Reichsdruckerei Berlin (January 21, 1944), as well as the General Administration of the KWS (Bollmann) to the Offizin Haag – Drugulin Leipzig, (November 23, 1944), MPG-Archiv, Abt. I, Rep. 1A, Nr. 802/1 and Nr. 802/3.

[64] The fundamental conflicts that developed between members of the SA and the "National Socialist Factory Organization" (*Nationalsozialistischen Betriebsorganisation*) faded away after the decapitation of the SA in 1934. The hard-line anti-Semitic ideology (that allowed no deviation) and the pressure to enforce rigorously the regime's anti-Semitic restrictions produced a contradictory response from the General Administration. The Haber commemoration in 1935 or the rather tepid protests against the planned dismissal of further institute directors were not protests against the anti-Semitic ideology in general; in the case of Fritz Haber, Planck and other leading scientists were indignant at the shabby treatment of an outstanding scientist who had served his country well. For a detailed discussion of this, see Hachtmann, *Wissenschaftsmanagement*.

way of thinking, finally led to a psychological self-mobilization. Pragmatism already implies self-mobilization because of the willingness to accept the guidelines of the state or rather state-associated institutions. In the long run, self-mobilization demonstrates the psychological effects of socialization; what initially had been pragmatic tactical cunning or acquiescence to a softer or stronger external pressure was internalized and gradually became normal behavior. The barrage of Nazi propaganda, which was inescapable in everyday life, equally formed or deformed minds and made committed Nazis out of the "half[-hearted]" ones.

Apart from Telschow, the individuals who until the last year of the war demanded unconditional affirmation of the goals and politics of the Nazi regime came from the ranks of the Kaiser Wilhelm Society – above all, Albert Vögler who was elected president in mid-1941. Following his assumption of office, the new KWS president issued this "instruction": "You have to be steeped in the belief, be downright obsessed with it, that the results of your research today are helping to guarantee tomorrow's victory."[65] The clear-cut priority, which the "national interests" of Germany, embodied by the Nazi regime, still possessed during the last year of war for Vögler in particular, was demonstrated in the KWS directors' meeting on November 9, 1943. There the president urged the heads of the institutes to "take ruthless action against defeatist attitudes and not to shrink from making a report in particularly blatant cases ... the only vital thing [is] the German victory." Nobody contradicted him.[66]

CONCLUSION

The Kaiser Wilhelm Society did not differ essentially from the entire German bourgeoisie in its willingness to become involved in the "national awakening" promised by the National Socialists in 1933. However, the involvement of the KWS had greater consequences because the majority of the Kaiser Wilhelm Institutes played a crucial role in the defense economy and scientific research for the war effort. The General Administration of the KWS in particular pursued a close relationship between the Society and the new regime. However, Glum, who since the late 1920s had developed a profound sympathy for Italian fascism and the "Conservative Revolution," could only accomplish this in a limited way. It was the more adaptive Telschow who succeeded in securing the new networks necessary for expanding resources and autonomy and linking the General Administration for the "benefit" of the whole Society in the closest possible way to the Nazi regime.

[65] From the annual report of the KWS 1941/42, *Die Naturwissenschaften* (1942), 609.
[66] Minutes of the KWS directors' meeting (November 9, 1943), MPG-Archiv, Abt. I, Rep. 44, Nr. 104 and BArch, R 26 III, Nr. 693.

This self-mobilization for the National Socialist dictatorship does not change the fact that Glum and even more so Telschow were very accomplished science managers. Adolf Butenandt, former manager of the Max Planck Society (for whom Telschow continued to work for two more years as personal advisor following his official resignation as "director general" of the MPS in 1960), eulogized the former KWS and MPS secretary general in 1988: "his administrative skills, his adaptability, his quick-mindedness even in the most complex issues, his tenacity in pursuing his goals" were Telschow's "special abilities."[67] Butenandt was absolutely right with this characterization – but that is precisely the problem. Such abilities are compatible with any political system, as proven by the unbroken continuation of Telschow's career after 1945. Yet they reveal little if anything about the political and moral substance of the individual in question.

---

[67] Butenandt's memorial address commemorating Ernst Telschow (October 31, 1988), MPG-Archiv, Abt. II., Rep. 1A, Personalakte Telschow, Nr. 11.

3

"No Time to Debate and Ask Questions" – Forced Labor for Science in the Kaiser Wilhelm Society, 1939–1945

Bernhard Strebel and Jens-Christian Wagner

As the British Royal Air Force stepped up their bombing attacks on the capital of the German Reich as part of the "Battle of Berlin" campaign, the General Administration of the Kaiser Wilhelm Society (*Kaiser-Wilhelm-Gesellschaft*, KWS) became increasingly concerned about the safety of the staff in their research institutes in Berlin-Dahlem.[1] After tough negotiations with the authorities, the KWS property department finally gained permission to convert the cellar of the Harnack House, the society's main meeting place and lecture hall and, as such, the representative heart of the KWS, into a bunker. As manpower was scarce, the General Administration was obviously glad when in early March 1944 a member of staff of the Kaiser Wilhelm Institute (KWI) for Physical Chemistry negotiated the placement of "further assistant workers … from a concentration camp."[2] Although it is not recorded whether concentration camp prisoners actually worked on the Harnack House, it speaks for itself that their forced labor on this symbolic place, so central to the corporate identity of the KWS, was even considered.

The subject of forced labor has not been dealt with, even peripherally, in most publications on the history of the KWS. The same is true of most

[1] The quotation in the chapter title is from KWS president Albert Vögler in response to the demands of "total war." It is taken from an appeal he made at a strategic discussion with all KWI directors concerning the relocation of institutes and is recorded in the minutes of the directors' conference on 9.11.1943, Federal German Archives (*Bundesarchiv*, BArch), R 26 III/693. For a more detailed discussion of this subject, as well as more detailed references to sources and literature, see Bernhard Strebel and Jens-Christian Wagner, "Zwangsarbeit für Forschungseinrichtungen der Kaiser-Wilhelm-Gesellschaft 1939–1945. Ein Überblick," *Ergebnisse. Vorabdrucke aus dem Forschungsprogramm "Geschichte der Kaiser-Wilhelm-Gesellschaft im Nationalsozialismus,"* No. 11 (Berlin: Forschungsprogramm, 2003; further quoted as *Ergebnisse*, No., and year).

[2] File entry by Forstmann (General Administration), 2.3.1944, Archives of the Max Planck Society, Berlin (*Archiv zur Geschichte der Max-Planck-Gesellschaft*, MPG-Archiv), Berlin, Abt. 1, Rep. 1A, Nr. 736/6.

publications on the history of the individual institutes. For this reason, this chapter will look into the extent of forced labor in the research institutions of the KWS. Further consideration will be given to interpreting more detailed information on the fate of the victims of forced labor and the role of the researchers, institute directors, and the General Administration of the KWS in the use of this workforce.

The forced labor deployed in the research institutions of the KWS can be divided into four categories or fields of activity. As one would expect, the highest number of foreign civilian workers was to be found in the Kaiser Wilhelm Institutes involved in agriculture in the broadest sense and working on experimental farms. Another field of activity was construction and unskilled manual labor. Then, in 1943–44, help was needed when a number of KWS research institutions had to be relocated as a consequence of heavy Allied bombing. Last, foreign scientists and academics were also made to work on KWS projects. For two of these fields, a complex network of collaboration existed that led to three Kaiser Wilhelm Institutes benefiting from the forced labor of concentration camp prisoners.[3]

The use here of "voluntary" and "forced" as clearly distinguished terms is problematic on several levels – particularly with regard to recruitment procedures.[4] Thus a historical study of forced labor must classify all foreign members of staff and distinguish among their very different living and working conditions in Germany. Workers can be classified in the following groups:[5]

1. Voluntary foreign civilian workers from Bulgaria, Italy (until autumn 1943), Croatia, Romania, Slovakia, Spain, Denmark, and Western and Southern Europe in the early war years.

---

[3] In this context, the forced labor of concentration camp prisoners on the "shoe testing track" in Sachsenhausen concentration camp should also be mentioned. This was an activity that the KWI for leather research in Dresden helped to organize and evaluate; see Anne Sudrow, "Vom Leder zum Kunststoff. Werkstoff-Forschung auf der 'Schuhprüfstrecke' im Konzentrationslager Sachsenhausen 1940–1945," in Helmut Maier (ed.), *Rüstungsforschung im Nationalsozialismus. Organisation, Mobilisierung und Entgrenzung der Technikwissenschaften* (Göttingen: Wallstein, 2002), 214–249.

[4] Ulrich Herbert's study, *Fremdarbeiter. Politik und Praxis des "Ausländer-Einsatzes" in der Kriegswirtschaft des Dritten Reiches* 2nd ed. (Berlin: Dietz, 1999), is a key work. A good overview, based primarily on research literature, is provided by Mark Spoerer, *Zwangsarbeit unter dem Hakenkreuz. Ausländische Zivilarbeiter, Kriegsgefangene und Häftlinge im Deutschen Reich und im besetzten Europa* (Stuttgart: DVA, 2001). Three anthologies that also stand out from the abundant research literature are Ulrich Herbert (ed.), *Europa und der "Reichseinsatz". Ausländische Zivilarbeiter, Kriegsgefangene und KZ-Häftlinge in Deutschland 1938–1945* (Essen: Klartext-Verlag, 1991); Dietrich Eichholtz (ed.), *Krieg und Wirtschaft. Studien zur deutschen Wirtschaftsgeschichte* (Berlin: Metropol, 1999); and Ulrike Winkler (ed.), *Stiften gehen. NS-Zwangsarbeit und Entschädigungsdebatte* (Cologne: PapyRossa-Verlag, 2000).

[5] See Spoerer, *Zwangsarbeit*, 9–20, esp. 16 ff.

2. Forced laborers with some influence on their living conditions; some came from the occupied territories (excluding workers from Poland and the Soviet Union) and others were prisoners of war from Belgium, France, Great Britain, and Yugoslavia.

3. Forced laborers with minimal influence on their living conditions; these were from Poland and the Soviet Union and some also were Polish and Italian prisoners of war.

4. Forced laborers with no influence on their living conditions; these were Polish-Jewish and Soviet prisoners of war, "work Jews" in forced labor camps and ghettos, and inmates of "Labor Education Camps" (*Arbeitserziehungslager* or AEL) and concentration camps.

A direct link can be drawn between the living and working conditions of the respective groups and their mortality rate: in group 1 the death rate was normal or only slightly higher than average; in group 2, significantly higher than average; and in groups 3 and 4, extremely high. According to recent estimates, the total number of people falling into these categories between 1939 and 1945 was roughly 13.5 million, of which 80 percent to 90 percent belonged to groups 2 to 4 and can therefore be considered forced laborers.[6] Note that recruitment procedures and levels of duress varied considerably, although on the whole, aggression toward these workers seems to have steadily increased as the war went on.

In August 1944, there were about 5.7 million foreign civilian workers and nearly 2 million prisoners of war on Reich territory. This means that almost a quarter of all employees of the German economy were foreign nationals in the last year of the war. In some economic sectors, such as the armaments industry and agriculture, they even made up a third of the number. About two thirds of foreign civilian workers came from the Soviet Union (38%) and Poland (29%), followed by France (11%), the Protectorate of Bohemia and Moravia and the Netherlands (each nearly 5%), Belgium (3.5%), and Italy (2.7%). The proportion of women among them was about a third and the majority of them (87%) came from the East (eastern Europe and the Soviet Union). Among the native countries of the prisoners of war, the Soviet Union (33%), France (31%), and Italy (22%) had the greatest representation. The number of Belgians (2.6%) and Poles (1.5%) was significantly less.[7] At the same time, the SS had a total of 524,000 – roughly 379,000 male

[6] The actual figures of those made to carry out forced labor are 8.4 million foreign civilian workers, 4.6 million prisoners of war, and 1.7 million concentration camp prisoners and German and Austrian Jews; see Spoerer, *Zwangsarbeit*, 219–225. The difference in the sum of individuals and the total number is a consequence of the fact that about 1.1 million people were included in two of the groups named, giving rise to an error margin of +/− 750,000 persons in the number of Soviet prisoners of war.

[7] Statistics for the period August 1994 taken from the journal *Der Arbeitseinsatz im Grossdeutschen Reich*, No. 10, dated 31.10.1944, published by the "Plenipotentiary for Labor

and 145,000 female – concentration camp prisoners in their power.[8] Their
potential as a workforce began to be appreciated in 1942, at the same time
the systematic mass killing campaigns began. From early 1943, this led to
an increasing number of concentration camp subcamps being set up near
armament factories.[9]

Extensive research, particularly over the last fifteen years, has shown that
there was hardly a sphere of German society that did not resort to using
some form of forced labor – albeit to varying extents. The spectrum ranged
from state institutions, such as the Volkswagen plant and Hermann Göring
works, to leading industrial groups, such as I.G. Farben, Daimler-Benz, and
Siemens, to agricultural businesses and small handicraft businesses, church
and municipal institutions, and private households.[10]

Just as recruitment procedures for the individual groups and nationalities varied, so did their living and working conditions in Germany. These
were not only dictated by ordinances regulating forced labor based on a
racist theory of hierarchy – particularly the "Polish decrees" of March 1940
and the "Eastern worker decrees" of February 1942 – but to a considerable
degree also by the behavior of their "employer."[11]

Unfortunately, the quantity of available source material can only be
described as meager. As the activities of nearly forty institutes were to be
examined, some of which had several locations and also went through a
series of relocations beginning in late 1943, the search for relevant documents was often like the proverbial search for a needle in a haystack.
Looking at the papers of the General Administration, one is struck by
the realization that files for the years 1939 onward become ever thinner.
Moreover, some documents contain indications that not all records were

Deployment," taken from Herbert, *Fremdarbeiter*, 314 ff.; for more detail on developments
up to 1944, see Herbert, *Fremdarbeiter*, 170–186 and 291–305.

[8] Internal communication from the SS Office of Economic Administration (*Wirtschafts-
Verwaltungshauptamt*, WVHA) with regard to the report on the state of prisoners and overview of prisoners' clothing, 15.8.1944, Nuremberg Document PS-1166, reprinted in *Trial
of the Major War Criminals before the International Military Tribunal, Nuremberg, 14
November 1945–1 October 1946*, vol. 27 (New York: AMS Press, 1971). The WVHA was
founded in February 1942 and was responsible for concentration camp administration.

[9] Also see Karin Orth, *Das System der nationalsozialistischen Konzentrationslager. Eine politische Organisationsgeschichte* (Hamburg: Hamburger Edition, 1999), 113–221, and articles
in Ulrich Herbert, Karin Orth, and Christoph Dieckmann (eds.), *Die nationalsozialistischen
Konzentrationslager. Entwicklung und Struktur*, 2 volumes (Göttingen: Wallstein, 1998),
vol. 2, esp. 533–751.

[10] In some cases extensive studies are now available; in many others there is still a considerable
need for research to be done. See the review of research since 1985 in Herbert, *Fremdarbeiter*,
416–433; and the articles published in Winkler, 10–168, and Eichholtz, 9–170.

[11] On the content and significance of these fundamental decrees, see Herbert, *Fremdarbeiter*,
85–93 and 178–182; on the individual nationalities, see the articles in Herbert, *Europa und
der "Reichseinsatz"*; Spoerer, *Zwangsarbeit*, 35–229.

kept.[12] Files that provide concrete information about the extent to which foreign civilian workers were used were kept in the institute itself in only one case. These files were not in the General Administration but in the "Rosenhof," a branch of the KWI for Breeding Research in Ladenburg. Yet, even these files are far from complete. The following account can therefore provide only a basic outline.

AGRICULTURAL WORK

German agriculture was the first economic sector to rely on a considerable number of foreign workers, having already employed some in the prewar years. In August 1944, the figure was 2.7 million foreign civilian workers and prisoners of war, making up 46 percent of the workforce.

Kaiser Wilhelm Institute for Breeding Research

A prominent example is the KWI for Breeding Research, headquartered in Müncheberg, which ran experimental farms in Ladenburg near Mannheim (Rosenhof) and in Laukischken in East Prussia. A total of 141 foreign workers, identifiable by name, can be proved to have worked at the Rosenhof between 1939 and 1945. As the work in question was mostly seasonal, no more than thirty foreign workers were ever employed at the Rosenhof at one time. They came from the following countries: Poland (42), Hungary (36, including six "ethnic Germans"), Yugoslavia (27, including 23 with Hungarian nationality),[13] Belarus (18), Ukraine (10), Italy (4), and France (3). The ratio of men to women was about 60 to 40. The youngest foreign workers employed on the Rosenhof were three female Hungarians aged fourteen and fifteen, who began working there in July 1942 and May 1943. The oldest were the Polish husband and wife Jozef and Zofia W.,[14] who were sixty-four and sixty-two, respectively, and were sent to the Rosenhof in May 1944 together with their adult daughter.[15]

This relatively well-documented example demonstrates that work here was done increasingly under duress. From spring 1940, the Rosenhof administration employed Croatian and Hungarian agricultural workers (some of

---

[12] See various communications from the KWI for Physical and Electrochemistry and the KWI for Breeding Research to the General Administration 1944–45, MPG-Archiv, I Abt., Rep. 1A, Nr. 1184, and Nr. 2634.

[13] Registered as "Croatians" in some documents until April 1941.

[14] The surnames of forced laborers may not be disclosed for reasons of data protection and archive requirements (in the case of judicial documents), except those of persons who can be assumed to be known or already mentioned in other publications.

[15] Data from registration certificates and other personnel documents in MPG-Archiv, I Abt., Rep. 51, Nr. 15–17. The nationality of one man with a Czech sounding name was not recorded.

German descent) each season. These could still be described as traditional migrant workers, some of whom returned to the Rosenhof in the 1941 season. Records show that in the case of one "ethnic German" family from Hungary, they very much saw themselves as German; the eldest son even enrolled with the armed division of the SS in April 1942.[16] It remains questionable, however, to what extent the twelve Polish men and women who joined the Rosenhof staff in 1940, nearly all of whom were from the same town, had come to work in Germany "voluntarily."[17] The same applies to the ten to fourteen Croatian workers who arrived in 1941 from an area that had been annexed by Hungary following the division of Yugoslavia. One communication records that they had been "transported to the Reich by the armed forces." It also notes that none of these workers was in possession of a passport.[18]

The situation at the Rosenhof significantly deteriorated with the employment of "Eastern workers" (Ostarbeiter), that is, women and men who had been forcibly recruited in the occupied territories of the Soviet Union and brought to Germany. The first Eastern workers (Ukrainians and Belarussians) were assigned to the Rosenhof in late 1941 and early 1942 by the relevant employment office. Some of them were obviously in such a bad state of health that they had to be hospitalized shortly after their arrival, and others never even made it to the Rosenhof.[19] The regulations made inferior provision for the Eastern workers. There is documentation of several, ultimately unsuccessful, attempts by the Rosenhof administration to negotiate with the relevant authorities for some improvement in the workers' condition, emphasizing that they were working eleven to thirteen hours a day.[20] A request for the normal soap ration for workers from the Soviet Union sheds more light on working conditions at the Rosenhof at harvest time:

With half the normal quantity that has so far been allotted, the people [the "Eastern workers"] are not able to keep themselves and their things clean. As the supervision

---

[16] The H. family to Fräulein Wolter (KWI for Breeding Research), 4.6.1942, MPG-Archiv, I. Abt., Rep. 51, Nr. 15.

[17] The date (May 1940) suggests that they were recruited in connection with the requirement that all Poles born between 1915 and 1925 must work in Germany, an order imposed by the administration of the Government General in late April 1940; see Herbert, *Fremdarbeiter*, 99 ff.

[18] KWI for Breeding Research to the Deutsche Bank (Abtl. Ausland 2), 14.7.1941, MPG-Archiv, I. Abt., Rep. 51, Nr. 15.

[19] Staatliches Gesundheitsamt Mannheim, with regard to fitness for work of Ukrainian agricultural worker Michael D., 9.1.1942, MPG-Archiv, I. Abt., Rep. 51, Nr. 15; KWI for Breeding Research to Mannheim employment office, 22.7.1942, MPG-Archiv, I. Abt., Rep. 51, Nr. 16.

[20] KWI for Breeding Research to Mannheim employment office, 22.7.1942, MPG-Archiv, I. Abt., Rep. 51, Nr. 16; KWI for Breeding Research to Kreisbauernschaft Heidelberg, 27.4.1942, MPG-Archiv, I. Abt., Rep. 51, Nr. 16.

of the Russians' cleanliness has been made our special duty by the public health department and 14 hours of dirty fieldwork mean the people have to wash often and thoroughly, the normal soap ration, as for German agricultural workers, is absolutely necessary. Moreover, at the moment our beds and blankets are so badly soiled that we ask for the situation to be remedied as soon as possible. [21]

In late July 1942, Hungarians finally replaced the workers from the Soviet Union. Mainly Hungarians were employed again in the 1943 season. They were intended to return the following year, but in May 1944 the institute was assigned fourteen Poles in their place. An institute communication reports "sudden conscription" at their previous workplace in Warthegau.[22] With them, the proportion of foreigners at the Rosenhof rose to 66 percent – 20 percent more than the general average in German agriculture.

Quite a few of the foreign workers were related to one another. There is evidence of a total of thirteen married couples working there. The birth of two Polish children at the Rosenhof is also recorded. The daughter of husband and wife Jan and Sofja J. was born in October 1941; the parents had been working at Rosenhof from the summer of 1939 through the 1941 season. In this first case, the institute took care of the infant.[23] In the second case (February 1944), the family was offered to the Mannheim employment office after months of unsuccessful "exchange attempts," "without attaching importance to their replacement or return."[24]

Reliable descriptions of the living and working conditions of foreign workers at the Rosenhof can hardly be gleaned from the scattered references in the documents that survive. Any mention of the personal experiences of the victims are even sketchier. In 1967, the Polish husband and wife Johann and Maria G. filed a petition for restitution. They had been forced to work at Rosenhof from May 1944 until May 1945. They maintained that they were mistreated by administrator Krötz and badly provided for.[25]

Very restrictive regulations applied particularly to civilian workers from the Soviet Union and Poland (the "Eastern worker decree" and "Polish decree"). Violation of these regulations was punishable by severe penalties. In mid-July 1942, the *Gestapo* arrested Ukrainian worker Wasyl S. (in all probability after notification from the institute), born in 1919, who had been

[21] KWI for Breeding Research to Wirtschaftsamt Mannheim, with regard to soap rations for civilian Russians (agricultural workers), 11.6.1944, MPG-Archiv, I. Abt., Rep. 51, Nr. 16.
[22] KWI for Breeding Research to Mannheim employment office, 26.6.1944, MPG-Archiv, I. Abt., Rep. 51, Nr. 16.
[23] KWI for Breeding Research to Wirtschaftsamt Mannheim, with regard to issuing of ration coupons for a Polish child, 14.4.1942, MPG-Archiv, I. Abt., Rep. 51, Nr. 17.
[24] KWI for Breeding Research to Mannheim employment office, 29.11.1944, MPG-Archiv, I. Abt., Rep. 51, Nr. 16.
[25] File entry KWI for Breeding Research, 31.5.1967, MPG-Archiv, I. Abt., Rep. 51, Nr. 15.

at Rosenhof since December 1941. Accused of "refusing to work," he was committed to the AEL at Oberndorf am Neckar. This camp, set up and run by regional Gestapo sections together with local companies, local authorities, and employment authorities, had existed since 1940. Its purpose was to discipline, intimidate, and terrorize not only its mostly foreign inmates but also, in a general preventive sense, the whole workforce. Conditions in these camps were often similar to those in concentration camps.[26] Wasyl S. was released after three months' imprisonment in the AEL and subsequently worked at Rosenhof again. In October 1943, the Gestapo arrested him once more. This time he was accused of stealing a pair of gloves. Once again he was admitted to an AEL but was released early because of the institute's appeal to the Gestapo citing the need for assistance with the approaching sowing work:

We can find no replacement for him and urgently need S. as a cart-driver. From autumn '42 he worked entirely to our satisfaction; perhaps it may be possible to release him earlier, as on the one hand his punishment and the deterrent effect on the other foreigners should now be achieved, and on the other hand, a German agricultural business is suffering damage due to the missing manpower. We ask you most courteously to consider whether a premature release may be possible for S.[27]

The main office of the KWI for Breeding Research in Müncheberg, led by Professor Wilhelm Rudorf, also employed a relatively large number of foreign workers on its two experimental estates, Brigittenhof and Rotes Luch. The total number, however, cannot be calculated from the source material available. The details of some female "Eastern workers" employed at the Rotes Luch estate, recorded in pay lists, indicate that they came from the neighboring resettlement camp run by the Ethnic German agency (*Volksdeutsche Mittelstelle* or VOMI). The VOMI served as an instrument of Himmler's "policy of fostering national traditions," which applied to about 10 million non-German residents who counted as "ethnic Germans" according to Nazi racial doctrine. The VOMI's function was to organize the transport of "ethnic Germans" into the "Reich," screen them for their "racial" and political suitability for settlement in the occupied territories in the East, and divide them into different categories of "ethnic Germans." The VOMI had its own camp system for this purpose, which included at the high point of its activities in 1940–41 between 1,500 and 1,800 transit, collection, and observation camps. Within this system, the VOMI camp in Rotes Luch, sometimes described as a concentration camp, fulfilled the function of a "reformatory camp," particularly for those "incorrigible" Slovenians, Alsatians, Lorrainers, and Luxembourgers who refused to be "Germanized."[28]

We know that from the early forties, the KWI for Breeding Research in Rotes Luch took leases on an ever-increasing area of land for experiments with the cultivation of the rubber-producing kog-sagyz plant.[29] There is also evidence that the VOMI repeatedly provided inmates of its camp at short notice for agricultural work connected to the KWI's kog-sagyz kog-sagyzcultivation experiments. In spring 1943, the KWI once again planned to considerably extend their cultivation experiments in Rotes Luch.[30] Dr. Richard Werner Böhme, commissioned to direct the cultivation experiments, applied to the VOMI for the permanent transfer of fifty workers for this purpose. Previously, ten female "Eastern workers" had been employed there for a period.[31] After some delay, the VOMI largely complied with Böhme's request. Since July 1943 at the latest, thirty-five Slovenian forced laborers, who had been transferred from a VOMI camp in Brandenburg due to their inability to be "Germanized," had worked in the KWI's experimental fields in Rotes Luch. Fifteen more Slovenians followed later, to stay there as "long-term regular staff."[32] The VOMI vacated the camp in Rotes Luch in the first half of 1944. However, according to a letter from Oswald Pohl, head of the SS office of economic administration (*Wirtschafts-Verwaltungshauptamt* or WVHA), enough workers were left in Rotes Luch to continue work on the kog-sagyz experimental site.[33]

In autumn 1944, the number of foreign agricultural workers and researchers in Rotes Luch steadily increased as the advance of the Red Army meant that ever more experimental estates in the East, where kog-sagyz plants had also been cultivated, were abandoned. The mainly Russian staffs of these estates were transported without further ado to Reich territory, including to Rotes Luch.[34]

---

[28] Valdis Lumans, *Himmler's Auxiliaries. The Volksdeutsche Mittelstelle and the German National Minorities of Europe 1933–44* (Chapel Hill: University of North Carolina Press, 1993), 188 and 201 ff.

[29] Draft by Böhme (KWI for Breeding Research) with regard to reorganization of the Rotes Luch estate, 29.3.1943, Federal German Archives (Bundesarchiv, BArch), NS 19/3920, 103 ff.

[30] Entry by Vogel (head of Office W5 in the WVHA) re kog-sagyz KWI in Müncheberg (discussion with Böhme), 6.4.1943, BArch, NS 19/3920, 101 ff.

[31] Böhme to Himmler, 17.5.1943, BArch, NS 19/1803, 15 ff.

[32] Werner Lorenz (head of the VOMI) to Rudolf Brandt (Pers. Stab RFSS), 27.7.1943, BArch, NS 19/1803, 24; Pers. Stab RFSS to Vogel (head of Office W 5 in the WVHA), 17.8.1943, BArch, NS 19/1803, 27 ff.

[33] Pohl to Brandt (Pers. Stab RFSS), 11.9.1944, BArch, NS 19/1803, 38.

[34] Entry by SS-Hauptsturmführer Berg (Pers. Stab RFSS), 26.10.1944, BArch, NS 19/1803, 40; Communication from VOMI to Pers. Stab RFSS, 1.12.1944, BArch, NS 19/1803, 42. Exact numbers are not given in the sources.

On the neighboring estate, Brigittenhof, the number of forced laborers also increased over the winter 1944–45 for various reasons, including the "evacuation" of Soviet workers who had previously been employed on the Laukischken branch estate in East Prussia.[35] A note by the KWS in April 1944 indicates that sixty-eight foreign civilian workers and ten Soviet prisoners of war worked in Laukischken. The deputy head of this branch and a research employee (Dr. Joachim Hackbarth and Frau Dr. Hertzsch) each temporarily employed a Russian woman for 0.50 Reichsmarks a day to see to their private needs.[36]

Furthermore, documents confirm the employment of Slovakian migrant workers, "Eastern workers," and a group of "half-Jews" on the Tuttenhof experimental estate (near Vienna), founded in 1943, that belonged to the KWI for Plant Cultivation Research. Foreign workers were probably also permanently deployed on the experimental estate near Trebnitz (Silesia), acquired by the Institute for Agricultural Manpower Studies in 1941, albeit not on the initiative of the institute's directors. Finally, the employment of foreign civilian workers and prisoners of war can also be proved for the KWI for Stockbreeding Research, founded in 1938, and its experimental estates in Dummerstorf and Hohen Schwarfs.[37]

CONSTRUCTION AND UNSKILLED MANUAL LABOR

Shortly after the outbreak of war and thereafter, a considerable amount of construction and conversion work took place on Kaiser Wilhelm Institute buildings. As "free" construction workers were increasingly less available, here too the KWS fell back on forced laborers. In many cases, forced laborers were not directly employed by the KWS but by the construction company, which acted as a kind of subcontractor. In other cases, individual KWIs put "their" forced laborers at the construction company's disposal. Often the question of who was actually responsible for employing forced laborers for KWS building projects can no longer be resolved with any certainty.

In 1940, the KWI for Stockbreeding Research in Dummerstorf near Rostock planned extensive conversion and extension work. Supported by Reich minister Richard Walther Darré and on the initiative of under-secretary Herbert Backe (both of the Reich Ministry for Food and Agriculture), the building project was entirely financed by Reich funds. The institute also had the backing of the KWS General Administration in Berlin. From the outset, Secretary General Ernst Telschow did what he could to ensure that

---

[35] Report by Erich Kühn (researcher for the KWI for Breeding Research) on the entry of the Red Army into Müncheberg, 24.5.1945, MPG-Archiv, Abt. I, Rep. 1A, Nr. 2606/4.

[36] Report for audit of the Laukischken branch by the General Administration, 27.4.1944, MPG-Archiv, Abt. I, Rep. 1A, Nr. 2723/2.

[37] Strebel and Wagner, "Zwangsarbeit," *Ergebnisse*, No. 11, (2003), 29–33.

the institute was allocated the necessary workers for the building project. In late July 1940, he applied to the Reich Ministry for Employment for the allocation of 120 prisoners of war for the construction work in Dummerstorf[38] – initially, however, without success. Two weeks later, the institute's director, Professor Gustav Frölich, complained in a letter to the General Administration:

As I am sure you can understand, I am extremely annoyed about the slow progress of the construction work.... With hundreds of thousands of prisoners of war available, it should be possible to release these important workers for a strategically important business as the institute is acknowledged to be.[39]

As the delay in the assignment of prisoners of war continued, the institute resorted to employing forty Danish construction workers, the first of whom arrived in January 1941 and who stayed until Christmas 1942. These workers came to Dummerstorf under regular work contracts and cannot be described as forced laborers.[40]

The first prisoners of war to be employed as construction workers (barely a few dozen men) probably arrived at the construction site in Dummerstorf in summer 1941. The use of twenty-three "Croatian prisoners" (June to October 1941), twenty French prisoners of war (July 1941), and fifty Russians (from October 1941) can also be proved. Other forced laborers also worked for subcontractors on the construction site. Formally speaking, these workers were assigned to work for the construction companies and subcontractors on site. However, their use actually stems from the intensive efforts of the KWS General Administration to have them assigned to the project. Still, the institute failed to get as many construction workers as desired, and the consequent requests for more are a recurring theme in the institute's files.[41]

Similarly, in the case of the KWI for Bast Fiber Research, which was relocated after the outbreak of war from Sorau (Brandenburg) to Mährisch-Schönberg (Sudetenland), fewer foreigners and prisoners of war were used than the General Administration recommended.[42]

---

[38] Telschow to Reich ministry for employment, 31.7.1940, MPG-Archiv, Abt. I., Rep. 1A, Nr. 2668/3.

[39] Frölich to the General Administration, 17.8.1940, MPG-Archiv, Abt. I., Rep. 1A, Nr. 2668/3.

[40] KWS (Forstmann) to Co. Müller (Bremen), 6.1.1941, with regard to delivery of ovens for the Danish barracks. MPG-Archiv, Abt. I, Rep. 1A, Nr. 2868/6; construction report by architect Kegebein, 22.12.1942, MPG-Archiv, Abt. I, Rep. 1A, Nr. 2873.

[41] Correspondence between KWI for Stockbreeding Research and KWS General Administration, 1941–42, MPG-Archiv, Abt. I, Rep. 1A, Nr. 2868–2872.

[42] Strebel and Wagner, "Zwangsarbeit," Ergebnisse, No. 11 (2003), 33 ff. and 36–39; see the above also for further examples of KWS research institutions that employed forced laborers in isolated cases. Records show that a greater number of forced laborers worked for the

RELOCATIONS

In view of the danger posed by Allied bombing attacks, in June 1943 Telschow informed the directors of all Kaiser Wilhelm Institutes of an order from Armaments Minister Albert Speer: preparations for the relocation of all institutes were to be made, particularly those engaged in strategically important work. The institute directors were to take the necessary measures themselves, although the General Administration, Telschow wrote, "is glad to put its knowledge of properties, for negotiations with the authorities, etc., at your disposal."[43] At a meeting in early November 1943, Brandenburg (north of Berlin) and the Stuttgart area were confirmed as the main areas for relocation.[44] In early April 1945, the total cost of relocating twenty-three Kaiser Wilhelm institutes amounted to nearly 2.4 million Reichsmarks. The cost was borne by the Reich ministry for science, education, and national instruction.[45]

Conversion and transport work was necessary for all relocations, albeit to varying extents, and was completed in very different ways, as shown by the quarterly accounting reports of the individual institutes to the General Administration.[46] The additional workers employed can be divided into two categories:

1. Regular tradesmen, removal companies, and soldiers of the German army
2. Civilian prisoners, prisoners of war, forced laborers, and concentration camp prisoners

The relocations of the KWI for Labor Physiology, the KWI for Biology, the KWI for Physics, the KWI for Iron Research, the German Entomological Institute, the Research Unit for Virus Research, the KWI for Silicate Research, and the KWI for Biochemistry were all completed with workers of both categories.[47]

The Case of Falkenhagen

In most cases, forced laborers were used on a small scale over a limited amount of time. One exception is the KWI for Physical Chemistry and its

---

aerodynamic research institute (AVA). The AVA was separated from the KWS in 1937 but remained closely linked to the neighboring KWI for Fluid Dynamics.

[43] Telschow to KWI directors, 10.6.1943, MPG-Archiv, Abt. I, Rep. 42, Nr. 55, Bl. 11.

[44] Minutes of the directors' meeting on 9.11.1943, BArch, R 26 III/693.

[45] File entry with regard to expenditure of the General Administration on the relocation of the Kaiser Wilhelm Institutes, 4.4.1945, MPG-Archiv, I. Abt., Rep. 1A, Nr. 380; Telschow to Reichsministerium für Wissenschaft, Erziehung und Volksbildung, 27.4.1944, MPG-Archiv, I. Abt., Rep. 1A, Nr. 380.

[46] MPG-Archiv, I. Abt., Rep. 1A, Nr. 379 and 380.

[47] Strebel and Wagner, "Zwangsarbeit," *Ergebnisse*, No. 11 (2003), 41 ff.

partial relocation to Falkenhagen, a small town east of Berlin, between Fürstenwalde and Frankfurt-Oder.

Since 1938, building work had been under way on a plant (codename: "Seewerk") intended for the manufacture and testing of the chemical warfare agent chlortrifluoride (codename: "Substance N"), an exceptionally aggressive incendiary agent that destroys almost anything it comes into contact with. Much of the works, covering an area of one hectare, were underground. The centerpiece was an extensive four-story bunker that reached about twenty meters into the ground.[48] The plant was built and run according to the so-called *Montan-Schema*. Behind this complex legal construction lay the army ordnance office (*Heereswaffenamt* or HWA) of the German Army's High Command (*Oberkommando des Heeres* or OKH) that used the misleadingly named Operating Company for Coal and Steel Industry Ltd. (*Verwertungsgesellschaft für Montanindustrie* GmbH), taken over as a front by the HWA in 1934 to produce weapons and munitions. The clients and owners of the operation were the OKH, represented by Montan – the short name for the coal and steel industry plan. The planners, architects, and operating authorities, however, were private companies that brought their technical expertise and qualified personnel to work on the production stage after the plant had been completed by the OKH.[49]

In Falkenhagen, the OKH cooperated with I.G. Farben. In September 1943, I.G. Farben and Montan founded Monturon GmbH (initially also called Turon GmbH) as a cover, each holding an interest of 50 percent.[50] For the construction work, I.G. Farben used their subsidiary company Luranil Baugesellschaft mbH, also founded exclusively for this purpose. Furthermore, from late 1943 to early 1944, plans existed to supplement the completed N-Substance plant in Falkenhagen with another production plant in which the nerve gas Sarin would be produced by I.G. Farben.[51] The OKH officially placed their order with I.G. Farben in late May 1944.

---

[48] For an overview, see Heini Hofmann's booklet, *Objekt "Seewerk." Vom Geheimobjekt des Dritten Reiches zum Einsatzgefechtsstand des Warschauer Vertrages* (Zella-Mehlis/Meiningen: Heinrich-Jung-Verlag-Gesellschaft, 2003).

[49] Barbara Hopmann, *Von der Montan zur Industrieverwaltungsgesellschaft (IVG) 1916–1951* (Stuttgart: Steiner, 1996), 21 ff. and 71–96. In mid-1943 over 120 armament companies with an investment value of more than 3 billion Reichsmarks were administered according to the *Montan-Schema*.

[50] Hopmann, *Montan*, 58. Hopmann speaks mistakenly of production plants for Sarin. Monturon acted initially as the operating company for the production of Substance N and took over responsibility for the Sarin plant on the works' premises in mid-1944; cf. statement by Jürgen von Klenck (asst. director of Seewerk), 3.9.1947, Staatsarchiv Nürnberg (SN), Nuremberg Document NI-10557.

[51] Memo from Otto Ambros, "Die deutsche Kampfstoffproduktion," Ludwigshafen, 1.2.1944, BArch, R 3/1894, p. 18; OKH to I.G. Farben, reconstruction contract for the Sarin II plant (Seewerk), 23.5.1944, SN, Nuremberg Document NI-4994.

Events, however, prevented the large-scale production of Sarin from ever taking place in Falkenhagen.[52]

From the outset, there were problems on the Falkenhagen construction site due to an insufficient number of workers, even though from September 1939 prisoners of war and from 1941 forced laborers from Belarus were also used on the site, some of them temporarily.[53] From October 1943, progress on the project was speeded up by the use of hundreds of concentration camp prisoners. They were housed in a specially converted subcamp of Sachsenhausen concentration camp. At six Reichsmarks for skilled work and four Reichsmarks for unskilled work a day, the concentration camp prisoners' pay was no more than the usual rate. Furthermore, the SS had agreed to exchange prisoners who were no longer fit to work for "fresh" inmates from the main camp. This meant that site managers could ruthlessly exploit prisoners without any consideration for their health or ability to work.[54] This quite common construction site practice of simply replacing exhausted prisoners and leaving them to face their fate – that is, death – meant that there was a considerable amount of fluctuation in the ranks of the camp's workforce.

Statements by surviving prisoners and former SS guards suggest that the workforce at the Falkenhagen subcamp (also called Briesen) varied between 300 and 800 men during its one-and-a-half year existence.[55] In one document referring to the camp's vacation and transfer of the inmates to the Sachsenhausen main camp in early February 1945, 500 prisoners are identified who worked in thirteen building work units and one metalwork work unit.[56] The majority of them were Russian, Polish, or French. There were also a few German prisoners who were mainly deployed in supervisory functions (as foremen or head of a block). One of the few reports by survivors tells us about the conditions there:

The overexploitation of the prisoners' ability to work is best demonstrated by the following: every 14 days 30 to 50 prisoners had to be taken from Sachsenhausen

[52] Christina Eibl, "Der Physikochemiker Peter Adolf Thiessen als Wissenschaftsorganisator (1899–1990). Eine biographische Studie," Ph.D. diss., University of Stuttgart (1999), 157.
[53] War diary Rüstungskommando Frankfurt-Oder 24.2.1939–31.12.1942, BArch, RW 21/20, Bd. 2.
[54] WVHA/D II (Gerhard Maurer) to the site managers in Falkenhagen, with regard to the use of prisoners, 31.7.1943, SN, Nuremberg Document NI-14291.
[55] Statement by Hans D. (former SS guard), 6.2.1967, Central Office of the Justice Administration for Investigation of NS Crimes in Ludwigsburg (*Zentrale Stelle der Landesjustizverwaltungen zur Aufklärung von NS-Verbrechen in Ludwigsburg*, ZSL), 406 AR-Z 40/71, pp. 19–24; statement by Daniel B. (former prisoner), 17.4.1967, ZSL, 406 AR-Z 40/71, 27–30. An internal Luranil communication from 18.9.1943 mentions a lost attachment applying for 1,000 prisoners for the Falkenhagen construction site (200 skilled workers and 800 unskilled workers), ZSL, 406 AR-Z 40/71, 243.
[56] File entry Arbeitsstatistik KZ Sachsenhausen, not dated (early February 1945), ZSL, 406 AR-Z 40/71, 78.

to replace those who had become unable to work in Briesen. Fatal accidents were very frequent. Clothing was unsatisfactory. Many prisoners had to work in deepest winter without an under-jacket or socks, with completely torn shoes.... How little we had to eat is best illustrated by the following incidents: prisoners tried to get leftovers of meat and bones that had been left for the dogs (even though they were beaten away with fists) and ate them. Yes, even leftovers that were in the pigs' containers were eaten.[57]

Surviving prisoners and former members of SS guard squads have also spoken of serious maltreatment, such as dogs being set on prisoners, and there are several reports of prisoners being shot on the march back to the camp from the construction site, usually because of trifles or allegedly attempting to escape.[58]

The minutes of a meeting on November 9, 1943, to discuss relocation record that the KWI for Physical Chemistry had been allocated the Falkenhagen property by the head of the HWA.[59] But the institute had already been directly involved with the "Seewerk" plant before its partial relocation. While Substance N had initially proved to be difficult to store due to its extremely dangerous nature, a doctoral thesis at the KWI for Physical Chemistry, supervised by institute director Professor Peter Adolf Thiessen,[60] had revealed a way to simplify the manufacturing process and make the substance easier to handle. In summer 1944, Thiessen drew up a report in cooperation with specialists from I.G. Farben, the results of which – "Danger! Highly explosive!" – called for costly conversion work to be done on the production plant. The SS ultimately took over the manufacture and testing of Substance N because of disputes over various areas of responsibility.[61]

The first concrete evidence for the activities of the KWI for Physical Chemistry in Falkenhagen dates from August 1943. In a letter to the German Research Foundation (*Deutsche Forschungsgemeinschaft* or DFG), institute

[57] K. (former prisoner), Report on Briesen subcamp, 24.5.1945, ZSL, 406 AR-Z 40/71, 698.
[58] Zentrale Stelle Ludwigsburg, Result of the preliminary investigation into the subcamp Briesen/Falkenhagen (KL Sachsenhausen), 24.3.1971, ZSL, 406 AR-Z 40/71, 730–751.
[59] Minutes of the meeting of KWI directors on 19.11.1943, BArch, R 26 III/963.
[60] Thiessen was director of the institute from 1935 and specialist branch director in the RFR from 1937; he was the most influential man with regard to the promotion of research in the field of chemistry. He also had a long, close friendship with Professor Rudolf Mentzel, SS brigade leader, president of the DFG, and from June 1942, vice president of the RFR; see Eibl, Thiessen, 144–153 and 180.
[61] Helmuth Fischer, "Erinnerungen, Teil II: Feuerwehr für die Forschung," *Quellenstudien der Zeitgeschichtlichen Forschungsstelle Ingolstadt*, 6 (1985), 56 ff.; see Eibl, Thiessen, 154 ff. From 1938 Fischer was in the RSHA, responsible for the supervision of scientific research. On responsibility being handed to the SS, see the Himmler-Speer correspondence, July 1944, SN, Nuremberg Document NI-4043; also Joseph Borkin, *Die unheilige Allianz der I.G. Farben. Eine Interessengemeinschaft im Dritten Reich* (Frankfurt am Main: Campus, 1981), 122 ff.

director Thiessen requests a company car for the director of the reconnais-
sance group in Falkenhagen (referred to here as "work group"), Dr. Georg
Graue, who had already been works manager in Dahlem.[62] A statement of
costs beginning that month also lists travel costs for a "Dutch convoy" for
September to October 1943, which was probably used to transport equipment.[63] The institute's first payments to Monturon and Luranil are dated
November 1943. Whether they related to the use of concentration camp
prisoners is unclear, but unlikely.[64]

By late February 1944, enough preliminary work had been done to proceed with the construction of three brick barracks as alternative premises.[65]
A letter from the Reich Research Council (*Reichsforschungsrat* or RFR) to
the head of the SS WVHA, Oswald Pohl, dated May 10, indicates that building work had not yet been completed three months later:

On the orders of Reich minister Speer, the Kaiser Wilhelm Institute for Physical
Chemistry and Electrochemistry, director Prof. Dr. Thiessen, is to establish a second
operation in Falkenhagen. These production plants will be engaged in the special
program for the production of Substance N, which is of crucial military importance.
In connection with this building project, Turon GmbH is erecting a larger plant
in Falkenhagen, for which it has been assigned a number of prisoners. In order to
proceed with the required production as quickly as possible, several of the prisoners employed by Turon GmbH are also being used on the second operation of the
Institute for Physical Chemistry.

The reason for this petition to the highest level was the threatened departure
of the SS guard men:

We kindly ask for authorization to provide if not four men as previously then at least
two men until completion of the works in eight–ten weeks. The tradesmen charged
with the work (two bricklaying firms and one carpentry firm) will not be able to
complete work in the designated time if we must lose the prisoners due to the guard
squads being withdrawn.[66]

The institute's quarterly statements of relocation costs, beginning in
August 1943, contain a number of expense reports by institute researchers
for trips to Falkenhagen.[67] For November and December 1944 there are

---

[62] Thiessen to Mentzel (DFG), 21.8.1943, BArch, R 26 III/214.
[63] Statement by the KWI for Physical Chemistry and Electrochemistry (removal costs),
17.4.1944, MPG-Archiv, I. Abt., Rep. 1A, Nr. 379.
[64] KWI for Physical Chemistry and Electrochemistry, with regard to the bill for relocation costs
1.1.44–31.3.44, 9.8.1944, MPG-Archiv, I. Abt., Rep. 1A, Nr. 380.
[65] KWI for Physical Chemistry and Electrochemistry to KWS, 28.2.1944, MPG-Archiv, I. Abt.,
Rep. 1A, Nr. 1184/2.
[66] RFR (Wolfram Sievers) to Pohl, with regard to guard squads at the Falkenhagen building
project, 10.5.1944, BArch, R 26 III/214; see Eibl, Thiessen, p. 56.
[67] MPG-Archiv, I Abt., Rep 1A, nos. 379 and 380.

many statements of travel expenses by institute staff claiming the purpose of travel as "building supervision, Falkenhagen."[68] Thiessen, the institute's director, also traveled to Falkenhagen at least five times between September and December 1944.[69] It can therefore be assumed that institute staff had direct experience of the conditions under which concentration camp prisoners were being forced to work there. The concentration camp prisoners were officially made available by the Luranil construction company, which in turn borrowed them from the SS.[70] According to Luranil's invoice documents and a letter from the RFR to the WVHA in May 1944, an average of about thirty-five to forty prisoners worked for the KWI for Physical Chemistry from early May at the latest, but probably from early March.[71] Taking into consideration a certain amount of fluctuation within the work units not least because of the practice of replacing exhausted and sick patients, a realistic figure is probably about 100 prisoners who were forced to work in Falkenhagen in the interests of the KWI for Physical Chemistry.

EMPLOYMENT OF FOREIGN SKILLED WORKERS AND SCIENTISTS

To a lesser degree, forced workers were also employed in research under the KWS. The reason for using forced workers to do research was, as in other fields, the increasing lack of manpower as the war progressed. By April 1942, 40 percent of all KWS employees had been conscripted into the army.[72] Like German industry, the KWS was faced with a development that ran contrary to its increasing personnel requirements as it tried not only to keep the status quo but to develop a considerable number of new projects and institutes it had acquired.

Secrecy regulations led the KWS generally to avoid taking any foreign scientists under regular work contracts, particularly in institutes involved in armaments. There were, however, some exceptions among employees whose

---

[68] MPG-Archiv, I Abt., Rep. 36, Nr. 18.

[69] Transport order to Falkenhagen for Thiessen, 8.9., 22.9., 27.10., 29.11. and 21.12.1944, BArch, R 26 III/214; see Eibl, Thiessen, p. 157.

[70] On the complex and initially vague clearing system for the use of prisoners for outside firms, see Luranil/Turon's internal correspondence, from the ISD archive in Arolsen, January–May 1944, in ZSL, 406 AR-Z 40/71, 244–253.

[71] Various invoices from Luranil to KWI for Physical Chemistry and Electrochemistry with regard to the prisoners' fees for the months July and August 1944 and January 1945, MPG-Archiv, I. Abt., Rep. 1A, Nr. 1190/5.

[72] Taken from Helmuth Albrecht and Armin Hermann, "Die Kaiser-Wilhelm-Gesellschaft im Dritten Reich," in Rudolf Vierhaus and Bernhard vom Brocke (eds.), Forschung im Spannungsfeld von Politik und Gesellschaft. Geschichte und Struktur der Kaiser-Wilhelm-/Max-Planck-Gesellschaft aus Anlass ihres 75jährigen Bestehens (Stuttgart: DVA, 1990), 356–406, here 400.

status as forced workers considerably restricted their freedom of movement. These included foreign students from occupied countries (no duress seems to have been applied to students from neutral countries or states allied to Germany). Yet, these were only isolated cases. Thus, some of the over 3,000 Dutch students who had been deported to Berlin in late 1943 to work as forced laborers were employed at KWS institutions, such as the KWI for Cell Physiology in Liebenberg and the KWI for Biology in Berlin.[73] The question remains as to the extent the Dutch students were employed under duress. Institute documents convey the impression of regular working arrangements and hardly any statements have survived from the students themselves.

The same applies for a number of Western European prisoners of war who worked for the KWS during the war. Among the French soldiers who were captured by the Germans in 1940, for instance, there were many scientists and academics. Some of the prisoners in the POW camps had made professional visits to Kaiser Wilhelm Institutes before the war and now contacted German colleagues with whom they had worked. Occasionally, German scientists were able to help their French colleagues by getting them released or posted as prisoners to Kaiser Wilhelm Institutes where they could work as scientists. Again, these were only isolated cases; records survive of this occurring in the KWS Hydrobiological Institute in Plön[74] and the KWI for Biology in Dahlem and its branch office in Hechingen.[75] Some French prisoners of war were released from captivity to work for the KWIs for Biology and Physical Chemistry in Dahlem, not as experts but as unskilled workers, performing gardening and laboratory duties.[76]

Scientifically qualified forced workers were also employed by the research institutes of the KWS in the occupied territories of Poland and the Soviet Union. Of particular significance here is the activity of various KWS scientists on committees that had been set up to coordinate the exploitation of academic resources in the occupied territories. The Head Office for Research in the East (*Zentrale für Ostforschung*, ZFO), which came under the Reich ministry for the occupied territories in the East, is the most prominent case of this. As head of a team of specialists for agriculture, Dr. Klaus von Rosenstiel of the KWI for Breeding Research played a major

---

[73] KWI for Cell Physiology correspondence and audit, 1943, MPG-Archiv, I. Abt., Rep 1A, nos. 2806/6 and 2806/7, and correspondence between the KWI for Biology and the Berlin employment office (31.5–12.7.1944) and private work contract for W., MPG-Archiv, I. Abt., Rep. 8, nos. 19 and 20.

[74] Thienemann's correspondence with the General Administration, December 1941, MPG-Archiv, I. Abt., Rep. 1A, Nr. 1084 and Franz Ruttner to Telschow, 10.9.43, MPG-Archiv, I. Abt., Rep. 1A, Nr. 1085.

[75] KWI for Biology, correspondence, 1943, MPG-Archiv, I. Abt., Rep. 8, nos. 18 and 19.

[76] KWI for Physical Chemistry to General Administration, 11.5.1944, MPG-Archiv, I. Abt., Rep. 1A, Nr. 1184/2; and Wettstein to General Administration, 6.5.1944, MPG-Archiv, I. Abt., Rep. 1A, Nr. 1564/2.

role in the ZFO.[77] Personnel and institutional links between the ZFO, the RFR, and the Army Economic Panel for the East (*Wehrwirtschaftsstab Ost*) of the OKW (Rosenstiel, for example, was simultaneously head of department for the chief group assigned to nutrition and agriculture in this panel) made it easier for KWS employees to gain access to research institutes in the occupied territories as well as to their staff. Thus, the KWS Hydrobiological Institute in Plön took over the Limnological Station at Lake Wigry in occupied Poland, and the KWI for Breeding Research worked in close cooperation with the former Soviet experimental plant for fruit and vegetable cultivation near Minsk.[78] In some cases, however, takeovers faltered at the planning stage as the KWS could not always win out over its (pseudo) scientific competitors, such as the SS *Ahnenerbe* (Research Division for German Ancestry) and the Rosenberg task force, which also showed great interest in the research institutions and cultural assets of the occupied territories.[79]

The records of the KWI for Silicate Research provide one instance of the KWS successfully gaining access to scientific personnel in the occupied territories. From mid-1942, the director of this institute, Professor Wilhelm Eitel, was particularly interested in the Ukrainian scientific research institute for fireproof materials in Charkov (also called the Silicate Institute). After Eitel had personally inspected the Silicate Institute in Charkov in July 1943, he was appointed to the research team of the ZFO in August 1943 and made head of a team of specialists for silicate research.[80] At the same time, as the Red Army was advancing, it was agreed that the research institute should be moved from Charkov to Kiev, and Eitel was to take over as scientific director, responsible for selecting the research staff to be "evacuated."[81] In mid-August, Eitel reported to Vögler, the president of the KWS:

I am glad to say I have managed to secure the most valuable local scientific members of staff from the Charkov Institute; our team of employees is further supplemented by the inclusion of specialists from the silicate department of the chemical-technological institute of Charkov Technical College. Furthermore I have involved

[77] List of specialist groups and group leaders set up by the Zentrale für Ostforschung as of August 1943, MPG-Archiv-Archiv, I. Abt., Rep. 42, Nr. 43, 18 ff.; see Susanne Heim, *Kalorien, Kautschuk, Karrieren. Pflanzenzüchtung und landwirtschaftliche Forschung in Kaiser-Wilhelm-Instituten 1933–1945* (Göttingen: Wallstein, 2003), 229 ff.

[78] Ute Deichmann, *Biologen unter Hitler. Porträt einer Wissenschaft* (Frankfurt-Main: Fischer Taschenbuch Verlag, 1995), 182 ff., Heim, *Kalorien*, 44 and 71.

[79] Heim, *Kalorien*, 232.

[80] Eitel's appointment to ZFO research team, 5.8.1943, MPG-Archiv, I. Abt., Rep. 42, Nr. 43, p. 5; on his two inspections, see Eitel's report from 29.7.1943, MPG-Archiv, I. Abt., Rep. 42, Nr. 43, 6–16.

[81] Telex from Wirtschaftstab Ost to Wirtschaftsinspektion Süd (Abt. Wissenschaft), 2.8.1943, BArch, RW 31/528.

the Mineralogical Institute of Kiev Technical College in our research activity that I consider to be important in the field of silicates.[82]

Eitel's "securing" of Russian scientists was – not unproblematically – linked to the "Reich deployment" of Russian scientists under the direction of the economic panel for the East, which took place in close cooperation with I.G. Farben. In the course of these "enlistments," a total of 1,111 Russian scientists and engineers were brought to Germany between April 1942 and March 1944 via the Heydebreck-Bierau transit camp in Upper Silesia. Special regulations applied to these highly qualified employees that provided for them to be treated as foreign nationals and issued aliens' passports, and that they be better fed than "Eastern workers," significantly better paid, and not housed in a camp.[83] More in-depth research would have to be conducted to ascertain the extent to which the work of these scientists was forced.

Employment of Qualified Concentration Camp Prisoners

The employment of scientifically qualified concentration camp prisoners as forced workers has hitherto been the subject of little research. Strictly speaking, the medically trained prisoners who served as doctors and nursing staff for the inmates in concentration camps also come under this category. Some of them were enlisted to take part in activities relating to medical experiments on prisoners. One well-known example is the Hungarian-Jewish pathologist Dr. Miklós Nyiszli who had to assist Dr. Josef Mengele with his experiments, including those that Mengele conducted for the director of the KWI for Anthropology, Professor Otmar Freiherr von Verschuer, and his colleague Karin Magnussen.[84] Existing documents record the concrete considerations of the "racial studies" department of the institute as to whether to employ scientifically qualified staff from the Sachsenhausen concentration camp. These concentration camp prisoners were to evaluate a series of anthropological experiments on Soviet prisoners of war, which their director, Professor Wolfgang Abel, conducted between 1942 and 1943 in close cooperation with the SS *Ahnenerbe*. Files were kept until mid-1943, when the last entry records Abel's suggestion that two

---

[82] Eitel to Vögler, 16.8.1943, MPG-Archiv, I. Abt., Rep. 42, Nr. 43, 22 ff.

[83] Rolf-Dieter Müller (ed.), *Die deutsche Wirtschaftspolitik in den besetzten sowjetischen Gebieten 1941–1943. Der Abschlussbericht des Wirtschaftsstabes Ost und Aufzeichnungen eines Angehörigen des Wirtschaftskommandos Kiew* (Boppard am Rhein: Boldt, 1991), 332 ff.

[84] Miklós Nyiszli, *Im Jenseits der Menschlichkeit. Ein Gerichtsmediziner in Auschwitz* (Berlin: Dietz, 1992), esp. 40–47; see Benno Müller-Hill, "Das Blut von Auschwitz und das Schweigen der Gelehrten," in Doris Kaufmann (ed.), *Geschichte der Kaiser-Wilhelm-Gesellschaft im Nationalsozialismus. Bestandsaufnahme und Perspektiven der Forschung*, 2 vols. (Göttingen: Wallstein, 2000), vol. 1, 189–227.

prisoners be made to work in the institute building in Dahlem rather than in Sachsenhausen.[85]

Concentration camp prisoners were used in greater numbers for the research into kog-sagyz mentioned above at the KWI for Breeding Research in Rajsko, a subcamp of Auschwitz. Research involving the kog-sagyz plant and its capacity for providing small amounts of rubber was driven by National Socialist efforts at achieving self-sufficiency and the increased wartime demand for rubber (particularly for tires) as an alternative or supplement to synthetic rubber (buna). Since 1943, the kog-sagyz program had been headed by the SS, and ultimately answerable to it were employees of the KWI for Breeding Research and the KWI for Chemistry, along with representatives of the chemicals industry, the German Labor Front, the authorized agent of the motor vehicle industry, the general agent for special questions concerning chemical production, the Reich ministry of nutrition, and the Reich farming authority.[86]

In June 1943, a decisive conference was held, attended by several representatives of the breeding research and the chemical institutes. At this conference the director of the KWI for Breeding Research, Professor Wilhelm Rudorf, presented a schedule for the work program. As responsibilities were subsequently allocated, all questions of rubber chemistry and technology were assigned to the overall control of Professor Kurt Hess of the KWI for Chemistry (rubber research department); pure research relating to cultivation was to be conducted by Professor Rudorf and Dr. Richard Werner Böhme of the KWI for Breeding Research.[87] Böhme was the only German scientist to have worked on the cultivation and processing of kog-sagyz as early as 1938 and had already inspected kog-sagyz plantations in Uman (Ukraine) by order of the German army (the economic panel for the East) in autumn 1941.[88]

From their inception, these cultivation experiments with kog-sagyz relied heavily on the forced labor of concentration camp prisoners. In autumn 1941, the first seeds imported from the occupied Soviet territories were sown and transplanted in greenhouses on the experimental estate that was part of Ravensbrück concentration camp and run by the SS German experimental institute for nutrition and alimentation (*Deutsche Versuchsanstalt*

[85] Brandt to Sievers, 23.6.1943, SN, Nuremberg Document NO-3751; Abel to Sievers, 23.7.1943, BArch, SS personal file on Abel.

[86] Pohl to Himmler, with regard to kog-sagyz, 12.2.1943, BArch, NS 19/2686, 1 ff.; see in more detail Heim, *Kalorien*, 126–152.

[87] Joachim Caesar, report on works conference on 25.6.1943, BArch, NS 19/1802, 56–62. Rudorf was an NSDAP member and had openly declared his support for National Socialism; see Deichmann, *Biologen*, 361.

[88] Herbert Backe (Reich minister for food and agriculture and senator of the KWS) to Himmler, 10.3.1943, BArch, NS 19/1802, p. 25; see Böhme's report on his inspection trip to Uman (19.9.-5.10.1941), not dated, BArch, NS 19/3929, 98–109.

für Ernährung und Verpflegung, DVA). Already at this stage, female prisoners from Ravensbrück concentration camp were probably brought in to
carry out the necessary work. In spring 1942, the seedlings were taken to
Rajsko in the immediate vicinity of Auschwitz concentration camp, where
a broad expanse of agricultural land had existed since September 1941 and
been farmed since February 1942 by SS Obersturmbannführer Dr.
Joachim Caesar, who was an experienced farmer.[89] Like the DVA, this came under the
control of the W 5 Office in the WVHA, which was responsible for SS agriculture. On May 10 and June 20, 1942, at least ten female Polish specialists
(biologists, chemists, and gardeners) were taken from Ravensbrück concentration camp to Auschwitz to assist with the transport of seedlings.[90]

In Auschwitz, they formed the core of the plant cultivation workforce.
In late March 1944, this work unit comprised eleven qualified members
of staff and twenty-five unqualified workers, probably all female prisoners.[91] By June 1944, the number of prisoners employed in the workforce
had risen to 100.[92] As well as the Polish women from Ravensbrück, there
were other, mostly Polish, women who had been deported via Krakow
directly to Auschwitz, some Czech women, and Polish-Jewish women
from various ghettos and Jewish women of other nationalities, particularly French.[93]

The prisoner-scientists were initially accommodated in the women's
section of the Auschwitz main camp, then from early August 1942, in the
women's camp in Auschwitz-Birkenau. In his autobiographical notes, even
commanding officer Rudolf Höss described the conditions in these two
camp sections as "in every respect the worst"[94] from their establishment. In
June 1943, the SS finally transferred the prisoners of the plant cultivation
workforce to a specially constructed subcamp in Rajsko. Apparently, the
conditions in this camp, made up of two barracks, were better than in the

[89] Anna Zięba, "Nebenlager Rajsko," *Hefte von Auschwitz*, 9 (1966), 75–108; see statement
by Joachim Caesar, 14.11.1961, ZSL, 402 AR-Z 45/73, 43–49; BArch, SS personal file on
Joachim Caesar.
[90] Danuta Czech, *Kalendarium der Ereignisse im Konzentrationslager Auschwitz-Birkenau
1939–1945* (Reinbek: Rowohlt, 1989), 209 ff. and 232; see statement by Maria Raczyńska,
19.11.1969, ZSL, 409 AR-Z 80/72, 234 ff.; statement by Anna Laskova, 14.12.1970, ZSL,
402 AR-Z 45/73, 253 ff.; report by Zofia Grochovalska (née Abramoviczova), in Lore
Shelley (ed.), *Criminal Experiments on Human Beings in Auschwitz and War Research
Laboratories. Twenty Women Prisoners' Accounts* (San Francisco: Mellen University Press,
1991), 222–230.
[91] KL Auschwitz, list of agricultural work units, 23.3.1944, copy in ZSL, 402 AR-Z 77/73, 103.
[92] Caesar to WVHA (Office D II), 20.5.1944, facsimile in Zięba, *Nebenlager Rajsko*, 91.
[93] Statements by survivors in ZSL, 402 AR-Z 45/73; account by Dr. Claudette Kennedy, in
Shelley, *Criminal Experiments*, 153–174; Eva Tichauer, *I Was No. 20832 at Auschwitz*
(London: Mitchell Vallentine, 2000).
[94] Martin Broszat (ed.), *Kommandant in Auschwitz. Autobiographische Aufzeichnungen des
Rudolf Höss* (Munich: DTV, 1989), 117 ff.

main camp at Auschwitz and Birkenau. Survivors' reports all agree that in Rajsko it was possible to wash regularly, that they had clean clothing, and that the accommodation was relatively bearable.[95] The reason for this, and for their transfer to Rajsko, was probably to prevent the spread of contagious diseases, as no regular selections for the gas chamber were made in Rajsko, unlike in Birkenau. Yet, even though no direct fatalities in the Rajsko subcamp are recorded, the female prisoners were still subjected to arbitrary punishments and serious maltreatment by SS women guards and men.[96] The relative safety of the camp remained only provisional, as sick prisoners were sent back to Birkenau.[97] The same applies for the execution of severe punishments. This is illustrated by the case of Slovakian-Jewish prisoner Lilli Tofler who was shot in Birkenau in September 1943 for smuggling a secret message.[98]

The exact date of Böhme's first appearance in Auschwitz is not recorded. We know, however, that he was admitted into the SS as a specialist leader in the rank of storm trooper on May 1, 1943, and transferred to Auschwitz in April 1944 to run the botanical laboratory.[99] This decision, partly by institute director Rudorf, was an effort to speed up results that had hitherto been hampered by the poor condition of the soil and lack of manpower in Müncheberg.[100] Eva Tichauer, a concentration camp survivor, described Böhme's behavior in Auschwitz-Rajsko thus:

His springy, silent footsteps force us to be constantly on our guard. He is continually on our backs, trying to control everything and insisting that it is our duty to cooperate honestly and to attain full production capacity. He pushes this perverse logic to its extreme by explaining to us that if he were a prisoner of the Soviets, he would act in the same way.[101]

When the Auschwitz camp complex was vacated on January 18, 1945, the prisoners of the plant cultivation workforce were marched westward along

---

[95] Statement by Jozefa K., 1.7.1971, ZSL, 402 AR-Z 45/73, 218–221; statement by Maria K., 5.8.1971, ZSL, 402 AR-Z 45/73, 232 ff.; statement by Helena H., 1.7.1971, ZSL, 402 AR-Z 45/73, 238 ff.

[96] Statement by Jozefa K., 1.7.1971, ZSL, 402 AR-Z 45/73, 218–221; statement by Ludmila R., 11.1.1971, ZSL, 402 AR-Z 45/73, 256–259; Tichauer, No. 20832, 68. Among the SS men described as feared was Thies Christophersen, who later wrote the revisionist publication "Die Auschwitz-Lüge" (1972).

[97] Rajsko sickbay ledger, where the names of three female prisoners suffering from typhus fever are marked with the note "to Birkenau," facsimile print in extracts in Zięba, Nebenlager Rajsko, 92 ff.

[98] Czech, Kalendarium, 604 f.; see Heim, Kalorien, 189 ff.

[99] BArch, SS personal file on Werner Böhme. The file gives his employer as "Abtl. Kautschukpfl. Kaiser-Wilhelm-Inst. Müncheberg."

[100] Heim, Kalorien, 169 ff.

[101] Tichauer, No. 20832, 69.

with the other prisoners, and several exhausting days later, they reached the already overcrowded Ravensbrück concentration camp.[102]

The kog-sagyz phase in Auschwitz-Rajsko preceded the broader employment of scientifically qualified concentration camp prisoners in which the KWI for Physical Chemistry also participated at a later stage. In May 1944, Himmler ordered the systematic "scientific deployment of prisoners":

> Among the Jews who we now have coming from Hungary, as well as among other concentration camp prisoners, there are doubtless a great number of physicists, chemists and other scientists. I instruct SS Obergruppenführer Pohl to set up a scientific research site in a concentration camp in which the specialist knowledge of these people can be put to use on the humanly demanding and time-consuming calculation of formulae, the construction of individual models, and on pure research.[103]

Himmler charged the Institute for Applied Army Research (*Institut für wehrwissenschaftliche Zweckforschung*, IWZ), under the umbrella of the SS *Ahnenerbe*, with the task of taking on commissions that the scientific world and armaments industry considered urgent, in cooperation with the SS Reich Security Main Office (*Reichssicherheitshauptamt*, RSHA). General responsibility was placed in the hands of the chief of the WVHA, Oswald Pohl, and the scientific running of the project was assigned to vice secretary general of the SS German ancestry office, SS Oberführer Walter Wüst.[104]

Two initiatives emerged later in Berlin and Krakow, which continued to develop independently from each other until the end of the war. In Berlin, a representative of the RSHA (Dr. Helmuth Fischer) suggested setting up a mathematical calculation institute in Sachsenhausen concentration camp, which began operation with ten prisoners in mid-November 1944.[105]

The second initiative, which the KWI for Physical Chemistry also took advantage of, came from senior SS leader and police chief in the General Government, SS Obergruppenführer Wilhelm Koppe. In early summer 1944, he arranged for another mathematicians' taskforce, a chemists' taskforce, and an engineers' and inventors' taskforce to be put together, manned by prisoners in Płaszów concentration camp. On an organizational level, they were linked with the Institute for German Work in the East (*Institut für deutsche Ostarbeit* or IDO) in Krakow.[106] Responsibility for the two

---

[102] Statements by survivors in ZSL, 402 AR-Z 45/73; Zięba, *Nebenlager Rajsko*, 94.

[103] Himmler to Pohl, 25.5.1944, SN, Nuremberg Document NO-640.

[104] For more on the SS-funded IWZ, see Michael H. Kater, *Das "Ahnenerbe" der SS, 1935–1945. Ein Beitrag zur Kulturpolitik des Dritten Reiches* 2nd ed. (Munich: Oldenbourg, 1997), 227–264.

[105] Karl-Heinz Boseck (head of the "mathematical department" in Sachsenhausen), November and December reports, 29.11.1944 and 28.12.1944, SN, Nuremberg Document NO-640.

[106] The Institute for German work in the East (*Institut für deutsche Ostarbeit*, IDO) was founded in 1940 in the defunct Polish university of Krakow. From spring 1943, the IDO

scientists' taskforces was given to chemist Dr. Hans-Paul Müller, deputy head of the Chemistry section of the IDO from 1943, and "representative of the OKW (General Armed Forces Office/Science Department) and Reich Research Council" at the IDO, Dr. Erich Pietsch, who supervised their organization.[107] In early September 1944, when the IDO was moved from Krakow to Schloss Zandt in the Upper Palatinate due to the advance of the Red Army, Himmler authorized the relocation of the chemists' taskforce and the engineers' and inventors' taskforce (altogether fifty-three largely Polish-Jewish prisoners) to Flossenbürg concentration camp; this move occurred in mid-October 1944.[108]

The research in Flossenbürg was concerned, among other things, with a collaboration between the Supreme Command of the Navy (*Oberkommando der Marine* or OKM) and the KWI for Physical Chemistry to construct a device named E O 2. In mid-December, Pietsch informed the institutions and persons involved, including Professor Thiessen as head of the specialist branch in the RFR and Professor August Winkel as head of department in the KWI for Physical Chemistry, that after extensive talks with the commanding officer of Flossenbürg concentration camp, work had begun on the prototype.[109] At a meeting attended by Pietsch and Thiessen in December 1944, it was stressed that "as intensive a use as possible of the scientific prisoners in the Płaszów concentration camp (or Krakow city) and Flossenbürg" was desired.[110] According to the memoir of the survivor George Topas, in January 1945 "a mousy-looking German civilian of small stature made an appearance in our shop [in Flossenbürg], sent from the Kaiser Wilhelm Institute in Berlin to supervise and speed up the completion of the project.

took on research commissions relating to military economics from the army. At the same time, it became a gathering place for numerous military-scientific institutes that were relocated to the General Government from Soviet territories near the front line; see, for example, Michael Burleigh, *Germany Turns Eastwards. A Study of Ostforschung in the Third Reich* (Cambridge: Cambridge University Press, 1988), 253–290.

[107] Hans-Paul Müller (born 1902), manager of the I.G. Farben plant in Eberfeld 1928–1935; Nazi Party member from 1937; instructor in chemical warfare from 1935; 1942–43 Wehrmacht (army medical facility Berlin); see personal record sheet on Hans-Paul Müller, BArch, R 52 IV/70, 277–285, and Eibl, *Thiessen*, 160 ff. On Pietsch's position, see an agreement between Pohl and Koppe (copy in excerpts), not dated, BArch, NS 21/845.

[108] Brandt to Koppe (communication of Himmler's assent), 9.9.1944, BArch, NS 19/2586, 6; Nummernbuch KL Flossenbürg, copy in Flossenbürg memorial.

[109] Pietsch, update on the scientific prisoner groups in KL Flossenbürg, 16.12.1944, BArch, NS 21/845; see Eibl, Thiessen, 160. The participation of Winkel, an expert on chemical warfare, suggests research connected to poison gas. The fact that the construction plan for the device mentions air filters, air distributors, reaction mass, and filler material suggests that EO2 was a gas protection filter.

[110] Entry by Pietsch, with regard to prisoners in scientific employment, 6.1.1945, BArch, NS 21/845; see Eibl, Thiessen, 161.

His presence put an end to our relative privacy and set up a gloomy and silent atmosphere."[111]

Finally, in mid-April 1945, the twenty-two remaining scientific prisoners in Flossenbürg were sent away on a transport together with other Jewish prisoners.[112] At least one member of the chemists' work unit was shot by the SS for being "unfit to march" before American troops liberated the completely exhausted group of prisoners some days later.[113]

CONCLUDING REMARKS

To summarize, we emphasize that the account presented here can only serve as an initial overview. With an extreme lack of source material, it was possible to reconstruct to only a minimal degree the social reality of forced labor and the attitudes and experiences of those directly affected.

Where numbers are concerned, we arrived at the following results: taking all possible uncertainties and the fragmentary nature of surviving documents into consideration, it seems realistic to assume that a total of about 1,000 persons (minimum) were forced to work for the KWS and its institutes between 1939 and 1945. Distinguishing among the individual institutes, the following numbers can be verified: KWI for Breeding Research – about 400 forced workers (including 100 concentration camp inmates); KWI for Stockbreeding Research – at least 224; KWI for Physical Chemistry – about 120 (concentration camp inmates); Institute for Agricultural Manpower Studies – 60; and KWI for Plant Cultivation Research – 16.[114]

Assessing the attitude of the General Administration of the KWS is hindered by the extreme lack of documents. Nevertheless, we have found that in several cases the General Administration explicitly recommended the use of forced labor and assisted with its good connections to senior Reich authorities when required. Thus, it can be assumed that the staff of the General Administration were on the whole aware of the extent and manner of forced labor used in research institutes of the Kaiser Wilhelm Society and did not raise any objections.

The major discrepancies between the individual institutes' handling of forced labor – even between those dealing with the same or similar fields of

---

[111] George Topas, *The Iron Furnace. A Holocaust Survivor's Story* (Lexington: University Press of Kentucky, 1990), 236. According to conservative estimates, at least twenty "prisoner scientists" must have been working in Flossenbürg on the E O 2 device.

[112] The majority of the other prisoners were either sent back to Płaszów on 13.11.44 or to Kirchham, a subcamp of Flossenbürg; see Nummernbuch KL Flossenbürg, copy in Flossenbürg memorial.

[113] Henry Orenstein, *I Shall Live. Surviving the Holocaust 1939–1945* (Oxford: Beaufort Books, 1988), 262 ff. Orenstein's brother Felek was one of the prisoners who were shot.

[114] The relocations are not included in this result – with the exception of Falkenhagen – as no concrete figures are available on which precise estimates could be made.

research – point to the fact that they enjoyed relative autonomy. It is notable that the forced labor of concentration camp inmates was limited to two institutes and quite obviously motivated by their directors and other influential scientists. Thus, the use of concentration camp labor at the KWI for Physical Chemistry would hardly have been imaginable without their director, Professor Peter Adolf Thiessen, who as head of the specialist branch in RFR had a great deal of influence as well as long-standing, excellent relations with the SS. The director of the KWI for Breeding Research, Professor Wilhelm Rudorf, and his assistant, Dr. Richard Werner Böhme, entered into a similarly close cooperation with Himmler's personal staff for their work on rubber research.

In the case of most institutes, records show that the attitude of members of staff toward forced workers was essentially shaped by how useful the workers were for their institute. There are only a few occasions on file of a head of an institute trying to improve the unenviable situation of his non-German employees. Moral or political scruples on the part of institute directors and the General Administration cannot be inferred from the records. On the whole, they bear witness to a certain apathy and moral indifference.

In this respect, the KWS and its research institutes were no different from other organizations, state institutions, and private enterprises in Germany at that time. While this emerges as the basic outcome of our investigation, the cases of Rajsko, Falkenhagen, and Flossenbürg should be noted as urgent reminders that scientists' ethical responsibility includes consideration of the conditions and context in which their research takes place.

4

Adolf Butenandt between Science and Politics: From the Weimar Republic to the Federal Republic of Germany

Wolfgang Schieder

Whether it makes sense to investigate the political views and behaviors of a natural scientist is a valid question. Certainly it does not do justice to the lifetime achievement of a natural scientist to look at him first and foremost as a homo politicus. However, the opposite is also true: scientific research is located in a social and political context, which conditions this research in any number of different ways. Without any reference to the political situation in which scientists work, the historical dimension of their scientific activity cannot be sufficiently understood.

In the history of German science, this is especially true for the period of the fascist-totalitarian dictatorship of National Socialism. There is a common misconception that National Socialism was hostile to science. In fact, this regime offered previously inconceivable opportunities for professional development to scientists, or at least to those who were not ostracized or driven out of the country.[1] Of course, the Nazi dictatorship also tempted scientists to disregard ethical principles and even to participate in research directly connected to the regime's crimes against humanity.

Therefore, it is legitimate to conduct a biographical investigation of Adolf Butenandt's political posture during the National Socialist period. Between

[1] On this, see Michael Grüttner, "Wissenschaftspolitik im Nationalsozialismus," in Doris Kaufmann (ed.), *Geschichte der Kaiser-Wilhelm-Gesellschaft im Nationalsozialismus. Bestandsaufnahme und Perspektiven der Forschung*, 2 vols. (Göttingen: Wallstein, 2000), vol. 2, 557–585; also Kristie Macrakis, *Surviving the Swastika: Scientific Research in Nazi Germany* (New York: Oxford University Press, 1993); Notker Hammerstein, *Die deutsche Forschungsgemeinschaft in der Weimarer Republik und im Dritten Reich. Wissenschaftspolitik in Republik und Diktatur* (Munich: Beck, 1999); Herbert Mehrtens, "Kollaborationsverhältnisse. Natur- und Technikwissenschaften im NS-Staat und ihre Historie," in Christoph Meinel and Peter Voswinkel (eds.), *Medizin, Naturwissenschaft, Technik und Nationalsozialismus. Kontinuitäten und Diskontinuitäten* (Stuttgart: GNT Verlag, 1994), 13–32; Monika Renneberg and Mark Walker (eds.), *Science, Technology and National Socialism* (Cambridge: Cambridge University Press, 1994).

1933 and 1945, Butenandt experienced a spectacular scientific ascent. As a biochemist and director of one of the most important institutes of the Kaiser Wilhelm Society (*Kaiser-Wilhelm-Gesellschaft*, KWS), he was one of the leading natural scientists of the Third Reich.[2] After 1945, he advanced to become probably the most successful scientist in the science policy of the Federal Republic. In terms of his public reputation, he probably could be compared only to Werner Heisenberg, yet he was superior to Heisenberg in terms of his organizational skills and personal assertiveness.

In science, too, however, the higher they climb, the harder they fall. Butenandt appeared to be threatened by this danger in the 1980s when the geneticist Benno Müller-Hill confronted him with an episode from his scientific activity during the final phase of the Third Reich.[3] Müller-Hill claimed that through his colleague and neighbor in Dahlem, Otmar Freiherr von Verschuer, the director of the Kaiser Wilhelm Institute for Anthropology, Butenandt had collaborated with Josef Mengele in Auschwitz. Rather than publicly contesting these accusations, Butenandt refused any serious discussion of the issue. Thereafter he was spared any further attacks on his reputation for the rest of his life. Nevertheless, once the nasty suspicion that he might have been involved in experiments with human material from Auschwitz had been uttered, it never went away. Angelika Ebbinghaus and Karl Heinz Roth even went so far as to declare that Butenandt had stood "at the center of German research on war and annihilation."[4] Therefore, it is time to subject Butenandt's role in the Third

---

[2] On Butenandt's biography, see the valuable, yet uncritical biography based primarily on conversations with Butenandt by Peter Karlson, *Adolf Butenandt. Biochemiker, Hormonforscher, Wissenschaftspolitiker* (Stuttgart: Wissenschaftliche Verlagsgesellschaft, 1990), countered demonstratively by the article by Robert N. Proctor, "Adolf Butenandt (1903–1995). Nobelpreisträger, Nationalsozialist und MPG-Präsident. Ein erster Blick in den Nachlass," *Ergebnisse. Vorabdrucke aus dem Forschungsprogramm "Geschichte der Kaiser-Wilhelm-Gesellschaft im Nationalsozialismus,"* No. 2 (Berlin: Forschungsprogramm, 2000; further quoted as *Ergebnisse*, No., and year). Rich in material but of questionable interpretation, Angelika Ebbinghaus and Karl Heinz Roth, "Von der Rockefeller Foundation zur Kaiser Wilhelm/Max-Planck-Gesellschaft: Adolf Butenandt als Biochemiker und Wissenschaftspolitiker des 20. Jahrhunderts," *Zeitschrift für Geschichtswissenschaft*, 50 (2002), 389–418. Recently on a single aspect: Lothar Mertens, "Nur 'zweite Wahl' oder Die Berufung Adolf Butenandts zum Direktor des KWI für Biochemie," *Berichte zur Wissenschaftsgeschichte*, 26 (2003), 213–22.

[3] Credit for raising this question for the first time with reference to Butenandt is undoubtedly due to Benno Müller-Hill, *Tödliche Wissenschaft. Die Aussonderung von Juden, Zigeunern und Geisteskranken* (Reinbek bei Hamburg: Rowohlt, 1984); English edition: *Murderous Science: The Elimination of Jews, Gypsies and Others in Germany 1933–1945* (Oxford: Oxford University Press, 1988). See also Benno Müller-Hill, "Das Blut aus Auschwitz und das Schweigen der Gelehrten," in Kaufmann, 189–227. Also revealing is the correspondence between Müller-Hill and Butenandt in Butenandt's papers, in the Archives of the Max Planck Society, Berlin (*Archiv zur Geschichte der Max-Planck-Gesellschaft*, MPG-Archiv), Abt. III, Rep. 84/2, NL Butenandt, Nr. 357.

[4] See Ebbinghaus and Roth, 410 f.

Reich to serious historical research and end the "silence of the scholars" so rightly criticized by Müller-Hill.

Butenandt hailed from a small-town, rather lower-middle-class background. He attended a Prussian secondary school rather than a classical academy. Moreover, as he was fond of emphasizing himself, he was the first academic in his family. This explains why he felt so unsure of himself at the beginning of his studies in Marburg in 1921 and was glad to be inducted into the Philippina Student Club through friends from school. His socialization in this fencing students' corps, in whose male bonding rituals he enthusiastically participated, imparted to him the social group consciousness that was to remain important to him throughout his life. To anyone who belonged to the inner circle of his family, of his group of friends, of the institute, or of the Kaiser Wilhelm Society, he remained steadfast and loyal.[5]

In keeping with this, Butenandt's style of leadership entailed treating his staff like one big family. Butenandt placed a high value on rituals that encouraged a sense of community. For this reason, birthdays and engagements were celebrated at the institute as well as Carnival and Summer Festivals; he also organized music evenings and once, even an institute horseback ride from Berlin to Grunewald.[6] Thus, Butenandt was more than just a normal doctoral advisor or institute director for his students and staff, even before he received the Nobel Prize. He understood himself to be the "*Führer*" (Leader) of his followers at the institute, and this feeling was more than just his way of conforming to the times.[7] He did not challenge his biographer's designation of him as a "patriarch in the best sense of the word."[8] Both epithets

---

[5] For example, see, MPG-Archiv, Abt. III, Rep.84/1, NL Butenandt, Butenandt to his parents of 30 April 1921: "I just came back from the dueling competition, which lasted a whole 8 hours. ... The duels were extremely heated and interesting," as well as his letter to his parents of 5 May 1922: "Of the glory of the fight, you, my dear 'anxious ones,' can have no idea. ... I soon stabbed my opposing driller, for I succeeded in inflicting upon him large head gashes and finally to cut the cheek from the top through to the mouth. About this glorious success everyone in Marburg is in great cheer."

[6] For example, see MPG-Archiv, Abt. III, Rep.84/2, NL Butenandt, Butenandt to his parents of 1 August 1942: "Last Sunday we had a wonderful music evening with 24 persons. At 6 o'clock we began; by nice weather 1 cup of tea was drunk in the garden and then there was Mozart, Bach and Brahms, later Reger as well"; and MPG-Archiv, Abt. III, Rep.84/2, NL Butenandt, Butenandt's letter to his parents of 18 October 1941: "Have I already told you of the plan to ride through Grunewald with all of the riders in the institute? Last Wednesday we did it! With Erika and myself we were 9 riders – a respectable group. ... The mood was very gay. Certainly there has never been such a thing, that a 'company outing' took place on horseback."

[7] For example, see the letter of 24 August 1943 to his parents in the MPG-Archiv, Abt. III, Rep. 84/2, NL Butenandt: "One must first of all get to it, move things around and reinforce air raid protection, but I have to set an example of this for the people here – that is why I am their leader"

[8] Karlson, 275.

signaled that he wanted to set an example not only as a scientist but also as an educator in all aspects of life. As a social climber who had needed to work hard for most of his social habitus, he was convinced that purely academic success was not sufficient for scientific advancement. Therefore, his patriarchal ministrations were intended to impart to his pupils more than mere scientific knowledge.

In the student corps in Marburg, Butenandt found more than just a sense of security and belonging, however. The German national ideology predominant there also corresponded to the vague political ideas he had adopted from his parents and his schooling. Although nominally a Protestant, he was rather distant from the church and sought a personal contingency in the arts and in nature.[9] The letters he wrote to his parents from the university feature lyrical reports about the kinds of nature hikes characteristic for the contemporary youth movement.[10] In the arts, his first preference was for music, above all, German classical and Romantic composers from Beethoven to Brahms. His literary taste, too, spanned the conventional framework from the German classics all the way to Wilhelm Raabe and Theodor Fontane.[11] Yet, back in his school days he was already an enthusiastic fan of the dull, nationalistically inclined writer Friedrich Lienhart;[12] he designated himself Lienhart's "disciple" in Marburg in 1922, sitting at the feet of this "master" in Göttingen.[13] Thus, it comes as no surprise that he ultimately developed decidedly antimodern taste in art, a remarkable contrast to the young chemist's strong faith in science. Characteristically, he regarded Fritz Lang's film *Metropolis* in 1927 as "kitsch to the greatest degree, hardly worth seeing."[14]

From his upbringing he also appears to have picked up certain anti-Jewish prejudices. These became virulent whenever he felt personally attacked or provoked, as when his parents came into conflict with Jewish neighbors or when he disapproved of readings of contemporary poetry. More alarming was his reaction to critical questions by Bernhard Zondek, a professor of gynecology in Berlin, on the occasion of his first lecture at the Kaiser Wilhelm

[9] Tellingly, on 8 November 1924 he wrote to his parents about a religious service he had attended "that was so beautiful that I found God in the church again for the first time in ages"; see MPG-Archiv, Abt. III; Rep. 84/2, NL Butenandt. That religiousness was "an important aspect of his being" and that he had "drawn power in difficult hours" from his devoutness, as Karlson, 276, asserts, is rather improbable.

[10] For example, see the letters to his parents of 19 May 1921, 9 November 1923, and 15 December 1923, MPG-Archiv, Abt. III, Rep.84/2, NL Butenandt.

[11] See Karlson, 20.

[12] See Karlson, 20.

[13] MPG-Archiv, Abt. III, Rep.84/2, NL Butenandt, Butenandt to his parents, 5 February 1922 and 27 June 1925.

[14] MPG-Archiv, Abt. III, Rep.84/2, NL Butenandt, Butenandt to his parents, 12 November 1927, 5 February 1922, and 27 June 1925.

Society; Butenandt described him in a letter to his parents as a "disgusting Jew," accusing him of a "certain arrogance."[15] He also reacted particularly stubbornly in 1935 to "new polemics by the Jew Ružicka,"[16] the very man with whom he was later awarded the Nobel Prize. As early as 1926 he had participated in a "protest rally against the disgusting Lessing," putting him in the ranks of the Germany-wide academic campaign that ultimately drove the pacifistic Jewish philosopher Theodor Lessing to commit suicide.[17]

In contrast, in January 1933, he was pleased to dine with the Jewish Nobel laureates Otto Warburg and Otto Meyerhof.[18] Further, there is proof that in 1942, he emphatically supported granting Warburg the same rights as the "German-blooded."[19] And last, it has been authenticated that in the 1930s he protected a Jewish member of his staff as long as he could.[20] His behavior toward his predecessor at the Kaiser Wilhelm Institute for Biochemistry, Carl Neuberg, whose Jewish background served as grounds for his forced dismissal in 1934, was somewhat more ambivalent. While he had no objections to a laboratory being set up for Neuberg in an annex to the institute, he insisted that the institute should carry none of the costs for the laboratory.[21]

Whenever it appeared useful for his career, or at least did no harm, Butenandt apparently had no objection at all to personal association with Jews. It was not "the" Jews in and of themselves against whom he objected; rather, his anti-Jewish prejudice emerged only in cases of conflict. This corresponds to the fact that he, in contrast to his colleagues Verschuer, Fischer, and Rüdin, for example, never got carried away with anti-Semitic tirades in public. He was by no means a militant anti-Semite. This behavior was

[15] The complete quote reads: "The only discordance was brought in by Zondek, a quite disgusting Jew – who attempted, with a certain arrogance and in an ironic tone, to belittle the importance of my work and its correctness. I responded with an answer that made the whole auditorium laugh heartily and put Mr. Zondek at a loss for words." See MPG-Archiv, Abt. III, Rep. 84/2, NL Butenandt, Butenandt to his parents, 18 January 1930.

[16] MPG-Archiv, Abt. III, Rep. 84/2, NL Butenandt, Butenandt to his wife Erika, 1 May 1935.

[17] MPG-Archiv, Abt. III Rep. 84/2, NL Butenandt, Butenandt to his parents, 18 June 1926.

[18] MPG-Archiv, Abt. III, Rep. 84/2, NL Butenandt, Butenandt to his parents, 14 January 1933: "In Berlin I spent the evening with the two Nobel laureates, O. Warburg and Meyerhof; I was Warburg's guest and it was terribly nice."

[19] See MPG-Archiv, Abt. III, Rep. 84/1, NL Butenandt, Nr. 598, REM to Butenandt, 4 September 1942, and Butenandt to the Reich Minister, 8 September 1942.
    See the sworn statement by Dr. Heinz Cobler of 11 June 1948, MPG-Archiv, Abt. III, Rep. 84/1, NL Butenandt, Nr. 211. On this, see Proctor, 13.

[20] See the sworn statement by Dr. Heinz Cobler of 11 June 1948, MPG-Archiv, Abt. III, Rep. 84/1, NL Butenandt, Nr. 211. On this, see Proctor, 13.

[21] On this, see Proctor, 31–33, and Ute Deichmann, "Chemie – Innenansicht einer Wissenschaft 1933–1945. Chemie und Biochemie an deutschen Universitäten und Kaiser-Wilhelm-Instituten; Entlassung und Exil jüdischer Chemiker und Biochemiker," *Habilitationsschrift*, University of Cologne (1998), 519–525.

hardly singular in the Third Reich. Indeed, it corresponded quite precisely to the conventional everyday anti-Semitism that had become so common within the upper middle class since the late imperial period, before the radical National Socialist type of anti-Semitism prevailed.

As far as Butenandt's political views are concerned, he rejected the Versailles blueprint for peace, as his vehement critique of French and English postwar policy shows.[22] In his private correspondence, he spoke of "French beasts" and "cursed Englishmen."[23] From this, it was clear that he aligned himself with the parties of the political right, which advocated a strict revisionist foreign policy. We know that in the Reichstag election of May 4, 1924, he vacillated between voting for the "German nationals or the *Völkisch* Socialists." While in this election he still voted for the German National Party of the *Volk*, from then on he drifted increasingly toward the *völkisch* orientation.[24]

From 1925 on, Butenandt had belonged to the *Jungdeutscher Orden* (Order of Young Germans), which had emerged from one of the many paramilitary Freikorps in 1920.[25] Like all *völkisch* ideologues, the founder and self-appointed leader of the order, Artur Mahraun, rejected "party democracy."[26] Instead, he envisioned a "*Führer* democracy," the basis of which was to be a kind of communitarian People's Community ("Volksgemeinschaft").[27] This movement, which was organized, typically, not as a party but as an "order," was supposed to assemble the leadership reserves of the future republic. The *Jungdeutscher Orden* accorded with other völkisch groupings

[22] See the enthusiastic birthday letter to his mother of 17 January 1923, MPG-Archiv, Abt. III, Rep. 84/2, NL Butenandt; he took the occasion of the occupation of the Rhineland by French troops to draft the vision of a nationalist future with a kind of German uprising. This letter includes passages like "thrilled, one glimpses the abrogation of Versailles and the strengthening of the German armies."

[23] See Butenandt to his mother, 17 January 1923, MPG-Archiv, Abt. III, Rep. 84/2, NL Butenandt, and Butenandt to his parents, 6 October 1925, MPG-Archiv, Abt. III, Rep. 84/2, NL Butenandt.

[24] See MPG-Archiv, Abt. III, Rep. 84/2, NL Butenandt, Butenandt to his parents, 3 May 1924.

[25] General information on the *Jungdeutscher Orden* from Kurt Finker, *Jungdeutscher Orden* (Jungdo) 1920–1933, in *Lexikon zur Parteigeschichte*, vol. 3 (Leipzig: Bibliographisches Institut, 1985), 138–148. The only major portrayal available is the older, rather apologetic one by Klaus Hornung, *Der Jungdeutsche Orden* (Düsseldorf: Droste, 1958).

[26] Artur Mahraun, *Das Jungdeutsche Manifest* (Berlin: Jungdeutscher Verlag, 1927), 61 ff. and 81 ff.

[27] For example, see MPG-Archiv, Abt. III, Rep. 84/2, NL Butenandt, Butenandt to Walter Hagenah, 31 October 1925: "The perfect person is the one who complies with his duty in life to the very extreme in the sense of the greatest capacity for humanity over *Volk* and fatherland"; MPG-Archiv, Abt. III, Rep. 84/2, NL Butenandt, Butenandt to his parents, 19 November 1927: "The fire of enthusiasm, the will to perform one's duties, this commitment of our entire life for one idea – that will never have been for nought."

in its militant nationalism and its anti-Semitic attitude. As such, it belonged to the camp of enemies of the Weimar Republic.

There is no doubt that Butenandt found in the *Jungdeutscher Orden* that "community" that the Philippina Student Club in Marburg had offered him. Although he was quite wrapped up in his exams and dissertation at the time, he was extremely active in the political work of the *Jungdeutscher Orden*. In numerous remarks, he revealed himself to be entirely of Mahraun's mind in rejecting the predominance of the parties in the Weimar state and wanting to replace it with an elitist leadership.

As long as bringing about this *Führer* state remained a utopian program for the future, however, Butenandt had to deal with the detested political present. He could do this only by emphasizing the notion of *duty*, which was one of the central categories of Mahraun's political philosophy. From Mahraun, Butenandt adopted the idea that one had to be loyal toward any political system, even if it did not correspond to one's own ideals. "Performing one's duty" thus became a secondary political virtue, which remained valid independent of the individual's personal value orientation. This dogmatization of the notion of duty probably carries the key to under-standing Butenandt's political behavior, not only in the Weimar Republic but especially in the Third Reich, and perhaps even after World War II. In any case it is documented that in situations during his career when he was required to make important decisions, he found orientation in this highly politicized idea of duty.

His veneration of his "*Führer*" Mahraun did not mean that Butenandt was treading a direct path to National Socialism. On the contrary, until 1933 the *Jungdeutscher Orden* strongly opposed the National Socialists. The main thing that separated these organizations was the fascist habitus of violence. It was no coincidence that the *Orden* welcomed the ban of the SA imposed by the government of the Reich in May 1932.[28] Thus, there can be no doubt that Butenandt kept a clear distance from National Socialism dur-ing the years of his active membership in the *Jungdeutscher Orden*. As late as the presidential election in March 1932, he signed an appeal supported by the *Jungdeutscher Orden* in Göttingen with the slogan "We are voting for Hindenburg, not Hitler."[29]

Through his appointment in early January 1933 to a chair for organic chemistry at the Technical University of Danzig, Butenandt initially

---

[28] See Hornung, 129.
[29] See the complete text of this appeal from the *Göttinger Tageblatt* of 5–6 March 1932, reprinted in Proctor, 14: "Hindenburg embodies us: German history, German character, German unity. Hindenburg, the first in war, the first in peace, the guarantor of Germany's future! Hindenburg knows only one thing: Service to the fatherland! *Volk* against party! We are voting for Hindenburg!" Of course, this had nothing to do with a "development toward becoming a democrat," as Karlson, 17, asserts.

remained out of the line of fire politically after Hitler took power.[30] The Free State of Danzig was under the control of a High Commissioner appointed by the League of Nations, who prevented an immediate National Socialist *Gleichschaltung*.[31] Yet, Butenandt was highly dependent on German financial support, most of which failed to materialize after 1935 for lack of hard currency. Thus, almost his entire stay in Danzig was characterized by a struggle for money, personnel, and premises. However, he contrived to receive not only research funding from the Rockefeller Foundation but also a stipend for travel to the United States and Canada.[32]

The two-month trip to America, for which he departed in March 1935, can be regarded as the most important research trip Butenandt ever undertook.[33] He was literally passed around among the most outstanding hormone research centers of the United States and Canada, met all of the esteemed luminaries of his field, and was able to establish how superior American biochemistry was to German – and to the field anywhere in Europe, thanks to its teamwork, its interdisciplinarity, and its mutual transparence. Quite early during this trip it dawned on him that such pains were being taken on his behalf to lure him from Germany to the United States. A few months after his return to Germany, he did indeed receive an offer of a chair at Harvard University.[34]

At the age of thirty-two, Butenandt thus faced the same decision that had confronted Heisenberg during the Third Reich: he could have left the Nazi state quite legally. Why did he not do so? The answer is quite simple: he never even seriously considered it. When he informed his wife on March 31, 1935, about the possibility of an offer from Harvard, he added the following: "Look, dear – I did not reject it in principle; I am waiting for the terms. At the moment there is nothing more opportune than an important offer from abroad. ... It is a trump – and I have the courage to use it against Berlin, if they want me. The question as to whether we fight for the German spirit here or there does not depend on me or on Harvard; it rests entirely with Germany."[35]

[30] On 22 December 1933 he wrote to his parents, "Today I see more and more that with the appointment to Danzig luck grasped me with both hands at the last second! Private instructors today have to undergo many new regulations, have to leave work to run through military sports, academy, etc. His achievements there determine his suitability."

[31] On this and the following, see Gotthold Rhode, "Die Freie Stadt Danzig," in Theodor Schieder (ed.), *Handbuch der europäischen Geschichte*, vol. 7 (Stuttgart: Klett-Cotta, 1979), 605–618.

[32] See Ebbinghaus and Roth, 394.

[33] For a detailed description of the trip based on Butenandt's letters to his wife Erika, see Karlson, 83–94. See also Ebbinghaus and Roth, 394, for supplementary information.

[34] See Karlson, 87.

[35] MPG-Archiv, Abt. III, Rep. 84/2, NL Butenandt, Butenandt to Erika Butenandt, 31 May 1935.

The offer from Harvard thus came along just at the right moment for Butenandt to return to the Reich from Danzig. Not a word of his response speaks of any consciousness that moving to the United States would have liberated him from all of the political constraitäten to which he had been subjected in Danzig. Not until 1985, in a television interview with Peter Koslowski, did he allow that he "did not recognize until much later ... that the appointment in Harvard also was intended to imply an opportunity for me to escape the political events in Germany, or anywhere in Europe."[36] While Butenandt did not feel beholden to National Socialism in 1935, his political commitment to the *Jungdeutscher Orden* had reinforced in him an emphatically charged nationalism, which, as he frequently expressed, bound him to his "beloved fatherland."[37] In late September, he therefore decided to reject the offer from Harvard and, as he said with great pathos, "persevere loyal to his post up to the very last day." Yet instead of the great offers he hoped for in Germany, he had to content himself with the fact "that the Technical University remains."[38]

In April 1936, however, he learned that the post of director at the Kaiser Wilhelm Institute for Biochemistry in Dahlem was to be his. He received a handwritten letter from Max Planck offering him the position in Berlin on May 1, 1936.[39] In 1933, Butenandt initially had assumed that he would be able to remain true to his party-hating convictions and avoid formally joining the NSDAP. Like so many others with national conservative leanings, he succumbed to the fatal error that it would be possible to act as a "nationalist" in the Third Reich without becoming a National Socialist. His name is found in the "Public Declaration of the Professors at German Universities and Colleges to Adolf Hitler and the National Socialist State," which was published on the evening before the National Socialist plebiscite of November 12, 1934.[40] At nearly the same time, he was asked to submit a short personal biography for a propaganda work the Nazi government was

---

[36] Transcript of the television interview with Peter Koslowski on ZDF in the "Witnesses of the Century" ("Zeugen des Jahrhunderts") series, MPG-Archiv, Abt III, Rep. 84/1, Nr. 199.

[37] For example, see MPG-Archiv, Abt. III, Rep. 84/2, NL Butenandt, Butenandt to Erika Butenandt, 13 April 1935: "America and England have received so many scientific greats that it makes one worry. And I love Germany so much." Note the allusion to the scientists expelled from Germany, several of whom he had met in the United States.

[38] MPG-Archiv, Abt. III, Rep. 84/2, NL Butenandt, Butenandt to his parents, 31 October 1935.

[39] On Butenandt's appointment in Berlin, see Mertens, 215–219.

[40] *Bekenntnis der Professoren an den deutschen Universitäten und Hochschulen zu Adolf Hitler und dem nationalsozialistischen Staat. Überreicht vom Nationalsozialistischen Lehrerbund Deutschland/Sachsen* (Dresden: NSLB, 1933), 132. On this, see the older work by Karl-Dietrich Bracher, Wolfgang Sauer, and Gerhard Schulz, *Die nationalsozialistische Machtergreifung. Studien zur Errichtung des totalitären Herrschaftssystems in Deutschland 1933/34*, 2nd ed. (Cologne: Westdeutscher Verlag, 1962), 318.

to publish under the title *Die Männer des neuen Deutschlands* ("The Men of the New Germany"). Tellingly, he agreed to be included in this political compendium because he had been requested to do so as a nonmember of the party.[41] If one were to define this behavior more precisely, it could be designated as a nonidentification with National Socialism. Butenandt held to the illusion that he could serve the Nazi regime without actually belonging to it.

Yet as early as 1935, it became clear that he would not be able to stay this course for the duration. The first time his name came into consideration for a position at the Kaiser Wilhelm Institute for Biochemistry, there were explicit reservations against him in the Reich Ministry of Education and Science (*Reichserziehungsministerium*, REM), "for political reasons." Thus Butenandt's abstinence from party politics could no longer be sustained.[42] When he was summoned to join the NSDAP by the head of the Danzig district, *Gauleiter* Forster, along with around 250 other personages of Danzig, he therefore submitted an application for party membership.[43] His explanation of why he relinquished his previous strategy of collaboration in the National Socialist state without party affiliation was not terribly convincing: he pointed out that he had not taken the initiative of joining but had been requested to do so by the party. This squares with his assertion ever since that his acquiescence to submit an application made him only an aspirant, but not actually a regular member of the NSDAP.[44] In truth, there is no doubt that he was listed on the party rolls from May 1, 1936, as party member No. 3716562.

It may be a coincidence that this was the precise day on which he received the appointment to the Kaiser Wilhelm Institute in Berlin. However, it is more likely that there was a connection – that Butenandt received the posting only because he joined the party at the same time. In any case, the significant political opposition against his appointment can only have been dissipated by the news that REM was at least informed of his application for membership in the NSDAP. Again, he deceived himself that he had received the appointment "without joining the party," as his party admission was "not yet known in Berlin."[45] However, it is apparent that his application for

[41] See the letter to his parents of 10 November 1933, MPG-Archiv, Abt. III, Rep. 84/2, NL Butenandt, as well as the *Deutsches Führerlexikon 1934/35* (Berlin, 1934), 82 f.

[42] See Karlson, 100, who cites an Administrative Committee protocol of the Kaiser Wilhelm Society of 9 April 1935. More recently, on the basis of the same files, also see Mertens, 215 f.

[43] See MPG-Archiv Archive, Abt. III, Rep. 84/2, NL Butenandt, Butenandt to E. Abderhalden, 9 January 1947: "In the year 1936 I was summoned by the Danzig *Gauleiter*, along with around 250 personages of Danzig's public sphere, to have my name accepted on the list of aspirants to NSDAP membership, in order to profess to Germanness. After thorough consideration I agreed to do so and thus became a party aspirant from 1936 on."

[44] MPG-Archiv, Abt. III, Rep. 84/2, Butenandt to his parents, 12/5/1936.

[45] See Federal German Archives (*Bundesarchiv*, BArch), NSDAP-Zentralkartei, Parteistatistische Erhebung 1939, Butenandt, Adolf.

membership in the NSDAP, which was nothing if not politically opportunistic, was the prerequisite for his appointment in Berlin – and the reason that it came about.

By 1939, Butenandt had joined a number of National Socialist suborganizations, but remarkably, not the SA or the SS.[46] It is further worth emphasizing that Butenandt, in contrast to many of his colleagues in the KWS, did not hold a leadership position in the party. However, he also consistently distanced himself from all public discourse about race policy, euthanasia, or Jewish policy. He was by no means the "red-hot Nazi" Thornton R. Hogness, a representative of the Rockefeller Foundation, believed he had met during a fleeting visit to Berlin in 1937.[47] On the other hand, he was more than a nominal member of the NSDAP. From 1937 on, his legacy certainly does include traces of his activity in the Dahlem chapter of the NSDAP.

Overall, Butenandt's activity in the NSDAP can be regarded as relatively insignificant. However, his ideological warming toward Hitler must be assessed as more problematic than his party activity, as the *Führer*'s foreign policy successes blinded Butenandt, like so many other Germans of the national conservative persuasion. At the time Hitler seized power, Butenandt took an extremely reserved position toward not only the NSDAP but also toward Hitler. Yet, when Hitler had apparently fulfilled the foreign policy program of the national right by 1939, he increasingly met with Butenandt's approval. While Hitler was still not the *Führer* Butenandt had dreamed of while in the *Jungdeutscher Orden*, Hitler's foreign policy appeared to agree more and more with the objectives of national revisionism. Butenandt, like most other Germans, did not comprehend that Hitler was aspiring to much more than the revision of "Versailles" and that Danzig was "not the objective"; rather, he aspired to the "consolidation of life space in the East."[48]

Butenandt spoke out positively about Hitler for the first time on May 17, 1933, when Hitler held the first of his so-called foreign policy peace speeches. Yet he was not "quite thrilled" until the German "*Anschluss*" (connection) of Austria.[49] When Hitler then had the armed forces Wehrmacht march into the defenseless Czech Republic on March 15, 1939, Butenandt spoke with praise about the "dynamic of events." The "European worldview" had "changed in accordance to the will of the *Führer*," he wrote to his parents. And for the first time he declared his "complete admiration for the man's

---

[46] See BArch, NSDAP-Zentralkartei, Parteistatistische Erhebung 1939, Butenandt, Adolf.

[47] This is used, but without any explication, by Ebbinghaus and Roth, 397, which merely repeats the designation "red-hot Nazi" found in the report.

[48] See the well-known protocol of Hitler's meeting with the military leaders of 23 May 1939 produced by Oberstleutnant G. Schmundt, for example, in Walther Hofer, *Der Nationalsozialismus. Dokumente 1933–1945* (Frankfurt: Fischer, 1957), 227.

[49] MPG-Archiv, Abt. III, Rep. 84/2, NL Butenandt, Butenandt to his parents, 12 March 1939.

genius," as Hitler had "achieved the increase of the Reich bloodlessly, in a way never before experienced."[50]

As we see from these remarks, Butenandt's opinion of Hitler changed gradually because Hitler had accomplished all of these foreign policy successes peacefully. He failed to recognize Hitler's threats and extortion as well as his one-page opt-out from the Munich Agreement, joining instead the collective self-deception of the German people. Consequently, his shock was tremendous at the beginning of the war on September 1, 1939. "Full of horror," he pictured "what else [might] conceivably come."[51] Yet, in the meantime, he had thoroughly fallen for Hitler's foreign policy *Führer* myth, as he laid the entire blame for the war on the English and French. "My disgust against the English mentality is great; all the more ardently does my heart beat for the *Führer* and his course."[52]

There can be no doubt that Butenandt continued to be thrilled to the utmost by Germany's military successes, although his concern about the political future and his hope for a rapid peace were also on his mind. Yet, as the war progressed, something in him changed decisively. Butenandt no longer praises Hitler's supposed political genius but only the military strength of the armed forces Wehrmacht. Never again does he speak as emphatically of Hitler as he had at the beginning of the war. What had happened?

On November 10, 1939, Butenandt was informed by a telegram from Stockholm that he and his colleague in Zurich, Leopold Ružička, had been awarded the Nobel Prize for Chemistry for his experiments with sex hormones.[53] Butenandt's joy was understandably great. It was thoroughly spoiled for him, however, when REM informed him that he would not be permitted to accept the Nobel Prize – the same fate encountered by the physiologist Gerhard Domagk and the chemist Richard Kuhn, the two German researchers who had been honored with Nobel Prizes in the previous year.[54] Not even the form of rejection was left up to Butenandt. Rudolf Mentzel of the Reich Ministry for Education and Science presented him with two

---

[50] MPG-Archiv, Abt. III, Rep. 84/2, NL Butenandt, Butenandt to his parents, 18 March 1939.
[51] MPG-Archiv, Abt. III, Rep. 84/2, NL Butenandt, Butenandt to his parents, 8 September 1939.
[52] MPG-Archiv, Abt. III, Rep. 84/2, NL Butenandt, Butenandt to his parents, 8 September 1939.
[53] MPG-Archiv, Abt. III, Rep. 84/1, NL Butenandt, Nr. 1161: telegram of 9 November 1939: "I have the honor to inform you that the royal Swedish Academy of Sciences has decided to award you and Professor Ruzicka the Nobel Prize for Chemistry of 1939. Letter to follow. Henning Pleijel, Secretary." Also see Pleijels letter to Butenandt of 17 November 1939, in which the Nobel Prize is designated "as a reward for your experiments about sex hormones." For the entire process, see Karlson, 105 f.
[54] See on this and the following, Political Archives of the Foreign Office (*Politisches Archiv des Auswärtigen Amtes*), Botschaft Stockholm, Box 627, Kult. 9, 1937–1944. I thank Florian Schmaltz for discovering these files.

draft letters, one of which he was to sign. The version he ultimately selected described the award of the Nobel Prize, because the Nobel Peace Prize had been awarded to Carl von Ossietzky, as an "insulting demonstration against the German Reich" and as an attempt to place him "outside the German People's Community."[55] Ossietzky was a well-known leftist journalist, had been an outspoken opponent of the National Socialists, and was imprisoned in a concentration camp. When he received the 1935 Nobel Peace Prize, it was an embarrassment for the regime, with the result that Hitler forbade Germans from accepting the prize.

The reference to the "People's Community" makes clear what Butenandt would have faced if he had accepted the Nobel Prize. Mentzel had intimated that the rejection of a command from the *Führer* could have consequences for him and his family.[56] Thus, what should have been a special tribute to Butenandt the scholar ended up presenting him with at least a potential existential threat. No wonder he was completely devastated. It was also the only time he ever expressed clear criticism of National Socialist government policy in his private correspondence: "What a shame, what an infinite shame, that my joy is so tarnished! Why did this unhappy development have to come about? How different it was when Windaus received the prize in 1927, what a zenith in the life of the nation! And now, in the midst of the war, in the hateful song of the peoples, three Germans are honored by the world; the foreign press reports it, 100 journals all over the world speak of their esteem before our work ... and Germany remains silent and forbids any direct response from us scholars!"[57]

Not only was he forced to reject the award but even a public announcement of the prize was prohibited.[58] As he wrote, he went through some "difficult days, so difficult that I often believed they would be my undoing," adding: "And some kind of blithe belief within me also must have perished."[59] Although he took care not to pronounce it in a letter, there can

[55] See the copy of an undated "draft of a response for Professor Kuhn," as well as a copy of the identical letter by Butenandt to the Royal Swedish Academy of Sciences of 25 November 1939, MPG-Archiv, Abt. III, Rep. 8/1, NL Butenandt, Nr. 233.
[56] See the credible portrayal in Karlson, 106, where it is also reported that Telschow, Alfred Kühn, and Fritz von Wettstein sought out Butenandt to convince him to sign.
[57] MPG-Archiv, Abt. III, Rep. 84/2, NL Butenandt, Butenandt to his parents, 17 November 1939. See also the folder with congratulations on the Nobel Prize in the MPG Archive, Abt. III, Rep. 84/2, Nr. 201.
[58] When Butenandt contacted the Swedish Academy of Sciences in 1948, he was informed on 27 December 1948 that he would receive the medal and the certificate for the Nobel Prize after the fact, but that payment of the prize money was no longer possible. The Swedish Consulate in Frankfurt then reported on 13 July 1949 that the consul had presented him the medal and the certificate.
[59] MPG-Archiv, Abt. III, Rep. 84/2, NL Butenandt, Butenandt to his parents, 24 November 1939.

be no doubt that with this he could only have meant his belief in Hitler, whose foreign policy successes had cast their spell on him up to the beginning of the war. From this exact point on, we find no further flowery phrases of devotion to the *Führer* in his private correspondence; indeed, Hitler is hardly ever mentioned at all.

In the context of the Nobel Prize incident, Butenandt had to acknowledge personally the totalitarian reality of the fascist regime, a reality he had been able to ignore for the most part. In 1933, he had first attempted to collaborate with the National Socialist state as a biochemist without joining the NSDAP. When this was no longer possible in 1936, he appears to have rationalized his conduct as loyal to the regime with the fact the Hitler had accomplished by peaceful means all of the demands for national revision so important to him. Not until the ban on accepting the Nobel Prize affected him so personally in 1939 did the political justification for his activity as a scientist in National Socialism vanish. Consequently, only "pure science" itself could legitimate his cooperation with the regime. In reality, of course, the "pure science" he claimed to restrict himself to during the National Socialist period did not stand in opposition to National Socialist science policy in the war but was indeed one of its pillars. Without the outstanding contributions of science, the Nazi regime would not have been able to launch the war or keep it up for so long. Moreover, Butenandt certainly worked to help meet the scientific demands of the war. He continued to comport himself loyally toward the Nazi regime, which he served dutifully to the bitter end. This is the only explanation for the fact that he received the War Merit Cross, Second Class, on November 19, 1942, and even the First Class medal on December 6, 1943.[60]

During the war, Butenandt understood better than anyone how to portray his research as applied, although the majority of his work was anything but contract research of military relevance. On March 15, 1940, for instance, he asserted that "all applied science ultimately has its roots in theoretical research." In this context he demonstratively praised National Socialist science policy because at the start of the war, despite "new tasks of the day," the policy had not restricted its plans for long-term research.[61] On January 23, 1941, he commented at greater length in a lecture at the Prussian Academy of Sciences on "Biological Chemistry in the Service of the Health of the Volk" (*"Die biologische Chemie im Dienste der Volksgesundheit"*).[62]

---

[60] MPG-Archiv, Abt. III, Rep.84/2, Butenandt to his parents, 12 November 1942, 6 December 1943.

[61] MPG-Archiv, Abt. III, Rep. 84/1, NL Butenandt, Nr. 154, handwritten lecture manuscript of 15 March 1940 titled "Virus Research as a Border Area of Biology and Chemistry."

[62] Adolf Butenandt, "Die biologische Chemie im Dienste der Volksgesundheit. Festrede am Friedrichstag der Preussischen Akademie der Wissenschaften am 23.1.1941," *Preussische Akademie der Wissenschaften, Vorträge und Schriften*, No. 8 (1941).

Proceeding from the observation that the "application of scientific work [had] never [been] demanded to such a great extent for the solution of tasks relevant to the present day," he moved the scientist up next to the soldier on the "first front lines of our struggle for survival." Yet, he insisted that in this situation chemistry had taken on such great importance for the "people's health" only because its work had been allowed to proceed without any presuppositions.[63]

Of course, it cannot be presumed that Butenandt was able to keep up this research concept during the war without any restrictions, no matter how subjectively he may have been convinced of its value. The biochemical research he performed had direct reference to practice for the very reason that a great deal of it was prescribed by industry. From 1929 on, when his mentor Windaus had placed him at the Schering-Kahlbaum Company in Berlin, he was closely linked, via Walter Schoeller, the director of the main laboratory, to a complex system of mutual dependence that lasted until 1945.[64] Through Heinrich Hörlein, he had also been associated with the I.G. Farben concern since 1937.[65] Moreover, this did not exclude sponsorship by the DFG or the Reich Research Council. On the contrary, the more successfully Butenandt solicited funds from industry, the more state funding flowed as well. To that extent, it was altogether appropriate when Butenandt declared in his lecture of 1943 that his research work during the war, "in terms of the tasks assigned," had "hardly experienced a change from the last decades of peace."[66] Even during the war, he actually did perform work that was primarily "theoretical research," which was supported by industry for the purpose of direct application. This alliance can be described as a scientific-industrial complex, whose volume, in terms of both the number and the scope of study projects, actually increased during the war.

Yet, this is not the whole truth either. During the war Butenandt also had direct military contract research performed in his institute in Dahlem, as even Peter Karlson admits.[67] The scientific importance and the results of this war research cannot be assessed here. What will be discussed, however, are a number of projects for which there is suspicion that Butenandt crossed ethical boundaries in their performance and thus may have associated himself with the crimes of the Third Reich.

[63] Butenandt, Die biologische Chemie, 20 f.
[64] On this, see Jean-Paul Gaudillière, "Biochemie und Industrie. Der 'Arbeitskreis Butenandt-Schering' im Nationalsozialismus," in Wolfgang Schieder and Achim Trunk (eds.), *Adolf Butenandt und die Kaiser-Wilhelm-Gesellschaft. Wissenschaft, Industrie und Politik im "Dritten Reich"* (Göttingen: Wallstein, 2004), 198–246.
[65] See Karlson, 93. Butenandt's relationship with the I.G. Farben concern has yet to be investigated.
[66] MPG-Archiv, Abt. III, Rep. 84/1, NL Butenandt, Nr. 154, Die Bedeutung der Wissenschaft im Kriege.
[67] See Karlson, 113, although only a compound against louse infestation is mentioned here.

As is known thus far, two features distinguished the "strategic" research contracts taken on by Butenandt. First, they consisted of such a thoroughly incidental collection of projects that their description as a "general store" is quite justified.[68] Second, it can be established that these projects generally were not delegated to Butenandt but that he himself proposed the majority of them. As both features corresponded to the reality of National Socialist science policy at the time, Butenandt need take no special credit. There was no central science policy decision center in the Third Reich. Thus, if it is possible to speak of a polycratic system anywhere, it is especially so in science policy, where various political channels competed against each other for access to natural science research. For many scientists this resulted in an entirely new latitude they were able to use to their advantage. They, and not the political or military channels they were serving, remained masters of the process and were able to seek out their cooperation partners themselves. The freer they were in their decisions, of course, the greater the responsibility they had to bear for their research projects.

Butenandt can be regarded as the prototype for such self-mobilization of science policy, with the consequence that he was primarily responsible for the projects required by various military offices. Nevertheless, one can make him responsible only for the projects he worked on himself. And this was seldom the case for the war projects that are particularly controversial in contemporary historical research because of their potential ethical transgressions. These tended instead to be projects conducted by his staff under the direction of or in collaboration with other researchers, without Butenandt in any position to exert any scientific control.

A first project of this kind emerged in 1942 from Butenandt's collaboration with Theodor Benzinger, the Air Force doctor and director of the physiological institute of the *Luftwaffe* (air force) Test Station in Rechlin. The point of departure for this collaboration was the shared "scientific interest regarding hemopoietines."[69] The *Luftwaffe* was facing the problem of oxygen deficiency among aviators during a sudden drop in pressure at high altitudes. Butenandt's research interest in the subject was dedicated to a potential hormonal solution to the problem of physiological adjustment to heights through the multiplication of red blood cells using this hemopoietine. Aside from the fact that this project clearly constituted war research, suspicion has arisen that Butenandt may have conducted it using unethical methods. As Benzinger was the leading expert in Germany on the utilization of vacuum chambers, it appeared that he could be connected with the homicidal human experiments performed by Sigmund Rascher in

---

[68] Ebbinghaus and Roth, 404
[69] See MPG-Archiv, Abt. III, Rep. 84/1, Nr. 627: sworn statement by Butenandt for submission as evidence at the American Military Court I in Nuremberg of 3 July 1947.

Dachau.[70] In truth, however, Benzinger expressly rejected experiments on human subjects "because of the extraordinary mortal danger."[71] Butenandt therefore had no reason to reproach himself for working with Benzinger.

The same cannot be said about Gerhard Ruhenstroth-Bauer, however, to whom he entrusted the project work for this scientific collaboration. Ruhenstroth-Bauer had taken his own initiative to develop from this project a further one in which he actually performed questionable human experiments in a vacuum chamber. They were part of a joint project with the departmental direction of the Kaiser Wilhelm Institute for Anthropology under Hans Nachtsheim.[72]

This project concerned whether an oxygen deficiency induced by negative pressure could contribute to the elucidation of the pathogenesis of epilepsy. As has been known for some time, six underage children from the State Psychiatric Hospital in Brandenburg-Görden were used as subjects for experiments in a vacuum chamber in Berlin performed in September 1943. Although the children apparently survived these experiments unharmed, according to later testimony by Ruhenstroth-Bauer, there is no question that the experiments had a medically impermissible coercive character.[73] Nor can it be forgotten that Görden was a center of the National Socialist murder program known as "euthanasia."[74]

Yet Butenandt was not responsible for these questionable experiments. After becoming a staff physician of the Air Force (Luftwaffe) from 1942 on, Ruhenstroth-Bauer no longer reported to him. Nachtsheim, not Butenandt, procured the research funds for the joint project. Above all, however, Ruhenstroth-Bauer did not publish his questionably obtained research results jointly with Butenandt, which was a condition upon which the latter insisted for all projects in which he participated. However, as Ruhenstroth-Bauer continued to occupy a position in Butenandt's institute after becoming a staff physician, it is likely that he had informed the director of his

---

[70] For the most recent account of this, see Karl Heinz Roth, "Tödliche Höhen. Die Unterdruckkammer-Experimente im Konzentrationslager Dachau und ihre Bedeutung für die luftfahrtmedizinische Forschung des 'Dritten Reiches,'" in Angelika Ebbinghaus and Klaus Dörner (eds.), *Vernichten und Heilen. Der Nürnberger Ärzteprozess und seine Folgen* (Berlin: Aufbau-Verlag, 2001), 110–151.

[71] Cited in Roth, "Tödliche Höhen," 118.

[72] For an extensive discussion of this, see Alexander von Schwerin , *Experimentalisierung des Menschen. Der Genetiker Hans Nachtsheim und die vergleichende Erbpathologie 1920–1945* (Göttingen: Wallstein, 2004). See also the earlier study by Paul Weindling, "Genetik und Menschenversuche in Deutschland, 1940–1950. Hans Nachtsheim, die Kaninchen von Dahlem und die Kinder vom Bulenhuser Damm," in Hans-Walter Schmuhl (ed.), *Rassenforschung an Kaiser-Wilhelm-Instituten vor und nach 1933* (Göttingen: Wallstein, 2003), 245–274.

[73] For a thorough discussion of this, see von Schwerin, *Experimentalisierung*, which utilizes all known documents as well as the later testimony provided by Ruhenstroth-Bauer.

[74] For the most recent account of this, see Hans-Walter Schmuhl's chapter in this book.

experiments in the vacuum chamber. Therefore, Butenandt could have known something about the project, even if he had nothing to do with it.

There was also a second case of a former pupil of Butenandt, namely Ulrich Westphal, and his research methods while serving in the military. As with Ruhenstroth-Bauer, the work probably had to do with hemopoietines.[75] However, Westphal was interested in their presumed effect in adaptation not to high altitudes but to low temperatures. In summer 1944, as he wrote to Butenandt, he performed "a series of metabolic experiments on humans ... conversion values in cold (cold bath) before and after the injection of cortisone or testovirone, respectively" in the cryogenics laboratory of the Army Mountain Warfare School in St. Johann, Austria.[76] Whatever was behind these experiments, it is remarkable how casually Westphal spoke of experiments on humans. This shows that he obviously had been caught up in the scientific dynamic of medical research in the Third Reich, which led everywhere to the stealthy transition from animal to human experiment and thus all too often to ethical transgressions. But he was no more instructed to perform these experiments by Butenandt than was Ruhenstroth-Bauer; rather, Westphal took the step toward medical irresponsibility on his own. However, in this case Butenandt was expressly informed.

Finally, there was also a third, especially controversial, case in which a member of Butenandt's staff became active in a questionable research context. Otmar Freiherr von Verschuer, director of the Kaiser Wilhelm Institute for Anthropology, was responsible for the project in question.[77] Verschuer had the ambitious goal of an experimental method to allow a serological diagnosis to identify human "races." He was convinced that in this manner he could eliminate what was probably the most sensitive gap in Nazi ideology, namely, the inability of the National Socialists to define the concept of race precisely. The research project was questionable because it was to be performed using "blood samples from over 200 persons of various racial extraction," which had been supplied to him by his pupil Josef Mengele in Auschwitz.[78]

[75] See MPG-Archiv, Abt. III, Rep. 84/1, Nr. 207, diary calendar of 1942, entry of 27 October 1942: "Besprechung bei Lang Mil. Ärztl. Akademie über Hämopoietine."

[76] MPG-Archiv, Abt. III, Rep. 84/2, NL Butenandt, Westphal to Butenandt, 22 August 1944.

[77] For this and the following, see Müller-Hill, *Tödliche Wissenschaft*; Ebbinghaus and Roth; Carola Sachse and Benoit Massin, "Biowissenschaftliche Forschung in Kaiser-Wilhelm-Instituten und die Verbrechen des NS-Regimes. Informationen über den gegenwärtigen Wissensstand," *Ergebnisse*, No. 3 (2000); Proctor; Hans-Peter Kröner, *Von der Rassenhygiene zur Humangenetik. Das Kaiser-Wilhelm-Institut für Anthropologie, menschliche Erblehre und Eugenik nach dem Kriege* (Stuttgart: Fischer, 1998).

[78] There is no authoritative biography on Mengele. See, however, Gerald L. Posner and John Ware, *Mengele. The Complete Story* (New York: McGraw-Hill, 1986); Helena Kubica, "Dr. Mengele und seine Verbrechen im Konzentrationslager Auschwitz-Birkenau," *Hefte von Auschwitz*, 20 (1997), 369–455: Zdenek Zofka, "Der KZ-Arzt Josef Mengele. Zur

As biochemical problems emerged in the production of substrates of these blood samples, Verschuer requested Butenandt's assistance. In response, in late summer 1944, after he himself had already moved to Tübingen along with most of his institute, Butenandt assigned Verschuer Günter Hillmann, one of the members of the institute who was still in Berlin.[79] Since Hillmann provided his scientific assistance exclusively at his home institute, the Kaiser Wilhelm Institute for Biochemistry, there is indeed justification to ask about the extent to which Butenandt, too, was responsible for the questionable project. Yet, since Butenandt was not at all interested in the content of the project, and in a sense only had Hillmann provide technical support, one cannot blame him. The scientific responsibility for the Auschwitz project lay exclusively with Verschuer.

Nevertheless, it must be presumed that Butenandt was informed about the provenance of the blood samples from Auschwitz. Verschuer made no secret of this, not even after the war. That was serious in this case to the extent that Hillmann, in contrast to Westphal and Ruhenstroth-Bauer, did not place himself in an ethically questionable research context on his own initiative but through Butenandt's direct agency. This connection, from Auschwitz to Verschuer to Hillmann to Butenandt, makes it understandable that Butenandt endeavored to keep Verschuer out of the Max Planck Society after the war.[80]

According to the evidence, and although to date not all of his research projects in the period of National Socialism are fully known, Butenandt cannot be linked directly to the National Socialist extermination policy. In his case, there were neither scientific grounds nor any ideological motivation for ethically impermissible experiments with humans. Finally, one can assume, without any further elaboration here, that he also did not participate in research about the manufacture of biological weapons. However, although he was not scientifically responsible for them, he definitely was informed about the questionable scientific projects performed by Westphal, Ruhenstroth-Bauer, and especially Hillmann. Given his understanding of science, Butenandt actually should have warned his staff members about crossing the boundary to what is impermissible according to the ethics of science. Yet this definitely did not happen here. This is what constitutes Butenandt's real moral failure.

Typologie eines NS-Verbrechers," *Vierteljahrshefte für Zeitgeschichte*, 34 (1986), 245–267, as well as the recent work by Achim Trunk, "Zweihundert Blutproben aus Auschwitz. Ein Forschungsvorhaben zwischen Anthropologie und Biochemie (1943–45)," *Ergebnisse*, 12 (2003), 9–16, 61–67, translated as a chapter in this book.

[79] See Müller-Hill, *Tödliche Wissenschaft*, 162 f.
[80] On this, see Carola Sachse, "Adolf Butenandt und Otmar von Verschuer. Eine Freundschaft unter Wissenschaftlern (1942–1969)," in Schieder and Trunk, 286–319.

His knowledge of others performing ethically questionable research appears not to have been a matter of particular concern to Butenandt during the period of the Third Reich. He probably preferred not to know all that he actually could have known. Tellingly, as a witness in the Nuremberg I.G. Farben trial against Heinrich Hörlein in 1947, he claimed that he knew the names of only Dachau and Oranienburg. "I had never heard of Buchenwald, Belsen, Auschwitz. I did not know what took place in the camps; whenever I heard allusions to what was going on there during trips abroad, I gave no credence to the rumor, because they were located completely beyond the realm of my imagination."[81] While it is theoretically possible that he did not know the name Auschwitz, because of his collaboration with Verschuer this claim must be ruled out as implausible. Butenandt apparently had repressed his unwelcome memories so intensively that he may not even have told the truth in court.

It can no longer seem surprising that Butenandt did not see any occasion immediately after the collapse of the Third Reich for a self-critical confrontation with his political past. His withdrawal to "theoretical research," to which he had committed himself since the outbreak of the war, seemed after the fact to legitimate his behavior as a natural scientist in the Third Reich. Since he had performed only "pure" science and thus presumably protected himself against any political instrumentalization, he believed, like most of the natural scientists of his rank, to have remained politically "pure." This behavior thoroughly corresponded to the scientific strategy of self-justification generally advanced by the natural science elite in West Germany after 1945.

The only thing that troubled Butenandt politically after 1945 was the fact that his name was listed as wanted in the American zone and was not removed until June 23, 1947.[82] Yet, he could comfort himself with the fact that the French Military Administration in Tübingen treated him quite differently. "Everyone is obliging and cooperative to the Nobel laureate," he wrote his parents in June 1945.[83] Although internally he was certainly assessed as a National Socialist, the French occupation power granted him political probation. As early as 1946 he was invited to Paris to meet with a member of the *Académie de Médecine*.[84] The French Military Administration

[81] MPG-Archiv, Abt. III, Rep. 84/1, NL Butenandt, Nr. 211: Butenandt's testimony of 5 July 1947, 6.

[82] See the effusive letter of thanks he wrote to the Commander of the CIC in Stuttgart on 5 August 1947 after his name was stricken from the list of those to be arrested on 23 June 1947, MPG-Archiv, Abt. III, Rep. 84/2, NL Butenandt, Nr. 620.

[83] MPG-Archiv, Abt. III, Rep. 84/2, NL Butenandt, Butenandt to his parents, 6 June 1945.

[84] See the handwritten entry on this list of his foreign trips, MPG-Archiv, Abt. III, Rep. 84/1, NL Butenandt, Nr. 1332: "Personal invitation" as "guest of Dr. Fouché, Paris" ("*Gast von Dr. Fouché, Paris*"). A report about this trip is found in the letter to his parents of 23 September 1946, MPG-Archiv, Abt. III, Rep. 84/2, NL Butenandt. See further the Archives

also protected him from the grasp of the Americans on several occasions.[85]
As early as November 1945, he was in Basel for two days of negotiations
with the La Roche Company about possible employment.[86] In September
1948, despite tempestuous public discussions in Switzerland, he was even
offered a chair at the University of Basel; however, he turned down this offer
in January 1949.[87]

There is no question that his preferential treatment by the French occupying power, like the lucrative offers from politically neutral Switzerland,
must have reinforced Butenandt's subjective perception that he had nothing
to reproach himself for politically. How was he supposed to subject himself
to political self-critique when he was courted so intently immediately after
the end of the Third Reich? This behavior should not be criticized too hast-
ily. The assumption that the Germans would have better mastered the path
from the murderous dictatorship into a free democratic future after 1945 if
they had immediately and wholeheartedly faced up to their past is based on
pure speculation. On the contrary, it is no coincidence that some time was
needed before most Germans even took notice of the balance of the Third
Reich's crimes, in part because they were not aware of the full extent of these
crimes and in part because their entire devastating impact was too much for
many people to comprehend. Yet, it remains very difficult to accept the fact
that during this period of overwhelming speechlessness, all too many people
self-righteously sought refuge in the role of victim, with the result that most
of the true perpetrators escaped punishment.

This chapter could close here and diagnose Butenandt as a normal case
of the German "inability to mourn." There is a second conclusion, however. Just as the political stance of many Germans regarding the past of the
Third Reich gradually changed in a period characterized by the politics of
memory, for Butenandt, too, there appears to have been a kind of political
shift in memory. Butenandt appears to have at least recognized that the
mere fact that he played such an outstanding role as a natural science expert
in demand during the Third Reich was a political liability, even though he
believed there was no reason to reproach himself for moral failings.

In any case, it can be established that around 1949 Butenandt began to
speak out in a clearly self-critical tone about his past in the Third Reich. In
March 1949, for instance, in the context of a discussion about the founding

of the Occupation of France by Germany and Austria (*Archives de l'occupation française en
Allemagne et en Autriche*), Colmar, Affaires culturelles 70, Cabinet: de Recherche scienti-
fique, letter of 21 August 1946. On Fouché, see Karlson, 159.

[85] See Karlson, 149; MPG-Archiv, Abt. III, Rep. 84/2, NL Butenandt, Butenandt to his parents,
15 March 1947.
[86] MPG-Archiv, Abt. III, Rep. 84/2, NL Butenandt, Butenandt to his parents, 4–10 November
1945; 15 December 1945.
[87] On the entire process, see MPG-Archiv, Abt. III, Rep. 84/1, NL Butenandt, Nr. 1283.

of a German Research Council, he stated his belief that setting up such an institution was important because it would allow the failings of the past to be corrected: "We would then not suffer from the accusations we always face now, that we did not bring our sense of responsibility to bear."[88] Especially revealing in this regard is another lecture, which he held in 1968 on the occasion of the presentation of the Theodor Heuss Prize to Karin Storch, a witness in the concentration camp trials. In this speech he explicitly criticized the fact that the "criminals ... from the period of ignominy [who] continue to live among us" still had not been punished. He spoke up for the rights of Polish residents in the formerly German territories east of the Oder-Neisse line "for the loss of which we are to blame."[89]

In the interview Peter Koslowski conducted with him in 1985, as part of the ZDF "Witnesses of the Century" ("*Zeugen des Jahrhunderts*") series, he again expressed himself quite clearly on the subject of Germans' "collective guilt." He rejected the concept with regard to the Third Reich, yet spoke of "guilt" because "we all did not do enough. One probably could have done more." In this context, he is reminded of a conversation he conducted with his teacher Windaus at the very beginning of the Third Reich. They had agreed that one would have to wait until the storm had passed. And he added, "As we know, this prevalent opinion was utterly wrong. I believe stronger opposition could have prevented some of what happened."[90]

Finally, it must be pointed out that Butenandt, along with Alfred Kühn and above all Georg Melchers, was one of the few leading lights of the young Max Planck Society who perceived from a very early point in time that action had to be taken to make up for the injustices perpetrated against the expelled members of the Kaiser Wilhelm Society. As early as April 1947, he suggested to Otto Hahn, albeit unsuccessfully, that the society encourage James Franck to return to Germany from the United States. He regarded this effort to reconcile with Franck to be "a wonderful possibility" to make up for "an injustice that is burdensome to us all."[91]

Certainly, there were no precise confrontations with Butenandt's own past in the Third Reich. That he was a science policy collaborator on the highest level, with changing rationalizations for his participation, is something he never actually acknowledged. And Butenandt never took the position that

---

[88] MPG-Archiv, Abt. III, Rep. 84/1, NL Butenandt, Nr. 338.

[89] See the manuscript – unfortunately, only partially preserved – in the MPG-Archiv, Abt. III, Rep. 84/1, NL Butenandt, Nr. 1643. The manuscript is undated, but from an allusion to the year 1955, "thirteen years ago almost to the day," it is clear that it must have been written in 1968.

[90] Transcript of the television interview with Peter Koslowski on ZDF, MPG-Archiv, Abt. III, Rep 84/1, Nr.199, 65 f.

[91] Butenandt to Otto Hahn, April 1947, MPG-Archiv, Abt. III, Rep. 14a, Nr. 529. I thank Michael Schüring for bringing this letter to my attention.

the Max Planck Society as an institution should confront its dark past during the Third Reich as the Kaiser Wilhelm Society. In all fairness, and this must be stated clearly, there was never any demand from within the society that he do so. But his scattered pronouncements do reveal that Butenandt ultimately did take a clear position on the collective process of German memory. Apparently, the clear conscience that carried him without reflection from the Third Reich into the immediate postwar period clouded over the years. To this extent, Butenandt did confront his personal responsibility before history, albeit more through his political activity than through self-critical reflection.

SECTION II

RACIAL RESEARCH

5

Brain Research and the Murder of the Sick: The Kaiser Wilhelm Institute for Brain Research, 1937–1945

Hans-Walter Schmuhl

On 14 June 1946, Professor Julius Hallervorden, director of the Section for Histopathology at the Kaiser Wilhelm Institute for Brain Research (*KWI für Hirnforschung*, KWIHF), experienced the surprise of his life. Completely unexpectedly, the neurologist and psychiatrist Professor Leo Alexander, a Jew who had been forced to leave Germany in 1933[1] and was now conducting numerous interviews with German neurologists, psychiatrists, and neuropathologists on behalf of the American military government, appeared in Dillenburg, Hessia, where Hallervorden had landed with his department in 1944. Believing Alexander to be an ally in the struggle to preserve the KWIHF, Hallervorden threw caution to the wind and acknowledged forthrightly that in his department he had studied hundreds of brains that came from mentally ill and mentally disabled patients who had been killed in the course of the Nazi "euthanasia" program.[2]

---

[1] Leo(pold) Alexander was born in Vienna in 1905. After studying medicine at the University of Vienna, he worked at the City and University Clinic for the Emotionally Disturbed and Mentally Ill (*Städtische und Universitätsklinik für Gemüts- und Nervenkranke*) in Frankfurt am Main from 1929 to 1933, initially as an intern and then as an assistant. Suspended in February 1933, he was granted a Rockefeller scholarship, which took him to Beijing, China, as a visiting lecturer. After the National Socialists seized power, he lost his position in Frankfurt and immigrated to the United States in late 1933, where he became a successful neuropathologist. Having become a U.S. citizen in 1938, he was a member of the U.S. Army Medical Corps from 1942 until 1946. In 1945 Alexander investigated medical research institutions in the Allied zones for the Combined Intelligence Objectives Sub-Committee (CIOS). From November 1946 to June 1947 he testified as a medical expert for the U.S. prosecutor's office in the Nuremberg Doctors' Trials. See the brief biography in Angelika Ebbinghaus and Klaus Dörner (eds.), *Vernichten und Heilen. Der Nürnberger Ärzteprozess und seine Folgen* (Berlin: Aufbau-Verlag, 2001), 620 f. In 1928 Alexander had visited the KWIHF as an observer. Information according to Jürgen Peiffer, *Hirnforschung in Deutschland 1849 bis 1974. Briefe zur Entwicklung von Psychiatrie und Neurowissenschaften sowie zum Einfluss des politischen Umfeldes auf Wissenschaftler* (Berlin: Springer, 2004), 1051.

[2] See Jürgen Peiffer, *Hirnforschung im Zwielicht: Beispiele verführbarer Wissenschaft aus der Zeit des Nationalsozialismus* (Husum: Matthiesen, 1997), 41–45.

As far as his visitor's intentions were concerned, Hallervorden could not have been more wrong. Alexander's mission was to investigate the state of research achieved in National Socialist Germany; at the same time, he was collecting material to prepare charges in the Nuremberg Physicians' Trial. While no preliminary proceedings against Hallervorden were opened and he was not charged, his remarks in conversation with Alexander resulted in his role in "euthanasia" becoming public, so that in the aftermath – for instance, in connection with the Fifth International Congress of Neurology in Lisbon in 1953 – intense controversies about Hallervorden's wartime activities erupted on numerous occasions. Later, Hallervorden vehemently denied using the formulations cited by Alexander, but confirmed the facts – the investigation of hundreds of brains obtained through the mass murder of the mentally ill and disabled. What is clear is that the KWIHF was definitely involved in the research accompanying Nazi "euthanasia." This must be the point of departure for any history of the institute: Which factors caused, made possible, or favored the institute's drifting off into that gray area of research on the perimeter of the "euthanasia" program?

A number of works on the history of the KWIHF are already available.[3] They have laid an empirical foundation upon which further research can build. These works fall short with regard to the epistemological questions formulated above, however, because they proceed from a quite narrow institutional history approach, placing the primary emphasis of their depiction on the life and work of Oskar Vogt. Thus, the period from 1937 to 1945 – that is, precisely the phase during which the "euthanasia" program was prepared and executed – is treated only very briefly. This final point is also true for the dissertation by Helga Satzinger,[4] which nevertheless opens up a broad history of science perspective and thus exposes long-term lines of continuity in the institute. General historians, with Götz Aly[5] at the forefront, have taken a different approach in studying the involvement of the KWIHF in the Nazi "euthanasia." The focus of this work goes beyond the analysis of the scope and the forms brain research assumed as it became involved in

[3] Jochen Richter, "Das Kaiser-Wilhelm-Institut für Hirnforschung und die Topographie der Grosshirnhemisphären. Ein Beitrag zur Institutsgeschichte der Kaiser-Wilhelm-Gesellschaft und zur Geschichte der architektonischen Hirnforschung," in Bernhard vom Brocke and Hubert Laitko (eds.), *Die Kaiser-Wilhelm-Gesellschaft/Max-Planck-Gesellschaft und ihre Institute* (Berlin: de Gruyter, 1996), 349–408; Heinz Bielka, *Die Medizinisch-Biologischen Institute Berlin-Buch. Beiträge zur Geschichte* (Berlin: Springer, 1997).

[4] Helga Satzinger, *Die Geschichte der genetisch orientierten Hirnforschung von Cécile und Oskar Vogt (1875–1962, 1870–1959) in der Zeit von 1895 bis ca. 1927* (Stuttgart: Deutscher Apotheker-Verlag, 1998).

[5] Götz Aly, "Der saubere und der schmutzige Fortschritt," *Beiträge zur nationalsozialistischen Gesundheits- und Sozialpolitik*, 2 (1985), 9–78; Götz Aly, "Forschen an Opfern. Das Kaiser-Wilhelm-Institut für Hirnforschung und die 'T4'," in Götz Aly (ed.), *Aktion T4, 1939–1945* (Berlin: Hentrich, 1987), 153–160.

Nazi medical crimes. Instead, it is directed primarily toward the scientific preparation, control, and evaluation of the mass murder of the sick and disabled in order to investigate the character of the "euthanasia" program as a means of *social engineering* based on the biological sciences. In this case, brain research is portrayed as part of the scientific substructure upon which the murders rested, thus appearing as a quasi-appendage of psychiatry and anthropology. Great credit is due to Jürgen Peiffer[6] for having brought these two research orientations closer together. Yet Peiffer's interpretation remains beholden to a biographical approach. Certainly Julius Hallervorden must be at the core of the analysis if the point is to investigate the involvement of the KWIHF in the murder of the mentally ill and disabled. However, focusing on Hallervorden results in making his department seem like a foreign body within the institute, which could give the false impression that the research performed on the brains of "euthanasia" victims there was entirely disconnected from the "normal research" performed at the institute.

In contrast, this chapter advances the thesis that the institute became involved in the research accompanying mass murder as a logical consequence of the personnel, institutional, and conceptual changes taking place within the KWIHF from 1937 on, and that research in the slipstream of the "euthanasia" campaign dovetailed with the institute's research program developed before the war. Replacing Oskar Vogt with Hugo Spatz as director of the institute marked a caesura whose importance has been underestimated as regards the murder of the mentally ill. It must be added forthwith that – in addition to these course settings on the eve of annihilation – there were also long and continuous lines leading to this murderous program. Indeed, these can be traced back further than the change of epochs in 1933 – all the way back to the era of Oskar Vogt.[7] It was a bundling of long-term developments in the conception of brain research combined with short-term changes in institutional structures and personnel constellations that brought the institute onto the slippery slope.

---

[6] Peiffer, *Hirnforschung im Zwielicht*; Jürgen Peiffer, "Neuropathologische Forschung an 'Euthanasie'-Opfern in zwei Kaiser-Wilhelm-Instituten," in Doris Kaufmann (ed.), *Geschichte der Kaiser-Wilhelm-Gesellschaft im Nationalsozialismus. Bestandsaufnahme und Perspektiven der Forschung*, 2 vols. (Göttingen: Wallstein, 2000), vol. 1, 151–173.

[7] See Michael Hagner, *Geniale Gehirne. Zur Geschichte der Elitegehirnforschung*, 2nd ed. (Göttingen: Wallstein, 2005), 235–287; Michael Hagner, "Im Pantheon der Gehirne. Die Elite- und Rassengehirnforschung von Oskar und Cécile Vogt," in Hans-Walter Schmuhl (ed.), *Rassenforschung an Kaiser-Wilhelm-Instituten vor und nach 1933* (Göttingen: Wallstein, 2003), 99–144; Helga Satzinger, "Krankheiten als Rassen. Politische und wissenschaftliche Dimensionen eines internationalen Forschungsprogramms am Kaiser-Wilhelm-Institut für Hirnforschung (1919–1939)," in Schmuhl, *Rassenforschung*, 145–189. See also Hans-Walter Schmuhl, "Hirnforschung und Krankenmord. Das Kaiser-Wilhelm-Institut für Hirnforschung 1937–1945," *Vierteljahrshefte für Zeitgeschichte*, 50 (2002), 559–609, here 575–582.

THE REORGANIZATION OF THE INSTITUTE IN 1937/38

The KWIHF was a creation of the scientist couple Oskar and Cécile Vogt. Its nucleus was the Neurological Center (*Neurologische Zentralstation*), a private institute the Vogts founded in Berlin in 1898 with financial support from the Krupp family; the center was formally associated with the Physiological Institute of the Charité as the Neurobiological Laboratory of the Berlin University in 1902. During 1914–1919, the Senate of the Kaiser Wilhelm Society (*Kaiser-Wilhelm-Gesellschaft*, KWS) resolved to set up a KWIHF, initially specifying that this institute should be accommodated in the Neurobiological Laboratory. In fact, this meant that the two institutions, both of which were directed by Oskar Vogt, were practically identical. On February 24, 1930, after two years of construction, the institute moved into its new quarters in the immediate vicinity of the City Hospitals in Berlin-Buch. Thus the KWIHF advanced to become the world's largest and most modern institute for brain research of its day.[8]

The political spectrum represented within the staff extended from the extreme left to the outmost right. In 1933 the inner circle surrounding Oskar Vogt exploded, with latent tensions erupting in a series of fierce conflicts. Vogt was trapped in a thicket of intrigues and denunciations from which escape was all but impossible and ultimately he could not be retained. In late 1935 it was definitively clear to everyone that Oskar and Cécile Vogt would leave the KWIHF.[9] It was agreed that Oskar Vogt should continue to serve as acting director of the institute until 1 April 1937. His anointed successor was Hugo Spatz, the assistant to Munich psychiatrist Professor Oswald Bumke and director of the Neuropathological Laboratory at the Psychiatric and Neurological Clinic in Munich.

The new leadership went hand in hand with a far-reaching restructuring, as even a cursory glance at the structure of the institute shows: dissolved immediately were the Department for Neurochemistry – its director, Dr. Marthe Vogt, a daughter of Cécile and Oskar Vogt, emigrated to England – as well as the Department for Psychology directed by Dr. Wolfgang Hochheimer. Dr. Jan Friedrich Tönnies, who had directed the Department for Physical Technology under Dr. Vogt, was working at the Rockefeller Institute for Medical Research in New York from 1936 to 1939 and thus was not in Berlin at the time of the power shift. Upon his return to Germany, he did not go back to the KWIHF, although he was listed as a visiting scientist until 1940. His department was taken over by his staff member Dr. Johann Albrecht Schaeder as a subdivision of the Department for Experimental Physiology under Professor Alois Kornmüller.

[8] Richter, 355–388; Bielka, 18–25; Satzinger, *Geschichte*, 82–91.
[9] See Richter, 388–392; Bielka, 31–33; Satzinger, *Geschichte*, 93–95; Schmuhl, "Hirnforschung," 562–569; Hagner, "Pantheon," 125–131.

Through negotiations with the Reich Ministry for Education and Science (*Reichserziehungsministerium*, REM), Spatz was able to spin off the Department for Psycho-Phonetics under Dr. Eberhard Zwirner, which had distanced itself ever further from the research program of the institute since 1933, and the Department for Experimental Genetics under Nikolaj Vladimirovich Timoféeff-Ressovsky. In fact, the Psycho-Phonetics Department was dismantled in 1938.[10] This was not so simple in the case of the internationally renowned Genetics Department. While Spatz initially had pushed insistently for the rapid spinoff of the department he regarded as a "foreign body" in the institute, pressure from REM convinced him to change his position. Timoféeff-Ressovsky had been offered a position with the Fundamental and Scientific Research Program at the Carnegie Institution of Washington. Since attempts to incorporate the Genetics Department into the KWI for Biology foundered on the resistance of the institute's director, Professor Fritz von Wettstein, the ministry resolved to maintain the Genetics Department and Timoféeff-Ressovsky on the campus of the KWIHF, although it became completely independent in terms of administration and financing.[11]

The new Department for Experimental Pathology and Tumor Research was established. Its director was Professor Wilhelm Tönnis, a specialist in brain surgery, who had held a professorship in Würzburg until that time and now was appointed extraordinary professor at the University of Berlin – despite opposition from the Medical Faculty – and chief surgeon of the Hansa Hospital. Tönnis was also to take over part of the Clinic for Nervous Diseases of the KWI.[12] Also new was the Department for General Pathology under Professor Hans E. Anders, whose main position was director of the Neuropathological Institute in Berlin, which was located at the Department of Pathology of the Sanatorium and Hospital in Berlin-Buch. With the appointment of Anders, Spatz as head of the institute hoped that

[10] Gerd Simon and Joachim Zahn, "Nahtstellen zwischen sprachstrukturalistischem und rassistischem Diskurs. Eberhard Zwirner und das 'Deutsche Spracharchiv' im Dritten Reich," manuscript (available by request at http://www.homepages.uni-tuebingen.de/gerd.simon).

[11] See Bernd Gausemeier, *Natürliche Ordnungen und politische Allianzen. Biologische und biochemische Forschung an Kaiser-Wilhelm-Instituten 1933–1945* (Göttingen: Wallstein, 2005), 150–186. For a biography, see Helga Satzinger and Annette Vogt, "Elena Aleksandrovna Timoféeff-Ressovsky (1898–1973) und Nikolaj Vladimirovich Timoféeff-Ressovsky (1900–1981)," in Ilse Jahn and Michael Schmitt (eds.), *Darwin & Co. Eine Geschichte der Biologie in Portraits*, 2 vols. (Munich: Beck, 2001), vol. 2, 442–470.

[12] Notes concerning the Kaiser Wilhelm Institute for Brain Research, 26 March 1936, Archives of the Max Planck Society, Berlin (*Archiv zur Geschichte der Max-Planck-Gesellschaft*, MPG-Archiv), Abt. I, Rep. 1 A, 1581; Glum to Spatz, 26 May 1936, MPG-Archiv, Abt. I, Rep. 1 A, 1582; Tönnis to General Administration of the KWS, 12 March 1937, MPG-Archiv, Abt. I, Rep. 1 A, 1598. Spatz/Tönnis to von Bohlen, 29 July 1937, Krupp Historical Archive, Essen (*Historisches Archiv Krupp*, HA Krupp), FAH, 4 E 271.

"brain research would find the necessary connection with the pathological research of the other bodily organs."[13]

Both the KWIHF and the Department of Pathology of the Sanatorium and Hospital in Buch hoped that their cooperation would provide a powerful stimulus to intensify the relations between the researchers at the institute and the physicians in Berlin's district sanatoriums and hospitals in Buch, Herzberge, Wuhlgarten, and Wittenau. A cooperation of this nature had been initiated back in 1920 and was given a new contractual foundation in 1928 – in connection with the new building for the institute and the establishment of the research clinic.[14] Yet, the cooperation appears to have lacked any momentum before 1933. An indication of both sides' initial lack of interest in collaboration is demonstrated by the fact that there was not even sufficient demand among physicians to fill the workplaces for advanced training stipulated in the contract.[15]

Under the conditions of the Third Reich, on the one hand, exterior political and economic pressure on the clinic grew, while on the other, this development also generated impetus for the expansion and intensification of its work. There was significantly increased interest from the KWI in collaborating more closely with the city's sanatoriums and hospitals. Such forms of cooperation were targeted for expansion in the Spatz era. Consequently, the visiting scientists at the KWIHF in 1938 included no fewer than seven physicians from Berlin, among them Dr. Wolfgang Goetze of the Buch Hospital and Sanatorium, Senior Physician Dr. Karl Balthasar of the Herzberge Hospital and Sanatorium, and Senior Physician Dr. Otto Reisch of the Robert Koch Hospital. Also, in subsequent years, physicians from sanatoriums and hospitals in Berlin were regularly represented among the guests at the institute.[16] Being a visiting scholar at the KWIHF endowed these residents with a unique identity and mentality. Because of its isolated location and cramped quarters – the residents of the campus in 1939 included eleven families of scientists with a total of nineteen children[17] – a very tight coherence emerged in both the professional and private spheres, a development that was directly encouraged by Spatz, for instance, by introducing sport activities for all residents.[18]

---

[13] Spatz to Glum, 3 June 1936, MPG-Archiv, Abt. I, Rep. 1 A, 1582.

[14] Contract between the city of Berlin and the KWS of 20 July 1928, Berlin State Archives (*Landesarchiv Berlin*), Rep. 03–04/1, 136. See the exposé on Oskar Vogt, sent by von Harnack to Deputy Assistant Undersecretary Donnevert at the Reich Ministry of the Interior on 13 January 1928, Federal German Archives (*Bundesarchiv*, BArch), R 1501/26787.

[15] See Mayor/Ges. IV/4, to Buch Hospital and Sanatorium, 8 August 1933, Berlin State Archives, Rep. 03–04/1, 135.

[16] Identified according to the overviews in the journal *Die Naturwissenschaften*.

[17] Denkschrift über die Wohnungsverhältnisse am KWI für Hirnforschung, Hugo Spatz, 26 January 1939, MPG-Archiv, Abt. I, Rep. 1 A, 1636.

[18] Spatz to von Cranach, 22 April 1937, MPG-Archiv, Abt. I, Rep. 1 A, 1632.

The exceedingly close coherence was manifested not least in a number of marriages between scientific staff members of the institute. Close networks emerged among the scientists who worked at the institute in the years from 1937 to 1945, extending far beyond the German borders to places like Scandinavia, southeastern Europe, Italy, Spain, and Chile, and outlasted the epochal change of 1945.

An additional channel for scientific exchange with the medical profession in Berlin was the Bucher Tag, an annual symposium, to which prominent speakers from other locations were invited.[19] The great interest Spatz showed in the Buch Hospital and Sanatorium in particular was apparent when, in 1940, the closure of the facility was planned; Spatz lobbied City Medical Councillor Dr. Theobald Sütterlin intensely for the preservation of the institution or at least for a Special Station for Psychoses of Particular Scientific Interest.[20] What is certain is that the politics of the new institute director served to create a tightly meshed fabric of relationships between the KWIHF and Berlin's institutions for the mentally ill. Initiated here were networks of personnel and institutional interactions that became important in the execution of the "euthanasia" program.

The network of relationships soon extended well beyond the borders of Berlin into the province of Brandenburg. The expansion of ties was a direct consequence of the reopening of the Department for Histopathology, which had been shut down temporarily after the dismissal of Max Bielschowsky in 1933. This department played quite a central role in the plans for the future. Even when Spatz was negotiating his acceptance of the directorship, he had energetically urged that the department be headed by an "independent and recognized scientific personality."[21] And here Spatz's decision was for Hallervorden.

Julius Hallervorden[22] had worked as an assistant and then as senior physician at the Landsberg/Warthe Hospital and Sanatorium since 1913, where he operated a small neuropathological laboratory in addition to performing his clinical activities. In 1921, Professor Walter Spielmeyer procured a scholarship for him at the German Research Institute for Psychiatry (*Deutsche Forschungsanstalt für Psychiatrie*), where Hallervorden also befriended Spatz – in 1922 the two men classified the condition that

[19] For example, see the invitation to the Bucher Tag on 16 December 1937, MPG-Archiv, Abt. I, Rep. 1 A, 1583.

[20] Spatz to Sütterlin, 8 July 1940 (quote); Sütterlin to Spatz, 10 July 1940, MPG-Archiv, Abt. I, Rep. 1 A, 1583. Spatz's intervention was emphatically supported by Hallervorden. See Hallervorden to Spatz, 25 September 1940, MPG-Archiv, Abt. II, Rep. 1 A, PA Hallervorden, 5.

[21] Spatz to Telschow, 28 July 1937, HA Krupp, FAH, 4E 271.

[22] See Peiffer, *Hirnforschung im Zwielicht*, 14 f., and MPG-Archiv Archives, Abt. II, Rep. 1 A, PA Julius Hallervorden, 1.

bears their names, Hallervorden–Spatz disease. Although his scientific achievements attracted international interest and he maintained a lively correspondence with Spielmeyer, Spatz, and Bielschowsky, Hallervorden stayed at the Hospital and Sanatorium in Landsberg. In 1928, he declined Oskar Vogt's offer to switch to the KWIHF and take over part of the planned research clinic. Not until 1929 was he released from his clinical position to assume direction of the Central Pathological Department of the psychiatric institutions of the Brandenburg province. This pathological department was relocated to Potsdam in 1936. Dr. Hans Heinze had directed the hospital there since 1934. Heinze was the first scientifically interested, prominent, and committed psychiatrist to enter the service of the Brandenburg Province Association, and he breathed new life into the group. Hallervorden was thrilled:

This man has created a downright fantastic clinical operation worthy of a university clinic and thus it is conceivable that the two of us will be attracted to each other like magic. This is how the matter came about and considering the central location, there is hope of pepping up my laboratory in a way very different than has been possible so far.[23]

In 1937, when Spatz offered him the positions of director of the Histopathological Department and deputy director of the KWIHF, Hallervorden initially expressed strong reservations, as he did not want to give up the Department of Pathology in Potsdam. Against this backdrop, the plan matured to merge the Potsdam Department of Pathology with the Histopathological Department of the KWI. As Spatz argued to Ernst Telschow, the Secretary General of the KWS, this would not only solve the question of staffing the Department for Histopathology "but at the same time it would link with the KWIHF a state institution that is ripe for expansion. A bounty of brain material – coming from greater Berlin and the Brandenburg province – thus could be investigated from both Buch and Potsdam according to uniform aspects. It would be possible to undertake far-reaching scientific investigations through the collaboration of combined forces."[24] The plan was implemented quickly, so that Hallervorden was able to join the KWIHF on 1 January 1938. He retained his position as director of the Pathological Department of the Brandenburg state psychiatric institutions. The Department of Pathology, still funded by the provincial association, was officially transferred to the KWIHF in Berlin-Buch; from that point on, the laboratory at the state institution in Potsdam was an outpost of the KWI, financed by the KWS

---

[23] Hallervorden to Spatz, 29 November 1935, cited in Peiffer, *Hirnforschung im Zwielicht*, 22.
[24] Spatz to Telschow, 6 August 37, HA Krupp, FAH, 4 E 271.

and represented by an assistant, first by Dr. Oskar Ammermann, and later by Dr. Werner-Joachim Eicke.[25] In 1938, it moved to the state hospital in Brandenburg-Görden, which was soon to become one of the centers of the "euthanasia" program. Thus, the KWIHF outpost in Brandenburg-Görden became the most important link between the murder of diseased patients and brain research in Berlin.

The founding of these new departments – along with the modified tasks of Department I – showed the shift in emphases experienced by the research program of the KWIHF in 1937.[26] For, in his department, Spatz continued the Vogts' research on brain architectonics only marginally.[27] He pursued markedly pathological interests, primarily related to the pathology of the nucleus caudatus (striary system), the clinical and pathological anatomy of systematic atrophy of the cerebral cortex (Pick's disease), the pathological anatomy of circulatory disturbances of the brain, studies on brain injuries, and the propagation of the various forms of encephalitis.[28] In some points, these interests coincided with those of Hallervorden, who was interested above all in the pathogenesis of multiple sclerosis and on the investigation of "idiocy" that was congenital or manifested at a young age.[29] The research emphasis of the KWIHF shifted clearly from the *healthy* to the *diseased* brain, the pathogenesis of individual diseases and disabilities moved into the foreground, and the question as to disposition and heredity became considerably more important. Even in the address he gave the staff of the institute upon taking office, Spatz referred explicitly to the Law for the Prevention of Genetically Diseased Offspring.[30]

---

[25] Vereinbarung zwischen dem Provinzialverband der Provinz Brandenburg und der KWG, 1/12/1937+23/1/1938, Archives of the Berlin-Brandenburg Academy of Sciences (*Archiv der Berlin-Brandenburgischen Akademie der Wissenschaften*), KWG, 74. Peiffer, *Hirnforschung im Zwielicht*, 33. On the physicians in the Department of Pathology: Personalbogen Oskar Ammermann, MPG-Archiv, Abt. II, Rep. 20 B, 121; service evaluation of Werner-Joachim Eicke, 1 April 1944, BArch, H 20/425.

[26] This was also apparent in the changed membership of the board of trustees. See Schmuhl, "Hirnforschung," 582–587.

[27] On this, Spatz to the General Administration of the Kaiser Wilhelm Society (*Kaiser-Wilhelm-Gesellschaft*, KWS), 14 November 1936, HA Krupp, FAH, 4 E 271; Hugo Spatz, "Von den Zielen des KWI für Hirnforschung. Denkschrift an die Generalverwaltung der KWG," 23 March 1945, p. 2, MPG-Archiv, Abt. II, Rep. 20 B, 120.

[28] Working plans for the Kaiser Wilhelm Institute for Brain Research in Berlin-Buch, starting on 1April 1937, MPG-Archiv, Abt. I, Rep. 1 A, 1598; Protocol of the Meeting of the Board of Trustees of the Kaiser Wilhelm Institute for Brain Research on 1 November 1937 and 20 December 1938, MPG-Archiv, Abt. I, Rep. 1 A, 1590.

[29] Peiffer, *Hirnforschung im Zwielicht*, 16 f.

[30] Ansprache des Betriebsführers des Kaiser-Wilhelm-Instituts für Hirnforschung in Berlin-Buch, Professor Hugo Spatz bei Übernahme der Direktion am 1.4.37, MPG-Archiv, Abt. I, Rep. 1 A, 1582.

The start of World War II marked a further rupture in the institute's history. A parallel military structure emerged, comprised of three complexes: the Special Office for the Research of War Damage to the Central Nervous System (*Sonderstelle zur Erforschung der Kriegsschäden des Zentralnervensystems*) under Julius Hallervorden, the External Department for Brain Research (*Aussenabteilung für Gehirnforschung*) of the Aviation Medicine Research Institute (*Luftfahrtmedizinisches Forschungsinstitut*) under Hugo Spatz, and the Research Office for Brain, Spine and Nervous Injuries (*Forschungsstelle für Hirn-, Rückenmark- und Nervenverletzte*) under Wilhelm Tönnis.[31] The installation of military structures alongside the civilian ones certainly ensured the preservation of the institute in the short term, but in the long term it threatened to choke the civilian research sector. The institute was soon financially dependent on infusions from the military. Contract research for the military actually did overlap with the civilian research program in some areas, but other emphases of the institute's work in the prewar period – especially the studies on "idiocy" that was congenital or manifested at a young age – no longer could be continued. Involvement in the research accompanying the "euthanasia" program now presented an opportunity to continue this research orientation even under war conditions. At the same time, it opened up the possibility of obtaining outside financing independent of the military and thus at least maintaining the bare bones of the civilian research program.

BRAIN RESEARCH AND MURDER OF THE SICK

In the ideas held by the staff of psychiatric experts, which played a decisive role in the planning, preparation, and execution of the mass murder of the mentally ill and mentally disabled in the Third Reich, healing and annihilation were closely linked. These doctors, many of whom had risen to prominence in the Weimar Republic as advocates of a fundamental reform of psychiatry, regarded "euthanasia" as a chance to implement their concept of reform in reality: in the course of the "euthanasia" program the bulk of the chronically ill and disabled patients, who had failed to respond to any of the forms of therapy known at the time, were to be annihilated. In thus doing away with the "ballast existences," the program would clear the way to restructure clinical psychiatry, with the separation of healing institutions from institutions of care at the core. Then, on the basis of this reorganization of the system of psychiatric institutions, the new forms of therapy developed in the 1920s and 1930s could be implemented on a broad

---

[31] There are indications that at the External Department for Brain Research, examinations were also performed on the brains taken from victims of the low-pressure experiments "for rescue from great heights," which Dr. Sigmund Rascher had carried out at Dachau concentration camp from February through May 1942. See Schmuhl, "Hirnforschung," 588–594.

scale: the "more active treatment of the ill" along with insulin coma, car-
diazol shock, and electric shock therapies. The dovetailing of institutional
practice and theoretical research promised even further refinement of the
therapeutic instruments. Self-confidently, it was proclaimed "that psychiatry
today is a medically healing discipline in the true sense of the word."[32] There
was optimism that the possibilities of therapy would be expanded considerably further in the near future. In the therapy of hereditary diseases and
disabilities, eugenics always constituted a complementary element; through
sterilization, genetic defects were to be "eliminated" in coming generations.

The triad of therapy, eugenics, and "euthanasia" moved psychiatric
genetic research into the focus of interest. The staff of medical experts at
the head of the "euthanasia" apparatus was well aware that the diagnostic
possibilities available at the time were hardly sufficient to illuminate with
any certainty the inheritance of mental illnesses and mental disabilities. The
murder of these patients actually opened up new possibilities for psychiatric
research. Some people who were sorted out for elimination in the course of
the selection process carried out by the "euthanasia" headquarters represented "interesting cases" that attracted the scientists' attention; these individuals could first be observed clinically and then murdered so their brains
could be dissected for pathological examination. Of course, the prerequisite
for this was that the researchers involved would flout elementary norms of
general and professional ethics. As would become apparent, many scientists
had no problem with this – it appears that once the basic categorization of
patients as "worthy of life" or "unworthy of life" was accepted, the flood-
gates were opened.

In early 1941 – probably on 23 January – Reich University Teachers'
League *Führer* (Leader) Walter Schultze held a conference at which a large-
scale research plan linked with the "euthanasia" program was drafted.
Fourteen of the thirty anatomical institutes of the German Reich were
to take part in the planned mass examinations. While the course of the
war prevented the realization of this ambitious plan, from 1942 on, the
"Euthanasia" Headquarters maintained two research departments: one
directed by Professor Hans Heinze at the Brandenburg-Görden Clinic (from
January 1942), the other under the direction of Professor Carl Schneider in
the Wiesloch Clinic in Baden (from late 1942) or at the Heidelberg University
Clinic, respectively (from August 1943). The brains of patients who had been
killed were sent to various neuropathological laboratories, including that of

[32] Schlussbemerkungen. Wissenschaftliche, wirtschaftliche und soziale Bedeutung und Zukunft
der psychiatrischen Therapien, BArch, R 96 I/9. These remarks were made by Carl Schneider
and intended as the final paragraphs of a lecture about the therapy of endogenous psychoses
to be given at the 1941 Convention of the Society of German Neurologists and Psychiatrists
(*Tagung der Gesellschaft deutscher Neurologen und Psychiater*) – which ultimately did not
take place.

the German Research Center for Psychiatry (*Deutsche Forschungsanstalt für Psychiatrie*, DFA) in Munich, via the Pathological Department at the Eglfing-Haar Clinic under Professor Hans Schleussing[33] to which it reported, and that of the KWIHF via the Department of Pathology at the state clinic in Brandenburg-Görden.

In the course of a reorganization of the clinics administered by the Mark Brandenburg province, the Potsdam Clinic had been dissolved in 1938 and the majority of children and teenage patients had been brought to the Brandenburg-Görden State Hospital.[34] At the same time, Heinze took over as director in Görden, bringing his staff with him. Under Heinze, the clinic, which counted 2,600 beds at the start of World War II, 1,000 of them for children and teenagers, emerged as one of the centers of the "euthanasia" campaign. It became the headquarters of the first Specialized Pediatric Department of the German Reich. From 1940 this department, which had sixty to eighty beds and was generously equipped, served as the "Reich training station" for physicians being groomed as directors of further Specialized Pediatric Departments. The pioneering function of Brandenburg-Görden in the "euthanasia" of children was no coincidence: Heinze belonged to the Reich Committee for the Scientific Registration of Serious Hereditary and Constitutional Conditions (*Reichsausschuss zur wissenschaftlichen Erfassung schwerer erb- und anlagebedingter Leiden*) and was thus directly involved in the consultations about the "euthanasia" of children. Moreover, he was a member of the three-man board of experts that made the decisions about the life and death of the selected children. It is uncertain how many children and teenagers were killed in Görden. Hans-Hinrich Knaape indicates that children were carried off in five waves of transports, in May and June 1940, to the gas chambers of the so-called Brandenburg Mental Hospital set up in the penitentiary in the city of Brandenburg, where they met their death.[35]

The Brandenburg-Görden Hospital also played an important role in Aktion T4, the mass gassing of around 70,000 psychiatric patients from January 1940 through August 1941. This was no accident. In this case, Heinze was also on the staff of medical experts concerned with the planning

---

[33] Volker Roelcke, "Psychiatrische Wissenschaft im Kontext nationalsozialistischer Politik und 'Euthanasie'. Zur Rolle von Ernst Rüdin und der Deutschen Forschungsanstalt für Psychiatrie/Kaiser-Wilhelm-Institut," in Kaufmann, *Geschichte*, vol. 1, 112–150; Peiffer, "Neuropathologische," 166–170.

[34] On the role of Görden in the "euthanasia" program, see: Hans-Hinrich Knaape, "Euthanasie in der Landesanstalt Görden 1939–1945." Lecture given at the conference "'Eugenik' und 'Euthanasie' im sog. Dritten Reich," Diakonisches Werk der Evangelischen Kirche in Lobetal, 28 October–1 November 1989, unpublished manuscript; Sabine Hanrath, *Zwischen "Euthanasie" und Psychiatriereform. Anstaltspsychiatrie in Westfalen und Brandenburg: Ein deutsch-deutscher Vergleich (1945–1964)* (Paderborn: Schöningh, 2002), 136–148.

[35] Knaape, "Euthanasie," 6.

of the murders. In Aktion T4, Brandenburg-Görden functioned as an intermediary. It is not clear how many patients were sent from here to the Aktion T4 annihilation centers. Knaape declares that seven transports with approximately 550 patients departed Görden for the Brandenburg Mental Hospital, and that eighteen more transports with around 1,100 adult patients went to Bernburg. Beyond this, between May 1940 and November 1943, an additional 1,100 patients of all ages were moved to the clinics in Eichberg, Hadamar, and Meseritz-Obrawalde.[36] Also unclear is whether three more transports in January, February, and September 1944, which brought a total of 161 patients to the Ansbach Clinic in Bavaria, were connected with the "euthanasia" program.[37]

In September 1941, the medical director of Aktion T4, Professor Hermann Paul Nitsche, suggested making the hospital useful for research by moving "the cases of congenital idiocy and epilepsy" from the surrounding institutions to Görden, "to then forward them to one of our [killing] institutions after performing the necessary examinations."[38] From November 1941 through January 1942, a number of preliminary discussions between Nitsche and Heinze took place, concluding on 24 January 1942 with a discussion between Nitsche, Schneider, Heinze, and the doctors called upon to work in the research department at Görden: Dr. Ernst Schmorl, Dr. Wilhelm Schumacher, and Dr. Arnold Asmussen. Due to an agreement between the Reich Consortium for Institutions of Healing and Care (*Reichsarbeitsgemeinschaft Heil- und Pflegeanstalten*) and the Provincial Association of the Mark Brandenburg province of 20–26 February 1942, eighty beds at the Görden hospital were available to the research department from 26 January 1942 on. Originally 160 beds had been planned, but half of the beds had to be relinquished to the armed forces Wehrmacht. On 6 July 1942, half of the slots available to the research department, again, were ceded to the armed forces, so that research had to be restricted to comparatively few cases. By September 1942, ninety-seven patients had been examined in the Görden research department; one year later, in September 1943, the number had risen to 135.

In a research report submitted by Heinze to the "Euthanasia" Headquarters on 9 September 1942, two research emphases emerge: on the one hand,

---

[36] Knaape, "Euthanasie," 7. Sabine Hanrath, based on a transport list reconstructed in 1948, arrives at different numbers. Hanrath, "Euthanasie," 143 f.

[37] Hanrath, "Euthanasie," 147. On Ansbach today, see Reiner Weisenseel, "Heil- und Pflegeanstalt Ansbach," in Michael von Cranach and Hans-Ludwig Siemen (eds.), *Psychiatrie im Nationalsozialismus. Die bayerischen Heil- und Pflegeanstalten zwischen 1933 und 1945* (Munich: Oldenbourg, 1999), 143–157. It also remains unclear whether and if so, how many patients were murdered on site in the Brandenburg-Görden State Hospital after the conclusion of Aktion T4. Heinze rejected an unregulated procedure.

[38] File note by Nitsche of 20 September 1941, BArch, R 96 I/5.

Heinze was concerned with the nosology of forms of idiocy. As part of this, the "trainability of low-level idiots" was also investigated. As early as 15 April 1941, in a letter to Chief Administrative Officer Viktor Brack, Heinze reported that he had set up a "school of life" at Brandenburg-Görden Hospital, in which "imbecile" children, whose theoretical intelligence was too low to learn such skills as reading and writing, but whose practical intelligence was sufficient for them to perform manual tasks, were trained as laborers. Heinze's other research emphasis was the diagnostic distinction between congenital forms of idiocy and various forms of dementia.[39]

While these two emphases corresponded with Heinze's genuine research interests, the expansion of the research program to the field of nervous diseases points to the lateral links between the observation and research department in Görden and the KWIHF.[40] The scientific exchange between Heinze, Hallervorden, and Spatz had the consequence that people who suffered from athetosis[41] found themselves in the sights of the "euthanasia" planners, who voiced considerations about expanding the murder of the mentally ill to include this group of patients. Heinze repeatedly turned his attention to groups of patients who also occupied the KWIHF. In his research report of 9 September 1943, he established, as the result of comparative clinical and anatomic studies, "that the heterodegenerative diseases, among which are conditions like amaurotic idiocy and Hallervorden–Spatz disease, play a significantly greater numerical role than had previously been supposed."[42] In this manner, the ties between the KWIHF and Brandenburg-Görden State Hospital affected the selection criteria of the "euthanasia" planners.

Yet, the links were not limited to indirect reciprocal actions resulting from the institute's involvement in a shared research context. As early as

[39] In some cases Heinze abused the children designated for "euthanasia" as guinea pigs, by using them to test a scarlet fever vaccine. See Wentzler to the Reich Committee/Blankenburg, 17 October 1942, BArch, NS 11/94. In 1942, Professor Hans Nachtsheim of the KWI for Anthropology and Dr. Gerhard Ruhenstroth-Bauer of the KWI for Biochemistry used six epileptic children from the research and observation station at Brandenburg-Görden for a low-pressure experiment concerning the importance of oxygen deprivation in triggering epileptic fits. On this – with more extensive references to older literature – see Alexander von Schwerin, *Experimentalisierung des Menschen. Der Genetiker Hans Nachtsheim und die vergleichende Erbpathologie, 1920–1945* (Göttingen: Wallstein, 2004), 302–319; Hans-Walter Schmuhl, *Grenzüberschreitungen. Das Kaiser-Wilhelm-Institut für Anthropologie, menschliche Erblehre und Eugenik, 1927–1945* (Göttingen: Wallstein, 2005), 431–436; English edition, *The Kaiser Wilhelm Institute for Anthropology, Human Heredity and Eugenics, 1927–1945: Crossing Boundaries* (Heidelberg: Springer, 2008).
[40] Heinze, Bericht über die bisherige Tätigkeit der Beobachtungs- und Forschungsabteilung bei der Landesanstalt Görden, 9 September 1942, BArch, R 96 I/5.
[41] A clinical term for various diseases with continuous, involuntary, writhing movements of the hands and/or feet.
[42] Heinze, Bericht über die Arbeit der Beobachtungs- und Forschungsabteilung bei der Landesanstalt Görden im 3. Halbjahr ihres Bestehens, 9 September 1943, BArch, R 96 I/5.

1940, the KWIHF was involved directly in the research accompanying the "euthanasia" program. On 29 April 1940, Julius Hallervorden – along with other professors – was *officially* informed about Aktion T4 (of course, it is more than probable that he knew about the "euthanasia" program from Heinze much earlier).[43] As early as 15 May 1940 – in the context of the children's "euthanasia" – he received the first brains of children killed at Brandenburg Penitentiary. These deliveries continued well into the fall. Dr. Heinrich Bunke, a physician responsible for the killings in Brandenburg from August through October 1940, testified that during his service around 100 children from Görden – presumably in two transports – were moved to Brandenburg Penitentiary where they were gassed. On 28 October 1940, the final transport left Görden with fifty-six children and teens for the gas chamber in Brandenburg. The brains of around forty children from this transport are found in Hallervorden's collection. The notebook of the physician responsible for the killings in Brandenburg at the time, Dr. Irmfried Eberl, records that Hallervorden and Heinze participated in the autopsies of these children on the premises.[44]

Even after fall 1940, Hallervorden and Spatz received the brains of "euthanasia" victims, some from the Department of Pathology in Brandenburg-Görden, some from the killing hospitals in Bernburg and Sonnenstein, and some from the Leipzig-Dösen Hospital and other hospitals; since Aktion T4 had warmed up, the brains of adults were also included in these deliveries. Dr. Heinrich Bunke, a physician participating in Aktion T4 who had met Hallervorden during the autopsies at Brandenburg Penitentiary in October 1940, established the contact to Bernburg. After the dissolution of the gas chambers at Brandenburg in late 1940, their staff was moved to Bernburg. In May or June 1941, Bunke spent four weeks training at the KWIHF and subsequently went to Bernburg to remove the brains of gassed patients that he presumed "would be of interest in Buch."[45] Dr. Irmfried Eberl, director of the T4 institutions in Brandenburg and Bernburg, later commander of Treblinka, had worked as a medical officer in the main health office of Berlin in the 1930s – it can be presumed that he was already acquainted with Hallervorden and Heinze before he encountered them at the T4 institute in Brandenburg.[46] A further contact to Bernburg could have been established

---

[43] This is Peiffer's hypothesis, *Hirnforschung im Zwielicht*, 23, 35.

[44] Peiffer, *Hirnforschung im Zwielicht*, 37; Aly, "Fortschritt," 69.

[45] Cited in Aly, "Fortschritt," 69. See Dietmar Schulze, *"Euthanasie" in Bernburg. Die Landes-Heil- und Pflegeanstalt Bernburg/Anhaltische Nervenklinik in der Zeit des Nationalsozialismus* (Essen: Verlag die Blaue Eule, 1999), 137 f., 157–160; Peiffer, "Neuropathologische," 166. During his short training period in Berlin-Buch Bunke – like all visiting scientists – lived in the house of its director, Hugo Spatz.

[46] Schulze, *Bernburg*, 137, 155–157; Ursula Grell, "'Gesundheit ist Pflicht.'" Das öffentliche Gesundheitswesen Berlins 1933–1939," in Arbeitsgruppe zur Erforschung der Geschichte der Karl-Bonhoeffer-Nervenklinik (ed.), *Totgeschwiegen 1933–1945. Zur Geschichte der*

through Dr. Otto Hebold, who had previously worked at the Brandenburg state hospitals in Eberswalde and Teupitz and thus was certainly acquainted with Heinze and Hallervorden. In 1940, Hebold was appointed as a T4 assessor, someone who decided on who lived and who died, and occasionally employed to perform killings in Bernburg from April 1941 until March 1943.[47] Through a stint as visiting scientist at the KWIHF in late spring 1941, he established contact with another physician employed to perform killings in Bernburg, Dr. Kurt Borm, who occasionally substituted for Bunke. In the main, however, Borm was employed to perform killings as part of Aktion T4 in Sonnenstein, which therefore also fell into the network linked to the KWIHF.[48]

The hospital in Leipzig-Dösen collaborated with the KWIHF and the children's clinic of the Leipzig University Hospital. Here the connection to Berlin ran through Dr. Georg Friedrich,[49] who had taken over the Department of Pathology in Leipzig-Dösen (responsible for the state hospitals in Saxony) in 1936 and had come to the KWIHF temporarily as a visiting scientist in 1938. In August 1939, he was appointed military surgeon at the Outpost of the Military Surgical Academy for the Study of War Damage to the Central Nervous System (*Militärärztliche Akademie zur Erforschung der Kriegsschäden des Zentralnervensystems*) under Hallervorden – with the result that no physician was available for the Department of Pathology in Leipzig. In spring 1940, however, Nitsche managed to get leave for Friedrich once every two weeks to work in the Department of Pathology in Leipzig. Spatz and Hallervorden vigorously advocated maintaining the research office in Leipzig-Dösen.[50] When the Specialized Pediatric Department was opened in Leipzig-Dösen in October 1940, Friedrich took over the pathological examination of the children murdered there and presumably also was in charge of the victims of the Specialized Pediatric Department in the

Wittenauer Heilstätten, seit 1957 Karl-Bonhoeffer-Nervenklinik, 2nd ed. (Berlin: Hentrich, 1989), 49–76, here 72. The main health office in Berlin exerted influence on the KWIHF via the board of trustees. In December 1936, Dr. Leonardo Conti was appointed to the board of trustees in his capacity as City Medical Councilor of Berlin. He appointed a close staff member, Dr. Theodor Paulstich, director of the Department for the Care of Heredity and Race in the main health office of Berlin, as his permanent representative.

[47] Schulze, *Bernburg*, 138 f.; Joachim S. Hohmann and Günther Wieland, *MfS-Operativvorgang "Teufel." "Euthanasie"-Arzt Otto Hebold vor Gericht* (Berlin: Metropol, 1996).
[48] Schulze, *Bernburg*, 138; Thomas Schilter, "Die 'Euthanasie'-Tötungsanstalt Pirna-Sonnenstein 1920–1941. Ein Beitrag zur Geschichte der Psychiatrie im Nationalsozialismus," Ph.D. diss., Humboldt University of Berlin (1997), 198–202.
[49] Peiffer, *Hirnforschung im Zwielicht*, 39; Aly, "Fortschritt," 66. On this also see Benno Müller-Hill, *Tödliche Wissenschaft. Die Aussonderung von Juden, Zigeunern und Geisteskranken 1933–1945*, 2nd ed. (Reinbek: Rowohlt, 1988), 171.
[50] Spatz to de Crinis, 22 May 1940, Archives of the Humboldt University of Berlin (*Archiv der Humboldt-Universität zu Berlin*), NL de Crinis, 224. I thank Volker Roelcke for alerting me to this document's existence.

children's clinic of the Leipzig University Hospital. In this he worked closely with Hallervorden and Professor Werner Catel of the children's clinic. From mid-1940 on, Friedrich also examined the brains submitted by the T4 hospital in Sonnenstein. Despite his regular service in Leipzig-Dösen, Friedrich was barely able to handle the material accumulating in his department. In October 1942, the Reich Committee thus requested that Friedrich be released from his other duties.[51] In point of fact, Friedrich was detached from Berlin-Buch to Leipzig-Dösen before the end of the year.[52] Moreover, at the same time Dr. Fritz Kühnke (who was also involved in the murder of children in Eglfing-Haar and Wiesloch) was transferred to Leipzig as a military doctor, right near the children's clinic of the University Hospital. He was to assist Professor Werner Catel in the study of poliomyelitis.[53]

Jürgen Peiffer's hypothesis appears to be correct – that only a minor share of the brain deliveries sent to the KWIHF were a consequence of central planning, whereas most came through the networks of persons into which the institute and its staff were integrated. These networks included T4 doctors in the killing institutions, who were trained for their service at the KWIHF or in Brandenburg-Görden, extracted brains, and sent them to Berlin on their own initiative; and the physicians at the core institutions with which the KWIHF was in contact, who authorized the autopsies in the killing institutions.[54] The KWIHF had no need to "order" brains; a network of collegial relationships saw to it that the supply of new specimens to Berlin continued without the need for brain researchers in Berlin having to lodge specific requests. For instance, a great number of the brains transferred from Bernburg to Berlin originated in the hospitals of the Schleswig province. As a possible explanation for this circumstance, in September 1941, Dr. Erna Pauselius, the first director of the Specialized Pediatric Department in Schleswig-Stadtfeld, had been briefed in Görden on her duties by none other than Heinze.[55] The connection to Westphalia was of a similar nature. Back in 1939 Dr. Wilhelm Holzer, senior physician at the province hospital in Dortmund-Aplerbeck, had come to the KWIHF as a visiting scholar. Later, the directors of the Westphalian Specialized Pediatric Departments were sent to the Reich Training Station in Brandenburg-Görden for "further education." In September 1941, Medical Councilor Dr. Werner Sengenhoff,

---

[51] Wentzler to Reich Committee/Werner Blankenburg, 17 October 1942, BArch, NS 11/94. See Aly, "Fortschritt," 65.

[52] On this, see also Christiane Roick, "Heilen, Verwahren, Vernichten. Die Geschichte der sächsischen Landesanstalt Leipzig-Dösen im Dritten Reich," Ph.D. diss., University of Leipzig (1998), 142 ff.

[53] Wentzler to Reich Committee/Blankenburg, 17 October 1942, BArch, NS 11/94. See Aly, "Fortschritt," 65 ff.

[54] Peiffer, "Neuropathologische," 166 f.

[55] Peiffer, "Neuropathologische," 166 f.

director of the Specialized Pediatric Department in Niedermarsberg, and in May 1942, Senior Physician Dr. Theodor Niebel, head of the Specialized Pediatric Department in Dortmund-Aplerbeck, spent several days in Görden.[56] In Saxony, the contact to the Hospital and Sanatorium in Arnsdorf, an intermediary institution for Sonnenstein, had been established before the war; in 1938, Dr. Woldemar Hammerbeck had spent time at the KWIHF. Personal connections also existed between Hallervorden and Dr. Leppien of the Lörchingen Sanatorium in Lorraine, which sent a large number of brains to Berlin.[57]

The connections to the sanatoriums in Berlin were especially close. In at least one case, Dr. Karl Balthasar, senior physician at the Herzberge Hospital and Sanatorium, who had worked as a visiting scientist at the KWIHF in 1938, authorized the dispatch of the brain of a "euthanasia" victim to the KWI.[58] Dr. Gertrud Soeken, senior physician at the research clinic of the KWI, after the clinic was converted to a reserve military hospital on 28 August 1939, took over a pediatric station for infectious diseases at the Ludwig Hoffmann Hospital.[59] Appointed chief surgeon shortly thereafter, according to her own testimony she cooperated with the Reich Committee for the Scientific Research of Serious Hereditary Diseases.[60] This title was the cover for the bureaucratic apparatus of the program for the "euthanasia" of children.[61]

---

[56] Bernd Walter, *Psychiatrie und Gesellschaft in der Moderne. Geisteskrankenfürsorge in der Provinz Westfalen zwischen Kaiserreich und NS-Regime* (Paderborn: Schöningh, 1996), 650; Franz-Werner Kersting, *Anstaltsärzte zwischen Kaiserreich und Bundesrepublik. Das Beispiel Westfalen* (Paderborn: Schöningh, 1996), 300–305, 327–330. On this, see also Franz-Werner Kersting and Hans-Walter Schmuhl, "Einleitung," in Franz-Werner Kersting and Hans-Walter Schmuhl (eds.), *Quellen zur Geschichte der Anstaltspsychiatrie in Westfalen, vol. 2: 1914 – 1955* (Paderborn: Schöningh, 2004), 1–64, here 38–48.

[57] Peiffer, "Neuropathologische," 168.

[58] Oral information from Herbert Loos. Balthasar first switched from Herzberge to Meseritz-Obrawalde, later – holding the rank of an SS Squad Leader – he ran an SS military hospital in Giessen. Oral information from Jürgen Peiffer. On Herzberge, see Herbert Loos, "Die Heil- und Pflegeanstalt Berlin-Herzberge während der Jahre des Zweiten Weltkrieges," in Sabine Fahrenbach and Achim Thom (eds.), *Der Arzt als "Gesundheitsführer." Ärztliches Wirken zwischen Ressourcenerschliessung und humanitärer Hilfe im Zweiten Weltkrieg* (Frankfurt am Main: Mabuse-Verlag, 1991), 129–134.

[59] Hallervorden to Spatz, 18 September 1939, Jürgen Peiffer's private archive. I thank Jürgen Peiffer (+) for making these documents available.

[60] Soeken to Oskar Vogt, 30 December 1942, Vogt-Archiv Düsseldorf. I thank Jürgen Peiffer for referring me to this document.

[61] It is unclear how many patients of the Research Clinic of the KWIHF were caught in the gears of the "euthanasia" campaign. "We keep an eye on the ill," Hallervorden wrote to Spatz after the dissolution of the Research Clinic. In this connection, Hallervorden also mentioned Dr. Wolfgang Goetze of the Buch Hospital and Sanatorium, who was listed as a visiting scientist at the KWIHF from 1938 to 1941. Hallervorden to Spatz, 18 September 1939 (Peiffer's private archive). Various documents on patient transfers (Berlin State Archives, Rep. 03–04/1,

There were also ties between the KWIHF and the T4 Research Department in Wiesloch/Heidelberg. Thus Dr. Hans-Joachim Rauch, who examined the brains of victims in Heidelberg, had interned in Buch. Dr. Heinrich Gross, too, director of the Specialized Pediatric Department at Spiegelgrund in Vienna, took part in a course in Görden in June/July 1941. Since he had scientific interests – he produced specimens of brains and spinal cords of the majority of the 800 children killed at Spiegelgrund – one can assume that he also maintained contact with the KWIHF via the External Office of the Department of Pathology in Görden.[62] Finally, there were close connections between Hallervorden and Dr. Berthold Ostertag, who worked as head of the Department of Pathology at the Berlin-Buch Hospital and Sanatorium from 1925 until 1933, before replacing Professor Rudolf Jaffé as chief surgeon at the Pathological Institute of Moabit City Hospital. In 1935, Ostertag finally was assigned the largest department of pathology in Berlin, at Rudolf Virchow Hospital. In the framework of the children's "euthanasia" program, Ostertag and his senior physician Dr. Hans Klein performed the autopsies of the victims killed in the Specialized Pediatric Department Wiesengrund in Berlin-Wittenau.[63]

Various lines of connectivity – by no means only the collaboration between Hallervorden and Heinze – lead from the KWIHF to the "Euthanasia" Headquarters at Tiergartenstrasse 4. Several T4 assessors had a direct or indirect relationship with the KWI: Dr. Walther Kaldewey had worked as an assistant at the KWIHF in 1930/31 until confrontations with Oskar Vogt resulted in his dismissal. Kaldewey, who thereafter

---

136) list the names of thirteen children who were transferred from the dissolved children's hospital in Buch or from the Hospital Buch-Mitte to the Research Clinic in 1934. Two of these names appear in the list Jürgen Peiffer compiled of the brains examined in the KWIHF between 1940 and 1945. One of these two patients – Georg D., born in 1915, diagnosis: athetosis – was probably one of the murder victims.

[62] Herwig Czech, "Dr. Heinrich Gross, Die wissenschaftliche Verwertung der NS-Euthanasie in Österreich," *Dokumentationsarchiv des österreichischen Widerstandes, Jahrbuch* (1999), 53–70, here 55.

[63] For a comprehensive account, see Peiffer, *Hirnforschung im Zwielicht*, 72–96; Martina Krüger, "Kinderfachabteilung Wiesengrund. Die Tötung behinderter Kinder in Wittenau," in *Totgeschwiegen*, 151–176. In early 1945, Klein examined lymph nodes from the armpits of twenty Jewish children who were subjected to criminal human experiments on tuberculosis research by Kurt Heissmeyer, senior physician at the SS Sanatorium Hohenlychen, in the period from December 1944 to April 1945 at the Neuengamme concentration camp near Hamburg, and who finally were murdered at the school on Bullenhuser Damm. In the period during which Klein was detached to Hohenlychen with a part of the Pathological Institute of the Rudolf Virchow Hospital, he also collaborated – in the framework of a research project on a hereditary blood anomaly of the rabbit – with Hans Nachtsheim, director of the Department for Experimental Genetic Pathology at the KWI for Anthropology, Human Genetics and Eugenics Berlin-Dahlem. This network is discussed in Paul Weindling, "Genetik und Menschenversuche in Deutschland, 1940–1950. Hans Nachtsheim, die Kaninchen von Dahlem und die Kinder vom Bullenhuser Damm," in Schmuhl, *Rassenforschung*, 245–274.

served as director of the Westphalian province hospitals in Eickelborn
and Niedermarsberg and worked at the Psychiatric Clinic in Bremen, was
an assessor of Aktion T4 in 1940/41 and also took part in the discussions
on a "euthanasia" law in 1940.[64] Professor Friedrich Panse, managing
physician of the Rhine Province Institute for Psychiatric and Neurological
Genetic Research in Bonn from 1936 and previously senior physician at
the psychiatric department of the Wittenauer Heilstätten, was also a T4
assessor in 1940. From 1937 on, there is evidence that he had regular
contact with Hallervorden.[65] In this connection – referring to Götz Aly –
the directors of the four hospitals in Berlin had been intimately involved
in the preliminary planning for Aktion T4 in August and September
1939.[66] Dr. Ernst Hefter, director of the Specialized Pediatric Department
Wiesengrund at the Berlin City Neurological Clinic for Children and
Teenagers, became a T4 assessor, as did Dr. Wilhelm Bender, director of
the Buch Hospital and Sanatorium from 1934 until its dissolution on 31
October 1940.[67] Dr. Ernst Wentzler became a Reich Committee Assessor
and set up a Specialized Pediatric Department in his private children's
clinic in Frohnau.

As is apparent, the KWIHF was interwoven with the "euthanasia" apparatus in manifold ways. Of particular weight in this context was ultimately
the connection to Maximinian de Crinis, full professor for Psychiatry and
Neurology and director of the Clinic for Psychiatric and Neurological
Diseases at the Charité, who also sat on the board of trustees at the KWIHF
from 1938 on. In 1940, de Crinis also became a ministerial aide in the
Science Office of the Reich Ministry for Education and Science. At the same
time he advanced to become "elder statesman" in the planning staff of the

[64] Gerda Engelbracht, *Der tödliche Schatten der Psychiatrie. Die Bremer Nervenklinik 1933–1945* (Bremen: Donat, 1997), 76–85; Kersting, *Anstaltsärzte*, passim.
[65] On this, see the correspondence in the MPG-Archiv, Abt. III, Rep. 55, 5. See Uwe Heyll, "Friedrich Panse und die psychiatrische Erbforschung," in Michael G. Esch (ed.), *Die Medizinische Akademie Düsseldorf im Nationalsozialismus* (Essen: Klartext-Verlag, 1997), 318–340. Professor Reisch, also listed as a T4 assessor, could be the same Dr. Otto Reisch who was senior physician at the Robert Koch Hospital and visiting scientist at the KWIHF in 1938.
[66] Götz Aly, "Die "Aktion T4" und die Stadt Berlin," in *Totgeschwiegen*, 137–150, here 146 f.
[67] Wilhelm Bender initially worked in Berlin-Wittenau before succeeding Professor Karl Birnbaum as director of Berlin-Buch; Birnbaum had been dismissed in accordance with the Law for the Restoration of the Professional Civil Service. In July 1939, Bender took part in a meeting on the preparation of the "euthanasia" program, at which he declared his willingness to cooperate. He played a special role in the murder of the Jewish psychiatric patients in summer 1940, as his institute served as a collection point for such patients. In 1946, Bender became director of Ueckermünde Hospital and Sanatorium. Heike Bernhardt, *Anstaltspsychiatrie und "Euthanasie" in Pommern 1933 bis 1945. Die Krankenmorde an Kindern und Erwachsenen am Beispiel der Landesheilanstalt Ueckermünde* (Frankfurt am Main: Mabuse-Verlag, 1994), 140.

"Euthanasia" Headquarters.[68] This accumulation of offices presented Spatz with the opportunity to submit to de Crinis an informal application for a subsidy of 10,000 Reichsmarks in November 1940. Departmental director Professor Julius Hallervorden earmarked the funds for purposes including "the studies on the organic foundations of congenital idiocy (based on a great amount of material of cases of idiocy)." It must have been clear to de Crinis that this meant research accompanying the "euthanasia" program. Nevertheless, he enthusiastically approved Spatz's request and ensured that the application, after being rejected by the General Administration of the KWS,[69] was forwarded to the German Research Foundation (*Deutsche Forschungsgemeinschaft*, DFG).[70] In fact, funds from the DFG were routed to the Brandenburg Department of Pathology in Brandenburg-Görden.

On 8 May 1944, Hallervorden's department was moved from Berlin-Buch to Dillenburg to escape the bombing attacks in the capital.[71] According to his own account, up to this time Hallervorden had "received 697 brains including those which I once removed myself in Brandenburg. Those in Dösen are included in the count."[72] Jürgen Peiffer concluded that of the 1,179 brains studied in Hallervorden's and Spatz's departments between 1939 and 1944, 707 certainly or probably came from "euthanasia" victims.[73] A file memo from the state hospital in Görden from July 1945 attests that to this point – the Red Army had long since occupied the hospital – Hallervorden was receiving material from the Department of Pathology in Brandenburg-Görden.[74] The murder of patients had come to an end, but the accompanying research was just hitting its stride.[75]

[68] Hinrich Jasper, *Maximinian de Crinis (1889–1945). Eine Studie zur Psychiatrie im Nationalsozialismus* (Husum: Matthiesen, 1991).
[69] See file note R. (?) of 22 November 1940, MPG-Archiv, Abt. I, Rep. 1 A, 1600.
[70] BArch, R 4991 – formerly R 21 – 11.065. See Jasper, 92–101.
[71] A bombing on 7 April 1944 had caused serious damage to the institute building. See MPG-Archiv, Abt. I, Rep. 1 A, 1633.
[72] File note by Hallervorden, BArch, R 96 I/2.
[73] Peiffer, "Neuropathologische," 162 f.
[74] Archive of the Brandenburgische Landesklinik Görden. I thank Sabine Hanrath for referring me to this document. Dr. Friederike Pusch of Blankenburg/Harz was listed as an employee of the Reich Committee from 1941 on. See vH/S. (signed by Brack) to Heinze, 22 December 1941, BArch, NS 11/94.
[75] See also Jürgen Peiffer, "Assessing Neuropathological Research carried out on Victims of the 'Euthanasia' Programme," *Medizinhistorisches Journal*, 34. (1999), 339–356.

6

Two Hundred Blood Samples from Auschwitz: A Nobel Laureate and the Link to Auschwitz

Achim Trunk

As the 1939 Nobel Laureate and subsequent president of the Max Planck Society, Adolf Butenandt represented Germany's first-class research of his time like nobody else[1] and received many honors during his lifetime. Yet, in recent years he has met increasingly with public criticism: he has been blamed for several things – in particular, his conduct during the National Socialist era. The most severe of these reproaches will be the issue of this essay: according to this charge, Butenandt had been at least aware of, if not actually involved in, the human experiments conducted by SS physician Josef Mengele in the Auschwitz death camp.

The first suggestion for a connection between Butenandt's institute and Auschwitz was detected by molecular biologist Benno Müller-Hill. This connection consisted in a project conducted by a colleague of Butenandt, the hereditary pathologist and physical anthropologist Otmar von Verschuer, for which he received blood samples that Mengele had acquired from

---

[1] For Butenandt's life and work, see Peter Karlson, *Adolf Butenandt. Biochemiker, Hormonfoscher, Wissenschaftspolitiker* (Stuttgart: Wissenschaftliche Verlagsgesellschaft, 1990); Robert Proctor, Adolf Butenandt (1903–1995). Nobelpreisträger, Nationalsozialist und MPG-Präsident. Ein erster Blick in den Nachlass," *Ergebnisse. Vorabdrucke aus dem Forschungsprogramm "Geschichte der Kaiser-Wilhelm-Gesellschaft im Nationalsozialismus,"* No. 12 (Berlin: Forschungsprogramm, 2000; further quoted as *Ergebnisse*, No., and year). Angelika Ebbinghaus and Karl-Heinz Roth, "Von der Rockefeller Foundation zur Kaiser Wilhelm/Max-Planck-Gesellschaft. Adolf Butenandt als Biochemiker und Wissenschaftspolitiker des 20. Jahrhunderts," *Zeitschrift für Geschichtswissenschaft,* 50 (2002), 389–418; and Wolfgang Schieder and Achim Trunk (eds.), *Adolf Butenandt und die Kaiser-Wilhelm-Gesellschaft. Wissenschaft, Industrie und Politik im "Dritten Reich"* (Göttingen: Wallstein, 2004).

This essay is based on an abridged and revised version of the following article: Achim Trunk, "Zweihundert Blutproben aus Auschwitz. Ein Forschungsvorhaben zwischen Anthropologie und Biochemie (1943–45)," *Ergebnisse*, 2 (2000).

Auschwitz. Müller-Hill then tried to reconstruct this venture.[2] Though universally accepted, his reconstruction leaves some questions unanswered. Therefore, this chapter will first describe the key sources for the project so as to place this project and its personnel in historical context. Subsequently, Müller-Hill's reconstruction will be described and analyzed before an alternative reconstruction is introduced. Finally, some thoughts on the evaluation of this project will be offered.

THE KEY DOCUMENTS

The controversial project, named "Specific Proteins" (*Spezifische Eiweisskörper*), was funded by the German Research Foundation (*Deutsche Forschungsgemeinschaft*, DFG) and classified as "war critical." Otmar Freiherr von Verschuer (1896–1969), director of the Kaiser-Wilhelm-Institute (KWI) for Anthropology, had started the project in 1943. Like their private residences, his institute was located close to the KWI for Biochemistry directed by Butenandt in Berlin-Dahlem. Thus Butenandt and Verschuer were not only colleagues but also neighbors.

Firsthand information regarding the project is scant. It consists only of Verschuer's brief project reports to the DFG as well as some short passages in his letters, not least in his correspondence with Butenandt. Verschuer's successful application to the DFG for support has not been preserved. The first reference to the purpose of this project can be found in Verschuer's preliminary report to the DFG in September 1943.[3] Since the project was classified as war critical, it received special assistance – for instance, where materials procurement was concerned. However, it was not categorized as top priority.[4]

The key phrase used was "specific proteins." In the files of the Reich Research Council (*Reichsforschungsrat*, RFR), the venture was also cited under its full title "Experimental research aimed at finding out the heredity of specific proteins, thus serving as a base for hereditary and racial

---

[2] This reconstruction has been portrayed in a series of publications: Benno Müller-Hill, *Tödliche Wissenschaft. Die Aussonderung von Juden, Zigeunern und Geisteskranken* (Reinbek bei Hamburg: Rowohlt, 1984), 71–75; English edition: *Murderous Science: The Elimination of Jews, Gypsies and Others in Germany 1933–1945* (Oxford: Oxford University Press, 1988), 70–74; Benno Müller-Hill, "Genetics after Auschwitz," *Holocaust and Genocide Studies*, 2 (1987), 3–20; Benno Müller-Hill, "The Blood from Auschwitz and the Silence of the Scholars," *History and Philosophy of the Life Sciences*, 21 (1999), 331–365, here 344–349; and Benno Müller-Hill, "Genetics of Susceptibility to Tuberculosis. Mengele's Experiments in Auschwitz," *Nature Reviews Genetics*, 2 (2001), 631–634, here 632 f.

[3] Kennwort: Spezifische Eiweisskörper, Federal German Archives (*Bundesarchiv*, BArch), R 73/15.342, Nr. 55.

[4] The *"Spezifische Eiweisskörper"* project had been approved by the *Wehrmacht* and classified under category "S," the lowest priority level, as can be gathered from the *Wehrmacht* assignment number of the report heading.

research."[5] Obviously, Verschuer was interested in specific differences between proteins. His description was this:

After all the material required to conduct this research had been finally delivered, first preliminary examinations began and the method was tested in consultation with Abderhalden. By transferring this branch of research to the institute's reception post in Beetz, work had been interrupted, but now the laboratory there has been completely equipped. Work can be continued.[6]

The most important clue in these lines is that the project was obviously based on a method that was a popular, yet not uncontroversial one in Germany at that time: Abderhalden's Defense Enzyme (*Abwehrfermente*) theory. The basic theoretical assumption of this method was that an animal organism can recognize and destroy invading alien protein – for instance, that of bacteria in case of an infection – by producing enzymes that specifically decompose this alien protein.

An enzyme is a protein that catalyzes a biochemical reaction: it multiplies the reaction rate in order to supply the organism with a sufficient quantity of the reaction product. In doing so, it is neither consumed nor changed. Molecules, which are converted in such a reaction by enzymes, are called substrates.

Abderhalden's correspondence does suggest that he instructed one of Verschuer's medical-technical assistants, Irmgard Haase, in his methodology.[7] And a second report to the DFG, written by Verschuer half a year later, confirms without doubt that this method was meant to be the basis of the project:

New difficulties occurred in testing this method, which have been resolved in consultation with Abderhalden. Rabbit series are being screened to trace animals suited for the test devoid of spontaneously produced enzymes. My assistant Dr. med. and Dr. phil. Mengele has entered this branch of research as a staff member. He is on post as *Hauptsturmführer* and camp physician in Auschwitz concentration camp. Authorized by the *Reichsführer* SS anthropological tests are being carried out in the diverse racial groups of this concentration camp and the blood samples are delivered to my laboratory.[8]

---

[5] "Experimentelle Forschung zur Feststellung der Erbbedingtheit spezifischer Eiweissköper als Grundlage von Erb- und Rassenforschung." See also the Reich Research Council file, BArch, R 26 III, Nr. 6, 82.

[6] Kennwort: Spezifische Eiweisskörper, BArch, R 73/15.342, Nr. 55. Verschuer sent biannual reports on his projects to the DFG. This report dates from September or October 1943.

[7] Verschuer to Abderhalden, 23 November 1943, Archives of the Leopoldina, Halle (*Archiv der Leopoldina*) Abderhalden papers, 390/3, mentioned in Michael Kaasch, "Sensation, Irrtum, Betrug? Emil Abderhalden und die Geschichte der Abwehrfermente," *Vorträge und Abhandlungen zur Wissenschaftsgeschichte* (1999/2000), 145–210, here 186.

[8] Kennwort: Spezifische Eiweisskörper (Bericht für den Zeitraum vom 1. Oktober 1943 bis zum 31. März 1944), sent by Verschuer on 20 March 1944 together with all the other reports to the DFG, BArch, R 73/15.342, 64.

It is especially important that Verschuer called the SS physician Josef Mengele (1911–1979)[9] his assistant and introduced him officially as a member of the project staff. Moreover, he was completely aware of Mengele's operational location and agreed to receive blood from Auschwitz for the examinations. The venture obviously required numerous blood samples to be taken from members of "various racial groups." The extent of the planned investigation can be derived from Verschuer's third (and last) report from October 1944:

This research has been further advanced. Blood samples of more than 200 people of most diverse racial provenience have been processed and blood plasma substrates produced. Further research will be continued with Dr. Hillmann, staff member of the Kaiser Wilhelm Institute for Biochemistry. Dr. Hillmann is a biochemical expert on protein research. With his aid the original Abderhalden Method has been perfected, so that the actual rabbit test can henceforth begin.[10]

Apparently, the experiments had unearthed further method difficulties, and Verschuer called in the biochemist Günther Hillmann (1919–1976) for assistance. Because at that time Hillmann worked at Adolf Butenandt's institute in Dahlem, for the first time a connection is mentioned to the KWI for Biochemistry and, if only circumstantially, to its director Adolf Butenandt.

Simultaneous with this project, the DFG approved another of Verschuer's submitted research projects, this one carrying the code name "Tuberculosis" (*Tuberkulose*). Certain rabbit strains showed more tuberculosis resistance than others. The goal of this project was to determine why. The researchers assumed that there was inherited resistance. Since this project, conducted by the tuberculosis physician Karl Diehl (1896–1969), who at the same time directed a department at Verschuer's institute, also called for a biochemical analysis, cooperation with the Butenandt institute was likewise initiated.

The correspondence between Verschuer and Butenandt represents another source for the Specific Proteins project. Almost all the letters can be found in the Butenandt papers, as well as several of the letters exchanged between Butenandt and Hillmann. Though part of the correspondence with Butenandt is available in Verschuer's papers, one looks in vain for letters exchanged between Verschuer and his assistant Mengele. What happened to

[9] For Mengele, see, for example, Zdenek Zofka, "Der KZ-Arzt Josef Mengele. Zur Typologie eines NS-Verbrechers," *Vierteljahreshefte für Zeitgeschichte*, 34, no. 2 (1986), 245–267; Gerald L. Posner and John Ware, *Mengele. The Complete Story* (New York: McGraw-Hill, 1986); in German: *Mengele. Die Jagd auf den Todesengel* (Berlin, Aufbau-Verlag, 1993); Ulrich Völklein, *Josef Mengele. Der Arzt von Auschwitz* (Göttingen: Steidl, 2002).

[10] Kennwort: Spezifische Eiweisskörper (Bericht für den Zeitraum vom 1. April bis zum 30. September), sent by Verschuer on October 4, 1944, together with other project reports to the DFG, BArch, R 73/15.342, 47.

the remainder of Verschuer's documents concerning his project and, above all, his correspondence with Mengele, is unknown.

ROOTS

To shed light on both the personnel and science contexts of the project, we have to answer the following questions: How did Verschuer acquire a research assistant in Auschwitz? Who was Hillmann? What was the Abderhalden reaction all about?

Verschuer and His Student Mengele

In 1935, at the age of twenty-four, Josef Mengele earned a doctorate in anthropology at the University of Munich with a dissertation on racial differences in the structure of the lower jaw.[11] His supervisor, the physical anthropologist Theodor James Mollison (1874–1952), was also very interested in comparative morphological issues. Moreover, he had concentrated for some time on how to identify a person's racial affiliation (*Rassenzugehörigkeit*) with a serological test. His goal was to prove the existence of race-specific proteins in human serum.[12] Though Mengele was working on a different branch of "racial science," we can safely assume that he was well informed about his teacher's research approach.

After completing his Ph.D., Mengele went to the University of Frankfurt am Main to work with Verschuer, a physician who specialized in human racial biology, in particular hereditary pathology, and was head of the Frankfurt Institute of Hereditary Biology and Racial Hygiene. Mengele, who had also passed the state examination in medicine in Munich, now also obtained a doctorate in medicine supervised by Verschuer[13] and

---

[11] See Josef Mengele, "Rassenmorphologische Untersuchung des vorderen Unterkieferabschnitts bei vier rassischen Gruppen," *Morphologisches Jahrbuch*, 79 (1937), 60–117. Also see his 1935 doctoral thesis for the University of Munich.

[12] See, for example, Theodor Mollison, "Serodiagnostik als Methode der Tiersystematik und Anthropologie," in Emil Abderhalden (ed.), *Handbuch der biologischen Arbeitsmethoden*, IX/1 (Munich: Urban and Schwarzenberg, 1923), 553–584, 553 f. and 570 f.; Emil Abderhalden, "Serologische Verwandtschaftsforschung am Menschen und anderen Primaten," in *Tagungsberichte der Deutschen Anthropologischen Gesellschaft. Bericht über die allgemeine Versammlung der Deutschen Anthropologischen Gesellschaft* (Augsburg: Filser, 1926), 88–92. Already during World War I Ludwik and Hanna Hirszfeld had determined the frequency distribution of blood factors A and B in members of different ethnic groups and thus established significant differences; see Ludwik Hirszfeld and Hanna Hirszfeld, "Serological Differences between the Blood of Different Races," *Lancet*, 180 (1919), 675–679.

[13] See Josef Mengele, "Sippenuntersuchungen bei Lippen-Kiefer-Gaumenspalte," *Zeitschrift für menschliche Vererbungs- und Konstitutionslehre*, 23 (1939), 17–43 (also see his 1938 doctoral thesis for the University of Frankfurt am Main).

subsequently became his assistant. Obviously Verschuer regarded Mengele as a promising junior scientist and helped him accordingly. In Frankfurt, Mengele also worked mainly in the anthropo-morphological field.[14] Moreover, Verschuer increasingly entrusted him with the task of providing morphological-anatomical expert opinions on paternity. However, their objective was more often than not to determine the "racial" status of a person.

When Verschuer was appointed director of the KWI for Anthropology, he intended to bring Mengele as an assistant to his new institute.[15] Mengele, who joined the SS in 1938 and was drafted by the armed forces (Wehrmacht) in 1940, volunteered for the *Waffen-SS* and was placed in the medical division (*Sanitätsinspektion*). [16] It appears that he was then transferred to the Central Emigration Office (*Einwandererzentralstelle*) in Posen (Poznań) where he used his race biological expertise to judge the "racial value" of ethnic German (*volksdeutsche*) settlers.[17] Thereafter, he was apparently stationed with a reserve medical corps in Prague. In November 1940, Mengele was transferred to the SS Main Race and Settlement Department (*Rasse- und Siedlungshauptamt der SS*, RuSHA).[18] There he worked in Department II of the Racial Office (*Sippenamt*) in charge of Hereditary Hygiene (*Erbgesundheitspflege*) and the corresponding examinations (*Erbgesundheitsprüfungen*).[19]

During 1941, Mengele was drafted again and placed as a troop physician with the SS Division *Wiking* on the Eastern front.[20] He participated from the very beginning of the war of aggression against the

[14] See Josef Mengele, "Zur Vererbung der Ohrfistel," *Der Erbarzt*, 8 (1940), 59–60.

[15] Verschuer to Lehmann, 11 June 1942, Archives of the University of Münster (*Universitätsarchiv Münster*), Verschuer papers, quoted from Niels C. Lösch, *Rasse als Konstrukt. Leben und Werk Eugen Fischers* (Frankfurt am Main: Lang, 1997), 405.

[16] Records of Josef Mengele, BArch, SS-Offiziers-Personal-Akte Mengele (SSO Mengele), 395. For Mengele's SS career prior to his transfer to Auschwitz, see Sven Keller, *Günzburg und der Fall Josef Mengele. Die Heimatstadt und die Jagd auf den NS-Verbrecher* (Munich: Oldenbourg, 2003), 18–26.

[17] *Tätigkeitsbericht Dr. Heidenreich, Posen*, 7 October 1940, BArch, R 69/455, 18–23, here 18. See Götz Aly and Susanne Heim, *Vordenker der Vernichtung. Auschwitz und die deutschen Pläne für eine neue europäische Ordnung* (Frankfurt am Main: Fischer Taschenbuch Verlag, 1993), 164; English version: *Architects of Annihilation: Auschwitz and the Logic of Destruction* (Princeton: Princeton University Press, 2002).

[18] *Sanitätsinspektion der Waffen-SS an das Rasse- und Siedlungshauptamt (RuSHA)*, 5 November 1940, BArch, R 69/455, 18–23, here 403. For RuSHA see Isabel Heinemann, *Rasse, Siedlung, deutsches Blut. Das Rasse- und Siedlungshauptamt der SS und die rassen-politische Neuordnung Europas* (Göttingen: Wallstein, 2003).

[19] See the undated organigram of the *Sippenamt* in the RuSHA, BArch, NS 2, Nr. 167, 1.

[20] Though the main record of Mengele's dossier (BArch, SSO Mengele, 395) gives 30 January 1942 as the date, he is already mentioned in a recommendation for promotion from 24 November 1941 as "Arzt SS-Division, Wiking" BArch, SSO Mengele, 404 and 405. Obviously his enlistment took place earlier.

Soviet Union.[21] In July 1942, he was formally transferred to the Berlin-based bureau of the Chief SS and Police Medical Officer (*Reichsarzt SS und Polizei*)[22] – that is, the very institution in charge of controlling the concentration camps and the human experiments performed there. Yet, it is questionable whether Mengele actually reported there for duty, for he evidently stayed with the *Wiking* division. He was still recorded as troop physician there in October 1942 and received another recommendation for promotion owing to his merits.[23] Likewise, a letter from Verschuer to his colleague and former mentor Eugen Fischer suggests that Mengele did not return from the Eastern front to Berlin until January 1943.[24] In February 1943, he was then – possibly due to an injury – assigned to the SS Infantry Reserve Battalion East, stationed in Berlin.[25]

Formally, Mengele remained affiliated with the Frankfurt University until the end of the war.[26] Hence, he never became an official employee of the Kaiser Wilhelm Society but rather began working as a guest researcher at Verschuer's institute. Perhaps Verschuer, who obviously considered Mengele a candidate for an academic career, planned joint projects with him during his stay at the institute. Mengele's institute-related activities ended, however, in late May 1943, when he became camp physician at Auschwitz.[27] Whether he was "posted" in Auschwitz "against his will"[28] (as Verschuer later insisted), or whether he actively applied for the post or was even placed there by Verschuer,[29] cannot be established beyond any doubt. Whatever the

---

[21] Keller, 20 f., provided some evidence for this and also referred to a massacre Mengele's division committed against Jews.

[22] *Personalbefehl des SS-Führungshauptamtes, SS-Sanitätsdienst vom 17. Juli 1942*, BArch, SSO Mengele, 406.

[23] *Vorschlag zur "Beförderung in der Waffen-SS,"* 13 October 1942, BArch, SSO Mengele, 412; *Beförderungsmitteilung an Mengele*, 16 April 1943, BArch, SSO Mengele, 408.

[24] Verschuer to Fischer, 25 January 1943, Universitätsarchiv Münster, Verschuer papers, quoted from Lösch, 405.

[25] SS-Führungshauptamt, Amtsgruppe D, an den Reichsarzt SS und Polizei, 14 February 1942, BArch, SSO Mengele, 407.

[26] See excerpts from the calendar of Frankfurt University up to the winter term 1943/44, published in Gerhard Koch, *Humangenetik und Neuropsychiatrie in meiner Zeit (1932–1978). Jahre der Entscheidung* (Erlangen: Palm and Enke, 1993), 130 f.

[27] The transfer note reads as follows: "*Betr.: Versetzungen. Bezug: Ohne. Anlg.: Keine. [...] Der SS-Hauptsturmführer d.R. Josef Mengele, geb. 16.3.1911, SS-Inf.Ers.Btl. ,Ost', wird mit Wirkung vom 30.5.1943 zum W.u.V.-Hauptamt, Amtsgruppe D III versetzt. Inmarschsetzung nach Übergabe der Dienstgeschäfte an SS-Sturmbannführer Lack. Inmarschsetzung zum K.L. Auschwitz b. Kattowitz, Meldung beim Lagerkommandanten.*" SS-Führungshauptamt to SS-Infanterie-Ersatz-Bataillon "Ost," 24 May 1943, BArch, SSO Mengele, 409.

[28] Affidavit by Verschuer concerning the reproaches made against him in the *Neue Zeitung* from 3 May 1946 and 10 May 1946, Archives of the Max Planck Society, Berlin (*Archiv zur Geschichte der Max-Planck-Gesellschaft*, MPG-Archiv), Abt. II, Rep. 1A, Personalia Verschuer, Nr. 5, 2 ff.

[29] For instance Zofka considers that a likely possibility, 255. Posner and Ware share this opinion, 37, German edition.

case, Mengele assumed his new position in Auschwitz on May 30, 1943. He kept in touch with Verschuer during his time in Auschwitz and also visited Verschuer's institute.[30]

Verschuer apparently seized the opportunity to make use of the camp's anthropological "research potential" by obtaining otherwise difficult to acquire human organs through his assistant. Last, the concentration camp held the prospect of acquiring the blood of people alien to the German "race" (*Fremdvölkische*), a good that had become almost unattainable by normal channels (that is, especially cooperation with local hospitals) owing to the absence of such people in the German *Reich* in 1943. It is unclear whether the prospect of receiving blood from the Auschwitz concentration camp served right from the start as grounds for project planning, or whether Mengele's transfer to Auschwitz made this potential apparent and feasible. According to preliminary reports, Mengele did not enter the project until October 1943,[31] leading to the conclusion that he had not been mentioned in the original (missing) application.

During Mengele's stay in Berlin, that is, beginning in February 1943, the opportunity arose to revive his scientific relationship with Verschuer, including renewed activity as an expert for the KWI.[32] Whether Mengele notified Verschuer *expressis verbis* about his real functions in the death camp or not also remains open. During a dinner, he allegedly told Verschuer's wife Erika that his job in Auschwitz was "atrocious" but that he could not talk about it.[33] After the war, Verschuer claimed that he had asked Mengele on a similar occasion if there was some truth to the rumors concerning the procedures in Auschwitz. Mengele had allegedly denied this and talked instead about the big factories where the inmates worked, about the camp infirmary where they were made fit for work again, and about his grateful patients.[34]

---

[30] Thus Koch, 130, reports that he had run into Mengele – probably in July 1943 – in the library of the KWI for Anthropology.

[31] Verschuer to DFG, 20 March 1944, BArch R 73/15.342, Nr. 64.

[32] Note from Verschuer to the KWS regarding his institute's revenues in the fiscal year 1942 derived from institute employees furnishing expert opinions, 29 June 1943, MPG-Archiv, Abt. I, Rep. 1A, Nr. 577.

[33] Erika von Verschuer remembered that Mengele made such a statement, as her son, Helmut von Verschuer, recalls. See the memory protocol of Benno Müller-Hill's interview with Helmut von Verschuer; Müller-Hill, *Murderous Science*, 116–119, here 118.

[34] This can be concluded from a statement Verschuer made in a letter from 20 February 1947, which Karl von Lewinski had sent on 23 December 1946 to Wolfgang Heubner that dealt with the "Affair Verschuer"; MPG-Archiv, Abt. II, Rep. 1A, Personalia Verschuer, Nr. 5, 2. Verschuer made a similar statement when questioned by U.S. Military officials on 13 May 1947; interrogation protocol, Spruchkammerakte Verschuer, Hauptstaatsarchiv Wiesbaden, Abt. 520/F FZ5261, quoted by Hans-Peter Kröner, *Von der Rassenhygiene zur Humangenetik. Das Kaiser-Wilhelm-Institut für Anthropologie, menschliche Erblehre und Eugenik nach dem Kriege* (Stuttgart: Urban and Fischer Verlag, 1998), 129.

Günther Hillmann – From Guest Researcher to Butenandt's Stand-In

Günther Hillmann was likewise concerned with a serological diagnosis: since 1941, the DFG had promoted his dissertation project, which dealt with cancer-related biochemical changes in blood serum.[35] His boss, the cancer researcher Karl Hinsberg, was a professor at the Berlin Charité. When Allied bomb raids left his institute in a state unfit for work, Hinsberg left Berlin for Freiburg in January 1944. Yet prior to that he had dismissed his doctoral student Hillmann, with whom he had had a falling out.[36] The DFG, however, was obviously interested in continuing Hillmann's project. Remarkably (and for reasons unknown) DFG president Rudolf Mentzel approached Butenandt on behalf of Hillmann. Thus on October 6, 1943, Hillmann was asked to introduce himself to Butenandt. After the meeting Butenandt noted in his diary that "Dr. Hillmann" – he'd obviously been left in the dark regarding the latter's qualification – was going to enter the Institute "as a guest."[37] Hillmann, on his part, informed the DFG that "Thanks to Prof. Dr. Mentzel's recommendation, Prof. Dr. Butenandt has agreed to offer me a workplace at his institute."[38] He was now working "at the Kaiser Wilhelm Institute for Biochemistry directed by Prof. Butenandt," he said.[39] The DFG expressly confirmed this.[40] Maybe Butenandt's proper interest in cancer research facilitated his admission of Hillmann.[41] In any case, Butenandt provided Hillmann with a workplace in his laboratory from October 1943 on. Space was available, since the transfer of part of the institute to Tübingen, a Southern German university town hardly affected by air raids, had already begun by summer 1943.

For the time being, Butenandt himself remained basically in Berlin. He was undoubtedly aware of Hillmann's activities, since Butenandt managed the institute with a firm hand and was generally well informed about the

---

[35] DFG to Hillmann, *Bewilligung eines Stipendiums für "Untersuchungen über den Chemismus der serologischen Krebsreaktion,"* 3 September 1941, BArch, R 73/11.807, Nr. 23.

[36] Hinsberg reported to the DFG that on his (Hinsberg's) request, Hillmann no longer worked in his department; Hinsberg to the DFG, 30 September 1943, BArch, R 73/11.807, Nr. 15. Hillmann explained his departure to the DFG as due to "personal disagreements"; Hillmann to DFG, 10 October 1943, BArch, R 73/11.807, Nr. 14.

[37] Entry made by Butenandt in his diary on 6 October 1943: "Vorstellg Dr. Hillmann, der als Gast ins Institut eintritt"; MPG-Archiv, Abt. III, Rep. 84/1, Nr. 208.

[38] Hillmann to DFG, 10 October 1943, BArch, R 73/11.807, Nr. 14.

[39] Hillmann to DFG, 10 October 1943, BArch, R 73/11.807, Nr. 14.

[40] DFG to Hillmann, 26 Oktober 1943, BArch, R 73/11.807, Nr. 12.

[41] Butenandt's cancer research proceeded from a completely different approach: he looked for possible "derailments" of steroids in metabolism, that is, he assumed that the body could transform steroid hormones into carcinogenic substances. Butenandt had already published results of this approach in several articles, all of which are published in his collected works. See Adolf Butenandt, *Das Werk eines Lebens*, Vols. 1 and 2 (Göttingen: Vandenhoeck and Ruprecht, 1981). This basic assumption, however, following his long-standing research on human sex hormones, later proved to be wrong. See Karlson, 128.

work of his employees. Even when Butenandt also moved to Tübingen, accompanied by the better part of the Berlin-based "institute entourage" (*Institutsgefolgschaft*) – the standard expression the "leader principle" (*Führerprinzip*) of the Nazi work rules applied for the scientific institutes – and only returned occasionally to Berlin, he was certainly informed about who researched what in his Berlin annex. That applied as well (or in particular) if this employee held some kind of a special status – as did Hillmann. After all, Butenandt applied twice for a renewal of Hillmann's DFG grant.[42] Furthermore, a work report prepared by Hillmann for Butenandt has survived, depicting Hillmann's efforts in the field of amino acid racemate, a section of his dissertation.[43] This is a clear indication that by now Butenandt acted – at least pro forma – as a supervisor of Hillmann's doctoral thesis.

On what terms were Butenandt and Hillmann? It remains to be seen whether the relationship between the institute's director and his employee can accurately be called a "close friendship" – as denominated by Robert Proctor[44] – given that this characterization mistakes the distinctive functionality of their connection. As a matter of fact, Hillmann turned into a very important person for Butenandt the moment Butenandt's assistant Ulrich Westphal, whom he had left as a representative at the institute in Dahlem, first went to the institute's branch (which had been moved to Göttingen) and then to the Mountain Medical School of the Army (*Gebirgssanitätsschule des Heeres*) in St. Johann, Tyrol, to pursue his military-medical research.[45] In Dahlem, only part of the technical staff remained as well as a few students.

Hillmann, henceforth the "highest-ranking" male scientist of the institute, became the stand-in for the absent institute director.[46] Thus, Butenandt was by now reliant on Hillmann, since through him Butenandt maintained a small "toehold"[47] in the evacuated Berlin institute. This allowed Butenandt to maintain a continuous tenure, important both for a possible return and for safeguarding equipment, furniture, books, journals, and other fixtures. Since not all of that could be transferred to Tübingen, there was the permanent threat of loitering, confiscation, or other forms of appropriation by third parties in Dahlem. Hillmann obviously rather enjoyed his new position as

---

[42] Butenandt to DFG, 6 March 1944, BArch, R 73/11.807, No. 10; Butenandt to DFG, 28 March 1944, BArch, R 73/11.807, No. 8.

[43] Work report from Hillmann, 19 February 1945, MPG-Archiv, Abt. III, Rep. 84/1, No. 836.

[44] Proctor, 22, and likewise on 24.

[45] See Bernd Gausemeier, "An der Heimatfront. "Kriegswichtige" Forschungen am Kaiser-Wilhelm-Institut für Biochemie," in Schieder and Trunk, 134–168.

[46] Westphal, however, provided a detailed set of guidelines regarding the running of the institute prior to leaving; Hillmann to Butenandt, 20 February 1945, MPG-Archiv, Abt. III, Rep. 84/2, No. 2508.

[47] Butenandt chose exactly the same expression (*Brückenkopf*, i.e. "toehold") both in a letter to Hillmann, 14 March 1945, MPG-Archiv, Abt. III, Rep. 84/2, No. 2508, and in a letter to Westphal, 15 March 1945, MPG-Archiv, Abt. III, Rep. 84/2.

the director's "representative"[48] in Dahlem, regardless of his repeated written affirmations that he was by no means going to play the hero or, possibly, aggrandize himself – he was only acting out of responsibility for the institute, he claimed.[49]

Abderhalden's Method

So, what was the Abderhalden method, employed in the Specific Proteins project, all about? Swiss biochemist Emil Abderhalden (1877–1950), who spent the better part of his scientific career in Germany,[50] went public in 1909 with an apparently groundbreaking discovery: he had injected a test animal subcutaneously with foreign protein, then taken a blood sample from which he obtained the serum and observed that the serum now was capable of disintegrating the foreign protein. Serum of the same animal, however, which had been obtained prior to the protein injection, did not possess this capacity.[51] He concluded that the organism of the test animal must have produced enzymes. These enzymes evidently catalyzed a protective reaction against the intruded foreign protein without, however, disintegrating the autologous proteins. Abderhalden introduced the term "defense enzyme" for his discovery. Moreover, Abderhalden discovered that this reaction proceeded in a rather specific way: only the foreign protein that had been added was disintegrated whereas other proteins remained intact, according to his observation. Hence he concluded that the intrusion of foreign proteins triggered the creation of highly specific enzymes, disintegrating the intruded substance.

Defense enzymes are defunct now, since their existence actually never proved true. Even so, the new research branch experienced a boom for several decades. In particular, Abderhalden himself went on unperturbed to develop his theoretical and methodical construct based on a self-delusion. Hence, in 1930 he believed he had discovered that the kidneys excreted the defense enzymes, thus it got into the urine.[52] From that moment on,

---

[48] With a note from 14 March 1945 Butenandt appointed Hillmann as his representative "*in allen Direktorialgeschäften für das Dahlemer Mutter-Institut und den dort verbliebenen Teil der Institutsgefolgschaft*"; MPG-Archiv, Abt. III, Rep. 84/2, No. 2508.

[49] Hillmann to Butenandt, 20 February 1945, MPG-Archiv, Abt. III, Rep. 84/2, No. 2508.

[50] The first ones to bring up the story of Abderhalden and the *Abwehrfermente* were Benno Müller-Hill and Ute Deichmann, "The Fraud of Abderhalden's Enzymes," *Nature*, 393 (1998), 109–111. Material to the argumentation pursued in this article was Kaasch.

[51] See Emil Abderhalden and Ludwig Pincussohn, "Über den Gehalt des Kaninchen- und Hundeplasmas an peptolytischen Fermenten unter verschiedenen Bedingungen. 1. Mitteilung," *Hoppe-Seyler's Zeitschrift für physiologische Chemie*, 61 (1909), 200–204.

[52] See Emil Abderhalden and Severian Buadze, "Die Verwendung von Harn an Stelle von Serum zum Nachweis der Abderhaldenschen Reaktion," *Fermentforschung*, 11 (1930), 305–344; Emil Abderhalden and Severian Buadze, "Vereinfachter Nachweis von Abwehrproteinasen im Harn," *Fermentforschung*, 14 (1933/1935), 502–521.

standard extraction of defense enzymes proceeded by using urine instead of blood samples; infections of the wound might trigger the creation of new defense enzymes, thus contaminating the results of a second blood sample, but any number of urine samples could be taken.

Now, the Abderhalden reaction seemed to become a promising technique for diagnosing cancer, infections, and even psychoses. It promised, among other things, to open up new paths in heredity and racial research.[53] This was a rather appealing perspective for the hereditary and racial researcher Verschuer. In 1940, Verschuer and Abderhalden exchanged some letters. Abderhalden apparently asked Verschuer to examine the results of the defense enzyme reaction in twins as well. Verschuer declined, however, explaining the difficulty of obtaining blood samples: this was out of question without the willing consent of the blood donor, he claimed; nobody should be scared away. Twin research would have to wait until after the war, he wrote.[54]

Another important field of research where the Abderhalden reaction inspired great expectations was cancer diagnosis. Even Butenandt seems to have harbored no serious doubts concerning Abderhalden's method; at least, he appreciated its potential contribution to cancer research in 1940.[55] Like Butenandt, many other acknowledged researchers regarded Abderhalden's theory as valid, though their assessment was certainly biased by Abderhalden's standing and reputation. Be that as it may, in 1943, the year the Specific Proteins projects was initiated, the Abderhalden reaction had not yet been proved definitely wrong, despite numerous negative results.

Reconstructions

Now the course of the project will be examined. Benno Müller-Hill has provided the authoritative reconstruction of the project up until now. It will be described here and critically analyzed in order to suggest an alternative reading.

Reconstruction I: Race-Specific Susceptibility for Tuberculosis

Müller-Hill linked Mengele's already known human experiments with the so-far discounted research of his academic tutor Verschuer. He reconstructed

[53] See, among many others, Emil Abderhalden, "Rasse und Vererbung vom Standpunkt der Feinstruktur von blut- und zelleigenen Eiweissstoffen aus betrachtet," *Nova Acta Leopoldina. Neue Folge*, 7 (1939), 59–79.

[54] Verschuer to Abderhalden, 26 October 1940, Archives of the Leopoldina, Halle, Abderhalden papers, No. 478. Quote by Kaasch, 183 f.

[55] Adolf Butenandt, "Neuere Beiträge der biologischen Chemie zum Krebsproblem," *Angewandte Chemie*, 53 (1940), 345–352; here page 520 of the off-print version.

an experimental pattern for the whole project, whereby Mengele systematically infected "gipsy" twins as well as Ashkenazi and Sephardic Jews
with tuberculosis – a death sentence in this camp. According to Müller-
Hill, Mengele then took blood samples of the subjects and delivered them
to Berlin-Dahlem. The method had first been established there with animal models and was now to be applied to the human sera. Allegedly, the
objective had been to observe the Abderhalden reactions that varied in their
strength in the blood serum of the different test persons. It was assumed
that the more tuberculosis-resistant Eastern European Jews possessed additional or more active defense enzymes against the proteins of the tuberculosis germ.[56] The plan was to possibly concentrate and isolate these specific
defense enzymes to be able to conduct a tuberculosis therapy on a molecular
basis with them later.[57] The Abderhalden method had been improved with
the help of Günther Hillmann, and Müller-Hill argues that Hillmann also
planned to perform the crucial tests. Müller-Hill regards it as obvious that
Butenandt had at least been informed about his employees' activities, if he
indeed had not actively participated in initiating the cooperation.

This reconstructed connection is plausible because of a series of facts. It
was already known immediately after the war that Mengele had killed twins
in Auschwitz and sent part of their organs – for instance, heterochromatic
eyeballs – to Dahlem, evidently to Verschuer's institute.[58] The experiments
performed by Mengele on twins in Auschwitz also included blood samples.
One of the few survivors, Eva Mozes Kor, recalls:

Three times a week we walked to the main Auschwitz camp for experiments. These
lasted six to eight hours. We had to sit naked in a room. Every part of our body
was measured, poked and compared to charts and photographed. Every movement
was noted. I felt like an animal in a cage. Three times a week we went to the blood
lab. There we were injected with germs and chemicals, and they took a lot of blood
from us.[59]

---

[56] In Müller-Hill, *Tödliche Wissenschaft*, 74, only deliberate typhoid infections are mentioned.
Müller-Hill postulates the connection with Verschuer's tuberculosis research for the first time
in Müller-Hill, "Genetics after Auschwitz," 5, saying the project had dealt with "resistance
against typhoid, typhus and tuberculosis." The possibility of epidemic typhus infections was
again suggested in Müller-Hill, "Blood from Auschwitz," 346.

[57] See Müller-Hill, "Blood from Auschwitz," 345.

[58] See a book written by Hungarian pathologist Miklós Nyiszli about his time in Auschwitz,
where he was forced by Mengele to assist him; Miklós Nyiszli, *Auschwitz. A Doctor's
Eyewitness Account* (New York: Fell, 1960); German edition: *Im Jenseits der Menschlichkeit.
Ein Gerichtsmediziner in Auschwitz* (Berlin: Dietz, 1992), 41–47 (the Hungarian original
was published in 1946).

[59] Eva Mozes Kor, "Heilung von Auschwitz und Mengeles Experimenten," in Carola Sachse
(ed.), *Die Verbindung nach Auschwitz. Biowissenschaften und Menschenversuche an Kaiser-
Wilhelm-Instituten – Dokumentation eines Symposiums* (Göttingen: Wallstein, 2003), 59–70,
here 65. Also see her report in Eva Mozes Kor and Mary Wright, *Echoes from Auschwitz. Dr.
Mengele's Twins – The Story of Eva and Miriam Mozes* (Terre Haute: Candles, 1996), 106 f.

Furthermore, it has been proven that Mengele infected twins intentionally with typhoid germs in order to observe the physical reactions. Shortly afterward he sent them to the gas chambers.[60] The testimony of another camp physician documents that he tested the different susceptibility of Ashkenazi and Sephardic Jews to typhus fever: he infected both groups and watched how the latter ones died within days from the disease.[61] Müller-Hill considers it probable that Mengele, who had also shown an interest in typhus fever in Auschwitz, conducted similar experiments.[62] Verschuer himself had explicitly stated in his textbook on racial hygiene that there was a lower "racial disposition" (*Rassendisposition*), that is a lesser susceptibility of Jews in general to tuberculosis due to race.[63] It is safe to assume that he was also interested in the molecular basis of this phenomenon.

Moreover, the connection is made feasible by chronology: Mengele assumed office in Auschwitz on May 30, 1943. About the same time, Müller-Hill assumes,[64] Verschuer applied for research grants for the Specific Proteins and Tuberculosis projects. Here Müller-Hill uses the date of approval and normal duration of the DFG process to make his estimate. Approval of the Tuberculosis project was given on August 18, 1943,[65] thus making a late-May application realistic. In the case of the Specific Proteins project, the exact dates of application and approval are unknown, yet the time frame should be quite similar. This suggests an internal connection between Mengele's and Verschuer's projects.

This thesis receives additional support from the fact that at that time scientists were trying to obtain a secure diagnosis for other infective diseases, like scarlet fever, by using the Abderhalden method.[66] After all, the same order (first developing an animal model, then testing the results found with human beings) was maintained at the KWI for Anthropology when exploring epilepsy. In that case, rabbit model strains with a lower seizure threshold (that is, that developed epileptic seizures more rapidly) were traced and subsequently tested in the low-pressure chamber to trigger such a seizure. Finally,

---

[60] Testimony of Dr. Jan Češpiva in the Frankfurt Auschwitz trial on 5 April 1960, Oberstaatsanwaltschaft Frankfurt am Main, Auschwitz-Verfahren, Strafsache 4 Js 444/59, 4.829 f., quoted by Ernst Klee, *Auschwitz, die NS-Medizin und ihre Opfer* (Frankfurt am Main: Fischer, 1997).

[61] See Max Weinreich, *Hitler's Professors: The Part of Scholarship in Germany's Crimes against the Jewish People*, reprint edition (New Haven: Yale University Press, 1999), 198.

[62] See Müller-Hill, "Blood from Auschwitz," 346.

[63] See Otmar von Verschuer, *Leitfaden der Rassenhygiene* (Leipzig: Thieme, 1941), 162 and 127.

[64] See Müller-Hill, "Blood from Auschwitz," 346.

[65] This information comes from a letter of Verschuer to the RFR dated 25 February 1944; BArch, R 73/15.342, Nr. 92.

[66] See Emil Abderhalden, *Abwehrfermente (Die Abderhaldensche Reaktion)*, 6th ed. (Dresden: Steinkopff, 1941), 47–51.

children were subjected to low pressure.[67] A strong point for the viability of Müller-Hill's hypothesis is that organs that Mengele had extracted from assassinated inmates were also examined at Verschuer's institute.[68]

For these reasons, Müller-Hill's reconstruction of the overall project has been universally well received by both experts and the public.[69] However, if one takes the sources seriously and proceeds on the assumption that they do not employ any camouflage terms, then the following three crucial inconsistencies result, shaking the plausibility of this reconstruction.

1. The reconstruction proceeds on the assumption that the enzymes were to be examined. Yet both the DFG reports as well as the correspondence of Verschuer and Butenandt always refer to substrates. For instance, Verschuer's third DFG report says: "Blood samples [...] were processed and blood plasma substrates produced."[70] In February 1945 Verschuer wrote to Butenandt, telling him he had been forced to leave Berlin and in doing so had merely been able to take along the "particularly precious and irrecoverable protein substrates."[71] Therefore Verschuer had not been interested in human defense enzymes, but had converted the human blood into dried substrates. The distinction between enzyme and substrate is fundamental for experts, thus making it almost inconceivable that a biochemist or some other bioscientist would confuse the two terms by mistake or intentionally – all the less when both substances belong to the chemical class of proteins.

2. The reconstruction continues to reduce the Tuberculosis project to mere preliminary tests of the Specific Proteins venture. But as a matter of fact, the Tuberculosis research had been classified as the more urgent and war-critical one, that is, in category "SS" and not merely "S," like the research on Specific Proteins. This can be explained with the high military impact of the widespread disease for "front" and

---

[67] For more on this, see Alexander von Schwerin, *Experimentalisierung des Menschen. Der Genetiker Hans Nachtsheim und die vergleichende Erbpathologie 1920–1945* (Göttingen: Wallstein, 2004), 281–328. See also Ute Deichmann, *Biologen unter Hitler. Vertreibung, Karrieren, Forschung* (Frankfurt am Main: Campus, 1992), 269–276; English edition: *Biologists under Hitler* (Cambridge, Mass.: Harvard University Press, 1996).

[68] See Carola Sachse and Benoît Massin, "Biowissenschaftliche Forschung an Kaiser-Wilhelm-Instituten und die Verbrechen des NS-Regimes. Informationen über den gegenwärtigen Wissensstand," *Ergebnisse*, No. 3 (2000), 23 f.

[69] For example, see Peter Weingart, Jürgen Kroll, and Kurt Bayertz, *Rasse, Blut und Gene. Geschichte der Eugenik und Rassenhygiene in Deutschland* (Frankfurt am Main: Suhrkamp, 1988), 422; Paul Weindling, *Health, Race and German Politics between National Unification and Nazism, 1870–1945* (Cambridge: Cambridge University Press, 1989), 563 and 579; Ute Deichmann, "An Unholy Alliance," *Nature*, 405 (2000), 739; Ebbinghaus and Roth, 410 f.; Proctor, 21–25.

[70] Verschuer to DFG, 4 October 1944, BArch R 73/15.342, Nr 47.

[71] Verschuer to Butenandt, 19 February 1945, MPG-Archiv, Abt. III, Rep. 84/2, scientific correspondence.

"homeland." The Tuberculosis project must actually be regarded as an independent, self-coherent research program that differed notably in several points from the protein project.

    a. At no time did blood play a part in the Tuberculosis project; researchers worked with tissue lysate instead.

    b. The Abderhalden method was never employed.

    c. The objective of the research project cannot have been to isolate defense enzymes against tuberculosis germ proteins; otherwise, researchers would have tried to isolate them from the unproblematic and plentiful urine of Diehl's patients.

    d. The Tuberculosis project continued along the same path begun in 1943 until the end of the 1950s, whereas the Specific Proteins project was aborted in 1945.

3. Finally, Müller-Hill's reconstruction requires *blood* samples where state-of-the-art science would have called for *urine* samples. Supposedly it was possible to isolate defense enzymes from urine without any difficulty, whereas a blood sample was regarded as a potential cause of defect: it might induce other defense reactions – with micro-infections in the wound or the coagulation reaction. In other words, had the objective been an examination of human defense enzymes against tuberculosis germs, researchers would definitely have taken urine samples. Only if they were not interested in defense enzymes at all, rather in their substrates, does the use of blood make sense: substrates were not isolated from urine.

Reconstruction II: Serological Diagnosis of Race

Bernd Gausemeier suggests an alternative view of the Specific Proteins project's objective: the project aimed to determine the "racial" affiliation of individuals.[72] The following reconstruction of the project's course is based on this assumption – starting from the idea that blood could either be sampled to trace defense enzymes or to form defense enzymes against the proteins it contains. This second possibility will be taken up here.

In 1940, Verschuer was deeply impressed by Abderhalden's experiments to diagnose the race of mammals.[73] His objective then became the "determination of racial specificity of proteins" in humans. We know which human "races" were to be analyzed, in part thanks to Müller-Hill's research: in the early 1980s he succeeded in locating and interviewing Irmgard Haase,

---

[72] See Bernd Gausemeier, "Rassenhygienische Radikalisierung und kollegialer Konsens. Verschuer, Butenandt und die Blutproben aus Auschwitz," in Sachse, 178–199.

[73] See Otmar von Verschuer, "Emil Abderhalden, Rasse und Vererbung vom Standpunkt der Feinstruktur von blut- und zelleigenen Eiweissstoffen aus betrachtet," *Nova Acta Leopoldina. Neue Folge*, 7, No. 46 (1939); *Der Erbarzt*, 8 (1940), 91 f.

former technical assistant to Verschuer, who was supposed to conduct the experiments. Müller-Hill himself wrote the minutes from memory of this meeting.[74] According to this account, Irmgard Haase had spent at first three months with Abderhalden in Halle to learn the defense enzyme reaction in order to analyze the blood of "gipsy" twins, Russians, Uzbeks, and Kyrgyzes. In a first step the involuntary blood donors were racial-anthropologically classified[75]: such anthropometrical race determinations were required in order subsequently to be able to connect the desired blood analysis results (that is, the race-specific proteins) to a precise type of "race." Citrating their blood made it incoagulable; it was then sent to Dahlem. Haase declared that since mid-1943, several deliveries, each containing 30 ml samples of citrated blood, had arrived at the institute, yet she had been unaware of their origin.[76] From this, blood substrates were obtained, as indicated, for instance, from Verschuer's third report to the DFG.[77]

An October 1944 letter from Verschuer to his friend, the Frankfurt pediatrician Bernhard de Rudder, also shows that the blood samples were processed to substrates. But what is more, Verschuer provides the greater scientific context in this letter. He was going to give a talk on the subject of the heredity of infective diseases, Verschuer wrote, and then turned to Diehl's research as well as the Specific Proteins project:

Diehl has gained new, and I believe, basically rather important results in his tuberculosis research. I cannot yet report about them, since publication is reserved to him. I think that the whole problem is also connected to my research on the issue of heredity of specific proteins. Plasma substrates have been produced from more than 200 people of the most diverse races, twin-pairs and some clans. The Abderhalden method has been exercised and is to be completed with a new method, invented by Hillmann (added on the staff). Hence work on the actual experiment can be started in the next future. My efforts are no longer aimed at establishing the impact of hereditary influence on some infectious diseases, but how it works and what are the processes happening along the way.[78]

This also confirms the scale of the project: 200 test persons implies a large-scale project with considerable objectives. It also becomes evident that the "actual test" was not to take place prior to but following the taking of blood samples. Verschuer would have hardly chosen those words if it had been only a matter of testing the proteinase activities of the sera in Berlin – as postulated in Müller-Hill's reconstruction. But most of all we now know that for Verschuer, the "actual test" meant the one involving the rabbit. On the

[74] See Müller-Hill, *Murderous Science*, 155 f.
[75] Verschuer to DFG, 20 March 1944, BArch R 73/15.342, Nr 64.
[76] See Müller-Hill, *Murderous Science*, 155.
[77] Verschuer to DFG, 4 October 1944, BArch R 73/15.342, Nr 47.
[78] Verschuer to de Rudder, 4 October 1944, BArch R 73/15.342, Nr 47. Emphasis in the original.

other hand, it is also clear that, as postulated by Müller-Hill, the connection between protein and tuberculosis research was indeed of great importance to Verschuer. This connection, however, did not refer to their combination in one single project but to Verschuer's basic theoretical concept: according to this, "single genes [decided] on the resistance or susceptibility" of an individual to infectious diseases.[79] That also brought "race," defined as a "group of men sharing the possession of certain hereditary dispositions, absent in other groups of men,"[80] into the focus of infection biology.

The project was in need of test animals whose sera did not degrade foreign protein prior to being vaccinated with it. Hence, "rabbit series [were] checked so as to trace animals suited for the test devoid of spontaneously produced enzymes," Verschuer reported.[81] After dry preparations were produced from the blood sera, the rabbits were vaccinated with the individual substrates; the rabbits were injected subcutaneously with the dried substrates and the researchers waited for them to develop defense enzymes against the assumed race-specific proteins from the human blood. Haase's testimony also confirms this procedure, which does not feature in Müller-Hill's reconstruction but is indispensable if one wants to evoke the formation of defense enzymes in rabbits.[82]

Subsequently, the defense enzymes, allegedly formed by the rabbits against the race-specific human proteins, had to be isolated. Since they were supposed to be excreted with the urine, the rabbit urine had to be gathered and processed. Rabbit hutches with special appliances were used for this. In fact, Verschuer complained to Butenandt in February 1945 that his technical assistant had been obliged to leave the "laboratory equipment with the special rabbit hutches for collecting the urine"[83] in Berlin. The urine of the rabbits was examined for the defense enzymes one expected to find there. The fact that the project pursued a large-scale comparison follows from another letter of Verschuer to de Rudder from January 1945. Also in this letter, only human substrates are mentioned, not enzymes.[84] Verschuer specifically emphasized that his point was the comparison of a large variety of people of different races; "blood sera from more than 200 persons of varied racial origin" were now available for examination, he wrote.

---

[79] Verschuer provided a detailed outline of this concept in a talk he gave in November 1944 in the Preussische Akademie der Wissenschaften. See Otmar von Verschuer, "Die Wirkung von Genen und Parasiten," *Ärztliche Forschung*, 2 (1948), 378–388, here 382; however, this was not published until three years after the war.

[80] Thus Verschuer's definition of the term in Otmar von Verschuer, *Erbanlage als Schicksal und Aufgabe* (Berlin: de Gruyter, 1944), 14.

[81] Verschuer to DFG, 20 March 1944, BArch R 73/15.342, Nr 64.

[82] See Müller-Hill, *Murderous Science*, 155 f.

[83] Verschuer to Butenandt, 19 February 1945, MPG-Archiv, Abt. III, Rep, 84/2.

[84] "Inventar des Laboratoriums mit den Spezial-Kaninchen-Käfigen zum Auffangen des Urins" Verschuer to de Rudder, 6 January 1945, Archives of the University of Münster, Verschuer papers.

Abderhalden described in numerous articles and books the standard test arrangement, its course, and how to evaluate it.[85] Therefore, the planned experimental course for this precise case can be deduced: the blood sample of the concentration camp inmate should be transformed into a protein substrate and injected under the skin of a rabbit. According to theory, the rabbit now ought to produce defense enzymes against this protein, to be excreted with the urine from which they could be isolated. Then one solution of such defense enzymes was to be laced with the injected protein and another with substrates prepared from additional blood samples from Auschwitz. One expected the enzyme solution to degrade the injected substrate rather well; the other substrates, however, were to degrade only insofar as they were similar to the first one. The corresponding formula was this: the stronger the substrate degradation, the bigger the chemical similarity of the proteins and thus the genetic affinity of the individuals from whom the blood was taken.

A complete implementation of the project would have required inoculating 200 rabbits each with a substrate so as to be able to produce as many defense enzyme specimens. Then each one of these defense enzymes could have been used against each of the 200 original dry substrates. The alleged strength of the project consisted in this large sample, supposed to capture human "racial" heterogeneity. By improving the identification of the products of the Abderhalden reaction, one expected to come closer to an exact determination of a relationship. In this context, samples of twins (monozygotic as well as dizygotic) and "clans" (*Sippen*) were of particular importance.

But why call in Hillmann? Obviously, Verschuer had described the biochemical difficulties in conducting this project to his neighbor and colleague Butenandt. One methodical problem consisted in identifying the substrate's degradation products. Hillmann had developed a new method for this, and Butenandt cooperatively referred him to Verschuer. Hence in September 1944, Hillmann actively joined the project, which by then had been under way for almost a year and a half. One can only speculate when exactly Butenandt and Verschuer agreed to Hillman's participation. Verschuer had been in Dahlem since autumn of 1942. The first letters exchanged between Verschuer and Butenandt date from November 1943 and show the beginning of a mutual interest in each other's research.[86] They exchanged lecture scripts and off-prints, and they probably considered cooperation in fields of mutual interest. That included not only the tuberculosis research, but the Specific Protein venture as well. Evidently during the months that followed, the two

[85] For example, see Emil Abderhalden, "Kleine Mitteilung: Abwehrproteinasekristalle," *Nova Acta Leopoldina. Neue Folge*, 13 (1942), 517–521.
[86] Verschuer to Butenandt, 13 November 1943, MPG-Archiv, Abt. III, Rep. 84/2; Butenandt to Verschuer, 18 November 1943, MPG-Archiv, Abt. III, Rep. 84/2.

men came to an agreement. At any rate, Verschuer informed Butenandt in late September 1944: "Recently Herr Hillmann has spent a day with me in Beetz for a first collaboration. I am rather satisfied with the success. At his recommendation some methodical improvements will be made and then it can go on."[87]

How far the project actually progressed can also be reconstructed. According to Irmgard Haase, she herself (in spite of being employed at Verschuer's institute) had worked "from the end of November 1944 until February 1945 in the KWI of Biochemistry, where Hillmann gave me technical advice."[88] When the project was aborted, Haase had "just sensibilized the first rabbits with the dried sera."[89] The state of the war prevented this project from progressing further. In view of the approaching Red Army, Verschuer moved with part of his institute to the Hessian town of Solz, where his family owned an estate.

In February 1945, he contacted Butenandt from there regarding "my problem child, the protein research." He informed Butenandt that he had put his technical assistant on leave and that he had missed the chance to talk to Hillmann. He asked "if there was a chance for Frau Haase to continue her work with Herr Hillmann in Tübingen." The laboratory equipment was still stored at the KWI for Biochemistry in Dahlem, he wrote. "I have taken along only the so particularly precious and irrecoverable protein substrates."[90] Butenandt replied that Hillmann still remained in Dahlem and for the time being, work could be continued there (i.e., at the laboratories of the Institute for Biochemistry). For the time afterward, he had no solution, Butenandt wrote, as laboratory space in Tübingen did not suffice to house Verschuer's project as well.[91] Verschuer never abandoned his hope to continue the project.[92] Butenandt penned the last written reference known thus far. In October 1945, he wrote to Verschuer: "It's a pity that our mutual work schedule cannot be continued for the present, but I am putting my hopes on a later date."[93] In letters exchanged between Butenandt and Hillmann at the same time, the project went unmentioned.

CLASSIFICATION

To what extent can the reconstructed project be classified as criminal science? What was its political perspective? Who had been responsible? And what was Butenandt's part in this project in particular?

[87] Verschuer to Butenandt, 30 September 1944, MPG-Archiv, Abt. III, Rep. 84/2.
[88] Müller-Hill, *Murderous Science*, 155.
[89] Müller-Hill, *Murderous Science*, 163.
[90] Verschuer to Butenandt, 19 February 1945, MPG-Archiv, Abt. III, Rep. 84/2.
[91] Butenandt to Verschuer, 28 February 1945, MPG-Archiv, Abt. III, Rep. 84/2.
[92] Butenandt to Verschuer, 25 September 1945, MPG-Archiv, Abt. III, Rep. 84/2.
[93] Butenandt to Verschuer, 18 October 1945, MPG-Archiv, Abt. III, Rep. 84/1, Nr. 601.

Perspective of the Project

The first question arising here is, to what extent did conducting the project require criminal acts? It is safe to assume that the majority of the approximately 200 people serving as blood donors were later killed in Auschwitz. Yet, it is important to determine whether they were killed by an injection with tuberculosis germs in Mengele's lab or by forced inhalation of prussic acid in the gas chambers. Did these people fall victim to science without moral boundaries, or do they have to be addressed as victims of the Nazi desire to exterminate in a wider sense? The blood samples were taken without the consent of the people concerned, which not only violated their right to physical inviolability but also imperiled the already debilitated health of the concentration camp inmates even more if carried out on a large scale. Moreover, the samples were obtained as a by-product of the mass deportations and organized killing in Auschwitz. The fact – certainly known to the scientists involved – that without the deportations the involuntary blood donors would have been out of their reach makes the use of the blood samples already condemnable. However, taking blood samples did not require the death of the person concerned, which is different from the use of eyes, for instance. And artificial infections or similar violations of the victims made no sense for the project's scientific logic.[94]

Therefore, we have a case of using illegally acquired sample material, one that becomes more serious as it appears more plausible that the project director had been aware of how the material was obtained. Sachse's and Massin's assessment, that Otmar von Verschuer more than anybody else must have been able to recognize the character of the camp in Auschwitz, is

---

[94] However, this statement has recently been questioned again: Hans-Walter Schmuhl does not exclude the possibility that the blood samples of deliberately infected people had been sent to Berlin as well; see Hans-Walter-Schmuhl, *Grenzüberschreitungen. Das Kaiser-Wilhelm-Institut für Anthropologie, menschliche Erblehre und Eugenik 1927–1945* (Göttingen: Wallstein, 2005), 521 f.; forthcoming English edition: *The Kaiser Wilhelm Institute for Anthropology, Human Heredity and Eugenics, 1927–1945: Crossing Boundaries* (Heidelberg: Springer, 2008). The Specific Proteins project appears analogous to research carried out by the Austrian researcher Karl Horneck (on this, see Schmuhl, *Grenzüberschreitungen*, 511–521). Horneck examined serological reactions in people of different "races" with infectious diseases, though admittedly not until his actual aim, to develop a serological race diagnosis based on the so-called Precipitine Reaction (*Präzipitin-Reaktion*), had failed; see Karl Horneck, "Über den Nachweis serologischer Verschiedenheiten der menschlichen Rassen," *Zeitschrift für menschliche Vererbungs- und Konstitutionslehre*, 26, No. 3 (1942), 309–319, especially 316 f. Horneck's research with sick people resulted from his desire to continue working (and receive funding) in the "racial serological" field even after this failure. However, Verschuer had not yet failed and was rather optimistic regarding the success of his method, which argues against this analogy. Moreover, and as already explained above, in Verschuer's project infections might have disturbed the actually desired reactions. Hence they were to be avoided and by no means intentionally induced.

valid.[95] If, thanks to his relationship with Mengele as well as several other employees, Verschuer had actually been aware of the so-called Final Solution of the Jewish Question (*Endlösung der Judenfrage*), then using such blood samples means no less than consciously benefiting from genocide.

Regarding the issue of research, the project was by all means state of the art. It was very reasonable for a German human biologist of that time to expect to find something resembling a geographical frequency scale for specific proteins in human blood. The basic assumptions of the project reflect the state of development and thinking of a science (i.e., an anthropology shaped by the race concept) as developed in Germany. Notwithstanding the elevated position of "racial science" in a political system based on racism, the project's classification as "critical for the war and state" requires an explanation. After all, the project promised no contribution whatsoever in achieving the final victory (*Endsieg*). So what was expected of it? In the first place, one surely would have to mention what the project would have meant for both racial science and hereditary pathology if its initial hypotheses had proved true. As a matter of fact, the connection postulated by Müller-Hill regarding the project and Verschuer's main interest with genetics cannot be dismissed – albeit in modified form: if Verschuer really wanted to examine the influence of heredity and, in association, "race" on resistance against infective diseases, that primarily required an absolutely reliable racial diagnosis. Even more, strictly speaking it constituted an indispensable "base for hereditary and racial research," as already indicated in the long version of the project title.[96]

Furthermore, it is safe to assume that the project's findings would have been likewise channeled into direct application beyond anthropologic and genetic research: conducting a scientifically authorized racial diagnosis would have hardly gone unnoticed in a regime where "blood" and "race" were the defining categories determining affiliation to the "people's community" (*Volksgemeinschaft*) – and thus determining life and death. One possible field of application was the proof of paternity. That is, the "hereditary-biological expert opinions on parentage" (*erbbiologischen Abstammungsgutachten*) often served not merely to ascertain the father but also the racial categorization of the person examined. Verschuer and his employees, including Mengele, rendered such expert opinions in great numbers. Verschuer's expert opinions were always impartial, regardless of whether they helped or harmed the person affected.[97] A serological race diagnosis could have been applied in numerous ways in this field.

[95] See Sachse and Massin, 26.
[96] See the data in RFR file, BArch, R 26 III, Nr. 6, 82.
[97] Kröner, 42–44, describes a case when Verschuer insisted on his different expert opinion to the disadvantage of the person affected. On Verschuer's work as an expert, also see Alexandra Przyrembel, "*Rassenschande*". *Reinheitsmythos und Vernichtungslegitimation im Nationalsozialismus* (Göttingen: Wallstein, 2003), 350–352.

However, the demand for racial expertise in the national socialist state was compelling; bear in mind the Nazi population policy in the so-called Integrated Eastern Territories (*Eingegliederte Ostgebiete*) – that is, the parts of Poland annexed by Greater Germany from Eastern Upper Silesia to the *Warthegau*. With great effort, bureaucrats decided whether the people living there were to be treated as "Germans," as "people suited for Germanization," (*Eindeutschungsfähige*) or as "Racial Aliens" (*Fremdrassige*). Race-biological examinations were sometimes performed to determine the degree to which an individual should be regarded as "German-blooded" (*deutschblütig*). Such examinations, for example, might confirm the person's "capability of being germanized" (*Eindeutschungsfähigkeit*) by assessing the person as "R.u.S. III"[98] and issuing the green certificate of suitability. "R.u.S." refers here to the SS Main Race and Settlement Department, that is, the very same institution for which Mengele delivered hereditary biological opinions as well.

Yet, even more important is his assignment as a race biological expert for the Central Immigration Office in Posen in 1940. This part of Mengele's career, which has not been adequately considered up until now (after all, his job as a physician already consisted in a kind of selection[99]), had familiarized him rather well with the difficulties of evaluating the "racial quality" based on classical techniques. If the working hypothesis underlying Verschuer's project had actually worked, a scientifically established, definite racial diagnosis would have found extensive fields of application: the desired racialist reorganization of the annexed territories concerned almost 10 million people and – according to Isabel Heinemann's estimates – the RuSHA planned to perform race biological examinations on about 2 million people.[100] Thus, seen in the context of its time, the project represented scientific work profoundly relevant for Nazi racial policy – with potentially extensive, destructive consequences for the people affected by this policy.

Butenandt's Responsibility

Concluding with a few words concerning Butenandt's part in this project seems appropriate. After all that has been said, he has to be assessed as a minor character and not as an initiator or even as the moving force. To be sure, if it had not been for taking on Hillmann, a graduate student with knowledge of the Abderhalden reaction, the cooperation between Butenandt and Verschuer would never have happened. The project never had even remotely the same significance for Butenandt as for Verschuer. Butenandt

---

[98] For example, see *Documenta Occupationis*, 11, No. 1–47, 123 and 127.

[99] Heinemann, 595, points this out: "Auch zukünftige Praktiker der 'Endlösung' wie der spätere Lagerarzt von Auschwitz, Josef Mengele, sammelten bei der rassischen Bewertung der Volksdeutschen erste Erfahrungen in 'praktischer Auslese'."

[100] Heinemann, 268.

merely accommodated Verschuer by lending him an employee and placing adequately equipped laboratories at his disposal. Nevertheless, under the prevailing circumstances even this form of support – a kind of neighborly help, in a manner of speaking – was for a project that, if it had been successful, would certainly have facilitated Nazi population and racial policy.

Butenandt was quite adept at getting money for his research; time and again he successfully convinced others to classify employees of his institute as "indispensable for the war effort" and his projects as "critical for the war." In many cases, he achieved this by touting the possible applications of his research work. Could he really have overlooked the obvious possible applications of the Specific Proteins project? This would at least point to great political naiveté. Or did he object to racial research and its political implications? There is every indication to believe that he did not. Butenandt obviously perceived this venture as "normal" science, thus justifying Müller-Hill's verdict that Butenandt had taken his selective perception too far and suppressed more than is admissible in an era of outrageous injustice.[101]

The accusation that Butenandt had been an "accomplice" to the Holocaust is inappropriate for the case at hand. But had he been an "accessory"? Had he been aware that the blood samples originated from an extermination camp? His correspondence with Verschuer testifies that Butenandt had been informed about the project's crucial stages. Hence, he must have known that the blood samples originated from either a prisoner of war or a concentration camp. That is the closest one gets in answering the question about Butenandt's knowledge of the blood samples' origin.

Within the historical community, it is widely acknowledged that the majority of adult Germans were in the position to be aware of the Holocaust, and that people were much better informed than they were willing to admit after the war.[102] To what extent this applied to Adolf Butenandt remains a matter of speculation: based on the sources, the question cannot be answered.[103] When in 1948 Butenandt testified in the I.G. Farben trial on behalf of an influential mentor of German science, I.G. Farben director Heinrich Hörlein, he actually admitted that when he was traveling abroad and had heard rumors regarding crimes in the concentration camps (thus acknowledging

[101] Benno Müller-Hill, "Selective Perception. The Letters of Adolf Butenandt Nobel Prize Winner and President of the Max-Planck-Society," in Giorgio Semenza and Anthony J. Turner (eds.), *Comprehensive Biochemistry, Volume 42, Selected Topics in the History of Biochemistry. Personal Recollections, VII* (Amsterdam: Elsevier Science, 2003), 548–580, especially 577.

[102] On this, see in particular David Bankier and Arnold Harttung (eds.), *Die öffentliche Meinung im Hitler-Staat. Die "Endlösung" und die Deutschen – eine Berichtigung* (Berlin: Verlag Spitz, 1995).

[103] Even with the members of a group of perpetrators, like Gestapo officials who conducted the deportation of German Jews, it is difficult to actually prove their knowledge about the mass murders in the gas chambers. See Holger Berschel, *Bürokratie und Terror. Das Judenreferat der Gestapo Düsseldorf 1935 bis 1945* (Essen: Klartext-Verlag, 2001), 423–428.

that this had indeed been the case), he had disbelieved them, since they had been beyond his imagination.[104]

Butenandt's work during the Nazi years is taken as an exemplar for assessing the role of first-class science in the National Socialist era. So what is the contribution of the Specific Proteins project to this? First, it should be stated that there was actually a connection between the Nobel laureate and Auschwitz. The fact that such a connection existed indicates the structural proximity of the scientific elite to National Socialist political power.

Second, the Specific Proteins project was not an example of science that exceeded all ethical limits and culminated in murderous human experiments. For a long time, the debate on science in general and Butenandt's role in particular during the National Socialist era has focused on scandalous transgressions of moral boundaries (*Entgrenzungen*) – medical crimes, but also the development of weapons of mass destruction. This focus unnecessarily constricts our perspective. In fact, it obstructs the crucial fact that a scientific community that respected the conventional ethical boundaries could and did succumb to the demands of National Socialist warfare.

Finally, this case illustrates how potential applications can be subsequently injected into an experimental scheme that had been conceived from "pure cognitive interest." Given the Nazi policy of violence, the findings that this "basic research" project was supposed to deliver would most likely have been applied with disastrous consequences for innumerable people. Thus the Specific Proteins project proves, probably as empathically as no other single project, the importance of considering the social, political, and cultural contexts when assessing research.

---

[104] See Butenandt's handwritten answers on the questionnaire for his military court interrogation, MPG-Archiv, Abt. III, Rep. 84/1, Nr. 1159. Also see Center for Research on Anti-Semitism, Berlin (*Zentrum für Antisemitismusforschung*), Militärgerichtshof Nürnberg, Die Vereinigten Staaten von Amerika gegen Krauch und andere (Fall 6), Wortprotokoll, hearing on 2 February 1948, interrogation of Adolf Butenandt, 6229–6257, here 6245.

7

Racial Purity, Stable Genes, and Sex Difference: Gender in the Making of Genetic Concepts by Richard Goldschmidt and Fritz Lenz, 1916 to 1936

Helga Satzinger

In 1936, the geneticist Richard Goldschmidt (1878–1958) was forced to relinquish his position as director at the Kaiser Wilhelm Institute (KWI) for Biology in Berlin Dahlem due to National Socialist anti-Semitism. His emigration to the United States at the age of nearly fifty-eight meant leaving behind excellent working conditions, his editorship of important journals, and a highly influential position in German-language genetics. He was never able to achieve a comparable status in the United States.[1] His position at the KWI in Berlin was assumed by Alfred Kühn (1885–1968). Goldschmidt and Kühn were representatives of different genetic concepts; the forced personnel change thus also meant a change on the scientific level.

Toward the end of World War II, Kühn collaborated with the biochemist Adolf Butenandt (1903–1991) to develop, supported by their staff, a model of the relation between gene and character. This model is valid even today as part of the "one gene-one enzyme hypothesis" and thus constitutes an

[1] Curt Stern, "Richard Benedikt Goldschmidt (1878–1958): A Biographical Memoir," in Leonie K. Piternick (ed.), *Richard Goldschmidt. Controversial Geneticist and Creative Biologist. A Critical Review of His Contributions with an Introduction by Karl von Frisch, Experienta Supplementum*, vol. 35 (Basel: Birkhäuser, 1980), 68–99; see Richard B. Goldschmidt, *In and Out of the Ivory Tower. The Autobiography of Richard B. Goldschmidt* (Seattle: University of Washington Press, 1960); Michael R. Dietrich, "On the Mutability of Genes and Geneticists: The "Americanization" of Richard Goldschmidt and Victor Yollos," *Perspectives on Science*, 4 (1996), 321–346.

This chapter is a translation, with minor changes, of the German paper "Rasse, Gene und Geschlecht. Zur Konstituierung zentraler biologischer Begriffe bei Richard Goldschmidt und Fritz Lenz, 1916–1936," *Ergebnisse. Vorabdrucke aus dem Forschungsprogramm "Geschichte der Kaiser-Wilhelm-Gesellschaft im Nationalsozialismus,"* No. 15 (Berlin: Forschungsprogramm, 2004). This text is also part of my book on the history of genetics from the perspective of gender studies: *Differenz und Vererbung. Geschlechterordnungen in der Genetik und Hormonforschung 1890–1950* (Köln: Böhlau, 2009). I wish to thank Felix von Reiswitz, London, for his help with the final version of the translation.

important element of molecular genetics.[2] The model concurred with the "theory of the gene" developed after 1914 by the school of Thomas Hunt Morgan (1866–1945), which prevailed in further research including the mapping of the human genome. According to this theory, genes are corpuscular units, lined up in the chromosome like pearls on a string, each of which can be defined precisely with respect to their molecular size. Through enzymes, these units determine the hereditary characters of the cell.[3] Although the history of how Goldschmidt's work was received in Germany after 1945 has not been studied yet, it is clearly apparent that little reference to Goldschmidt and his genetic concepts was made – as, for example, in the 1973 edition of Kühn's genetics textbook.[4]

Goldschmidt developed the most important alternatives to Morgan's gene model in the first half of the twentieth century.[5] His work has to be divided into different phases. Starting shortly before World War I, Goldschmidt

---

[2] Hans-Jörg Rheinberger, "Ephestia: The Experimental Design of Alfred Kühn's Physiological Developmental Genetics," *Journal of the History of Biology*, 33 (2000), 535–576.

[3] I use the term "character" (*Merkmal*) in the sense of Mendelian genetics in the 1920s. Here "characters" were morphological or physiological units, supposedly determined by respective genes and transmitted to the next generation according to the Mendelian laws of heredity. However, the use of the term does not imply that I approve this meaning.

[4] Alfred Kühn, *Grundriss der Vererbungslehre*, 6th ed. (Heidelberg: Quelle and Meyer, 1973), here 156–157, 264; 1st ed. Leipzig, 1939.

[5] The following textbooks are good examples: Thomas H. Morgan, *The Physical Basis of Heredity* (Philadelphia: Lippincott, 1919), German: *Die stoffliche Grundlage der Vererbung* (Berlin: Gebrüder Borntraeger, 1921); Thomas H. Morgan, *The Theory of the Gene* (New Haven: Yale University Press, 1926); Richard Goldschmidt, *Die quantitative Grundlage von Vererbung und Artbildung. Vorträge und Aufsätze über Entwicklungsmechanik der Organismen* (Berlin: Springer, 1920); Richard Goldschmidt, *Physiologische Theorie der Vererbung* (Berlin: Springer, 1927); Richard Goldschmidt, *Physiological Genetics* (New York: McGraw-Hill, 1939); Richard Goldschmidt, *Theoretical Genetics* (Berkeley: University of California Press, 1955); German: *Theoretische Genetik* (Berlin: Akademie-Verlag, 1961); Garland E. Allen, "Opposition to the Mendelian-Chromosome Theory: The Physiological and Developmental Genetics of Richard Goldschmidt," *Journal of the History of Biology*, 7 (1974), 49–92; Scott F. Gilbert, "Cellular Politics: Ernest Everett Just, Richard B. Goldschmidt, and the Attempt to Reconcile Embryology and Genetics," in Ronald Rainger, Keith Benson, and Jane Maienschein (eds.), *The American Development of Biology* (Philadelphia: University of Pennsylvania Press, 1988), 311–346; Michael R. Dietrich, "From Gene to Genetic Hierarchy: Richard Goldschmidt and the Problem of the Gene," in Peter J. Beurton, Raphael Falk, and Hans-Jörg Rheinberger (eds.), *The Concept of the Gene in Development and Evolution. Historical and Epistemological Perspectives* (Cambridge: Cambridge University Press, 2000), 91–114; Michael R. Dietrich, "Richard Goldschmidt: Hopeful Monsters and Other 'Heresies,'" *Nature Reviews Genetics*, 4 (2003), 68–74. See also the critical discussion by Goldschmidt's scientific colleagues: as described in Piternick, Leonie. On Morgan in particular, see Garland E. Allen, *Thomas Hunt Morgan: The Man and His Science* (Princeton: Princeton University Press, 1978); Robert E. Kohler, *Lords of the Fly. Drosophila Genetics and the Experimental Life* (Chicago: University of Chicago, 1994).

drafted a concept of genes that could not be depicted through chromosome maps. He crossbred various populations of the *Lymantria dispar* moth and used the inheritance and the development of sex difference, or "sex determination," as the paradigmatic problem of genetics. Far from the clear-cut genes that caused the same characters always and everywhere, in his conception they derived their function, as we would formulate it today, only in the context of the entire genome of an organism.[6] Starting in 1937 after his emigration to the United States, Goldschmidt continued to question Morgan's gene concept on the basis of new experimental findings. From 1944 on, he argued that chromosomes consisted of five hierarchical and overlapping levels. Their orderly interaction in complicated temporal sequences was supposed to cause the development of the hereditary characters over the course of the individual organism's development.[7] Goldschmidt also used his genetic concepts to develop a theory of evolution, which he submitted in 1940 as an alternative to the "modern synthesis" developed around the same time;[8] however, it did not become a dominant theory and neither did the genetic concepts themselves. Not until the 1980s did Goldschmidt's work receive renewed attention.[9] To this extent, the National Socialist attack against Goldschmidt's scientific career can certainly be interpreted as an influential factor for the development of genetics and the theory of evolution after 1945.

From the plethora of interactions between politics and scientific development, this chapter will single out one aspect that is distinguished by a sort of paradoxical relationship. Richard Goldschmidt's genetic work in the 1920s was linked directly with the politically explosive issues of racial purity and miscegenation, and with the unambiguousness of sexual identity, or at least the highly contentious attribution of social tasks for man and woman. Goldschmidt's investigations of the inheritance and determination of sex in insects was seized upon by his contemporaries in the 1920s as experimental proof for the racist and anti-Semitic idea that "race mixtures" (*Rassenmischungen*) among humans must lead to the loss of a clear binary

---

[6] Not yet at issue here was the so-called position effect, according to which a chromosomal unit "gene" receives its function depending on its location in the chromosome. See Dietrich, "Gene," 92–93.

[7] Goldschmidt, *Theoretical*; Dietrich, "Gene," 91–114.

[8] Richard Goldschmidt, *The Material Basis of Evolution* (New Haven: Yale University Press, 1940); Richard Goldschmidt, *The Material Basis of Evolution*, 2nd ed. (New Haven: Yale University Press, 1982), with an introduction by Stephen Jay Gould; Michael R. Dietrich, "Richard Goldschmidt's 'Heresies' and the Evolutionary Synthesis," *Journal of the History of Biology*, 28 (1995), 431–461.

[9] Dietrich, "Heresies"; Dietrich, "Gene"; Stéphane Schmitt, "L'oeuvre de Richard Goldschmidt: un tentative de synthèse de la génétique, de la biologie du développement et de la théorie de l'évolution autour du concept d'homéose," *Revue d'histoire des sciences*, 53 (2000), 381–401; Steven J. Gould, "Introduction," in Goldschmidt, *Basis* (1982), xiii–xlii.

gender order and thus to degeneration. However, Goldschmidt's genetic concept, based on his experimental blurring of a binary sex-difference, was not adopted. Genes with the attributes postulated by Goldschmidt seemed useless for the aim of a new racial anthropology based on genetics. Especially if the genes were studied in the context of the population or "race" to which the given organism and its genes belonged, no universal, context-independent, and reliable relationship between genes and characters would result.[10] In particular, the leading racial hygienist of National Socialism, Fritz Lenz (1887–1976), formulated this as a critique of Goldschmidt in the 1920s, while at the same time – and based on Goldschmidt's experiments – he alleged that there was a direct connection between miscegenation, degeneration, and the disintegration of a binary gender order.[11]

This chapter will first introduce Goldschmidt's genetic concept of the 1920s – also in comparison with Morgan – as well as his interpretation of sex determination. The contrasting receptions of Goldschmidt's work by the gynecologist Paul Mathes on the one hand and the racial hygienist (*Rassenarzt*) Fritz Lenz on the other are then used to reconstruct two different possibilities of applying his concepts to humans. Moreover, comparing the genetic concepts of Fritz Lenz with Richard Goldschmidt's makes apparent what inherent logic the genes had to follow if they were to substantiate claims to racial superiority. For Fritz Lenz, the conceptions of racial purity, Nordic supremacy, and a clearly separated and hierarchically ordered masculinity and femininity were compatible only with Morgan's concept of the gene, and not with Goldschmidt's. It will be shown how the conceptions of race, genes, and sex difference were mutually constitutive and how gender was part of their making; also, it will be demonstrated how the premises of racial and sexual politics determined the acceptance of a particular genetic concept. However, explicit reference to anti-Semitic stereotyping such as the contentious phrase of "racial defilement" (*Rassenschande*), which was used openly from 1933 onward to attack the newly defined "Germans" and "non-Aryan, Jewish" people who entered into sexual relationships with each other, are not to be found in the investigated texts from the 1920s.[12]

---

[10] The term "race" was used in the sense of taxonomists of the 1920s; later evolutionary synthesis saw races or geographic populations as incipient species. In the following I use the term in this sense.

[11] I use the term "gender order" to indicate that it is a social process that defines various "sexes" and "intersexes." I do so even in the case when the author I am dealing with thinks that he is talking of a "natural" entity. However, I still use the terms "sex difference" and "sex determination" when referring to the efforts in biology and genetics to deal with a difference in reproductive capacities. The German term "*Geschlecht*" refers to both the social and the biological/corporeal, thus it does not lead to the Butlerian gender trouble in the use of "sex" or "gender," which is inevitable in the English language.

[12] On this, see Alexandra Przyrembel, *"Rassenschande." Reinheitsmythos und Vernichtungslegitimation im Nationalsozialismus* (Göttingen: Wallstein Verlag, 2003).

Nevertheless, considering how closely anti-Semitic *topoi* were entangled with questions as to the desired or abominated gender identity at the time, it must be presumed that the authors presented here were aware of an invisible subtext that provided the setting not only for their arguments but also for their everyday lives.[13]

Sex Determination and Genetics

During the 1920s, the inheritance and development of sex difference was a central topic of genetic research at the Kaiser Wilhelm Institute for Biology in Berlin Dahlem. Since the characters many organisms signifying "male" or "female" were understood as hereditary in the terms of Mendelian genetics, the inheritance of sex difference (*Vererbung des Geschlechts*) became the paradigmatic case. Three of the institute's first five departmental directors had divided up the territory: Carl Correns (1864–1933) dealt with botany, Max Hartmann (1876–1962) chose the unicellular organisms, the "protists," and Richard Goldschmidt studied sex determination in zoology.[14] By the end of the 1920s, he had developed his concept of the genetic material and its mode of action on the basis of his own studies on the inheritance and determination of sexual characters in the *Lymantria dispar* gypsy moth, and a broad knowledge of contemporary findings in biology. His ideas were launched in a summary work, the monograph published in German in 1920 and then translated into English and Russian, *Mechanismus und Physiologie der Geschlechtsbestimmung* (The Mechanism and Physiology of Sex Determination). The 528-page book *Die sexuellen Zwischenstufen* (The

---

[13] See Ute Planert, "Reaktionäre Modernisten. Zum Verhältnis von Antisemitismus und Antifeminismus in der völkischen Bewegung," *Jahrbuch für Antisemitismusforschung*, 11 (2002), 31–51.

[14] For example, Carl Correns, "Geschlechterverteilung und Geschlechtsbestimmung (bei Pflanzen)," *Handwörterbuch der Naturwissenschaften*, vol. 4 (Jena: Fischer, 1913), 975–989; Carl Correns and Richard Goldschmidt, *Die Vererbung und Bestimmung des Geschlechts. Zwei Vorträge gehalten in der Gesamtsitzung der naturwissenschaftlichen und der medizinischen Hauptgruppe der 84. Versammlung deutscher Naturforscher und Ärzte in Münster am 19.9.1912* (Berlin: Bornträger, 1913); Goldschmidt, *quantitative*. Subsequently Hartmann developed his own theory of sexuality; see Max Hartmann, *Die Sexualität* (Jena: Fischer, 1943). The determination of sex was of central importance in the biology of the day for many reasons. What was sought was not only an explanation for how the different sexes came into being, but also how the number of male and female progeny could be influenced. See Richard Goldschmidt, "Das Problem der Geschlechtsbestimmung," *Die Umschau. Übersicht über die Fortschritte und Bewegungen auf dem Gesamtgebiet der Wissenschaft und Technik, sowie ihrer Beziehungen zu Wissenschaft und Kunst*, 14 (1910), 201–205; W. E. Ankel, "Gerichtete und willkürliche Geschlechtsbestimmung," *Natur und Museum, Senckenbergische Naturforschende Gesellschaft*, 6 (1929), 273–374. On the situation in the United States, see Jane Maienschein, "What Determines Sex? A Study of Convergent Research Approaches, 1880–1916," *Isis*, 75 (1984), 457–480.

Intermediate Sexual Forms or "sexual intermediacy") of 1931 presented the then current state of knowledge about sex determination in zoology.[15]

The development of Goldschmidt's genetics until the late 1920s is pains-takingly depicted in an unpublished dissertation by Marsha Richmond from 1986.[16] On the basis of Goldschmidt's scientific publications, she traces the significant stages and modifications to his concept between 1909 and 1934. In this period, around eighty articles including four monographs appeared.[17] Richmond shows that Goldschmidt's genetic counter-draft to the genetics developed at the same time by the school of Thomas Hunt Morgan in the United States must be accorded its own scientific rationality and logic. In so doing, she blazes the first path through the thicket of previous standard assessments by geneticists and biologists of the "modern synthesis," along with many a historian of science, who saw Goldschmidt as "obstructionist" and held his concepts to be highly speculative, if not downright wrong.[18] Richmond makes clear that Richard Goldschmidt's genetic ideas fulfilled a set of conditions placed on scientific consistency: any explanation of a hereditary process had to include the problem of onto-genesis and phylo-genesis as well; cytological findings about the behavior of chromosomes and gametes had to concur with the results of the Mendelian breeding experi-ments; and concepts from physical chemistry and enzyme chemistry had to help develop hypotheses about the properties of the materials that were supposed to act as the gene. In contrast, Morgan and his school defined the permissible questions and interpretations to be made within a narrow framework that could be addressed by their experimental system using *Drosophila melanogaster*, declaring every hypothesis that extended beyond it "fictive" or even "metaphysical."[19]

It is not enough to describe the difference between the two approaches as merely the difference between transmission genetics in the sense of Morgan, and a genetics that treats the problem of heredity simultaneously as a prob-lem of the organism's development and of the transmission of genes to the next generation. While Goldschmidt belongs to the typical representatives of the "comprehensive style" so common in Germany of that time, the group

---

[15] Richard Goldschmidt, *Mechanismus und Physiologie der Geschlechtsbestimmung* (Berlin: Bornträger, 1920); Richard Goldschmidt, *Die Sexuellen Zwischenstufen* (Berlin: Springer, 1931).

[16] Marsha Richmond, "Richard Goldschmidt and Sex Determination: The Growth of German Genetics, 1900–1935," Ph.D. diss., Indiana University (1986).

[17] Richmond, 381, counts circa 100 publications.

[18] Richmond, 490. The paper is also notable to the extent that Richmond turns against the dominant position in the U.S. history of genetics of the early 1980s, which itself remained in the framework of Morgan's paradigm and did not concede any "major breakthroughs" to the German-language genetics of the first three decades of the twentieth century that might have led to an improved "understanding of the nature of heredity," Richmond, 6.

[19] Richmond, 483.

around Morgan has been categorized more appropriately as belonging to the "pragmatic style." Another part of the difference between the research approaches of Goldschmidt and Morgan, however, is a fundamental difference between two different experimental systems.[20] Goldschmidt used specimens of the *Lymantria dispar* gypsy moth collected in various geographical regions of Europe and Imperial Japan, and his experiment's basic units were geographically defined wild populations. The character he investigated, which followed Mendelian rules, was male or female sex. The group around Morgan used inbred strains of the fruit fly *Drosophila melanogaster*, which they had produced in the laboratory. The experiments, upon which Morgan constructed the "theory of the gene," began with flies that exhibited sex-linked characters such as white eyes. These were inherited along with the character "female sex" in accordance with the Mendelian rules and remained unchanged across the next generations.

As Richmond demonstrates, the differences in Morgan's and Goldschmidt's gene concepts had already become clear by 1917, at the time of Goldschmidt's first, involuntary stay in the United States due to the war. By this time, the essential elements that distinguished the respective genetic theories of both approaches had been worked out.[21] According to Morgan, genes were corpuscular, discrete, and usually stable units on the chromosomes, which did not influence each other.[22] These genes could be assigned to certain locations on the chromosomes by means of mathematically analyzing series of hybridizations to produce chromosome maps.[23] The very

---

[20] Jonathan Harwood, *Styles of Scientific Thought. The German Genetics Community 1900–1933* (Chicago: University of Chicago Press, 1993); Ludwik Fleck, *Entstehung und Entwicklung einer wissenschaftlichen Tatsache. Einführung in die Lehre vom Denkstil und Denkkollektiv* (Frankfurt am Main: Suhrkamp, 1994); on the relevance of the experimental system, see Hans-Jörg Rheinberger, *Toward a History of Epistemic Things. Synthesizing Proteins in the Test Tube* (Stanford: Stanford University Press, 1997), here 24–37.

[21] Richmond, 381–382; Thomas H. Morgan et al., *The Mechanism of Mendelian Heredity* (New York: Holt, 1915); Richard Goldschmidt, *Einführung in die Vererbungswissenschaft*, 2nd ed. (Leipzig: Engelmann, 1913).

[22] These conceptions were modified in the following years without abandoning the basic assumption of the autonomous gene. In 1925, Sturtevant showed the so-called position effect on *Drosophila* for the first time, according to which the location of a gene was decisive for its function. Richmond sees in this the first evidence against Morgan's gene model; see Richmond, 437. Dietrich, in contrast, holds the mid-1930s to be the decisive period in the conflict about the importance of the position effect, when Goldschmidt declared that the new findings meant Morgan's gene was "dead as a dodo." In 1927, the idea of stability of the genes was suspended by H. J. Muller, who produced mutations by subjecting genes to X-ray radiation, which manifested themselves in modified characters. These mutated genes did keep their stable position in the chromosome, however, and for this reason made it possible to further differentiate chromosome maps. See Dietrich, "Goldschmidt," 92–102.

[23] The basis for the calculations of the gene locations was the frequency of "crossing over," that is, how often characters, normally linked and inherited together, thus supposedly located on the same chromosome, were transmitted separately to the next generation. It was postulated

design of the experiments stipulated that the genes were to be understood as units that appear unchanged in following generations. The only question was how frequently they occurred together with other genes, so that they could be mapped together on one chromosome. Neither environmental conditions nor an organism's genetic context, determined by the population it belonged to, were studied as potential influences on the mode of action of the individual genes, but instead were excluded by the experimental design. Furthermore, the genes initially studied by the Morgan group were distinguished by their sex-linked inheritance, that is, they could be attributed to the very chromosome that was also seen to be responsible for the female sex. In this manner it became possible to map the sex-linked genes to discrete locations on that chromosome. Accordingly, the heredity of sex did play a significant role for Morgan. However, female or male sex was not the primary character investigated but rather an auxiliary construction that was to remain stable to trace other hereditary traits through the generations.

In opposition to this, the genes Goldschmidt developed on *Lymantria* were not portrayed as discrete units on chromosome maps. In crossings of certain geographical populations, or – in the terminology used by Goldschmidt – in certain racial hybrids, individuals were created that showed a combination of characters from both sexes. In 1915 Goldschmidt called these experimentally produced animals "intersexes."[24] The species *Lymantria dispar* received its name for precisely that reason, that male and female specimens turn out so differently that close observation of their behavior was required to categorize them as a single species: male and female animals vary greatly with regard to their body size, wing pigmentation, structure of antennae, genitals, and other characters. In the moths designated as intersexual, these differences in characters were no longer distributed so strictly between two sexes.

By crossing various European and Japanese populations or races of *Lymantria dispar*, it was possible to breed animals whose chromosome differences made them identifiable as male or female but whose morphology exhibited a mixture of male and female characteristics. Richard Goldschmidt published the results of his first stay in Japan in the Archive for Racial and

---

that this effect was due to a break in the chromosomes and an exchange of pieces during meiosis. The more frequently crossing over between two traits of the same "linkage group" or chromosome occurred, the greater should be their distance on their original common chromosome. The purely mathematic-geometric production of the gene maps becomes especially clear in the textbook by Morgan's pupils: Alfred H. Sturtevant and George W. Beadle, *An Introduction to Genetics* (Philadelphia: W. B. Saunders, 1939). On the dynamics of *Drosophila* genetics as a nearly autocatalytic generator of experimental results and further questions, see Kohler, *Lords*.

24 Richmond, 382. In this Goldschmidt demarcated these mixed forms from the "gynandromorphs."

Social Biology (*Archiv für Rassen- und Gesellschaftsbiologie*) during World War I, while staying in the United States:

Through the correct crossing-breeding of the races I am familiar with, I am now able to generate any intermediate sexual form (*"geschlechtliche Zwischenform"*) I desire, which extend in a seamless series from a female to a male and vice versa. And further, I can, of course, also achieve the extreme that all animals, which are to be females in terms of their constitution, become actual males. The reversed extreme, the transformation of all males into females, has not been achieved so far.[25]

Goldschmidt interbred the various races of *Lymantria dispar* according to all the rules of Mendelian genetics: crossing two races in the parent generation, that is, creating hybrids; sorting the first successive generation by males, females, and intersexes; categorizing the intersexes according to their degree of sexual ambiguity; then crossing these animals with each other, sorting them, crossing them with a representative of the parent generation, and so on. Over the years and additional research stays in Japan, he and his assistants produced test series counting hundreds of thousands of animals. The studies were extended by means of cytology and histology, determining chromosomes, and describing the development of the antennae, the gonads, and other organs at various stages in order to investigate the differences correlated with sex difference.

In this, Goldschmidt considered "male" and "female" as units of Mendelian heredity, each responsible for an entire group of characters. In the hybridization experiment these characters could be distributed on a scale and located between fully "male" and fully "female." In his interpretation of sex determination, Goldschmidt revived the old embryological concept of the bisexual potential of organisms, by postulating the sex-determining factors M for male and F for female characters, which together and in a given balance within the organism, led to the development of a male or a female animal. These factors were present in the fertilized egg, they were inherited in accordance with the Mendelian rules, and they could vary in their intensity. In Goldschmidt's view, the intensities of the factors determining maleness or femaleness differed in the various geographic populations or races. Genes were supposed to be substances, the amounts of which determined whether and how they produced a certain effect in an organism.

With his new interpretation of the inheritance and determination of sex, Goldschmidt hoped to resolve a problem that had caused considerable headaches in previous years. In the first decade of the twentieth century it had been a dramatic proposition to link the heredity of sex to the number of

---

[25] Richard Goldschmidt, "Die biologischen Grundlagen der konträren Sexualität und des Hermaphroditismus beim Menschen," *Archiv für Rassen- und Gesellschaftsbiologie*, 12 (1916), 1–14 [off-print pagination], here 5–6.

the chromosomes present in the given organism and rule out the influence of factors like nutrition or the metabolism of the mother organism.[26] This meant that fertilization, with the chromosomes distributed by chance, determined whether the fertilized egg would develop into a male or a female individual. The correlativity of sex difference and chromosome difference even became proof for the chromosomal theory of heredity, claiming that the chromosomes were the sites of Mendelian genes. However, over the course of research a great wealth of contradictory chromosomal differences became apparent, each of which was supposed to be responsible for the development of maleness and femaleness.[27] By postulating the inheritable sex determination factors M and F, Goldschmidt dissolved the correlation between sex determination and the number of chromosomes, offering a model that could be applied flexibly to the many contradictory findings obtained from different species. In *Lymantria*, the females were supposed to possess 2 F and 1 M, the males 2 F and 2 M. The combined strength of 2 M had to outperform the 2 F in order to produce an unambiguous male, while the effect of 2 F merely needed to be greater than 1 M for a female to develop.

According to Goldschmidt's experiments, the balance between F and M required for a binary sex difference to develop was given within each race; the strengths of the sex-determining factors conformed to this balance. If certain race mixtures produced "intersexual" animals that combined male and female sex characters, this could be explained through the interplay of female and male factors of different intensity. Consequently, when these factors were combined, neither sex was able to develop unambiguously. For instance, when European moth females were crossed with Japanese males, normal males and intersexual females resulted. Inversely, when a Japanese female was crossed with a European male, the progeny were unambiguous males and unambiguous females. The factors that determined maleness in the Japanese populations were thus stronger than the corresponding factors in the European moths. Nevertheless, crossing "races" still did not produce "intersexuals" in all cases. Other scientists' subsequent findings allowed doubt to be cast on Goldschmidt's interpretation; however, he did not integrate these into his interpretation of sex determination.[28] The initial finding that intersexual animals could also be produced through incest was not investigated any further.[29]

---

[26] The work of Nettie Maria Stevens (1861–1912) is particularly important; see Stephen G. Brush, "Nettie M. Stevens and the Discovery of Sex Determination by Chromosomes," *Isis*, 69 (1978), 163–172; Marilyn Bailey Ogilvie, "Nettie Marie Stevens (1861–1912)," in Louise S. Grinstein, Carol A. Biermann, and Rose K. Rose (eds.), *Women in the Biological Sciences. A Bibliographical Sourcebook* (Westport: Greenwood Press, 1997), 517–523.

[27] Franz Schrader, *Die Geschlechtschromosomen* (Berlin: Bornträger, 1928).

[28] Stern, here 75.

[29] Goldschmidt, "Grundlagen," here 9.

Until the late 1920s, Goldschmidt championed the idea that genes were enzymes that became active during the development of an individual. He explained the development of the intersexual animals by postulating that the development of an organism took place according to its chromosomal sex up to a certain "turning point" (*"Drehpunkt"*), but that the strength of the given opposite factor became decisive thereafter. Thus, under the effect of this factor, those parts of the body that developed after the "turning point" could then develop the characters of the other sex.[30] This interpretation, existing in principle in 1917, was subsequently buttressed by experiments and then applied to all genes in his *Physiological Theory of Heredity* of 1927.[31] The development of an organism was bound to its genes acting in precise coordination, with a specific quantity operating at a particular speed.[32] However, on the basis of his gene concept – and this deserves particular emphasis – Goldschmidt certainly saw breeding and eugenic applications as possible.[33] In the 1920s, he was involved in the drafting of a law on voluntary eugenic sterilization.

Toward the end of World War I, the theories of Morgan and Goldschmidt differed from each other essentially through their different gene concepts. For Goldschmidt, the genes had their exact place in the life period of an organism and were part of a complex interaction.[34] The chromosome meant merely the assembly of genes or enzymes at the point of fertilization and cell division. The chromosome was only produced on the occasion of cell division, for which there must also be forces or causes in the cell.[35] A cell's inventory of genes was, accordingly, always also a product of cellular processes.[36] Goldschmidt's model postulated a dual property of genetic material: it was responsible for the manifestation of the characters and, beyond this, for its own organization.[37] Genes were chemical substances, variable with regard to

[30] Richmond, 386–390. "Turning point" is Goldschmidt's term in his English publications.

[31] Richmond, 380–431; Goldschmidt, *Physiologische Theorie.*

[32] Richmond, 400–415.

[33] Richard Goldschmidt, "30 Jahre Vererbungswissenschaft des schwedischen Getreidebaues," *Wissenschaftliches Korrespondenzbüro "Akademia"* 2, [special issue] *Lebendige Wissenschaft* (1929), 4–5.

[34] These concepts are easier to understand by considering that *Lymantria* is an animal that hatches from an egg as a caterpillar, grows and finally changes its form completely during pupation, and then continues its life as a butterfly. These features of the experimental animal directly suggest various phases of development and of genetic activity, and the conception of a "turning point" of development, but only when the phenomena to be explained by the function of the gene cover the entire life phase of an organism. After all, *Drosophila* also has a pupa stage, yet Morgan's group did not regard the ontogenetic metamorphoses of its experimental animal as relevant for its study of the genes.

[35] Richmond, 315, 322.

[36] Richmond, 395–399.

[37] For 1917, see Richmond, 390–391. This concept has older roots in the cytology of the "chromodial apparatus"; see Richmond, 94–136.

their quantity, but not as easy to pin down as chromosome maps suggested. In the early 1920s, the significant differences between the two gene concepts were apparent. Therefore, it was not emigration that turned Goldschmidt into a pronounced opponent of Morgan and his school.[38]

After World War I, not everyone in Germany followed Goldschmidt's approach.[39] Members of Germany's genetics community criticized Goldschmidt, with express reference to Morgan's theory. This critique was connected to the work on sex determination in *Lymantria* in a highly contradictory manner. First, Goldschmidt's concept of "fluctuating" genes or genes of variable power to effect a certain character was not accepted. Second, the intersexual moths served the anti-Semitic and racial rhetoric that racial miscegenation in humans inevitably will lead to degeneration. In this rhetoric, the concept of a clear binary sex difference was a key characteristic of the supposedly highest developed group, namely, the Nordic race. The blurring of a difference between men and women was perceived as a severe threat to Nordic superiority. Thus, multiple aspects of Goldschmidt's experimental production of sexually ambiguous individuals on the basis of crossbreeding different races harbored dynamite for the sociopolitical realm.

Impurities: Sex/Gender and Race

In 1916, Goldschmidt used his experimental results to interpret the human gender order.[40] Referring to the moths, he argued that homosexuality was also a form of "biological intersexual," and thus natural. He further postulated a genetic cause for the occurrence of hermaphrodites. He argued that humans with ambiguous sex characters should not be assigned an unambiguous sexual identity by law, since they did not have one. In these cases, the supposedly clear chromosomal status did not determine their identity as a man or a woman. Homosexuality in humans, he continued, was merely a nonpathological variant of sexuality and about as irrelevant to health as red-green color blindness. These statements place Goldschmidt in the same group of biologists and physicians who, like one of the founders of sexology (*Sexualwissenschaft*) Magnus Hirschfeld, argued that social policy should be liberalized and homosexuality should no longer be a punishable offense,

---

[38] Michael R. Dietrich argues that the results of Sturtevant and Dobzhansky were the first to allow Goldschmidt to critique the corpuscular gene in the mid-1930s on the basis of the position effect. However, Dietrich does not regard the work on *Lymantria* as a contribution to Goldschmidt's concept of the gene. He does not see the work on the sex determination as belonging to genetics. See Dietrich, "Gene," 93–102, 110.

[39] Richmond, 366.

[40] Goldschmidt, "Grundlagen"; Michael R. Dietrich, "Of Moths and Men: Theo Lang and the Persistence of Richard Goldschmidt's Theory of Homosexuality, 1916–1960," *History and Philosophy of the Life Sciences*, 22 (2000), 219–247.

precisely because homosexuality was inherited and nonpathological.[41] However, and it is important to emphasize this here, Goldschmidt did not assume that miscegenation was the cause of homosexuality; for him homosexuality and intersexuality, although both inherited, did not have the same causes. In this Goldschmidt referred to Hirschfeld's assumption that it was inbreeding that led to homosexuality, as its frequent occurrence in Courland Germans or in the mountains of Upper Bavaria would suggest.[42]

The intersexual moths did not remain in Goldschmidt's laboratory, silently acquiescent to the development of a "physiological theory of heredity." In the 1920s, they populated nearly every kind of scientific and popular science literature that dealt with the inheritance and determination of sex. Meyer's Encyclopedia listed them, as did the sex education texts of Paul Kammerer and Julius Schaxel, two biologists active on the political left.[43] Kammerer emphasized in his 1927 pamphlet *Geschlecht, Fortpflanzung, Fruchtbarkeit* (Sex, Reproduction, Fertility) that no two fundamentally different sexes existed, but that all humans were hermaphrodites, a "dual sex" that developed into one direction or the other, woman or man.[44] In contrast, Julius Schaxel attempted to maintain that a binary order of the sexes was the primordial one – the man in the forest, the woman at home – which, according to Friedrich Engels, was the norm at the beginning of human history. Schaxel used Goldschmidt's moths to pathologize sexual ambiguity as due to "abnormal mixtures resulting from the combination of unbalanced nuclei."

These biological debates took place in the social setting of the Weimar Republic, where the social gender order was being renegotiated in provocative public confrontations.[45] Signs and symbols previously used unambiguously to identify men or women were now combined in new ways; women usurped male territory ranging from political suffrage through professional work, including academic positions, to the rejection of women's "sole vocation as wife and mother" (*alleiniger Lebensberuf als Ehefrau und Mutter*).

[41] At this time the postulate that homosexuality was congenital was not a means of criminalizing or pathologizing it, but rather of liberalization. See the opposite view, unfortunately an ahistorical account, which is also rather imprecise in other respects: Florian Mildenberger, "Ein Zoologe auf Abwegen. Richard B. Goldschmidt (1878–1958) als Sexualforscher und seine Rezeption im Dritten Reich," *Sudhoffs Archiv*, 85 (2001), 64–81.

[42] Goldschmidt, "Grundlagen," 9.

[43] *Meyers Konversationslexikon*, 7th ed. (Leipzig: Verlag des Bibliographischen Instituts, 1927); Julius Schaxel, *Das Geschlecht, seine Erscheinungen, seine Bestimmung, sein Wesen bei Mensch und Tier* (Jena: Urania-Verlag-Gesellschaft, 1926); Paul Kammerer, *Geschlecht. Fortpflanzung. Fruchtbarkeit. Eine Biologie der Zeugung (Genebiotik)* (Munich: Drei Masken-Verlag, 1927), here 81–88. Kammerer translates Goldschmidt's sex determination genes as a "man-substance" (*Mannstoff*) and a "woman-substance" (*Weibstoff*).

[44] Kammerer, here 81–88.

[45] Ute Planert, *Antifeminismus im Kaiserreich. Diskurs, soziale Formation und politische Mentalität* (Göttingen: Vandenhoeck and Ruprecht, 1998).

However, everyday life for the majority of young women was distinguished primarily by a heavy workload, as the responsibility for domestic duties was not at all evenly divided between men and women.[46] Artists, both male and female, reinvented themselves as androgynous chimeras. Thus the poet Else Lasker-Schüler had created for herself the literary figure Prince Jussuf of Thebes before World War I. Theater, film, and cabaret played with image of the ambiguous woman; just to name a few: Asta Nielsen, Claire Waldoff, Erika Mann, and Marlene Dietrich. The Dadaists of the 1920s created portraits mismatching pieces of males and females. The art historian Katrin Hoffmann-Curtius commented derisively that Hannah Höch's parodistic confusion of the binary gender system could even be "read as a strategic proposal in the spirit of Judith Butler."[47]

In this cultural context, Goldschmidt's moths showed that mixed forms combining male and female features could be produced biologically. Thus, they served the cause of liberalization, providing counter-arguments against the claim that these hybrid forms were unnatural.[48] Goldschmidt's interpretation of the heredity of sex was based upon the older "one-sex model" of embryology, according to which there is a bisexual potential of organisms with every male or female organism manifesting characters of both to an extremely variable degree. According to this model, there was no clear male or female identity:

For me there is neither the concept of a sex gene, in the sense that there is one gene for the development of the organs of one or the other sex; nor is there the concept of the realizer (*Realisator*) … , which suppresses the effect of the opposite sex gene. [All] cell[s] … of each and every organism have to decide at a certain moment whether they pursue the female or male route of development, differentiation; they have an alternating norm of reaction. Which of the two happens depends on the

---

[46] Christiane Eifert, "Die neue Frau. Bewegung und Alltag," in Manfred Görtemaker (ed.), *Weimar in Berlin: Porträt einer Epoche* (Berlin: be.bar-Verlag, 2002), 82–103. On the tremendous effort to reorganize the division of labor in the family at women's expense, see also Karin Hausen, "Mütter, Söhne und der Markt der Symbole und Waren: Der deutsche Muttertag 1923–1933," in Hans Medick and David Sabean (eds.), *Emotionen und materielle Interessen. Sozialanthropologische und historische Beiträge zur Familienforschung* (Göttingen: Vandenhoeck and Ruprecht, 1984), 473–523.

[47] Kathrin Hoffmann-Curtius, "Geschlechterspiel im Dadaismus," *Kunstforum*, 128 (October–December 1994), 166–169.

[48] It is inappropriate in this case to indulge in the general suspicion that biology always strives for biopolitical control in Foucault's sense. See the unpublished dissertation by Christopher S. W. Kohler, "The Sex Problem: Thomas Hunt Morgan, Richard Goldschmidt, and the Question of Sex and Gender in the Twentieth Century," Ph.D. diss., University of Florida (1998). Nevertheless, the credit goes to Kohler for investigating for the first time the important connection between extensive biological research about sex determination and the social problem of the gender order, the "new woman," and the issue of homosexuality in the first decades of the twentieth century. I would like to thank Kohler for sending me his work.

presence of sex-differentiating substances whose production constitutes the essence of the sex genes F and M.[49]

With this concept of sex determination, no clear dichotomous order could be produced; there was merely a scale between the end points "completely male" and "completely female," with any number of "intermediate sexes" in between. This very concept of sexuality was provocative.[50] Because of its experimental prerequisite, "miscegenation," the discourse about biological causes of the blurring sexual identities bore additional tinder. For its very biological justification, the discourse about intersexuality could be integrated into the discourse about the degeneration of the race cultivated in the racist right-wing (*völkisch*) circles.

Two examples of the reception and discussion of Goldschmidt's ideas about genes and sex determination will show how the experimental effects of miscegenation in moths was used as a scientific explanation for the unrest on the gender front, and what differences in the reception were still possible in the 1920s. These examples are two physicians, the gynecologist Paul Mathes and the racial hygienist Fritz Lenz.

Reception 1: The Gynecologist

In 1924, Paul Mathes, professor at the women's hospital of the University of Innsbruck, published a chapter over 100 pages long in the standard textbook of gynecology, *Biologie und Pathologie des Weibes* (The Biology and Pathology of the Woman), entitled "Die Konstitutionstypen des Weibes, insbesondere der intersexuelle Typus" (The Constitutional Types of Woman, Especially the Intersexual Type).[51] Goldschmidt's work on moths served Mathes as a model through which a certain portion of his clientele could be described as intersexuals. To do this, however, he had to completely modify one significant aspect of Goldschmidt's genetic model. The strict sequence that Goldschmidt had observed in the development of the organs up to the "turning point" could not be found in the development of sex characters of woman. Mathes boldly asserted that in contrast to *Lymantria*, the sequence in the development of the various

---

[49] Richard Goldschmidt, "Geschlechtsbestimmung im Tier- und Pflanzenreich," *Biologisches Zentralblatt*, 49 (1929), 641–648, here 643.

[50] This concept is no postmodern invention of the late twentieth century, as contemporary works suggest. See Katrin Rieder, "XX gleich Frau, XY gleich Mann? Die Kategorie Geschlecht in der Entwicklung der Genetik," *Ariadne, Forum für Frauen- und Geschlechtergeschichte*, 41 (2003), 8–18.

[51] Paul Mathes, "Die Konstitutionstypen des Weibes, insbesondere der intersexuelle Typus," in Josef Halban and Ludwig Seitz (eds.), *Biologie und Pathologie des Weibes*, Vol. III (Berlin: Urban and Schwarzenberg, 1924), 1–112.

physical and mental traits in woman was not at all fixed. Indeed, for him its "irregularity" was rather striking.[52]

Mathes's remarks illuminate what kind of medical invention "woman" was, where the line between the pathology and normality of the woman was drawn, and what kinds of fantasies about femininity and masculinity were opened up by Goldschmidt's sex-determining factors. With reference to Otto Weininger's *Geschlecht und Charakter* (Sex and Character), Mathes also saw both sexes realized in both men and women, and this in a great variety of manifestations since so many combinations of the sex characters were possible.[53] Mathes was astoundingly open when he admitted that "woman" corresponding to the female set of chromosomes was a "fiction," a "mental abstraction," an idea in the Platonic sense. He explained the contradiction between reality and fiction using the example of women's legs, which contemporary fashion were just revealing to public view: "By a ratio of 143:64, hairy legs are usual, the norm, among woman, and nevertheless we will never regard a woman with hairy legs as the normal type of woman." On the contrary, the "creative eyes of the artist" were the "appropriate tool" to find and determine the ideal type:

It would be welcomed if here, too, an authoritative organization, in this case it could be the *Deutsche Gesellschaft für Gynäkologie* (German Society for Gynecology), would take on the task of formulating a norm, a canon of the woman for all phases of life, and to designate as the normal constitution of woman that condition of the chromosomes which leads to the development of the ideal.[54]

In this case the chromosomes turned out to be the ideal substratum for phantasmagorical femininity.

Mathes explained the emergence of the intersexual woman by referencing Goldschmidt's concept that the different strengths of the hereditary factors M and F determined the different grades of masculinity and femininity in one organism. In this he even imagined the development into a woman as a swimming competition of the sex-determining factors. He obviously imagined femininity as a serious threat:

Let us assume that in a fertilized egg, which we imagine to be infinitely enlarged, all hereditary dispositions (the chromosomes) sit very close to each other, ready and able to unfold. The sex-determining factors are located at a specific position – in

[52] How many indicators for female sex the physicians had to keep in mind is shown in the review by Robert Hofstätter, "Unser Wissen über die sekundären Geschlechtscharaktere," *Zentralblatt Grenzgebiete der Medizin und Chirurgie*, 16 (1912/13), 37–420. Here 2,324 relevant publications are considered in order to come to terms with the confusing phenomenon "woman" (*Frau und Geschlechtlichkeit*). Hofstätter also forgoes the attempt to set a sequence in which the sex characters occur during the development of the individual. I thank Karin Hausen for referring me to this work.

[53] Mathes, 72, 75.

[54] Mathes, 9.

the case of an egg that is determined as female they are initially just a large F and a very small m. Now the work of development begins; ever more increasing streams of colloidal plasma flow here and there; the streams stagnate in places, here and there islands consolidate in the current, which increase through apposition; these are the individual organs beginning to form. Flowing along everywhere in the currents are the progeny of the large F and the small m, furnished with their own energy. ... The large F's are always faster than the small m's; presumably they also reproduce more rapidly. Thus they are able to take possession of the organ islands, always and everywhere, the small m's always arrive too late, and if some do occasionally land on such an island they are immediately repelled back into the current by the large F's, which have already hoisted their flag there. They then drift defenseless, injured by the blow, or even drown. The entire organism becomes female throughout when the large F's are always stronger and faster than the small m's. ... Thus a kind of race unfolds between the large F's and the small m's, which the large F's always win – the most ideal case, but the least probable one.[55]

Mathes's text reveals a high degree of ambivalence regarding the ideal, superior woman and her deviation, the intersexual. After all, the latter at least referred to the existence of a strong m determining masculinity that overcame F and did not drown. In cases where the intersexual woman was too far removed from the male ideal, Mathes advocated surgical correction.

Mathes included working women in his definition of intersexuals:

... women for whom rationality completely outweighs emotion. In such a woman nothing wells from the depths of her being. Reasonable deliberation dominates her action and inaction; emotions do not occur or are intentionally suppressed. She rejects the man as a sexual object, sees in him the companion, and presumably also the competitor, to whom she feels superior because her reason is less inspired by imagination, works more steadily, remains more strictly focused on the goal and therefore is more apt than many men's to complete a certain workload. We find her most often in the teaching profession ... we find her as a reliable, loyal and competent employee in commercial and scientific professions, or in administrative positions.[56]

For Mathes, the intersexuality of the woman, measured by the hairiness of her legs, was certainly one of the causes of the contemporary decline in birth rate, just as infertility among Goldschmidt's moths increased along with the degree of intersexuality. Nevertheless, this condition was not necessarily a pathological one. Especially the intersexual woman in menopause, as long as she was

of great mind and strong intellectual and artistic talent ... [was] the center of the circle of men ... who revere and admire in the brilliant aged woman the combined masculine energy and the feminine grace of her intellect.[57]

[55] Mathes, 73–74.
[56] Mathes, 80.
[57] Mathes, 84.

Mathes counted among these women Schopenhauer's mother, Empress
Elisabeth of Austria, Charlotte von Stein, and the women of the French
Ancien Régime. For him, the male intersexuals included, for instance,
Johann Wolfgang von Goethe, Leonardo da Vinci, and Michelangelo. The
intersexual woman fascinated him; she was the woman of the future –

with all of her charms, with the gradually proceeding blurring of the sex characters, with her slim, narrow, high figure, the brilliant, problematically beautiful, sharp
facial features and with her abrupt temperament and diminished capability to conceive and bear children.[58]

Following Goldschmidt's results with the moths, Mathes saw the cause
for intersexuality in "miscegenation." At the moment, he continued, "the
differentiation of the sexes was regressing in civilized humanity"; in large
cities this process was widespread, and also "especially in Tyrol, a country which has been known since time immemorial as a gateway between
North and South, the stomping grounds of diverse races and clans."[59] Yet,
Mathes did not believe it necessary to impose marital prohibition. "Despite
the efforts of the eugenicists we are not in the position of the breeding cre-
ator and never will be; everyone takes, as from time immemorial, *what he
pleases.*"[60] Indeed, using eugenics to realize the ideal of perfect femininity
would have deprived Mathes the gynecologist of his professional activity
and Mathes the man of any erotic variety. Obviously, contemporary women
could make men feel insecure, and the prospect of genetically typing various
women and creating a therapeutic order was a fascinating one for physicians like Mathes.

Reception 2: The Racial Hygienist

The case is different for the physician who had dedicated himself to making race, not the individual, the target of therapy: Fritz Lenz. In the 1920s,
he was an aspiring racial hygienist, member of the German Racial Hygiene
Society (*Deutsche Gesellschaft für Rassenhygiene*) and the Aryan racist
(*völkisch*) Midgard Bund, and also editor of the journal *Archiv für Rassen-
und Gesellschaftsbiologie* (Archive for Racial and Social Biology). Lenz,
along with Erwin Baur and Eugen Fischer, co-authored the leading textbook on human heredity, *Grundriss der menschlichen Erblichkeitslehre
und Rassenhygiene,* four editions of which were published between 1921
and 1936, with an English translation, *Human Heredity* in 1931. Lenz
became one of the most influential representatives of human genetics and

[58] Mathes, 84.
[59] Mathes, 75–76.
[60] Mathes, 77. Original emphasis.

racial hygiene during National Socialism.[61] In 1933 he was appointed director of the Department for Eugenics at the Kaiser Wilhelm Institute for Anthropology in Berlin. Lenz contributed to the efforts of those actively promoting the political implementation of racial hygiene in the form of compulsory sterilization.[62]

In the early 1920s, Lenz connected the discourse of intersexuality with that of degeneration and scenarios of racial doom. He used as evidence Goldschmidt's experiments on *Lymantria* about the dissolution of a clear sexual duality through crossbreeding. However, he did not apply Goldschmidt's concept of genes, which was based on precisely these experiments, but rather criticized them decisively. This contradiction demonstrates clearly that different concepts of the gene were compatible with different political concepts of human society.

Lenz was openly antifeminist; he placed the highest value on the improvement of the (Nordic) race.[63] He condemned the employment of women as pernicious counter-selection, for, through their refusal of an exclusively maternal existence, "the ladies of emancipation" threatened "the Nordic race" in particular. Through the collective performance of the "brain lady" (*Gehirndame*), this "most masculine race on Earth" was in danger of being eradicated more quickly than through the emancipation of women, a movement which ultimately, but nevertheless unfortunately too late, would itself have to die out as the feminists refused to give birth and thus could not pass on their own rebellious characteristics.[64] Lenz perceived the Nordic race as the most highly evolved. This superiority was guaranteed by the highest possible difference between men and women and the highest possible birth rate, visible above all in a pronounced division of labor between the domestic mother of numerous children and the male breadwinner.[65] This circular

---

[61] Heiner Fangerau, "Der 'Baur-Fischer-Lenz' in der Buchkritik 1921-1940: Eine quantifizierende Untersuchung zur zeitgenössischen Rezeption rassenhygienischer Theorien," *Medizinhistorisches Journal*, 38 (2003), 57–81.

[62] Renate Rissom, *Fritz Lenz und die Rassenhygiene* (Husum: Matthiesen, 1983); Paul Weindling, *Health, Race and German Politics between National Unification and Nazism, 1870–1945* (Cambridge: Cambridge University Press, 1989); Peter Weingart, Jürgen Kroll, and Kurt Bayertz, *Rasse, Blut und Gene. Geschichte der Eugenik und Rassenhygiene in Deutschland* (Frankfurt am Main: Suhrkamp, 1988); Gabriele Czarnowski, *Das kontrollierte Paar. Ehe- und Sexualpolitik im Nationalsozialismus* (Weinheim: Deutscher Studienverlag, 1991); Gisela Bock, *Zwangssterilisation im Nationalsozialismus. Studien zur Rassenpolitik und Frauenpolitik* (Opladen: Westdeutscher Verlag, 1986).

[63] Rissom, 57–60; Weindling, 302–303.

[64] Fritz Lenz, *Über die krankhaften Erbanlagen des Mannes und die Bestimmung des Geschlechts beim Menschen. Untersuchungen über somatische und idioplasmatische Korrelation zwischen Geschlecht und pathologischer Anlage mit besonderer Berücksichtigung der Hämophilie* (Jena: Fischer, 1912), here 160–161. See also Rissom, 51–60.

[65] See the illustrated book reissued for over forty years, Carl Heinrich Stratz, *Die Rassenschönheit des Weibes* (Stuttgart: Enke, 1901), 21st ed. 1941.

axiomatic also allowed him to reinvent himself as a man of the elite, despite the fact that his background was neither upper middle class nor nobility.[66]

Fritz Lenz began his scientific career in 1912 with a medical doctoral dissertation about sex determination and sex-linked heredity of diseases in humans, *Über die krankhaften Erbanlagen des Mannes und die Bestimmung des Geschlechts beim Menschen* (On the Pathological Genetic Disposition of the Male and Sex Determination in Humans).[67] In 1922 he published *Erfahrungen über Erblichkeit und Entartung an Schmetterlingen* (Experiences about Heredity and Degeneration in Butterflies); this book was the basis of his "Habilitation" in medicine in 1919.[68] Experimenting on *Lymantria dispar* to investigate the question of sex determination, he explicitly referred to Goldschmidt's work. Initially he defined "degeneration" as the "occurrence of hereditary characters, which make the achievement of general life objectives more difficult or impossible." Besides diseases, this included all kinds of "dysfunction ... of normal sexual characters caused by hereditary factors," including the "sexual instincts." For, according to Lenz, "nothing is more important for the preservation of the race than healthy procreation and its conditions." Lenz rejected any differentiation between primary and secondary sex characters in humans; for him "all features by which sex can be recognized [were] sex characters, and every normal sex character serves procreation directly or indirectly."[69] Back in 1912 Lenz had already identified the turbulences in the gender order (literally: "*Unordnung des Geschlechtswesens*") and "degeneration" as being two sides of the same coin, which had to be fought simultaneously.[70] In 1922, Lenz applied the results of his findings on butterflies to humans. To him, the blurring on the heterosexual gender front, embodied by the "intermediate sexes," represented "degeneration in its most intrinsic sense," and was attributable to the same cause for butterflies and humans, namely, interbreeding. The differences between butterfly races could be equated with those between groups of humans: "The outward differences between Negroes, Mongolians and Europeans of the Nordic race are even much more pronounced than the differences between races of butterflies. Even within

---

[66] Rissom, 15. According to this account Lenz was from a Pomeranian farm estate; his mother was an elementary school teacher.

[67] Fritz Lenz, *Erbanlagen*.

[68] Fritz Lenz, "Erfahrungen über Erblichkeit und Entartung bei Schmetterlingen," *Archiv für Rassen- und Gesellschaftsbiologie*, 14 (1922), 249–301. In the German university system a "*Habilitation*" is the precondition for being appointed as a professor.

[69] Lenz, "Erfahrungen," 251, 275, 277.

[70] Lenz, "Erbanlagen," 167. Lenz dedicated his dissertation to Paul J. Möbius, who is known even today for his antifeminist best-seller *Der physiologische Schwachsinn des Weibes* (Munich: Matthes and Seitz, 1977), facsimile of the 1905 8th ed.; an English translation of the title would be *The Physiological Feeblemindedness of Woman*.

the European human population, the racial differences are presumably no smaller than those between the various Japanese gypsy moth races." In 1922, Lenz called the "interbreeding of significantly different human races a contributing cause of those phenomena of degeneration ... which we observe to such an extensive degree in our populations."[71]

Drawing on his own experiments, Lenz criticized Goldschmidt's genetic model and analysis of intersexuality based on developmental to physiology.[72] Particularly, Lenz did not accept Goldschmidt's idea that genes were enzymes that varied in their quantity and thus could not always unambiguously produce a particular character. He supported the gene model conceived by the Morgan group. These genes were supposed to be unambiguous units that were "morphologically individualized" and provided a "pure" and proper Mendelian segregation."[73] For Lenz, heredity was the transmission of stable traits from one generation to the next; the existence of races was dependent on this: "For the essence of race lies in the genes."[74] A "fluctuation of genes" as postulated by Goldschmidt undermined Lenz's construct of an inalterably hereditary, and thus racial, identity; for, according to Goldschmidt, what a gene could ultimately achieve depended on the given population or race in which it was active. Crossbreeding different butterfly races not only confused a binary sexual order but it also showed that the genes were not individualized and autonomous, and that they by no means caused the same effect in all possible circumstances.

The heredity of sex, or rather the properties of the postulated genes for male or female characters, were also an extremely important issue for Lenz because for him the difference between two sexes was essentially greater than the difference between different races. In the late 1920s, Lenz formulated his concept of sex difference, which was contrary to Goldschmidt's in every way:

There is no doubt that the two sexes differ with reference to anatomical, physiological and psychological characters even more than do recognized races. ... As there are no human races that differ from each other as strongly as men and women in their primary sexual function, one can also say that the two sexes are two different forms of organism, which merely live in a sort of symbiosis.[75]

In the face of such a desire for difference, any conception that men could have female and women male characters must have seemed sinister indeed. However, if the genes for male or female sexual characters could vary in

---

[71] Lenz, "Erfahrungen," 291–299.
[72] According to Curt Stern, looking back from the vantage point of 1980, his critique was correct on one point of Goldschmidt's interpretation of the development of intersexual animals. However, Goldschmidt never responded to this criticism. Stern, 80.
[73] Lenz, "Erfahrungen," 293.
[74] Lenz, "Erfahrungen," 299. In his terms: "das Wesen der Rasse liegt ja in der Erbmasse."
[75] Quoted in Rissom, 57.

strength and lacked an unambiguous effect, as Goldschmidt claimed, and if this "fluctuation" was supposed to be valid for all genes, then the genes for individual racial characters must also vary in strength and lose their definitude, precisely in the case when it mattered, that is, in the case of miscegenation or crossbreeding. One can conclude that in Lenz's eyes, such genes were not suitable for the project of a new racial anthropology which aimed at "cleanly separating" races on the basis of stable, hereditary characters like hair structure or the shape of the nose.[76]

In 1922, Lenz formulated his unease with regard to Goldschmidt by accusing him of the greatest possible heresy conceivable in the genetics of the time: Goldschmidt's ideas, if they were true, would "shake the foundations of modern Mendelian genetics."[77] For Lenz, and equally so for his co-authors on human genetics and racial hygiene, Eugen Fischer and Erwin Baur, Morgan's genes offered by far the better foundation upon which to establish the irreconcilable differences between humans, which allocated them into men and women or different races, thus creating social hierarchies.

Lenz, nine years younger than Goldschmidt and initially hoping for a university career, doubtlessly had a weak starting point in his endeavor to do experimental genetic research. He banked on the newly developing field of racial hygiene. In 1922, shortly before he was appointed as the first – extraordinary – professor for racial hygiene in Germany, he sketched a research program for a new anthropology. Its "main task ... of the future" would be to study the "consequences of crossbreeding among humans," understood to be degeneration. Eugen Fischer, he stated, had already started down the "path of finding suitable bastards."[78] In this, Lenz was referring to Fischer's studies of the so-called Rehoboth bastards, performed before World War I on the children of European colonizers and African women in what is now Namibia. The next group of "bastards" on which these racial anthropologists trained their sights were the children of German women and members of the French army of African extraction, who were born in the early 1920s after the occupation of the Rhineland. Under the Third Reich and with the cooperation of Lenz and Fischer, official experts on the Committee for Population and Racial

---

[76] On the simultaneous plan by the important racial anthropologist Eugen Fischer to define Mendelian racial characters, see Niels C. Lösch, *Rasse als Konstrukt. Leben und Werk Eugen Fischers* (Frankfurt am Main: Lang, 1997); Benoit Massin, "Rasse und Vererbung als Beruf. Die Hauptforschungsrichtungen am Kaiser-Wilhelm-Institut für Anthropologie, menschliche Erblehre und Eugenik im Nationalsozialismus," in Hans-Walter Schmuhl (ed.), *Rassenforschung an Kaiser-Wilhelm-Instituten vor und nach 1933* (Göttingen: Wallstein Verlag, 2003), 190–244, esp. 205–210.

[77] Lenz, "Erfahrungen," 291. This accusation is absurd, as Goldschmidt was one of the first biologists using Mendelian genetics in his experiments and writing textbooks in genetics. See Richard Goldschmidt, *Der Mendelismus* (Berlin: Parey 1920), 2nd ed. 1927.

[78] Lenz, "Erfahrungen," 299.

Policy (*Reichsausschuss für Bevölkerungs- und Rassenpolitik*) in the Reich Ministry of the Interior, these "Rhineland bastards" were subjected to compulsory sterilization.[79]

Goldschmidt: Attempted Resistance

In the late 1920s, Richard Goldschmidt attempted to counter the racist and antifeminist interpretation of his works on intersexuality. In 1927, in the very year the Kaiser Wilhelm Institute for Anthropology was opened in Berlin under the directorship of Eugen Fischer, he published a strictly Mendelian paper in *The Natural Sciences* (*Die Naturwissenschaften*), an extremely prominent periodical and the "organ" of the Kaiser Wilhelm Society: "The Descendants of the Old Settlers on the Ogasawara Islands" (*Die Nachkommen der alten Siedler der Bonininseln*).[80] Goldschmidt had visited these islands on his travels to Japan; the descendants of the settlers were "bastards" in the racial anthropology sense defined by Lenz. Both the contents of Goldschmidt's paper and its placement can be understood as an open challenge to the research premises of the new institute located in his immediate vicinity.

Men of various geographical origins had settled in the Ogasawara Islands only in 1830; the women, however, all came from Polynesia. Goldschmidt first outlined the early history of this group of people in the altogether jovial gesture of a patriarch: "here there is murder and manslaughter, robbery and the abduction of women on the part of landing whalers, political intrigues ... all in all, though, the small, isolated colony did well."[81] He treated the kinship relations of the descendants of these settlers encountered in the 1920s as a zoological crossbreeding experiment, concluding that the children who had resulted from marriages between

whites ... Negroes, Polynesians and Japanese ... pass [the tests] with honor throughout, both physically and above all, morally. ... Judging from the success, which several of those who left the islands had in life, they are presumably no different from other groups of people in terms of intellect either.[82]

With this article, Goldschmidt explicitly formulated that he saw no reason to conjure up apocalyptic scenarios caused by marriages between persons of those groups that his contemporaries so earnestly wanted to keep separate as the main races of humanity.

---

[79] Reiner Pommerin, *Sterilisierung der Rheinlandbastarde. Das Schicksal einer farbigen deutschen Minderheit 1918–1937* (Düsseldorf: Droste, 1979); Weingart, Kroll, and Bayertz, 460–464; Bock, 82, 85, 354.

[80] Richard Goldschmidt, "Die Nachkommen der alten Siedler der Bonininseln," *Die Naturwissenschaften*, 15 (1927), 449–453.

[81] Goldschmidt, "Nachkommen," 449.

[82] Goldschmidt, "Nachkommen," 450, 453.

A second German-language publication of 1931 can be read as a further attempt by Goldschmidt to banish the ghosts that had been scared up by his intersexual moth bastards in the past years. The essay *"Intersexualität und menschliches Zwittertum"* (Intersexuality and Human Hermaphrodism) appeared in the *Deutsche Mediznische Wochenschrift* (German Medical Weekly). By this time, the first sex hormones, characterized as the products of human gonads, had been isolated in a chemically pure form. Goldschmidt included these findings in his new concept of sex determination in humans.[83] According to Goldschmidt, men and women were supposed to come about through the effect of substances of the first, second, and third order, and were usually defined by the number of chromosomes upon fertilization: two x chromosomes for the women, but only one for the men. The first direct products of the "sex genes" in the "proper F:M proportion [were supposed] to ensure that one of the two possible paths of embryonic development to male or female gonads is taken."[84] If the proportion was not correct, an intermediate sexual form resulted. The second-order substances were supposed to be produced by the sexually differentiated gonads and effect a tissue differentiation similar to the "organizers" in embryology. Only the third-order substances were identical to the sex hormones of medical science. These substances were supposed not to differentiate the organs themselves sexually but only affect their respective functions, such as the monthly cycle and "the psychosexual characteristics." According to Goldschmidt, intersexuality encompassed only the developments that affected the first step, that is, the development of the gonads due to the effect of the genes. At this level, intersexes existed that ranged from female-looking humans to those who appeared completely male. Male intersexuals who looked completely female were not supposed to occur. Goldschmidt thus restrained "intersexuality" onto the physical level of the genitalia. The imaginative application of his concept to the behavior of women, as conducted by Mathes and Lenz, was thus ruled out. Goldschmidt explicitly rescinded his assertion of 1916 that homosexuality was a form of intersexuality and left open whether it was "a purely hormonal phenomenon ... or something entirely different."[85]

It is striking that Goldschmidt's article in the *Deutsche Medizinische Wochenschrift* did not use the term "race," unlike in his "Analysis of Intersexuality in the Gypsy Moth," which appeared in the United States in the same year.[86] The words "miscegenation" (*Rassenmischung*) or

[83] Richard Goldschmidt, "Intersexualität und menschliches Zwittertum," *Deutsche Medizinische Wochenschrift*, 57 (1931) [12 pages, pagination of off-print].

[84] Goldschmidt, "Intersexualität," 7.

[85] Goldschmidt, "Intersexualität," 10.

[86] Richard Goldschmidt, "Analysis of Intersexuality in the Gypsy Moth," *Quarterly Review of Biology*, 4 (1931), 125–142.

"crossbreeding" (*Rassenkreuzung*) were not mentioned, merely an "abnormal" F:M ratio that could lead to the given degree of intersexuality, or "insufficiently balanced quantities of F and M."[87] This cautious language in a publication that was widely propagated within the German medical community can be interpreted as an attempt by Goldschmidt to extract the problem of intersexuality and homosexuality from the discourse on miscegenation. In so doing, he tried to remove sexual relationships between people of different origin and the new life plans of working women from the realm of medical diagnosis and pathology.

In 1933, the discourse of degenerative miscegenation became openly anti-Semitic politics. When the Nuremberg Laws were decreed in 1935, Richard Goldschmidt and his family became the targets of accusations of "racial defilement" (*Rassenschande*); as the son of a German-Jewish Frankfurt family, Richard Goldschmidt lost his political rights as a German citizen. His wife Elsa Kühnlein was not Jewish according to National Socialist terminology and both their grown children suddenly faced marriage bars.[88] By his own account, it was the Nuremberg Laws that ultimately gave him the deciding impetus for emigration.[89] The family survived the Holocaust in the United States.[90] Fritz Lenz, in contrast, had a splendid career in the Kaiser-Wilhelm-Society during National Socialism and in 1946 was appointed the first professor for human genetics at a university in postwar West Germany.

CONCLUSION

The comparison between Richard Goldschmidt and Fritz Lenz makes apparent how during the Weimar Republic the central biological concepts of race, genes, and sex difference were created in mutual interdependences and in two different ways, incorporating two different concepts of the political order, including the gender order. For Goldschmidt, there was no separation of humans into unambiguous races that were to be kept pure, nor were there two mutually exclusive sexes as the foundation of the utopia of male, Nordic supremacy by birth. He could imagine a sexual identity where "each sex also includes all the characteristics (*Eigenschaften*) of the other."[91] In his view, genes could be blurred to a certain degree. For Lenz, however, irreconcilable differences were essential to privileged people of his kind and of his sex. Races, genes, and the two sexes always had to be clearly separated from each other; without such separation, his project of establishing

[87] Goldschmidt, "Intersexualität," 3, 9.
[88] Stern, 88.
[89] Goldschmidt, *Ivory Tower*, 274, 300.
[90] Goldschmidt, *Ivory Tower*, 293, 303.
[91] Goldschmidt, "Grundlagen," 4.

a hierarchy for humans, based on racial and sexual policy and founded in biology, would fall apart. For this project, the gene concept developed by Morgan and his school appeared more suitable than Goldschmidt's.

It is somewhat paradoxical that the use of Morgan's gene concept in Germany after 1945 made it possible to avoid referring to genetics and racial hygiene during National Socialism. These genes were especially "racially pure," and not only in the strict biological sense because they had been developed by inbred laboratory animals. They also did not show that they had helped make possible a genetic definition of human races and thereby legitimate the politics of racial purity.

EASTERN RESEARCH, LIVING SPACE,
BREEDING RESEARCH

8

Kog-Sagyz – A Vital War Reserve

Susanne Heim

Long after the end of the Second World War, many Germans still regarded the *Autobahn* network and the *Volkswagen* car as representative of the positive achievements of the Nazi period. Both were elements of the *Führer's* Motorization Program, which eventually laid the foundations for mass motorization in Germany but originally formed part of the preparations for war. One vital aspect of this program was an attempt to produce rubber for vehicle tires inside the Reich or in the conquered territories without using imported raw materials. A number of studies have investigated the research into Buna, a synthetic rubber. But there has been very little study so far of the *kog-sagyz* (caoutchouc) project, an attempt to grow natural rubber for industrial purposes on lands under German control.[1] This project combined research, practical trials, processing, and marketing for a single product in a research network that was politically protected by the highest levels of government and made use of all the powers available under the Nazi regime. The project included the use of slave labor for scientific purposes in the Auschwitz concentration camp and plans to grow natural rubber in partisan-dominated territory for strategic military reasons.

This chapter will first investigate the development of rubber plant research in Germany and its expansion following the German invasion of the Soviet Union. It will also examine the differing and often, conflicting interests of the institutions involved in the *kog-sagyz* project. Furthermore, this article

---

[1] One example is Alexander Schlichter, "Forschung im 'Dritten Reich' – Taraxacum kok-sagyz. Ein Fallbeispiel," *Diplom* thesis, Fachbereich Biologie, University of Oldenburg (1999). See also Thomas Wieland, "Die politischen Aufgaben der deutschen Pflanzenzüchtung," in Susanne Heim (ed.), *Autarkie und Ostexpansion. Pflanzenzucht und Agrarforschung im Nationalsozialismus* (Göttingen: Wallstein Verlag, 2002), 35–56, here 50–54; Susanne Heim, "Forschung für die Autarkie," in Heim, *Autarkie*, 145–177, here 169–173.

An extended version of this article has been published in Susanne Heim, *Plant Breeding and Agrarian Research in Kaiser-Wilhelm-Institutes 1933–1945* (Boston: Springer 2008).

will outline how rubber plant research was pursued further in the Auschwitz concentration camp: in 1944, the Kaiser Wilhelm Institute for Breeding Research moved its *kog-sagyz* research center to Auschwitz. Finally, we will discuss what the history of this rubber plant research project can tell us about science and the organization of science in the Nazi era. Did rubber-plant research fail to live up to the expectations placed in it because it was a hopeless venture that had only been launched for ideological reasons in the first place? (The military undertones are deliberate.) Or did the project fail because of limits placed on academic freedom under the conditions of dictatorship? Or was the reason the lack of efficient research coordination in the chaos of multiple competencies that characterized the Nazi state? We will also investigate the specific contribution that Kaiser Wilhelm Society (*Kaiser-Wilhelm-Gesellschaft*, KWS) researchers made toward developing this ambitious project and the role they played in its failure.

GROWING DEMANDS

Until the late nineteenth century, most natural rubber that was sold overseas came from Brazil.[2] In 1876, an Englishman, Henry Wickham, managed to smuggle a large number of rubber tree seeds from Brazil home to England. Within a few years rubber tree plantations were established in several countries in eastern Asia and in Cameroon. By 1913, more rubber was being harvested from these plantations than from wild rubber trees. But almost all of them were located in colonies controlled or under the influence of Great Britain and the Netherlands, which had succeeded in breaking the Brazilian monopoly.

In the early twentieth century, the increasing importance of rubber for motor vehicles, together with the dependence on foreign producers, also gave impetus to efforts to create synthetic rubber. Such efforts were undertaken more or less successfully and with slightly different methods in the United States, the Soviet Union, and Germany.[3] But no matter how it was produced,

---

[2] Background information on the topic of natural rubber is given on a Web page entitled "Entdeckung des Kautschuks," belonging to the travel company "brasilien.de ReiseService," version of 3 September 2002. On the following passage, see also Ulrich Giersch and Ulrich Kubisch, *Gummi – Die elastische Faszination* (Berlin: Nicolai, 1995); also Wolfgang Jünger, *Kampf um Kautschuk* (Leipzig: Goldmann, 1942), 63 ff; Stefan Reiner, *Kautschuk-Fibel. Einführung in die Chemie und Technologie der natürlichen und synthetischen Kautschukarten*, 2nd ed. (Berlin: Union, 1942); Lothar Frantzke, *Vom Kautschuk zum Buna* (Berlin: Limpert, 1939); Paul Erker, "Die Rolle der Forschung bei der Ersatzstoff-Produktion. Das Beispiel Continental AG/Reifenindustrie," in Doris Kaufmann (ed.), *Geschichte der Kaiser-Wilhelm-Gesellschaft im Nationalsozialismus. Bestandsaufnahme und Perspektiven der Forschung*, 2 vols. (Göttingen: Wallstein Verlag, 2000), vol. 1, 411–425.

[3] Peter Hayes: *Industry and Ideology. IG Farben in the Nazi Era* (Cambridge: Cambridge University Press, 2001); Gottfried Plumpe, *Die IG-Farbenindustrie-AG: Wirtschaft, Technik und Politik 1904 – 1945* (Berlin: Duncker and Humblot, 1990).

for a long time synthetic rubber was inferior to natural rubber. In any case small amounts of natural rubber had to be added to the synthetic rubber Buna to enable the products made from it to meet minimum quality standards. It was impossible to produce durable truck tires using synthetic rubber alone.

During the first few years of the Nazi regime, the *Führer's* Motorization Program brought about a large increase in Germany's rubber requirements. By 1933, the country imported 55,000 tons, and by 1937 this increased to 100,000 tons, some 55 percent of which was used for manufacturing tires.[4] A Monitoring Body for Caoutchouc and Asbestos, set up in 1933 under the Reich Ministry of Economic Affairs, strictly regulated the use of all rubber, both synthetic and natural.[5] A few months before the war started, German annual rubber requirements were estimated to be 120,000 tons,[6] of which 26,000 tons was to be met by domestic Buna production. The remainder was to be imported in the form of natural rubber, at least for the first few years.

However, because the majority of this natural rubber had to come "from British areas of cultivation in exchange for cash payment in foreign currencies,"[7] and because it was feared that transport routes from rubber-producing countries could be blocked in the event of a war, the Four-Year Plan prescribed that imports of natural rubber should be reduced as far as possible, and that the German economy should cease to be reliant on them by 1943.[8] State-guaranteed prices for Buna[9] and the opportunity of accessing new markets in the Greater European Area led to a drastic scaling-up of production plans. In September 1940, it was estimated that the Central European Economic Area needed a total of 300,000 tons of rubber per year. Most of these needs were to be met by German-produced Buna.[10]

[4] "The Rubber Economy in the Four-Year Plan." Unpublished memorandum dating from 1937/38," no author given, Federal German Archives (*Bundesarchiv*, BArch), R 3112/170, diagrams 2 and 6.

[5] On the work done by this Reich body, see BArch, RW 19/3097, 3098 and 3211; Wilhelm Treue, "Gummi in Deutschland zwischen 1933 und 1945," *Wehrwissenschaftliche Rundschau*, 5 (1955), 169–185.

[6] Working report by Dr. Carl Krauch, Plenipotentiary General to Minister President [Premier] General Field Marshal Göring for Special Issues in Chemicals Production, submitted to the General Council of the Four-Year Plan, Berlin, 20/21 April 1939, BArch, R 3112/14.

[7] Working report by Dr. Carl Krauch, Plenipotentiary General to Minister President [Premier] General Field Marshal Göring for Special Issues in Chemicals Production, submitted to the General Council of the Four-Year Plan, Berlin, 20/21 April 1939, BArch, R 3112/14.

[8] "The Rubber Economy in the Four-Year Plan." Unpublished memorandum dating from 1937/38, no author given, BArch, R 3112/170, 15 and diagram 12.

[9] Jochen Streb, "Technologiepolitik im Zweiten Weltkrieg. Die staatliche Förderung der Synthesekautschukproduktion im deutsch-amerikanischen Vergleich," *Vierteljahrshefte für Zeitgeschichte*, 50 (2002), 367–397, here 388.

[10] Minutes on the meeting of the Technical Committee of IG Farben Industry on Thursday, 26 September 1940 in Frankfurt am Main, Unternehmensarchiv Filmfabrik Wolfen, Nr. A 5192, fo. 171, cited in Florian Schmaltz, "Die Entstehung des Konzentrationslagers

Limited amounts of natural rubber were still imported during the war, with the help of blockade-runners or transport submarines. In addition, the *Wehrmacht* (armed forces) seized all the rubber reserves of the countries it occupied. But after a short period, rubber actually had to be exported from the Reich to the occupied territories to prevent a collapse of transport. The needs of the armed forces itself for truck tires increased continuously throughout the war. Serious shortages loomed on a number of occasions. In late January 1941, the armed forces estimated that its rubber reserves, needed for tires and shoe soles, would last only another month. After this, it claimed, the only hope was very unreliable imports.[11]

In other words, over the course of the war, the shortage of rubber became ever more acute; appeals to conserve rubber and thoughts of rationing it became increasingly urgent. And by invading the Soviet Union, the armed forces actually cut off one of its own supply routes for natural rubber, that from eastern Asia.[12]

THE *KOG-SAGYZ* NETWORK

In the spring of 1938, attempts to breed rubber plants commenced in the Kaiser Wilhelm Institute for Breeding Research in Müncheberg, about seventy kilometers east of Berlin. Richard Werner Böhme (1903–1945) headed a small department of "special cultures" (as the group was described in the institute's literature),[13] working mainly on *Taraxacum kog-sagyz*. Soviet breeding researchers had been studying this dandelion-like plant since the early 1930s, after the discovery that its roots contained latex, as did those of the related *Taraxacum krim-sagyz* and *tau-sagyz*.[14] However, the project to grow rubber plants on German soil and under German climate conditions initially was seen to have little chance of success. Only in 1941, in the context of the German invasion of the Soviet Union, did a real boom on *kog-sagyz* research start in Germany. In the spring of 1941, the director of the Müncheberg institute, Wilhelm Rudorf, planned to travel to the Soviet

---

Auschwitz-Monowitz, historische Magisterarbeit im Fachbereich Geschichte," Ph.D. diss., Free University of Berlin (1999), 68 f.

[11] Franz Halder, diary entry of 28 January 1941, cited in Treue, 181.

[12] Franz Halder, diary entry of 28 January 1941, cited in Treue, 181.

[13] *Kaiser-Wilhelm-Institut für Züchtungsforschung Müncheberg (Mark)* (Müncheberg: Kaiser-Wilhelm-Institut für Züchtungsforschung, 1938), 20.

[14] Assertions about the actual latex content vary considerably. With regard to the *kok-sagyz* plant, which contains the highest amount of latex of all the *sagyz* species, the literature gives figures ranging from 2 percent to 20 percent. Soviet seed producers received a one-time bonus of 30,000 rubles for producing strains with 3 percent latex content in the root; if it reached 5 percent, they received a bonus of 100,000 rubles. Author unknown, "Anbau von Kautschukpflanzen in der UdSSR. Ein Versager des Sowjet-Systems," *Die chemische Industrie*, 27/28 (1941), 374–378, here 375.

Union in May and June of that year to gather information on *kog-sagyz* cultivation.[15] Rudorf's plans coincided with a period in which the armed forces' rubber reserves were being used up, as described above, and in which preparations for the invasion of the Soviet Union were in full swing. This may be the reason the leaders of the Nazi state now suddenly began to show interest in the rubber plant research project.

In March 1941, Heinrich Himmler, the *Reichsführer-SS*, instructed Heinrich Vogel[16] of the SS Office of Economic Administration (*Wirtschafts-Verwaltungshauptamt*, WVHA) to produce detailed information on *kog-sagyz* and on the plant seeds "which we will then reproduce as fast as possible."[17] He mentioned that the *Führer* had asked him about the rubber plant. The seeds were then "reproduced" quickly after the invasion of the Soviet Union on 21 June 1941 by seizing the Soviet Union's stocks. In early September 1941, two SS brigade leaders were ordered to search out *kog-sagyz* plantations and the documentation belonging to them, because this rubber plant was "of the greatest importance for the German war economy."[18] During their trip, they discovered "many hundredweights of seed," "numerous Russian specialists," and relevant literature, and they transferred as many of their finds as possible to the German Reich, where the experts were to be employed as advisors, the seeds sown, and the specialist literature translated as fully as possible into German.[19] Careful attention was paid to ensuring that "at all events ... the priority of the SS with regard to this find is secured." For this reason, news about the discovery of plants and documents was "reported directly to the *Reichsführer-SS*, bypassing the armed forces."[20]

In the period that followed, the resources captured in the occupied Soviet territories were used to intensify the scientific investigation of *kog-sagyz*. Shortly after the invasion of the Soviet Union, Hitler had listed the regime's goals for the German-dominated region and had demanded that, in addition to an increase in cattle herds, "400,000 hectares of rubber plants [were to be

---

[15] Heinrich Vogel (WVHA) to the Reichsführer-SS, 7 April 1941, Institute for Contemporary History, Munich (*Institut für Zeitgeschichte*), MA 343, frame 2669558, also BArch, NS 19/3920, frame 137–139.

[16] Heinrich Vogel (1901–1958) was the head of the W 5 – Agriculture, Forestry and Fishing office in the WVHA.

[17] Himmler to Vogel, 29 March 1941, BArch, NS 19/3920, frame 140, published in Helmut Heiber (ed.), *Reichsführer! ... Briefe an und von Himmler* (Stuttgart: DVA, 1968), 84 f.

[18] Klingemann (Commander of the SS Junker School in Tölz) to Rudolf Brandt (Personal Staff of the RFSS), 18 July 1943, BArch, NS 19/3923, frame 138 ff.

[19] Brandt to Oswald Pohl (head of the WVHA), 7 April 1942, BArch, NS 19/1802, frame 15. In addition to the SS, the Chemical Industry group commissioned expert reports on the progress made by rubber research in the Soviet Union. The first of these is dated July 1941, the second in the summer of 1942, BArch, RW 19 Anh. I/1499, 1506, 1507.

[20] Klingemann to Brandt, 18 July 1943, BArch, NS 19/3923, frame 138 ff.

provided] to meet our needs."[21] From 1941 onward, a variety of state institutions, industrial manufacturers, and scientific research centers expressed
great interest in the rubber plant used by the Soviets, in controlling the cultivation areas, in the processing units, and in the seed stocks and academic
literature held by the occupied territories.

The KWI for Breeding Research was one of the institutes involved in
the race to capture Soviet research resources. Rudorf's plan to travel to the
Soviet Union in May/June 1941 was thwarted by the German invasion. But
in September, Richard Böhme, the head of the KWI's Special Cultures division, traveled into occupied Ukraine to view *kog-sagyz* production in situ.
His trip coincided almost exactly with that of the SS brigade and included a
visit to a rubber factory in Uman.

This trip to Uman may have inspired Böhme to carry out experiments
on processing *kog-sagyz* roots in Rotes Luch in Brandenburg alongside the
research on plant breeding. In 1941, experiments with breeding and cultivating *kog-sagyz* were carried out by the KWI for Breeding Research on a
total of four hectares of land, some of it at their Müncheberg site and some
in Rotes Luch, six kilometers away. In the same year, a processing unit was
constructed in Rotes Luch, commissioned by the Plenipotentiary General
for Issues of Chemical Production (GBChem); it included a modern peeling
centrifuge and an apparatus for testing the plants' latex content. Böhme,
who also oversaw the work in this "technological large-scale testing center,"
drew up the plans for this unit.[22]

According to Böhme, the peeling centrifuge was used as the first stage in
the process and allowed approximately 90 percent of the raw latex to be
extracted.[23] This approach to rubber extraction, known as the "Müncheberg
method," was regarded as a development of the process used in Uman. In
mid-1943, Böhme reported that the "erection of three units on the same
principle [i.e., that developed by him] is under way in the occupied eastern
territories."[24]

In August 1942, another KWS researcher, Kurt Hess of the KWI for
Chemistry, had also visited the Uman plant with a delegation and had

[21] Henry Picker, *Hitlers Tischgespräche im Führerhauptquartier 1941–42* (Bonn: Athenäum-
Verlag, 1951), 197 (entry dated 2 August 1941, evening).

[22] Report, unsigned, "Re: Russian rubber plant kok-Sagyz," undated, BArch, NS 19/3929, frame
90–97, here frame 97. The report states that the facility would be completed in November
1941. In a letter written in May 1943, Böhme describes the facility in more detail; Böhme to
the Reichsführer SS, 17 May 1943, BArch NS 19/1803, frame 15–17.

[23] Short report on important progress in breeding research on agricultural plants in the Kaiser
Wilhelm Institute for Plant Breeding Research Müncheberg/Mark, 5 July 1943, BArch,
R 73/14093.

[24] Short report on important progress in breeding research on agricultural plants in the Kaiser
Wilhelm Institute for Plant Breeding Research Müncheberg/Mark, 5 July 1943, BArch,
R 73/14093.

studied the root processing and centrifuging methods used there.[25] Hess was known in the institute as a committed Nazi and was unpopular because he was angling for Otto Hahn's job as director of the KWI for Chemistry. In addition, he had informed on Lise Meitner on several occasions. Meitner was Jewish, but because she was an Austrian citizen, she was allowed to continue working at the KWI until the Austrian *Anschluss* (connection) in 1938.[26] From 1943 onward, Hess presented his research on *kog-sagyz* processing under the title of head of the Institute for Raw Material Supplies, an organization that had been set up for him by the German Labor Front (*Deutsche Arbeitsfront*, DAF) in Löwenberg in Silesia when bomb attacks on Berlin intensified.[27] The DAF was extremely eager to integrate this institute into the KWS.[28]

The DAF was interested in the *kog-sagyz* research because it owned the Volkswagen Works (*Volkswagenwerk*), the core piece of the motorization program. The DAF also maintained its own Research and Exploitation Company, working on developing the Russian *kog-sagyz* processing methods in its own laboratories. It had "overhauled and improved" the Russian methods and also managed to extract alcohol as well as rubber from the plant's roots. DAF experts believed that within a few years they would be capable of producing 12,000 tons of natural rubber per year.[29] In early 1943, the DAF set up a second laboratory, in Auschwitz.[30]

By late 1941, most of the institutions interested in *kog-sagyz* research had been bundled together to form the Plant Rubber Research and Cultivation Company (*Pflanzenkautschuk Forschungs- und Anbaugesellschaft m.b.H.*). The members of the company included the Hanover tire company Continental; the Four-Year Plan Authority, in the form of the Plenipotentiaries General for Automotive Affairs (*Bevollmächtigter für das Kraftfahrtwesen*, BdK)

[25] Report, unsigned, on plant rubber – cultivation and preparation, trip to Russia from 27 June to 10 August 1942, Archives of the Continental Gummi-Werke, Hannover, A 13, 6500, 1/69, 7 ff.

[26] Ruth Lewin Sime, *Lise Meitner. Ein Leben für die Physik* (Frankfurt am Main: Insel-Verlag, 2001), 237 and 262.

[27] See Hess to the Hitler Youth Niederschlesien, "Home and Shelter" section, 31 August 1943, BArch, NS 19/1803, frame 30. On Hess, see also Schlichter, 40 f.

[28] In March 1944, the DAF's "*Forschungs- und Verwertungsgesellschaft m.b.H.*" (Research and Utilization Company) sent Ernst Telschow, the Secretary General of the KWS, a draft contract regarding the integration of the institute into the KWS. The letter includes the dictation note "Dr. He" and may thus have been written by Hess himself; the Forschungs- und Verwertungsgesellschaft m.b.H. to Telschow, 4 March 1944, Archives of the Max Planck Society, Berlin (*Archiv zur Geschichte der Max-Planck-Gesellschaft*, MPG-Archiv), Abt. I, Rep. 1A, Nr. 972.

[29] Pohl to Himmler, 11 March 1942, BArch, NS 19/1802, frame 12 f. In this letter, Pohl reports on a conversation with Dr. Lafferentz "who manages the Forschungs- und Verwertungs-G.m.b.H. for Dr. Ley."

[30] Pohl to Himmler, 12 February 1943, BArch, NS 19/3920, frame 122.

and for Special Issues in Chemical Production (*Generalbevollmächtigter für Fragen der chemischen Erzeugung*, GBChem); as well as the DAF, the Reich Food Estate (*Reichsnährstand*, RNS), the Reich Ministry of Food and agriculture, the Kaiser Wilhelm Institute for Breeding Research, and the SS (or rather its Office of Economic Administration – WVHA).[31]

In early 1943, Himmler undertook an initiative to reorganize and centralize all matters concerning *kog-sagyz*. He received Böhme from the KWI for Plant Breeding together with SS-*Obersturmbannführer* Joachim Caesar, head of the agricultural research unit at Auschwitz concentration camp, and Hans Stahl, a Navy officer who had previously been director of the Krupp subsidiaries in the northern Caucasus and spoke fluent Russian. Stahl's task for the next eighteen months was to travel to various European countries on Himmler's orders to explore possibilities for cultivating *kog-sagyz*.

After his meeting with Himmler, Böhme drew up a plan for revamping the Rotes Luch estate near Müncheberg where, as previously mentioned, breeding trials on *kog-sagyz* had already been carried out. Rotes Luch was to be converted into a state-held estate "for the purpose of extending it to create a research institute for rubber plants."[32] According to Böhme's plans, the institute would consist of two branches, a research laboratory for chemical and technological work on *kog-sagyz* for processing, and an agricultural research center for plant-breeding work. Böhme estimated that this center would require 50 to 100 hectares of land, would cost 1.5 million Reichsmark to buy, and would need an annual budget of 202,000 Reichsmark. The KWS would administer the new research center.

Böhme explained his choice of location by saying that the forests surrounding Rotes Luch allowed research work to be done "almost completely in private." He also pointed out that it was close to other institutes belonging to the Kaiser Wilhelm Society, without naming these, and that "in any case use would have to be made" of their specialist researchers and facilities "if the task of turning a wild plant into a crop plant in accordance with the modern requirements of a planned economy is to be achieved in a short period." Böhme argued that this "centralized combination of the two most important areas [i.e., breeding and processing] at a single location, in the form of a new KWS research center" would bring together all

---

[31] Pohl to Himmler, 12 February 1943, BArch, NS 19/3920, frame 122. Members of the Administrative Board included Kurt Hess of the KWI for Chemistry, Klaus von Rosenstiel, formerly of the KWI for Plant Breeding Research, then of the Economic Staff (East) and now representing the Reich Ministry for the Occupied Eastern Territories, Joachim Caesar of the agricultural research unit at Auschwitz concentration camp, and Wilhelm Rudorf of the KWI for Plant Breeding Research.

[32] Draft dated 29 March 1943; BArch, NS 19/3920. This memo was intended for the Reich Office of Economic Development, the Reich Ministry of Food, and the Kaiser Wilhelm Society and was also sent by Böhme to the SS Economic and Administrative Main Office (WVHA), with a request that it be forwarded to the Reichsführer SS.

the "interested institutes in Germany and abroad." Evidently, Böhme's own institute in Rotes Luch was to become the center of this network of *kog-sagyz* research units. Thus Böhme further demanded to "be authorized not merely to enter into correspondence with the various research stations and units, but also to assign partial areas of the research to these and to monitor their implementation."[33]

Böhme's ambitious plans, however, were realized only in a small part. Actually, Joachim Caesar succeeded in ensuring that responsibility for *kog-sagyz* cultivation was transferred to him from the Ministry of Eastern Affairs. Joachim Caesar (1901–1974) had studied at the agricultural college in Bonn-Poppelsdorf and at the University of Halle, and had acquired his doctoral degree there in 1927. In 1931, he joined the SA and the Nazi party, and in 1933, the SS. He was a member of the Lebensborn project and was head of the Training Office of the SS Racial and Settlement Main Office for a number of years[34] before taking over the agricultural unit at Auschwitz. Step by step, Caesar had gained overall responsibility for *kog-sagyz* plant breeding in all research units in the occupied Soviet Union.[35] The decisive person to help him in receiving this authorization was Klaus von Rosenstiel, a former researcher in the KWI for Breeding Research who had been transferred to the Ministry of Eastern Affairs and like Caesar was a member of the SS. In May 1943, Caesar triumphantly reported to Himmler's personal assistant, Rudolf Brandt, that "Dr. v. Rosenstiel is making available the entire Ministry of Eastern Affairs' plant-breeding organization, led by him, for *kog-sagyz* breeding: I am being assigned as the representative for this matter and thus all the breeding stations are automatically under my control."[36]

Himmler arranged a working conference in the SS Main Office for June 25, 1943. During this meeting, the tasks related to *kog-sagyz* research were divided up between the institutions involved.[37] The participants were from a variety of research institutions, including the KWI for Breeding Research and the KWI for Chemistry[38] as well as several universities, ministries, armed forces and SS institutions, and the DAF. Most of those involved

[33] Head of office W-5 of the WVHA, note, 6 April 1943, BArch, NS 19/3920, frame 100–102.

[34] Research assignment on Caesar, Dr. Joachim, BArch Dahlwitz-Hoppegarten, Dok/P/366.

[35] Caesar, note (on headed paper of the Head of the W-5 office of the WVHA), 27 May 1943, BArch, NS 19/1802, frame 47: Von Rosenstiel, note, 28 May 1943, BArch, NS 19/3920, frame 53.

[36] Caesar to Brandt, 29 May 1943, BArch, NS 19/3920, frame 60–61. On Rosenstiel, see Heim, *Plant Breeding*.

[37] Report on the meeting of the parties interested in *kok-sagyz* rubber in the SS Main Office on 25 June 1943, written by Joachim Caesar, 1 July 1943, BArch, NS 19/1802, frame 56–62.

[38] Rudorf and Böhme represented the KWI for Plant Breeding Research, Hess, Dr. Wergin, and Dr. Steurer the KWI for Chemistry.

had already met at the regular meetings of the Plant Caoutchouc Research Society (*Planzenkautschuk-Forschungsgesellschaft*). The meeting took place under the auspices of the SS. Several research institutes that had not previously been involved were integrated into the research network for the first time.[39]

The Kaiser Wilhelm Society was strongly represented, making up five of the thirty participants, even though Klaus von Rosenstiel and Walter Hertzsch had not accepted their invitations. (Both had worked for the KWI for Breeding Research for a number of years, but they were invited as representatives of the Economic Staff of the High Command of the armed forces.) Four experts attended from Auschwitz.[40]

Wilhelm Rudorf, the director of the KWI for Breeding Research and, according to the minutes, the only person to give a talk at the conference, put forward a work program that was divided up into the different areas of research, focusing on breeding *kog-sagyz* plants. At the conference, four task areas were defined, two of which were assigned to KWS researchers. Kurt Hess of the KWI for Chemistry was to be responsible for all issues related to rubber chemistry and rubber technology. Rudorf, in cooperation with Böhme, was to be responsible for basic breeding research. They had to cooperate closely with Joachim Caesar, who was in charge of coordinating practical plant breeding. Friedrich Christiansen-Weniger was put in charge of cultivation issues, and the agricultural research unit at Pulawy, which was under his command, was to be made available to him for this purpose.[41]

KOG-*SAGYZ* CULTIVATION AND OCCUPATION POLICY

The conference can be seen as a joint attempt, initiated by the SS, to overcome the difficulties in cultivating *kog-sagyz* that the Germans had encountered during the first two years of occupation of the Soviet territories. These experiences had not been at all encouraging and stood in sharp contrast with the huge plans made in Berlin to extend the areas of cultivation to hundreds of thousands of hectares. The above-mentioned Naval officer Stahl, who on behalf of Himmler had traveled through the *kog-sagyz* cultivation areas in the occupied Soviet Union, reported the rather devastating results: the fields planted with *kog-sagyz* were divided into small plots. In many

---

[39] The *Gau* (Regional) Research Institute for Plant Physiology in Posen, the Botanical Institute of the Forestry College in Eberswalde, the Institute for Genetic and Breeding Research in Berlin-Dahlem, the Botanic Garden there and the Technical University of Dresden, the Agricultural Research Institute in Landsberg/Warthe were represented at the meeting, as well as the *Pflanzenkautschuk-Forschungsgesellschaft* and the Institute for Materials Research in Löwenberg, Silesia.

[40] Ruth Weinmann, Kudriawtzow, Heinz Schattenberg, and Caesar as head of the unit.

[41] Approximately one month later, Himmler ordered some changes in the assignment of work; letter from Himmler dated 23 July 1943, BArch, R 26 IV/33, 93.

places, they were full of weeds. Stahl criticized the poorly trained staff, the lack of monitoring of the Russian farmers, the low-quality seed, the shortage of workers, and the general "unwillingness of the population to work." The main problem, however, was the partisans carrying out attacks on the representatives of the German occupying forces – in particular, the agricultural control officers, the agricultural processing plants, and even the native farmers who were working for the Germans.[42]

The coordination of *kog-sagyz* research as it was organized at the conference in June 1943 was only one of the ways Himmler confronted the difficulties. He also reacted with the usual hard line. On July 9, 1943, Himmler was appointed Plenipotentiary for Plant Rubber. The day after, again citing instructions from Hitler, he ordered "that the entire population of the partisan-infested areas of northern Ukraine and central Russia is to be cleared out."[43] Men who were capable of working should be employed as forced laborers "but under the conditions applicable to prisoners of war." Effectively, this represented a death sentence for many men; Soviet prisoners of war were starving to death in droves in German camps.[44] Women, Himmler continued, were to be deported to the Reich as workers or should be housed in transit camps together with orphan children. The depopulated lands were to be used for agriculture where possible, some of this for *kog-sagyz* cultivation. "The children's camps" were, his decree states, "to be placed on the edge of these areas so that the children can be used as workers for growing *kog-sagyz* and for agriculture."

By late autumn 1943, the progress of the war and the German retreat had greatly reduced the amount of arable land under German control. Thus arguments developed about which crops should be grown on the limited amount of land still available. *Kog-sagyz* grew particularly well on soils that were also highly suitable for vegetable or tobacco cultivation. The decision on which type of crop was to be given priority caused a clash between the interests of Himmler, the Plenipotentiary for Plant Rubber, and those of Herbert Backe, who had overall responsibility for all issues related to food.[45] The armed forces also put its needs forward. It laid claim to workers who were needed for *kog-sagyz* cultivation[46] and placed "high demands for vegetables"

[42] See the various reports by Korvettenkapitän [naval officer] Dr. Stahl on his travels, BArch, NS 19/3922.

[43] The Reichsführer-SS to the Head of the Anti-Partisan Units, the HSSPF Ukraine, the HSSPF Russia-Center, SS-Obergruppenführer Berger, SS-Ogrf. Backe, 10 July 1943, BArch, NS 19/3922, frame 52; also National Archives, Washington, DC (NA), T-301/82.

[44] See Christian Streit, *Keine Kameraden. Die Wehrmacht und die sowjetischen Kriegsgefangenen 1941–1945* (Stuttgart: DVA, 1978).

[45] See Backe to Himmler, 20 December 1944, BArch, NS 19/1802, frame 288 f.

[46] See Report by *Korvettenkapitän* [naval officer] Dr. Stahl on the journey to the Wi In Mitte and the R. K. Ostland from 6 to 21 June 1943, 22 June 1943, BArch, NS 19/3922, frame 87–98, here frame 91.

on the farms in the occupied territories;[47] however, it was also interested in the cultivation of rubber plants and tobacco, irrespective of the food requirements of its troops. Finally, the interest of these Reich institutions clashed with those of the occupation authorities in the various regions.

For example, the heads of the Agriculture Group in the occupied areas of the Soviet Union and Poland stated that they could increase the area under cultivation with *kog-sagyz* as demanded only if fewer workers were deported to the Reich and if the plans to increase tobacco cultivation (as also demanded by Reich authorities) were partially reversed.[48]

The farther the German troops had to retreat from the occupied eastern territories, the more heated the arguments became about workers and the use of arable land. The actual effect of so much emphasis being placed on the *kog-sagyz* project was that the reign of terror to which the population in the occupied areas was subjected was intensified and differentiated. For the local population, the production of natural rubber in German-controlled areas, a "task of vital importance to the war effort,"[49] meant resettlement, forced labor, child labor, cultivation targets, and, in particular, raids against partisans, including the arbitrary imprisonments and executions that such raids usually involved.

The decision to grow *kog-sagyz* mainly in the occupied territories – often in areas with considerable partisan activity – and food crops mainly within the Reich was not primarily based on agricultural reasons, such as differences in soil characteristics. Rather, these priorities were in line with security considerations and with the hierarchical differences accorded to the nutrition of the various different population groups in German-controlled Europe. The farmers who were forced to grow *kog-sagyz* could make very little use of the plants themselves. On the other hand, if they grew food crops, although most of the harvest would be requisitioned for the needs of the German occupiers, the farmers could covertly siphon off some of the harvest to alleviate the hunger that was prevalent in much of the occupied territories. In contrast, growing vegetables and sugar beet (instead of rubber plants) on soils within the Reich benefited the food supply for the German population without taking up much transport capacity.

The Red Army's reconquest of large areas of the occupied territories reduced the scope of the rubber plant project. In spring 1944, Stahl's staff

[47] Report by *Korvettenkapitän* [naval officer] Dr. Stahl on his journey to the R. K. Ostland and the Wi In Mitte from 17 to 26 August 1943, 28 August 1943, BArch, NS 19/3922, frame 28–30, here frame 29.
[48] See memorandum by Karl Partry (Economic Staff [East], Group La [Agriculture]) for *Kriegsverwaltungschef* Riecke on a meeting about future cultivation of *kok-sagyz*, 3 July 1943, BArch, NS 19/3922, frame 73.
[49] Kok-sagyz Leaflet no. 1, published by the Reichsführer SS as Plenipotentiary for Plant Rubber, Cultivation and Trials Group, Autumn 1943, BArch, NS 19/3922, frame 21 f.

started to look for alternative cultivation areas in France and in Hungary. But it turned out to be more expensive to grow rubber there because not as much use could be made of confiscated resources as in the Soviet Union and compulsory targets were unenforceable. In fact, the French farmers would have to be offered bonuses for above-average performance in the form of either money or rubber goods (which were much in demand because of rationing). Under these conditions, the total cost of raw natural rubber grown in France would be too expensive.[50]

The loss of vital resources such as arable land and workers, combined with the low yields of the *kog-sagyz* fields still under German control, meant that the project lost much of its original attraction. The latent institutional conflicts and rivalries between the widely dispersed members of the research network intensified. In simplified terms, the botanists were in favor of expanding the *kog-sagyz* project, but their interests were in conflict with those of the chemists or of industry, who were involved in root processing but in general gave preference to research into Buna above research into plant rubber. The fault lines of the Buna/*kog-sagyz* dispute also ran through the Kaiser Wilhelm Society. Kurt Hess took the side of the rubber processing industry, while Rudorf and Böhme joined forces with Caesar and were a central part of Himmler's team in his role as Plenipotentiary for Plant Rubber.

In the beginning of 1944, the ties between the KWI for Breeding Research and the SS with its *kog-sagyz* research facilities in Auschwitz became even stronger. In February 1944, it was decided that *kog-sagyz* research should be transferred from Müncheberg to Auschwitz, or more precisely, to the Rajsko research unit belonging to the concentration camp and headed by Joachim Caesar. The memorandum states:

For the Auschwitz breeding station, the war-related form of cooperation chosen is regarded as a merger of one department of the Kaiser Wilhelm Institute for Breeding Research with the Auschwitz unit, i.e., scientific steering, advice and ideas will continue to be provided by the director of the Kaiser Wilhelm Institute for Breeding Research, Professor Rudorf, who, also acting as scientific head of the Breeding and Basic Research Group, is offering his services to the Office of the *Reichsführer-SS* as Plenipotentiary for Plant Rubber.[51]

Böhme was transferred to Auschwitz where he became head of botanic research on *kog-sagyz* and thus had to report to Joachim Caesar as head of

[50] Report on Lieutenant Bardenwerper's official trip to France, 5 April 1944, BArch, NS 19/1802, frame 254–259; report by *Korvettenkapitän* [naval officer] Hans Stahl on his official trip to France from 8 June to 22 June 1944, 25 June 1944, BArch, NS 19/1802, frame 268–275.

[51] Memorandum, signed by Rudorf, Stahl, Caesar, and Böhme, Müncheberg, 18 February 1944, BArch, NS 19/3919, frame 91–93.

the research unit. In practice, this meant an end to his plans of managing his own institute in Rotes Luch. Work also continued on rubber plants in the KWI.

PLANT BREEDING RESEARCH IN AUSCHWITZ

In the existing literature, the agricultural research unit in Rajsko, which was part of the camp complex, is usually treated as a minor issue. Most publications on Auschwitz mention little more than the name of the person in charge of the Rajsko unit, Joachim Caesar, and the fact that there were two work details, a market gardening detail, and a plant-breeding detail.[52] One of the reasons for this is, presumably, that the conditions at Rajsko were much better than in the main camp and a description of these conditions would not be representative of the situation in Auschwitz as a whole. It is a strange paradox that precisely this (relatively) favorable situation means that little information has survived. The following passages will describe not only the development of the agricultural research unit in Rajsko but also the conditions in which the prisoners belonging to the plant-breeding detail lived and the work they did.

In November 1940, Himmler first had a report prepared on the opportunities for agricultural development in the general area of the camp that had been set up at Auschwitz about six months previously. The camp commander, Rudolf Höss, later reported that Himmler had shown considerable interest in these plans. Auschwitz was to become "*the* agricultural research unit for the east"; it provided excellent conditions and an adequate supply of labor. "All agricultural trials needed must be carried out there. Large laboratories and plant-breeding divisions must be created. Animal breeding should include all the major types of animal and breeds."[53]

---

[52] Exceptions are the essays by Anna Zięba, "Das Nebenlager Rajsko," *Hefte von Auschwitz*, 9 (1966), 75–108 and "Die Geflügelfarm Harmense," *Hefte von Auschwitz*, 11 (1970), 39–72; Lore Shelley (ed.), *Criminal Experiments on Human Beings in Auschwitz and War Research Laboratories. Twenty Women Prisoners' Accounts* (San Francisco: Mellen University Press, 1991), and the published memoirs of Eva Tichauer, *I was No. 20832 at Auschwitz* (London: Mitchell Valentine, 2000). Shelley has collected reports by ten women who worked as prisoners in the plant-breeding detail. In the following passages I have abbreviated the surnames of prisoners who are not named in the existing secondary literature and whose names are only contained in unpublished documents because it was not possible to obtain their consent to being named.

[53] Memoirs of Rudolf Höss, cited in Zięba, "Nebenlager Rajsko," 77, emphasis in the original. See also Robert-Jan Van Pelt and Debórah Dwork, *Auschwitz. Von 1279 bis heute* (Munich: Pendo, 2000), 209 f.; Danuta Czech, *Kalendarium der Ereignisse im Konzentrationslager Auschwitz-Birkenau 1939–1945* (Reinbek: Rowohlt 1989), 64. On the agricultural research unit in Auschwitz, see also Sybille Steinbacher, *"Musterstadt Auschwitz." Germanisierungspolitik und Judenmord in Ostoberschlesien* (Munich: Saur, 2000), 238 and 247; Christoph Kopke, "Deutsche Versuchsanstalt für Ernährung und Verpflegung

In early March 1941, Himmler visited Auschwitz for the first time. On this occasion he ordered considerable extensions to the main camp.[54] "Within a few weeks, seven villages in the SS area of interest were empty, namely Plawy, Harmense, Broschokowitz, Budy, Rajsko, Babitz and Birkenau."[55] The inhabitants of Rajsko, for example, were almost all resettled, either to neighboring villages or to the General Government. They were allowed to take a maximum of 25 kilograms of hand luggage. The families who remained in Rajsko, some twenty in all, including the Polish owner of the Rajsko estate, were removed from their own houses and housed in different ones close to the farm.[56]

These extensive forced resettlements were a precondition for the creation of a variety of units within the "zone of interest of Auschwitz concentration camp": initially, a poultry farm,[57] a breeding center for small animals for scientific research, a fish breeding unit with a laboratory for studying aquatic plants and micro-organisms (making use of the fish ponds of the Polish Academy of Sciences),[58] the market garden and plant-breeding unit mentioned above, and the Hygiene Institute.[59] Pigs were fattened in Rajsko, a fruit tree nursery was created, and as in many other concentration camps, a large number of angora rabbits were bred to produce warm underwear for

im III. Reich. Eine Fallstudie zur Politik und Ökonomie der SS," *Diplom* thesis, Fachbereich Politische Wissenschaft, Freie Universität Berlin (1997), 72 ff.; Franciszek Piper, "Die Ausbeutung der Arbeit der Häftlinge," in Waclaw Długoborski and Franciszek Piper (eds.), *Auschwitz 1940–1945. Studien zur Geschichte des Konzentrations- und Vernichtungslagers Auschwitz*, vol. II: *Die Häftlinge. Existenzbedingungen, Arbeit und Tod* (Oswiecim: Verlag des Staatlichen Museums Auschwitz-Birkenau, 1999), 83–167, here 118–121.

[54] Zięba, "Nebenlager Rajsko," 77; Czech, 79. On the history of the construction of Auschwitz Concentration camp, see Rainer Froebe, "Bauen und Vernichten. Die Zentralbauleitung Auschwitz und die 'Endlösung.'" *Beiträge zur Geschichte des Nationalsozialismus*, 16 (2000), 155–209.

[55] Steinbacher, 217.

[56] Zięba, "Nebenlager Rajsko," 76.

[57] The poultry-breeding unit included a modern incubation room where thousands of chicken and duck eggs were incubated; see Joachim Caesar's memoirs, 8. I am grateful to Alexander Schlichter for supplying me with a copy of these memoirs, which consist of a hand-written transcript of a tape recording made in the early 1970s (cited hereinafter as Caesar, memoirs) and a copy of the pencil notes compiled by Caesar in Nuremberg in 1946, some of which have been typed up: Joachim Caesar, "Der landwirtschaftliche Grossbetrieb. Aufbau und Bewirtschaftung," Nuremberg 1946 (hereinafter cited as Caesar, Nuremberg notes – page numbering differentiates between the typescript and the handwritten notes).

[58] Zięba, "Geflügelfarm Harmense." Caesar later mentioned that the agricultural sections had also included a forestry unit, a tree nursery, and a sheep farm; interrogation of Caesar by the Oberstaatsanwalt at Konstanz District Court, 14 November 1961, Central Office of the Justice Administration for Investigation of NS Crimes in Ludwigsburg (*Zentrale Stelle der Landesjustizverwaltungen zur Aufklärung von NS-Verbrechen in Ludwigsburg*, ZSL) IV 402 AR-Z 45/73, 10528–10534, here 10530.

[59] Mieczyław Kieta, "Das Hygiene-Institut der Waffen-SS und Polizei in Auschwitz," *Die Auschwitz-Hefte*, 1 (1987), 213–217.

the U-Boot crews.[60] The expulsion of the Polish inhabitants created space for settling ethnic Germans and Germans from the Reich as part of the development of Auschwitz as a "model of settlement in the east."[61] At the center of this project was the construction of a Buna factory for the IG Farben[62] group, which had been decided on in late 1939. The workers in this factory were to be housed in the homes vacated by the Poles who had been evacuated. By October 1943, 7,000 Germans had moved from the Reich to Auschwitz, most of them employees of IG Farben.[63]

In addition, on the lands belonging to the Rajsko agricultural unit, some 3,800 hectares in total, the plan was to set up "model agricultural units for teaching young farmers at the educational and research institutes that will be linked." The agricultural units were to aim for an "exemplary level of production." "The commission was to be carried out with a view to simple conditions, so that the young farmers would be shown how to develop a farm with simple means, not using the model of highly mechanized agriculture. Part of this task was to investigate types of buildings, cereal strains, animal breeds, and types of farm suitable for the east."[64]

In March 1942, Himmler appointed Joachim Caesar head of the unit. Caesar lived in Auschwitz with his family. As the highest ranking SS officer in Auschwitz after the camp commander Rudolf Höss,[65] he had considerable powers, and shortly after his arrival he began to arrange for trials on the cultivation of *kog-sagyz*. On Caesar's instructions, the first five female prisoners were transferred from the Ravensbrück concentration camp to Rajsko on May 12, 1942. These were Polish scientists who were to be employed in the scientific work on the rubber plants.[66] These workers formed the core of the plant-breeding detail, as the *kog-sagyz* research unit was called.

In mid-July 1942, Himmler inspected the Auschwitz concentration camp for the second time. On this occasion, he also visited the Rajsko agricultural research unit that had been set up on his initiative. Caesar showed him

---

[60] Caesar, memoirs, 9 f. In his 1946 notes, Caesar states that some 4,000 angora rabbits were bred at Auschwitz. However, this project had been abandoned in 1944 because the climate was unsuitable; Caesar, Nuremberg notes, 3 (typescript) and 19 (handwritten).

[61] Karin Orth, *Das System der nationalsozialistischen Konzentrationslager. Eine politische Organisationsgeschichte* (Hamburg: Hamburger Edition, 1999), 80

[62] Florian Schmaltz and Karl-Heinz Roth, "Neue Dokumente zur Vorgeschichte des I.G. Farben-Werks Auschwitz-Monowitz. Zugleich eine Stellungnahme zur Kontroverse zwischen Hans Deichmann und Peter Hayes," 1999. *Zeitschrift für Sozialgeschichte des 20. und 21. Jahrhunderts*, 13, No. 2 (1998), 100–116.

[63] Steinbacher, 242 f.

[64] Caesar, Nuremberg notes, 1 (typescript).

[65] Hermann Langbein, *Der Auschwitz-Prozess. Eine Dokumentation* (Frankfurt am Main: Verlag Neue Kritik, 1965), 54.

[66] These were Wanda Dutczynska, Maria Raczyтska, Emilia Goszkowska, Janina Kukowska (who died in the camp of typhus on 12 September 1942), and an agriculturalist whose first name was Ada, surname unknown; Ziтba, "Nebenlager Rajsko," 84; see also Czech, 209.

the animal breeding units, tree nurseries, and plant-breeding station, among other features.[67] Shortly after this visit, a typhus epidemic was rampant in the camp. Caesar's wife fell victim to it and Caesar himself became seriously ill as well. He therefore had to leave the management of the *kog-sagyz* cultivation to a replacement. According to his postwar accounts, this was the reason the cultivation did not make as much progress as intended. In 1943 he married the chemist Ruth Weinmann, who was also working in the plant-breeding unit.[68]

In addition to *kog-sagyz* research, work in Rajsko also investigated the vitamin C content of gladioli bulbs,[69] and experiments were carried out on wheat and rye.[70] The annual report for 1942/43 written by Caesar also mentions that "comparative studies on vitamin research for Dachau" were carried out in the chemistry laboratory.[71]

The market garden detail in Rajsko was responsible for growing vegetables, flowers, and cereals in the camp greenhouses and in the fields belonging to Rajsko. "The vegetables were delivered to the SS kitchen, and most were taken away by car to meet the troops" requirements. The vegetables grown were of a high standard. The cucumbers were stamped with the initials of the place of cultivation and were sent to Berlin from April onward. "Flowers from Rajsko were known across Germany."[72] It was mainly female prisoners who worked in the market garden and plant-breeding details – several hundred in total.[73]

A Czech prisoner, Anni Binder, worked as Caesar's secretary.[74] She saw to it that the first people employed in the plant-breeding section, after the Polish women from Ravensbrück, were three French Jewish women who had had

---

[67] Czech, 250.

[68] From April 1945 to January 1949, the Americans held Caesar as a prisoner of war. In January 1949, a German denazification tribunal initially placed him in its Category II, "implicated, beneficiaries and activists" (*Belastete, Nutzniesser*, and *Aktivisten*), and later in Category III, "less implicated" (*Minderbelastete*); Interrogation of Caesar by the *Oberstaatsanwalt* at Konstanz District Court, 14 November 1961, ZSL, IV 402 AR-Z 45/73, 10528–10534, here 10530. Caesar later ran a laundry in Konstanz, in southern Germany.

[69] Zięba, "Nebenlager Rajsko," 90. Tichauer, *No.* 20832, 67 f., states that the prisoners involved in the study were happy to see flowers appearing in their laboratory and had sabotaged the results.

[70] Zięba, "Nebenlager Rajsko," 90.

[71] The Reichsführer SS as Plenipotentiary for Plant Rubber, Annual Report 1942/43 of the Breeding Group, Auschwitz, 19 January 1944, BArch NS 19/3919, frame 16–69, here frame 38;

[72] Zięba, "Nebenlager Rajsko," 81.

[73] Zięba, "Nebenlager Rajsko," 85, reports that the plant-breeding detail was constantly expanding and that toward the end, 150 women were employed there and about the same number in the market-garden detail.

[74] Anni Binder (later Urbanová, after her marriage) testimony, ZSL, IV 402 AR-Z 45/73, 38–42. In Lore Shelley, *Auschwitz – The Nazi Civilization* (Lanham, Md.: University Press of America, 1992), 44–61, she describes her life and her experiences in Rajsko.

scientific training. Because *kog-sagyz* research was perceived to be of major importance for the German war economy, the women in the plant-breeding detail managed over time to have more and more prisoners transferred to the detail, where the chance of survival was far higher than in the main camp. One of the first prisoners who worked as a scientist in Rajsko was the French biologist Claudette Bloch. She had managed to have herself sent to the camp by the German occupying forces in France because she wanted to find out what had happened to her husband. He had been deported to Auschwitz in late March 1942 and died there a short time later. She arrived in Auschwitz on June 22 and was transferred to the plant-breeding detail after about six weeks.

Bloch states that on one occasion when Caesar brought a microscope into the plant-breeding unit, she managed to persuade him that, given the appropriate equipment, she could make a scientific contribution to the research on rubber plants. Caesar then sent her to "Canada," the section of the camp where possessions stolen from the prisoners were kept, to find the equipment needed to set up a laboratory.[75] In this way, Claudette Bloch became the laboratory manager in Auschwitz. This role allowed her to ask for prisoners to be transferred from the main camp for use as specialized workers in *kog-sagyz* research. Some of those transferred did not have any training that would qualify them for research on *kog-sagyz*, but the relative safety of Rajsko saved them. In 1944, for example, Bloch stated that a trainee lawyer, Simone Floersheim, whose mother had been murdered in Auschwitz and whose sister had died of typhus, was a scientist. By this time, Böhme was in charge of deciding who would be hired for the laboratory. But as he did not speak French and Floersheim did not speak German, Bloch "interpreted" – not what Floersheim said, but what Böhme wanted to hear. She answered questions about Floersheim's scientific expertise with the answers needed.[76]

In addition to the prisoners, various other groups of people were employed in the plant-breeding unit. These were German scientists or *kog-sagyz* experts, Russian ones who were collaborating with the Germans, and

---

[75] See interview with Claudette Bloch(-Kennedy), National Sound Archive, London, C410/027/01–05. I am grateful to Paul Weindling, who informed me of the existence of the interview and also provided me with a second interview with Claudette Bloch held by him. However, the files of Auschwitz's central construction body reveal that in March 1942 there were already plans to build an agricultural laboratory in Auschwitz. It is thus possible that the decision to create a botanic laboratory was as coincidental as Bloch reports, but it had always been planned to carry out some form of research at the agricultural unit. The head of the SS Economic and Administrative Main Office to the Central Construction Office of the Waffen-SS and the Police at Auschwitz, 2 March 1942, United States Holocaust Memorial Museum, Washington, DC (USHMM), RG 11.001M.03, Reel 25, Folder 98 und Reel 43, Folder 338.

[76] Interview with Simone Floersheim on 22 April 2001.

SS men and women as guards. The German scientific staff was made up of Schattenberg, mentioned above, Ruth Caesar née Weinmann, and Böhme, who was in charge of managing cultivation and of the chemical and botanical labs. The Russian specialists did not live in the camp as prisoners but in the village of Rajsko, sometimes with their families,[77] in "Polish houses that had been vacated."[78] However, they were not allowed to leave Auschwitz.[79]

Initially, the prisoners had to walk three kilometers by foot, under guard, from the women's concentration camp in Birkenau to Rajsko to work at the unit. After the typhus epidemic that broke out in the camp in late July/early August 1942, Caesar campaigned for an improvement in the hygiene of the living conditions for the prisoners working in the plant-breeding detail. His goal was to reduce the danger of infection, as it was inevitable that these prisoners would come into contact with the German scientists and the guards.

The camp quarantine imposed as a result of the epidemic brought to a halt all work in the external work details. As a result, the members of various work details were later transferred out of the camp and housed at their places of work. In late September 1942, the women in the plant breeding detail were re-housed in the Rajsko Staff Office (*Stabsgebäude*) on Caesar's orders.[80] Some of the camp administration and clerks were also working in this building. This reorganization meant that the prisoners would be able to continue work if a new epidemic caused the camp to be quarantined again. For the prisoners, the move meant that they no longer had to march from Birkenau to Rajsko and back every day. It was also a considerable improvement in their living conditions in other ways. For Claudette Bloch, after spending months in Birkenau during which most of the French women with whom she had been deported to Auschwitz had already died, the idea of having her own bunk, a washroom, and three meals a day was an unimaginable luxury.[81]

In addition to the danger of infection, Caesar also stated that another reason to improve the prisoners' conditions was "the particular interest shown by a relatively broad scientific public" in the plant-breeding unit. In the summer months, in particular, the unit "was visited very frequently."[82] For this reason, he asked that the women working in Rajsko be supplied with

[77] Jozefa Kiwalowa in Shelley, *Criminal Experiments*, 218.
[78] Heinrich Vogel, report "Regarding kok-sagyz rubber plant," 21 January 1942, BArch, NS 19/1802, frame 5 f.
[79] According to Zięba, "Nebenlager Rajsko," 84.
[80] Evidently, at first only some of the plant-breeding detail was housed in Rajsko; the entire group was only transferred there from June 1943 onward; see Zięba, "Nebenlager Rajsko," 85.
[81] Claudette Kennedy (as C. Bloch called herself later after remarrying) in Shelley, *Criminal Experiments*, 161.
[82] Caesar to the SS Economic and Administrative Main Office (WVHA), 20 May 1944, reproduced in Zięba, "Nebenlager Rajsko," 102.

clothing belonging to Hungarian Jews who had been deported to Auschwitz and murdered there. The women also reported, later on, that the greenhouses and laboratories were often visited by interested scientists and officers and by "high-ranking German individuals."[83] One result of the relatively acceptable conditions in Rajsko was that the women imprisoned there had a certain amount of scope to develop cultural activities and to make contact with prisoners in other parts of the camp:

> Our minds were waking up. We chatted, recalling our past lives, and we endeavored to exercise our brains by undertaking intellectual activities. Anny [Anni Binder] taught me some German, which was so necessary to understand the orders we were given (as we couldn't understand what we were supposed to do or not do, the guards took us for imbeciles). I gave some talks on biology, but the most striking recollection I have of those evenings is the reading and translating of Goethe's *Faust* by Ella Schliesser, who had found a copy of it in the mud.[84]

The historian Anna Zięba also reports the existence of a "cultural life" with talks and texts being read aloud, dancing (mazurka), and a performance of Molière's *Imaginary Invalid*.[85] This performance was directed by the French writer Charlotte Delbo, who has described her experiences in Rajsko in her trilogy *Auschwitz and After*, a literary memorial to many of those who accompanied her there.[86] In addition to these cultural activities, the prisoners also developed political interests. Tichauer reported that her political beliefs had changed during her time in the camp. On January 21, 1944, she and a small number of others held a ceremony to mark the anniversary of Lenin's death; in the autumn of the same year, she asked to be admitted to the underground Communist Party of Rajsko.[87]

The prisoners in Rajsko managed to maintain contact with their fellow prisoners in the main camp and to smuggle vegetables as well as information. The vegetables were buried at pre-agreed locations in the greenhouses and were later collected by male prisoners who came from Auschwitz to

---

[83] Testimony by Jozefa Zofia Kiwala, née Kaleta, 1 July 1971, ZSL, IV 402 AR-Z 37/58, 218–212, here 219; see also the statements by Stanislawa Slowakiewicz, ZSL, IV 402 AR-Z 37/58, 227–231, and Claudette Bloch(-Kennedy) in Shelley, *Criminal Experiments*, 166.

[84] Claudette Bloch(-Kennedy), cited in Shelley, *Criminal Experiments*, 161 f.

[85] Zięba, "Nebenlager Rajsko," 92.

[86] Charlotte Delbo, *Auschwitz and After*, translated by Rosette C. Lamont, with an introduction by Lawrence L. Langer (New Haven: Yale University Press, 1995). The rehearsals are described on 168–171.

[87] Tichauer, *No. 20832*, 76. Eva Tichauer had emigrated with her family from Berlin to France in 1933 when she was young and had taken French citizenship, but the Vichy government under Henri Pétain withdrew it again. In 1942, her father was arrested and deported, and some months later, the same thing happened to her mother and herself. After two months at the Drancy camp, both were deported to Auschwitz. Immediately after their arrival, Eva Tichauer's mother was murdered in the gas chamber, on her fiftieth birthday. By this point her father was already dead.

Rajsko every day to work in the fields; they brought them back to the main camp on their return.[88] The same route was used to exchange information between the prisoners in Rajsko and other parts of the camp.[89]

Even in the plant-breeding detail in Rajsko, the prisoners were still at risk of being transferred back to the main camp if they became ill or committed even a minor offense. In the main camp, the chance of survival was low; they might even be sent to the gas chambers. Lili Tofler, who worked as a draftsperson in the plant-breeding detail, was reputed to be engaged to a prisoner in the main camp. She was murdered because of a letter she wrote to him that never reached its destination. Several different versions of her story have survived; all, however, state that she was arrested by SS men from the political section who pressured her to reveal the name of the person to whom the letter was addressed, and that she was then shot together with two male prisoners.[90]

A chemist called Berthe Falk was transferred to a punishment detail for six months after the SS guard Thies Christophersen had caught her writing a text about the approaching liberation of Paris, which she imagined happening on July 14, the French national day.[91] Her fellow prisoners believed that the reason she was not executed immediately was that she was working on Ruth Caesar's doctoral thesis and continued to do so during her punishment.[92]

All the former prisoners report that conditions in Rajsko were considerably better than in the main camp in Auschwitz-Birkenau. However, opinions of Caesar's behavior varied considerably, ranging from the claim that he was a "guardian angel" and a "savior" (Maria Ossowski)[93] to the

---

[88] Tichauer, *No. 20832*, 76. Tichauer reported that on one occasion Thies Christophersen had found out about a transfer of vegetables; afterward, he frequently looked for buried vegetables in the greenhouse to catch the prisoners in the act.

[89] See Jozefa Kiwalowa in Shelley, *Criminal Experiments*, 219. Henryk Świebocki, "Die lagernahe Widerstandsbewegung," *Hefte von Auschwitz*, 19 (1995), 5–187, here 85.

[90] See Delbo, 160–161. Langbein, 407 ff; Lore Shelley (ed.), *Secretaries of Death. Accounts by Former Prisoners Who Worked in the Gestapo of Auschwitz* (New York: Shengold, 1986), 350. See also the record of the testimony given by Irena S., née K., 25 March 1972, ZSL IV 402 AR-Z 37/58, 222–226, here 225.

[91] Testimony by Irena S., née K., 5 March 1972, ZSL, IV 402 AR-Z 45/73, 222–226, here 225; see also Marie-Elisa Cohen in Shelley, *Criminal Experiments*, 182.

[92] See Zięba, "Nebenlager Rajsko," 83; a similar account is given in the testimony by Irena S., née K., 25 March 1972, ZSL, IV 402 AR-Z 45/73, 222–226, here 225, and by Simone Floersheim in my interview with her on 22 April 2001. This thesis, which was to be submitted to Kurt Hess – although this never happened – was concerned with the latex content of kok-sagyz roots; the Reichsführer SS as Plenipotentiary for Plant Rubber, Annual Report 1942/43 of the Breeding Group, Auschwitz, 19 January 1944, BArch NS 19/3919, frame 16–69, here frame 38. According to Tichauer and Wanda Landniewska, Ruth Caesar's doctoral dissertation had been prepared by Marie-Elisa (Cohen), maybe in addition to Berthe Falk. Landniewska did the illustrations; see her account in Shelley, *Criminal Experiments*, 241.

[93] Interview with Maria Ossowski on 19 July 2000.

charge that he saw prisoners merely as tools, not as people (Stanislawa Slowakiewicz).[94] Many of the women believed that because the *kog-sagyz* project had been judged to be vital for the war effort, this decision had secured Caesar's position and prevented him from having to fight in the war. Either this self-interest or his lack of expertise in plant breeding was, according to this argument, the reason Caesar did not acknowledge that the Rajsko research was achieving very limited results.

While it is unclear whether Caesar did not see the inefficiency of the *kog-sagyz* research in Auschwitz or did not want to see it, the survivors' reports on Böhme are unequivocal. They state that he had noticed soon after arriving in Auschwitz that the prisoners were not carrying out "serious research" and had watched them suspiciously to try to prove them guilty of sabotage. Böhme harassed Claudette Bloch in particular, because he felt that as the head of the botanic laboratory in Rajsko, she was responsible for the poor results being achieved by the kog-sagyz research. Bloch reported:

He did the job wholeheartedly. Inevitably he found out that, if our work in the *Pflanzenzucht* [plant-breeding] lab was accurate, it was, to say the least, slow and not very original (in fact, when we received books we discovered that what we had done was already known in the Russian literature). Naturally, he held me responsible for the mediocrity of the work and developed a keen dislike for me. I suppose psychologists could find an explanation of his special hate for me, whose background was similar to his own. ... At every opportunity he reminded me of my prisoner status, while he was one of the masters.[95]

Although Böhme evidently had it in for Claudette Bloch in particular,[96] she was not the only one who was afraid of him. Of the German scientific staff in Rajsko, Eva Tichauer only remembers Joachim and Ruth Caesar and Richard Böhme. She had the impression, she said later, that Caesar had just wanted to hold on to his job so that he would not be called into active military service. Ruth Caesar, she remembers thinking, might have been a Jew and could have been attempting to cover this up by working for the SS. Of the three, Böhme had been much the worst because when he arrived, the prisoners first had the feeling "of having a scientist to deal with

[94] Testimony by Stanislawa Slowakiewicz, 22 June 1971, ZSL, IV 402 AR-Z 37/58, 227–231, here 228.
[95] See Claudette Bloch(-Kennedy) in Shelley, *Criminal Experiments*, 166 f.
[96] Interview with Simone Floersheim on 22 April 2001; see also Floersheim in Shelley, *Criminal Experiments*, 195. In my interview with her, Floersheim also reported that Böhme had not taken her (Floersheim herself) seriously as a scientist but had, however, treated her correctly.

who knew about our work and as a result was in a much better position to watch over us."[97]

His springy, silent footsteps force us to be constantly on our guard. He is continually on our backs, trying to control everything and insisting that it is our duty to cooperate honestly and to attain full production capacity. He pushes this perverse logic to its extreme by explaining to us that if he were a prisoner of the Soviets, he would act in the same way. On the eve of the evacuation of the camp, when we remind him of his words and promise to save him if he keeps us at Rajsko until liberation by the Red Army, this coward lets us take our place in the death march. The intelligent ones among the SS are worse than beasts. Until the very end they plan our deaths so that no witnesses will remain against them.[98]

As in Claudette Bloch's account, Eva Tichauer's report has undertones of astonishment that someone like Böhme, who had studied at the best universities, could deliberately agree to support the Nazi rubber plant-breeding project at Auschwitz and could offer his services to it. The women working in the laboratory, of whom Tichauer was the spokeswoman, believed that Böhme was an educated man; this led them to attempt to convince him by force of argument. "We tried to explain to him that we knew that we would probably never get back home and that for this reason we did not see any need to do good work. ... We said to ourselves that the SS men in the camp were better off than those on the eastern front. ... We were their security. Given a certain amount of cooperation we would stay there [i.e., in Rajsko], and so would they. We were always conscious that there was a risk that we could be gassed at the last moment."[99]

Böhme left Auschwitz on the day the camp was evacuated, wearing his SS uniform. He was killed shortly afterward before getting back to Germany.[100] The Russian scientists and the equipment in the plant-breeding unit were transported to Büschdorf, near Halle, probably in the hope of continuing the work by linking it to the university in Halle.[101] The women

---

[97] Interview with Eva Tichauer on 23 and 24 April 2001.

[98] Tichauer, *No. 20832*, 69.

[99] Interview with Eva Tichauer. Brigitte Ullrich, a colleague of Böhme in Müncheberg, recalls Böhme telling her that the "terrible treatment of the people" in Auschwitz and the large numbers of dead "got him down"; he felt incapable of doing work there; interview with Brigitte Ullrich on 26 April 2000. Overall, Ullrich describes Böhme as a "soft-hearted" man who had not really fit into the SS and who had taken it very hard that he had to send prisoners who were ill back to the main camp in the knowledge that they would be murdered there. But he does not appear to have voiced any such feelings to the prisoners.

[100] Interview with Brigitte Ullrich on 26 April 2000.

[101] Wieland, 54. After the capitulation, the American military who were controlling the town ordered Theodor Roemer, a professor at Halle, to continue the work on *kog-sagyz*, but he refused.

of the plant-breeding detail were sent – partly on foot and partly in cattle wagons – first to Ravensbrück concentration camp; from there to Malchow, an auxiliary camp; and finally to a camp in Leipzig. From there, they were sent on a second death march in mid-April. Ten days later, the Red Army liberated those who had survived.[102]

SCIENTIFIC PRODUCTIVITY AND TERROR

The *kog-sagyz* project failed. Not only were the tires produced by Continental using natural rubber not good enough for the *Reichsführer-SS*;[103] after the war, research on this plant was discontinued. Instead, natural rubber was imported from the tropics, making use of classic colonial structures, just as it had been before the war.

Failed projects are useful as screens onto which we can project our pre-existing ideas. They seem to substantiate the theory that science cannot function successfully in an authoritarian state because in such a state, the plurality of methods, the international exchange, or simply the overall freedom that science needs to thrive on are impossible. Implicitly, such a view would also confirm inherited beliefs according to which science was a victim of the Nazi regime, not a part of it.

What does the *kog-sagyz* project reveal about science and science policy in Nazi Germany? Research on rubber plants growing on European soils only became interesting under a rigid autarky policy – albeit one conceived as limited to the continent rather than to the nation state – and when imports from former colonies could not be relied upon. The real research boom started only in 1941 when natural rubber became difficult to obtain and stocks began to run out. Another factor was that research into Buna was not bringing the results expected. However, it was mainly the opportunity of accessing the resources of the occupied Soviet Union that speeded things up. Fact-finding missions and the transfer of seed stocks, literature, and scientists represented major inputs for research. A considerable amount of know-how on processing the roots of the plants was also taken from the occupied Ukraine, that is, from the processing unit in Uman.

As a result of this input, a variety of different institutes and bodies suddenly expressed an interest in the project. Initially, the SS had planned to keep possible rivals such as the armed forces out of this research, but within a few months – at the latest by late 1941 – a research network had been set up that included numerous representatives from scientific research, the processing industry, government authorities, and consumers. It included two Kaiser Wilhelm institutes. In this heterogeneous group, conflicts of

[102] See Tichauer, *No. 20832*, 78–89.
[103] Continental Gummiwerke, Direktion an Vorstand der Ges. f. Pflanzenkautschuk und Guttapercha m.b.H., 25.7.1944, BArch, NS 19/1803, frame 213.

interest developed mainly on issues related to hierarchies and authority and access to research resources, especially those in the east. The process of establishing Himmler as the Plenipotentiary for Plant Rubber went through several stages and took several months, but it did not meet with any real opposition.

In the early summer of 1943, rubber research was coordinated under Himmler's management. The transfer of the center of research on *kog-sagyz* to Auschwitz and the extension of research facilities there provide proof that funds were not simply thrown at projects that were then politically in fashion but were given to the institutions that were seen as the most successful. Evidently, Caesar managed to create the impression that Rajsko was successful more effectively than Böhme did for Rotes Luch. This is reflected in the fact that Böhme eventually had to report to Caesar. The reason for the failure of the *kog-sagyz* project lies elsewhere.

It is clear that everyone involved saw *kog-sagyz* research as promising only when it was based on large-scale expropriation of resources. This does not merely mean the misappropriation of knowledge and technical equipment; the cultivation of *kog-sagyz* stood a chance of being profitable only when it became possible to exploit the agricultural land and labor of the occupied Soviet Union for the project. After the German army had withdrawn from the most important cultivation areas, conditions in other regions such as France and Hungary were examined.[104] In regions where it did not seem feasible to control production strictly, to use forced labor, or to employ other forms of repression, growing natural rubber promised only very limited success.

The *kog-sagyz* research project failed not because the scientists involved on either the German or the Soviet side refused to cooperate, or because research in Nazi Germany was organized in an inefficient manner; it was because botanical experiments could not be forced into the pace dictated by the "production battle." A much longer lead-time would have been required to reduce the problems of seed reproduction, plant cultivation, and root processing to the level needed to produce natural rubber on a semi-industrial scale. In *kog-sagyz* processing, as in other innovative scientific projects, methods developed in the Soviet Union were to be transferred to Germany where they would be carefully studied and improved before being reexported to the areas under German occupation in the east. Böhme had intended something similar when he campaigned for rubber processing units to be constructed "in the east" where the Müncheberg method was to be used – itself based on the method used in Uman. But before these plans could be realized, the German troops had to give up most of the areas of *kog-sagyz* cultivation in the east.

---

[104] See Heim, *Plant Breeding*, 122.

Under the conditions of the early 1940s, the project was so susceptible to problems that there was no possibility of implementing it in an occupied country against the resistance of the local population or organizing research using slave labor in a concentration camp. From that point of view, using force to implement the project was both the hypothetical prerequisite for its success (cultivation would not have been profitable under market conditions) and the reason for its failure. Neither this failure nor the supposed inability of the dictatorship to initiate scientific innovation are specifically National Socialist–related elements of the *kog-sagyz* project. What is typical of the National Socialist regime is the use of forced labor, slave labor, and stolen resources. Without these, no attempt to produce natural rubber "domestically" would ever have been made.

For the botanic research and for the cultivation of hundreds of thousands of hectares of land, and given the low level of mechanization in botanic research and agriculture, large numbers of workers would have been needed to meet the ambitious production targets that had been set. It was not essential that most of these workers were experts, but they did need to be able to carry out various stages of the process by themselves once they had received a certain amount of training. This minimal level of training meant that while the workers were not irreplaceable, it did give them a certain level of protection – for example, in Auschwitz they were protected from being transferred to the main camp in an arbitrary manner. During Claudette Bloch's time as manager, the prisoners employed in the botanic laboratory merely had to pretend to be working diligently on the research. When Böhme took over, this relative security in the plant-breeding detail was seriously jeopardized.

Böhme came to Auschwitz at a time when the machinery of extermination was operating at full steam. He had adequate opportunity to inform himself about the camp in advance, both as a member of the Personal Staff of the *Reichsführer-SS* and through a colleague, who had been temporarily sent to the KWI for Breeding Research as part of the scientific exchange between the units at Auschwitz and at Müncheberg.[105] But this did not sway his decision to move there. After beginning work in Auschwitz, Böhme did articulate his unease with the working conditions that existed at the camp, in private conversation. But he himself was a prop of the camp regime – a scientist who went about his job in the belief that he was doing the right thing and attempting to achieve perfection, without worrying about the general conditions and consequences insofar as they were not related to science. He made use of the camp's regime of terror and the threat of returning prisoners to Birkenau as an instrument of discipline to force the prisoners to carry out "good science."

---

[105] See Heim, *Plant Breeding*, 128, 147.

Böhme and his boss, Wilhelm Rudorf, had embedded *kog-sagyz* research at the KWI for Breeding Research in an extensive network of different institutions. But the SS was granted a central role in this network with the appointment of Himmler as Plenipotentiary for Plant Rubber, if not before. Böhme's personal links with Himmler, his SS membership, and the fact that many members of the academic staff of the KWI for Breeding Research were also members of the SS ensured that even after the *Reichsführer-SS* became Plenipotentiary for Plant Rubber, the KWI continued to have a leading role in *kog-sagyz* research. With the failure of Böhme's own plans to set up a *kog-sagyz* research institute in Rotes Luch and his move to Auschwitz, the cooperation between that concentration camp and the Kaiser Wilhelm Institute became the main axis of this research.

9

Raw and Advanced Materials for an Autarkic Germany: Textile Research in the Kaiser Wilhelm Society

Günther Luxbacher

"Everything in the soldier's armor that is not iron is chemistry – even the tunic."[1]

PRELIMINARY REMARKS

Materials research and armaments research generally evoke images of artifacts made of iron and metallic materials. Although metals research represents a considerable portion of such work, over history both types of research have covered a constantly growing catalog of raw materials.[2] The introductory quotation, a common saying at the Reich Ministry of Economics (*Reichswirtschaftsministerium*, RWM) during the National Socialist period, points to the importance of the chemical industry, and within this sector, expressly to the field of synthetic fibers and plastics. Research into raw and advanced materials is highly relevant for industry in all mass consumption societies, and even more so for national economies lacking raw materials. The greatest trade expense for industrialized European countries during the nineteenth and early twentieth centuries was always the import of textile raw materials, amounting to around one third of the cost of all commercial and industrial imported raw materials. Despite numerous successful innovations in the area of advanced textile materials research during World War I,

---

[1] Popular saying in the RWM during War II. Cited in Willi A. Boelcke, *Die deutsche Wirtschaft 1930–1945. Interna des Reichswirtschaftsministeriums* (Düsseldorf: Droste, 1983), 238.

[2] See the articles in Helmut Maier (ed.), *Rüstungsforschung im Nationalsozialismus. Organisation, Mobilisierung und Entgrenzung der Technikwissenschaften* (Göttingen: Wallstein, 2002).

The submitted text is an extensively abridged version of a sixty-nine page article, Günther Luxbacher, "Roh- und Werkstoffe für die Autarkie. Textilforschung in der Kaiser-Wilhelm-Gesellschaft," *Ergebnisse. Vorabdrucke aus dem Forschungsprogramm "Geschichte der Kaiser-Wilhelm-Gesellschaft im Nationalsozialismus,"* No. 18 (Berlin: Forschungsprogramm, 2004; further quoted as *Ergebnisse*, No., and year).

by the end of the Weimar Republic more than 90 percent of all textile raw materials still had to be imported from abroad. While in times of peace a substantial portion of these were refined and then reexported for profit, alleviating the problem in terms of the national economy, the shortage remained unsolved in strategic terms. This was particularly true for cotton, which had been introduced for cultivation in southeastern Europe back in the early nineteenth century – however, with poor results.[3]

Many industrial companies in Germany as well as private and state institutions carried out basic and applied research on natural, semisynthetic, and fully synthetic fibers.[4] At Fritz Haber's urging,[5] the young Kaiser Wilhelm Society (*Kaiser-Wilhelm-Gesellschaft*, KWS) entered this research sector that was so relevant to armaments by founding the Kaiser Wilhelm Institute for Textile Fiber Research toward the end of World War I.[6] In the period between the wars, the new institute enjoyed moderate financial success until the undertaking was abandoned during the early phase of the National Socialist era. Not until 1938 did the KWS succeed in entering the field of textile research again. It used the policy of economic autarky in National Socialist Germany to further its own ends, taking over an existing research institute on natural fibers that was closely associated with industry. The resulting KWI for Bast Fiber Research (KWIBF), with a staff of around 150, was the largest institute for textile research in the Third Reich and the second largest institute in the whole of the KWS, right after the KWI for Breeding Research. The KWIBF performed research on the breeding, technical processing, and use of flax, hemp, jute, and other domestic bast fibers.

[3] Günther Luxbacher, "Massenproduktion wider Willen: der Rohstoff Baumwolle und die Maschinisierung der österreichischen Spinnerei," in *200 Jahre erste Baumwollmaschinen-Spinnerei in Sachsen* (Chemnitz: Selbstverlag des Chemnitzer Geschichtsvereins, 1999), 102–111.

[4] Karin Zachmann, "Die Entwicklung der deutschen Chemiefaserindustrie und ihre staatsmonopolistische Regulierung von 1900 bis 1933," Ph.D. diss., Technical University of Dresden (1983), 12–20; Gottfried Plumpe, *Die IG. Farbenindustrie AG. Wirtschaft, Technik und Politik 1904–1945* (Berlin: Duncker & Humblot, 1990), 296–324; Ulrich Marsch, *Zwischen Wissenschaft und Wirtschaft. Industrieforschung in Deutschland und Grossbritannien 1880–1936* (Paderborn: Schöningh, 2000).

[5] Margit Szöllosi-Janze, *Fritz Haber 1868–1934. Eine Biographie* (Munich: Beck, 1998).

[6] More precise depictions have been submitted by Bettina Löser, "Der Beitrag des Kaiser Wilhelm-Institutes für Faserstoffchemie in Berlin-Dahlem," *Mitteilungen der Fachgruppe Geschichte der Chemie*, 7 (1992), 50–61; Bettina Löser, "Zur Gründungsgeschichte des Kaiser Wilhelm-Institutes für Faserstoffchemie in Berlin-Dahlem," NTM-*Schriftenreihe Geschichte der Naturwissenschaft, Technik und Medizin*, 28, No. 1 (1991), 73–93; Bettina Löser, "Zur Gründungsgeschichte und Entwicklung des Kaiser-Wilhelm-Institutes für Faserstoffchemie in Berlin-Dahlem (1914/19–1934)," in Bernhard vom Brocke and Hubert Laitko (eds.), *Die Kaiser-Wilhelm-, Max-Planck-Gesellschaft und ihre Institute. Studien zu ihrer Geschichte: Das Harnack-Prinzip* (Berlin: de Gruyter, 1996).

Since the demand for equipment and arms for the troops in general climbed permanently from 1933 on, the overall consumption of fibers obviously needed to rise as well. However, because the second Four Year Plan, starting in 1936, called for a reduction of imported fibers, it was necessary to fall back on raw materials available within the German borders of the time (in case imports were blockaded).[7] Raw materials were recycled, such as by reprocessing wool; in addition, imported fibers were to be replaced primarily by natural animal and vegetable fibers (wool, flax, and hemp), semisynthetic fibers on the basis of cellulose (faux silk, spun rayon, synthetic jute), and increasingly from the 1940s on, fully synthetic fibers produced from polymerized carbon compounds (PC fibers, nylon). Moreover, the techniques of stop-gap utilization and research into stretching the existing inventories of raw materials by extending their useful life (*Gebrauchswertforschung*) shifted increasingly into the foreground as the war progressed.

The focus of research at the KWIBF was on material for soldiers' kit (caps, coats, uniform drill, belts, components of gas masks, haversacks, sheaths, flags, pennants, blankets, parachutes) and for equipping the troops in general (tent and truck tarpaulins, sail cloths, car seat covers, horse blankets, balloon cloth, flight tethers, jute sacks, packing tethers and other packing materials, bandages, cords, ropes, camouflage nets, pressed materials, filling agents, insulation and construction materials, tire tread, conveyor belts, ammunition belts, grenade lifting belts, cartridge pouches, tank hoses, cable casings, and the like). All these items were generally subject to very specific demands in terms of equipment technology and textile physics.

Although the new KWI was successful at first, over time its problems ballooned. Conflicts of interest emerged, related to both science organization and economic policy. The economic interest of the state and the military to reduce reliance on imported fiber by creating domestic materials contrasted with the business interests of the textile industry, which was interested predominantly in developing cost-effective methods for processing fibers. Against this conflict of interest, the institute increasingly found itself a casualty of the tensions between opposing interest groups, gradually disrupting its intended chain of research.

This chapter will first sketch the role of the KWS in German textile research between 1914 and 1938. Next the focus will shift to the KWIBF and

---

[7] "*Blockadefestigkeit.*" For general information, see, for example, René Erbe, *Die nationalsozialistische Wirtschaftspolitik 1933–1939 im Lichte der modernen Theorie* (Zurich: Polygraphischer Verlag, 1958), especially 24–28; Dieter Petzina, *Autarkiepolitik im Dritten Reich. Der nationalsozialistische Vierjahresplan* (Stuttgart: DVA, 1968), especially 30–36; Lotte Zumpe (ed.), *Wirtschaft und Staat in Deutschland 1933 bis 1945* (Vaduz: Topos-Verlag, 1980); Eckart Teichert, *Autarkie und Grossraumwirtschaft in Deutschland 1930–1939: aussenwirtschaftspolitische Konzeptionen zwischen Wirtschaftskrise und Zweitem Weltkrieg* (Munich: Oldenbourg, 1984).

its integration into the national innovation system of the Nazi regime. This system centered on the growing field of armament research, which was to be administered by a comprehensive central institute covering all levels of production. This meant the KWS had to embed the institute into state entities like the Reich Ministry for Education and Science (*Reichserziehungsministerium*, REM), the Reich Aviation Ministry (*Reichsluftfahrtministerium*, RLM), the RWM, the Reich Office for Economic Expansion (*Reichsamt für Wirtschaftsausbau*, RWA), the Reich Research Council (*Reichsforschungsrat*, RFR),[8] military authorities like the Supreme Command of the Armed Forces (*Oberkommando der Wehrmacht*, OKW), and the Supreme Command of the Air Force (*Oberkommando der Luftwaffe*, ObdL) as well as private industry, along with its numerous associations and groups.

In terms of science organization, this political and institutional integration was supposed to create an unbroken chain of research extending from the raw materials to the completed product. The participants described this conglomerate of interests as a "nexus" (*Konnex*). Yet, it soon became apparent that the colliding spheres of interest of the various participants increasingly threatened this nexus. The conflict of objectives, which came to a head from 1942 on, sheds light on how the Nazi system of rule operated.

ATTEMPTS TO INSTITUTIONALIZE FIBER MATERIALS RESEARCH IN THE KAISER WILHELM SOCIETY FROM 1914 TO 1938

The first attempts to found a KWI for textile or fiber materials research took place during the founding phase of the KWS, but initially representatives of the Wilhelmian government, the interested states, industry, and the KWS were not able to agree on the location, status, and financing of such an entity. This situation did not change until the war.

Even then, circumstances were complicated by a fundamental conflict of objectives. In terms of national policy, the potential fault lines ran between the interests of the military and those of industry. In terms of science organization, these fell between breeding researchers, cellulose chemists, and textile engineers. Added to these were the particular interests of some federal states in attracting Reich funding to establish research institutions in these fields. The paper and textile industry wanted a research institute to focus on the technological issues commercially relevant to their needs. Because of the blockade and the resulting discourse about substitute materials, the Reich government was interested above all in raw materials technology.

---

[8] The author is currently working on a study of industrial raw materials and advanced materials research in the German Research Foundation (*Deutsche Forschungsgemeinschaft*, DFG) and the Reich Research Council from 1920 to 1970.

This was especially true of Lieutenant Colonel Joseph Koeth, who from 1916 on directed the Department for War-Related Raw Materials in the Armed Forces Ministry, which always collaborated closely with Haber, and of Friedrich Schmidt-Ott, the responsible official in the Prussian Ministry of Science and one of the central state actors in the late Wilhelminian and Weimar organization of science.[9] If the idea was to support the institutions *processing* raw materials, the textile industry would have been the right strategic partner; but if the concentration was to be on the institutions *creating* raw materials, one had to choose among the cultivation sciences, breeding research, and the chemical raw materials industry. To untangle this complex situation, at least on the level of science organization, Koeth and Schmidt-Ott requested an expert opinion from KWS President Adolf von Harnack.

At the KWI for Physical Chemistry, Fritz Haber and his departmental director Reginald Oliver Herzog were already prepared for the new field of work. Haber had brought the Viennese chemist, who was pursuing an academic career in Karlsruhe, back to his institute when the war broke out, establishing a Department for Textile Research especially for him.[10]

A number of German states had already set up their own kinds of fiber materials institutes, which they hoped to expand using state funds.[11] Only two examples are mentioned here, namely, the German Research Institute for the Textile Industry in Karlsruhe and the Textile Technology Center of Dresden Technical University. However, it appears that the KWS had the better hand from the outset, thanks to its location near the Berlin government offices. After difficult turf battles, a solution emerged during 1918 based on Harnack's expert opinion that both a biochemical KWI in Berlin-Dahlem and a technological institute in Dresden would be founded, both of them directly responsible to a joint board of trustees.[12]

The separation into an institute for raw materials chemistry (Berlin) and an institute for textile technology (Dresden) ultimately meant an institute for "fundamental biochemical" matters[13] and one for "applied"[14] matters. The

---

[9] Both Koeth and Haber were members of the "German Society of 1914" (*Deutsche Gesellschaft 1914*). On this, and on the later role of Koeth, see Szöllösi-Janze, 307, 410–413; Ruth Sime, "Otto Hahn und die Max-Planck-Gesellschaft: zwischen Vergangenheit und Erinnerung," *Ergebnisse*, No. 14, (2004), 18.

[10] Szöllösi-Janze, 343f.; Adolf von Harnack (ed.), *Handbuch der Kaiser-Wilhelm-Gesellschaft zur Förderung der Wissenschaften* (Berlin: Hobbing, 1928), 53.

[11] A historical study summarizing the genesis of the association for the research on fiber materials technology in twentieth-century Germany is urgently needed.

[12] On Dresden, see Rolf Sonnemann et al., *Geschichte der Technischen Universität Dresden 1928–1988*, 2nd ed. (Berlin: Deutsche Verlag der Wissenschaften, 1988), 137; on Karlsruhe, see the letter from Ubbelohde to "Gluhn" [Glum], 25 October 1933, and attachments, Archives of the Max Planck Society, Berlin (*Archiv zur Geschichte der Max-Planck-Gesellschaft*), MPG-Archiv), Abt. I, Rep. 1A., Nr. 535/3, Bl. 50–56.

[13] Harnack quoted in Löser, "Gründungsgeschichte und Entwicklung," 285.

[14] Quoted in Löser, "Gründungsgeschichte und Entwicklung," 285.

idea that research on the chemical questions of raw and advanced materials processing was *basic research* and research concerned with technological questions was *applied research* was reinforced over the years, appearing again and again during the Nazi period as terminology used (and at the same time functionalized) in later discussions at the KWIBF.

The institution in Berlin, planned as a war institute, initially had to demonstrate its value in times of peace. Not until 1920 did the founding of the KWI for Textile Fiber Research under Director Herzog take place in the planned alliance with Dresden, along with the long list of other textile research institutions that had been pushed back into the second tier for funding. The groundwork for the institute's founding was laid by an application from the Reich Economic Office, once again under Koeth, which expressly called for "continuing to build on the experiences acquired in the war."[15]

Yet, both the cellulose and the textile industries were interested in results that could be utilized immediately. For this reason, the model they pursued – concentrating biochemical fiber research in Berlin and textile-technology research in Dresden, but also in associated institutes in Karlsruhe, Krefeld, Aachen, Mönchengladbach, Stuttgart-Reutlingen and Sorau/Brandenburg (today Żary, Poland) under the informal umbrella of the KWS – failed to meet expectations. After only five years, losses due to inflation and the death of the most important private donor resulted in the dissolution of the organization responsible for organizing the institute in 1925. Due to the lack of funds, it was forced to cede some of its facilities to the KWI for Silicate Research in 1926.[16]

Against this background, it is hardly surprising that the General Administration of the KWS was relieved to dissociate itself from this institute and its limited economic success after the National Socialists seized power, especially considering that its director, Herzog, was of Jewish origin.[17] Subsequent to a ruling by the Reich Ministry for Food and Agriculture (*Reichsministerium für Ernährung und Landwirtschaft*, RMEL) on 30 September 1933, with reference to the Law for the Restoration of the Professional Civil Service, Herzog retired effective 1 October 1933.[18]

During the following years, the KWS tried on several occasions to found a new institute. However, it was forced to recognize that because of the propagated "independence of raw materials" and the policy of autarky advocated by the Commissioner for German Raw and Advanced Materials,

---

[15] Koeth quoted in Löser, "Gründungsgeschichte und Entwicklung," 289; for Koeth, see *Reichshandbuch der Deutschen Gesellschaft* (Berlin: Deutsche Wirtschaftsverlag, 1930), 974.

[16] Plumpe, 313 ff.

[17] Letter from Glum and Telschow to the Reich Minister of the Interior (*Reichsminister des Innern*), 16 June 1933, MPG-Archiv, Abt. I, Rep. 1A, Nr. 535/3, Bl. 32–34.

[18] Letter from RE *Reichshandbuch der Deutschen Gesellschaft* M (on behalf of Stuckart) to KWS, 30 September 1933, MPG-Archiv, Abt. I, Rep. 1A, Nr. 535/3, Bl. 62.

Wilhelm Keppler, and the head of its textile division, Hans Kehrl, a fiercely contested "research market" had emerged.[19] For this reason, any attempt by Ernst Telschow, at the time still working under KWS Secretary General Friedrich Glum, to establish a new institute was doomed to failure. Around 1936, Telschow and the president of the Office for Materials Testing, with the support of a newly founded Working Committee for Textile Research, attempted to found a KWI for Cellulose Fiber Research. One of the reasons the project failed was that the parallel attempt to upgrade the Office for Materials Research into a Reich Office for Raw Materials was also unsuccessful.[20]

In early 1937, the prominent macro-molecular chemist Hans Staudinger attempted to found a KWI for Wood and Cellulose Research in Freiburg with an emphasis on rayon, and even his effort did not meet with success.[21] In June 1937, Glum ensured Staudinger that the KWS had "great interest" in its plans.[22] Yet, high-ranking experts argued that such an application-oriented institute "[could] obtain funds elsewhere" in the framework of the Four Year Plan.[23] In early 1938, Staudinger received a conclusively negative response from the KWS Senate, stating that the RWA planned to consolidate the Chemical Institute in Heidelberg under Karl Freudenberg and the two institutes under Georg Jayme and Walter Brecht at the Darmstadt Technical University into a Special Institute for Wood and Cellulose Research (later a Four-Year Plan institute).[24]

In late 1937, the chemist Kurt Hess, who directed a guest department financed by I.G. Farben at the KWI for Chemistry, made another unsuccessful attempt to realize a KWI for Wood and Cellulose Research.[25] The chairman of the Board at I.G. Farben, Carl Duisberg, supported Hess's department. Despite this backing, however, Hess was ultimately rejected

---

[19] Hans Kehrl, *Krisenmanager im Dritten Reich. 6 Jahre Frieden-6 Jahre Krieg. Erinnerungen* (Düsseldorf: Droste, 1973), 74–86; Rolf-Dieter Müller, *Der Manager der Kriegswirtschaft. Hans Kehrl. Ein Unternehmer in der Politik des Dritten Reiches* (Essen: Klartext-Verlag, 1999), 37–46.

[20] Various letters and file notes, for example, file note of 22 April 1936, MPG-Archiv, Abt. I, Rep. 1A, Nr. 2397.

[21] Letter from Staudinger to Planck, 4 March 1937, and supplemental manuscript "Die Gründung eines Kaiser Wilhelm-Instituts für Holz- und Cellulose-Forschung," MPG-Archiv, Abt. I, Rep. 1A, Nr. 967/1.

[22] Letter from Glum to Staudinger, 15 June 1937, MPG-Archiv, Abt. I, Rep. 1A, Nr. 967/4.

[23] Quote in letter from Debye (KWI for Physics) to Planck, 26 May 1937, MPG-Archiv, Abt. I, Rep. 1A, Nr. 967/4. In his assessment Debye emphasizes that he had coordinated his response to this issue with Hahn and von Wettstein.

[24] Letter from Telschow to Staudinger, 10 January 1938, MPG-Archiv, Abt. I, Rep. 1A, Nr. 967/5; on this, see Gottfried Jayme (ed.), *50 Jahre Cellulosechemie an der Technischen Hochschule Darmstadt 1908-1958* (Darmstadt: Institut für Cellulosechemie, 1958), 9–25.

[25] Quoted in Hermann Klare, *Geschichte der Chemiefaserforschung* (Berlin: Akademie-Verlag, 1985), 100f.

with the same argument used a few months later with Staudinger, that is, reference to the imminent expansion in Heidelberg/Darmstadt.[26]

Glum was therefore unable to open up this promising research market of the future for the KWS. Telschow was subsequently successful due to his double capacity as KWS Secretary General and RWA Liaison and Director of Research. He recognized that the research market for (semi-)synthetic fibers was full, saw that duplicated labor must be avoided, and thus shifted his focus to natural fibers and breeding research, an area the KWS had great hopes for in the 1930s.

BAST FIBER RESEARCH

The Austrian plant physiologist Julius Wiesner wrote the first comprehensive work on the value of natural fibers for the processing industry. In 1873, he published his sensational volume *The Raw Materials of the Plant Kingdom* (*Die Rohstoffe des Pflanzenreiches*), based on microscopic analysis, which remains the standard work on industrial plant materials even today.[27] The institutional implementation of Wiesner's proposals was left up to the Association of German Linen Manufacturers, founded in 1877. In 1916, the Association founded the nonprofit Research Station of the Association of German Institutions for Bast Fiber, Retting and Processing in the middle of the flax-producing region of Brandenburg. The driving forces behind this undertaking were Curt Oesterhelt, later to become the station's managing director, and Georg Müller, industrialist and board member of the Reich Association of German Manufacturers (*Reichsverband Deutscher Industrieller*, RDI). The research station was accommodated in a textile school that had been run by the city of Sorau since 1886; its purpose in the framework of the Department for War-Related Raw Materials was to optimize the provisioning of the army with textiles – above all, with articles made of linen.[28]

The botanist and flax specialist Ernst Carl Magnus Schilling, who had been a department chief at the institute since 1920, was appointed director in 1930. Immediately thereafter the Bast Fiber Institute received a modern new building next to the textile school. Schilling left his mark on the

[26] Letter from Telschow to Hess, 25 November 1937, MPG-Archiv, Abt. I, Rep. 1A, Nr. 1146.
[27] On the explanation of technical raw materials theory by Wiesner, see Günther Luxbacher, "Die technologische Mobilisierung der Botanik. Konzept und Wirkung der Technischen Rohstofflehre und Warenkunde im 19. Jahrhundert," *Technikgeschichte*, 68, No. 4 (2001), 307–333.
[28] Charter of the nonprofit German Research Institute for Bast Fibers (*Satzung des Deutschen Forschungs-Institutes für Bastfasern e.V.*) of 1 July 1932; quoted in *50 Jahre Preussische Höhere Fachschule für Textilindustrie* (Sorau: Forschungsinstitut Sorau, 1936), 10; quoted in Curt Oesterhelt, "Erinnerungen an Georg Miller Oerlinghausen," unpublished manuscript, Gert Müller Collection, Oerlinghausen, 19.

institute like no other director in its long history, and his influence extended until its final closure in 1957. Schilling, born in 1889, earned his doctorate under his predecessor Friedrich Tobler and the subsequent director of the KWI for Biology, Karl Correns. Tobler was probably the most prominent propagandist in Germany for using substitute materials in the area of textile fibers.[29] Schilling was one of the first volunteers for the war in 1914 but emerged from it as an invalid to become the director of the breeding department in Sorau in 1920. Like most botanists, he saw himself in the tradition of Julius Wiesner.[30]

Before 1933, work oriented toward the autarky of the German textile economy played no role at the institute. This changed in 1933/34, when official government offices declared their main objective to be "the provision of the entire German cultivation area with German-bred seed,"[31] and in 1934, when the "Fabric Law" (*Spinnstoffgesetz*) took effect, laying the foundation for the Nazi policy of autarky. Ever larger portions of the budget of the KWIBF were borne by the RMEL, until State Secretary Herbert Backe announced in 1937 that the institute would be assimilated into the circle of KWIs, an event that took place on 1 April 1938.[32] Although it was restricted to domestic plant fibers, or perhaps because of this fact, the institute was expanded to become the largest textile research institute in Germany.[33]

The Bast Fiber Institute was conceived as a central research institute, which thus necessarily involved fields ranging from breeding research, biochemistry, chemical technology, and mechanical technology all the way to research on laundry and extending the useful life of materials.[34] The breeding department was taken over by the director, Dr. Ernst Schilling; the fiber production department by Dr. Max Lüdtke; the spinning department by the engineer Waldemar Rohs (deputy institute director); the weaving department by the engineer Georg Scheithauer; the chemistry department by Dr. Walter Kind; the fiber product conservation department also by Kind;

[29] Friedrich Tobler, *Textilersatzstoffe* (Dresden: Globus, 1917); Friedrich Tobler, *Deutsche Faserpflanzen und Pflanzenfasern* (Munich: Lehmann, 1938).

[30] Ernst Schilling, *Die Faserstoffe des Pflanzenreiches* (Leipzig: Hirzel, 1924).

[31] Quoted in *Geschäftsbericht der Deutschen Flachsbau GmbH* (1934/35), 3.

[32] Quoted in Niederschrift Senatssitzung KWS, 4 November 1937, 11, MPG-Archiv, Abt. I, Rep.1A; Niederschrift Verwaltungsratssitzung Dt. Forschungsinstitutes für Bastfaserforschung, 8 February 1939, MPG-Archiv, Abt. I, Rep. 1A, 2200/3; Vermerk über Mitgliederversammlung des Dt. Forschungsinstitutes für Bastfaserforschung e.V., 1 March 1939, MPG-Archiv, Abt. I, Rep. 1A, Nr. 2200/3, Bl. 2.

[33] Wilhelm Rudorf, "Max-Planck-Institut für Züchtungsforschung," *Jahrbuch der Max-Planck-Gesellschaft* (1961), 848; Niederschrift Senatssitzung KWS 30.5.1938, 7, MPG-Archiv, Abt. I, Rep. 1A; on the research office and its size, see Walczyk and Werzmirzowsky, "Das Kaiser-Wilhelm-Institut für Bastfaserforschung," *Deutsche Textilwirtschaft*, No. 1 (1941), 6.

[34] Letter from Telschow to Schilling, 28 May 1938, MPG-Archiv, Abt. II, P. A. Ernst Schilling, vol. 1.

and the material testing department also by Scheithauer.[35] The institute was sustained by an eighteen-member board of trustees, including high-ranking representatives of the KWS (among them Wilhelm Rudorf of the KWI for Breeding Research), the RMEL, the REM, the RWM, the RWA, the "Reich Food Estate" (*Reichsnährstand*, RNS), the German Labor Front (*Deutsche Arbeitsfront*, DAF), and the Reich Textile Foundation, along with a number of industrialists and military officers. The ten members of the Scientific-Technical Council included the prominent Peter Adolf Thiessen of the KWI for Physical Chemistry as well as several military officers.[36]

Telschow, as both the KWS Secretary General and an RWA liaison and director of that body's research department, was very interested in taking over the institute.[37] Conceived for a staff of ten to twelve in the early 1930s, the institute was now slated for expansion to dimensions that practically dwarfed its location in Sorau. After the occupation of Czechoslovakia, the RMEL saw a chance to enlarge the KWIBF, since it had just secured a test estate with 150 hectares in the middle of the flax-growing region of Mährisch-Schönberg (Šumperk, Moravia). A large new complex was to be built there, funded by the RMEL, the RWM, and industry, whose staff of 150 did in fact make the KWIBF the largest textile research institute in the Third Reich.[38] Yet, the institute did not manage to complete the move from Sorau to Mährisch-Schönberg before the war ended.

THE KAISER WILHELM INSTITUTE FOR BAST
FIBER RESEARCH AND ITS CONTRACT RESEARCH FOR
THE WAR ECONOMY

Ernst Schilling and several members of his staff were integrated from the outset into a Research Alliance for the War Economy, which had been initiated by Carl Krauch, who was the de facto I.G. Farben Chairman of the Board, director of the RWA, and General Plenipotentiary for Chemical Production.[39] When Krauch chaired the first workshop of the Working

---

[35] Organization chart KWIBF, MPG-Archiv, Abt. I, Rep. 1A, Nr. 2211/4, Bl. 38 ff.

[36] For details, see Luxbacher, "Roh- und Werkstoffe," 32 ff.

[37] Letter from Telschow to Bosch, 21 March 1938, MPG-Archiv, Abt. III, Rep. 83, 31.

[38] Niederschrift Senatssitzung 4.4.1939, 9, MPG-Archiv, Abt. I, Rep. 1A; Niederschrift Senatssitzung KWS 23.5.1939, 5 f., MPG-Archiv, Abt. I, Rep. 1A; Telschow intercede personally with Todt to obtain a building permit. On this, see Schilling to *Generalverwaltung*, 25 May 1940, MPG-Archiv, Abt. I, Rep. 1A, Nr. 2202/3, Bl. 25 and 48 ff.; Rudorf, 848.

[39] On this in general, see Karl-Heinz Ludwig, *Technik und Ingenieure im Dritten Reich* (Düsseldorf: Droste, 1974), 224 f.; although Karl Krauch succeeded Carl Bosch as chairman of the Board of Directors of I.G. Farben, it was decided that for reasons of politics and economic strategy, he would hold this office in abeyance for the duration of the war. Even so, Krauch, in his simultaneous capacity as a state official at the RWA, had access to information that he could exploit to his advantage at I.G. Farben, and vice versa. Even Petzina recognized

Group on Textile Fibers on 28 June 1940, Ernst Schilling was one of the invited representatives of his institute.

Other institute staff members were also integrated into the far-reaching Raw Materials Innovation System. Max Lüdtke, for example, was on the staff of Krauch's Working Group on Cellulose.[40] Moreover, he and his colleague Scheithauer also worked under Krauch in the Working Group on Textile Fibers. At the same time, Scheithauer was on the staff of the RWA, which was also represented in this working group by the director of the organization's textile department, O. Eisenhuth. This last group also included Telschow and his assistant Walter Forstmann; Thiessen of the KWI for Physical Chemistry; Walther Schieber, the later privy counselor and chairman of the board of directors of Thüringische Zellwolle AG; Fritz Gajewski, director of the Fibers Department of I.G. Farben; and the chemists Hess and Jayme, mentioned earlier.[41]

In a confidential activity report in 1941, Schilling pointed out the war's impulse in stimulating research as well as the importance of basic research – which he oversimplified by defining as breeding research, behind which applied research had to take a back seat: "By its very nature, the situation the war has created in the area of fibrous materials also had far-reaching effects on our institute. Our projects on flax, hemp and other fibers received a powerful impetus, from cultivation all the way to consumer research .... We are pleased that we were able to make a number of contributions to strengthening the German defense economy. At the same time scientific research remains the actual mission of our institute." As early as September 1939, the institute was declared to be a "supply station of the first order" and worked on contracts in the area of fabrics not only for the RWA and the RMEL but also for the OKW.[42] On the one hand, this secured its financing; on the other, portraying the institute's work as militarily relevant became ever more important.

Since Schilling's highest priority was breeding research, he attempted to steer as much money and interest as possible toward "his" field. But he could pursue these long-term research interests only as long as they were not too constrained by the generally short-term interest in the defense economy

that over the course of its existence, the Four-Year Plan increasingly became "practically an 'IG Plan.'" On this, see Peter Hayes, *Industry and Ideology. IG Farben in the Nazi Era* (Cambridge: Cambridge University Press, 1987), 337, and Dieter Petzina, *Autarkiepolitik im Dritten Reich. Der nationalsozialistische Vierjahresplan* (Stuttgart: Deutsche Verlagsanstalt, 1968). Quote on 123.

[40] *Chemische Berichte. Arbeitsgemeinschaft Zellstoff* (Berlin: Reichsamt für Wirtschaftsausbau, November 1941), 6.
[41] *Chemische Berichte. Arbeitsgemeinschaft Textilfasern* (Berlin: Reichsamt für Wirtschaftsausbau, 1940), 5 ff.
[42] Letter from Telschow, 29 August 1939; letter from OKW to Schilling, 23 September 1939, MPG-Archiv, Abt. I, Rep. 1A, Nr. 2201/4.

pursued by the given contractor.[43] He did his best to promote his case by emphasizing the importance of "basic research" for the war. In so doing, he again implied tacitly that basic research on natural fibers was restricted to work located at the beginning of the extremely long production and utilization chain in the area of fiber materials. Thus, according to the definition of the institute director, who was at the same time departmental director, only the creation of a specific raw material could be designated as basic research, not the study of its processing and utilization. In this way, Schilling denied that there could be anything like basic research at the departments for the mechanical and chemical technology of fabrics, which were actually on an equal footing within his institute.

His pattern of argumentation is reminiscent of that during the founding phase of the KWI for Textile Fiber Research. At that time, the strategy was to claim that basic research on textiles was biochemical research on the pulping of cellulose rather than genetic research on fiber plants. In this way, the basic research studies located further down the research chain were implicitly devalued, including any work of a chemical or mechanical-technological nature, and thus the functional concept of "basic research" was shaped toward his understanding.

After all, the leading personalities of the elitist KWS did not view technical scientific research as their main task. That kind of work, so ran the assumption, was the domain of the industrial institutes, the army testing stations, the technical universities; true scientists did not have to dirty their hands with such tasks. At least for the concerns of his institute, Schilling thus consistently employed the concept of basic research as a synonym for his breeding projects; he argued that all other departments (which, strictly speaking, did not belong in the KWS properly at all, according to his conception) performed applied research.[44] Yet, the more heavily state pressure came to bear on industry from 1943 on, and the further the "Final Victory" slipped from Germany's grasp, the less promising his protracted projects on breeding research must have seemed, since they yielded no more than one to two harvests a year.

Nevertheless, the powerful RWA preferred to sponsor technical science projects.[45] In 1939/40, the total worth of its contracts to the KWIBF amounted to around 130,000 Reichsmarks. The institute sought an optimized process

---

[43] See Helmut Maier, "'Wehrhaftmachung' und 'Kriegswichtigkeit': zur rüstungstechnologischen Relevanz des Kaiser-Wilhelm-Institutes für Metallforschung in Stuttgart vor und nach 1945," *Ergebnisse*, No. 5, 2002), 22–27.

[44] Vertraulicher Tätigkeitsbericht 1.4.1938–31.3.1941, MPG-Archiv, Abt. I, Rep. 1A, Nr. 2206/3.

[45] At a meeting in Sorau in 1940 it was remarked that the RWA was the driving force in turning the KWIBF into a Central Research Institute for the Area of Bast Fiber; see Tätigkeitsbericht 18. Geschäftsjahr, 1.4.1937–31.3.1938, MPG-Archiv, Abt. I, Rep. 1A, Nr. 2204/3, Bl. 2.

for impregnating sailcloth, a material needed for the navy, truck tarpaulins, tents, assembly and conveyor belts, and perhaps even for airplane wings. The chemical department worked on contracts for dyeing the green flax standard army colors (sulfuric black, indanthrene field gray, and naphthol dyes).[46] In 1940 the KWIBF received a research contract for the extraction of bast fibers from wild nettles or corn bract (substitute fibers for flax and jute).[47] Further contracts concerned experiments to prepare ramie and nettle stalks.[48] The institute also took on research contracts that were not exclusively concerned with bast fibers. The background for this was not the duplication of labor but rather the fact that cotton or cellulose was generally added to bast fibers (and vice versa) to stretch scarce stocks.[49] From 30 September 1944, the RLM financed a project on refueling aircraft entitled Experiments on Hoses; the president of the Reich Research Council supported a project called Bast Fiber Short Fiber Spinning starting on 15 July 1943.[50]

Schilling headed up around a dozen research projects for the RFR on chemical investigations of linseed and flax: (1) determining how far the useful life of textiles could be extended through utility research and recycling, and (2) "decisive for the war" (*kriegsentscheidend*) projects on rationalizing the spinning process.[51] The research on extending the life of materials also included washing and wearing experiments on selected textiles. Thus the annual report for 1937/38 described tests performed for the RWA in which garments made of cellulose were distributed to 400 test wearers, along with washing instructions, to obtain findings for the construction of a machine that would simulate actual wear and tear.[52] In 1944, the institute ordered "extensive wearing tests" on drill made of various linseed yarns.[53] Laundry

[46] Sitzung des Technisch-Wissenschaftlichen Beirats in Sorau am 15.11.1939, MPG-Archiv, Abt. I, Rep. 1A , Nr. 2210/3.

[47] Letter from Schilling to *Generalverwaltung*, 24 October 1940, MPG-Archiv, Abt. I, Rep. 1A, Nr. 2203/6 fol. Bl. 127; Schilling to *Generalverwaltung*, January 1941, MPG-Archiv, Abt. I, Rep. 1A, Nr. 2205/1, Bl. 159.

[48] Letter from Scheithauer to Forstmann, 26 July 1941, MPG-Archiv, Abt. I, Rep 1A, Nr. 2205/6; letter to *Generalverwaltung*, 9 December 1942, MPG-Archiv, Abt. I, Rep. 1A, Nr. 2207/1; letter from Forstmann to RWA, 10 October 1941, MPG-Archiv, Abt. I, Rep. 1A, Nr. 2206/1; letter from Scheithauer to *Generalverwaltung*, 22 January 1942, MPG-Archiv, Abt. I, Rep. 1A, Nr. 2206/4

[49] Finishing process in accordance with Schubert.

[50] *Versuche an Schläuchen* and *Bastfaser-Kurzfaserspinnerei*; list of "Forschungsaufträge des KWIBF" (no date, presumably late 1944/45), MPG-Archiv, Abt. I, Rep. 1A, Nr. 2207/6.

[51] Federal German Archives (*Bundesarchiv*, BArch), R 73, 14292; 14293; BArch, R 26, III. No. 8; BArch, R 26, III, No. 16, No. 18; BArch, R 26, III, No. 6, No. 16.

[52] Tätigkeitsbericht KWIBF über das 18. Geschäftsjahr, 1.4.1937–31.3.1938, p. 26, MPG-Archiv, Abt. I, Rep. 1A, Nr. 2204/3.

[53] Vertraulicher Tätigkeitsbericht KWIBF über 6. (24.) Geschäftsjahr, 1.4.1943–31.3.1944, BArch, R 10 I/99, 24.

experiments were performed on extending the life of materials, starting in 1943/44 with an emphasis on removing bloodstains from textiles.[54]

By April 1942, the OKW had renewed a first "S" contract (medium degree of urgency) for the KWIBF, one in the form of a "general research contract" for all areas of work. With this the institute continued to be a permanent supplier of war-crucial information regarding the demand for fabric to equip the army. From the available sources it can be inferred that this enduring collaborative relationship had been extended far beyond the period of the report (April 1, 1942–March 31, 1943).[55] As further evidence of the continuing relationship, the OKW was mentioned as an important contractor repeatedly from 1942 until 1945. A total of seven concrete research contracts were brought to the institute from external contractors during this period.[56]

FIRST CONFLICTS OVER OBJECTIVES

Telschow and Schilling pursued similar research strategies, placing their emphasis on breeding research. Telschow did this for institutional reasons, Schilling out of scientific interest. Telschow calculated that the breeding research competence of the KWS would continue to expand in the course of the bast fiber boom, oriented as it was toward economic autarky. He recognized that the demand was so great that the KWS would be able to set up a second, more or less fully fledged breeding research institute in Mährisch-Schönberg, and moreover, one that would receive permanent funding. Thus, for Schilling to equate basic research with breeding research came in very handy for Telschow. Yet, in contrast to the KWS Secretary General, Schilling was hardly assertive or skilled at strategic argumentation and weak in building personnel and institutional networks. Conflicts on the institutional level were therefore inevitable and were already becoming clearly visible by 1940.

Beginning in 1940, the bast fiber industry, represented on the Board of Trustees of the KWIBF, saw endangerment for the "nexus" between breeding research and technology extending the useful life of material. In his capacity as representative of the bast fiber industry, Karlgustav Hartung, managing director of the Sector Group for Bast Fiber Processing in the Reich Association of Bast Fibers (*Reichsvereinigung Bastfaser*, RVB), feared that

---

[54] Vertraulicher Tätigkeitsbericht KWIBF über 6. (24.) Geschäftsjahr, 1.4.1943–31.3.1944, BArch, R 10 I/99, quote on 30.
[55] Vertraulicher Tätigkeitsbericht KWIBF 1.4.1942–31.3.1943, June 1943, 1–5, MPG-Archiv, Abt. I, Rep. 1A, Nr. 2210/7; Besprechungsvermerk Forstmann vom 28.9.1942, MPG-Archiv, Abt. I, Rep. 1A, Nr. 2212/4.
[56] Forschungsaufträge des KWIBF (no date, presumably late 1944), MPG-Archiv, Abt. I, Rep. 1A, Nr. 2207/6.

this research chain was in danger of degenerating. To solve this problem, representatives of the industry proposed a meeting in Mährisch-Schönberg, together with Schilling. According to the ideas of the bast fiber industry, the missing nexus was supposed to be restored by making the department head Lüdtke its own scientific consultant. Forstmann and Telschow rejected this proposal, pointing out the institute's obligations to perform general scientific work.[57]

At the subsequent meeting in Sorau, Helmke, director of Gräben Flax Works, who was simultaneously chairman of the Sector Group for Bast Fiber Processing, attempted another foray in this direction. Since it was clear, he argued, that new, large-scale machine assemblies would have to be tested by KWIBF staff and that these could not be mounted in Mährisch-Schönberg for the time being, at least one delegate should be authorized for this task.[58]

Other representatives of the industry also found the personnel and the work of the institute wanting and even threatened to discontinue their payments if no compromise solution could be found.[59] Hartung, who apparently had advanced to become a sort of speaker for all of the industry's interests in matters concerning the institute, declared that if at least one of the many smoldering conflicts could be resolved, the bast fiber industry would provide an additional sum to erect the chemical-technical facility planned for the expanded institute in Mährisch-Schönberg. It was also conceivable, he continued, that the KWIBF might receive additional research funding from the Sector Group, as did the research institutes in Reutlingen (Technical School for the Textile Industry) and Dresden (Textile Institute at Dresden Technical University). The Sector Group for Bast Fiber Processing also wanted to join the KWS as a legal entity – another indication of the industry's fear that it would not be able to exert enough influence on the bodies steering the course of the KWIBF.[60] In general, the strategy of the textile industry representatives was to purchase influence so that it would enjoy a larger voice in formulating the institute's research objectives.

A further measure to secure the "nexus" between industry and the KWIBF was the application by the Sector Group for Bast Fiber Processing to set up

[57] Aktenvermerk Forstmann, 17/10/1940, MPG-Archiv, Abt. I, Rep. 1A, Nr. 2203/5, Bl. 122 ff.; Obviously the metal industry is a parallel case of a missing nexus between basic and applied research. See Günther Luxbacher, "Wertarbeit mit Ersatzstoffen? Ausstellungen als Bühne deutscher Werkstoffpolitik 1916 bis 1942," *Dresdner Beiträge zur Geschichte der Technikwissenschaften* (2006), 3–24.
[58] Aktenvermerk Forstmann, 16 November 1940; Sitzung Fachuntergruppe Bastfaseraufbereitung 6.11.1940, both in MPG-Archiv, Abt. I, Rep. 1A, Nr. 2204/1, Bl. 2–10.
[59] Aktenvermerk Forstmann, 17 October 1940, MPG-Archiv, Abt. I, Rep. 1A, Nr. 2203/5, Bl. 122 ff.
[60] Aktenvermerk Forstmann, 17 October 1940, MPG-Archiv, Abt. I, Rep. 1A, Nr. 2203/5, Bl. 122 ff.

experimental retting equipment in Mährisch-Schönberg at a total estimated cost of 350,000 Reichsmarks. The Sector Group urged that the 125,000 Reichsmarks it contributed to the total project in Mährisch-Schönberg (2.2 million Reichsmarks for construction costs, 700,000 of which was raised by industry) should furnish a new experimental retting system of this type. Furthermore, their offer continued, they would finance a scientific assistant for Lüdtke. However, at the same time the Sector Group hoped it would be able to procure from the Bast Fiber Institute in Sorau the old experimental retting system located nearby in Christianstadt am Bober, at a book value of 100,000 Reichsmarks.

The Sector Group for Weaving Mills tendered a similar offer. It held out the prospect of 150,000 Reichsmarks as its contribution for a new weaving factory in Mährisch-Schönberg, which the General Administration accepted.[61] Such tempting financial support did not fail to have the desired effect on the General Administration, no less than did threats from those staff members at the KWIBF who were associated with the industry. Scheithauer and his assistant Kling, for instance, who were both also on the staff at the RWA, threatened to leave the institute because they had been offered more lucrative positions. Just as the debate about additional funding came to a head (and, naturally, at a strategically advantageous time for Hartung and Helmke), Scheithauer received an offer to take over the laboratory of a cellulose factory run by Phrix AG. It was probably no coincidence that at the same time Kling received an offer from I.G. Farben to head up its fiber pulping laboratory.[62]

These offers must be viewed against the backdrop of the new Research Group on Textile Fibers founded by Carl Krauch. In addition to Institute Director Schilling, Scheithauer was also invited to the first annual conference of this organization on 28 June 1940. By this time Scheithauer was already exercising his dual function, which reflected the institute's structural problems. While the unprinted list of participants still registers Scheithauer as the representative of the KWIBF,[63] in the printed version he suddenly appeared exclusively in his capacity as representative of the RWA.[64]

Although Schilling was still the superior of department head Scheithauer, this formal hierarchy only counted within the KWS. In almost any external

[61] Aktenvermerk Forstmann, 16 November 1940; Sitzung FU Bastfaseraufbereitung, 6 November 1940, both in MPG-Archiv, Abt. I, Rep. 1A, Nr. 2204/1, Bl. 2–10.
[62] Letter from Forstmann to Telschow, 16 October 1941, MPG-Archiv, Abt. I, Rep. 1A, Nr. 2212/1.
[63] Teilnehmer an der Arbeitsgemeinschaft "Textilfasern," 28 June 1940, MPG-Archiv, Abt. I, Rep. 1A, Nr. 2002/4.
[64] RWA, Arbeitsgemeinschaft Textilfasern, 4; in the RWA's schedule of responsibilities of 1941, Scheithauer appears in Abt II Text as an unsalaried staff member under Eisenhut's direction in Dez. II Text 3 "Extraction and Processing of Natural Fibers." On this, see Geschäftsverteilungsplan vom 15.5.1941, 18, MPG-Archiv, Abt. I, Rep. 1A, Nr. 229.

relations cultivated by the institute, Scheithauer had an advantage over Schilling because the two men found themselves in a different, informal and parallel hierarchy. One of these parallel hierarchies was the informal network of the subgroups of the RVB; the other consisted in its somewhat more formal integration into the RWA, where Scheithauer had become an officially registered honorary staff member in 1941 at the latest, but presumably long before. Schilling, in contrast, could rely only on Telschow and Fritz Lorenz, the textile industrialist he had known for a long time, who also occupied positions of leadership in the RWA, although not in "Textile Department II," the section responsible for textile issues.

For these reasons, it is necessary to reevaluate the various positions of power the institute staff enjoyed through their membership in the "hybrid communities" (*Hybridgemeinschaften,* as Helmut Maier has called them), newly created lateral associations like the chemical working groups founded by Krauch. Thus in late 1940, the General Administration was forced to take the interests of the processing industries into closer consideration than it originally might have planned. Both Kling and Scheithauer were induced to stay by the offer of salary increases, thus preserving its "central institute" character.[65]

Around 1941, a general understanding of the necessity of collaboration apparently emerged, especially since other German research stations in Stuttgart and Dresden had begun to take an interest in bast fibers. In November 1940, a resolution was passed that, beginning in 1941, Schilling alone would take over the technical editorship of *Die Bastfaser* ("The Bast Fibers"), the most important trade journal, a manifest sign of harmony.[66] Yet, this did not last long, for industry soon set out in its own directions. Parallel to establishing the KWIBF, the managing director of the RVB and Ostfaser GmbH, Czaya, and several subgroups of the RVB, in consultation with Kehrl and Hans Croon, head of the Economic Group for the Textile Industry, established a professorship for bast fiber machine construction at the Technical University in Breslau "in extension of the Kaiser Wilhelm Institute for Bast Fiber Research."[67] At the same time, Phrix AG, which had made a name for itself with successes such as the invention of "cell jute," a substitute fiber for jute, provided 4 to 5 million Reichsmarks to establish a new Institute for Fabric Chemistry at the Breslau Technical University.[68]

[65] Geschäftsverteilungsplan RWA vom 15.5.1941, 19, BA Berlin R 3112/324; note to Telschow, 16 October 1941, MPG-Archiv, Abt. I, Rep. 1A, Nr. 229, Bl. 2212/1.
[66] File note by Forstmann, 16 November 1940, Sitzung Fachuntergruppe Bastfaseraufbereitung, 6 November 1940, MPG-Archiv, Abt. I, Rep. 1A, Nr. 229, 2204/1. This was a supplement to *Der Leinenindustrielle* ("The Linen Industrialist"), edited by Curt Oesterhelt.
[67] Copy of a letter of 23 July 1941, MPG-Archiv, Abt. I, Rep. 1A, Nr. 2205/6.
[68] File note by Scheithauer for Forstmann, MPG-Archiv, Abt. I, Rep. 1A, Nr. 2206/7.

There was also discontent in the Subgroup for the Jute and Hard Masonite Industry. At the third meeting of the Technical-Scientific Council in January 1942 in Sorau, criticism of Schilling became loud. In the name of the director of the local Subgroup for the Bast Fiber Industry, which had contributed 270,000 Reichsmarks to the institute, Oesterhelt threatened to demand the reimbursement of this amount unless the emphasis of the institute's work changed toward industrial research. He directed his displeasure at the journal edited by Schilling, which, according to Oesterhelt, was long-winded and not up-to-date; he denounced the journal's strong emphasis on biological and breeding topics and the lack of attention to topics of industrial research. The Berlin textile manufacturer Gustav Winkler supported Oesterhelt by pointing out that cooperation functioned better between the cotton industry and the Stuttgart-Reuttlingen Technical School, where cottonized bast fiber was another topic of study. Schilling's response was fairly awkward, stating that such projects on cultivation and breeding were also important, and that it was not always possible to offer something for industry.[69]

At this juncture, Fritz Lorenz came to the aid of Schilling and his lack of argumentation skills, countering Winkler and Oesterhelt by indicating that work on hemp issues was indeed of use for the jute and hard masonite industry. He further offered Oesterhelt an additional seat on the scientific-technical council, which he was glad to accept. Thus, Lorenz fended off the conflict temporarily, but Schilling was weakened, as he was not the one who had tendered the compromise.[70] However, the KWS had one advantage that it could wield in the struggle with the associations over the orientation of the institute's work: the imminent sale of the retting facility in Christianstadt near Sorau.[71] That the purchase price of this object still had not been settled after years of negotiations is indicative of the vehemence of the deteriorating conflict.[72]

Also critical of Schilling and of the KWIBF's orientation was one who actually should have been closer to Schilling: the representative of the Reich Food Estate in the Scientific-Technical Committee, Agricultural Advisor and Reich Farmer Leader Koch, who was responsible for research and testing on

[69] See, for instance, Otto Johannsen, "Verarbeitung des Flockenbastes," *Mitteilungen des Deutschen Forschungsinstitutes für Textilindustrie in Reuttlingen-Stuttgart* (July 1940), 1–34.

[70] Niederschrift 3. Sitzung des Technisch-Wissenschaftlichen Beirates 23 January 1942, MPG-Archiv, Abt. I, Rep. 1A, Nr. 2210/5; for Winkler, see Rudolf Vierhaus and Bernhard vom Brocke (eds.), *Forschung im Spannungsfeld von Politik und Gesellschaft. Geschichte und Struktur der Kaiser-Wilhelm-/Max-Planck-Gesellschaft aus Anlass ihres 75jährigen Bestehens* (Stuttgart: DVA, 1990), 57.

[71] Czaya (Reichsvereinigung für Bastfasern) to Schuster (REM) and Telschow, 7 September 1939, MPG-Archiv, Abt. I, Rep. 1A, Nr. 2211/2, Bl. 19–19a.

[72] The dispute began in 1939 and apparently dragged on until the end of the war. See the annotation by Forstmann, 18 November 1939, MPG-Archiv, Abt. I, Rep. 1A, Nr. 2211/2, Bl. 20.

flax and hemp by the state farming associations. He addressed what must
have been the most delicate aspects of breeding research in the advanced
phase of the war, expressing his skepticism that Schilling would be able to
conduct the planned projects at all and admonishing him to concentrate on
short-term projects important for the war. From the perspective of the Reich
Food Estate, he advocated that Schilling conduct more urgent work, with
a focus on breeding substitute fibers and flax for eastern Europe. In this
context, Koch came out in favor of assessing militarily conquered genetic
resources as quickly as possible, with research in progress relegated to a
lower priority.

Thus Schilling's ambitious research program was put into question not
only by industry but also by a representative of the agricultural sciences.
Koch advised concentrating on oil flaxes from the Kujavia region (northern
Poland), which, according to Koch, also provides a good cottonized bast
fiber. Also important, he continued, was exploring flax from the district of
Zichenau (before 1939 and after 1945: Ciechanów) and Białystock, concentrating on flaxes for eastern Prussia, and studying substitute fibers like
yucca and cotine, and fibers from herbaceous perennials.[73] In accordance
with these ideas, in 1943 Koch – in his capacity as staff member of the
Reich Food Estate – had the state farming association of Saxony-Anhalt perform extensive cultivation experiments with varieties from the Soviet Union.
Koch's great hopes in these experiments were disappointed.[74]

Schilling agreed with some of Koch's suggestions but remained skeptical.[75]
However, he did not pass up the opportunity to get a firsthand impression
of the situation in the occupied parts of the Soviet Union. In mid-March,
Schilling and his assistant Wanjura traveled around Latvia and Russia for
several weeks.[76] Schilling's trip to the Soviet Union was not his first to the
occupied territories, however. Right after the annexation of the classic flax
country of Belgium he had sat in an office on the premises of the Belgian
Flax Association, along with Oberländer, the Special Commissioner of the
Textile Department of the Military Commander in Belgium and northern
France.[77] Yet, the experiments Schilling performed in 1943, using fiber

[73] Niederschrift 3. Sitzung des Technisch-Wissenschaftlichen Beirates, 23 January 1942, MPG-
Archiv, Abt. I, Rep. 1A, Nr. 2210/5.
[74] Circular from Reichsbauernführer to Landesbauernschaften, 18 February 1943, BArch R
10 I/5; unfortunately these sources do not include information as to whether the KWIBF
attended to these experiments.
[75] Schilling wanted to keep an eye on the area only because of systematic botanical interests;
see Schilling to RWA: "Erforschung der zusätzlichen Faserpflanzen," 5 August 1940, MPG-
Archiv, Abt. I, Rep. 1A, Nr. 2203/2, Bl. 80a.
[76] Letter from Schilling to Forstmann, 2 March 1943; Schilling to Forstmann, 10 March 1943,
both in MPG-Archiv, Abt. I, Rep. 1A, Nr. 2207/2.
[77] On the cooperation between Oberländer and Schilling ("Shilling") in Belgium, see Andre
Verhenne, 65 jaar Belgisch Vlasverbond Kortrijk 1920/1985, Allgemeen Belgisch Vlasverbond

sources that the institute had annexed into its collection from the Baltics and northwestern Russia, Spain, Portugal, and the occupied areas of Poland (General Government), remained largely unsuccessful.[78]

Schilling wanted to breed his own varieties of flax and hemp. He tried to assert his special research interests repeatedly by pointing out that the reduction in personnel due to military conscription made it impossible to place the requisite emphasis on analyzing eastern European resources. The argument was a rather unfortunate one, however, as Schilling's institute had lost relatively few staff to conscription. And this time, Lorenz did not come to his aid. On the contrary, he took the same line as Koch, pointing out the necessity to fortify a concentration on the "Eastern tasks" and admonishing that possibilities for cultivating hemp on mineral soils must be investigated "once new cultivation areas are created in the East."[79] Since Lorenz, too, now wanted to see breeding research projects oriented especially to Eastern expansion, Schilling's breeding plans were forced on the defensive. In the context of a future meeting, Koch reinforced his demand even further. He insisted that the institute concentrate its work even more intensively on the practical demands of the war, declaring that the institute must "not perform basic research alone." Schilling and Lorenz, rallied by this statement into a unified defense of the spirit of the KWS, responded that basic research must be performed as well, although during the war "the projects important for the practical demands of the war" had to predominate. [80]

Although Schilling was attacked from all sides for being too little oriented toward practice and applied research, he regarded his own work as more than basic research. He believed his projects were also essential for the war; indeed, they constituted war-essential applied research but happened to concern the area of genetics and breeding. This could be deduced clearly from the content and guiding principles of his work. His main problem consisted in the simple fact that verifiable results – new, more fertile seeds – took years to mature[81] because experimental work with subsequent generations and varieties was simply inextricably bound to seasonal cycles. The construction

Krotrijk (1985), 120; on the Netherlands, see Ernst Schilling, "Weissblühender Flachs in den Niederlanden," *Die Bastfaser* (1941), 58–61.

[78] Vertraulicher Tätigkeitsbericht KWIBF über das 6. (24.) Geschäftsjahr, 1 April 1943–31 March 1944, Schonberg Moravia, BArch, R 10 I/99, 8.

[79] Niederschrift 3. Sitzung des Technisch-Wissenschaftlichen Beirates, 23.1.1942, MPG-Archiv Archive, Abt. I, Rep. 1A, Nr. 2210/5.

[80] Niederschrift 4. Sitzung des Technisch-Wissenschaftlichen Beirates in Sorau, 14 January 1943, 4, MPG-Archiv, Abt. I, Rep. 1A , Nr. 2210/6.

[81] For the optimization of the flax harvest on optimum soils, the large-scale cultivation planning of the RVB in 1940 calculated with a time horizon of "3 to 5 years at the earliest." For the quote, see the undated manuscript (around 1940/41) "Planung für die zur Deckung des Kriegs- und Friedensbedarfes erforderliche industrielle Erzeugung und Rohstoffbeschaffung," 5, Reichsstelle für Textilwirtschaft, BArch, R 8/196.

of a greenhouse, where it would at least be possible to harvest twice a year, mitigated the pure conflict only slightly. Opponents of extensive basic breeding research argued: Why bother with long-term research planning in the middle of the war when any advances that could be expected might already be in the hands of the armed forces through its annexation of the Soviet breeding institutes? Why pursue long-term breeding research when seeds for specific soils and climates were needed?

In 1943, the industrialist Gustav Winkler also reiterated that the KWIBF should constitute the "headquarters" for the former Soviet institutes working in the area of bast fibers. Winkler even asked Schilling to write an exposé on this subject and offered to submit this document personally to the president of the Reich Research Council Rudolf Mentzel. Apparently, he spoke for all interested parties, for he closed with the words, "Those present are of the opinion that the Kaiser Wilhelm Institute for Bast Fiber Research must not exclude itself from dealing with pertinent issues in the Eastern Space (Ostraum)."[82]

Other institute staff members were also interested in the resources of the occupied countries, including Georg Scheithauer. An honorary RWA staff member, Scheithauer had been declared by the KWS to be indispensable as a researcher, a status that relieved him of military service. From 1939 to 1944, he took numerous trips funded by the KWIBF and the RWA to "annexed" retting and bast fiber processing facilities, first in Austria and then in Czechoslovakia. In August 1941, Erste Deutsche Ramie-Gesellschaft Emmendingen and the RWA paid for him to travel through occupied Bulgaria. There he located possibilities for cultivating ramie in the Southern Maritza valley and the Black Sea Region and established relations with the Agricultural Research Institute in Plovdiv, Bulgaria. Between 1941 and 1944 he served the KWS and the RWA as consultant with the Cracow government's Department for Food and Agriculture and its district Central Agricultural Office as well as for bast fiber factories in Zyradow, Krosno, and Częstochowa. In 1942/43, he made several trips to Spain to review ramie cultivation issues; from 1942 to 1944, he made many trips to Denmark, where he was contracted by the KWS to investigate short flax fiber processing in several factories and to test a new spinning procedure he had helped develop (a special sort of coagulation spinning, called "KS" process).[83]

THE MISSING "NEXUS"

With the imminent military defeat, the smoldering old conflict over objectives – the missing "nexus" – came to a head. Now that the economic

[82] Niederschrift 4. Sitzung des Technisch-Wissenschaftlichen Beirates in Sorau 14.1.1943. All quotes on 3, MPG-Archiv, Abt. I, Rep. 1A, Nr. 2210/6.
[83] Fragebogen Dr. Scheithauer, MPG-Archiv, Abt. II, P.A. Ernst Schilling, vol. 1.

groups and the Reich associations had forced the industrial companies to achieve the highest possible rationalization and productivity, acting in the framework of Speer's "combing out campaign" for reducing inefficiency in the war economy, the next step was to deploy even minor idle production capacities like unused machines. The two RWA and KWS staff members Kling and Scheithauer showed great skill in exploiting this precarious situation in the armaments economy for their scientific and private interests.

In a letter to Schilling in June 1944, the RVB announced that it intended to confiscate several machines from the chemical-technical experimental hall for the purpose of industrial production: "As far as we are informed, [the machines] have been stored unmounted for months, while precisely these special machines are urgently needed in war-essential industry." The RVB proposed that these special machines be mounted in the region's textile factories "on loan" for a fee, "for the duration of the war."[84]

However, the institute staff members Scheithauer and Kling were the ones pulling the strings in this campaign. Both were frequently consulted by the RWM and RWA on questions concerning companies like those of the cottonized bast industry.[85] The two men wanted to introduce the "KS" process for cottonized bast, which they had developed and patented, into industrial practice. Using this rational process, the bast was broken down into fibers of the maximum length that could be fed into a three-cylinder cotton spinning mill. About this Schilling reported, "The importance to the war of using the KS cottonized flax lies in its capacity to be spun out so thinly that it is possible to produce blended yarns of the fineness required for tarpaulin fabrics. Such a fineness has never before been possible using cottonized flax in a cotton three-cylinder spinning mill."[86]

Schilling had already suspected that the realization of the patent would be considered more important than the official duties of the two engineers. In June 1944, he wrote a "private!" letter to Telschow, reporting that

---

[84] Quote in copy of Appendix 1 to Schilling's letter to Telschow, 23 June 1944, MPG-Archiv, Nr. 2207/4.

[85] Vertraulicher Tätigkeitsbericht KWIBF 1.4.1942–31.3.1943, Juni 1943. Quote on 19, MPG-Archiv, Abt. I, Rep. 1A, Nr. 2210/7. The work was conducted in collaboration with H. Stein, Berlin.

[86] "Die Kriegswichtigkeit der Verwendung des K-S-Flockenflachses liegt darin, dass es bei dieser hohen Ausspinnbarkeit möglich ist, Mischgarne von einer Feinheit herzustellen, wie sie für Zeltbahnstoffe erforderlich sind. Bisher war eine solche in der Bw-Dreizylinder-Spinnerei mit Flockenflachs nicht möglich." Here "Bw" stands for *Baumwolle* (cotton); quote in Vertraulicher Tätigkeitsbericht KWIBF über das 6. (24.) Geschäftsjahr, 1.4.1943–31.3.1944, Mährisch-Schönberg, BArch, R 10 I/99, 14, quote on 21; letter from Schilling to Telschow, 23 June 1944, MPG-Archiv, Abt. I, Rep. 1A, Nr. 2207/4; since Helmke had also developed a cottonized bast process, it was decided to test both in parallel experimental operation. See Vermerk über die Besprechung in Reutlingen betreffend K-S- und Helmke-Verfahren, 2 February 1944 and 24 February 1944, BArch, R 10 I/116.

Scheithauer and Kling were "obstructing the acting deputy manager Rohs and myself, forcing a clear-cut decision. For if conditions in Sorau persist, I can no longer bear the responsibility of the director of the institute as a whole, of the work on the priority level 'SS,' and for the military service exemptions [*UK-Stellung*] of the two gentlemen."[87]

The opposition of interests became so severe that Schilling attempted to convince Telschow to revoke his two staff members' exemptions from military service, even at the danger of disrupting all mechanical-technological projects for the duration of the war. In so doing, Schilling clearly called the entire concept of his central institute into question (if only in a private message to Telschow, whom he could presume to be sympathetic), and this at an extremely critical point in time. Had this correspondence become known, it would inevitably have led the industrial associations to withdraw their financial support. This, in turn, would have endangered the institute's financing from the Ministry of Finance, which had provided funding only with the prerequisite that industry pay part of the cost.

As mentioned above, both Kling and Scheithauer had been honorary staff members of the RWA since 1938 at the latest. Scheithauer was even formally released from his duties at the KWIBF for this office.[88] For this reason alone, it may be presumed that both maintained good relations with the president of the RVB, Gruber, and perhaps with Czaya as well. With these two institutions giving them cover, they began demounting the machines in Mährisch-Schönberg against Schilling's protests. In a KWS committee meeting, the two men had been promised a "financial profit" from their patented process for spinning, which they endeavored to realize by any means as quickly as possible.[89] Because of this expected income, Kling and Scheithauer were interested in their invention being introduced to industry as fast as possible, yet this was thwarted by the sluggish expansion of the technological department in Mährisch-Schönberg/Šumperk as a field for experiments – if this expansion was seriously planned at all by this time.

In light of this affront from his own staff members, Schilling felt challenged and overextended, and he requested help from the General Administration. He deployed all of his authority as institute director. Schilling stated that because Scheithauer and Kling were spending so much time getting the KS process implemented into practice, which required them to travel a great deal, they were no longer performing enough work for the KWIBF, thus making regular operation of the institute impossible. Further, he continued, the five commandeered machines constituted the "centerpiece" of

[87] Level "SS" was the abbreviation for the highest priority level in research; letter from Schilling to Telschow ("Privat!"), 23 June 1944, MPG-Archiv, Abt. II, P. A. Schilling, vol. 1.

[88] Letter from Schilling to MPG-Archiv, 22 August 1951, MPG-Archiv, Abt. II, P.A. Ernst Schilling, vol. 1.

[89] Letter from Schilling to Telschow, 23 June 1944, MPG-Archiv, Abt. I, Rep. 1A, 2207/4.

the newly constructed chemical-technical hall. The actions of Kling and Scheithauer would have adverse consequences because after the machines in question were removed, the hall from which they were taken would be empty and would immediately be confiscated for armaments production. Schilling asked Telschow to intervene with the RVB and the RWA to reach a settlement.[90]

Schilling's deputy in Sorau, Waldemar Rohs, viewed the circumstances the same way Schilling did. In his opinion as well, the difficulty was "that through the dual posts, above all of Dr. Scheithauer, there are, so to speak, two souls dwelling in one breast, which make it impossible for him to fully share the institute's point of view; he or his office is probably just as responsible for the campaign to deploy the machines in production as it is for the introduction of the KS process."[91]

Thus, Rohs addressed the core of the problem – that the two staff members were working for the RWA and the KWIBF at the same time. In June 1944, Telschow approached KWS President Albert Vögler with the dilemma. Vögler responded with irritation and reproach, but apparently was also at a loss: "In my view we cannot permit that machines which belong to an institute of the KWS be confiscated by the Reich Association for Bast Fibers. If what Mr. Schilling relates is true, it seems Messrs. Scheithauer and Kling intend to make use of the machines for their personal developments. In this case I do not recommend giving in under any circumstances. I will bring the matter up with the minister personally. For his part, Mr. Schilling unfortunately does not appear to enjoy the necessary authority to keep the department heads in line."[92]

By appealing to the next higher level of the hierarchy, Vögler was doing exactly what he had reproached Schilling for. In any case, a few days later the KWS was forced to abandon its plans for a central institute, which it never had pursued very vigorously. Schilling and the RVB reached an unsatisfying compromise that prevented the KWIBF from ever achieving its long-sought "nexus." The decision was that the machines would remain in Mährisch-Schönberg and "only applied to the purposes of production to the extent to which they have free capacity." KWS Administrator Müller indicated expressly that this solution (all of a sudden) also corresponded with the opinion of Vögler, who presumably wanted to dispose of the troublesome

---

[90] Letter from Schilling to Telschow, 23 June 1944, MPG-Archiv, Abt. I, Rep. 1A, 2207/4.

[91] "dass durch die doppelte Stellung vor allen Dingen des Dr. Scheithauer in seiner Brust gewissermassen 2 Seelen vorhanden sind, die es ihm nicht möglich machen, sich völlig auf den Instituts-Standpunkt zu stellen, da ja die Aktion für den Einsatz der Maschinen in der Produktion ebenso wahrscheinlich auf seine eigene Veranlassung oder die seines Amtes zurückgeht, wie auch die Einführung des KS-Verfahrens." Copy of a letter from Rohs to Schilling, 19 June 1944, MPG-Archiv, Abt. I, Rep. 1A, Nr. 2207/4.

[92] Transcript from Vögler's Presidium File, Dortmund, 3 July 1944 to Telschow, MPG-Archiv, Abt. I, Rep. 1A, Nr. 2207/4.

matter through this decision, but at the same time gave up the idea of a central institute once and for all.[93]

Scheithauer and Kling implemented their KS process in a number of large flax spinning mills in Germany and Denmark, and in 1945 Schilling succeeded in having the majority of German cultivation areas planted with his two flax varieties, Sorauer Roland and Lusatia. In this sense, at least, the activities of the KWIBF did have consequences for the German military economy. However, the goal of a central institute for bast fiber research in Germany was never achieved.

CONCLUSION

This chapter investigates the development of textile research with special emphasis on fiber research and the relevant institutes of the KWS during the first half of the twentieth century. In the center of this stood the Kaiser Wilhelm Institute for Bast Fiber Research, founded in 1938, and with 150 staff members the largest German textile research institute at the time. It made an important contribution to the research on raw and advanced materials, first, in the context of National Socialist efforts to achieve autarky, and later in the defense industry. The focus of this chapter was on the research policy of the institute, which had to contend with interest groups from both the state and private economic sectors.

Since the founding of the KWS in 1911, there had been attempts to create a textile institute under its roof. But serious efforts came first during the second half of the First World War from the director of the KWI for Physical Chemistry, Fritz Haber, and others to create such a research institute as a KWI for Textile Chemistry. The main motive was the need to find replacements for natural fibers because of the shortage of textile raw materials during the blockade of Germany by the Allies, for not only were iron, metal, and rubber important for the war but also uniforms, tents, tire cord, belts, and the like. For various reasons, the KWI for Textile Chemistry was realized only after the war in 1920, with the chemist Reginald Oliver Herzog as director. The German state encouraged the institute to continue the wartime research for replacement materials. Meanwhile, the German textile industry once again had access to the world market in cotton and was less interested in textile research oriented toward raw materials. For this reason, the textile industry withheld most of the planned financial support from the institute, so that the new institution had already closed by the middle of the 1920s. Thus, there was no continuity in the German textile research between the First and Second World Wars.

---

[93] Letter from KWS Administrator Dr. Erwin Müller to Schilling, 6 July 1944, MPG-Archiv, Abt. I, Rep. 1A, Nr. 2207/4. On Müller's rank, see Vierhaus and vom Brocke, 425.

Despite this failure, the KWS continued to try to gain a foothold in textile research. However, there was little activity until 1938 when the new KWS Secretary General and RWA official Ernst Telschow took over as head of the KWIBF, which had been founded by the bast fiber industry in 1916 as the Research Center of the Union of German Bast Fiber. New facilities for the institute, located in Sorau, Brandenburg, were now to be built in the traditional flax-growing region of Mährisch-Schönau (Šumperk) in occupied Czechoslovakia. It was supposed to be a central institute concerned with both plant breeding and chemistry and with machine processing of native – that is, blockade-independent – fibers, like flax and hemp. Its dual purpose was not only to increase the output of fibers but also the production of linseed oil in order to reduce the national shortage of fat. Because of the ever-worsening shortage of raw materials, the institute was considered a very important institution within the National Socialist war economy. It received a series of research contracts from RWA and from different sectors of the military. Even though its staff was reduced periodically by military call-ups, it was able to replace them and even to increase its personnel until 1943 and become the largest textile institute in Germany and the second-largest KWI. The institute's work was greatly enhanced when it acquired genetic and knowledge resources from the occupied areas in the west and east. However, there were fundamental problems with the internal structure of the institution.

The botanist and breeding researcher Ernst Schilling became the leader of the KWIBF. Schilling was a follower of Julius Wiesner, who had founded the technical science of raw materials, and with Schilling's appointment, Telschow saw the chance to further strengthen breeding research within the KWS. Just as during the First World War, breeding research was designated as basic research under the National Socialist science system because of the central position given to raw materials research. It was thus distinguished from scientific work on processing technology (threads, spinning, weaving, etc.) and on extending the useful life of materials, including utility research and recycling, which were considered applied or goal-directed research; these procedures were to be used only for the further processing of materials produced through breeding research. This ideal conception of a research chain was designated as a "nexus"; however, from the beginning, this chain existed only on paper. The idea of a research assembly line did not correspond to reality but proved useful for the Ministry's autarky policy, Schilling's career aspirations, and Telschow's desire for power. Beginning in 1940 industry protested against the concept, just as it had when the KWI for Textile Chemistry was established. Industry did support National Socialist research policies, including the research into plant breeding and extending the life of materials. After all, the largest part of the financing came from the state and only a small part from private sources. But the bast fiber industry did not want their own interests neglected and they threatened to withdraw their financial support for the institute outside the KWS.

The institute was advised by an eighteen-member advisory board on which, along with state representatives, chemists, and military and agricultural organizations, the German textile and bast fiber industry was strongly represented. Schilling and the botanists at the institute used most of the resources provided to them by the state to advance their careers through long-term breeding research carried out on extended experimental fields. But as early as 1940, the representatives of the Reich Food Estate both warned Schilling and threatened him with sanctions if he did not do more applied research than biological and genetic basic research – and to make the shift immediately. He was urged to curtail his deep scientific ambitions for breeding his own plant varieties and instead to use resources plundered by the armed forces from Soviet institutions of breeding research. At the same time, the fiber industry was clamoring for increased technical and scientific research that would help it. Yet, with Telschow's support, Schilling insisted that his botanical work was basic research important for the war effort – indeed, the actual research that needed to be done. Because of this conflict, the research chain that was formally being attempted, the "nexus," moved into the background and in the middle of 1944 first began to show signs of falling apart.

The departments for technology – for research into extending the life of materials, material analysis, and cleaning research – received only meager resources; additionally they had to move from Sorau to Mährisch-Schönau (Šumperk), a transition that was never finished. From the beginning, the staff of the technological department, who were never in agreement with Schilling's course, knew how to take advantage of their multiple functions as KWIBF department heads and staff members of state and industrial institutions – for example, within the "textile threads" working group led by I.G. Farben and RWA manager Carl Krauch, for their own ends. Beginning in 1944, they even used their positions in this parallel hierarchy to remove machines from their own KWIBF in order to have better access to them. The RWA and bast fiber industry supported this removal, despite protests from Schilling. And when Telschow and Schilling asked KWS President Albert Vögler for help, they were forced to recognize that he too could do nothing against the industrial interests.

10

Political Networking and Scientific Modernization: Botanical Research at the KWI for Biology and Its Place in National Socialist Science Policy

Bernd Gausemeier

Since National Socialism was an essentially dictatorial system, many historians assume that it tried to impose total control and ideological alignment on all fields of scientific research. Some main features usually attributed to National Socialist science policy are the primacy of race ideology, closing off international exchange, and, above all, the rejection of "pure research" in favor of research that was "useful" for the nation.[1] Ironically, references to research fields that allegedly remained untouched by these ideological guidelines complement rather than contradict this view. Because the Nazi research administration was utterly incompetent and disorganized, some historians claim, there were "free spaces" enabling scientists to pursue their research in relative independence.[2] According to Kristie Macrakis, the Kaiser Wilhelm Institute for Biology (KWIB) in Berlin was such an island of excellence and "normal" research in an ocean of rigorously politicized science. Under the astute direction of Fritz von Wettstein, Macrakis claims, it was not only able to conduct "pure genetic research untainted by the needs of the government" but also served as a refuge for dissident scientists.[3] It is, however, rather questionable whether "pure research" in the Third Reich was such a heroic endeavor as this interpretation suggests. As Ute Deichmann has shown, research funding was by no means distributed only according to party memberships and "ideological" preferences. The support for the biological sciences was especially generous, and large parts

[1] Michael Grüttner, "Die deutschen Universitäten unter dem Hakenkreuz," in John Connelly and Michael Grüttner (eds.), *Zwischen Autonomie und Anpassung: Universitäten in den Diktaturen des 20. Jahrhunderts* (Paderborn: Schöningh, 2003), 67–100, here 94f.
[2] Margit Szöllösi-Janze, "National Socialism and the Sciences: Reflections, Conclusions and Historical Perspectives," in Margit Szöllösi-Janze (ed.), *Science in the Third Reich* (Oxford: Oxford University Press, 2001), 1–35, here 11.
[3] Kristie Macrakis, *Surviving the Swastika: Scientific Research in Nazi Germany* (Oxford: Oxford University Press, 1993), 116 and 123.

of it were distributed to the elite institutes of the Kaiser Wilhelm Society (*Kaiser-Wilhelm-Gesellschaft*, KWS).[4]

Does this imply that the KWIB was, in contrast to Macrakis's view, particularly open to the "needs of the government"? The more appropriate question seems to be how these needs were defined. If science had to be of practical use, who decided what was useful? Did scientists pay lip service to National Socialist goals only to further their personal interests or did they willingly align themselves with the aims of the regime? To answer these questions, we have to reconstruct both the political structures in which the institute was embedded and the actual content of its research. This portrayal of the research agenda of the KWIB's botanical department aims to analyze the National Socialist research system at the level of scientific practices. It seems especially interesting to look at an institute that can, with some reservations, be labeled a "basic research" institute – at least in comparison with an institute like the KWI for Breeding Research (KWIBR), which had been founded with the aim of raising agricultural yields and held a central place in Nazi agricultural politics.[5] How did an institute like the KWIB, which was not bound to a certain field of applied science, position itself in the political landscape of the Nazi regime?

FRITZ VON WETTSTEIN AND THE POLITICAL POSITIONING OF THE KWI FOR BIOLOGY

Like most institutes of the KWS, the situation of the KWIB changed substantially in 1933, though not only due to the National Socialist seizure of power. Its first director, Carl Correns, died in February 1933; its second director, Richard Goldschmidt, was hindered by his Jewish descent before he finally had to emigrate in 1935.[6] The leadership vacuum was resolved by the appointment of Fritz von Wettstein (1895–1945), a former assistant of Correns and son of a renowned Austrian family of botanists. By moving into the position of the first director at the KWIB, Wettstein also became a dominant science organizer and policy maker for the entire KWS and the German biological community. Even before the complications of his appointment

---

[4] Ute Deichmann, *Biologists under Hitler* (Cambridge, Mass.: Harvard University Press, 1996), 97–99, calculates that during the war years, Kaiser Wilhelm Institutes took in around half of all the funding distributed by the German Research Foundation in the area of biology; on the research of the KWIB, also see Deichmann, 206–210.

[5] For a structural comparison of KWIB and KWIBR, see Jonathan Harwood, "Eine vergleichende Analyse zweier genetischer Forschungsinstitute: die Kaiser-Wilhelm-Institute für Biologie und für Züchtungsforschung," in Bernhard vom Brocke and Hubert Laitko (eds.), *Die Kaiser-Wilhelm-/ Max-Planck- Gesellschaft und ihre Institute. Studien zu ihrer Geschichte: Das Harnack-Prinzip* (Berlin: de Gruyter, 1996), 331–348.

[6] For the post-1933 situation of the KWIB, see Bernd Gausemeier, *Natürliche Ordnungen und politische Allianzen* (Göttingen: Wallstein, 2005), 39–52.

had been sorted out,[7] he interceded in the negotiations about the succession of Erwin Baur, the influential director of the KWIBR who had died in December 1933. With the backing of KWS General Secretary Friedrich Glum, Wettstein lobbied for Gustav Gassner, the society's favored candidate, in the Prussian Science Ministry; nevertheless, he was unable to prevent the appointment of Wilhelm Rudorf, who was promoted by the ministry.[8]

In May 1934, Wettstein was asked by Max Hartmann, the interim director of the KWIB, to join him and Max Planck for a discussion with several leading representatives of the new regime; Hartmann saw this as a unique chance to advance the cause of scientific research "not only in the interest of the Kaiser Wilhelm Society, but ... of all German science."[9] For Wettstein to be urged to take immediate responsibility for science policy at the relatively young age of thirty-eight is an indication of not only the power vacuum in the Society's scientific leadership at the time but also his own extraordinary reputation as a science manager. Destined as the "natural" new leader of the most prestigious German biological institute, he gave the memorial lecture for his teacher and predecessor Carl Correns in December 1933.

In this address, Wettstein proved a virtuoso at painting an ideal image of the pure researcher, who was ahead of his time and whose research projects pressed ahead in all directions; he presented Correns's life as a consummate work of art, created from the willingness to pursue a cause for its own sake. But he also made Correns into a national hero, well aware of the important status accorded to his science in the "new age":

And when today a nation competes for its international standing in the final biological battle for the Earth, when it attempts to bring out all of the potential that still slumbers in this people with a courage and a joyful will to sacrifice never before witnessed, when it takes on the enormous fight to stop in the nick of time the enduring, harrowing loss of the most valuable genetic material, which has occurred among the civilized nations over and again, and to turn itself from an old nation into a young one again, then our entire nation should never forget that it was Correns who made it possible for us to approach this task at all, who gave us the science from which the courage became deed.[10]

---

[7] Wettstein's appointment dragged on for more than a year. Initially delayed by the bureaucratic dilatoriness of the Prussian Ministry of Culture, Wettstein was close to retaining his professorship in Munich before he finally decided to move to Berlin in July 1934; see Correspondence March 1933–July 1934 in Archives of the Max Planck Society, Berlin (*Archiv zur Geschichte der Max-Planck-Gesellschaft*, MPG-Archiv), Abt. II, Rep.1a, PA Wettstein

[8] Glum to Wettstein, 9 February 1934, MPG-Archiv, Abt. II, Rep.1a, PA Erwin Baur, Nr. 7, Bl. 43; Wettstein to Glum, 7 August 1934, MPG-Archiv, Abt. I, Rep. 1a, Nr. 1549, Bl. 243. Gassner had political difficulties after confrontations with Nazi students in Brunswick.

[9] Hartmann to Wettstein, 31/5/1934, MPG-Archiv, Abt. III, Rep. 47, Nr. 33, Bl. 24/25.

[10] Fritz von Wettstein, "Gedächtnisrede auf Carl E. Correns," *Die Naturwissenschaften*, 22 (1934), 2–8, here 8.

Clearly, Wettstein used the reference to racial hygiene to affirm his institute's usefulness to the new regime. But he also sought to vindicate "pure research" as a patriotic matter and a foresighted guidepost of national policy. Thus, the statement provided an example of political alignment as well as the claim for a free space for research. The quote shows that Wettstein not only promoted his positions by using "quiet, elastic, but in principle rigid methods," as his pupil Georg Melchers put it, but also through quite explicit language.[11] However, Melchers was well aware that his longtime boss paid more for the scientific and political success than mere lip service, even though he claimed in postwar eulogies that Wettstein had maintained the "freedom" of his institute without becoming a party member or making any political compromises.[12] When Melchers tried to persuade his former colleague Hans Stubbe to leave his post as the head of the major East German institute for plant genetics in the early 1950s, he reminded him of Wettstein's behavior in the Nazi state. Constant collaboration with the representatives of a totalitarian state, he warned, would create a "situation of partial dependence" which inevitably bore consequences "not only purely externally ... but also in feeling and thinking as a whole" due to the stealthy adoption of an "authoritative nature."[13]

This statement indicates that Wettstein was by no means a dissident bystander in National Socialist science policy. In fact, he took a committed and influential part in it. Herbert Mehrtens has pointed out that National Socialist science policy was characterized by informal networks and a climate of "uncivilized civility."[14] For high-ranking scientists, closeness to important decision makers could mean privileged sponsorship and liberation from onerous bureaucratic controls. Wettstein had a direct line to the regime's most important framer of biological research policy, the SS officer and agronomist Konrad Meyer. In addition to his well-known responsibility for Generalplan Ost, Meyer was also chairman of the Research Service (*Forschungsdienst*), the central organization of the German agricultural sciences, as well as director of the Sector for Agricultural Sciences and General Biology in the Reich Research Council (*Reichsforschungsrat*, RFR) from 1937 on.[15] In this double function, he

[11] Georg Melchers, "Fritz von Wettstein 1895–1945," *Berichte der Deutschen Botanischen Gesellschaft*, 100 (1987), 396–405, here 399.
[12] Georg Melchers, "Max-Planck-Institut für Biologie in Tübingen/Abteilung von Wettstein," *Jahrbuch der Max-Planck-Gesellschaft* (1961/II), 111–134, here 128.
[13] Melchers to Stubbe, 4 March 1952, MPG-Archiv, Abt. III, Rep. 75, Nr. 4.
[14] Herbert Mehrtens, "Wissenschaftspolitik im NS-Staat- Strukturen und regionalgeschichtliche Aspekte," in Wolfram Fischer (ed.), *Exodus von Wissenschaften aus Berlin. Fragestellungen-Ergebniss-Desiderate. Entwicklungen vor und nach 1933* (Akademie der Wissenschaften zu Berlin, Forschungsbericht 7), (Berlin: de Gruyter, 1994), 245–266, here 250f.
[15] On Meyer, see Götz Aly and Susanne Heim, *Vordenker der Vernichtung* (Frankfurt am Main: Fischer Taschenbuch Verlag, 1993), 156ff; Irene Stoehr, "Von Max Sering zu Konrad Meyer- ein

merged the sponsorship tasks of the RFR with the coordinating activities of the Research Service.[16]

Consequently, biology was incorporated into a research apparatus that was one of the most generously funded and best organized in the Nazi science system. Meyer appointed Wettstein and his co-director Alfred Kühn, both of whom had been his university teachers in Göttingen, to direct working groups in the area of general biology. Thus, it is not surprising that the comprehensive support of the DFG for the KWIB continued even after the war started, despite Meyer's announcement that funding would be restricted to "projects that are especially urgent or of importance to the war and to the state."[17] Kühn's postwar perception of Meyer suggests how good his relations to the KWIB must have been. Although Kühn was no enthusiastic producer of denazification certificates and was quite familiar with Meyer's role as a Nazi pioneer in Göttingen, he praised him as a man of "good character," "entangled" in Nazism but doing his best for "pure" science "in the framework of the party." Meyer's good character could be derived from his acting for "quality and objectivity" in science, promotion of nonparty members, and efforts at saving good scientists from the front.[18] If one takes Kühn at his word, the KWIB owed its "survival" during the war largely to an SS *Oberführer*. Actually, this circumstance is hardly surprising: like most Nazi science functionaries, Meyer did not expect vows of allegiance from his leading researchers but professional commitment in their domain. And there was no lack of this among the scientists of the KWIB.

MODERNIZED STRUCTURES, MODERNIZED GENETICS

After taking office in summer 1934, Wettstein forcefully pressed forward with the modernization of his department and of the entire institute. His agenda was to concentrate on forward-looking biological research programs in order "to maintain, in at least one place in Germany, an institute that is able to study biological problems, as they are now being promoted

"machtergreifender" Generationenwechsel in der Agrar- und Siedlungswissenschaft," in Susanne Heim (ed.), *Autarkie und Ostexpansion. Pflanzenzucht und Agrarforschung im Nationalsozialismus* (Göttingen: Wallstein, 2002), 57–90.

[16] Thomas Wieland, "'Die politischen Aufgaben der deutschen Pflanzenzüchtung.' NS-Ideologie und die Forschungsarbeiten der akademischen Pflanzenzüchter," in Heim, *Autarkie*, 35–56, here 42f. As early as 1935 Meyer worked to have applications to the research service processed by the DFG; see Meyer to Stark, 15 July 1935, as well as Meyer to Wolff/DFG, 20 July 1935, Federal German Archives (*Bundesarchiv*, BArch), R 73 Nr. 11051. When he became sector director within the RFR in 1937, the two organizations were effectively merged.

[17] Meyer to Wettstein and Kühn, resp. 12 July 1939, MPG-Archiv, Abt. I, Rep. 8, Nr. 14, Bl. 18 and 20; Circular by Meyer 10 November 1939, MPG-Archiv, Abt. I, Rep. 8, Nr. 14, Bl. 34.

[18] Kühn to Telschow, 18 July 1946, MPG-Archiv, Abt. II, Rep. 1a, PA Meyer, Bl. 35.

primarily in America, in a competitive manner."[19] The first step in preparing for the transatlantic competition was the technical upgrade of the "somewhat backward institute." Wettstein's entire research strategy can be viewed as a response to the American challenge. He saw the emerging superiority of large-scale research in the United States as both a financial and a structural problem. The traditional unity of instruction and research in Germany, he elaborated in 1940, prevented the concentration of the country's best forces on the most important research problems.

Wettstein criticized the German academic structures as too hierarchical and uncooperative. Though he made some conservative objections to the "narrowness" of American specialization, he recommended American-style working groups of highly qualified specialists as a necessary supplement to the conventional organization of German institutes.[20] For Wettstein, the United States was at the same time adversary and model. When he traveled the country on a lecture tour in 1938, he was not only interested in collecting insights into the American research system but also in the political situation. In his travel report to the Reich Ministry for Education and Science (*Reichserziehungsministerium*, REM), he submitted proposals for countering "anti-German propaganda" and establishing understanding for "our defensive movement" – as he termed the anti-Semitic racial policy. Wettstein recommended an "unobtrusive" cultural propaganda, especially an intensification of scientific exchange.[21]

In his own institute, Wettstein pushed ahead with the technical upgrade of the laboratories. A central element in this undertaking was the acquisition of climate chambers for physiological and genetic experiments on higher plants. After extensive negotiations, the DFG provided the 38,000 Reichsmarks for the system. Wettstein emphasized that the new technology was indispensable in two respects: first, the determination of the temperature and light dependencies of various plant races was important "for practice"; second, it allowed the advancement of the German "specialty" in genetics, the study of how genes act in the organism.[22]

---

[19] Wettstein, Report for KWIB board, 23 February 1937, MPG-Archiv, Abt. I, Rep. 1a, Nr. 1556, Bl. 30b-d.

[20] Fritz von Wettstein, "Über deutsches und amerikanisches Forschen," in *Das Jahrzehnt 1930–1940 im Spiegel der Arbeit des Stifterverbandes der Deutschen Forschungsgemeinschaft (Notgemeinschaft der Deutschen Wissenschaft)* (Berlin: Deutsche Forschungsgemeinschaft, 1940), 171–179.

[21] Wettstein to RMWEV, 27 July 1938, MPG-Archiv, Abt. I, Rep. 1a, Nr. 1059, M. 3. I thank Sheila Weiss for alerting me to the existence of this document.

[22] Wettstein to KWS administration, 24 October 1936, BArch, R 73 Nr. 15654; Wettstein to DFG, 4 May 1937, BArch R 73 Nr. 15654; see also Fritz von Wettstein and Karl Pirschle, "Klimakammern mit konstanten Bedingungen für die Kultur höherer Pflanzen," *Die Naturwissenschaften*, 28 (1940), 537–543.

Wettstein hereby referred to Kühn's conception of "physiological genetics," which aimed at a physiological and chemical analysis of the pathways between genes and external traits. When Kühn came to the KWIB in 1937, his working group was equipped with a highly developed experimental system based on the flour moth *Ephestia*. By using transplantation techniques, his team had come close to identifying the substances that control eye coloration in *Ephestia* and other insects.[23] To translate this approach from the field of zoology into botany, suitable experimental objects and analog techniques were required.

In 1934, Wettstein's staff member Karl Pirschle found a mutation in petunias, which was manifested in yellow-spotted leaves and inhibitions in growth. The starting point appeared to correspond to the "deficiency mutants" at the core of Kühn's *Ephestia* studies, a strain of moths exhibiting a lighter eye color as well as other changes to its pigmentation. The gene in question was "pleiotropic," – that is, it affected multiple traits – and influenced a coloring process. While in the *Ephestia* studies, the transplantation of tissue parts was used to trace the "effect of the gene," here the two botanists applied a common horticultural technique, namely, grafting. Wettstein and Pirschle conceded that transplantation in insects and grafting in plants were not actually comparable.[24] Yet, in the interpretation of the results they clearly oriented themselves on the *Ephestia* model. Wettstein and Pirschle presumed that the mutated plants suffered from a dysfunction in chlorophyll production, which also resulted in the growth inhibitions. Experiments in which "normal" petunias were grafted onto "mutated" ones showed that the "deficient" characters were transmitted from the mutated plants to the normal ones, while the inverse approach led to a slight regeneration of the mutated plants. The researchers interpreted these results as an indication that the deficiencies were produced by the "long-range effect" of a "genetic substance."

Since the effect seemed to proceed from the mutated plant, the substance in question apparently did not induce the production of chlorophyll but rather inhibited it.[25] Pirschle further demonstrated by grafting that the petunia mutant also exerted its effects on tobacco and tomato plants, so the "genetic substance" was apparently not typal – an insight that implied the possibility of experimenting with various species, as was successfully

[23] On Kühn's research, see Jonathan Harwood, *Styles of Scientific Thought: The German Genetics Community, 1900–1933* (Chicago: University of Chicago Press, 1993), 87–95; Hans-Jörg Rheinberger, "Ephestia: The Experimental Design of Alfred Kühn's Physiological Genetics," *Journal of the History of Biology*, 33 (2001), 535–576; Gausemeier, 94–122.

[24] Fritz von Wettstein and Karl Pirschle, "Über die Wirkung heteroplastischer Pfropfungen und die Übertragung eines genbedingten Stoffes durch Pfropfung bei *Petunia*," *Biologisches Zentralblatt*, 58 (1938), 123–142.

[25] Wettstein and Pirschle, "Wirkung," 139.

done in the insect experiments of the Kühn group.[26] The grafting experiments, however, provided no clues about the formation and accumulation of the presumed "chlorophyll-inhibitor." Yet, Wettstein remained optimistic that it would be possible to produce extracts and to investigate the biochemical processes causing the phenotypic changes. The perspective was alluring, for the petunia experiments concerned the genetics and the physiology of one of the most important vital processes in the plant kingdom.

Wettstein apparently planned to set up a larger project on the biosynthesis and function of chlorophyll, which, similar to Kühn's research program, would combine genetics, plant physiology, and biochemistry. In 1937, he hired the chemist Hans Gaffron, an established specialist for the biochemistry of photosynthesis.[27] Wettstein also hoped to cooperate with Otto Warburg's KWI for Cellular Physiology and Adolf Butenandt's KWI for Biochemistry.[28] But these plans were never realized. As the experimental objects provided no suitable way into the "gene activity chain" of chlorophyll production, the project was given up by 1940.

There was, however, another promising approach for "physiological genetics." Using two strains of the black henbane *Hyoscamus niger* that bloomed in a one-year and a two-year rhythm, Georg Melchers attempted to unravel the physiological basis of florescence. Similar to the petunia experiments, the technique of reciprocal grafting suggested the transfer of a substance that triggers blooming, since the genetically "biennial" forms of the plant allowed themselves to be inspired by the coadunation with "annuals" into unscheduled blooming. But the physiology of florescence was much more complex: it was also possible to make "biennial" plants bloom through the application of intense cold. Trying to make sense of these phenomena, Melchers hypothesized that there was a genetically dependent "blooming hormone" circulating in the plant that could be inhibited by genetic factors (namely, the "biennial gene") while the inhibiting effect was neutralized by the external factor temperature.[29]

Melchers's project promised to shed light on essential problems of plant physiology. The existence of vegetable "hormones" that controlled growth and blooming had been a subject of discussion for quite some time; in the 1930s, the essential vegetable growth substances appeared to have been

[26] Karl Pirschle, "Ist der 'd-Stoff' von *Petunia* artspezifisch?" *Biologisches Zentralblatt*, 60 (1940), 318–326.

[27] Wettstein to Planck, 1 June 1937, MPG-Archiv, Abt. I, Rep. 1a, Nr. 1538, Bl. 193.

[28] F. B. Hanson Diary, 29 December 1937, RAC RG 12.1. Box 25. In early 1940 Butenandt was still considering a "possible new working program" about the genetics and physiology of chlorophyll formation. See Butenandt's pocket calendar, 13 January 1940, MPG-Archiv, Abt. III, Rep. 84/1, Nr. 205.

[29] Georg Melchers, "Die Wirkung von Genen, tiefen Temperaturen und blühenden Pfropfpartnern auf die Blühreife von *Hyoscamus niger* L.," *Biologisches Zentralblatt*, 57 (1937), 568–614, here 610ff.

found: the "auxins."[30] Melchers emphasized that his genetically grounded experimental model could provide a new foundation for plant hormone research in this area. Now it would be possible, "in analogy to the advances of zoological and medical hormone physiology and the great successes of auxin research," to work toward the isolation and chemical identification of a substance that induces blossoms.[31] The allusion to Kühn's "insect hormones" and the advances of sex hormone research was not merely a superficial ploy. It shows how strongly the scientific horizon of the biologists in Dahlem was determined by the concept of hormones, which were held to be the molecular key to understanding the most important processes of life. And as the example of hormone therapies in human medicine showed, it opened up unimagined, novel possibilities for application.

The project was related to two physiological problems of great "practical" importance. The first was the sensitivity of plants to light and temperature. Since breeding research was dealing with base material from different climatic zones, it was constantly confronted with the problem of photoperiodism, the phenomenon that particular plants grow well only with a certain span of daylight. At the KWIBR, for instance, intensive study was dedicated to the genetics of photoperiodism in wild potatoes collected in South America, most of which did not thrive well in European light conditions.[32] The second problem concerned the effect of temperature on the plants' development. It was known that "germination attunements" using low or high temperatures sometimes allowed the adaptation of useful plants to certain climatic conditions. By far the best-known example for manipulating seeds with cold was provided by a Russian plant breeder by the name of Trofim Denisovich Lyssenko, who used this method successfully to allow fall wheat to be sown in the spring. While his name later was to become a synonym for Soviet pseudo-science, in the 1930s the practical importance of his method of "vernalization" made it quite appealing also to Western scientists – for example to Wilhelm Rudorf, the staunch National Socialist at the head of the KWIBR.[33]

Melchers's studies sought to clarify the material processes responsible for these phenomena and connect them with a concept of vegetable "hormonal effects." However, their main objective, the determination of a "blooming hormone," proved to be an extremely intricate endeavor. Melchers and his

[30] See Ekkehard Höxtermann, "Zur Geschichte des Hormonbegriffes in der Botanik und zur Entdeckungsgeschichte der 'Wuchsstoffe,'" *History and Philosophy of the Life Sciences*, 16 (1994), 311–337.

[31] Melchers, "Wirkung," 570.

[32] Joachim Hackbarth, "Versuche über Photoperiodismus bei südamerikanischen Kartoffelklonen," *Der Züchter*, 7 (1935), 95–104.

[33] Wilhelm Rudorf, "Pflanzenphysiologische Untersuchungen (Keimstimmung, Photoperiodismus usw.)," *Der Forschungsdienst, Sonderheft* 8 (1938), 192–197; for the reception of Lysenko in the 1930s, see Nils Roll-Hansen, "A New Perspective on Lysenko?" *Annals of Science*, 42 (1985), 261–278.

coworker Anton Lang tried to localize the "hormone" by studying the effects
of various extracts from plant organs on the "biennial" form of *Hyoscamus*,
but positive results failed to appear.[34] Lang suggested that the actual "blooming hormones" were stored in the taproots after demonstrating that blooms
were formed even on defoliated *Hyoscamus* plants that had been kept in
the dark.[35] Yet, their formation seemed to take place in the leaves, under the
influence of light. Soon this view was disproved by experiments indicating
that the photoperiodic rhythm was completely independent of light but was
based on temperature-dependent processes in the leaves.[36] The more connections between photoperiodism, temperature influences, and florescence that
Melchers and Lang established, the more it became apparent that the experimental system was too complex for an application of Kühn's approach of
physiological genetics. Ultimately, even the existence of blooming hormones
appeared to be doubtful.[37] This did not end the search for active agents that
trigger blooming, however. It was to become a lifelong mission for Lang,
who became one of the most influential plant physiologists in the United
States after the war.[38]

The KWIB was able to continue the experiments during the war with
the help of its climate chambers, equipment which no other botanical institute in Germany had at its disposal.[39] For Melchers, there was no reason
to raise unrealistic expectations or to gloss over the difficulties entailed
in a novel approach. In his reports to the DFG, he always categorized his
project as "theoretical research essential for plant cultivation and plant
breeding."[40] However, he did not fail to mention that he often advised
breeders "in matters of the physiology of flowering plants," sometimes even
"by conducting methodical preliminary experiments."[41] Even if Melchers
overemphasized the interest of the "practitioners," his project – like most
of the research in Wettstein's department – implied the constant possibility of building connections to agricultural "praxis": either by forwarding

---

[34] Georg Melchers and Anton Lang, "Weitere Untersuchungen zur Frage der Blühhormone,"
Biologisches Zentralblatt, 61 (1941), 16–39, here 29f.

[35] Anton Lang, "Über die Bedeutung von Licht und Dunkelheit in der photoperiodischen
Reaktion von Langtagspflanzen," *Biologisches Zentralblatt*, 61 (1941), 427–432.

[36] Georg Melchers, Arbeitsbericht an RFR, Abt Landbau, 6 January 1942, BArch R 73 Nr.
13053.

[37] Anton Lang, "Entwicklungsphysiologie," *Fortschritte der Botanik*, 12 (1942–48), 340–441,
here 382.

[38] Anton Lang, "Some Recollections and Reflections," *Annual Review of Plant Physiology*, 31
(1980), 1–28.

[39] The equipment was responsible for extremely high electricity bills, which were covered by
the DFG as an extraordinary cost. See Melchers to DFG, 2 February 1943, BArch, R 73
Nr. 13053.

[40] Melchers, Report for RFR, 6 January 1942, BArch, R 73 Nr. 13053.

[41] Melchers, Report for RFR, 12 December 1942, BArch, R 73 Nr. 13053.

technical knowledge and skills or by passing on experimental objects of interest to the breeder.

This was also apparent in another research area, which extended even more directly into the problems of plant breeding, namely the study of polyploid plants. Polyploids, plants with cells containing sets of more than two homologous chromosomes, are fairly common among cultivated plants, even in their "natural" forms, the most important example being wheat. Polyploidy had been Wettstein's preferential research topic before his term as KWIB director. He regarded polyploids as ideal objects for "physiological genetics" because they offered insights into the mechanism of gene action and into the foundations of Mendelian dominance and recessiveness.[42] His researches on heteroploid mosses (furnished with "asymmetrical" sets of chromosomes) were based on the assumption that a "duplicated" set of chromosomes must also induce correspondingly intensified gene effects. Wettstein also believed that more attention should be devoted to polyploidy as an aspect in the evolution of species.[43]

At the KWIB, Wettstein and his assistant Joseph Straub conducted new investigations of polyploidy on his favorite object, the tree mosses. These also concerned an essential problem for breeding practice. The observation that polyploid plants generally show more robust growth led to an intensive search for a reliable method of producing them artificially.[44] In 1937, American botanists discovered that the alkaloid colchicin was an ideal agent for manipulating cell nuclei. The production of polyploids at will seemed to open up boundless possibilities for breeding. When Wettstein portrayed the research potential of his institute to State Secretary Herbert Backe of the Reich Ministry of Agriculture, he mentioned that "numerous practitioners [asked] over and again," whether, for example, "more sugar [might be] expected from a polyploid sugar beet."[45] However, he emphasized the multitude of unsolved problems concerning the consequences of polyploidy for the plant's resistance, nutrition, and growth. Polyploidy, thus, was a case for "basic research" – further advances in breeding initially required fundamental physiological studies.

In fact, it turned out that new polyploid forms of useful plants were by no means necessarily bigger and more robust than the basic forms, and they often tended to produce undesirable side effects. In 1942, KWIB researcher Karl Pirschle pointed out that "the optimistic attitude regarding the

[42] Fritz von Wettstein, "Über plasmatische Vererbung und über das Zusammenwirken von Genen und Plasma," *Berichte der Deutschen Botanischen Gesellschaft*, 46 (1928), 32–49.
[43] Fritz von Wettstein, "Die natürliche Formenmannigfaltigkeit," in Theodor Roemer and Wilhelm Rudorf (eds.), *Handbuch der Pflanzenzüchtung*, Vol. I.: *Grundlagen der Pflanzenzüchtung* (Berlin: Parey, 1941), 8–45.
[44] Franz Schwanitz, "Experimentelle Erzeugung polyploider Pflanzenrassen," *Der Forschungsdienst*, 4 (1937), 455–463.
[45] Wettstein to Backe, 9 December 1939, MPG-Archiv, Abt. I, Rep. 1a, Nr. 2963.

problem of polyploidy has, owing to failed hopes, turned into ... pessimistic resignation."[46] The main problem was that the "quantitative" advantages of "artificially" generated polyploids were often accompanied by qualitative disadvantages like sterility and "diluted," oversized cells (a phenomenon all too familiar from greenhouse tomatoes). Wettstein and Straub asked why polyploid forms in nature more frequently assert themselves without such concomitant phenomena. Their results suggested that oversized cells were not necessarily a by-product of enlarged nuclei, but rather were dependent on specific genetic factors. As smaller forms of cells exhibited faster growth, they assumed that these forms were favored by natural selection.[47]

This view implied that the disadvantages of polyploidy could be handled by way of selective breeding. But these insights were still not directly applicable to breeding. As Pirschle stressed, it took not only a broad range of genetic experiments to find really "useful" cases of polyploidy but also careful investigations into the physiological qualities of polyploids, especially their content of certain nutrients.[48] Straub took one step in this direction by demonstrating that flowering plants with double, triple, and quadruple sets of chromosomes contain a correspondingly higher amount of pigments such as carotene.[49] The immediate "practical" value of these results – Straub alluded to potential consequences for the breeding of ornamental plants – may have been negligible. Like the experiments on "plant hormones," the research on polyploids was still in a primary, tentative state. Nevertheless, the experimental techniques used allowed it to establish relations to breeding praxis. In 1941, Straub published a manual directed to breeders about techniques of polyploidy generation in various useful plants.[50]

The field of polyploidy research, thus, was a hybrid field between cutting-edge cytogenetics and agricultural application. What separated the scientific practices of the KWIB botanists from those of breeding researchers was primarily the use of model objects rather than useful plants. In this respect, polyploidy was an object that corresponded perfectly with Wettstein's research philosophy. Wettstein defined the role of the "basic researcher" as that of a pathfinder, who, "from the edge of research," enjoyed the best overview of which practical problems were on the agenda. "In this survey, and always during our work, with every step forward and every disappointment, we are accompanied by the questions as to how this can be effective in the

[46] Pirschle, Report to RFR, 10 December 1942, BArch, R 73 Nr. 13647.
[47] Fritz von Wettstein and Joseph Straub, "Experimentelle Untrsuchungen zum Artbildungsproblem III. Weitere Beobachtungen an polyploiden *Bryum*-Sippen," *ZIAV*, 80 (1942), 271–280.
[48] Pirschle, Report to RFR, 10/12/1942, BArch, R 73 Nr. 13647.
[49] Joseph Straub, "Quantitative und qualitative Verschiedenheiten polyploider Pflanzenreihen," *Biologisches Zentralblatt*, 60 (1940), 659–669.
[50] Joseph Straub, *Wege zur Polyploidie. Eine Anleitung zur Herstellung von Pflanzen mit Riesenwuchs* (Berlin: Borntraeger, 1941).

broad area of application, how it can be useful."[51] To do justice to this task, however, the reciprocal connection between geneticists, breeding researchers, and breeders had to improve. While his institute endeavored to comply with this demand, the relationship to the "practitioners" was anything but unproblematic.

MUTATION GENETICS AND EXPANSION PLANS

Wettstein's statements clearly show that he claimed a leading role for the botanist in agricultural research: in his professional hierarchy, the farsighted "basic researchers" ranked above the crop geneticists and the plant breeders. But this also implied that the borders with breeding research were blurred. In fact, Wettstein's department had moved closer to the working areas of the KWI for Breeding Research, although both institutes clearly differed in scope and structure. The KWIB and the KWIBR, as Jonathan Harwood has shown, can be regarded as typical representatives of Kaiser Wilhelm Institutes for "basic" and for applied research.[52] While Erwin Baur's institute had been founded with considerable support by the agricultural industry and was focused on the genetics of agricultural crops, the content of research at the mainly state-funded KWIB remained entirely at the discretion of the department directors.

The two institutes also differed with regard to the way the scientists saw their professional roles, their political views, and their research styles. Yet, there were always overlaps in personnel and research topics. Baur's pupil Hans Stubbe switched to the KWIB in 1936, while several botanists who had trained under Wettstein worked at the KWIBR.[53] In addition to the departments for the breeding of various cultivated plants, the KWIBR also maintained "theoretically" oriented departments for mutation research, for cytogenetics, and for cell physiology. At the last of these, Peter Michaelis spent over three decades working on plasmatic or "non-chromosomal" heredity in *Epilobium* (willowherb), a problem vigorously discussed in plant genetics. Although Michaelis occasionally tried to prove the opposite, these experiments were quite far removed from application in breeding; yet they did fit into an agricultural institute because they consumed a great deal of time and space.[54]

Despite – or because of – these convergences of interest, the relationship between the botanical department of the KWIB and the KWIBR was always

[51] Fritz von Wettstein, "Was ist aus der neueren Vererbungsforschung für die Pflanzenzüchtung zu verwerten?" *Der Forschungsdienst, Sonderheft*, 14 (1941), 116–130, here 129.

[52] Harwood, "Analyse," 331–348.

[53] See the directory of Wettstein's doctoral students in Melchers, "Wettstein," 404f.

[54] On Michaelis and the discussion about plasmatic heredity, see Jan Sapp, *Beyond the Gene. Cytoplasmatic Inheritance and the Struggle for Authority in Genetics* (New York: Oxford University Press, 1987), and Harwood, *Styles*, Chap. 9.

tense. In 1939, a serious conflict arose when Wettstein began planning a genetic institute for the collection and adaptation of wild plants. KWIBR Director Rudorf regarded this, with some justification, as an attack on "his" territory and protested to all dignitaries against the "competing enterprise." For Rudorf, the point was not only that the questions involved were the ones already being dealt with at his institute but also that the new institution would treat them less effectively, because the classificatory interest of the botanist could "never substitute for the passion of the scientific breeder" to collect material relevant for breeding research.[55]

Wettstein could defy Rudorf, the director of the most heavily staffed and financed institute of the KWS, because he was confident of Backe and Meyer's backing.[56] The conflict between the KWIB and the KWIBR was a long-term struggle grounded in both politics and science. It extended well into the postwar era, when Melchers and Straub attacked Rudorf and his team as the worst National Socialist liabilities of the young Max Planck Society.[57] The political differences had already become apparent in the confrontations surrounding Hans Stubbe, who directed the KWIBR Department for Mutation Research. After 1933, Stubbe found himself under fire from the faithful National Socialists at the institute; he, along with two colleagues, was ultimately dismissed after Rudorf took office in 1936.[58] Wettstein was not interested in the accusations of political unreliability raised against Stubbe and took him in at his institute, thus obtaining the leading German expert in the area of mutation research in plants.

The feud between Wettstein and Rudorf was not about Stubbe's political attitude but the working material he wanted to transfer to Dahlem.[59] Stubbe's stock of *Antirrhinum majus* (snapdragon) strains was one of the most comprehensive experimental objects in plant genetics. Besides *Drosophila* and corn, it was the model organism whose genetics were known best; by 1933 the location of 179 genes had been identified.[60] The exclusive access to this material made it possible to constantly develop new research approaches. Stubbe was one of the first plant geneticists systematically using (X-ray or radium) radiation to produce mutations on a large scale. Radiation genetics promised direct practical effects for plant breeding. Since it made the

---

[55] Rudorf to Bosch, 11 January 1940, MPG-Archiv, Abt. I, Rep. 1a, Nr. 2963/4.

[56] Wettstein to Telschow, 24 June 1939, MPG-Archiv, Abt. I, Rep. 1a, Nr. 2963/2.

[57] On this Michael Schüring, "Ein 'unerfreulicher Vorgang.' Das Max-Planck-Institut für Züchtungsforschung in Voldagsen und die gescheiterte Rückkehr von Max Ufer," in Heim, *Autarkie*, 280–299.

[58] Susanne Heim, *Kalorien, Kautschuk, Karrieren. Pflanzenzüchtung und landwirtschaftliche Forschung in Kaiser-Wilhelm-Instituten 1933–1945* (Göttingen: Wallstein, 2003), 208–210.

[59] Glum to Rudorf, 5 June 1936 and 19 June 1936, MPG-Archiv, Abt. III, Rep. 1a, Nr. 1563, Bl. 280 and 283.

[60] Rudolf Schick and Hans Stubbe, "Die Gene von *Antirrhinum majus* III.," *ZIAV*, 66 (1934), 425–462.

generation of a great number of mutations possible, the researchers seemed justified in hoping that in the future it would be easier to obtain new, advantageous traits in cultivated plants. Stubbe offered a representative expression of this optimism:

One gets the impression that, if experiments are carried out on a sufficiently large scale, everything that is developmentally possible for a given object can be generated. The fact of parallel variation, or of a homologous variation series, also makes very probable that attributes of a wild form that are valuable for breeding, but which, like in the genus Lupinus, cannot be transmitted to the cultivated form, can also occur in the latter.[61]

Yet, these hopes were disappointed for the most part. In 1941, Edgar Knapp, Stubbe's successor in Müncheberg, was able to announce in a survey report many corresponding experiments on useful plants but no certain beneficial results.[62]

Stubbe did more than use radiation genetics as a method for generating beneficial mutations, however. His ambition was to use *Antirrhinum* to elucidate the foundations of the origination of mutation and thus also the structure of the genetic material itself. The methods of radiation genetics were first developed for use with the *Drosophila* fly. In Germany, Nikolai Timoféeff-Ressovsky at the KWI for Brain Research opened up this area of research. After initial fears of competition, Stubbe and Timoféeff-Ressovsky established a friendly relationship.[63] The basic idea of radiation genetics was to establish a clear, "physically exact" relation between a precisely defined external stimulus (the dose of radiation) and the biological reaction (the mutation) in order to obtain inferences about the nature of the mutation process. In *Drosophila* genetics there were highly elaborate methods of determining the rate of mutations occurring in a generation. A correspondingly quantitative approach in higher plants was in fact problematic. In a plant like *Antirrhinum* the cycle of generations was significantly slower than in flies, and the number of experimental objects was necessarily smaller; above all, the detection of new traits due to mutation was extremely difficult.[64] Nevertheless, Stubbe was able to present quantifiable results about the effect of X-ray radiation on the frequency of mutation.

---

[61] Hans Stubbe, *Spontane und strahleninduzierte Mutabilität* (Leipzig: Thieme, 1937), 150.

[62] Edgar Knapp, "Züchtung durch Mutationsauslösung," in Roemer and Rudorf, 541–562. The first spectacular success was achieved in 1942, when Rudolf Freisleben, a plant geneticist from Halle, produced a blight-resistant variety of barley; see Wieland, 46.

[63] On the beginnings of Stubbe's mutation experiments, see Edda Käding, *Engagement und Verantwortung. Hans Stubbe, Genetiker und Züchtungsforscher. Eine Biographie* (Müncheberg: ZALF, 1999), 19ff and 31f. For Timoféeff's radiation experiments on Drosophila, see Gausemeier, 165–186.

[64] Hans Stubbe, "Entwicklung und Stand der Mutationsforschung in der Gattung Antirrhinum," *Die Naturwissenschaften*, 22 (1934), 260–264.

Like the *Drosophila* geneticists, he found a positive correlation between the dosage and the rate of mutation, although his results did not show a precise linear increase.[65]

Like most geneticists, Stubbe was an advocate of eugenics, a fact that enabled him to improve his relations with the National Socialist system.[66] His mutation research also profited indirectly from increased interest in eugenic research, since his radiation experiments were temporary funded within a DFG program on the endangerment of "genetic health" through medical and technical radiation effects.[67] Stubbe soon altered his line of research to experiments on the mutagenic effect of natural toxins and of pharmaceutical products. In a proposal written for the DFG Department for Medicine, Stubbe emphasized the necessity of investigating pharmaceuticals because "in addition to their therapeutic effect, they have an effect that triggers mutations, which – so far unrecognized – could be of grave importance for the genetic health of our nation."[68] Even during the boom in eugenically oriented research it was unusual to perform such investigations on plants. This circumstance shows how well Stubbe had mastered the transformation of *Antirrhinum* into an object of versatile utility, compatible with various areas of interest.

By the late 1930s, Stubbe turned away from radiation genetics because he held that "today the main features in [this] area ... can be regarded as complete."[69] Radiation genetics, primarily through the work of Timoféeff-Ressovsky, had generated a theoretical model of gene structure which now had to be extended by means of other approaches.[70] Parallel to his research on chemically induced "genetic damages," Stubbe took up experiments about the influence of deficiencies or surpluses of certain soil minerals on the mutation rate. As a botanist, he regarded it as an obvious possibility that the substrate of a plant, which contained its nutrients, could affect its genetic material. His studies indicated that varying amounts of phosphorus, nitrogen, or sulfur in the soil in fact elevated the mutation rate. Stubbe concluded that the lack of one of these nutrients caused "disharmonies in the

[65] Hans Stubbe, "Untersuchungen über experimentelle Auslösung von Mutationen bei *Antirrhinum majus* IV. (Über die Beziehung zwischen Dosis und Genmutationsrate nach Röntgenbestrahlung männlicher Gonen)," *ZIAV*, 64 (1933), 181–204.

[66] Heim, *Kalorien*, 206f.

[67] Stubbe and Jaeger, application to DFG, 15 July 1936, BArch, R 73 Nr. 15057. On the radiation damage project of the NG/DFG, see Section 3.2. On Stubbe's involvement in the eugenic discussions in this regard, see Käding, 33.

[68] Stubbe to DFG, 11 June 1937, BArch, R 73 Nr. 15057.

[69] Hans Stubbe, "Der Einfluss der Ernährung auf die Entstehung erblicher Veränderungen," *Angewandte Chemie*, 52 (1939), 599–602, 599

[70] An influential biophysical theory of the gene was developed in Nikolai Timoféeff-Ressovsky, Karl G. Zimmer, and Max Delbrück, "Über die Natur der Genmutation und der Genstruktur," *Nachrichten von der Gesellschaft der Wissenschaften zu Göttingen, Math.-Nat. Klasse, Fachgruppe VI, N.F.*, 1 (1935), Nr. 13.

metabolism" that produced mutations.[71] Since the composition of the genes apparently changed in correspondence to the "supply" of certain elements, he postulated that this line of research might allow conclusions about the chemical structure of the genetic substance.

Generally, Stubbe held that the cell plasma played an important role for mutagenesis since it was an "external factor," which provided "the 'nourishment' of the genes." He argued that it was time to overcome "the old dispute about nucleus or plasma" as the main carrier of genetic material and "to regard the cell and all of its components as a unit, and to study the major questions of genetics on this basis."[72] This view reflects that botanists, in contrast to Drosophila geneticists, were more inclined to regard the complex physiology of the cell as an aspect of genetics.

An observation supporting this perspective was the increase in the mutation rate as the seed aged, which Stubbe interpreted as a result of chemical disintegration. If such physiological processes affected the state of the gene, he concluded, it could not be ruled out that certain chemical influences triggered specific mutations. Stubbe posed the provocative question as to whether "perhaps there was a grain of truth" to the old presumption that changes in environmental conditions induced certain mutations.[73] In the context of his experiments on chemically induced mutations, Stubbe even formulated the hope of "finding compounds acting specifically, that is, substances through which definite mutations can be generated with certainty."[74]

This idea of "directed" mutations, which was proscribed as "Lamarckian" among the majority of geneticists, was extremely attractive in the context of plant breeding. Wettstein, who had never entirely dismissed the idea of a heritability of acquired characters,[75] skillfully exploited its propagandistic implications. Both in public and in reports to the ministry of agriculture, he suggested that through experiments like Stubbe's it might soon be possible to find ways of generating new forms of plants upon request and thus place plant breeding on an entirely new foundation.[76]

The idea of "steering" mutations, however, remained an episode in Stubbe's career. With Wettstein's help he hit upon a field that was to become his scientific future – namely, the genetics of "wild" plants. This topic had shifted into the focus of plant genetics research since the Russian botanist

---

[71] Stubbe, "Einfluss der Ernährung," 600.

[72] Hans Stubbe, "Über den Einfluss artfemden Plasmas auf die Konstanz der Gene," *ZIAV*, 70 (1935), 161–169, here 168.

[73] Hans Stubbe, "Weitere Untersuchungen über Samenalter und Genmutabilität bei *Antirrhinum majus*," *ZIAV*, 70 (1935), 533–537, 537.

[74] Stubbe, application to DFG, 6 February 1937, BArch, R 73 Nr. 15057.

[75] Melchers, "Max-Planck-Institut," 131f.

[76] "Erbwunder der Pflanze. Ein Gespräch mit Prof. Wettstein, dem neuen Leiter des Kaiser-Wilhelm-Instituts für Biologie," *Deutsche Allgemeine Zeitung* (1 November 1934); Wettstein to Backe, 9 November 1939, MPG-Archiv, Abt. I, Rep. 1a, Nr. 2963/3.

Nikolai Vavilov had propagated his theory of "gene centers" in the late 1920s.[77] According to Vavilov, all cultivated plants had a home region in which they could be found in a particularly diversified form. While agricultural crops underwent increasing standardization during migration and domestication, their entire genetic wealth was still stored in the wild forms of the original habitat: recessive genes with many valuable attributes for breeding. The theory had profound consequences for the praxis of plant breeding. Botanists from various nations organized collection expeditions to the supposed gene centers – the Caucasus region was held to be especially important for grain, and the Andes for potatoes – and competed to acquire the best material. Stubbe's teacher Erwin Baur filled the institute in Müncheberg with varieties from South America and Turkey; Vavilov himself built up an organization for collection and breeding that covered the entire Soviet Union.[78]

In early 1939, Wettstein submitted an application to the KWS for the erection of a "Central Office for Wild Forms and Primitive Races of Cultivated Plants" (*Zentralstelle für Wildformen und Primitivrassen der Kulturpflanzen*). In order to use the plant material collected during the expeditions in a methodical way, he claimed, an office was required that "continually preserved it, sifted through it, and made it available for all breeding questions."[79] The conditions for the plan were favorable, as the German industry was just launching a new foundation for sponsoring science. Funding was provided, as the KWS treasurer and later president Albert Vögler expressly stated, "not for actual applied research" but for "purely scientific research ... presumably because it is assumed that funds for what is known as applied research could be raised from other sources."[80]

The outbreak of the war delayed the plan considerably but also lent it new urgency. However, Wettstein advertized it less by referring to its potential for plant breeding in the autarkic war economy than by stressing the need to preserve precious resources for future researchers and breeders:

On the one hand, the martial procedures implicate that we can already collect materials in many countries where it could become more difficult again at a later date. But they also imply that through military events, resettlements, etc., there is a great danger that some of the wild and primitive forms will disappear again.[81]

[77] Nikolaj I. Vavilov, "Geographische Genzentren unserer Kulturpflanzen," *ZIAV Suppl.* 1 (1928), 342–369.

[78] On the implications of Vavilov's ideas and the first German expeditions, see Michael Flitner, *Sammler, Räuber und Gelehrte. Die politischen Interessen an pflanzengenetischen Ressourcen 1895–1995* (Frankfurt am Main: Campus Verlag, 1995), 52–62 and 74–80.

[79] Wettstein to KWS/President, 26 March 1939, MPG-Archiv, Abt. I, Rep. 1a, Nr. 2963/1.

[80] Vögler to Telschow, 25 August 1939, MPG-Archiv, Abt. I, Rep. 1a, Nr. 2963/2.

[81] Wettstein to Ministry of Agriculture, 21 March 1941, MPG-Archiv, Abt. I, Rep. 1a, Nr. 2963/4.

The war offered the chance to collect plant resources unchallenged, and it was precisely this activity that provided Stubbe with the opportunity to move into the area of "cultivated plant research." Stubbe led two collection expeditions to occupied territories: in summer 1941, through the Balkans, and in the following summer to the Greek mainland and Crete. Both expeditions were planned as military operations and, especially in Greece, took him to areas that suffered under a particularly brutal German occupation regime.[82]

The foundations for the genetic analysis of "wild forms" were thus given, but Wettstein and Stubbe hoped to receive material from the Soviet Union as well, especially from the institutes of the research organization set up by Vavilov. Wettstein explicitly suggested the "takeover" of the Russian plant-breeding institutes. Based on the information that Vavilov had vanished in Stalin's camps, Wettstein declared the institutes to be endangered cultural assets that had to be "saved" from the Soviets. The robbery he incited was thus not merely the addition of valuable seed material but also a "cultural mission of particular rank."[83]

Wettstein wanted to integrate the Russian institutes into a research empire covering all of Europe – a network of institutes that extended from marine biology stations in the Mediterranean all the way to the tundra.[84] His aim was not only to establish an effective collection of "plant material" for breeding purposes but also to create structures that would place the study of evolution on a new basis. The new "Wild Plants Institute" was designated to form the center of this organization. It appeared that Greater Germany would make Wettstein's dreams of a new form of large-scale biological research a reality.

Wettstein and Stubbe never came into direct contact with the Soviet institutes, but it is possible that they benefited from a 1943 raid by Heinz Brücher, a member of the SS and a botanist.[85] The SS research organization *Ahnenerbe* had also become interested in plant resources and planned its own institute under the aegis of the "Tibet expert" Ernst Schäfer. The KWS's plan was not endangered by this, for Schäfer – with Himmler's assent – and Wettstein reached an agreement to pursue the project jointly under the umbrella of the KWS. Schäfer was even willing to accept the politically burdened Stubbe as its director, if his complete rehabilitation by the SD (SS *Sicherheitsdienst*, Security Service) could be achieved.[86] Ultimately, the SS

[82] Heim, *Kalorien*, 216f.
[83] Wettstein to Vögler, 13 October 1941, MPG-Archiv, Abt. I, Rep. 1a, Nr. 2963/4.
[84] Wettstein's proposals for "taking over" Russian institutes are described in Deichmann, 126f, and Macrakis, 139f. Even before the war Wettstein had worked out the plan for a (Western) European alliance of institutes; see Wettstein to KWS/President, 29 March 1939, MPG-Archiv, Abt. I, Rep. 1a, Nr. 969, Bl. 41.
[85] Heim, *Kalorien*, 222f.
[86] File note by Telschow 1 November 1942, MPG-Archiv, Abt. I, Rep. 1a, Nr. 2963/4.

opted instead to make its own use of the seed material stolen in Russia and open up an institute of its own in Lannach, Austria.[87]

The new KWI for Cultivated Plant Research was finally set up in Vienna in 1943. Rudorf's interventions against its establishment were reasonable to the extent that it formed another institute for studying the genetics of useful plants. However, it was supposed to be significantly different from the existing plant-breeding institutes. Wettstein did not envisage a mere breeding station for especially exotic base material. Cultivated plant research, in his understanding, was a "*border area*, in which genetics and evolution research, metabolic physiology and biogeography, prehistory and history are linked in the most interesting manner and can come together for concerted research."[88] The phrase "prehistory and history" referred to the history of cultivated plants, which Wettstein labeled as a field of the "most general cultural-historical interest."

The institute comprised an independent department devoted to this field which was led by Elisabeth Schiemann, another KWIB researcher who had experienced political difficulties. Schiemann initially had been slated as director, but after Stubbe's successful collection journeys she was relegated to the second rank.[89] Departments were also planned for plant physiology, cytology, plant geography, and taxonomy, thus comprising an institute that grouped various botanic subdisciplines around a new object. The theory of the "gene centers" provided a most attractive conceptual basis for the new institute exactly because it represented a key to the theory of evolution, a model of cultural history, and new possibilities for plant breeding at the same time. For Wettstein, there was no contradiction between the demands of a self-sufficient economy and the establishment of an innovative and comprehensive scientific concept. Rather than seeing the new institute as a consequence of a brutal war of conquest, he regarded its erection as a "cultural mission."

The KWI for Cultivated Plants Research was able to pursue its actual goal of research only to a limited degree. In 1943, the institute took up its work in the famous Vivarium on Prater Island; in early 1944, it moved, with some difficulty, to Tuttenhof Manor near Vienna. Already in the fall preparations began to move its entire material stock to the east of the Harz region, where Stubbe eventually set up the most important plant genetics institute of the communist German Democratic Republic. Because of the difficult external circumstances, Stubbe primarily continued with his previous experiments during the period in Vienna.

---

[87] On this in detail, Deichmann, 216f and 258–264.

[88] Wettstein to Vögler, 13 October 1941, MPG-Archiv, Abt. I, Rep. 1a, Nr. 2963/4.

[89] Wettstein, application concerning "Central Office for Wild Forms and Primitive Races" to president of the KWS, 26 March 1939, MPG-Archiv, Abt. I, Rep. 1a, Nr. 2963/1; for Schiemann, see Elvira Scheich, "Elisabeth Schiemann (1881–1972), Patriotin im Zwiespalt," Heim, *Autarkie*, 250–279.

Nevertheless, Stubbe's *Antirrhinum* material allowed him to pursue a research program very few German botanists could compete with. His experiments included the production of haploid forms (plants with a single set of chromosomes), studies of the heterosis effect (the phenomenon that crosses of two different strains often produce unusually tall and robust offspring), and new mutation experiments with various useful plants.[90] Stubbe's impressively broad research agenda demonstrates how a well-developed experimental system allows the constant generation of new projects and the development of a strong professional position. However, it also shows that the Third Reich offered unusual opportunities for a dynamic "basic researcher" – provided he had the backing of influential scientists and the willingness to cooperate with powerful institutions.

SELF-ASSERTION AND SELF-MOBILIZATION

During the Third Reich, the KWIB was not only able to pursue its research continuously but even managed to expand. Three years after the war, Georg Melchers wistfully stated "how good we had it" in Dahlem.[91] For him, the situation did not really deteriorate until after it was moved to Tübingen in late summer 1943; for a botanist whose experiments were set up for the long term and depended on buildings like greenhouses, discontinuity meant more than any other difficulties caused by the war.

Yet, the war certainly did have consequences for the institute's capacity to work. Even the powerful organization in the area of agricultural research was not able to completely eliminate conflicts of interest, especially with military offices. In early 1942, Wettstein complained that "enlistments were raining" on the institute, and that "all possible officials ... repeatedly [had] implied clearly that no one really appreciated why our institute, as a purely scientific institute without tasks decisive for the war, should receive continued support."[92] However, Wettstein was not alone in his determination to "counter [this danger] immediately with full force." The leadership of the KWS was able to persuade the Armed Forces to grant the large majority of its staff reserved status.[93] In fact, there were only a few – and most of them temporary – enlistments of assistants at the KWIB, whereas the technical personnel was affected more frequently.[94]

---

[90] Stubbe, Report to RFR, 29 January 1943, 27 June 1943 and 28 January 1944, BArch, R 73 Nr. 15058.

[91] Melchers to Maria Lange-de la Camp, 7 June 1948, MPG-Archiv, Abt. III, Rep. 75, Nr. 1.

[92] Wettstein to Hartmann, 26 January 1942, MPG-Archiv, Abt. III, Rep. 47, Nr. 1575, Bl. 9.

[93] Vögler to directors of the KWI, 20 May 1942; MPG-Archiv, Abt. I, Rep. 29, Nr. 101.

[94] List of KWIB staff called up, 6 December 1941, MPG-Archiv, Abt. I, Rep. 1a, Nr. 1564/1. On the problems surrounding enlistment and reserved status, see Helmut Maier, "Einleitung," in Helmut Maier (ed.), *Rüstungsforschung im Nationalsozialismus. Organisation, Mobilisierung und Entgrenzung der Technikwissenschaften* (Göttingen: Wallstein, 2002), 7–29, here 26.

Toward the end of the war, the situation nevertheless became more critical. In September 1944, Wettstein stated with resignation that the institute
had "no longer any great momentum; we are not important enough for the
war."[95] In this situation he sought direct contact to the military in order to
erect additional safeguards. For the Supreme Command of the Navy, the
institute studied the "marine phosphorescence" caused by the alga *Noctiluca
miliaris*, a phenomenon regarded as potentially relevant for submarine warfare. The scientists "secured" by this project were certainly aware that their
personal advantage was much greater than any possible military benefit of
the project.[96] Yet, Wettstein found the marine biological "war research" anything but absurd; after the successful conclusion of the contract he fretted
that the expert knowledge of his institute had not been mobilized earlier and
more effectively. In consideration of the imminent German defeat, for him
the question arose as to "why did they not come to us with this six years
ago? For many things it is too late now."[97] Wettstein was not a scientist
who reacted only to crises in his own institute. He was concerned with how
German science would be able to master the "enormous tasks" that fell to
it during the war.[98] For him, commitment to his own institute and mobilization for the national mission were not mutually exclusive. Ultimately, his
tireless efforts to bring the KWIB more or less unscathed through the final
battles of the Third Reich were to become Wettstein's doom; on February 12,
1945, he died of an untreated case of pneumonia at his family estate at the
Brenner Pass.

Even the disintegration during the final stage of the war could not under-
mine the stable position of the KWIB. The institute was never forced to give
up its identity as an institute of "basic research," which does not mean that
its research remained "pure" and untouched by political and economic interests. It is utterly naive to assume that scientists only referred to the possible
"utility" of their work in order to satisfy clueless Nazi officials.[99] But it is also
misleading to view the generous support for the KWIB as a political reward
for Wettstein's rhetorical "acceptance and support" for National Socialist

---

[95] Wettstein to Hartmann, 13 September 1944, MPG-Archiv, Abt. III, Rep. 47, Nr. 1576, Bl.
    15/16.
[96] One of the scientists involved was Straub; see his retrospective account in Straub to E. Stein,
    14 December 1953, MPG-Archiv, Abt. III, Rep. 30, Nr. 195, and Georg Melchers, Joseph
    Straub. Lehrer, Forscher, Wissenschaftspolitiker. Laudatio zum 70. Geburtstag, 8.5.1981, in
    MPG-Archiv, Abt. II, Rep. 1a, PA Straub neu., Bl. 14. Before he was granted "indispensable"
    status in summer 1944, Straub had been detached to the High Command of the Navy, where
    he was able to continue his KWIB research; see Straub to RFR, 28 April 1944, BArch, R 73
    Nr. 15026.
[97] Wettstein to Telschow, 27 August 1944, MPG-Archiv, Abt. I, Rep. 1a, Nr. 1538, Bl.
    318–322.
[98] Wettstein to Hartmann, 27 June 1941, MPG-Archiv, Abt. III, Rep. 47, Nr. 1575, Bl. 5.
[99] Macrakis, 154.

policy (like his plans for "taking over" Russian institutes).[100] Both positions, in their own way, rest upon the assumption that National Socialism was a regime under which "purely" scientific ventures could only survive either by servility or by camouflage. The history of the KWIB contradicts this view.

Influential Nazi science policy makers like Konrad Meyer and Herbert Backe shared Wettstein's idea of "basic" biological research as the most advanced form of agricultural science. These patrons of the institute – both trained in botanical research – were not short-sighted bureaucrats expecting short-term results from science, but men with a long-term vision for a Greater German empire that would be based on a highly rationalized agriculture. This vision provided a favorable environment for a research strategy like Wettstein's, which aimed at structural and technical modernization.

His group focused on the adaptation of new research technologies and objects. The programmatic framework, provided by the concept of "physiological genetics," implied a closer connection to biochemistry – a perspective also reflected in the tobacco mosaic virus project that was pursued in collaboration with the KWI for Biochemistry.[101] This trend toward a more "technicized" and "molecularized" style of biological research bears striking resemblance to the trends prevailing in the leading American institutes at the same time.[102] This is also true for the other key feature of KWIB research, the considerable orientation toward research problems – polyploidy, photoperiodism, wild plants genetics – that were closely connected with current problems in plant breeding. The blurring of the boundaries between "pure" botany and breeding research was clearly promoted by the autarky policy, but it was by no means a peculiarity of the Third Reich. Above all, it was not a development imposed on science by politics but rather resulted from experimental possibilities that were furnished with a certain political meaning by the scientists themselves.

The National Socialist regime, after all, was not only a dictatorship aiming at total political control at all social levels but also a highly dynamic system that was able to integrate and to mobilize the most diverse social groups – not least the sciences. Doubtlessly, scientists in the Nazi state were under great pressure to prove professional commitment and political reliability. Yet, the KWI, designated to fulfill their traditional role as cutting-edge

[100] Deichmann, 119f.
[101] On this project, see Hans-Jörg Rheinberger, "Virusforschung an den Kaiser-Wilhelm-Instituten für Biochemie und für Biologie," Doris Kaufmann, (ed.), *Geschichte der Kaiser-Wilhelm-Gesellschaft im Nationalsozialismus. Bestandsaufnahme und Perspektiven der Forschung*, 2 vols. (Göttingen: Wallstein, 2000), vol. 2, 667–698; Gausemeier, 221–254; Jeffrey Lewis, "From Virus Research to Molecular Biology: Tobacco Mosaic Virus in Germany, 1936–1956," *Journal of the History of Biology*, 37 (2004), 259–301.
[102] For a comprehensive picture of the American development, see Lily E. Kay, *The Molecular Vision of Life. Caltech, the Rockefeller Foundation, and the Rise of the New Biology* (Oxford: Oxford University Press, 1993).

laboratories of German research, enjoyed extraordinary political liberties. Few other academic institutions in Germany would have been able to promote scientists like Stubbe and Schiemann, who had fallen out of favor with the Nazi party. Wettstein's tolerant attitude, however, was complementary to his closeness to power. The hierarchical world of the Third Reich was an advantageous setting for an assertive and prestigious research manager who, even though not conforming to all of the regime's ideological principles, was committed to the German quest for a self-sufficient war economy and political hegemony.

SECTION IV

MILITARY RESEARCH

I I

Ideology, Armaments, and Resources:
The Kaiser Wilhelm Institute for Metal Research
and the "German Metals," 1933–1945

Helmut Maier

Since 1933, and even more so during this war, here in Germany we differentiate between domestic materials and thrift materials. The domestic metals include, first of all, iron and steel in all their forms, followed by the light metals aluminum and magnesium as well as the highly valued, most important heavy metal, zinc. ... In this German team of metals, aluminum and magnesium are the weighty forwards and halfbacks who decide the number of victorious goals.[1]

Because of the experience of World War I, a main focus of National Socialist economic and technology policy was the erection of a blockade-proof "armed state."[2] Since the availability of raw materials was especially poor with regard to the metals important for armaments, considerable efforts were made to extract metallic substitutes from domestic natural resources.[3] Of the nonferrous metals, the application of zinc, aluminum, and magnesium was pushed in order to replace such metals as copper, bronze,

---

[1] Max Haas, "Die europäische Rolle des Aluminiums," *Berichte der Gesellschaft von Freunden der Technischen Hochschule Berlin zu Charlottenburg e. V.*, 1, No. 2 (1942), 67–76, here 67.

[2] Georg Thomas, "Wehrkraft und Wirtschaft," in Richard Donnevert (ed.), *Wehrmacht und Partei*, 2nd ed. (Leipzig: J. A. Barth, 1939), 152–166, here 154. Major General Thomas (1890–1946) was head of the Defense Economy Staff in the Armed Forces Supreme Command.

[3] Wilhelm Jungermann and Herbert Krafft, *Rohstoffreichtum aus deutscher Erde. Eine Darstellung unserer Rohstoffwirtschaft* (Berlin: Verlag für Sozialpolitik, Wirtschaft u. Statistik, 1939).

I am indebted to Linda and Mark Walker, who greatly improved the English version of my article. For further reading relating to the history of technoscientific research and development during National Socialism, including personal data of the mentioned individuals, see Helmut Maier, *Forschung als Waffe. Rüstungsforschung in der Kaiser-Wilhelm-Gesellschaft und das Kaiser-Wilhelm-Institut für Metallforschung 1900–1945/48* (Göttingen: Wallstein 2007), and Helmut Maier (ed.), *Gemeinschaftsforschung, Bevollmächtigte und der Wissenstransfer. Die Rolle der Kaiser-Wilhelm-Gesellschaft im System kriegsrelevanter Forschung des Nationalsozialismus* (Göttingen: Wallstein 2007), with further examples for materials research.

and brass in armaments production.[4] Beyond calculations about materials strategy, National Socialist technology ideologues stylized the philosophy of substitute materials as an element of their "techno-policy."[5] Moreover, in this process the research of German metals scientists served as proof of the superiority of "German technology."

The alloys connoted by the disagreeable term "substitute material" (*Ersatzstoff*) were assigned the ideologically correct term "domestic material" (*Heimstoff*) which could be extracted from the "soil of the home country" (*Heimatboden*) or the "native clod" (*heimische Scholle*). The utilization of "German metals" gave a key role to the Kaiser Wilhelm Institute for Metal Research (KWIMT), for the technological properties of the new families of alloys had to be at the very least comparable with those of the standard metals they were to replace. On the other hand, all production and working processes such as smelting, casting, forging, machining, milling, and splicing had to be adapted to accommodate the newly introduced metallic materials.[6] In contrast, the armaments industry was confronted with the problem of exchanging tried and true materials for newly developed substances, and their initial experiences left these engineers dubious about the chances for success.

The effect exerted by the "domestic materials" ideology will be investigated through the example of the KWIMT. How did engineers, chemists, and physicists react to the symbolism of "national" metals imparted by

[4] On the utilization of iron and steel as substitutes for copper alloys, see also Andreas Zilt, "Rüstungsforschung in der westdeutschen Stahlindustrie. Das Beispiel der Vereinigte Stahlwerke AG und Kohle- und Eisenforschung GmbH," in Helmut Maier (ed.), *Rüstungsforschung im Nationalsozialismus. Organisation, Mobilisierung und Entgrenzung der Technikwissenschaften* (Göttingen: Wallstein, 2002), 183–213.

[5] In the course of the discourse on technology during the 1930s, the economist, sociologist, and economic historian Werner Sombart (1863–1941) advanced the demand for state-directed "technopolicy" so that the consequences of new technologies could be directed toward cultural progress; see Torsten Meyer, "Zwischen Ideologie und Wissenschaft: 'Technik und Kultur' im Werk Werner Sombarts," in Burkhard Dietz, Michael Fessner, and Helmut Maier (eds.), *Technische Intelligenz und "Kulturfaktor Technik". Kulturvorstellungen von Technikern und Ingenieuren zwischen Kaiserreich und Bundesrepublik Deutschland* (Münster: Waxmann, 1996), 67–86, here 86; beginning in 1935 the journal *Deutsche Technik* adopted the concept in its subtitle: "Technopolitische Zeitschrift der Architekten, Chemiker, Ingenieure, Techniker," when it took on the function of the official party organ of the "Office for Technology" (*Amt für Technik*) of the NSDAP; on this and on National Socialist technology policy in detail, see Andrea Brinckmann, "Nationalsozialistische 'Technikideologie.' Eine Analyse der technopolitischen Zeitschrift *Deutsche Technik* (1933–1943)," MA thesis, University of Hamburg (1999), 13; Helmut Maier, "Nationalsozialistische Technikideologie und die Politisierung des 'Technikerstandes.' Fritz Todt und die *Deutsche Technik*," in Dietz, 253–268.

[6] For a practical example from the metal industry based on the case of magnesium and the comprehensive adaptations to technical processes required to introduce this new material, see the voluminous manual by Adolf Beck (ed.), *Magnesium und seine Legierungen* (Berlin: Springer, 1939).

National Socialist technology ideologues, which seemed to lack any connection at all to their "apolitical" conception of themselves or professional methodology? Were the efforts to transfer the "techno-political" concept of materials from the "native clod" to the combat airplane via the lathe in the armaments industry ultimately successful? Did the armaments industry use these new alloys to a significant degree?

THE "DEFENSE ECONOMY" AND THE "IDEOLOGY OF MATERIALS"

But all the strata of the German nation recognize more and more – and foreign countries will have to accept this – that the Four Year Plan is more than just an emergency measure to bridge over difficulties conditioned by politics, namely, that it is a first major stage on the path to a socialist economy independent of international Jewry, alien racketeers and monopolists, to a *defense economy* subservient only to our nation.[7]

Beginning in 1934 at the latest, a dramatic shift took place in the area of raw and processed materials, with respect to both politics and ideology and technology and business. Policy makers demanded quite openly the conversion to such metals "for which the supply situation [is] more secure."[8] Industry was called upon to utilize "exchange materials" (*Austausch-Werkstoffe*);[9] the Association of German Engineers (*Verein Deutscher Ingenieure*, VDI) committed itself to the "native" generation of industrial raw materials,[10] and participants at the "First District Day of Technology" (1. *Gautag der Technik*) in Stuttgart in 1935 were recruited for the "conversion of the metalworking industry to native raw materials."[11]

The origins of the propaganda campaigns were, first of all, the negative experiences with substitute materials during World War I, which were anchored firmly as a "child of necessity" in the collective consciousness of the 1930s. It was necessary to overcome significant and legitimate distrust among consumers and construction engineers. The materials propaganda picked up on this distrust and attempted to convey the impression that the technological problems in this regard had long since been surmounted:

But that word, the term "substitute material" (*Ersatzstoff*), which earned its bad reputation during the war, has already disappeared from our vocabulary. The

---

[7] Jungermann and Krafft, 10; emphasis in original.
[8] Otto Eisentraut, "Zur künftigen Entwicklung der deutschen Metallgewinnung," *Deutsche Technik* (1933/34), 316 f.
[9] "Vernünftige Werbung für Austausch-Werkstoffe!" *Metallwirtschaft*, 13 (1934), 876.
[10] "Deutsche Technik und Rohstoffwirtschaft," *Zeitschrift des Vereins Deutscher Ingenieure*, 78 (1934), 1285–1290, here 1285.
[11] Arthur Kessner, "Umstellung der metallverarbeitenden Industrie auf heimische Rohstoffe," *Deutsche Technik*, 3 (1935), 217–220.

generation of artificial raw materials during the war with very little technical or economic preparation, and launched under especially difficult circumstances, has left such an enduring negative impression not only among German consumers, but also in German industry, that even the best raw and processed materials had to survive an often difficult struggle against the resistance of the fabricator and the consumer. Yet this aversion – the "substitute material" psychosis – has long since been overcome.[12]

Second, the goals of autarky and rearmament that started in 1933 could not have been carried out without utilizing the "native" materials. The most important journal for nonferrous metals, *Metall-Wirtschaft, -Wissenschaft, -Technik*, edited by Dr. Georg Lüttke (1884–1963), also placed itself in the service of the new materials policy. Lüttke, who had joined the National Socialist German Workers Party (*Nationalsozialistische Deutsche Arbeiterpartei*, NSDAP) in October 1931, before the National Socialists came to power, had held important offices in metals associations since the 1920s and was active in the Commission for Metal Research in the Emergency Association of German Science.[13] In early 1934, he publicized the National Socialist concept of autarky, cited here according to the words of the member of the Party Directorate of the NSDAP, Werner Daitz (1884–1945):[14]

The NSDAP understands "autarky" to designate the right of every nation to shape its economy such that, for the people it is like a castle in which they cannot be starved out and deprived of supplies when trade, currency, or even military conflicts occur. ... Thus autarky does not mean closing the borders for economic reasons, rather merely classifies needs in accordance with defense policy.[15]

Thus Daitz, who became prominent because of his propaganda in the service of the imperialist pipe dreams of German industry in World War I, and later of the National Socialist "Greater Regional Economy" (*Grossraumwirtschaft*),[16] made perfectly clear, just one year after his party assumed power, what the new economic policy was intended to do, and therefore what the tasks of the "metalworkers" in this regard would be.

---

[12] Jungermann and Krafft, 14 f.
[13] Protocol of the meeting of the Commission for Metals Research in the Emergency Association on 24 March 1933, attendance list, Archives of the Max Planck Society, Berlin (*Archiv zur Geschichte der Max-Planck-Gesellschaft*, MPG-Archiv), Abt. I, Rep. 1A, Nr. 926, fol. 15 f.; Georg Lüttke's membership book, Mitgliedsbuch No. 671217, Federal German Archives (BArch), party card file.
[14] From 1933 to 1945, Werner Daitz, a chemical engineer, headed the office for foreign trade in the office for foreign policy of the NSDAP; see in detail Joachim Lilla, *Statisten in Uniform. Die Mitglieder des Reichstags 1933–1945* (Düsseldorf: Droste, 2004), 86 f.
[15] "Metallwirtschaft und Weltwirtschaft im Jahre 1933," *Metallwirtschaft*, 13 (1934), 13.
[16] Karl-Heinz Ludwig, *Technik und Ingenieure im Dritten Reich* (Düsseldorf: Droste, 1974), 428 f.; Achim Bay, "Der nationalsozialistische Gedanke der Grossraumwirtschaft und seine ideologischen Grundlagen," Ph.D. diss., University of Erlangen-Nürnberg (1962).

The National Socialist ideology of materials was realized systematically. Techno-scientific research and development were included as part of the comprehensive program of measures. Thus, the annual report of the VDI for 1935 reflected the concept of converting the entire spectrum of raw and processed materials to the "native materials." In the section on "scientific papers," the VDI presented its contribution "to improving the raw materials situation of our economy," namely, the "economization of foreign raw materials in all application sites, development and utilization of native materials," and the "development and utilization of higher quality alloys." A suborganization of the VDI was the German Society for Metal Science (*Deutsche Gesellschaft für Metallkunde*, DGM), which participated with its affiliated "Committee for Specialized Norms for Non-Ferrous Metals" (*Fachnormenausschuss für Nichteisenmetalle*) in the "projects to convert to the increased utilization of native raw materials."[17] The DGM aggregated "the primary leading personnel in the factories and in the research institutes, laboratories, and experimental stations of the metal-producing and metal-consuming industries" as well as scientists at the universities and institutions of technical higher education.[18]

The only raw materials in abundant supply in Germany were coal, potash, and magnesium ore. With the exception of zinc, 70 percent to 100 percent of all metals had to be imported. For instance, German copper ores, of particular importance to the armaments industry, accounted for only 14 percent of the copper demand in 1934.[19] Henceforth in hundreds of articles, many of them appearing in technical and scientific publications, readers were urged to learn the lessons of World War I and convert the economy to "German metals." This lent timely importance to the wealth of experience accumulated through measures directed at the armaments industry and armaments technology, which the VDI had presented to the public in a comprehensive manual in 1921.[20] In fact, such appeals were only the beginning. In early 1934, "coordination" (*Gleichschaltung*)

[17] All quotes from Georg Garbotz, "Der Verein deutscher Ingenieure im Jahre 1935. Geschäftsbericht, erstattet vom Direktor des VDI," *Zeitschrift des Vereins Deutscher Ingenieure*, 80 (1936), 317–331, here 319.
[18] Werner Köster, "50 Jahre Deutsche Gesellschaft für Metallkunde. Festvortrag am 27. Mai 1969," *Metall*, 23 (1969), 661–666, here 662.
[19] On the importance of copper to the armaments industry, see Helmut Maier, "'Wehrhaftmachung' und 'Kriegswichtigkeit.' Zur rüstungstechnologischen Relevanz des Kaiser-Wilhelm-Instituts für Metallforschung in Stuttgart vor und nach 1945," *Ergebnisse. Vorabdrucke aus dem Forschungsprogramm "Geschichte der Kaiser-Wilhelm-Gesellschaft im Nationalsozialismus*," No. 5 (Berlin: Forschungsprogramm, 2002; further quoted as *Ergebnisse*, No., and year), 17.
[20] Arthur Kessner, *Ausnutzung und Veredlung deutscher Rohstoffe*, 3. Aufl. des Buches "*Rohstoffersatz*" (Berlin: Verlag des Vereines Deutscher Ingenieure, 1921).

and "aryanation" *(Arisierung)* were enforced in the metal industry.[21] As part of this "reorganization of the economy,"[22] economic groups *(Wirtschaftsgruppen)* were created for each economic sector. Retired Senior Mining Engineer Otto Fitzner (1888–1945) was appointed director of the economic group for the nonferrous metal industry – that is, the subgroup responsible for the "German metals." Fitzner was the technical director of the most important German producer of zinc, the Bergwerksgesellschaft Georg von Giesches Erben of Breslau,[23] and had been a member of the NSDAP and SA *(Sturmabteilung,* Storm Troopers) since October 1931.[24] Karl Eychmüller (1892–1981),[25] director of the Wieland-Werke AG, Ulm, one of the most important manufacturers of semifinished light metal products, became his deputy.

In March 1934, the Reich Ministry of Economics issued a set of regulations that mushroomed steadily in the following period. The "Decree on Base Metals" *(Verordnung über unedle Metalle)* was intended to improve the balance of raw materials and hard currency by regulating "transactions with industrial raw materials and semifinished manufactures." A meticulous list of banned materials regulated the use of metal down to the last paper clip. The use of copper for "festival badges, insignia, advertising, and office articles" was prohibited.[26] To enforce the new regulations and rationing measures, the "Supervisory Board for Base Metals" *(Überwachungsstelle für unedle Metalle)* was created, to which Georg Lüttke was appointed as

[21] On the legal measures over the course of the autarky economy and early economic activity on armaments, see the "Gesetz über den Verkehr mit industriellen Rohstoffen und Halbfabrikaten" of 22 March 1934; the "Verordnung über die Errichtung von Überwachungsstellen" of 4 September 1934; the "Gesetz über die Übernahme von Garantien zum Ausbau der Rohstoffwirtschaft" of 13 December 1934; Werner Sörgel, *Metallindustrie und Nationalsozialismus. Eine Untersuchung über Struktur und Funktion industrieller Organisationen in Deutschland 1929 bis 1939* (Frankfurt am Main: Europäische Verlag-Anstalt, 1965), 73 f.
[22] For a comprehensive account of the "coordination" *(Gleichschaltung)* and "Aryanization" of the metal industry through the "Law on the Preparation of the Organic Construction of the German Economy" *(Gesetz zur Vorbereitung des organischen Aufbaues der deutschen Wirtschaft)* of 27 February 1934, see Sörgel.
[23] Alfred Marcus, *Die grossen Eisen- und Metallkonzerne* (Leipzig: S. Hirzel, 1929), 55–64; Daniel Stone, "The Giesche Company: Anaconda Copper's Subsidiary in Interwar Poland," *Slavic Review,* 56 (1997), 679–697; "Zinklegierungen bei Giesche," *Metallwirtschaft,* 21 (1942), 143.
[24] Hermann Teschemacher (ed.), *Handbuch des Aufbaus der gewerblichen Wirtschaft,* 3 vols., Vol. 1: *Reichsgruppe Industrie, Reichsgruppe Energiewirtschaft, Reichsgruppe Banken, Reichsgruppe Versicherungen* (Leipzig: Lühe, 1936), 34 f.
[25] On Eychmüller, see Deutsche Gesellschaft für Metallkunde (ed.), *50 Jahre Deutsche Gesellschaft für Metallkunde e. V. im Spiegel der Zeitschrift für Metallkunde* (Stuttgart: Riederer-Verlag, 1969), 82.
[26] Günther Brandt, *Vorschriften zur Metallbewirtschaftung. Eine Zusammenfassung mit Erläuterungen,* 2nd ed., vol. 2 (Berlin: Lüttke, 1936), IXA/1.

first director and "Reich Commissioner." [27] Violations of prohibitions on use were treated not as mere pecadillos but rather as legal corpus delicti of "raw material crime." In 1938, the engineer and SS Oberführer Paul Zimmermann, member of the staff of the Reich Directorate of the SS since 1937, took over the position of Reich Commissioner. [28] In 1938, his Supervisory Board threatened any violator:

Both the "Inspection Service" (*Revisionsdienst*) and the "penal authorities" (*Strafbefugnisse*) of the Supervisory Board are deployed ... to achieve the goal of order and cleanliness in the German metal industry, the defense against vermin. ... Even today the instruments of power at the board's disposal are exercised with leniency and understanding for mere mistakes, although considering that most of the regulations have been in force for around four years, inadequate knowledge of them can no longer be excused. Where, however, ill will and a disposition hostile to the economy are behind an offense, we will not refrain from alerting the public prosecutor, and the German courts have long since disposed of any undue leniency in the sentencing of raw material crimes. [29]

This administrative pressure led to significant efforts to utilize the "German metals" in science and technology as well. A new system of concepts and classifications was developed for the materials. By 1942, the VDI was able to announce that conversion had been successful in many areas of machine and apparatus construction. The example of the manufacture of industrial fittings offers a clear illustration of how this conversion was to proceed. The left side of Figure 11.1 shows the "thrift materials," that is, cast iron, tin, nickel, lead, zinc, and copper and its alloys. Thrift materials were defined as those materials "of which a country, whether because of insufficient hard currency or policies to restrict access to the economy, does not have sufficient supply and thus must carefully use the stocks still available." The "exchange materials" are shown in the middle and at the right of the figure: steel and aluminum, heavy ceramics, glass, plastics, wood, and zinc. The "exchange materials" designated those that, according to the economic and technical policies pursued in Germany at the time, had to replace thrift materials due to their equal or even higher quality. [30] The "great line in the movement of materials" ran from left to right. Products that traditionally had been produced using materials in the left column were to be replaced by "exchange materials" from the middle and right columns. In the

---

[27] Schriftleitung und Verlag der "Metallwirtschaft," "Glückwunsch und Abschied," *Metallwirtschaft*, 13 (1934), 223.

[28] Reichsbeauftragter SS-Oberführer Dipl.-Ing. Paul Zimmermann, *Metallwirtschaft*, 17 (1938), 785.

[29] E. Wieprecht, "Die Bewirtschaftungsmassnahmen der Überwachungsstelle für Metalle," *Metallwirtschaft*, 17 (1938), 1175–1180, here 1180, emphases in original.

[30] Max Haas, "Neue Anwendungsgebiete für Leichtmetalle in Deutschland," *Schweizer Archiv für angewandte Wissenschaft und Technik*, 1 (1935), 71.

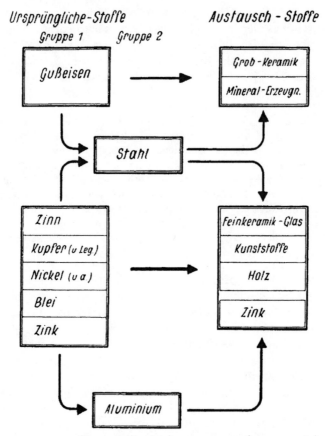

FIGURE II.I. The great line in the movement of raw materials

Source: Originally published in Helmut Maier (ed.), *Rüstungsforschung im Nationalsozialismus. Organisation, Mobilisierung und Entgrenzung der Technikwissenschaften* (Göttingen: Wallstein, 2002), 365.

construction of industrial fittings, for instance, this meant implementing anodized aluminum instead of the traditional brass used for water faucets; other examples included substituting the lead bell and the copper floater in toilet tanks with ceramics and plastics.[31]

The techno-politicians of the Third Reich had no problems integrating "native materials" into their ideology. From the "racial" point of view,

---

[31] Max Mengeringhausen, "Werkstoffumstellung im Armaturenbau," in Verein Deutscher Ingenieure (ed.), *Konstruieren in neuen Werkstoffen. Erfahrungen und Beispiele der Werkstoffumstellung im Maschinen- und Apparatebau* (Berlin: VDI-Verlag, 1942), 81–86, here 86.

one could read in 1936, "technology in the broadest possible sense [is] a creation of the Aryan race."[32] Every science, even those that deal "essentially with the determination of facts," as another author stated, was "conditioned by race."[33] "The *völkisch* (racial) economy" was a "well-fortified economy," and the freedom of sufficient food (*Nahrungs-Freiheit*) and raw materials (*Rohstoff-Freiheit*) were elements of this. Only "economic freedom" (*Wirtschaftsfreiheit*) could make self-defense and thus the "freedom of defense" (*Wehrfreiheit*) possible. As Daitz propagandized in *Deutsche Technik*, the central techno-political organ of the National Socialist Federation of German Technology (*Nationalsozialistischer Bund Deutscher Technik*),[34] only if "the iron ration of industrial raw materials, which protects a nation from surrender to a boycott or siege, are extracted in the country itself," would "such a soldierly posture by the economy back up the armed forces so that it could then truly provide external protection of German living space [*Lebensraum*]."[35] The major successes, which had already been realized by the "native materials," gave further reason to hope that "German spirit and German ingenuity" would, after all, be superior to the "Asian brain." The vital question was thus: "Who has the greater technical, scientific genius, the white man or the yellow one?"[36]

German metals occupied a key role in the calculus of the National Socialist armaments strategists. As articulated by Dr.-Ing, Max Haas (1897–1965), director of the Berliner Aluminium-Zentrale G.m.b.H. quoted at the beginning of this chapter[37] and someone who was dubbed by his contemporaries the "aluminum Goebbels,"[38] magnesium, zinc, and aluminum were considered the most important "German metals." While all of the magnesium and most of the zinc could be extracted using German ores, the designation "German metal" appears absurd for aluminum, as Germany had very insignificant bauxite deposits at its disposal. However, according to Haas, aluminum was nevertheless a "German metal" because its import amounted to only 7 percent of the total costs, "such that 93% of German aluminum

---

[32] Georg Nonnenmacher, "Technik – rassisch gesehen," *Deutsche Technik*, 4 (1936), 534 f.

[33] Christian Mergenthaler, "Staat und Partei sind eins geworden. Unsere Grundsätze verwirklicht," *Vier Jahre Aufbau in Württemberg, Stuttgarter NS-Kurier*, special edition (30 January 1937), 21–23, here 22. Mergenthaler (1884–1980) was prime minister and minister of culture in Württemberg.

[34] On the propagation of "freedom of defense and economic freedom" and on the importance of the journal *Deutsche Technik*, see the comprehensive work by Brinckmann.

[35] Werner Daitz, "Völkische Wirtschaft ist wehrhafte Wirtschaft," *Deutsche Technik*, 4 (1936), 255–257.

[36] Gustav A. Langen, "Die Bedeutung der Heimstoffe für das Exportgeschäft," *Deutsche Technik*, 3 (1935), 284 f.

[37] Haas, "Europäische."

[38] Paul Rosbaud to Walther Gerlach, 11 August 1947, Archives of the German Museum, Munich (*Archiv des Deutschen Museums*, ADM), estate of Walther Gerlach.

[consisted of] good German labor."[39] This reference back to parts of National Socialist ideology – in this case decoupling the light metal so elementary to armaments technology from bauxite, its raw material of origin – illustrates precisely the strategy of "politicizing the technical guild."[40] In the case of aluminum, the idea was to create a symbolism more deeply German, especially as bauxite was named after Les Baux in France, near where it was found. In the collective symbolism of national stereotypes, since its industrialization in the nineteenth century Germany had been connected in the material realm with the heaviness of iron, while France was associated with the lightness of aluminum.[41]

In the utopian literature read by a broad audience, especially among the technical intelligentsia, the light metals were mentioned as one of the technical-scientific technologies of the future almost as frequently as electricity.[42] For a German Reich whose collective consciousness since the turn of the century had been transformed into a "nation of flyers,"[43] in which an aeronautics industry had sprung up out of nowhere since 1933,[44] aluminum, particularly in the form of duralumin, had moved into the ranks of the most important materials.[45] Duralumin owed its key position in aeronautics to the fact that it was as stable mechanically as structural steel with about one third of steel's specific weight.[46] Due to these properties, before 1918 it was first used on a large scale in zeppelin construction, so that it was connected symbolically with "German" aviation – although not necessarily in terms of the pure statistics of consumption.[47] Although Germany was a latecomer to aluminum production and did not catch up until the end of

---

[39] Max Haas, "Aluminium und seine Legierungen im Wiederaufbauplan," *Deutsche Technik*, 2 (1934), 533 f.

[40] See Maier, "Todt."

[41] Ute Gerhard and Jürgen Link, "Zum Anteil der Kollektivsymbolik an den Nationalstereotypen," in Jürgen Link and Wulf Wülfing (eds.), *Nationale Mythen und Symbole in der zweiten Hälfte des 19. Jahrhunderts. Strukturen und Funktionen von Konzepten nationaler Identität* (Stuttgart: Klett-Cotta, 1991), 16–52, here 44.

[42] David E. Nye, *Electrifying America: Social Meanings of a New Technology, 1880–1940* (Cambridge, MA: MIT Press, 1990), 149.

[43] Peter Fritsche, *A Nation of Fliers: German Aviation and the Popular Imagination* (Cambridge, MA: Harvard University Press, 1992).

[44] See in detail Lutz Budrass, *Flugzeugindustrie und Luftrüstung in Deutschland 1918–1945* (Düsseldorf: Droste, 1998).

[45] H. Lennartz, "Der Flugzeugbaustoff Duralumin," *Junkers Nachrichten*, 8 (1934), 85–118.

[46] "Duralumin (dur = hard = hard aluminum). Composition: besides aluminum, around 4% copper, up to 1% manganese and 0.5% magnesium, usually even smaller amounts of silicium. It can be milled, drawn, compressed and also hardened, but is difficult to weld and solder. Its strength more or less corresponds to S[iemens]M[artin] steel, yet its corrosion resistance is low." Arthur Schulenburg, *Giesserei Lexikon* (Berlin: Schiele and Schön, 1958), 128.

[47] Helmut Maier, "'New Age Metal' or 'Ersatz'? Technological Uncertainties and Ideological Implications of Aluminium Up to the 1930s," *ICON*, 3 (1997), 181–201, here 188.

World War I, it was a perfect fit for the technology ideologue Haas that this highly cultivated "flight material" duralumin had been discovered by the German chemist and metallurgist Alfred Wilm (1869–1937). With the help of numerous publications on the history of aluminum, Haas succeeded in projecting flying, the aeronautics industry, and duralumin as collective symbols[48] of the Third Reich.[49] Indeed, capacity was increased to such a degree[50] that in 1940 Germany was the leading producer of refined aluminum, with 26.1 percent of the world's production, ahead of the United States with 23.9 percent, Canada with 12.6 percent, France with 7.9 percent, and Norway with 3.5 percent.[51] Thus at the outbreak of war Haas was able to announce credibly that Germany had overtaken even the United States in per capita consumption – as propagandistically shown in Figure 11.2.[52]

METAL RESEARCH AND "GERMAN METALS"

Of the metals, what we are lacking almost completely are the very important metals used to make bronze. We are lacking copper, except for a very small amount provided by our own soil. ... In contrast to these, what are the things of which we really have a surplus? The list is infinitesimally short. ... But this list is extended by something quite essential. ... That is, first of all, the special capability and aptitude of Germans for chemistry and the high and ancient tradition in this field. Second, it is *the fanatic will to embark upon what is humanly possible and even seemingly impossible with that which we are given.*[53]

With the far-reaching restrictions on using heavy metals, the pressure increased on metal researchers to provide corresponding substitute alloys. The frequency of scientific publications on German metals increased

[48] For an in-depth discussion of the concept and systematics of collective symbolism, see Link and Wülfing.

[49] Haas, "Aluminium"; Haas, "Anwendungsgebiete"; Max Haas, "Alfred Wilm, der Erfinder des Duralumins," *Aluminium*, 17 (1935), 502–509; Max Haas, "Wie das Duralumin erfunden wurde," *Aluminium*, 18 (1936), 366 f.; Max Haas, "Alfed Wilm und die Duralumin-Erfindung," *Aluminium*, 19 (1937), 511–522; Max Haas, "Austauscherfolge durch Aluminium an Stelle von Schwermetallen in Deutschland," *Aluminium*, 21 (1939), 643–649; Max Haas, "Wie Hans Christian Oersted dem Aluminium den Weg bahnte," *Aluminium*, 21 (1939), 681–687, 811–823; Max Haas, "Unser Alfred Wilm," *Aluminium*, 22 (1940), 497–501.

[50] For German production statistics, see Gottfried Plumpe, *Die I.G. Farbenindustrie AG. Wirtschaft, Technik und Politik 1904–1945* (Berlin: Duncker und Humblot, 1990), 414; on the administrative measures, see Plumpe, 701–740.

[51] *United States Department of Commerce, Business and Defense Services Administration, Materials Survey, Aluminum* (Washington: U.S. Dept. of Commerce, November 1956), II-22.

[52] Haas, "Austauscherfolge."

[53] Speech by Peter Adolf Thiessen in NSD-Dozentenbund (ed.), *"Wissenschaft und Vierjahresplan." Reden anlässlich der Kundgebung des NSD-Dozentenbundes Gau Gross-Berlin, am Montag, dem 18. Januar 1937, in der Neuen Aula der Universität Berlin* (Berlin: NSD-Dozentenbund, 1937), 4–17, here 5, emphasis in original.

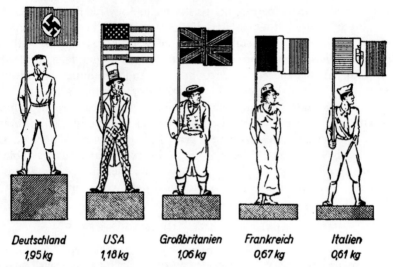

	Deutschland	USA	Großbritanien	Frankreich	Italien
	1,95 kg	1,18 kg	1,06 kg	0,67 kg	0,61 kg

FIGURE 11.2. Aluminum consumption per capita in various countries in 1939

Source: Originally published in Helmut Maier (ed.), *Rüstungsforschung im Nationalsozialismus. Organisation, Mobilisierung und Entgrenzung der Technikwissenschaften* (Göttingen: Wallstein, 2002), 369.

significantly over the course of the 1930s. Laboratories began working on the problem, and research institutions were expanded and new ones opened.[54] Starting in 1933, the laboratory of the Metallgesellschaft in Frankfurt began concentrating on the "domestic material" zinc; from 1937 it also worked on aluminum-zinc alloys.[55] In 1936, I.G. Farben began setting up the most modern laboratory for light metals in Bitterfeld, which became the focus of magnesium research.[56] The materials institutes of the expanding field of aeronautics research also began experimenting with the "German metals."[57] In 1936, the "Materials Department" of the German

[54] See a list of more than twenty new or expanded institutes for metal research in Helmut Maier, *Forschung als Waffe. Rüstungsforschung in der Kaiser-Wilhelm-Gesellschaft und das Kaiser-Wilhelm-Institut für Metallforschung 1900–1945/48*, 2 vols. (Göttingen: Wallstein Verlag, 2007), 889–891.

[55] Günter Wassermann and Peter Wincierz (eds.), *Das Metall-Laboratorium der Metallgesellschaft AG 1918–1981* (Frankfurt am Main: Metallgesellschaft, 1981), 25–50.

[56] Gustav Siebel, "Die technischen Magnesiumlegierungen und die magnesiumhaltigen Aluminiumlegierungen. Zusammenfassender Bericht über die Forschungs- und Entwicklungsarbeiten der I.G.-Farbenindustrie AG, Bitterfeld von 1920 bis 1945," *Zeitschrift für Metallkunde*, 43 (1952), 238–244, here 238.

[57] Karl Schraivogel, "Heimwerkstoffe im Flugzeug- und Flugmotorenbau," *Luftfahrt-Forschung*, 14 (1937), 224–227.

Experimental Station for Aviation (*Deutsche Versuchsanstalt für Luftfahrt,* DVL) was upgraded to the "Institute for Materials Research of the DVL" (*Institut für Werkstofforschung der DVL*).[58] In September 1937, the Allied Aluminum Works (*Vereinigte Aluminium-Werke AG*, VAW) in Lauta, Lower Lusatia, inaugurated a generous new building for its research station.[59] As another indication of the increased importance of metal sciences in the four-year plan, the Reich Ministry for Education and Science (REM) transformed the chair for inorganic chemistry at the University of Göttingen into a chair for metal sciences in 1938.[60] This position was occupied by Georg Masing (1885–1956), an industrial chemist from Berlin. The journal *Aluminium* reported that the work of the DVL institute constituted "an important contribution to the struggle for economic freedom on the foundation of the four-year plan."[61]

In 1933, the renowned KWI for Metal Research was closed at its location in Berlin-Dahlem and reopened in Stuttgart in 1934 under a new director, the physical chemist Werner Köster (1896–1989).[62] Köster also dedicated himself to the triumvirate of "German metals"[63] and justified this with Germany's necessity, supposedly imposed from abroad, to become autarchic. While not quite so superficial and vocal as those of his colleague Peter Adolf Thiessen (1899–1990),[64] Fritz Haber's successor as director of the KWI for Physical Chemistry and a member of the NSDAP,[65] Köster's comments, too, reflect the infiltration of techno-scientific ideology. Thus, he claimed it was physical

[58] Joachim Brämer, "Aus der Geschichte der Deutschen Versuchsanstalt für Luftfahrt," *Metallwirtschaft*, 16 (1937), 382 f.

[59] Hans Röhrig and Lothar Lux, "Ein neues Heim für die Forschungs- und Entwicklungsarbeit der Vereinigte Aluminium-Werke Aktiengesellschaft," *Aluminium*, 19 (1937), 658–664.

[60] For a comprehensive account of the events surrounding the rededication and orientation to "industry-related practical research" as well as the conspiratorial activities concerning these matters undertaken by Rudolf Mentzel (1900–1987), president of the German Research Foundation (*Deutsche Forschungsgemeinschaft*, DFG) and SS Brigade Führer, and Peter-Adolf Thiessen, director of the KWI for Physical Chemistry, see Ulrich Majer, "Vom Weltruhm der zwanziger Jahre zur Normalität der Nachkriegszeit. Die Geschichte der Chemie in Göttingen von 1930–1950," in Heinrich Becker, Hans-Joachim Dahms, and Cornelia Wegeler (eds.), *Die Universität Göttingen unter dem Nationalsozialismus*, 2nd ed. (Munich: Saur, 1998), 589–629, here 609–613; on Masing, see Claus Priesner, "Georg Masing," in *Neue Deutsche Biographie*, vol. 16 (Berlin: Duncker and Humblot, 1990), 354 f.

[61] "Ernennungen und Beauftragungen," *Aluminium*, 20 (1938), 287.

[62] On the history of the metals institute from its founding in 1921 until 1948 and the events surrounding the relocation to Stuttgart, see Maier, *Forschung als Waffe*.

[63] See the comprehensive account in the "Verzeichnis der Veröffentlichungen des Kaiser Wilhelm-Instituts für Metallforschung 1921–1949," in Werner Köster and Hans von Schulz, *25 Jahre Kaiser Wilhelm-Institut für Metallforschung 1921–1946* (Stuttgart: Riederer, 1949), 121–166.

[64] For Thiessen, see Florian Schmaltz's chapter in this book.

[65] Michael Grüttner, *Biographisches Lexikon zur nationalsozialistischen Wissenschaftspolitik* (Heidelberg: Synchron, 2004).

chemistry that had provided those few metals "with which Germany, scooping from its own soil," could supply itself.[66] Shortly after the four-year plan was proclaimed in September 1936, Köster was announced as a speaker at the scientific workshop of the Economic Group for the Non-Ferrous Metals Industry at the Berlin Technical University (*Technische Hochschule*); his paper was titled "Research Goals to Alleviate the Raw Materials Situation under the Führer's Four-Year Program."[67]

Compared with the laboratories for aeronautics research and those at the universities and institutes of technology, the KWIMT enjoyed a special status because the lion's share of its funding was provided by the metals industry. Through the 1930s, the Economic Group of the Non-Ferrous Metals Industry in particular supported the institute, providing considerable funds for apparatus and equipment and to expand the building. The number of staff increased from twenty-two in 1936 to more than 100 in 1945.[68] Director Köster reported to the board of directors and cooperated with that body in determining the topics of research; the board controlled and steered the institute. A look at the membership of this board reveals how particular interests were able to influence the emphases of the institute's work. Among the members were high-ranking representatives of the leading companies in the nonferrous metals industry, a number of whom also held positions in various economic groups and their subgroups within the Reich Industry Group (*Reichsgruppe Industrie*). By this time, the Jewish industrialist Dr. Alfred Merton (1878–1954), Metallgesellschaft A.G., one of the "most active and most influential patrons" from the outset and also a member of the board of the institute in Stuttgart from 1934 on, had departed.[69] Members of the board in the final year of peace before World War II are listed in Table 11.1.[70]

In earlier years, the main sponsors of the institute from the nonferrous metals industry had traditionally dominated the board of trustees; by 1939, however, there was considerable "insourcing of Reich authorities and research centers," meaning that representatives of competing industrial and state research institutions were now included. At the board meeting in

---

[66] Werner Köster, "Die Bedeutung der physikalischen Chemie für die Metallindustrie," *Zeitschrift für Elektrochemie*, 41, No. 7a (1935), 386–393, here 387.

[67] *"Forschungsziele zur Erleichterung der Rohstofflage unter dem Vierjahres-Programm des Führers,"* program of the "wissenschaftliche Arbeitstagung," 16 October 1936, MPG-Archiv, Abt. I, Rep. 1A, No. 1891, fol. 123; to date the manuscript of the lecture has not been located.

[68] See chart 2.4 in Maier, *Forschung als Waffe*, 957.

[69] See Ulrich Marsch, *Zwischen Wissenschaft und Wirtschaft. Industrieforschung in Deutschland und Grossbritannien 1880–1936* (Paderborn: Schöningh, 2000), 408.

[70] Meeting of the Board of Trustees of the Kaiser Wilhelm Institute for Metal Research in Stuttgart, 1 November 1938, MPG-Archiv, Abt. I, Rep. 1A, No. 1893, fol. 245; also see in more detail Maier, *Forschung als Waffe*.

TABLE 11.1. *Board of Trustees of the Kaiser Wilhelm Institute for Metal Research in 1939*

Lieutenant Colonel Ernst Becht (1895–1959)	Head of the Raw Materials Department in the Defense Economy Staff[a]	Defense Economy and Armaments Office in the Supreme Command of the Armed Forces[a]
Director Adolf Beck (1892–1949)	IG Farbenindustrie, Bitterfeld	Director of the Light Metals Department[b]
Director Dr.-Ing. Rolf Borchers (1889–1958)	Board of Directors of Hüttenwerke Kayser AG, Berlin-Niederschöneweide	Director of the "Metal-Producing Industry" section; "inner council" of the Economic Group for the Non-Ferrous Metals Industry[c]
Dr. Otto Dahl (1899–1962)	Director of the "Metallurgy" Department of the Research Institute of AEG, Berlin[d]	Deputy of Director Dipl.-Ing. Otto Koehn (1891–1955), Board of Directors of AEG, Berlin
Dr. Max Ditt	"Research and Development" division, "Dept. F 19 Institutes, Universities, Testing Centers" of the Reich Office for Economic Expansion[e]	Deputy Director of the KWI for Physical Chemistry under Peter Adolf Thiessen until 1937; employed in the department of its director Ernst Telschow (1889–1988), Secretary General of the Kaiser Wilhelm Society[f]
Director Wolf von Eichhorn	Zinc Department of the Technical Division, Metallgesellschaft AG, Frankfurt am Main; deputy member of the Board of Directors[g]	Member of the Technical-Scientific Committee of the Economic Group of the Non-Ferrous Metals Industry[h]
Director Karl Eychmüller (1892–1981)	Chairman of the Board, Wieland-Werke AG, Ulm	Deputy Director of the Sector Group of the Non-Ferrous Metals Industry[i]
Retired Senior Mining Engineer Otto Fitzner (1888–1945)	Director of Bergwerksgesellschaft Georg von Giesches Erben, Breslau	Director of the Economic Group of the Non-Ferrous Metals Industry; Senate of the Kaiser Wilhelm Society[k]
Undersecretary Hermann Forkel	Reich Ministry of Economics	Consultant for Metals[l]

TABLE 11.1 (continued)

Professor Dr. Richard Glocker (1890–1978)	Director of the Institute for Metal Physics at the KWIMT	Institute of Technology, Stuttgart
Professor Dr. Georg Grube (1883–1966)	Director of the Institute for the Physical Chemistry of Metals at the KWIMT	Institute of Technology, Stuttgart; editor of the *Zeitschrift für Elektrochemie* (organ of the Deutsche Bunsen-Gesellschaft)[m]
Retired Mines Supervisor Paul Ferdinand Hast (1890–1973)	Ober- und Unterharzer Berg- und Hüttenwerke, Goslar	Director of the "Metals Ore Mining" section of the Mining Economic Group; "inner council" of the Economic Group of the Non-Ferrous Metals Industry[n]
Professor Dr. Werner Köster (1896–1989)	Managing Director of the KWIMT and Director of the Institute for Applied Metal Science at the KWIMT	Institute of Technology, Stuttgart; member of the Technical-Scientific Committee of the Economic Group of the Non-Ferrous Metals Industry; Director of the Subdivision for Non-Ferrous Metals in the Reich Research Council[o]
Professor Dr. Georg Masing (1885–1956)	Chair for General Metal Science, University of Göttingen[p]	Director of Metallography, Electrochemical Laboratory, Siemens & Halske, Berlin, until 1937[q]
Director Dr. Theodor Menzen	Vereinigte Aluminiumwerke AG (VAW), Lautawerk, Lusatia	Member of the VAW Board of Directors, Berlin[r]
Dr. Erich Puff (1900–1967)	Chief Executive Officer of the Economic Group of the Non-Ferrous Metals Industry[s]	Reich Commissioner and Director of the Non-Ferrous Metals Industry Control Office[t]
Riem	Economic Group of the Non-Ferrous Metals Industry	
Director Dr. phil. Wilhelm Rohn (1887–1943)	Board of Directors,[u] Heraeus-Vakuumschmelze, Hanau	Chairman of the German Society for the Science of Metals (DGM) in the VDI

Professor Erich Schönhardt (1891–1979)	Rector of the Institute of Technology, Stuttgart	Former Director of the Lecturers' Corps at the University of Tübingen[v]
Dipl. Volkswirt Hans von Schulz (1903–1979)	Economic Group of the Non-Ferrous Metals Industry	Representative of the Economic Group of the Non-Ferrous Metals Industry in the Commitee of the Lead Research Center[w]
General Director Bernhard Unholtz (1877–1951)	First Member of the Board, Vereinigte Deutsche Metallwerke A.G., Frankfurt/Heddernheim	Director of the "Subsection for Semi-Finished Light Metal Products"; Council of the Economic Group of the Non-Ferrous Metals Industry[x]
Air Staff Engineer Dr.-Ing. Anton Väth (1903–1973)	Head of Division for Materials Research of the Reich Aviation Research Department of the Reich Aviation Ministry	Permanent Representative of Undersecretary Adolf Baeumker (1891–1976), Reich Aviation Ministry, on the Board of Trustees of the KWI for Metal Research[y]
SS Oberführer Dipl.-Ing. Paul Zimmermann	Reich Commissioner for Metals	Director of the Supervisory Board for Base Metals

[a] Georg Thomas, *Geschichte der deutschen Wehr- und Rüstungswirtschaft (1918–1943/45)*, ed. Wolfgang Birkenfeld (Boppard: Harald Boldt Verlag, 1966), 66.

[b] *50 Jahre Deutsche Gesellschaft für Metallkunde*, 56 f.

[c] Teschemacher, 53 f.

[d] Burghard Weiss, "Rüstungsforschung am Forschungsinstitut der Allgemeinen Elektricitäts-Gesellschaft bis 1945," in Maier, *Rüstungsforschung*, 109–141.

[e] Geschäftsverteilungsplan der Reichsstelle für Wirtschaftsausbau, 21 March 1938, MPG-Archiv, Abt. I, Rep. 1A, No. 228, fol. 42.

[f] Christina Eibl, "Der Physikochemiker Peter Adolf Thiessen als Wissenschaftsorganisator (1899–1990)" (Ph.D. thesis: University of Stuttgart, 1999), 138 f.

[g] Metallgesellschaft Aktiengesellschaft, Frankfurt am Main, Bericht über das Geschäftsjahr vom 1. Oktober 1935 bis 30. September 1936 [Geschäftsbericht zur Generalversammlung 1937], MPG-Archiv, Abt. I, Rep. 1A, No. 1891; Wassermann and Wincierz, 38.

[h] Wirtschaftsgruppe Nichteisenmetall-Industrie (ed.), *Bericht der Wirtschaftsgruppe Nichteisenmetall-Industrie über die Jahre 1936/37 und 1937/38* (Berlin: Wirtschaftsgruppe Nichteisenmetall-Industrie, 1938), 2.

(continued)

TABLE 11.1 (continued)

i Teschemacher, 53. On additional offices held by Eychmüller, see "Die faschistischen Wehrwirtschaftsführer in der westdeutschen Wirtschaft," *Berichte des deutschen Wirtschaftsinstituts*, 5, No. 9/10 (1954), 1–64, here 21.

j Teschemacher, 34 f.

k *Bericht der Wirtschaftsgruppe Nichteisenmetall-Industrie*, 6.

l Paul C. W. Schmidt (ed.), *Wer leitet? Die Männer der Wirtschaft und der einschlägigen Verwaltung 1941/42* (Berlin: Hoppenstedt, 1942), 240.

m Peter Adolf Thiessen, "Georg Grube zum 60. Geburtstag," *Zeitschrift für Elektrochemie*, 49 (1943), 193–198, here 194. On Grube's activities in the Bunsen-Gesellschaft, see also Walther Jaenicke, *100 Jahre Bunsen-Gesellschaft 1894–1994* (Darmstadt: Steinkopff, 1994).

n Teschemacher, 48, 53.

o *Bericht der Wirtschaftsgruppe Nichteisenmetall-Industrie*, 2. On the role of techno-scientists as research-managers of the Reich Research Council, see Sören Flachowsky, *Von der Notgemeinschaft zum Reichsforschungsrat. Wissenschaftspolitik im Kontext von Autarkie, Aufrüstung und Krieg* (Stuttgart: Franz Steiner, 2008).

p *50 Jahre Deutsche Gesellschaft für Metallkunde*, 57 f.

q Majer, 613.

r From 1918 until 1 January 1949; I thank Peter Belli for this information. On Menzen's career, see "Dr. phil. Theodor Menzen 60 Jahre alt," *Aluminium*, 21 (1939), 86.

s Teschemacher, 54. Dr. Erich Puff was a member of the NSDAP.

t *Bericht der Wirtschaftsgruppe Nichteisenmetall-Industrie*, 2.

u On Rohn's techno-scientific work, see the numerous mentions in Walter Kaiser and Norbert Gilson, *Heraeus – Pioniere der Werkstofftechnologie. Von der Hanauer Platinschmelze zum internationalen Technologieunternehmen* (Munich: Piper, 2001); on his political ideas, *50 Jahre Deutsche Gesellschaft für Metallkunde*, 51 f.

v On the events surrounding the appointment of the Director of the Lecturers' Corps and National Socialist German Teachers' Association of the University of Tübingen, the mathematician Professor Dr. Erich Schönhardt, as rector of the Technical University of Stuttgart, see Helmut Heiber, *Universität unterm Hakenkreuz, Teil II: Die Kapitulation der Hohen Schulen, vol. 2: Das Jahr 1933 und seine Themen* (Munich: Saur, 1994), 54–58.

w *Bericht der Wirtschaftsgruppe Nichteisenmetall-Industrie*, 6; also see this document for additional offices.

x Teschemacher, 53.

y Udet [Reich Aviation Ministry] to the Managing President of the KWS, 1 November 1938, MPG-Archiv, Abt. I, Rep. 1A, No. 1303, fol. 161. Ernst Udet (1896–1941) was General Inspector of the Air Force Fighter Division.

Stuttgart on November 1, 1938, the director of the Supervisory Board, SS Oberführer Zimmermann, noted that his monitoring offices would give the board of trustees and the institute a "further look at what is necessary... especially to the extent that it is conditioned politically or by economic policy."[71] Zimmermann's role meant that the KWIMT was controlled by a member of the staff of the Reichsführer SS but at the same time promised considerable funding from the ample resources of the Supervisory Board. His indication of the "politically necessary" made clear that he was not satisfied with previous research and development endeavors. Moreover, the board of trustees now included representatives of those state offices that planned and executed the establishment of the "defense economy," making the economy autarchic and driving rearmament: the Reich Ministry of Economics, the Reich Office for Economic Expansion, the Superior Command of the Armed Forces, and the Reich Aviation Ministry (*Reichsluftfahrtministerium*, RLM).

The *Gleichschaltung* (coordination) of the board of trustees can be regarded as one of many administrative measures to implement the ideological concept of the "German metals," and one can ask how the scientists themselves reacted to the propaganda about utilizing native materials and to the increased business activity in the fields of aluminum, magnesium, and zinc research. A partial answer can be found in records of the joint working convention of the Sector Group of the Non-Ferrous Metals Industry and the KWIMT in October 1937. On this occasion, the staff presented a humorous publication on a witty evening in a Swabian wine village. Several inches of column in the so-called *Mundelsheimer Merkur* were used to lampoon the "executive orders" from the governmental control authorities. The fictive "919th Executive Order for the Uniform Regulation of German Metal Consumption" shows that the regulations themselves were a source of humor:

Paragraph 1. The only German metal for the coming millennium is and remains ALUMINUM. ... In order to ensure a smooth conversion of the consumption regulation for metals to aluminum, it is imperative that by 1 January 1939, *iron and steel* production amount to no more than 50% of the aluminum production. ... Effective immediately, a commission is to be established with the task of reviewing the specific weight of *magnesium*, which is still a partial obstacle on the path to founding the aluminum age, and to adjust it to that of aluminum by revoking ordinance 7 of the story of the Creation, Chap. I ... § 5. In future *zinc* is to be treated as a non-German metal because of its excessive specific weight.[72]

[71] All quotes from the meeting of the Board of Directors of the Kaiser Wilhelm Institute for Metals Research in Stuttgart, 1 November 1938, MPG-Archiv, Abt. I, Rep. 1A, No. 1893, fols. 246 f.

[72] *Mundelsheimer Merkur* of 5 November 1937, MPG-Archiv, Abt. I, Rep. 1A, No. 1892, emphasis in original.

Apparently, assigning the national character "German" to a metal – besides making the economy autarchic and the country "well-fortified," the central ideological construct of National Socialist policy on materials – was the source of considerable merriment among techno-scientists. These scientists did not oppose the national economy policy concept of becoming autarchic nor object to the supposedly outstanding German characteristic of being particularly gifted in the fields of chemistry and technology; but this historical source showing their mentality and the reception they gave the ideology of "German technology" as a whole indicates that they apparently considered the "national symbolism of metals" to be nonsense.

"GERMAN METALS" ALL THE WAY TO
THE LATHE OF THE ARMAMENTS INDUSTRY?

Re: Fw 190 Konstructal Planes. As requested, we are providing you with an excerpt from the reports of the troops about damage to the 10 deployed planes made of konstructal. ... The machines had up to 300 starts under their belt. No damages to any of the machines were reported which could be ascribed to the use of konstructal. No cases of corrosion damage or fissuring occurred. ... The findings indicate in particular that great demands were placed on [the planes] mentioned, not only by enemy flights, but also during training and practice flights, and that even after a number of very hard landings there were no complaints about the airframe.[73]

Although the metal researchers did not accept the ideology attached to the objects of their research in its extreme form, on the institutional level, the KWIMT did indeed present a united front with the offices responsible for the armaments industry and technology. Above and beyond this, how successful was the conversion to "German metals"? Did the leading institutes of metal research succeed in developing suitable substitute alloys using the three "German" metals? Proceeding from the narrowness of this raw materials basis, were the metal researchers able to extend the war economy's meager raw materials at the decisive junctures? Due to the great number of applications in which aluminum alone was implemented as a replacement metal, it is not possible to strike a complete quantitative balance here. Not even consideration of the production and consumption of the nonferrous metals can clarify the scope, let alone the special areas in which conversion

---

[73] Focke-Wulf Flugzeugbau G.m.b.H., Sorau/L., to Dr. Brenner, Vereinigte Leichtmetall-Werke, Hannover-Linden, 1 February 1944, Main Brandenburg State Archives (*Brandenburgisches Landeshauptarchiv*, BLA), Pr. Br. Rep. 75, VAW Lautawerk, emphasis in original. I thank Peter Belli for alerting me to the existence of these files. Dr.-Ing. Paul Brenner (1897–1962) was head of the Research Institute of the VAW.

took place.[74] As the following example makes clear, it seems that each conversion project had its own biography.[75]

The aluminum-zinc-magnesium (Al-Zn-Mg) alloys represent a prominent example of the attempt to introduce "German metals." Composed of the "triumvirate" of the "German metals," they were the ideal form of an "ideologically correct" alloy. Although investigations of this ternary system had been undertaken in the 1920s, because of its higher susceptibility to stress corrosion as compared to duralumin[76] it failed to achieve practical importance.[77] Nonetheless, like duralumin it could be hardened, a very attractive property.[78] For forging, too, the Al-Zn-Mg alloys were excellent "because the yield pressures required for forging were up to 15% lower" than for duralumin.[79] In 1940, Duralumin, "at 40–50,000 t, constituted the main allocation of airplane alloys." In terms of the armaments industry, the Al-Zn-Mg-alloy had the decisive advantage that the "German" zinc could

[74] A comprehensive study about the conversion to different raw materials in the area of metal substitute materials has yet to be carried out.

[75] Compare a number of successful examples in cooperation with Army Ordnance (artillery fuses), the Navy (torpedoes) and the Air Force (bearings) in Maier, *Forschung als Waffe*.

[76] "Stress Corrosion – A term used in reference to the effect of stresses, whether residual or applied, on the rate of corrosion of a metal in a corrosive atmosphere. The corrosion rate may be increased, especially if the stress is fluctuating by breaking or by flaking off the protective skin that is formed as the result of the chemical action in corrosion. This exposes the underlying metal to further corrosive action. Stress corrosion failure may be intercrystalline in alloys that normally exhibit transcrystalline fracture." Arthur Douglass Merriman, *A Dictionary of Metallurgy* (London: MacDonald and Evans, 1958), 343. The German definition of stress corrosion of 1936: "Die einfachste und bekannteste Form des Spannungskorrosionsbruches ist die gewöhnliche interkristalline Korrosion, die auch unabhängig von der Spannung eintritt. Bekannt ist z. B. das Auftreten von Korngrenzenkorrosion bei Duralumin ... Das ... Material wird ... an den Korngrenzen angegriffen und dadurch der gesamte Gefügezusammenhalt aufgelockert, so dass trotz äusserlich oft nur mässig erscheinenden Korrosionsangriffs Festigkeit und Dehnung erheblich gelitten haben. Wenn die Probe während der Korrosion unter Spannung steht, verläuft dieser Vorgang noch rascher und führt schliesslich zum Bruch der Probe." In Kurt Matthes, "Über die Spannungskorrosion der Leichtmetalle," *Jahrbuch der Lilienthal-Gesellschaft für Luftfahrtforschung* (1936), 404–430, here 406 f.; for a comprehensive discussion of the problems with stress corrosion in duralumin, see Margaret B. W. Graham and Bettye H. Pruitt, *R & D for Industry. A Century of Technical Innovation at Alcoa* (Cambridge: Cambridge University Press, 1990).

[77] On this and the history of hardenable wrought alloys in general, see Rolf Grabow, "Zu einigen wissenschaftshistorischen Aspekten der Entwicklung aushärtbarer Aluminiumlegierungen," *NTM*, 17 (1980), 69–79.

[78] In detail, H. Hug, "Aluminium-Zink-Magnesium-Legierungen," in Dietrich Altenpohl (ed.), *Aluminium und Aluminiumlegierungen* (Werner Köster (ed.), *Reine und angewandte Metallkunde in Einzeldarstellungen*, 19) (Berlin: Springer, 1965), 770–785.

[79] Hubert Altwicker, "Schmieden von Aluminium- und Magnesiumlegierungen," in Max Hansen (ed.), *Metallkunde der Nichteisenmetalle* (*Naturforschung und Medizin in Deutschland 1939–1946), FIAT Review of German Science*, 32, No. 1 (Wiesbaden: Verlag Chemie, 1948), 166–170, here 167.

be used as the alloying addition instead of the "thrift metal" copper. Thus if the development of a substitute alloy with the same properties were successful, it would mean that Germany could expect to reduce its demand for copper by several hundred tons each year.[80] Just how urgent a reduction of copper consumption had become at this time is apparent in the drop in submarine production, where the navy was short by 400 tons.[81]

As early as the joint working convention of the Economic Group of the Non-Ferrous Metals Industry and the KWIMT in 1936, and well before the announcement of the four-year plan, Director Köster had presented his first results on the Al-Zn-Mg ternary system. The alloys were important, he wrote, because they were composed of those three raw materials of which Germany had an unlimited supply.[82] The study of ternary systems represented a decisive leap in metal science and also technology, because all technical alloys are ultimately multicomponent systems. Consequently, in that very year Dr. Max Hansen (1901–1978), director of the research institute at the Dürener Metal Works in Berlin, submitted a critical compilation of the binary alloys; this became one of the most important texts in the science of metals for decades worldwide. This work – most of which was produced at the pre-1934 location of the KWIMT in Berlin-Dahlem[83] – took on such decisive importance because it made possible the differentiation between alloys "within a binary system which can be applied to technical utilization, from those which are of no technical interest."[84]

The ternary Al-Zn-Mg system that appeared so desirable, both ideologically and in terms of armaments manufacture, was not exactly standard content in the textbooks of the 1930s. In fact, Köster, like Hansen before him, assigned himself the task of determining the technically utilizable area in the "aluminum corner" (see Figure 11.3). Again in 1949, Köster emphasized explicitly that their processing

was not an end in itself, but an imperative prerequisite for the understanding of the properties of a … group of alloys. This observation retrospectively underlines the great importance for metal technology of determining the constitution of a metal. A recorded picture of the status, reliable up to the last detail, is like a map, opening

---

[80] With the number of 40,000 metric tons named in the source and an average share of 4 percent copper in duralumin, around 1,600 metric ton of copper could have been substituted in 1940.

[81] Willi A. Boelcke (ed.), *Deutschlands Rüstung im Zweiten Weltkrieg. Hitlers Konferenzen mit Albert Speer 1942–1945* (Frankfurt am Main: Athenaion, 1969), 78.

[82] Workshop of the Kaiser Wilhelm Institute for Metals Research in Stuttgart, 19 May 1936, MPG-Archiv, Abt. I, Rep. 1A, No. 1904/3, fol. 21.

[83] Verzeichnis der Veröffentlichungen des KWI für Metallforschung 1921–1949, in Köster and von Schulz, 121–166.

[84] Max Hansen, *Aufbau der Zwei-Stoff-Legierungen. Eine kritische Zusammenfassung* (Berlin: Springer, 1936), V f.

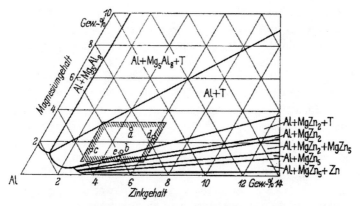

Aluminiumecke des Dreistoffsystems Aluminium-Zink-Magnesium bei Raumtemperatur (nach W. KÖSTER u. K. KAM [*19*]).

Schraffierter Bereich: Lage der gebräuchlichsten Handelslegierungen.

    a Leg. AlZnMg 3 Construktal 21/42;
    b Leg. AlZnMg 1 Construktal 21/51, Unidur;
    c Leg. A-Z4G Zicral 3, Scléral, MT 1, Superalumag T. 35;
    d Leg. A-Z6G Scléral MT 2, Superalumag T. 45, Strongal-6;
    e Leg. AlZnMg Unidal.

FIGURE 11.3. Aluminum corner of the Aluminum-Zinc-Magnesium ternary system

Source: Originally published in Helmut Maier (ed.), *Rüstungsforschung im Nationalsozialismus. Organisation, Mobilisierung und Entgrenzung der Technikwissenschaften* (Göttingen: Wallstein, 2002), 380.

up to the trained eye the correct route to interpreting the metal's behavior and to heat treatment, and protecting him from time-consuming detours, from experiments without a compass.[85]

From 1940 on, Köster's results and those of his collaborators – Wolf Wolf (1908–1984), Kurt Kam, and Walter Dullenkopf (1904–1976) – became the point of departure for systematic and intensive experimental activity by the largest aluminum producers, the air force suppliers, and the airplane producers themselves.[86]

The representatives of the participating companies and research institutions convened in March 1940 under the direction of Air Staff Engineer Dr.-Ing. Anton Väth to standardize an "aviation material" free of thrift

---

[85] Köster and von Schulz, 57.
[86] The authors referred most frequently to the works by Werner Köster and Wolf Wolf, "Das Dreistoffsystem Aluminium-Magnesium-Zink," *Zeitschrift für Metallkunde*, 28 (1936), 155–158; Werner Köster and Walther Dullenkopf, "Das Dreistoffsystem Aluminium-Magnesium-Zink," *Zeitschrift für Metallkunde*, 28 (1936), 309–312, 364–367; Werner Köster and Kurt Kam, "Über die Aushärtung von Aluminium-Magnesium-Zink-Legierungen und die Rückbildung der Kaltaushärtung," *Zeitschrift für Metallkunde*, 30 (1938), 320–322.

materials on the basis of Al-Zn-Mg. Proceeding from tests by the KWIMT, the following alloy combinations were proposed (Table 11.2):[87]

Aside from the alloys from IG Farben, all had a zinc share of 3 percent to 6 percent; chrome or vanadium had the function of "stabilizers," with which the dreaded stress corrosion was to be eliminated.[88] The "Al-Zn-Mg-Alloys Consortium" (*Arbeitsgemeinschaft Al-Zn-Mg-Legierungen*) was made up of the most prominent experts in the light metal technology of the day, thus documenting the high priority placed on developing aviation materials free of copper. Others present included representatives of "Junkers, Focke-Wulf, Heinkel, Messerschmitt, Fieseler and other aerospace companies."[89]

In March 1942, the "specifications"[90] were published for the aviation material 3425, designated "Konstructal 20/53." It was developed for processing into airfoils, rods, propeller roots, and compressed and free forged parts. At the same time, the RLM negotiated with Focke-Wulf (Fw), after ten planes already had been contracted, for the "production of 50 additional Fw 190 airplanes of konstructal and also for a plan to implement high-strength Al-Zn-Mg alloys in a new construction."[91] Despite inconsistent results in the test on stress corrosion, which initially caused Focke-Wulf to have only the first ten Fw 190s built of konstructal,[92] a suprising consequence of the intensive development activity was the realization that stress values could be raised by 10 percent using the Al-Zn-Mg alloy rather than duralumin. In January 1943, Väth reported that the head design engineer at Junkers, Heinrich Hertel (1901–1982), wished to build the long-range bomber Ju 290 out of a konstructal alloy of the highest stability in order to achieve a higher load capacity.[93] In April of the same year, however, at the meeting of

[87] Röhrig, VAW, to Dr. Menzen, file note, meeting at RLM, 12 March 1940, BLA Lautawerk. Hans Röhrig (1893–1946) was member of the Research Institute of the VAW, Lautawerk; see Peter Belli, *Lautawerk* (forthcoming).

[88] Hug, 770.

[89] Röhrig, VAW, to Dr. Menzen, file note, meeting at RLM, 12 March 1940, BLA Lautawerk; on the shifting fortunes of aluminum supply to the aviation industry, Lutz Budrass, *Flugzeugindustrie und Luftrüstung in Deutschland 1918–1945* (Düsseldorf: Droste Verlag, 1998).

[90] "Für jeden Werkstoff, wie er mit bestimmten Festigkeitseigenschaften sich aus seiner chemischen Zusammensetzung ergibt, ist ein 'Leistungsblatt' aufgestellt. Dieses Blatt enthält alle Angaben über die verlangten Eigenschaften des betreffenden Werkstoffes in den angegebenen Verarbeitungszuständen, ferner Angaben über seine Verwendbarkeit, Prüfung u. dgl." In Reichluftfahrtministerium (ed.), *Fliegwerkstoffe. Handbuch für die Auswahl der im deutschen Flugzeug-, Flugmotoren- und Luftfahrtgerätebau zu verwendenden Werkstoffe. Teil 1: Metallische Werkstoffe* (Berlin: Reichsluftfahrtministerium, 1942), 3. This is a looseleaf binder starting in 1935 through October, 1942. I thank Mr. Goers for providing this source.

[91] Brenner, Kostron, Vereinigte Leichtmetall-Werke AG, to Röhrig, Vereinigte Aluminium-Werke AG, 19/5/1942, BLA Lautawerk; Normblätter, BLA Lautawerk.

[92] Röhrig, file note, Betr. Reisebericht Metallgesellschaft Ffm, 21/8/1942, BLA Lautawerk.

[93] Väth, Protocol of the meeting on 29 January 1943 in Hanover, BLA Lautawerk.

TABLE 11.2. *Members of the Al-Zn-Mg-Alloys Consortium and the Composition of the Proposed Alloys (remainder aluminum)*

Company	Members			
Vereinigte Leichtmetall-Werke GmbH, Hannover	Dr.-Ing. Josef Schulte; Dr.-Ing. Paul Brenner	4–5% Zn	1–2.5% Mg	0.3–1% Mn 0.8% Si
Metallgesellschaft AG, Frankfurt	Prof. Dr. Ernst Schmid; Dr. phil. Günther Wassermann	similar to DVL		
Dürener Metallwerke AG	Dr. phil. habil. Max Hansen	4–5% Zn	2–2.5% Mg	0.5–0.8% Mn 0.6% Si
IG Farbenindustrie AG, Bitterfeld	Dr.-Ing. Erich Siebel; Dr. Menzel; Erich Rackwitz	1% Zn	9% Mg	
Deutsche Versuchsanstalt für Luftfahrt, Berlin	Dr.-Ing. Franz Bollenrath; Dr.-Ing. Walther Bungardt	3–4.5% Zn	2–2.5% Mg	0.3–0.6% Mn 0.6% Si 0.01–0.5% V
Vereinigte Aluminiumwerke AG, Lauta, Lausitz	Dr. Hans Röhrig	6% Zn	3% Mg	0.2% Cr or V, respectively

Source: Röhrig, VAW, to Dr. Menzen, file note, meeting at RLM, 12 March 1940, BLA Lautawerk.

the "Konstructal Community," the complete conversion of the Ju 288 to the aircraft construction material 3425 as originally planned was cancelled and restricted to airfoils and compressed parts. By this time the ten Fw 190s were stationed in southern France and subjected to the "strictest monitoring."[94]

The conversion to the new, high-strength construction material 3425 could not be done in the accelerated manner initially mandated by the RLM. So it was not possible to determine with any certainty the interactions between the various stabilizing components on the stress corrosion, or the optimum procedures from casting to half-finished products – from the raw ingot to the airfoil. Various airplane manufacturers complained over the uncertainty about stress corrosion, which they investigated by subjecting the delivered half-finished products to standard tests in their own facilities. Because of the high rate of rejection, use of the konstructal material 3425 from the Vereinigte Leichtmetall-Werke GmbH (VLW) was suspended and the RLM switched over to the alloy Hy 43, which had been developed by IG Farben and the DVL within the "Al-Zn-Mg Alloys Consortium." [95] Apparently the testing procedures of the participating producers of half-finished products and airplanes were not uniform, and even the simple sequence of preparing the test samples and the minor fluctuations in the chemical composition of the dipping baths had unexpectedly strong effects on the result.[96] In the dipping bath, a metal is "dipped" into a corrosive solution and thus, exposed to a high chemical stress in order to allow for a systematic while short-time investigation on its stress-corrosion properties. Since the consortium did not consider itself capable of reaching a solution to the complex problem, in 1943 it attempted to commission the KWIMT with testing "the influence of manganese on the solubility of $MgZn_2$," the metal compound that caused precipitation hardening in Al-Zn-Mg alloys. Köster had to refuse the offer, however, because of "other projects."[97]

Finally, in 1943, the production launch of the He 219, an airplane model by the Heinkel-Werke, was at risk. In this model, the "heavy spar boom sections" were to be made out of 3425.[98] This amounted to a quantum leap

[94] Feldmann, VLW, Hanover, file note, 12 April 1943, BLA Lautawerk.
[95] 4.5 percent Zn, 3.5 percent Mg, 0.15 percent Cr, 0.03 percent V, 0.08 percent Ti, 0.4 percent Cu; see Siebel, 241. The Hy alloys were a family of highly corrosion-resistant, aluminum-based cast alloys with magnesium as the main component, marketed under the "Hydronalium" brand name; magnesium alloys for special purposes also received this designation; Schulenburg, 298.
[96] Röhrig, Metall-Forschungsstelle der [VAW], "Über den Einfluss der Reihenfolge der Operationen Biegen und Warmverformen auf die Spannungskorrosion von Schlaufenproben aus Al-Zn-Mg-Legierungen," 14 July 1944, BLA Lautawerk.
[97] Brenner, file note. Meeting of the Al-Zn-Mg Consortium on 5 October 1943 in Frankfurt/Main, 7 October 1943, BLA Lautawerk.
[98] Brenner, Feldmann, VLW, Hanover, "Bericht über den Stand der Herstellung von schweren Al-Zn-Mg-Pressprofilen aus Fl.W. 3425," 13 September 1944, BLA Lautawerk.

in terms of production technology, for up until then spar booms of those dimensions had to be mill-cut – a procedure that was costly and wasted material. At the "Aluminum Alloys Meeting" of the Lilienthal Society for Aviation Research in November 1944, Hubert Altwicker of IG Farben Bitterfeld reported on the production of conic spar boom moldings for the models He 219 and He 177 using large wrought presses: "For a 10-m boom for the He 177, the amount of chipping drops from 66% to 11%, for the $5\frac{1}{2}$-m boom of the He 219, from 70% to 3%." For the case of the Ju 290, he estimated that forging would result in a reduction of 110 kg of completed weight per airplane and shorten the entire production time to 60 percent of its previous length. Savings of 700 kg alloyed steel, which previously required expensive cutting, were pitted against an increased demand of just 125 kg aluminum.[99]

Despite all the euphoria about being able to replace the duralumin "burdened with thrift materials," the program soon found itself in a raw materials predicament. The Al-Zn-Mg alloy required the aluminum from which it was produced be free of copper, or to have a very low copper content. With falling production of primary aluminum and the obligation to process the increasing amounts of airplane scrap containing copper, there was no way to make broad conversion feasible. The highest monthly production level reached was 520 t, the amount delivered to industry in October 1944.[100] Gustav Siebel (1900–1987), director of the Research Laboratory for Light Metals in Bitterfeld, estimated that a total of around 3,500 tons of the alloy were produced. Recovered aluminum from airplane scrap, used increasingly because of the lack of primary aluminum,[101] consequently had too high a copper content.[102] To avoid the increased stress corrosion resulting from this, as early as August 1944 Georg Masing of the University of Göttingen was contracted by the RLM to investigate the issue of plating – that is, rolling out – protective metals.[103] In the 1920s this method had been used successfully to eliminate the problem of stress corrosion in duralumin.[104] So finally, after nearly five years of research on stress corrosion within the Al-Zn-Mg

[99] Hubert Altwicker, "Grossschmiedeteile aus Leichtmetall," in Werkstoffe. *Bericht über die Sitzung Aluminiumlegierungen am 22. und 23. November 1944 in Weimar, Lilienthal-Gesellschaft für Luftfahrtforschung, Bericht 183*, 27–35, here 30–32, ADM.

[100] Walther Bungardt and Herbert Winter, "Al-Zn-Mg-Cu-Legierungen," in Hansen (ed.), Metallkunde, 117–126, here 118.

[101] In 1944, not less than around 38 percent of the German aluminum came from aircraft scrap; see Helmut Maier, "Flugzeugschrott und Suppentöpfe: Aluminium recycling in Deutschland vor und nach 1945," in Roland Ladwig (ed.), *Recycling in Geschichte und Gegenwart* (Georg-Agricola-Gesellschaft: Freiberg, 2003), 75–94, here 84.

[102] Siebel, 238.

[103] Feldmann, file note, Meeting of the "Konstructal" Consortium on 29 September 1944 in Göttingen, 17 November 1944, BLA Lautawerk.

[104] For a comprehensive account, see Graham and Pruitt.

Alloys Consortium, Franz Bollenrath (1898–1981), director of the Institute
for Materials Research of the DVL in Berlin-Adlershof, demanded "that
a recommitment to stress corrosion testing essentially return us to basic
research, and that the testing involved in the fabrication and the further utilization of our half-finished products in aviation construction be restricted
to a significantly lower level." With these setbacks, Air Staff Engineer Väth,
the responsible director of the RLM Consortium, argued, "The light metals industry and the aviation works can be proud that nothing has happened yet."[105] In fact, it appears that the relatively low utilization of the
aviation material 3425 was not only caused by the technical problem of
reproducibility in the laboratory but also the aviation industry's strict quality standards for materials. In any case, in early 1944 the ten konstructal
planes by Focke-Wulf, despite extreme operational demands and "strictest
monitoring," showed no signs at all of structural changes.[106]

SUMMARY

With gratification we can state that, even in the fourth year of war, German armaments manufacturing is capable of fulfilling all demands of the supreme command,
despite their significantly increased scope. Thanks to the exertions of industry we
have succeeded in overcoming the difficulties with the supply of raw materials,
something that the enemy even today, completely misjudging what German technical intelligence can do, still believes we cannot solve. We have managed to overcome
shortages through increased production and through conversion to substitute materials; through this, new weapons can be provided constantly to our combat troops in
even more effective design and to a degree not believed possible.[107]

The "conversion to substitute materials" constituted one of the central
ideological tenets of the National Socialist policy of autarky. Through the
mobilization of "native" metals it was largely successful in compensating
for shortages, maintaining and even increasing the flow of arms and munitions, as Minister of Armaments Speer noted in the *Jahrbuch der Metalle*
in 1943. Through a cross-alliance of institutions, metal science research for
armaments solved numerous application problems associated with utilizing
unfamiliar "substitute alloys." Even in late 1944, systematic, highly intense
research was still being performed to solve the problem of stress corrosion

---

[105] Debate about stress corrosion, in "Werkstoffe. Bericht über die Sitzung Aluminiumlegierungen
am 22. und 23. November 1944 in Weimar, Lilienthal-Gesellschaft für Luftfahrtforschung,
Bericht 183," 74–76, ADM.

[106] Focke-Wulf Flugzeugbau G.m.b.H., Sorau/L., to Herrn Dr. Brenner, Vereinigte Leichtmetall-
Werke, Hannover-Linden, 1 February 1944, BLA Lautawerk. On the development of
Al-Zn-Mg alloys into the 1960s, from the metal science and technological perspective, see
the comprehensive work by Hug.

[107] Albert Speer, Foreword, in "Hans von Schulz," *Jahrbuch der Metalle*, (1943), 9.

in copper-free aviation materials, seeking to relieve the permanent copper shortage of the war economy by producing ever-larger amounts of available alloys. As the example of the Al-Zn-Mg alloy demonstrates, the research and development programs involved here were executed politically and administratively, controlled by a "coordinated" board of trustees at the KWIMT, and/or performed in a consortium led jointly by science and the military.

For the metallurgists themselves, autarky, mobilization for the war, and metal technology methods to this end were familiar and well-established techno-policy concepts from World War I and the Weimar period.[108] Thus it is no surprise that they actively seized upon and further elaborated on them for their respective technical and scientific fields. It is possible that they adhered to the conception of the superiority of German technical intelligence based on reasons of race ideology, which, after all, amounted to flattery from the highest offices until 1944, but this is not at issue here. In any case, the materials specialists working in the research sections of industry, institutes of higher education, and the Kaiser Wilhelm Society picked up on the problems at hand and placed the results of their research in the context of utilization for the armaments industry. This is primarily a result of the close dovetailing of the KWIMT with the Economic Group of the Non-Ferrous Metals Industry. So the ideological concept of the "German metals" was not merely propaganda in the everyday work of the armaments industry or at the sites of metallurgical research and development. Despite their privileged position, the metal researchers were also confronted with strict requirements to economize.

The attribution of national characters in the material sphere reflects a deeply seated collective symbolism, and National Socialist ideologists of materials and technology endeavored to imply that a group of metals was "ideologically correct," associating them with the concepts of "home country" (*Heimat*), "soil," and "German." Among the techno-scientists, however, this evoked amusement at best. While these concepts can be found in the techno-political literature like the journal *Deutsche Technik* up to the early 1940s, there is no evidence of them in inter-institutional communication, that is, between the metallurgical research laboratories, the aviation industry, and the Reich Aviation Ministry.

The intensive study of the alloy families of the three "German" metals at precisely this time occurred in the context of making the economy autarchic, of supplying rearmament, and of overcoming the shortages in the war economy. The Al-Zn-Mg alloys had been considered extremely susceptible to stress corrosion even back in the 1920s. The large-scale replacement of duralumin with a "German" alloy ultimately failed because of the problems

---

[108] See Ulrich Marsch, "Von der Syntheseindustrie zur Kriegswirtschaft. Brüche und Kontinuitäten in Wissenschaft und Politik," in Maier, Rüstungsforschung, 33–51.

with stress corrosion and the limits of the raw materials economy during the second half of the war. An exact quantitative analysis of the conversion of the entire armaments production to "German metals" and other, nonmetal substitute materials has yet to be performed. The case introduced here, however, shows how the KWI for Metal Research, from the mid-1930s at the latest, and starting in 1940 along with the most important industrial leaders from the period, contributed to the acceptance of the ideological concept of materials from native ore, half-finished on the lathe in the armaments factory, all the way to the airplane on the front. Beyond this it becomes clear that in the Third Reich it was indeed possible to surmount departmental egotism and the boundaries of competing metals and aviation industry concerns to organize technical and scientific research and development in a directed and effective manner.

12

Calculation, Measurement, and Leadership: War Research at the Kaiser Wilhelm Institute for Fluid Dynamics, 1937–1945

Moritz Epple

The history of the sciences in National Socialism can be analyzed in a number of very different ways. These include the relationships between science and ideology, the interdependence of academic and state institutions, scientists' behavior toward persecuted colleagues, and the participation of scientists in the preparation and execution of the crimes of the Nazi state.[1] However, there is another dimension to this subject – one that concerns those sciences, or more precisely, techno-sciences, whose very research topics and structures were of keen interest to every modern state, especially to one with such a great military potential as Germany.[2]

---

[1] Instead of referring to the comprehensive body of literature, here I would like to mention only an outline of the questions asked in the "History of the Kaiser Wilhelm Society in National Socialism" research program; see Doris Kaufmann, "Wissenschaft im Nationalsozialismus," in Max-Planck-Gesellschaft zur Förderung der Wissenschaften e. V. (ed.), *Ethos der Forschung. Ethics of Research. Ringberg-Symposium October 1999* (Munich: Generalverwaltung der Max-Planck-Gesellschaft, 2000), 11–23.

[2] The relationship between technology and the sciences is historically complex. When the term "techno-sciences" (a plural) is used below, it is done to designate those modern sciences that were closely linked with the development of important technologies. The development of aerodynamics is just as inconceivable without the development of aeronautics as advanced flight technologies are without aerodynamic research. In such disciplines it is no longer possible to draw clear boundaries between "science" and "technology." For a critique of the inflationary use of the expression "techno-science" (in the singular), see also Hans-Jörg

This chapter is an abridged version of Moritz Epple, "Rechnen, Messen, Führen. Kriegsforschung am Kaiser-Wilhelm-Institut für Strömungsforschung 1937–1945" in Helmut Maier (ed.), *Rüstungsforschung im Nationalsozialismus* (Göttingen: Wallstein Verlag, 2002), 305–356. It relates several of the results of my archival work during a guest residency at the "History of the Kaiser Wilhelm Society in National Socialism" (Geschichte der Kaiser-Wilhelm-Gesellschaft im Nationalsozialismus) research program of the Max Planck Society in Berlin. I would like to extend my warmest thanks to all members of the working group for the stimulating and constructive atmosphere in which I was able to spend my time in Berlin. For their critical review of an earlier version of this essay, I thank especially Helmut Maier and Carola Sachse.

The integration of such sciences into the National Socialist state was therefore initially a question of neither ideology nor morality. Many of the actors – scientists, engineers, politicians – simply took this for granted, as have most historians in retrospective. Indeed, why should it be surprising or especially significant to find cooperation between aerodynamic scientists and aircraft design engineers or between research institutes and the air force, and to see scientists, industrialists, the military, and ministerial officials working together in the techno-sciences during the Nazi period?

A study of the literature published to the present shows two historiographic tendencies. First, a techno-science like aerodynamics and hydrodynamics has served to illustrate the supposedly deadlocked structures of the organization of science under National Socialism.[3] Second, the importance of hydrodynamics and aerodynamics research during the Nazi period has been understood as a chapter in a continuous, long-term development.[4]

According to this second perspective, the institutes of aerodynamics and fluid dynamics [5] in Göttingen, along with other, similar institutions, became the first institutions of large-scale scientific research in Germany. Perhaps the most important indicator of this long-term context (besides flows of financing and materials) may be the astonishing continuities in personnel in the areas of aerodynamics and aviation research. Scientific careers like those of Ludwig Prandtl, the director of the KWI for Fluid Dynamics (*KWI für Strömungsforschung*, KWIFD), and of his important pupil Albert Betz,[6] extended from the imperial period into the Federal Republic. This continuity guaranteed not only the handing down of theoretical approaches but also the transfer of the structures organizing research.

Rheinberger, *Toward a History of Epistemic Things. Synthesizing Proteins in the Test Tube* (Stanford: Stanford University Press, 1997), 31 f.

[3] See, for an example, Karl-Heinz Ludwig, *Technik und Ingenieure im Dritten Reich* (Düsseldorf: Droste, 1974).

[4] See especially Helmuth Trischler, *Luft- und Raumfahrtforschung in Deutschland, 1900–1970. Politische Geschichte einer Wissenschaft* (Frankfurt am Main: Campus Verlag, 1992); Helmuth Trischler, "'Big Science' or 'Small Science'? Die Luftfahrtforschung im Nationalsozialismus," in Doris Kaufmann (ed.), *Geschichte der Kaiser-Wilhelm-Gesellschaft im Nationalsozialismus. Bestandsaufnahme und Perspektiven der Forschung*, 2 vols. (Göttingen: Wallstein, 2000), vol. 1, 328–362.

[5] The literal translation of the German *Strömungsforschung*, an expression used both as a designation of the research field and in the names of the Göttingen institutes, would be the slightly awkward expression "flow research." In this paper *Strömungsforschung*, which included both theoretical and experimental approaches to all branches of hydro- and aerodynamics, will be translated as the more traditional fluid dynamics.

[6] From 1925 on, Betz was deputy director of the Aerodynamics Testing Institute (*Aerodynamische Versuchsanstalt*, AVA) in Göttingen, which he directed from 1937 on. After the war he became director of the successor institute to the KWIFD, namely, the Max Planck Institute for Fluid Dynamics Research in Göttingen.

More recently, however, scientific practice in a techno-science like aerodynamics and hydrodynamics during National Socialism has been interpreted in yet another way. Many years ago, Herbert Mehrtens suggested that the inefficiencies in the organization of science in fields like aviation research can be traced back not to the field's standards of neutrality or to the political and/or moral reservations of its scientists, but rather to "the essentially anarchistic political structure and dynamics" of the political institutions of the Nazi state.[7] To what extent such inefficiencies at the level of political organization actually restricted ongoing research activities in the institutes remains an open question.

If one examines the actual research rather than the innumerable memoranda, plans, decisions, and intrigues by ministerial officials, many of which worked at cross purposes, what emerges as historically significant is the overwhelming absence of friction in integrating scientific work into the technical and military structures of a criminal regime. It is not the difficulty but rather the ease with which everyday techno-science adapted to the conditions of military buildup and war that is striking at the level of research practice. The lack of any significant resistance to this convergence of the interests of scientists and technologists in state, industry, and military manifested itself in functioning research activity and illustrates, in National Socialist Germany more clearly than in other states, the complex of problems involved in a scientific structure when democratic and moral standards play no noticeable role. The result is a paradoxical thesis: the historical significance of the Nazi period of a techno-science like fluid dynamics is that, aside from minor disturbances, there was no significant break with tried and successful research practice.

Besides printed sources, the material basis of this chapter consists primarily of those files available in the Archive on the History of the Max Planck Society in Berlin Dahlem that involve the KWIFD.[8] A complete evaluation of the comprehensive material remains to be done. Many results of this study thus will allow further elaboration and contextualization.[9]

[7] "Die wesentlich anarchische politische Struktur und Dynamik," Herbert Mehrtens, "Kollaborationsverhältnisse. Natur- und Technikwissenschaften im NS-Staat und ihre Historie," in Christoph Meinel and Peter Voswinkel (eds.), *Medizin, Naturwissenschaft und Technik im Nationalsozialismus. Kontinuitäten und Diskontinuitäten* (Stuttgart: Verlag für Geschichte der Naturwisschaft und der Technik, 1994), 13–32, here 24.

[8] The two main stocks are the institute files in the Archives of the Max Planck Society, Berlin (*Archiv zur Geschichte der Max-Planck-Gesellschaft*, MPG-Archiv) Abt. I, Rep. 44, and the documents in the personal papers of Ludwig Prandtl in Abt. III, Rep. 61. Added to these are files of the General Administration (*Generalverwaltung*) of the KWS in Abt. I, Rep. 1A.

[9] Further historical research on aerodynamical war research in Germany is presently being performed by Florian Schmaltz. His studies focus on Göttingen's Aerodynamics Testing Institute.

EARLY HISTORY, STRUCTURE, AND PROFILE OF THE KAISER WILHELM INSTITUTE FOR FLUID DYNAMICS

Early History

The founding of the institutions for Fluid Dynamics in Göttingen – in particular, the Aerodynamic Testing Institute (*Modellversuchsanstalt*) and its expansion to an institute of the Kaiser Wilhelm Society (*Kaiser-Wilhelm-Gesellschaft*, KWS) – has been described repeatedly in the literature.[10] Several summarizing remarks on the period before 1933 should be sufficient here.

The first initiatives to establish aerodynamics research institutions in Göttingen came from the influential triumvirate of the "Göttingen Association for the Promotion of Applied Physics and Mathematics" (*Göttinger Vereinigung zur Förderung der angewandten Physik und Mathematik*): the mathematician Felix Klein; the director of the Bayer-Farbenwerke dye factories in Elberfeld Henry Böttinger; and the Prussian ministry official head Friedrich Althoff.[11] In 1904, the three succeeded in luring the young professor Ludwig Prandtl from Hanover to Göttingen. As Klein, especially, had recognized, Prandtl was on the verge of revolutionizing the theoretical landscape of hydrodynamics. He soon assembled other gifted young staff around him, including Theodore von Kármán, Otto Föppl, and Albert Betz.

The research interests of Prandtl and his staff shifted increasingly toward aerodynamics, not least under the influence of Klein, Böttinger, and Althoff. Even before World War I, a plan was conceived to create a Kaiser Wilhelm Institute in Göttingen dedicated to both areas of fluid dynamics: theoretical and experimental. The outbreak of World War I put these plans on

---

[10] The most important publications are Ludwig Prandtl, "Geschichtliche Vorbemerkungen," in Ludwig Prandtl (ed.), *Ergebnisse der Aerodynamischen Versuchsanstalt zu Göttingen, 1. Lieferung* (Munich: Oldenbourg, 1921), 1–7; Albert Betz, "Die Aerodynamische Versuchsanstalt Göttingen. Ein Beitrag zu ihrer Geschichte," in Walter Boje and Karl Stuchtey (eds.), *Beiträge zur Geschichte der Deutschen Luftfahrtwissenschaft und Technik* (Berlin: Deutsche Akademie der Luftfahrtforschung, 1941), 3–166; Julius C. Rotta, *Die Aerodynamische Versuchsanstalt in Göttingen, ein Werk Ludwig Prandtls. Ihre Geschichte von den Anfängen bis 1925* (Göttingen: Vandenhoeck and Ruprecht, 1990); Cordula Tollmien, "Das Kaiser-Wilhelm-Institut für Strömungsforschung verbunden mit der Aerodynamischen Versuchsanstalt," in Heinrich Becker et al. (eds.), *Die Universität Göttingen unter dem Nationalsozialismus*, 2nd ed. (Munich: Saur, 1998), 684–708; Trischler, *Luft- und Raumfahrtforschung*. In the following, details known from these works are not cited individually.

[11] On the "Göttingen Association" and the triumvirate mentioned, see Karl-Heinz Manegold, *Universität, Technische Hochschule und Industrie. Ein Beitrag zur Emanzipation der Technik im 19. Jahrhundert unter besonderer Berücksichtigung der Bestrebungen von Felix Klein* (Berlin: Duncker and Humblot, 1970); David E. Rowe, "Klein, Hilbert, and the Göttingen Mathematical Tradition," *Osiris*, 5 (1989), 186–213; Herbert Mehrtens, *Moderne – Sprache – Mathematik. Eine Geschichte des Streits um die Grundlagen der Disziplin und des Subjekts formaler Systeme* (Frankfurt am Main: Suhrkamp, 1990), chap. 5.

the back burner, but in their stead a concerted action by the Ministry of Culture, the KWS, and the Administration of the Army and Navy created what was called the "Model Experimental Institute for Aerodynamics" (*Modellversuchsanstalt für Aerodynamik*), which was to serve "the practical and military needs emerging from the situation of war."[12] At the end of the war, a highly modern research institute was nearly completed, with state-of-the-art wind tunnels and a number of additional elite staff; prominent among them was the young Max Munk, who emigrated to the United States right after the end of the war, contributing to the establishment of theoretical aerodynamics in that country.[13] The war years also saw a major theoretical breakthrough in aviation research in Göttingen, the "wing theory." Prandtl had conceived the first ideas of this theory shortly before World War I. By 1918, Prandtl and his staff, primarily Betz and Munk, had expanded this theory into a highly successful mathematical treatment of the forces acting on an airplane wing moving at subsonic speed.

The Weimar years, during which Germany was forbidden by the Treaty of Versailles to maintain an air force, resulted in a withdrawal of the military authorities from the institute in Göttingen and thus in a phase of delayed expansion. In 1925, the Testing Institute was finally converted into a double KWS institute: the Kaiser Wilhelm Institute for Fluid Dynamics linked with the Aerodynamic Testing Institute (AVA). Ludwig Prandtl was its director, Albert Betz its deputy director. Prandtl ran the Department for Fluid Dynamics and Betz directed the AVA, which now also conducted a great deal of contract research financed by private industry.

Not until the transition into the Nazi period were the aviation researchers in Göttingen able to resume the strong expansion of the World War I period. From its founding, the Reich Aviation Ministry (*Reichsluftfahrtministerium*, RLM) played the decisive role. New construction plans for experimental institutions and an expansion in staff size were approved right away in 1933. Showing the spirit of optimism during this period is a speech Prandtl gave at the groundbreaking celebration for the new wind tunnel of the AVA in May 1934. The following excerpts should be read with the solemn atmosphere of this event in mind:

Today construction is to begin on a facility that is fated to give aviation research in Germany new possibilities for development. ... Compared to other countries,

---

[12] Verständigung über die Errichtung einer Modellversuchsanstalt und deren Eingliederung in das zu errichtende Kaiser-Wilhelm-Institut für Aerodynamik und Hydrodynamik, draft of June 1915, cited in Rotta, 136 f.

[13] On Munk's career, see John D. Anderson Jr., *A History of Aerodynamics and Its Impact on Flying Machines* (Cambridge: Cambridge University Press, 1997), 289–292, as well as Michael Eckert, "Strategic Internationalism and the Transfer of Technical Knowledge: The United States, Germany, and Aerodynamics after World War I," *Technology and Culture*, 46 (2005), 104–131.

Germany has a great deal to catch up in this field. Quite aside from the handicaps brought by the Treaty of Versailles, the German postwar governments had no particular opinion on the sentence "Aviation is necessary." The situation did not change until after the NSDAP seized power, through the creation of a Reich Commissariat for Aviation, which later became the Reich Aviation Ministry. ... Our declarations that we could serve aviation much better if we were able to work, not with outdated, that is, essentially too small institutions, but rather with facilities enlarged and improved in keeping with the times, *now* fell on willing ears. Our wishes were by no means humble, but to our own gratification we were able to establish that, for the new Ministry, the best was barely good enough.[14]

The massive expansion of the AVA, which increasingly became a financial burden for the KWS, finally resulted in the separation of the AVA from the Department for Fluid Dynamics in 1937. The AVA, directed by Albert Betz, was placed under the direct control of the RLM and dedicated to military and industrial contract research, while the Department for Fluid Dynamics was transformed into a formally independent Kaiser Wilhelm Institute for Fluid Dynamics (*KWI für Strömungsforschung*, KWIFD). Compared to the AVA, the KWIFD had a rather humble budget and staff size.[15] This was presumably why historians' attention to the period from 1937 on has been directed primarily at the AVA.[16] In contrast, this chapter will concern itself more closely with the research activities at the KWIFD, to the extent that these can be reconstructed from the documents in Prandtl's papers. The AVA will be addressed only peripherally.

Structure

After the AVA was spun off, the KWIFD was expanded with the addition of new experimental facilities and new personnel. By the beginning of the war, its size had approximately doubled compared to the size of the previous Department for Fluid Dynamics within the double institute. In spring 1939, the institute employed a scientific staff of eighteen working on seven different projects as well as an unknown number of technicians, workers, and administrative staff.[17] As in earlier years, Prandtl made sure that his

[14] Rede von Professor Prandtl anlässlich der Feier des ersten Spatenstichs zum neuen Windkanal, 7/5/1934, MPG-Archiv, Abt. I, Rep.1A, Nr. 1476. Original emphasis.

[15] According to the balance sheets and asset statements of the AVA and the KWIFD (abbreviated in the table as KWI-S), MPG-Archiv, Abt. I, Rep. 1A, Nr. 1496–1503. See the detailed overview in Epple, "Rechnen, Messen, Führen."

[16] In addition to the mentioned works by Tollmien and Trischler, see also Burghard Ciesla, "Abschied von der 'reinen' Wissenschaft. 'Wehrtechnik' und Anwendungsforschung in der Preussischen Akademie nach 1933," in Wolfram Fischer (eds.), *Die Preussische Akademie der Wissenschaften zu Berlin 1914–1945* (Berlin: Akademie Verlag, 2000), 483–513.

[17] Tätigkeitsbericht des KWI für Strömungsforschung für 1938/1939, MPG-Archiv, Abt. I, Rep. 44, Nr. 43.

employees included skilled experimenters and technicians as well as adept mathematicians for the computational and theoretical tasks, allowing a division of labor characteristic for the scientific projects executed by the institute.

During the war, the content of the research performed at the KWIFD presumably was determined almost entirely by the contracts from ministries and sections of the armed forces, and (to a lesser extent) from private clients. From spring 1942 at the latest, Prandtl dedicated the majority of his time to overseeing research for the RLM; he turned seventy in February 1945 and increasingly left the active research to his leading staff members. Naturally, he continued to play a decisive role in the conception of the research projects, especially to ensure the continuity of his theoretical layout of hydrodynamics and aerodynamics.

The close links of the KWIFD to the AVA remained intact during the war. Prandtl's institute made its experimental equipment available for urgent projects by the AVA on orders of the RLM, and in turn used the AVA's in-house publishing facilities (including what were called the "AVA Reports"). The quite restrictive confidentiality regulations for the AVA (such as its inaccessibility to foreigners) were extended to the KWIFD to allow more open internal communication and mutual utilization of experimental facilities and knowledge resources.

Profile

What profile did Prandtl's institute project in the scientific landscape of the prewar and war years? In the literature, the research activities at the KWIFD after 1937 have often been described as fundamental research, a term the historical actors were happy to use themselves after the end of the war.[18]

It is correct that contract research for the military and for industry did not take place at the KWIFD on a scale comparable to the contracts of the AVA. Furthermore, the actual research done at the institute dealt with questions that were of fundamental theoretical or experimental interest for hydrodynamics and aerodynamics well into the war period. The theoretical emphasis of this work was investigating situations in which the internal friction of the fluid medium played a role, such as in the boundary layer of a flow in the direct vicinity of bodies around which the medium was flowing (airfoils, hull platings, tubes, the Earth's surface) or the turbulent movement of gases and liquids. Thermodynamic effects, in particular, were of fundamental interest to Prandtl and his staff; another central area of application was the field of meteorology. The experimental emphasis corresponded to these theoretical interests. In his investigations, Prandtl was especially

[18] See, for example, Trischler, *Luft- und Raumfahrtforschung*, 203. With more differentiation, but very briefly, in Tollmien, "Kaiser-Wilhelm-Institut," 697 ff.

concerned with studying not only the dynamics of air flows but also that of liquids, and with taking advantage of the reciprocal explanatory power of experiments in water canals and wind tunnels.

Yet, these fundamental interests did not exclude the possibility of dealing with very specific issues relevant to the war. On the other hand, and this is a particularly important point, it is misleading to set applied war research and so-called fundamental research in opposition to each other. The implicit assumption that fundamental research is distant from military applications and the war – perhaps because of its long-term time horizon – overlooks the fact that even concrete, technologically oriented war research always needs a "foundation." Projects like the development of a large-scale airplane; a fighter that could reach or break the speed of sound; a fast, self-steering torpedo; or a ballistic rocket required functioning scientific procedures, a bundle of reliable material, and epistemic techniques that could be used in industrial laboratories or in the research and development institutes of the Air Force, Navy, or Army.[19] In this sense, such techniques provided the scientific foundation of war research. The crucial point is that the more advanced military technological projects of World War II regularly lacked these techniques when they were started. They first had to be developed.

In many cases, the research designated fundamental research, both at the time and also retrospectively, was fundamental research in precisely this sense: it provided new or better material and epistemic techniques that were needed in technological development projects elsewhere. In any case, this was true for a large portion of the research activities at the KWIFD.[20]

CALCULATION AND MEASUREMENT: THE WAR CONTRACTS

Overview

The first contracts from the ministries of the Nazi government and from the Supreme Command of the Navy (*Oberkommando der Marine*, OKM) came in 1935 at the latest. In this year, the reorganized German Research Foundation (*Deutsche Forschungsgemeinschaft*, DFG) under the direction of Rudolf Mentzel withdrew its subsidies for the Department for Fluid Dynamics; these had amounted to around 30,000 Reichsmarks annually for research in the areas of turbulence, meteorology, and cavitation. Initially, Prandtl hoped that the KWS would increase his institute's budget and the KWS Secretary General Ernst Telschow suggested that they try to achieve this objective by writing a letter to Adolf Baeumker at RLM, pointing out

---

[19] Here I am picking up on the categories of Hans-Jörg Rheinberger; see in detail below.
[20] Another function of Prandtl's institute was to provide reviews and reports on various projects for the state, the military, and industrial companies, several of which were clearly of a military character. See Epple, "Rechnen, Messen, Führen."

the "importance of [Prandtl's] work in the interest of national defense."[21] This motif appears in Prandtl's application to the KWS, characteristically entangled with the key word "fundamental research":

The work [of the Department for Fluid Dynamics] is dedicated to general research in the fundamental laws of fluid dynamics. [This was followed by the thematic areas: turbulence, cavitation, gas dynamics, flows of viscous liquids.] The laws obtained have a broad area of application in technology and are also suited to instructively enriching applied research in the fields of aviation technology, ship building, jet engines and also ballistics. Therefore there is a general state interest, but especially a national defense interest, in sponsoring the work performed in the Department for Fluid Dynamics.[22]

However, the KWS did not immediately comply with Prandtl's request. The large-scale expansion of the AVA was already straining the KWS's financial support for the institutes in Göttingen. Not until the institute's separation from the AVA in the 1937/38 fiscal year did the KWS subsidy to the KWIFD increase again. At the same time, the financing granted by the ministries of the Nazi state rose to a sum that was already greater than the KWS subsidy of the previous fiscal year. The good contacts Prandtl had been cultivating since the late Weimar era – especially with Adolf Baeumker and the new state secretary of Göring's ministry and previous board member of Lufthansa, Erhard Milch – certainly helped in this regard. Of course, Prandtl's involvement in war research during World War I was also not forgotten.[23]

As the first activity reports for the Reich Aviation Ministry show, even at this early point the research projects were already marked by a clear ambivalence between general theoretical questions and the development of concrete calculation and measurement procedures for everyday aerodynamic research. In fall 1937, work was performed for the RLM on the following subjects, usually in collaboration with related projects at the AVA:[24] (1) methods of calculating the behavior of the laminar layer, managed at the KWIFD by Prandtl, Walter Tollmien, and the young mathematician Henry Görtler; (2) eddy water and resistance, a project that concerned experimental investigations, some of them turbulence measurements, overseen by Prandtl and Betz; and (3) investigations of fluctuations in turbulent flows, handled by Hans Reichardt and a doctoral student. In addition, an experimental program for determining the viscous drag of hull platings on ships

---

[21] See Prandtl to Baeumker in the RLM, 3 July 1935, and Prandtl to Generalverwaltung der KWS, 6 July 1935, both MPG-Archiv, Abt. I, Rep. 1A, Nr. 1499.
[22] Prandtl to Generalverwaltung der KWS, 6 July 1935, MPG-Archiv, Abt. I, Rep. 1A, Nr. 1499.
[23] On this, see Rotta, 117–197; Trischler, *Luft- und Raumfahrtforschung*, 101–106.
[24] See Vierteljahresbericht Nr. 2/37, 2 November 1937, MPG-Archiv, Abt. I, Rep. 44, Nr. 44.

had been in progress for the OKM since 1935; the experimental arrangement used for this was known as a "roughness canal" (*Rauhigkeitskanal*), which streamed water around models with defined roughnesses.[25] All of these investigations belong in the domain of boundary layers and turbulence research, which had characterized Prandtl's scientific orientation even back in the Weimar period. Only the third topic was aimed primarily at deepening the theoretical understanding of turbulence (the guiding questions were these: which conditions lead to the formation of more or less periodic patterns in turbulent movements and how can such patterns be detected?); the projects for the Navy, in contrast, had a clear practical orientation.

In October 1939, after the war broke out, the Aviation Ministry decreed: "During the war, the workforce and the material means of the Kaiser Wilhelm Institute for Fluid Dynamics [will] be [made] available to the Aerodynamic Testing Station in order to increase its efficiency."[26] Prandtl took this decree as an occasion to examine the "peace program" of the KWIFD for "war importance." At this time, the part of the turbulence experiments deemed "fundamental research" (namely, part 3) fell victim to the new priorities.[27] In exchange, Prandtl applied for funds to construct a small new wind tunnel, which was also to be used by the AVA. This was approved without delay.[28]

However, not even half a year later the turbulence issues found their way back into Prandtl's applications to the RLM. Of course, this time they were couched in new terms. What was to be investigated was, first, the laminar-turbulent transition of boundary layers, a question "that is already being worked on in many places, for which we, however, believe we can supply special contributions adapted to the nature of our research orientation." The main project staff included Hans Reichardt (managing), Fritz Schultz-Grunow, and Ludwig Prandtl; the sum applied for was 10,000 Reichsmarks. Prandtl asked for the exact same sum on a second occasion for the "development of devices to measure turbulence, mainly for the determination of turbulence intensity in wind tunnels." The staff members slated for this project were Reichardt and Biedenkopf. Finally, the mathematician Görtler was supposed to work on the laminar-turbulent transition (and also on transonic aerodynamics); a sum of 6,000 Reichsmark was earmarked for this.[29]

This revision of the research program immediately after the beginning of the war makes apparent how the theoretical competencies of the

[25] For more on this program, see below, the "Forms of War Research" section.
[26] Prandtl to Abt. LC 1 in the RLM, 20 October 1939, MPG-Archiv, Abt. I, Rep. 44, Nr. 45.
[27] See Prandtl to Abt. LC 1 in the RLM, 20 October 1939, MPG-Archiv, Abt. I, Rep. 44, Nr. 45.
[28] For this "KWI wind tunnel" Prandtl applied for 9,000 Reichsmarks and 270 kg of aluminum plates; see Prandtl to RLM, 20 October 1939, MPG-Archiv, Abt. I, Rep. 44, Nr. 45. The metal was approved on 3 November; see Prandtl to RLM, 25 May 1940, MPG-Archiv, Abt. I, Rep. 44, Nr. 45.
[29] All from Prandtl to RLM, 25 May 1940, MPG-Archiv, Abt. I, Rep. 44, Nr. 45.

institute were diverted. In particular, the most important staff member for the area of turbulence investigations, Reichardt, shifted his activities from general theoretical endeavors to the concrete issue of the laminar-turbulent transition and to the development of experimental technologies: building low-turbulence wind tunnels and the construction of devices to measure turbulence. Of course, both projects also involved important prerequisites for a general study of turbulence phenomena.[30]

Many of the research tasks carried out at the KWIFD for the AVA in the first year of the war were of direct technological importance for armaments; many were also oriented toward the improvement of necessary apparatus. Thus, among other projects, ballistic measurements were performed in the KWIFD "supersonic tunnel," which was well equipped with measurement instruments; an additional project involved improving the diffuser for high-speed wind tunnels and investigating the condensation and icing phenomena that occur within these tunnels.[31]

Over the course of the war years, two other topic areas gained increasing importance in the RLM research contracts for the KWIFD: the aerodynamics of compressible media at high speeds (gas dynamics) and cavitation. The first rudiments of work on gas dynamics go back to 1941, when the initial focus was on the processes in wind tunnels (the staff member in charge was Oswatitsch). By 1943 at the latest, the investigation of high-speed dynamics had become one of the emphases of the institute. Within this area, primarily theoretical and experimental problems that arose as a result of jet engines (high-speed airplanes, rockets, torpedoes) were the objects of several research contracts. For some, the KWIFD took over coordination duties and assigned partial contracts to other institutions. One contract refers to a collaboration with the companies Junkers, Focke-Wulf, Heinkel, Messerschmidt, Arado, and BMW as well as the test stations AVA and Erprobungsstelle Rechlin.[32] In the context of a further, more mathematically oriented contract by this group, there was a connection to the rocket project of the Army Munitions Office at the Army Experimental Station in Peenemünde.[33] Finally, the Navy granted contracts in the area of jet engines, with special concern for

---

[30] On this, too, see the details below in the section "Forms of War Research."

[31] See Draft report "RLM-Programm 1940," undated, MPG-Archiv, Abt. I, Rep. 44, Nr. 45.

[32] See War Contract of the RLM of 9 November 1943 and further associated correspondence, MPG-Archiv, Abt. I, Rep. 44, Nr. 46.

[33] A report by Prandtl to the RLM of 21 December 1943, MPG-Archiv, Abt. I, Rep. 44, Nr. 46, states, among other things, on the partial contract carried out by Oswatitsch and Wolfgang Rothstein "3) Development of Characteristics Processes for Non-Stationary Gas Flows" (*Entwicklung von Charakteristikenverfahren für nichtstationäre Gasströmung*): "Basic equations were advanced for one-dimensional stationary and non-stationary gas flows with combustion in a tube of variable cross section. For the computation of an example, results are being awaited from experiments which are currently being performed for this purpose at the OKH [Army Supreme Command], Army Ordnance Office."

jet-propelled torpedoes. The subject of cavitation also interested both the RLM and the OKM, as elaborated in detail below.

The KWIFD thus worked on research contracts for all three branches of the military, and many of these projects were closely linked to each other in terms of content. An illuminating note in Prandtl's files from January 1943 about "Projects in the Navy's area of interest " is reproduced here in full, because it provides evidence for this interconnectedness and shows clearly that much of the project had great topical relevance for the military:

Re: Projects in the Navy's Area of Interest
At the KWI various work is in progress which is located in Navy's area of interest:

1   Investigation of the physical foundations of cavitation.
2   Investigation of projectile bodies under water.
3   Construction of a new cavitation facility (the facility is especially intended for investigations on models of projectiles or torpedoes).

However, only No. 1 of these projects is being conducted by order of the Naval Command; No. 2 is an industrial contract and No. 3 is funded by the RLM.
Also to be mentioned are occasional consultations of the Naval Observatory in Greifswald about the dissipation of fog.
Reference to earlier projects:

a)   Fundamental investigations about cavitation on airfoils (work by Otto Walchner)
b)   Measurements of surface roughnesses (work by Karl Wieghardt).[34]

Most of the research activities begun in earlier projects were pursued further until the end of the war.

FORMS OF WAR RESEARCH

Were the war contracts mentioned in the previous section of serious military interest or did they have any effects on warfare? The titles of many of the partial projects mentioned in the applications and contracts could have been included in research programs during times of peace. Hence, the work actually performed must be investigated more closely. In the following, the adaptation of so-called fundamental research to the conditions of war will be analyzed by distinguishing between three forms of war-relevant research at the KWIFD: (1) finalized research with fundamental aspects,

---

[34] Confidential note of 22 January 1943, MPG-Archiv, Abt. I, Rep. 44, Nr. 46. The precise function of this file note is unclear. It could be an outline for a (not received) report of the KWIFD to the RLM or the OKM; see the parallel case of a note of August 1943, note 75.

(2) the development of computational techniques, and (3) the development of measurement techniques and apparatus. For each form, a detailed description of a typical example will be provided.

FINALIZED RESEARCH

The first discussion concerns a series of experimental investigations performed for the Navy between 1935 and 1941, namely, the above-mentioned "roughness experiments" on hull platings for ships. The formal initiative for these experiments came from the KWIFD after preliminary conversations with representatives of the Navy. In March 1935, Prandtl sent the Naval Command a project application whose essential details were worked out by his staff member Hermann Schlichting.[35] Various miniature patterns of hull platings with roughnesses integrated into their surface, like rivets or overlapping joints, were to be built into the walls of a specially designed water tunnel designed to measure the power of resistance occurring along the plating.

The previous scientific history of this project extends back to the Weimar period. Initially only the power of resistance of smooth platings could be calculated with any precision. As Prandtl and Schlichting emphasized in their application, in practice, roughnesses led to increases in resistance of up to 50 percent. In 1932, Prandtl had advanced initial proposals about the theoretical treatment of rough platings on the basis of measurements performed by his staff member Nikuradse on artificially roughened tubes. However, this experiment proceeded from very simple assumptions about the kind of roughness (essentially, that these roughnesses were like grains of sand).[36] This is precisely where the new project was supposed to pick up. Submitted along with the application was a collection of various designs for platings with different kinds of roughnesses to be investigated.

After numerous enquiries, the representative of the Naval Command, the ministerial official Burkhardt, was convinced of the importance of the tests. He initially expressed reservations as to whether the tests performed on a small scale could be translated to the actual dimensions of a ship or U-boat. Prandtl assured him that suitable translation procedures for this existed. Burkhardt decided that the experiments would be performed and that the Navy shipyards would produce the plates to be measured. The originally proposed list of roughnesses was changed in accordance with the needs of the Navy (e. g., round-head rivets were replaced by countersink

---

[35] Prandtl to Ministerialrat Burkhardt, 9 March 1935, MPG-Archiv, Abt. I, Rep. 44, Nr. 69.
[36] See Ludwig Prandtl and Hermann Schlichting, "Das Widerstandsgesetz rauher Platten," *Werft, Reederei, Hafen*, 15 (1934), 1–4; also in Ludwig Prandtl, *Gesammelte Abhandlungen*, ed. by Walter Tollmien, Hermann Schlichting and Henry Görtler, 3 vols. (Berlin: Springer, 1961), here vol. 2, 649–662.

rivets), and the first four plates arrived at the KWIFD in mid-October 1935. Around six weeks later, Prandtl sent the first report to the Navy shipyard in Wilhelmshaven.[37]

The project apparently was tailored from the outset to the very specific wishes of the Navy. The participation of the shipyards ensured that the data from the KWIFD could be utilized. In subsequent years, the investigation program was expanded continuously; new types of roughnesses were added to the program and studied. Finally, in summer 1938, the experimental facilities were expanded significantly and a new roughness wind tunnel was built that could also be used for aerodynamic investigations of side friction coefficients. Again, the surface to be investigated was built into the tunnel wall. In this case, however, the "opposite wall" was

constructed flexibly out of a great number of individual elements and can be configured so that any desired pressure history is generated on the experimental surface. The local frictional resistance is determined by means of a scale on which a piece of the surface to be investigated can be attached flexibly or through impulse measurements at the beginning and at the end of the section to be investigated. ... The actual measurements have yet to begin.[38]

The annual volume of contracts for the Navy project doubled, and the RLM, too, began to finance experiments in the new roughness tunnel.[39] Again, the Navy leadership was skeptical as to whether practically utilizable results were to be expected from the new experimental facilities and demanded preliminary experiments with plates previously measured in the water tunnel as a control group for the results.[40] In fact, only after the war began in 1939 was the new experimental arrangement worked to the Navy's satisfaction. One of the greatest problems in this regard was the production of an extremely low-turbulence wind flow in the new tunnel, since a turbulent tunnel flow would have prevented the results from being translated to the movement in water. In accomplishing this, Prandtl and his staff (by this time Karl Wieghardt was in charge) accumulated experience they were able to apply elsewhere to investigations of turbulence. Around the turn of the years 1939/40, new tables with roughness patterns arrived from the Naval Command, but this time the patterns were manufactured in-house by

[37] See Chef der Marineleitung to KWI für Strömungsforschung, 12 April 1935, and further correspondence, MPG-Archiv, Abt. I, Rep. 44, Nr. 69.

[38] Contribution to the Vierteljahresbericht April bis Juni 1938, Versuchseinrichtung zur Messung des Reibungswiderstandes strömender Luft an glatten und rauhen Oberflächen, undated, MPG-Archiv, Abt. I, Rep. 44, Nr. 44.

[39] Roughness investigations were often also illuminating for airplane constructions, for instance, for "Rows of Rivets, Joints, Window Slats and the Like," see Draft Report "RLM-Programm 1940," undated, MPG-Archiv, Abt. I, Rep. 44, Nr. 45.

[40] Lottmann, OKM, to KWI für Strömungsforschung, 2 November 1938, and subsequent correspondence, MPG-Archiv, Abt. I, Rep. 44, Nr. 70.

the KWIFD. In early 1941, the Navy Command finally halted the project "because of the strained labor situation that is also occurring in the area of experimentation."[41] Nevertheless, in the very same year Prandtl knitted together an even larger project for the Navy, as described below.

Even though this experimental program was oriented to the demands of the Navy, down to the most minor details, it also possessed aspects of general interest for the scientists at the KWIFD. The surface friction of a flowing medium along a body was a problem that was barely understood theoretically and hopelessly complicated in the pure mathematical sense. Only through precision measurements could one hope to obtain data that would also make theoretical progress possible. Carrying out such measurements at that time required the construction of suitable measuring tracks (wind tunnels with a very low degree of turbulence). In a clever game of alternately legitimating the projects toward the Navy and the RLM (the support of the other given authority served as an argument for the importance of the experiments), Prandtl and his staff succeeded in conveying their own scientific objectives in an almost completely finalized research project. This pattern of linking heteronomous (military) with autonomous knowledge interests also characterizes the research activities at Prandtl's institute described below.

CALCULATION

This section is devoted to the variety of types of "fundamental research" that produced methods of calculation that could be implemented elsewhere in projects relevant to the military. The war contracts of the KWIFD included several such projects. Some of them were concerned with the dynamics of boundary layers and some were related to the "method of characteristics" used to calculate supersonic flows. The latter were developed at the KWIFD above all for the case of air flows around rocket bodies; as mentioned, here a collaboration existed with the Army Experimental Station in Peenemünde. In general, the construction of similar calculation methods was one of the focal points of mathematicians' employment in the institutions of war research during World War II.[42]

This section picks out a number of endeavors pursued by Prandtl and his staff member Henry Görtler. This project, too, had already begun before the

[41] See serial correspondence on the roughness experiments, MPG-Archiv, Abt. I, Rep. 44, Nr. 70.

[42] On this in general, see Herbert Mehrtens, "Mathematics and War. Germany, 1900–1945," in Paul Forman and José M. Sánchez-Ron (eds.), *National Military Establishments and the Advancement of Science and Technology. Studies in the 20th Century History* (Dordrecht: Kluwer, 1996), 87–134; Moritz Epple and Volker Remmert, "'Eine ungeahnte Synthese zwischen reiner und angewandter Mathematik.' Kriegsrelevante mathematische Forschung in Deutschland während des II. Weltkrieges," in Kaufmann, *Geschichte*, vol. 1, 258–295.

war. It is mentioned in the research reports for the RLM for the first time in fall 1937, incorporated in a more comprehensive, partially experimental boundary layer project, involving elite staff at the AVA (Walchner, Lotz, Ritz, Flügge, and three doctoral students; the director of the entire project was Betz). This report states:

To date we are lacking a reliable calculation method that [in the case of two-dimensional flows] makes it possible to calculate the further development of a boundary layer for a given starting profile and given velocity plot outside the boundary layer. Such a method, which works with numerical and graphical methods, is to be developed up to "operation maturity" on the basis of a recently compiled work plan.[43]

Before the war began, an initial version of the method already had been completed. Yet Prandtl had to admit that it was a "practically utilizable, but nevertheless quite laborious method." In particular, the calculation supplied what was known as the delamination point and the course of the laminary boundary layer up to this position.[44] A description of this method by Görtler was published in 1939.[45]

However, this conclusion was not the end of the project. At the KWIFD, experiments were prepared to monitor the quality of the developed calculation method.[46] Yet, after the beginning of the war, this project, too, was "temporarily dropped as belonging to fundamental research."[47] In the following years, Görtler was entrusted with the theoretical investigation of the laminar-turbulent transition. In all probability, this work was probably little more than a relabeling of Görtler's work on the numerics of boundary layer processes.

In 1943, Görtler achieved a new breakthrough in the improvement of his calculation technique; at more or less the same time, the mathematician Kurt Schröder, working at the German Test Station for Aviation (*Deutsche Versuchsanstalt für Luftfahrt*, DVL) in Berlin-Adlershof, also submitted an improved method of calculating the boundary layer. After the war, Prandtl emphasized the decisive point of the improved method in a draft report for the investigation teams of the Allied Forces: it concerned the "advanced determination of the exact solution of any even boundary layer flows by means of a calculation scheme *that can be performed by subordinate assistants*."[48] What he meant here in particular were the young female

[43] Vierteljahresbericht Nr. 2/37, 2 November 1937, MPG-Archiv, Abt. I, Rep. 44 Nr. 44.
[44] Contribution to Vierteljahresbericht Juli bis September 1938, Verfahren zur Berechnung der laminaren Grenzschicht, MPG-Archiv, Abt. I, Rep. 44, Nr. 44.
[45] Henry Görtler, "Weiterentwicklung eines Grenzschichtprofils bei gegebenem Druckverlauf," *Zeitschrift für angewandte Mathematik und Mechanik*, 19 (1939), 129–140.
[46] Contribution to Vierteljahresbericht 1/39/40, Verhalten der Grenzschicht, MPG-Archiv, Abt. I, Rep. 44, Nr. 44.
[47] See Prandtl to RLM, 25 May 1940, MPG-Archiv, Abt. I, Rep. 44, Nr. 45.
[48] Draft of a Report for the Allies about the War Work of the Kaiser Wilhelm Institute for Fluid Dynamics, MPG-Archiv, Abt. I, Rep. 44, Nr. 49, 6. Author's emphasis.

"computers" without special mathematics training, considerable numbers of whom were deployed at the AVA and elsewhere to perform numerical tasks in war research. In a sense, Görtler wrote a "program" for such human calculation staff.[49]

The importance of a method developed up to "operation maturity" like the one by Görtler becomes apparent in the events surrounding a "war convention" held by the German Association of Mathematicians (*Deutsche Mathematiker-Vereinigung*, DMV) in Würzburg in September 1943. At a confidential meeting before selected university mathematicians, Schröder and Görtler were supposed to report about their new numerical method for boundary layer calculation. Even this went too far for some officials at the RLM. On short notice, Görtler's results were classified by the Research Directorate at the RLM as "a confidential command matter," and Görtler was forbidden to participate in the DMV convention. Only after an intervention by Prandtl (who was already chairman of the Research Directorate by this time, see below) was this extremely restrictive posture revised, Görtler's method reclassified as "only for official use," and his participation in the convention permitted; after all, the method was supposed to be deployed elsewhere as well.[50]

MEASUREMENT

Perhaps even more than through the construction of calculation techniques, the KWIFD contributed to the infrastructure of war research through the development of measurement methods. This section includes a series of projects that were at the research front of the experimental techniques available at the time: the work on cavitation in liquid flows.

The phenomenon of cavitation (i.e., the formation of hollow spaces behind bodies with media flowing past them) had not yet been the subject of much experimentation in the early 1930s. It occurred above all at high speeds – for instance, in ballistics and in very fast movements in water. Back in 1932, the initial investigations of cavitation were performed on airfoils at the AVA.[51] With the construction of rockets and high-velocity airplanes, the

---

[49] A more detailed historical investigation of the role of these female "computers" in World War II is still lacking. On the deployment of female calculation personnel in the decoding project of Bletchley Park, for example, see the scattered remarks in Andrew Hodges, *Alan Turing: The Enigma* (New York: Simon and Schuster, 1989), chaps. 4 and 5.

[50] Various correspondence of the Research Directorate in the RLM, 21 August–7 September 1943, MPG-Archiv, Abt. III, Rep. 61, Nr. 2119. A background of the events, which is beyond the scope of this discussion, presumably also involved factionalism in the Office of Research Directorate in the RLM. On the War Convention of the DMV in 1943 and the Görtler's later role, see Epple and Remmert, 277 f.; also the references to further sources there.

[51] For example, see Otto Walchner, "Profilmessungen bei Kavitation," in Günther Kempf and Ernst Foerster (eds.), *Hydromechanische Probleme des Schiffsantriebs*, vol. 1 (Munich:

phenomenon became ever more important in terms of aerodynamics. Since theoretical treatment required not only considerations about continuum mechanical but also thermodynamics, an experimental approach appeared more important in the short term.

In March 1942, Prandtl and Reichardt submitted to the RLM an application for the construction of new cavitation equipment.[52] As the roughness experiments for the Navy were coming to a close, the OKM was also informed about the new plans; it immediately indicated its interest.[53] Construction of the new system was begun in the very same year. The apparatus was a free water jet, projected horizontally, in a space that could be evacuated. Into the water jet, a model could be placed, along which cavitation bubbles would form. Hydraulic pressure balances were then inserted into these bubbles, and the entire process was either photographed or filmed with a slow-motion camera. The apparatus was constructed (entirely in keeping with Prandtl's line of experimental flow mechanics) so that it could be used for the analysis of movements in both water and (with corresponding conversions) air.[54]

The cavitation system was completed by October 1942, but the first work performed with it showed that an even stronger pump was necessary for the water jet.[55] Such a pump did not arrive at the KWIFD until early 1943. In April, Prandtl was able to inform the RLM that the operation of the completed system was to be launched in a few weeks. From this time onward, the work on the new equipment enjoyed the highest priority.[56] Even before the system was finally completed, the first experiments contracted by industry were performed:

With the provisional system, three-component measurements were performed on projectile bodies on behalf of the Henschel Aircraft Works. At the close of these

Oldenbourg, 1932), 256–267; Otto Walchner and Adolf Busemann, "Profileigenschaften bei Überschallgeschwindigkeit," *Forschungen aus dem Gebiet des Ingenieurwesens*, 4 (1933), 87–92.

[52] See Bericht über Forschungsarbeiten 1942, 30 July 1942, MPG-Archiv, Abt. I, Rep. 44, Nr. 46.

[53] Prandtl to OKM, 25 April 1942, as well as Brandes, OKM, to KWI für Strömungsforschung, 12 June 1942, both MPG-Archiv, Abt. I, Rep. 44, Nr. 70.

[54] The description of the experimental arrangement is taken from various applications and reports; see especially the draft of a Report for the Allies about the War Work of the Kaiser Wilhelm Institute for Fluid Dynamics, MPG-Archiv, Abt. I, Rep. 44, Nr. 49, here 5.

[55] This shows a typical dynamic in the construction of new experimental apparatus. From the onset there were also considerations about even larger apparatus. Prandtl's Bericht an die Forschungsführung of 28 November 1942, MPG-Archiv, Abt. I, Rep. 44, Nr. 46, states: "In consideration of the need to create larger, more powerful cavitation systems, investigations have been started that involve the possibilities of designing such systems."

[56] Prandtl's Bericht an die Forschungsführung of 10 April 1943, MPG-Archiv, Abt. I, Rep. 44, Nr. 46. Among other things, here Prandtl reported that projects in the smaller laminar tunnel (also overseen by Reichardt) had "been discontinued in favor of stronger promotion of the urgent work on cavitation and the development of devices to measure turbulence."

investigations, the staff member [Reichardt] started his own research program on the hydrodynamics of projectile movement in water.... Further, experimental investigations about the process of the immersion of projectile modules into the surface of water are in preparation.[57]

Even the Navy weighed in. Apparently, the only contract with the priority level DE (*Dringende Entwicklung*, "urgent development") ever received by the KWIFD during the war referred to work on the cavitation system. A secret note of August 1943 states: "Currently DE investigations are in progress for the Chemical-Physical Testing Institute of the Navy and these involve the development of underwater projectiles with rocket propulsion."[58] The results the scientists in Göttingen obtained from the new system apparently made a great impression on the OKM.[59]

In fall 1943, the RLM, which had also financed the apparatus, had its own urgent contract research concerning the design of what were called "constant-pressure contours" carried out on the same cavitation apparatus. The idea here was to photograph the shape of artificially generated cavitation bubbles in order to shape engine nacelles for high-speed airplanes in accordance with this archetype, initially for wind tunnel models.[60]

The consonance of fluid mechanical and military research interests is clearly recognizable here as well. While the armaments engineers, as well as presumably most of the scientists, hoped to support the design of projectiles, airplane parts, and torpedoes, at the same time the scientists were able to press ahead with the investigation of a little-known empirical phenomenon. The common denominator was the apparatus that allowed "bi-perspective" use, sometimes in the very same experiments.[61] Furthermore, this is another impressive example of the alternating war-related legitimation of a research program at the KWIFD vis-à-vis the RLM and OKM.

---

[57] Prandtl's Bericht an die Forschungsführung of 10 April 1943, MPG-Archiv, Abt. I, Rep. 44, Nr. 46. The possibilities for designing larger cavitation systems continued to receive consideration.

[58] Confidential note about the cavitation system, signed by Hans Reichardt, 3 August 1943, MPG-Archiv, Abt. I, Rep.44, Nr. 46. The note was adopted word for word in Prandtl's Tätigkeitsbericht an die Forschungsführung of 9 August 1943, MPG-Archiv, Abt. I, Rep. 44, Nr. 51.

[59] Prandtl to Forschungsführung, 19 November 1943, MPG-Archiv, Abt. I, Rep. 44, Nr. 46. The cavitation investigations for the *Chemisch-Physikalische Versuchsanstalt der Kriegsmarine* are mentioned once again in Prandtl's Bericht an die Forschungsführung of 21 December 1943, MPG-Archiv, Abt. I, Rep. 44, Nr. 46.

[60] War contract of 10 November 1943, MPG-Archiv, Abt. I, Rep. 44, Nr. 51. More details on this and the other work performed on the cavitation system in the draft Report for the Allies, MPG-Archiv, Abt. I, Rep. 44, Nr. 48.

[61] For the importance of the multiperspective use of scientific apparatus for the networking of scientific and military research, see also the case study by Hans-Jörg Rheinberger, "Virusforschung an den Kaiser-Wilhelm-Instituten für Biochemie und Biologie," in Kaufmann, *Geschichte*, vol. 2, 667–698.

LEADERSHIP

Any study about Ludwig Prandtl's KWI during World War II would be incomplete without a reference to the central role Prandtl himself played in research organization in the sphere of the Reich Aviation Ministry. As the undisputed leading authority in the field of fluid mechanics, as the teacher of many aerodynamic experts who had since ascended to positions of leadership, and as a loyal citizen of the Nazi state, his participation was inevitable wherever the leading representation of scientists in research organizations was concerned. In this, his area of action was linked above all to the power structures in Göring's ministry and less to the often-competing infrastructure of the Reich Ministry for Education and Science (REM) on one hand and the RFR or DFG, respectively, on the other. Prandtl's representative offices included membership in the Presidium of the Lilienthal Society for Aviation Research (along with Adolf Baeumker and Carl Bosch) and on the committee of the Reich Academy for Aviation Research, founded in 1936 and presided over by Göring and Milch. Prandtl was also the first to receive the "Hermann Göring votive medal," awarded in 1938. Additional offices and honors followed.

Prandtl's most important role was doubtlessly that of chairman of the organization founded in early summer 1942, known as the "Research Directorate of the Reich Ministry of Aviation" (*Forschungsführung des Reichsluftfahrtministeriums*). This body was created in the general restructuring of the Nazi science organizations in 1942 by Göring (who had since also become *Generalluftzeugmeister*, or "General Master of Aircraft"). Other members included Baeumker; Walter Georgii, the director of the German Research Institute for Gliding (*Deutsche Forschungsanstalt für Segelflug*, DFS) in Ainring near Munich; and Friedrich Seewald, the provisional managing director of the DVL in Berlin-Adlershof. The supreme objective of the Research Directorate was to "make use of all of the workers and knowledge present in aviation research for air armaments"; its concrete tasks consisted of

1) planning and monitoring the performance of aviation research, 2) Regulation of the use of the funds, apparatus and equipments available to aviation research as well as of the research personnel, 3) Exchange of experience with science, industry and the front.[62]

To fulfill these tasks, the Research Directorate was granted the authority to allocate financial resources independently, to make personnel policy

[62] Rundschreiben des Reichsministers der Luftfahrt (signed by Erhard Milch on the Minister's behalf), an alle untergebenen Dienststellen, Oberkommando der Wehrmacht (OKW), OKH, OKM, verschiedene Ministerien, KWS usw. of 29 May 1942, MPG-Archiv, Abt. III, Rep. 61, Nr. 2109.

on the executive level, and to report directly to Milch, a right of which Chairman Prandtl often made use.[63] One marginal detail is that through this authority, among other things, Prandtl was responsible for approving his own research funds and monitoring his own institute's personnel policy.

Much has been written already about the Research Directorate of the Air Force, whether to show the importance of the research in Göring's imperium in the face of increasing strains from 1942 onward,[64] or to discuss how effectively the new model of "self-monitoring" scientific research, which the Research Directorate was supposed to implement in the area of the RLM, was still able to function up to the end of the war.[65] Little new information can be added to these discussions. Nevertheless, it is important to discuss how seriously the director of the KWIFD took his activity for the Research Directorate, and how his activities on this level related to those of everyday research at his institute.

If one delves into the comprehensive documentary evidence, at least one thing becomes clear: because of the existing, largely polycentric structures, the task that was supposed to be solved by the Research Directorate was anything but easy. A major problem was coordinating the work of a dozen large research institutions and a multitude of smaller ones, with specializations ranging from the aerodynamics of high velocities to engine construction, radio and radar research, all the way to aviation medicine. Research priorities had be defined for the area as a whole and decisions made about gigantic expansion plans, the most prominent of which was probably the "Aviation Research Munich" (*Luftfahrtforschung München*, LFM) directed by Baeumker, an institute complex completed by the end of the war, at which targeted studies were to address questions of high-velocity flight and its military utilization.[66]

When the four-man committee was deciding whether to support such expansion plans, all aspects of aviation research had to be considered, including the more awkward moral ones. Thus, the use of prisoners in the construction plans of the AVA and the LFM was discussed[67] as well as Baeumker's foolhardy plan (never implemented), contingent upon the approval of the Health Inspector of the Air Force, Erich Hippke, to open a new Institute for Biological Aviation Research in Munich.[68] Beyond this,

[63] Trischler, *Luft- und Raumfahrtforschung*, 246–261.

[64] See Horst Boog, *Die deutsche Luftwaffenführung 1935–1946. Führungsprobleme, Spitzengliederung, Generalstabausbildung* (Stuttgart: Deutsche Verlags-Anstalt, 1982), 36–76.

[65] Trischler, *Luft- und Raumfahrtforschung*, 246–261; Trischler, "Big Science."

[66] See Trischler, *Luft- und Raumfahrtforschung*, 264–269.

[67] For the AVA, see Prandtl to Seewald, 12 November 1942, MPG-Archiv, Abt. III, Rep. 61, Nr. 2115; for the LFM, for example, see Baeumker to Prandtl, 10 September 1943, and subsequent correspondence in the MPG-Archiv, Abt. III, Rep. 61, Nr. 2190.

[68] For more details, see Epple, "Rechnen, Messen, Führen."

the Research Directorate of the RLM also had to coordinate its work with research offices in other branches of the military (Army, Navy), some of which granted research contracts to the very same institutes as the LFM (such as the KWIFD).

A final permanent difficulty that the Research Directorate never completely overcame was coordinating state research with industrial research. In this case, Prandtl particularly defended the right of the research institutes to perform urgent war tasks, not through making institute facilities available to private companies but by executing research contracts of their own. "The Reich," he argued in a corresponding petition to Milch, "has a well-understood interest in research work proceeding unimpeded in its institutes and ensuring that they not be choked out by company interests, which to a certain degree always conflict with the interest of the Reich."[69]

It is no surprise that manifold special interests in this field had to be coordinated with each other, and that the Research Directorate found itself embroiled in a network of smaller and larger, vertical and horizontal conflicts, many of which were not easily resolved. In view of this situation, the four members of the body faced anything but a simple choice between intervention and laissez-faire. It can hardly be disputed that all four made every endeavor to fulfill their duties as well as possible. Prandtl's role in this often involved conciliation among the various interests within the Research Directorate.[70]

After studying the files, one cannot escape the impression that Prandtl attempted to the best of his ability to occupy the difficult role of chairman of the Research Directorate in a manner that served the interests of the scientists as well as those of the state. There was no contradiction between his role as a skilled organizer of war-oriented research at the KWIFD and effective moderator of the Research Directorate of the RLM. On the contrary, through his involvement in prioritizing decisions in aviation research and his wide variety of coordination tasks in the entire field of armaments research, Prandtl also knew the main lines of armament technology development during the war as well as the research questions the armaments industry and the armed forces wanted answered in armaments research.[71] Without a doubt,

---

[69] Prandtl to Milch, 14 Ovtober 1942, MPG-Archiv, Abt. III, Rep. 61, Nr. 2114.

[70] In particular, he attempted to curb the permanent tensions between Baeumker, a visionary who had a megalomaniac tendency, and the skeptical Seewald. When it became clear that Seewald was going to withdraw from the managing function, Prandtl did his best to find a suitable alternative. Among others, he turned to the Secretary General of the KWS, Ernst Telschow, who rejected the offer. Prandtl was glad when Georgii declared himself willing to take over management duties; Georgii's DFS had grown into a "model National Socialist operation" with a staff of over a thousand, in which research was conducted on a variety of the most modern jet-propelled airplane models. See Epple, "Rechnen, Messen, Führen."

[71] As exemplary evidence for Prandtl's intervention in questions of industrial armaments development, a position paper about the works of Ernst Lippisch and the brothers Reimar and

this knowledge helped Prandtl adapt the research activities of his institute optimally to the conditions of war. The fact that research was conducted at the KWIFD on two key technologies of armaments development at the time, high-speed flight and the torpedo, thus appears in a new light.

INSTEAD OF CONCLUSIONS: OPEN QUESTIONS

In his commentary to the "Armaments Research and 'War-Relevant' Research" section of the opening conference of the "History of the Kaiser Wilhelm Society in the National Socialist Era" research program, Wilhelm Deist objected to Mehrtens and others applying the historically loaded concept of collaboration to refer to the manifold types of cooperation between scientists and the Nazi state.[72] Ultimately, the choice of words is not important, however; what is important in the case presented here is that the interests of science, the development of military technology, and armaments policy converged in the area of hydrodynamic and aerodynamic research, and that structural incongruities between the research operations of the Weimar period and those of the rearmament phase and the war did not exist. It was easy for the fluid dynamics researchers to tailor their research programs to the war conditions, both rhetorically (before 1939) and in the area of actual research activities (from 1939 at the latest).

Note, however, that the interests of the military were not necessarily identical with those of developing military technology. More precisely, the convergence of interests existed between the scientists and those groups in the state and armed forces who had a genuine interest in the development of military technologies. As regards war research, there should probably be a differentiation among at least three groups of actors: the scientists, the armaments engineers, and the military waging the war. My assumption is that, to the extent that the inefficiencies of the "deployment" of the sciences

---

Walter Horten should be mentioned. Lippisch was the decisive developer of the successful jet-propelled fighter Messerschmitt Me 163; the Horten brothers also worked on high-speed airplanes. Prandtl advocated the continued development of both lines with arguments of military strategy: "Mr. Lippisch is developing a fighter, and they are working on fast, two-engine bombers and destroyers, and, in the longer perspective, also on a large high-speed bomber, and the high-speed bombers are at least as important in the fight against the English and Americans as the fighters," Prandtl to Baeumker, 11 March 1943, MPG-Archiv, Abt. III, Rep. 61, Nr. 2116. An example of an inquiry from another branch of the military for research support mediated by the Research Directorate is presented by the meeting held on 4 June 1943 at which the Supreme Command of the Navy (perhaps even Grand Admiral Karl Dönitz himself) requested "a collaboration regarding the improvement of detection and weapon effectiveness from within the U-boat"; see Lorenz (RLM) to Prandtl, 22 May 1943, as well as Prandtl to Lorenz, 24 May 1943, both MPG-Archiv, Abt. III, Rep. 61, Nr. 2117. Later correspondence proves that the meeting took place.

[72] Wilhelm Deist, "Rüstungsforschung und Wehrmacht. Ein Kommentar," in Kaufmann, *Geschichte*, 363–370, here 363 f.

in war can be spoken of at all, the majority of such inefficiencies have their roots in tensions between the last two of these groups while the interactions between scientists and armaments engineers were for the most part unproblematic. It would be worth examining whether the known phases of the Nazi science "policy"[73] might have been dependent on the shifting position of power of this intermediate group, which was so strongly influenced by the course of the war.

In any case, these phases are also reflected in the temporal development of the war contracts of the KWIFD. The material compiled in the third section makes four shifts clearly recognizable: (1) In the military buildup phase between around 1935 and 1939, the theoretically oriented research of the Weimar period was integrated into the rapidly growing networks of military contract research without any significant modification of the research topics. (2) The "Blitzkrieg phase" in 1939/40 is characterized by a short-term restriction of projects with a fundamental research orientation. (3) This was soon, or from 1941/42 on at the latest, superseded by a renewed expansion, whereby theoretical research projects were reworked to emphasize the aspect of providing and optimizing (computational, measurement, experimental) methods. (4) Toward the end of the war, a clear dynamic appeared in which the research projects were increasingly tailored toward new technologies like high-speed planes, rockets, torpedoes, and the like.

The central historical phenomenon elaborated in this chapter is the remarkably rapid and, in terms of science and technology, productive adaptations of the research program at the KWIFD to the changing circumstances of military buildup and war. Explaining these adaptations merely through the institute's dependence on its financial backers would be insufficient. As demonstrated by Prandtl's speech at the groundbreaking ceremony for the new wind tunnel of the AVA cited in the "Early History" section, state authorities had hardly threatened to cut off funds for research on fluid dynamics, and thus forced a reorientation of their research. On the contrary, for the new sponsors "the best was barely good enough" (see above). The RLM (and other offices) offered the scientists financial resources on an ever-increasing scale as long as they understood how to emphasize the importance of their works for armaments.

The adaptation of Göttingen's aerodynamics and hydrodynamics research to the conditions of National Socialism must thus also be understood as the result of active intervention by the scientists and their administrative allies. This intervention ultimately went so far that leading scientists like Ludwig Prandtl himself helped shape the conditions to which members of their discipline were subjected during the war. Here, at the latest, any words about the "adaptation" of science to the conditions of National Socialism and war lose

---

[73] For example, see briefly in Michael Grüttner, "Wissenschaftspolitik im Nationalsozialismus," in Kaufmann, *Geschichte*, vol. 2, 557–585, here 579 ff.

part of their meaning. The "environment" to which Prandtl and his colleagues adapted was configured in large part by these scientists themselves. This shifts the perspective away from conditions with which the state confronted scientists to conditions that made it possible for these scientists to render their active participation in adapting and configuring their work. What were the prerequisites that allowed Prandtl and his staff to participate so quickly and so successfully in the erection of the structures for armaments research? The following section hints at two possible answers to this question.

First, the mentality of the central actors, as far as it is known to us, provides relatively little reason to expect open resistance against the objectives of the Nazi state. A number of well-known facts about Prandtl's attitude after the regime change of 1933 offer sufficient illustration of this. Herbert Mehrtens pointed out that Prandtl, like the KWS president at the time, Max Planck, was one of those scientists who stood up for some of their Jewish colleagues but were not willing to hazard any serious consequences for their profession as a result.[74]

If these events speak for Prandtl's willingness to enter into an arrangement with the new circumstances, his correspondence with the leading British specialist on aerodynamics, Geoffrey Ingram Taylor, to which Cordula Tollmien has already referred, shows that he was also willing to defend the Nazi state.[75] At the International Congress for Applied Mechanics in Cambridge, Massachusetts, in 1938, Prandtl and Taylor had clashed about the politics of the Nazi state. As Prandtl was the most renowned German aerodynamics specialist, his position supporting Nazi policy apparently caused quite a sensation there. After this controversy, in October 1938, Prandtl attempted to convince Taylor by letter that Hitler may have "made a million people in Germany his bitter enemies, but in exchange [he had made] eighty million his most loyal and enthusiastic supporters." The battle that Germany had had to fight against the Jews (and their conspiracy with the Masons and communists), Prandtl continued, had been necessary for its own self-preservation. Prandtl invited Taylor to visit Germany to "convince yourself [with your own eyes] that we are indeed very well governed here." Even as late as August 1939, when the possibility of a war was already looming, in a further letter to Mrs. Taylor, Prandtl emphasized that Germany had done much for peace and only wanted to eliminate "the last remainders of the Treaty of Versailles."[76] Just a few months later, Prandtl was in the process of

---

[74] See the discussion of Prandtl's intervention with the Minister of the Interior at the time; Mehrtens, "Kollaborationsverhältnisse," 19–21. Also, for the sketch of Prandtl's behavior during the *Gleichschaltung* of the GAMM, see Herbert Mehrtens, "Die 'Gleichschaltung' der mathematischen Gesellschaften im nationalsozialistischen Deutschland," *Jahrbuch Überblicke Mathematik*, 18 (1985), 83–103, here 96 ff.

[75] On the following, see Tollmien, "Kaiser-Wilhelm-Institut," 696 f.

[76] The citations from Prandtl's letter to Taylor and his wife; Tollmien, "Kaiser-Wilhelm-Institut," 696 f.

gearing his institute's entire research program toward the war. Apparently, even under these conditions, he still considered his state worthy of defending. Realizing the support and the opportunities the state had granted to his discipline, this is not too surprising.[77]

The second layer of prerequisites that made possible the rapid adaptation of the KWIFD to the structures of war research are located in the ease with which what was called "fundamental" research could be shifted toward the development of basic methods for using apparatus and epistemology that were needed for military technology. As Hans-Jörg Rheinberger has proposed, research can be described as practice that moves in a field with two key dimensions. In every research episode, work takes place on certain "epistemic things" – on variable bundles of problems generated by a certain object of research. This can succeed only if material and epistemic techniques are available with which these bundles of problems can be made tractable and, at least in part, answerable. In applying these techniques to the problems generated by the research object, these are partially stabilized and gradually transformed.[78]

Among the research topics studied at the KWIFD were the "boundary layers" of bodies subjected to aerodynamic flows, and the phenomena "turbulence" and "cavitation." All of these topics involved more or less sharply delineated research objects that exhibited far more aspects that were not understood than ones that were – in particular, questions about the "basic laws" of fluid dynamics as well as the design of a whole range of technological objects (aircraft, wind tunnels, projectiles). Thus, we are dealing here with a branch of research whose epistemic things, from the very start, were in contact with militarily utilizable technologies. A thesis suggested by the material investigated here is that in adapting such a branch of research to the interests of war armaments, it is sufficient to have only a few problem-generating elements prescribed externally, or adjusted to external demands, without

---

[77] In view of the material brought together here, the following brief description of Prandtl's activities during the Nazi period, taken from what is currently the most detailed history of the discipline of aerodynamics, appears not only contradictory but altogether misleading: Prandtl "remained at Göttingen throughout World War II, engrossed in his work and seemingly insulated from the politics of Nazi Germany and the privations and destructions of the war. In fact, the German Air Ministry provided new equipment and financial support for Prandtl's laboratory"; see Anderson, 258.

[78] See Hans-Jörg Rheinberger, *Experiment – Differenz – Schrift. Zur Geschichte epistemischer Dinge* (Marburg: Basilisken-Presse, 1992), 69–72; Rheinberger, *Epistemic Things*, 28–31. To be able to analyze theoretical research activities (like mathematical ones) as well, in which material apparatus plays no central role, I depart slightly from Rheinberger's differentiation between epistemic and technical things; see Moritz Epple, *Die Entstehung der Knotentheorie. Kontexte und Konstruktionen einer modernen mathematischen Theorie* (Wiesbaden: Vieweg, 1999), 14 ff., and Moritz Epple, "Knot Invariants in Vienna and Princeton during the 1920s. Epistemic Configurations of Mathematical Research," *Science in Context*, 17 (2004), 131–164.

restricting the dynamics of research in any other way. Through merely setting the points of such external linkages, scientific activity shifts toward the
answer-generating dimension, that is, toward the use and the expansion of
the existing material and epistemic techniques that can do service in processing those problems generated by epistemic things with external linkages.

In the case presented here, the prescribed problem-generating elements
were, for instance, high-speed flight, or more precisely, certain research
objects that could be isolated within this complex of problems, like the high-
velocity flows around an airfoil, around the body of a rocket or torpedo, or
around a jet engine. These elements modified the epistemic things worked
on at the KWIFD. "Boundary layers" turned into "boundary layer processes
in gas dynamics"; from the bundle of problems called "turbulence," various relevant partial bundles were isolated like wind tunnel turbulence and
laminar-turbulent transition in (high-velocity) boundary layers; "cavitation"
became "constant-pressure contours of jet engines." The external links of
the epistemic things thus modified consisted not only of the relationships
of knowledge transfer in the field of armaments development but also of
the parameters of financing and time-economy. Through this, the scientists
were forced to shift the balance between problem generation and problem
solution in favor of solution, that is, in favor of deploying the material and
epistemic techniques at their disposal. In the words of Walter Georgii in
April 1944:

For in today's so serious situation, one thing must be kept in mind by all of your
staff at all times: *the research objects are not advanced in order to keep them busy*
during the war, but in order to *solve* them in the shortest time possible, that is, *to
produce results.*[79]

In the case of the KWIFD, this meant the use and optimization of adapted
procedures for calculation and measurement as well as relevant apparatus
(wind tunnels, cavitation systems, devices to measure turbulence).

Yet, in all of the cases examined here, the existing techniques or technologies were not sufficient for the very reason that the problem-generating
objects were bound to things outside the institute, that is, because these
objects were not at the free disposal of scientists over the course of their
research activity: it was not possible to divide them into pieces that could be
investigated easily using the existing techniques. This meant that the available procedures and apparatus needed to solve the problem at hand became
problematic in themselves, that is, they shifted to the other dimension of
research. New material and epistemic techniques had to be constructed;
the numerical method for calculating the boundary layer or the cavitation

---

[79] Circular by Walter Georgii, 18 April 1944, MPG-Archiv, Abt. III, Rep. 61, Nr. 2173. original
emphases.

system turned into epistemic things. Not until the moment when such methods or apparatus were brought to "operation maturity" (as Prandtl wrote
about Görtler's calculation method, see above), or, in Bruno Latour's words,
not until they became "black boxes" in other networks of research or development[80] did they resume the character of epistemic techniques.

Thus, the dynamic exchange between the two dimensions of research
remained intact, but it shifted toward a direction in which the main products of scientific research were methods and apparatus. Not only (military)
engineering recipients profited from this but also the scientists themselves,
albeit in many cases under conditions that had changed once more. For
along with their heteronomous, technological utility, the new methods also
bore a potential for autonomously generating still other new epistemic
things: with new devices to measure turbulence, it was possible not only to
improve high-speed wind tunnels but also to empirically investigate all the
fine structures present in turbulent flows; similar consequences were found
in the other cases. As a general rule, methods and apparatus can be used in
more than one way. What is important is that this adaptation mechanism
does not require any fundamental reconstitution of a research area whose
epistemic things already possess an initial affinity with technologies of military interest. It works, one could say, in the framework of the natural adaptation spectrum of the knowledge-producing "system" involved.

*

This study began by hinting that the history of war research at the KWIFD
can be told as a history of a remarkable absence of friction – disregard-
ing minor, but permanent turbulence in the boundary layer to the political
structures. Aside from the first one or two years of World War II, under the
conditions of military buildup and war, aviation research in Göttingen actually had better research resources at its disposal than during the Weimar
period. Since obstacles for participation in the state and military structures
of National Socialism existed neither on the level of the scientists' political-
moral attitudes nor on the level of research dynamics, the only thing that can
be surprising (if anything is) about the fact that Fluid Dynamics was integrated into these structures was the speed by which it was accomplished.

This raises a final question. Does not the history of war research at
the KWIFD (and at many other, similar institutions)[81] show that the most

[80] For example, see Bruno Latour and Steve Woolgar, *Laboratory Life. The Social Construction of Scientific Facts* (Beverly Hills: Sage, 1979), 148 f., 242.
[81] See in the framework of the research program especially Helmut Maier, "'Wehrhaftmachung' und 'Kriegswichtigkeit.' Zur rüstungstechnologischen Relevanz des Kaiser-Wilhelm-Instituts für Metallforschung in Stuttgart vor und nach 1945," *Ergebnisse. Vorabdrucke aus dem Forschungsprogramm Geschichte der Kaiser-Wilhelm-Gesellschaft im Nationalsozialismus*, Nr. 5 (Berlin: Forschungsprogramm, 2002).

significant aspect of the history of a techno-science like fluid dynamics during the Nazi period is less the emergence of specific structures that did not exist before or after the National Socialist era than the lack of structural elements that could have prevented a participation in this criminal regime? At the level of the social behavior of the individuals involved, this finding touches on the generation of moral indifference in modern societies, described emphatically by Zygmunt Bauman as one of the central factors that made the Holocaust possible.[82] At the level of the scientific discipline's structures, it is considerably more difficult to conceive what kind of elements could constitute a counterweight to the far-reaching adaptability of techno-scientific research to the military interest of any regime. This is a political and moral problem that persists even after 1945 and not only in Germany, and one whose intractability can have fatal consequences again in any technologically waged war.

[82] See Zygmunt Bauman, *Modernity and the Holocaust* (Ithaca: Cornell University Press, 1989).

13

Chemical Weapons Research in National Socialism: The Collaboration of the Kaiser Wilhelm Institutes with the Military and Industry

Florian Schmaltz

The development of chemical weapons in World War I is closely associated with the name of the Kaiser Wilhelm Society (*Kaiser-Wilhelm-Gesellschaft*, KWS). Chemical weapons of mass destruction were researched and developed in the laboratories of the Kaiser Wilhelm Institute for Physical Chemistry and Electrochemistry (*KWI für physikalische Chemie und Elektrochemie*, KWIPC) under the direction of Fritz Haber, and deployed by the German empire for the first time in Ypers in April 1915.[1] A number of comprehensive studies have examined the history of the research, development, and deployment of chemical weapons in World War I.[2] In contrast, very little is

[1] The importance of Fritz Haber and the KWI for Physical Chemistry has been investigated in several biographical studies; see Dietrich Stoltzenberg, *Fritz Haber. Chemiker, Nobelpreisträger, Deutscher, Jude* (Weinheim: VCH, 1994); Margit Szöllösi-Janze, *Fritz Haber 1868–1934. Eine Biographie* (Munich: Beck, 1998). On the history of the first deployment of chemical weapons, see Ulrich Trumpener, "The Road to Ypres: The Beginning of Gas Warfare in World War I," *Journal of Modern History*, 47, no. 3 (1975), 460–480.

[2] In a comparative international perspective, see Ludwig F. Haber, *The Poisonous Cloud. Chemical Warfare in the First World War* (Oxford: Oxford University Press, 1986) and Dieter Martinetz, *Der Gaskrieg 1914–1918. Entwicklung, Herstellung und Einsatz chemischer Kampfstoffe* (Bonn: Bernard und Graefe, 1996); Dieter Martinetz, *Vom Giftpfeil zum Chemiewaffenverbot. Zur Geschichte der chemischen Kampfmittel* (Frankfurt am Main: Thun, 1996). On the United States, see the early study by Augustin M. Prentiss, *Chemicals in War. A Treatise on Chemical Warfare* (New York: McGraw-Hill, 1937); Gilbert F. Wittemore Jr., "World War I, Poison Gas Research and the Ideals of American Chemists," *Social Studies of Science*, 5 (1975), 135–163; Daniel P. Jones, "Chemical Warfare Research during World War I: A Model of Cooperative Research," in John Parascondola and James C. Whorton (eds.), *Chemistry and Modern Society. Historical Essays in Honor of Aaron J. Ihde* (Washington: American Chemical Society, 1983), 165–185; Hugh R. Slotten, "Humane Chemistry or Scientific Barbarism," *Journal of American History*, 77 (1990), 476–498; Edward M. Spiers, "Gas and the North-West Frontier (Chemical Warfare in World War I)," *Journal of Strategic Studies*, 6, no. 4 (1983), 94–112. On Great Britain, see Gradon Carter, *Porton Down. 75 Years of Chemical and Biological Research* (London: Stationery Office Books, 1992); Donald Richter, *Chemical Soldiers. British Gas Warfare in World*

known about their further development during National Socialism at institutes of the KWS, the largest research organization in Germany outside of the universities. Military historians have asked why no chemical weapons were deployed in Europe during World War II.[3] The production of chemical weapons has also been studied from the perspective of economic history.[4] Yet, for a long time there was no comprehensive investigation into the research on chemical weapons in the Nazi regime. The following remarks are based on a study of all research projects at the Kaiser Wilhelm Institutes conducted during National Socialism on both developing chemical weapons and providing the protection against them required for their military implementation.[5]

Of the over forty institutes and research facilities of the KWS that existed during the National Socialist period, seven institutes were involved in research on chemical weapons and defending against them. This empirical finding is surprising because it also includes institutes that worked in areas outside of chemistry or medicine (see Table 13.1).

The seven institutes of the KWS listed in Table 13.1 can be divided into two groups. The first group includes institutes that performed individual contracts limited to a fixed period of time. Among these are the KWI for Labor Physiology (*KWI für Arbeitsphysiologie*), the KWI for Leather Research (*KWI für Lederforschung*), the KWI for Chemistry (*KWI für*

War I (Lawrence: University Press of Kansas, 1992); Roy MacLeod, "The Chemists Go to War: The Mobilisation of Civilian Chemists and the British War Effort, 1914–1918," *Annals of Science*, 50 (1993), 455–481. On Austria-Hungary, see Wolfgang Zecha, "*Unter die Masken.*" *Giftgas auf den Kriegsschauplätzen Österreich-Ungarns im Ersten Weltkrieg* (Vienna: öbv und hpt, 2000).

[3] See Frederic J. Brown, *Chemical Warfare. A Study in Restraints* (Princeton: Princeton University Press, 1981); Günther W. Gellermann, *Der Krieg, der nicht stattfand. Möglichkeiten, Überlegungen und Entscheidungen der deutschen Obersten Führung zur Verwendung chemischer Kampfstoffe im zweiten Weltkrieg* (Koblenz: Bernard und Graefe, 1986); Olaf Groehler, *Der lautlose Tod. Einsatz und Entwicklung deutscher Giftgase von 1914 bis 1945* (Reinbek bei Hamburg: Rowohlt, 1989). On the plans by the U.S. Army to deploy chemical weapons in the invasion of Japan, see John Ellis van Courtland Moon, "Project Sphinx: The Question of the Use of Gas in the Planned Invasion of Japan," *Journal of Strategic Studies*, 12, no. 3 (1989), 303–323, and strategic considerations in the United States overall during World War II, John Ellis van Courtland Moon, "United States Chemical Warfare Policy in World War II: A Captive of Coalition Policy?" *Journal of Military History*, 60, no. 3 (1996), 495–511.

[4] Gottfried Plumpe, *Die I.G. Farbenindustrie AG. Wirtschaft, Technik und Politik 1904–1945* (Berlin: Duncker und Humblot, 1990), 558–559; Groehler; Dietrich Eichholtz, *Geschichte der deutschen Kriegswirtschaft 1939–1945. Vol. III: 1943–1945* (Berlin: Akademie-Verlag, 1996), 205–208; Angelika Ebbinghaus, "Chemische Kampfstoffe in der deutschen Rüstungs- und Kriegswirtschaft, in Dietrich Eichholtz (ed.), *Krieg und Wirtschaft. Studien zur deutschen Wirtschaftsgeschichte 1939–1945* (Berlin: Metropol, 1999), 171–194.

[5] Florian Schmaltz, *Kampfstoff-Forschung im Nationalsozialismus. Zur Kooperation von Kaiser-Wilhelm-Instituten, Militär und Industrie* (Göttingen: Wallstein Verlag, 2005).

TABLE 13.1. *Research on Gas Defense and Chemical Weapons at Kaiser Wilhelm Institutes during National Socialism*

KWI for	Director	Period	Contents of Research
Labor Physiology (Münster branch)	Edgar Atzler	1932–1934	• performance limits of soldiers in continuous service with the gas masks GM 24 and GM 30 • ergonomic deficiencies in the construction of gas masks • physiological problems in wearing gas masks
Brain Research Genetics Department (Berlin-Buch)	Nikolai Timoféeff-Ressovsky	1939–1943	• studies of gas mask filters using radioactive isotopes as tracers • physiological problems in wearing gas masks
Chemistry (Berlin-Dahlem)	Otto Hahn	1940–1944	• studies of gas mask filters using radioactive isotopes as tracers
Leather Research (Dresden)	Wolfgang Grassmann	1943–1944	• effect of impregnation agents against "*Lost*" (mustard gas) on various kinds of leather for military footwear • detoxication agents for leather
Fluid Dynamics (Göttingen)	Ludwig Prandtl	1943	• processes for propagating fog camouflage and clouds of chemical weapons at sea
Physical Chemistry and Electrochemistry (Berlin-Dahlem)	Gerhart Jander (1933–1934) Peter Adolf Thiessen (1934–1945)	1933–1945	• aerosoles (dispersions, mist, smoke) • gas defense filters and surrogate filter materials • chemical weapon detectors • development of new chemical weapons: incendiary agent "N-Stoff" (chlorine triflouride) • physiological effect of chemical weapons
Medical Research (Heidelberg)	Richard Kuhn	(1938) 1941–1945	• nerve gases (Tabun, Sarin, Soman) and antidotes: (a) synthesization of nerve gases (b) physiological effect in animal experiments and on human brains • therapeutic agents against skin injured by "*Lost*" (mustard gas)

Chemie),[6] the KWI for Brain Research (*KWI für Hirnforschung*, KWIHF), and the KWI for Fluid Dynamics (*KWI für Strömungsforschung*, KWIFD). With the exception of the KWIHF, these received military research contracts with a clearly defined set of questions to be explored.

The institutes of the second group had independent departments for chemical weapons. They continuously used their scientific resources to develop chemical weapons and defenses against chemical attacks. Among the institutes of the second group were the KWIPC in Dahlem and the Institute for Chemistry at the KWI for Medical Research (*Institut für Chemie des KWI für medizinische Forschung*, KWIMR) in Heidelberg.

The problems addressed called for a wide spectrum of highly specialized methods and various disciplinary approaches. Under the pressure of the military deployment in World War I, it had still been possible to combine all the research on chemical weapons as interdisciplinary work at the KWIPC. This was no longer feasible after 1933 because of the continuing differentiation of research in the framework of the KWS. The decentralized organizational form of chemical weapons research in the Nazi regime at different institutes of the KWS corresponded, on the one hand, to the needs of the fields of science and, on the other, to military demands. The historically new organizational form was based on the experience of the German Armed Forces (*Reichswehr*), which had established a decentralized, concealed research network during the Weimar Republic as a means of evading the ban on researching chemical weapons specifically required by the Treaty of Versailles.[7] Locally scattered institutes ensured effective secrecy and made possible the flexible delegation of contracts to the institutes of the KWS even after 1933. The following section will first present the KWIHF and the KWIFD as two examples of contract research at institutes of the KWS. Next the KWIPC and the KWIMR, the two institutes that set up departments for chemical weapons in which continuous research was conducted, will be discussed.[8]

---

[6] Ruth Lewin Sime, "'Die "Uranspaltung" hat da die ganze Situation gerettet.' Otto Hahn und das Kaiser-Wilhelm-Institut für Chemie im Zweiten Weltkrieg," in Helmut Maier (ed.), *Gemeinschaftsforschung, Bevollmächtigte und der Wissenstransfer. Die Rolle der Kaiser-Wilhelm-Gesellschaft im System kriegsrelevanter Forschung des Nationalsozialismus* (Göttingen: Wallstein Verlag, 2007), 268–304, here 282–283 and Schmaltz, *Kampfstoff-Forschung*, 15–16 .

[7] "Treaty about the Peace Agreement between Germany and the Allied and Associated Powers of 28 June 1919, Part V: Military, Naval and Air Clauses, Section I: Military Clauses, Chapter II: Armament, Munitions and Material, Article 171," in "The World War I Document Archive," http://www.lib.byu.edu/~rdh/wwi/versailles.html (accessed on 31 October, 2008). On the reorganization of the secret research on agents of warfare from 1925 on, see the files of the Inspektion der Artillerie in the Federal German Archives (*Bundesarchiv*, BArch, RH 12-4/37 and RH 12-4/38 as well as Groehler, 69–74.

[8] For a full accounting of research on chemical weapons and protection against such weapons including the KWI for Labor Physiology and the KWI for Leather Research, see Schmaltz, *Kampfstoff-Forschung*.

PROJECT-SPECIFIC RESEARCH ON CHEMICAL WEAPONS
AND GAS PROTECTION AT KAISER WILHELM INSTITUTES

The KWI for Brain Research

The Genetics Department under Nikolai Timoféeff-Ressovski at the KWIHF
was the second KWI to perform research on gas masks, even beginning
before World War II.[9] The research projects conducted there were exceptional because they were carried out, not in collaboration with the military
but rather in conjunction with the largest German gas mask manufacturer,
the Auergesellschaft.[10] In early 1938 and at the request of the KWIHF, the
board of directors of the Auergesellschaft began efforts to obtain a neutron
generator for the Genetics Department.[11] In order to become familiar with
the neutron generator, Karl G. Zimmer, one of the scientific assistants of
the department, conducted a research trip to the Netherlands, which was
sponsored by the Office for German Raw and Basic Materials (*Amt für
deutsche Roh- und Werkstoffe*) using funds from the Four Year Plan.[12] The

[9] Hans-Walter Schmuhl, "Hirnforschung und Krankenmord," *Vierteljahrshefte für
Zeitgeschichte*, 50 (2002), 559–609; Jochen Richter, "Das Kaiser-Wilhelm-Institut
für Hirnforschung und die Topographie der Grosshirnhemisphären. Ein Beitrag zur
Institutsgeschichte der Kaiser-Wilhelm-Gesellschaft und zur Geschichte der architektonischen
Hirnforschung," in Bernhard vom Brocke and Hubert Laitko (eds.), *Die Kaiser-Wilhelm/
Max-Planck-Gesellschaft und ihre Institute* (Berlin: de Gruyter, 1996), 349–408, 388–394;
Helga Satzinger, *Die Geschichte der genetisch operierenden Hirnforschung von Cécile und
Oskar Vogt (1875–1962, 1870–1959) in der Zeit von 1895 bis ca. 1927* (Stuttgart: Deutscher
Apotheker-Verlag, 1998). On the controversial biography of Nikolai W. Timoféeff-Ressovsky,
see Karl Heinz Roth, "Schöner Neuer Mensch. Der Paradigmenwechsel in der klassischen
Genetik und seiner Auswirkungen auf die Bevölkerungsbiologie des 'Dritten Reichs,'" in
Heidrun Kaupen-Haas (ed.), *Der Griff nach der Bevölkerung. Aktualität und Kontinuität
nazistischer Bevölkerungspolitik* (Nördlingen: Greno, 1986), 1–63, here 29 ff.; Diane B. Paul
and Costas B. Krimbas, "Nikolai W. Timoféeff-Ressovsky," *Scientific American*, 2 (1992),
64–70; Diane Paul, "Die bemerkenswerte Karriere von Nikolai Wladimorivich Timoféeff-
Ressovsky," in Heinz Bielka and Ganten Detlev (eds.), *Festschrift anlässlich der Gründung des
Max-Delbrück-Centrums für Molekulare Medizin 1992 in Berlin-Buch* (Bernau: Blankenburg,
1993), 30–34; Wigbert N. W. Dorna, "Timoféeff-Ressovsky in Berlin-Buch 1925–1945. Sein
Beitrag zur Genetik und dessen Verhältnis zur nationalsozialistischen Erblehre," Ph.D. diss.,
Universität Münster (1995).

[10] To date, there is no comprehensive study on the history of Auergesellschaft during the
Nazi regime. A few important aspects are included in Bernhard Lorentz, *Industrieelite und
Wirtschaftspolitik 1928–1950: Heinrich Dräger und das Drägerwerk* (Paderborn: Schöningh,
2001), 148–157, 273–283; Groehler, 235–236, and Peter Hayes, "Die 'Arisierungen' der
Degussa AG. Geschichte und Bilanz," in Irmtrud Wojak and Peter Hayes (eds.), *"Arisierung"
im Nationalsozialismus. Volksgemeinschaft, Raub, Gedächtnis* (Frankfurt am Main: Campus,
2000), 85–123, 92–93; Peter Hayes, *From Cooperation to Complicity. Degussa in the Third
Reich* (Cambridge: Cambridge University Press, 2005), 79–83.

[11] Quasebart to Busemann, 1 January 1938, Degussa Company Archives, Frankfurt am Main
(*Unternehmensarchiv der Degussa*), IW 24.5/2–3.

[12] Breuer to Amt für deutsche Roh- und Werkstoffe, 10 June 1937, BArch, R 73/16017.

investment cost of the neutron generator, estimated at around 50,000 RM, corresponded to the entire annual budget for the Genetics Department.[13] In early 1938, the Auergesellschaft set up an outpost of its research department at the Genetics Department in Berlin-Buch.[14] A neutron generator was installed there at the Auergesellschaft's expense, supplied by the Dutch company Phillips. Thus, the institutional prerequisites were created for a stronger orientation of research toward questions relevant to the military. The large-scale equipment was ready for operation in Berlin-Buch as early as mid-1939, not in 1941, as historical research had previously assumed.[15]

The work on artificially radioactive isotopes using the Phillips neutron generator was supposed to initiate innovation and generate new products for the Auergesellschaft's Radiological Department that would satisfy the expected medical demand for radio-nuclides. Along with three research areas – the phenomenology of gene manifestation, experimental mutation research, and population genetics – from this point on the neutron generator directly served the military research of the Auergesellschaft. The continuing research collaboration between the joint working group of the Auergesellschaft and the KWI remained project-oriented contract research. Besides the radiation genetic mutation studies, there is also evidence of studies on gas mask filters as armaments technology by the Auergesellschaft up to 1943.

The results of the first studies by Hans J. Born and Karl G. Zimmer, who applied radioactive isotopes to gas mask filters in spring 1940, were published a few weeks later in the journal *Die Naturwissenschaften*.[16] In July 1940, another article by Born and Zimmer followed in *Die Gasmaske*, the "Newsletter of the Auergesellschaft."[17] In this elaborate paper, presented with photographs and graphic diagrams, the two authors introduced to a broader audience the new isotope method for testing gas mask filters. At the same time, the article was effective advertising, presenting the prestigious particle accelerator in a way that publicly credited both the Auergesellschaft and the KWIHF

---

[13] Haushaltsplan der Genetischen Abteilung des KWI für Hirnforschung für 1939, Archives of the Max Planck Society, Berlin (*Archiv zur Geschichte der Max-Planck-Gesellschaft*, MPG-Archiv), Abt. I, Rep. 1 A, Nr. 1599, fols. 133b-133d.

[14] Tätigkeitsbericht der Genetischen Abteilung des KWI für Hirnforschung für die Jahre 1937/1938, MPG-Archiv, Abt. I, Rep. 1 A, Nr. 1583, fol. 186d.

[15] Otto Hahn witnessed a demonstration of the functioning neutron generator in Berlin-Buch in the first week of June 1939; see Otto Hahn to Lise Meitner (copy), 12 June 1939, MPG-Archiv, Abt. Va, Rep. 9, Nr. 5. For the later date, see Burghard Weiss, "Harnack-Prinzip und Wissenschaftswandel. Die Einführung kernphysikalischer Grossgeräte (Beschleuniger) an den Instituten der KWS," in Bernhard vom Brocke and Hubert Laitko (eds.), *Die Kaiser-Wilhelm/Max-Planck-Gesellschaft und ihre Institute* (Berlin: de Gruyter, 1996), 541–560, here 546.

[16] Hans J. Born and Karl G. Zimmer, "Anwendung radioaktiver Isotope bei Untersuchungen über die Filtration von Aerosolen," *Naturwissenschaften*, 28 (1940), 447.

[17] Hans J. Born and Karl G. Zimmer, "Untersuchungen an Schwebstoff-Filtern mittels radioaktiver Stoffe," *Die Gasmaske*, 2 (1940), 25–29.

with applying the most modern research technologies.[18] The concrete object of study, on which Born and Zimmer demonstrated the practical relevance of the tracer method, was the "High-Performance Filter 89" (*Hochleistungsfilter 89*), sold by the Auergesellschaft from 1931 on, which was used by the Armed Forces (*Wehrmacht*) as a filter against chemical weapons.[19] The experiments at the KWIHF proved that the Auergesellschaft's High-Performance Filter 89 was "built correctly with regard to fluid mechanics."[20]

During the following war years, the KWIHF continued to use the neutron generator for contracts on gas mask research from the Army Ordnance Office (*Heereswaffenamt*, HWA) or the Auergesellschaft until 1943, as documented by working reports by Timoféeff-Ressovsky.[21] The military contracts from the army and the air force demanded "a considerable degree" of the Genetics Department's resources, as Zimmer emphasized in an activity report in 1943.[22] No documents have been found yet on the military contracts performed after 1943. The test method developed by Zimmer, which allowed the operating mode and construction of the Auergesellschaft's gas mask filters to be tested by means of radioactive isotopes, was qualitatively superior to the methods used up until that time, and further, was easy to combine with the other test methods already applied in the gas mask industry, such as using an artificial lung to simulate human respiration.[23] The studies were financed by grants from the German Research Foundation (*Deutsche Forschungsgemeinschaft*, DFG), the Reich Research Council (*Reichsforschungsrat*, RFR), and the Reich Office for Economic Expansion (*Reichstelle für Wirtschaftsausbau*, RWA).

During World War II, the third-party funds that flowed into the institute rose significantly, amounting to around one third of the entire budget at their

---

[18] On the presentation of the particle accelerator as prestigious large-scale equipment, see Maria Osietzki, "The Ideology of Early Particle Accelerators. An Association between Knowledge and Power," in Monika Renneberg and Mark Walker (eds.), *Science, Technology and National Socialism* (Cambridge: Cambridge University Press, 1994), 255–270.

[19] Auergesellschaft, "Ein neuer Hochleistungsfilter," *Gasschutz und Luftschutz*, 1 (1931), 92; Heinz Eisenbarth, "Atemfilter gegen Schwebstoffe," *Die Gasmaske*, 8 (1936), 72–77, 72; Heinz Eisenbarth, "Atemfilter gegen Schwebstoffe," *Kolloid-Zeitschrift*, 75, no. 2 (1936), 253–256, 254.

[20] Born and Zimmer, "Untersuchungen," 28.

[21] Timoféeff-Ressovsky to Reichsamt für Wirtschaftsausbau, 23 April 1941, MPG-Archiv, Abt. I, Rep. 1606, fol. 319. The funds were booked as special income; see KWI für Hirnforschung – Genetische Abteilung, Bericht über die Prüfung des Rechnungsabschlusses zum 31.3.1942, 27 August 1942, MPG-Archiv, Abt. I, Rep. 1 A, Nr. 1602, fol. 410; Bericht, signed by Timoféeff-Ressovsky (stamped received by the DFG on 13 March 1942); and Timoféeff-Ressovsky to DFG, 7 March 1942, both BArch, R 73/16017; Karl G. Zimmer, Tätigkeitsbericht über Untersuchungen an Neutronen und künstlich radioaktiven Stoffen, 30 November 1942, BArch, R 73/16017, fol. 1.

[22] Zimmer to Breuer (DFG), Tätigkeitsbericht, 24 July 1943, BArch, R 73/16017, fol. 1.

[23] Rudolf Sauer, "Künstliche Lungen," *Die Gasmaske*, 12 (1940), 7–14.

peak.[24] The example here shows that the collaboration between the RFR, the RWA, the Genetics Department of the KWIHF, and the Auergesellschaft functioned smoothly and in a goal-oriented fashion. The historical interpretation dominant up until now argues that the polycratic structure of competing institutions in National Socialism inevitably resulted in a confusing chaos of offices and undermined the successful sponsorship of research by the Nazi science policy. However, the example depicted here, of a successful transfer of foreign technology through cooperating scientific organizations, must at least qualify this view.

The KWI for Fluid Dynamics

In early 1943, at the initiative of the Greifswald Naval Observatory, the Naval Supreme Command contracted the KWIFD in Göttingen with the task of using experimental physics experiments in wind tunnels to develop a mathematical model that could predict the distribution of chemical weapons clouds and artificial fog camouflage at sea. The naval leadership had become concerned about this research desideratum because documents from the British research center for chemical weapons in Porton Down, which fell into Nazi hands in France, indicated that the Chemical Warfare Service had a special slide rule designed to determine the spread of poison gases.[25]

At the KWIFD, Karl Wieghardt, an assistant of Institute Director Ludwig Prandtl, conducted the corresponding studies, presumably between January and September 1943.[26] On the basis of measurements of turbulent model flows recorded in the wind tunnel, Wieghardt calculated relatively simple mathematical formulas and drafted nomograms. This yielded a calculation method that was simple enough even for mathematical laymen to handle and could predict the distribution of poison gas clouds at sea or artificial fog in surface wind. Immediately after submission of the final report in October 1944, scientific experts from the Armed Forces began evaluating the soundness of the experimental results from the KWIFD. The HWA assessed the study positively.

---

[24] Schmaltz, *Kampfstoff-Forschung* , 272–273.

[25] Karl Wieghardt, Über Ausbreitungsvorgänge in turbulenten Reibungsschichten, KWI für Strömungsforschung, September 1944, "Vorbemerkung," Imperial War Museum (London), Air Document Division Technical Intelligence, Microfilm Reel 3352, Frames 1200–1240.

[26] In the sources, "occasional consultations with the Naval Observatory in Greifswald about the dissolution of fog" are mentioned for the first time in January 1943; see file note, Betr.: Arbeiten im Interessenbericht der Kriegsmarine (Geheim!), 22 January 1943, MPG-Archiv, Abt. I, Rep. 44, Nr. 46, fol. 17; Moritz Epple, "Rechnen, Messen, Führen. Kriegsforschung am Kaiser-Wilhelm-Institut für Strömungsforschung 1937–1945," in Helmut Maier (ed.), *Rüstungsforschung im Nationalsozialismus* (Göttingen: Wallstein, 2002), 305–356, here 328, 341.

In principle, Wieghardt's formulas could also describe how a cloud of a chemical agent would spread. However, the constant used to calculate the lift in layers of air near the ground was uncertain, as Wieghardt himself had pointed out. Since the values of the constant, which were dependent on the weather conditions in the study, were based solely on the analysis of measurements performed by third parties, as a safeguard the HWA recommended conducting outdoor tests of its own under real conditions to increase the accuracy of the calculation method.[27] These experiments, planned by the Greifswald Naval Observatory and the Army Proving Ground in Raubkammer near Munster, could no longer be realized in the final months of the war. After the war the final report by Wieghardt was confiscated by the Allies in 1945 and sent for further analysis to Porton Down, where the British military had maintained a research center for chemical and biological weapons since World War I.[28] The research results apparently met with great interest there, for shortly after the British chemical weapons specialists from Porton Down presented their opinion on the tests, the British Intelligence Objectives Subcommittee (BIOS) sent a group of specialists to Göttingen to investigate more closely the German work in fluid dynamics on the meteorological effects on the spread of chemical weapons.[29]

INDEPENDENT CHEMICAL WEAPONS DEPARTMENTS AT KAISER WILHELM INSTITUTES

The KWI for Physical Chemistry

The first legal measures for the persecution of Jews were a decisive prerequisite for this institute's re-transformation into a research center focusing on chemical weapons. The "Law for the Restoration of the Professional Civil Service"[30] of April 1933 provided the opportunity to initiate the institute's

---

[27] Dictation signed W. (presumably Weinberg), (Heeresgasschutzlaboratorium Spandau – VIb L) to Verteiler im Hause, Betr.: Kurze Diskussion der Wieghardt'schen Formeln über die Ausbreitung von Nebel-(Kampfstoff-) Wolken der freien Atmosphäre, 26 October 1944, National Archives (NA) Washington, DC, RG 373, Entry 1 B, Box 156, EFT 550 G-2446.

[28] On the history of Porton Down, see Rob Evans, *Gassed: British Chemical Warfare Experiments on Humans* (London: House of Stratus, 2000), as well as Gradon Carter and Brain Balmer, "Chemical and Biological Warfare and Defence, 1945–50," in Robert Bud and Philip Gummett (eds.), *Cold War, Hot Science: Applied Research in Britain's Defence Laboratories, 1945–1990* (Amsterdam: Harwood, 1999), 295–338.

[29] M. L. Calder, P. A. Sheppard and C. L. Wheeler, "German War-Time Development in Fluid Turbulence with Particular Reference to the Lower Atmosphere and the Meteorology of Chemical Warfare," *BIOS Final Report 760* (Item No. 8), (London: H. M. Stationery Office, 1945).

[30] Gesetz zur Wiederherstellung des Berufsbeamtentums, in *Reichsgesetzblatt*, Teil I (1933), 175–177.

takeover by the group of National Socialist chemical weapons specialists and chemists from Göttingen centered around Gerhart Jander, Rudolf Mentzel, and Peter Adolf Thiessen. The Reich Ministry of Defense, the HWA, and the Prussian Ministry of Culture all supported their efforts.[31] After Fritz Haber was forced to resign in November 1933, all five of the department director posts were filled with members of the NSDAP, three of whom had participated in the party's founding in Göttingen back in 1922/23. With this high number of "old fighters" (*"Alte Kämpfer"*) of the NSDAP in functions of leadership, the KWIPC took a special position within the entire KWS. This is also true with regard to the dismissal of twenty-eight Jewish employees of the institute. At no other KWI were so many Jewish scientists ousted.[32]

The reaction of the General Administration of the KWS to the takeover was ambivalent. In accordance with his conservative German nationalism, KWS president Max Planck fundamentally endorsed placing science in the service of the Nazi regime's armament goals. However, like Fritz Haber, for reasons of military security Planck considered it inadvisable to establish a research center for chemical weapons in the villa quarter of Dahlem.[33] As an alternative location, Planck suggested the branch office of the KWI for Labor Physiology in Münster, but this suggestion was rejected by the military. Planck also regretted that Haber was forced to resign.[34] Despite the conflicts surrounding the Prussian Ministry of Culture's making personnel policy decisions without consulting with the KWS, he ultimately accepted the appointment of Jander as institute director in 1933 and of his successor Peter Adolf Thiessen.

Once Jander had replaced the entire staff and the institute had been converted to weapons research, he stepped down as provisional director in March 1935.[35] His resignation was motivated in part by an institutionalized conflict of authority.[36] Because of their appointment as heads

---

[31] Christina Eibl, "Der Physikochemiker Peter Adolf Thiessen als Wissenschaftsorganisator. Eine biographische Studie. Historisches Institut der Universität Stuttgart," Ph.D. diss., University of Stuttgart (1999), 71; Schmaltz, *Kampfstoff-Forschung*, 62–77.

[32] Michael Schüring, *Minervas verstossene Kinder. Vertriebene Wissenschaftler und die Vergangenheitspolitik der Max-Planck-Gesellschaft* (Göttingen: Wallstein, 2006), 103.

[33] Planck to Vahlen, 11 August 1933, Geheimes Staatsarchiv preussischer Kulturbesitz, Rep. 76, Vc, Sekt. 2, Tit. 23, Litt. A, Nr. 108, vol. IV, fol. 59; Donnevert, file note, 13 September 1933, BArch, R 1501/126790, fol. 50; Haber to Generalmajor Geyer, 15 May 1933, MPG-Archiv, Abt. Va, Rep. 5, Nr. 999.

[34] Niederschrift über die Sitzung des Kuratoriums des KWI für physikalische Chemie am 17.7.1933, Geheimes Staatsarchiv Preussischer Kulturbesitz, Rep. 76, Vc, Sekt. 2, Tit. 23, Litt. A, Nr. 108, vol. IV, fol. 8.

[35] Rust and Vahlen to the president of Göttingen University, 2 May 1935, Archives of the University of Göttingen (Universitätsarchiv Göttingen), Kuratorium – Mathematisch-Naturwissenschaftliche Fakultät, 4 Vc, Nr. 351, Personalakte Gerhart Jander, fol. 5.

[36] Gerhart Jander, Gutachten über Herrn Prof. Dr. R. Mentzel in wissenschaftlicher, pädagogischer und persönlicher Hinsicht, 2 December 1935, BArch, BMA, RL 3/56, fol. 98.

in the Science Branch of the Reich Ministry for Education and Science (*Reichserziehungsministerium*, REM) in June 1934, the department directors Mentzel and Thiessen, although subject to his authority at the institute, were authorized to issue him directives from the ministry.[37] Moreover, in spring 1935, the institute lost its status as the most important chemical weapons outpost of the HWA once the military had expanded its own institutions for chemical weapons research with the Army Gas Protection Laboratory Spandau (*Heeresgasschutzlaboratorium Spandau*) and the Munster Proving Ground (*Heereserprobungsstelle Munster*).[38]

In April 1935, Peter Adolf Thiessen was appointed Jander's successor.[39] One year after he took office, a part of the HWA staff working at the KWI moved to the newly completed Army Gas Protection Laboratory in the Spandau Citadel.[40] From this point on, research on chemical weapons at the KWI was continued in the department directed by August Winkel, who had been a member of the NSDAP since February 1931 and of the SS since October 1932.[41] In 1938, Mentzel and Winkel planned to connect their section of the KWIPC to the Faculty of Defense Technology (*Wehrtechnische Fakultät*, WTF) being set up at the Berlin Technical University as an Institute for Gas Chemistry.[42] Mentzel became director of the RFR founded in 1937, and president of the DFG.[43] In late August 1938, he resigned from his position as department head at the KWIPC.[44] Although the expansion of the Faculty of Defense Technology had to be deferred in March 1940 as a conse-

---

[37] Stuckart to Mentzel, file note, 11 June 1934, BArch, REM-Akte A-070, Rudolf Mentzel, fol. 11; Karl Fredehagen (Dean of the Philosophy School of Ernst-Moritz-Ernst-Arndt-Universität), Bericht der Habilitationskommission Dr. Mentzel, 12 November 1933, BArch, REM-Akte A-070, Rudolf Mentzel, fol. 11; Vahlen to Thiessen and Planck, 12 June 1934, BArch, REM-Akte A-070, Rudolf Mentzel, fol. 4.

[38] Liese (HWA) to the Allgemeine Heeresamt, 8 June 1934, BArch, RH 12–4/35; Heinrici (Allgemeines Heeresamt) to the HWA, 25 June 1934, BArch, RH 12–4/35.

[39] Thiessen took over the office in April, initially provisionally, and was appointed institute director in May; see Kunisch (REM) to Planck, 29 March 1935, MPG-Archiv, Abt. II, Rep. 1 A, Personalia Peter Adolf Thiessen, and Rust to Planck, 20 May 1935, MPG-Archiv, Abt. II, Rep. 1 A, Personalia Peter Adolf Thiessen.

[40] Sicherer to Thiessen, 6 July 1936, BArch, R 73/15171.

[41] Parteistatistische Erhebung 1939, August Winkel, 1 July 1939, BArch; Mitgliedsnummer 44.657 – SS Stab 75. SS-Standarte, BArch, SSO-Akte August Winkel, geb. 20.9.1902; and also BArch, Reichssippenamt-Akte August Winkel, G5372.

[42] Becker (Dean of the WTF), 21 July 1938, BArch, R 2/12497; Mentzel, Denkschrift zur Errichtung des Instituts für Gas-Chemie der Wehrtechnischen Fakultät an der Technischen Hochschule Berlin (copy), undated (date of receipt in the Reich Ministry of Finance, 21 December 1938), BArch, R 2/12497; Winkel to Thiessen, 23 March 39, BArch, R 73/15732.

[43] Notker Hammerstein, *Die Deutsche Forschungsgemeinschaft in der Weimarer Republik und im Dritten Reich. Wissenschaftspolitik in Republik und Diktatur 1920–1945* (Munich: Beck, 1999), 205–206.

[44] Thiessen to Bosch, 31 August 1938, MPG-Archiv, Abt. I, Rep. 1 A, Nr. 1174, fol. 100.

quence of the war, the Institute for Gas Chemistry received a regular budget from REM.[45] Thus, Winkel's department functioned de facto as a provisional institute for gas chemistry until the end of the war.

In subsequent years, Thiessen occupied an important position as a science manager in the area of chemical weapons research. In his position as head of the Division for Inorganic Chemistry in the RFR from 1937 until 1945, he sponsored numerous research projects investigating chemical weapon aerosols, gas mask filters, and the effect of chemical weapons on the organism. Not counting the projects at his KWI, he approved at least twenty-four research contracts at universities and technical academies as well as at the KWIMR.[46]

It is also worth emphasizing that the prerequisites for the large-scale technical production of chlorine trifluoride (ClF_3) were created at the KWIPC. The HWA had shown particular interest in this compound, also known under the code name "N-Stoff,"[47] since 1934 at the latest.[48] Because of its extremely escharotic properties, chlorine trifluoride was tested by the research department of the HWA for its potential military deployment as a priming compound or incendiary material.

In the framework of the dissertation he wrote under the supervision of Thiessen, Siegfried Glupe worked at the KWIPC to devise a method for the industrial-scale production of N-Stoff.[49] In June 1935, Glupe initially

---

[45] On the history of the construction of the WTF, see Dean of the WTF to REM (copy), 30 August 1940, BArch, R 2/12498, fol. 60; Hans Ebert and Hermann J. Rupieper, "Technische Wissenschaft und nationalsozialistische Rüstungspolitik. Die Wehrtechnische Fakultät der TH Berlin 1933–1945," in Reinhard Rürup (ed.), *Wissenschaft und Gesellschaft. Beiträge zur Geschichte der TH/TU Berlin 1879–1979* (Berlin: Springer, 1979), 469–491, 477. On the development of the budget of the Institute for Gas Chemistry, see REM to Reichshauptkasse, 5 January 1942, BArch, R 2/12496, fol. 44; REM to Reichshauptkasse, 23 September 1943, BArch, R 2/12496, fol. 81; and REM to Reichshauptkasse, 12 October 1944, BArch, R 2/12496, fol. 86.

[46] For more details, see Schmaltz, *Kampfstoff-Forschung*, 125–142.

[47] According to the testimony of the IG Farben manager Jürgen von Klenck, the term N-Stoff stood for "Normal-Stoff" ("normal substance"); see sworn statement by Jürgen von Klenck, 6 March 1947, Case I, Karl Brandt VDB, Addendum I, Document Karl Brandt Nr. 88, in Klaus Dörner, Angelika Ebbinghaus, Karsten Linne, Karl Heinz Roth, and Paul Weindling (eds.), *Der Nürnberger Ärzteprozess 1946/47. Wortprotokolle, Anklage- und Verteidigungsmaterial, Quellen zum Umfeld* (Munich: Saur, 2000), Abt. 4, fol. 02336.

[48] Becker (HWA), Weiterentwicklung der Kampfstoffe (Geheime Kommandosache), September 1934, BArch, RH 12–9/19, fol. 3.

[49] Werner Osenberg, Inquiry No. 45, 9 July 1945, Public Records Office, London (PRO), FO 1031/137, fol. 115. In interrogation by staff of the British Intelligence Objectives-Subcommittee (BIOS), Glupe confirmed this in 1945; see H. L. Green, "Vereinigte Flussspategruben G.m.b.H. at Stulln (United Fluorspat Mines)," *BIOS Final Report* 72 (Items 8, 22, 31), (London: H. M. Stationery Office, no date), 6. Glupe's dissertation, accepted by the TH Berlin and entitled "Untersuchungen auf dem Gebiete der Schmelzflusselektrolyse von Alkalisalzen" (Studies on the area of the electrolysis of molten masses of alkali salts),

became a staff member of the Central Office for Army Physics (*Zentralstelle für Heeresphysik*) in the HWA under Erich Schumann, which became the Research Department (WA Prüf 11) on 1 September 1935. In April 1936, Glupe was transferred to the Experimental Station East (*Versuchsstelle Ost*) in Kummersdorf as a scientific assistant.[50] Although the military usefulness of N-Stoff was controversial, in 1938, the commander-in-chief of the Army ordered the founding of an N-Stoff factory in Falkenhagen (60 km southeast of Berlin).[51] In 1940 Thiessen participated in the construction of scientific research institutions there.[52]

When parts of the KWIPC were relocated to Falkenhagen to escape the air attacks on Berlin, concentration camp inmates were forced to erect institute buildings from spring until August 1944 and again from early 1945. The prisoners were loaned to the KWS by a subsidiary of IG Farben.[53] In summer 1944, Thiessen intervened with the RFR to prevent the removal of SS guards, which would have resulted in an interruption of the prisoners' exploitation.[54] According to Strebel and Wagner's calculations, an average of around thirty-five to forty prisoners were forced to work for the KWIPC, and based on the exchange of sick and emaciated prisoners, it must be assumed that around one hundred prisoners were exploited under the

---

is documented bibliographically, but the original is missing. According to reports by Allied intelligence services, the process developed by Glupe was evaluated positively: Green, *BIOS Final Report* 72, 6; and W. Archer, W. J. V. Ward and O. S. Whitson, "Hydrofluoric Acid Vereinigte Flussspategruben G.m.b.H. Stulln," *BIOS Final Report* 261 (Item 22), (London: H. M. Stationery Office, no date), 3–4.

[50] Personnel form Siegfried Glupe, BArch, ZA V 3.

[51] Werner Osenberg, Inquiry No. 45, 9 July 1945, PRO London, FO 1031/137, fols. 115 f and HWA (Wa F) to Chef Wa J Rü, (December 1938), Geowissenschaftliches Institut der Universität Mainz, Johannes Preuss Collection, Falkenhagen Inventory (cited as Preuss Collection). On the history of the works, see Johannes Preuss and Frank Eitelberg, "Rekonstruktion der ehemaligen Fabrik zur Herstellung von Brand- und Kampfstoffen: N-Stoff und Sarin der Monturon GmbH in Falkenhagen," unpublished report, Universität Mainz (1994).

[52] Aktenvermerk über die Besprechung am 8.7.1940 im Sitzungssaal HWA, Bl. 1, Anlage 1 to the letter by Glupe (Wa F IIc) to Adenauer (Verwertungsgesellschaft für Montanindustrie), 16 July 1940, Preuss Collection (Konvolut 10L) and Aktenvermerk über die Besprechung am 8.7.1940 im Sitzungssaal HWA, Betr.: Sonder-Bauvorhaben MO/D/6, Bl. 1–3, Anlage 2, to the letter by Glupe (Wa F IIc) to Adenauer (Verwertungsgesellschaft für Montanindustrie), 16 July 1940, Preuss Collection (Doc. 25).

[53] Eibl, 154–159; Bernhard Strebel and Jens-Christian Wagner, "Zwangsarbeit für Forschungseinrichtungen der Kaiser-Wilhelm-Gesellschaft 1939–1945. Ein Überblick," *Ergebnisse. Vorabdrucke aus dem Forschungsprogramm "Geschichte der Kaiser-Wilhelm-Gesellschaft im Nationalsozialismus,"* 11 (Berlin: Forschungsprogramm, 2003), 47–48, translated in this book, and also Schmaltz, *Kampfstoff-Forschung*, 164–169.

[54] Entry of 10 May 1944, Tagebuch des Reichsgeschäftsführers der Forschungs- und Lehrgemeinschaft "Das Ahnenerbe," SS-Standartenführer Sievers, in Dörner, Ebbinghaus, Linne, Roth, and Weindling, Abt. 3, fols. 00796–00797.

brutal working and living conditions during the erection of the Chemical Weapons Department of the KWIPC at Falkenhagen.[55]

Above and beyond this, as a science manager in the RFR Thiessen bore a share of the responsibility for the exploitation of scientists imprisoned in the Płaszów and Flossenbürg concentration camps.[56] Reichsführer SS Heinrich Himmler had ordered on 25 May 1944 that any scientific potential in the concentration camps was to be exploited for German research and the armaments industry.[57] The director of the Gmelin Institute, Erich Pietsch, who had been appointed as Thiessen's representative for the RFR's Division for Inorganic Chemistry in summer 1943, functioned as one of the coordinators of the scientific deployment of prisoners. In this capacity Pietsch took over the confiscation and evacuation of apparatus and scientific equipment for the RFR as well as the recruiting of scientists for the purposes of German war research.[58] From early summer 1944 on, Pietsch worked with the acting director of the Chemical Section of the Institute for German East Labor (*Institut für deutsche Ostarbeit*), Dr. Hans-Paul Müller, in order to use prisoners with scientific expertise at the concentration camp in Płaszów for various contracts.[59] In summer 1944, Pietsch contacted staff of the SD and Reich Security Main Office (*Reichsicherheitshauptamt*) and recommended the establishment of a chemists' command.[60] In the Płaszów and Flossenbürg concentration camps, prisoners from what was known as the "construction command" then had to construct a chemical weapons detector for the Chemical Weapons Department at the KWIPC under August Winkel. The design work for the device was completed in November 1944. Once the prisoner scientists and engineers had been transferred to Flossenbürg, the construction of the device was to commence there in mid-December.[61] The exploitation of qualified inmates thus became a resource for chemical weapons research at the KWIPC in the final phase of the war.

[55] Strebel and Wagner, 48.

[56] Schmaltz, *Kampfstoff-Forschung*, 178–188. and Sören Flachowsky, *Von der Notgemeinschaft zum Reichsforschungsrat. Wissenschaftspolitik im Kontext von Autarkie, Aufrüstung und Krieg* (Stuttgart: Franz Steiner Verlag, 2008), 414–432.

[57] Himmler to Pohl, 25 May 1944, BArch, NS 21/96.

[58] Mentzel to Pietsch, 31 July 1943, NA, RG 319, Entry 82a, Box 17, Folder: Alsos RFR 255.

[59] On this, see the report by Wilhelm Coblitz, Stand der Aufbauarbeiten und Einsatzmöglichkeiten am Verlagerungsort des Instituts für Deutsche Ostarbeit in den Schlössern Zandt und Miltsch, 16 October 1944, NA, RG 319, Entry 82a, Box 17, Folder: Alsos RFR 255.

[60] Notation, Betr.: Errichtung einer wissenschaftlichen Forschungsstätte in einem Konzentrationslager lt. Befehl RFSS vom 25.5.1944, Besprechung am 13.7.1944, 28 July 1944, BArch, NS 21/96.

[61] Pietsch to Lorenz (OKM), Mentzel und Thiessen (both RFR), Winkel (KWI for Physical Chemistry), Dr. Beyer (OKW AWA Ag W Wiss), Bericht über den Stand der Arbeiten der wissenschaftlichen Häftlingsgruppen im Konzentrationslager Flossenbürg, 16 December 1944, BArch, NS 21/845.

The KWI for Medical Research

Richard Kuhn, one of the outstanding biochemists of the twentieth century, was born in Vienna on 3 December 1900 to the elementary school teacher Angelika Kuhn (née Rodler) and the hydraulic engineer and *Hofrat* Richard Clemens Kuhn.[62] He belonged to the generation whose youth was indelibly molded by World War I. After Kuhn graduated from secondary school, he enlisted as a volunteer, serving from March 1917 until November 1918 in the K.u.K Telegraphen Regiment in St. Pölten.[63] After the end of the war, he studied chemistry, first in Vienna, and then from 1919 with the Nobel laureate Richard Willstätter at the University of Munich. Despite his Austrian citizenship, from 1919 until 1920 he was a member of the *Zeitfreiwilligen Kompanie*, a paramilitary organization in Munich.[64] Willstätter realized Kuhn's extraordinary talent and in 1921, after only six semesters, allowed him to write his doctoral thesis "On the Specificity of Enzymes in Carbohydrate Metabolism." Three years later, Kuhn received his postdoctoral qualification after writing a paper on the mechanism of action of amylases.[65]

In late June 1924, a few months after the failed putsch by Hitler in Munich and in the face of growing anti-Semitism at the university, Willstätter tendered his resignation, which was accepted by the Ministry of Culture in February 1925.[66] When Willstätter received a call to the Eidgenössische Technische Hochschule (ETH) in Zurich in 1926, he declined but recommended his pupil Kuhn in his stead.[67] Willstätter achieved Kuhn's appointment "against some resistance."[68] In Zurich, Kuhn dedicated himself predominantly to stereochemical studies of carbohydrates and physico-chemical studies on the chemical composition of natural dyes.[69] Through his work in Switzerland, Kuhn developed an active collaboration with the chemical industry. He

[62] Personnel form Richard Kuhn, MPG-Archiv, Abt. II, Rep. 1 A, Personalia Richard Kuhn, vol. 1. For the biography of Kuhn, see Florian Schmaltz, "Richard Kuhn," in Noretta Koertge (ed.), *New Dictionary of Scientific Biography. Ibn Al-Haytham–Luria*, vol. 4 (Detroit: Thomson Gale, 2008), 167–170.

[63] Personnel form, Richard Kuhn, MPG-Archiv, Abt. II, Rep. 1 A, Personalia Richard Kuhn, vol. 1., and Gerhard Oberkofler and Peter Goller, *Richard Kuhn. Skizzen zur Karriere eines österreichischen Nobelpreisträgers* (Innsbruck: Archiv der Leopold-Franzens-Universität, 1992), 10.

[64] Otto Westphal, "Richard Kuhn zum Gedächtnis," *Angewandte Chemie*, 80 (1968), 13, 501–519, 502; Universität Heidelberg, Fragebogen über Militärzeiten und Parteimitgliedschaften, 14 September 1937, Archives of the University of Heidelberg (*Universitätsarchiv Heidelberg*), PA 4717.

[65] Facsimile of the habilitation of Kuhn in Westphal, 503; Richard Kuhn, "Der Wirkungsmechanismus der Amylasen. Ein Beitrag zum Konfigurations-Problem der Stärke," Habilitation Thesis, Universität München (1925).

[66] Richard Willstätter, *Aus meinem Leben* (Weinheim: Verlag Chemie, 1949), 342–346; further, Freddy Litten, *Der Rücktritt Richard Willstätters 1924/25 und seine Hintergründe* (Munich: Institut für Geschichte der Naturwissenschaften, 1999), 41 and 49.

[67] Oberkofler and Goller, 21.

[68] Willstätter, 351.

[69] Westphal, 505–506.

concluded contracts of cooperation with both IG Farben, which financed his assistant, and the Gesellschaft für Chemische Industrie Basel (Ciba).[70] In December 1928, Kuhn married the Swiss pharmacology student Daisy Hartmann.[71] Six months earlier, the KWS had offered him the directorship of the Institute of Chemistry at the KWIMR being founded at the time, a position he assumed in May 1928.[72]

In his first years in Heidelberg, Kuhn continued the studies of natural dyes he had begun in Zurich. Together with Edgar Lederer, he succeeded in 1931 in separating carotin into α and β carotin.[73] Kuhn's working group was successful in isolating and synthesizing a number of natural substances. Using chromatographic adsorption techniques they were able to elucidate the relationship between carotinoids and vitamin A.[74] During the 1930s, his work increasingly centered on vitamin research. Together with Paul György, who emigrated to the United States in 1933, Kuhn isolated lactoflavin (vitamin B_2) from whey.[75] The hypothesis that was later confirmed, that lactoflavin was a component of Otto Warburg's yellow enzyme in the body of animals, linked vitamin research with enzyme research, thus prompting further studies.[76] In cooperation with the Scientific Chemical Laboratory of IG Farben, in 1938 Kuhn and his staff achieved the crystallization of vitamin B_6, and in the following year, its synthesis.[77]

When Ludolf von Krehl was no longer able to continue his administrative tasks as director of the KWIMR for medical reasons, Kuhn was appointed its provisional managing director in March 1934.[78] The principle of rotating the duties among colleagues was abandoned after Krehl's death on 26 July 1937.

[70] Vertrag zwischen Richard Kuhn und der I.G. Farbenindustrie, 4 October 1926, MPG-Archiv, Abt. III, Rep. 25, Nr. 32 and Mitarbeitervertrag zwischen Richard Kuhn in Zürich und der Gesellschaft für Chemische Industrie in Basel, 4 October 1927, MPG-Archiv, Abt. III, Rep. 25–2, Box 8.

[71] Theodor Wagner-Jauregg, *Mein Lebensweg als bioorganischer Chemiker* (Stuttgart: Wissenschaftliche Verlagsgesellschaft, 1985), 39–40; and Daisy Kuhn-Hartmann 17.5.1907 bis 10. März 1976, private printing 1976, MPG-Archiv, Abt. III, Rep. 25–2, box Nr. 2.

[72] Warburg to Kuhn, 11 July 1927, MPG-Archiv, Abt. III, Rep. 25, Nr. 33; and Glum (KWS) to Kuhn, 11 July 1928, MPG-Archiv, Abt. III, Rep. 25, Nr. 33 and the contract between the KWS and Richard Kuhn, 6 May 1928, 24 May 1928, MPG-Archiv, Abt. III, Rep. 25, Nr. 33.

[73] Westphal, 508.

[74] Westphal, 508; and Heinz A. Staab, "50 Jahre Kaiser-Wilhelm-/ Max-Planck-Institut für Medizinische Forschung Heidelberg," *Heidelberger Jahrbücher*, 24 (1980), 47–70, 57.

[75] Petra Werner (ed.), *Vitamine als Mythos. Dokumente zur Geschichte der Vitaminforschung* (Berlin: Akademie-Verlag, 1998), 32 ff.; Ute Deichmann, *Flüchten, mitmachen und vergessen. Chemiker und Biochemiker in der NS-Zeit* (Weinheim: Wiley-VCH, 2001), 302.

[76] Westphal, 509–510.

[77] Richard Kuhn and Gerhard Wendt, "Über das aus Reiskleie und Hefe isolierte Adermin (Vitamin B_6)," *Berichte der Deutschen Chemischen Gesellschaft*, 71 (1938), 1118; Richard Kuhn, Gerhard Wendt, Kurt Westphal, and Otto Westphal, "Synthese des Adermins," *Die Naturwissenschaften*, 27 (1939), 469–470; Deichmann, *Flüchten, mitmachen, vergessen*, 304.

[78] Planck to Kuhn (copy), 6 March 1934, MPG-Archiv, Abt. III, Rep. 25, Nr. 39; and Carl Bosch to Kuhn, 16 September 1937, MPG-Archiv, Abt. II, Rep. 1 A, Personalia Richard Kuhn, vol. 1.

After lengthy negotiations and approval by the Senate of the KWS, in January 1938, Kuhn was appointed director of the KWIMR.[79] Kuhn was not a member of the NSDAP.[80] Yet, his political position with regard to the Nazi regime is the subject of controversy. In 1936, the chief of the NS-Dozentenschaft at the University of Heidelberg passed judgment on Kuhn, declaring that as an Austrian his politics had been "very reluctant." "However, his attitude toward National Socialism would seem to be rather positive."[81] Nothing about this assessment by party offices changed until the end of the war. In September 1944, Wilhelm Spengler, the leader of the Culture Group (Amt III SD Inland) under the chief of the Security Police and the SD, noted that Kuhn was well known "in his specialized area as an outstanding personality with an international reputation" and although politically he was "not prominent," he nevertheless should be "regarded as reliable."[82]

Kuhn avoided coming into conflict with the Nazi regime because of his loyal conduct toward the state. In contrast to his colleague Otto Meyerhof, director of the Institute for Physiology at the KWIMR, Kuhn did not try to keep the Jewish staff and doctoral students at his institute after the anti-Semitic "Law for the Restoration of the Professional Civil Service" was issued.[83] When it was brought to his attention in April 1936 through an "inquiry" by the Gestapo that there were "another three persons of non-Aryan extraction employed by Dr. Meyerhof at the institute," namely "Mr. Lehmann, Miss Hirsch and another lady," he forwarded the denunciation to the General Administration of the KWS in Berlin.

Instead of warning Meyerhof about the Gestapo spies, Kuhn asked the General Administration "to give Professor Meyerhof clear instructions to which he should adhere in the selection of his staff." Since this circumstance could entail "discussions about the Kaiser Wilhelm Society as a whole and about the Institute in Heidelberg in particular," Kuhn urged that the measures for persecuting the Jews be monitored more strictly and instructions given "not only in a letter to Professor Meyerhof, but in a circular to all local subsidiaries of the institute, although no similar cases are known."[84] The

[79] Telschow to Kuhn, 6 January 1938, MPG-Archiv, Abt. II, Rep. 1 A, Personalia Richard Kuhn, vol. 1.

[80] The documents of the former Berlin Document Center in the Bundesarchiv do not contain any indications of Kuhn's membership in the NSDAP or its organizations; see also Kuhn's own claims in Military Government of Germany, questionnaire Richard Kuhn, 8 January 1946, MPG-Archiv, III. Abt, Rep. 25, Nr. 57.

[81] Leiter der Dozentenschaft to Rektor der Universität Heidelberg, 13 January 1936, Universitätsarchiv Heidelberg, Generalia, PA 4717.

[82] Spengler to Osenberg, 26 September 1944, BArch, R 26 III/112, fol. 187.

[83] Kuhn to the KWS, 21 September 1933, MPG-Archiv, Abt. I, Rep. 1 A, Nr. 531, fol. 83; moreover, Benno Müller-Hill, Tödliche Wissenschaft. Die Aussonderung von Juden, Zigeunern und Geisteskranken 1933–1945 (Reinbek: Rowohlt, 1988), 31 and Schüring, 60–61 and 68–70.

[84] Kuhn to Glum, 27 April 1936, MPG-Archiv, Abt. I, Rep. 1 A, Nr. 540, fol. 196. In Petra Werner's view, the letter from Kuhn is "to be assessed more as a sign of insecurity than as an

measures proposed by Kuhn went too far even for the General Administration, which informed him in its response that the listed staff members of "non-Aryan extraction" were not employed by the KWS but were "at the institute as guests or doctoral students," which is why they would "not be subject to notification to the General Administration of the Kaiser Wilhelm Society."[85]

Even before World War II began, Kuhn held an impressive number of leadership positions in scientific societies, expert committees, and state research institutions. He was on the board of directors of the Emil Fischer Society, the primary purpose of which was to fund the budget of the KWI for Chemistry through contributions from IG Farben. In addition, he was a member of the board of directors of the Adolf Baeyer Society for the Promotion of Chemical Literature (*Adolf-Baeyer-Gesellschaft zur Förderung der chemischen Literatur*) and deputy chairman of the Justus Liebig Society founded in 1920, which awarded postdoctoral scholarships to German chemists.[86] He was also chairman of the Organic Chemistry Working Group in the Association of German Chemists (*Verein Deutscher Chemiker*) and vice-president of the *Union Internationale du Chimie* since 1936.[87] He belonged to the scientific committee of the Society of German Natural Scientists and Physicians (*Gesellschaft Deutscher Naturforscher und Ärzte*).[88]

Among his most important functions as a science manager was undoubtedly his appointment as president of the German Chemical Society (*Deutsche Chemische Gesellschaft*) in May 1938. He had participated actively in the "coordination" ("*Gleichschaltung*") of the Society after his appointment as member of the board in 1936.[89] In October 1939, one month after the beginning of the war, Kuhn also became the head (*Fachspartenleiter*) of the Specialized Section for Organic Chemistry in the RFR.[90] Although the remaining sources are fragmentary, for the years 1943/44 a total of eight projects sponsored by Kuhn as Section Leader can be verified in the area of chemical weapons and gas protection research (see Table 13.2).

expression of Kuhn's National Socialist disposition"; see Werner, 52.
[85] Glum to Kuhn, 29 April 1936, MPG-Archiv, Abt. I, Rep. 1 A, Nr. 540, fol. 199. Hermann Lehmann emigrated to England in 1936; see Deichmann, *Flüchten, mitmachen, vergessen*, 76.
[86] Walter Ruske, *100 Jahre Deutsche Chemische Gesellschaft* (Weinheim: Verlag Chemie, 1967), 112, 136.
[87] Dahnke (REM) to Planck, 21 October 1936, MPG-Archiv, Abt. II, Rep. 1 A, Personalia Richard Kuhn, vol. 1.
[88] In addition, he was on the staff of the Reich Health Office (*Reichsgesundheitsamt*) and was an assistant to the commissioner for the Medical and Health Service; see Kuhn questionnaire, 3, OMGUS RG 260/20/2 Kuhn, Institute for Contemporary History, Munich (*Institut für Zeitgeschichte*, IFZ).
[89] See the "Satzung der Deutschen Chemischen Gesellschaft vom 2. Februar 1936," *Berichte der Deutschen Chemischen Gesellschaft*, 69 (1936), Abteilung A, 57–66; further, Ruske, 164.
[90] Kuhn to Telschow, 6 October 1939, MPG-Archiv, Abt. II, Rep. 1 A, Personalia Richard Kuhn, vol. 1. Kuhn refers in his letter to the Secretary General of the KWS to a letter of appointment by the REM of 2 October 1939.

TABLE 13.2. *Reich Research Council – Specialized Section for Organic Chemistry (Head Richard Kuhn) Research Contracts on Chemical Weapons in the Years 1943/1944*

Duration	Research Contract	Institute/Location	Contractor
unknown	Characterization of organic phosphorous and arsenic compounds	Prof. Dr. Henry Albers Organic-Chemical Institute of the Technical University of Danzig – Four-Year-Plan Institute for Organic Chemistry[a]	REM
1943	Investigations of the chemical change in epithelial and connective tissue cells in skin sensations (effect of chemical agents on the skin)	Prof. Dr. Johann Daniel Achelis Physiological Institute of the University of Heidelberg[b]	RFR
1943/1944	Biochemical effect of chemical agents	Prof. Dr. Theodor Bersin Physiological-Chemical Institute of the University of Marburg[c]	RFR
1943/1944	Controlling phosphorus fires and constraining their poisonous effects on the organism	Prof. Dr. Theodor Bersin Physiological-Chemical Institute of the University of Marburg[d]	RFR
1943/1944	Biological and physical-chemical investigations of plasma-protein bodies with regard to how chemical weapons and bacterial poisons work	Prof. Dr. Otto Bickenbach Research Institute of the Medical Department of the "Reich University of Strasbourg"[e]	RFR Karl Brandt SS-Ahnenerbe

Duration	Research Contract	Institute/Location	Contractor
1943	Discovery of agents to protect against "*Lost*" (mustard gas), especially for impregnating leather	Prof. Dr. Wolfgang Grassmann KWI for Leather Research, Dresden[f]	RFR
1943/1944	Gas protection (animal experiments with the nerve gas Tabun and using atropin as an antidote)[g]	Prof. Dr. Ludwig Lendle Pharmacological Institute of the University of Münster and the University of Leipzig[h]	RFR
31/3–30/6/1944	Research and development (nerve gases)	Prof. Dr. Richard Kuhn KWI for Medical Research, Heidelberg[i]	RFR

[a] BArch, R 26 III/8.
[b] Kurzberichte über die die auf Anregung und mit Unterstützung des RFR durchgeführten wissenschaftlichen Arbeiten (July–December 1943), 16, NA, RG 319, Entry 82a, Box 19.
[c] BArch, R 26 III/6, fol. 35; and R 26 III/438.
[d] BArch, R 26 III/6, fols. 35–36.
[e] BArch, R 26 III/6, fols. 29; and 26 III/216, fol. 52.
[f] BArch, R 26 III/271, fol. 53; and R 26 III/6, fol. 30.
[g] Wolfgang Wirth, Betr.: Interrogation vom 27.11.1945, 29.11.1945, PRO London, FO 1031/1104, fol. 1.
[h] BArch, R 26 III/6, fol. 35; and Liste der DE-Stufen bis 15.11.1943, Fachsparte organische Chemie, BArch, R 26 III/6, fol. 50.
[i] Karteikarte Kuhn, BArch, R 26 III/21, fol. 72; and Karteikarte Kuhn, BArch, R 26 III/13, fol. 151.

In 1942, Kuhn, though not a member of the party, assumed an office in
an association affiliated with the NSDAP by accepting an appointment as
the first Senator of the Reich Sector for Chemistry of the National Socialist
League of German Engineers (*NS-Bund Deutscher Technik*, NSBDT).[91] In
the final months of the war, he was appointed to the executive staff of the
Defense Research Association (*Wehrforschungs-Gemeinschaft*) founded
on 7 September 1944, which coordinated top-secret projects for armaments research.[92] Kuhn served on this executive staff along with leading
officials of the security service of the SS, the chief of the Reich Office for
Economic Development Carl Krauch, leading officers of the Armed Forces,
and influential officials in the Reich Ministry of Armament and Munition.[93]
Hermann Göring had authorized the Defense Research Association to guarantee, above all, the "most urgent monitoring and concentration of research
on tasks dictated by the demands of future warfare."[94]

Previous historical research had dated collaboration between the KWIMR
and the chemical weapons experts of the HWA to the year 1940; however,
this is based exclusively on Kuhn's postwar testimony to the Allies.[95] Newly
discovered sources document that this collaboration already existed in 1938
during the preparation for the war. At this time, Kuhn's assistant Christoph

---

[91] Telschow, file note, 5 July 1942, MPG-Archiv, Abt. II, Rep. 1 A, Personalia Richard Kuhn,
vol. 2.
[92] On the tasks of the Wehrforschungsgemeinschaft, see Osenberg (Planungsamt
des Reichsforschungsrates) to Verteiler, Rundschreiben Nr. 5, Betr.: Bildung einer
Wehrforschungsgemeinschaft (Geheime Reichssache), 7 September 1944, BArch R 26
III/156; Osenberg to Spengler, 18 October 1944, both BArch R 26 III/112, fol. 212. On
the creation of the Wehrforschungsgemeinschaft, see Ruth Federspiel, "Mobilisierung der
Rüstungsforschung? Werner Osenberg und das Planungsamt im Reichsforschungsrat," in
Maier, 72–105, 97 ff. and Flachowsky, *Von der Notgemeinschaft zum Reichsforschungsrat*,
446–459.
[93] On this, see the list of participants in meeting of the Führungsstabes der
Wehrforschungsgemeinschaft on 17 November 1944, BArch, R 26 III/208.
[94] Göring to Rudolf Mentzel, Erlass zur Gründung einer Wehrforschungsgemeinschaft (copy),
24 August 1944, BArch, R 26 III/185.
[95] Ebbinghaus and Roth dated the start of the collaboration to early 1940 in connection
with the research on inhibitors of vitamin B_1 and their potential applicability as chemical weapons; see Angelika Ebbinghaus and Karl Heinz Roth, "Vernichtungsforschung: Der
Nobelpreisträger Richard Kuhn, die Kaiser Wilhelm-Gesellschaft und die Entwicklung von
Nervenkampfstoffen während des 'Dritten Reichs,'" *1999. Zeitschrift für Sozialgeschichte
des 20. und 21. Jahrhunderts*, 17, no. 1 (2002), 15–50, 21. Deichmann and Tucker date the
start of the research on nerve gases to early 1943; see Ute Deichmann, "Kriegsbezogene
biologische, biochemische und chemische Forschung an den Kaiser Wilhelm-Instituten für
Züchtungsforschung, für Physikalische Chemie und Elektrochemie und für Medizinische
Forschung," in Doris Kaufmann (ed.), *Geschichte der Kaiser-Wilhelm-Gesellschaft im
Nationalsozialismus. Bestandsaufnahme und Perspektiven der Forschung*, 2 vols. (Göttingen:
Wallstein, 2000), vol. 1, 231–257, here 252, and Jonathan B. Tucker, *War of Nerves. Chemical
Warfare from World War I to al-Qaeda* (New York: Pantheon Books, 2006), 53.

Grundmann was researching on behalf of the HWA, investigating what therapeutic properties vitamin B_6 possesses for the treatment of skin injuries caused by the chemical agent "*Lost*" (mustard gas). When Grundmann attempted to sell a patent to the Swiss chemical corporation Hofmann-LaRoche in March 1939, Kuhn accused his assistant of treason, denouncing him to the Gestapo so that Kuhn's collaboration with IG Farben and Merck AG in the area of vitamin research would not be put at risk. Grundmann was immediately dismissed and arrested.[96] The subsequent trial ended with acquittal. The accusation of treason was not valid because an application to patent a technique for synthesizing vitamin B_6 had already been submitted in the United States before Grundmann's arrest.[97] Further studies then showed that vitamin B_6 possessed no therapeutic effect for mustard gas injuries.[98]

The threshold from contract research to solidly institutionalized collaboration with the HWA was crossed with the subsequent establishment of a separate department for chemical weapons at the KWIMR. An essential prerequisite for this was the availability of space in the Institute for Physiology, which was directed by the Nobel laureate Otto Meyerhof. The intensified persecution of Jews in September 1938 forced Meyerhof to flee Germany.[99] Thus, the expulsion of a Jewish institute director also facilitated the establishment of the second chemical weapons department at a KWI. After lengthy negotiations, the Chemical Weapons Department was ultimately established as an outpost of the Gas Protection Department of the HWA in the context of preparations for the attack on the Soviet Union in January 1941.[100] The new department absorbed one third of the academic staff of the Institute for Chemistry (see Table 13.3).

Günther Quadbeck was a doctoral student of Kuhn, who, with interruptions, worked in the Chemical Weapons Department from mid-November 1942 until the end of the war.[101] Quadbeck pursued medical-pharmacological

[96] Kuhn, Meldung, 11 March 1939, MPG-Archiv, Abt. I, Rep. 29, Nr. 88, fol. 52.

[97] Der Generalstaatsanwalt beim Oberlandesgericht Stuttgart, OJs.30/39g – Verfügung (copy), 22 May 1939, MPG-Archiv, Abt. I, Rep. 29, Nr. 178.

[98] The letter from Wirth to Kuhn is mentioned in a letter from Kuhn to Waldmann, 17 June 1939, MPG-Archiv, Abt. I, Rep. 29, Nr. 178.

[99] David Nachmansohn, *German-Jewish Pioneers in Science, 1900–1933* (New York: Springer, 1979), 284; Kristie Macrakis, *Surviving the Swastika. Scientific Research in Nazi Germany* (New York: Oxford University Press, 1993), 65; Dorothee Mussgnug, *Die vertriebenen Heidelberger Dozenten. Zur Geschichte der Ruprecht-Karl-Universität nach 1933* (Heidelberg: Winter, 1988), 157.

[100] The initially slated appointment of the physiologist Hermann Rein and the establishment of an Aviation Medicine Research Center failed; see MPG-Archiv, Abt. II, Rep. 1 A, Personalia Hermann Rein. On the establishment of the weapons department in January 1941, see Kuhn to KWS, 16 April 1942, MPG-Archiv, Abt. I, Rep. 29, Nr. 101, fol. 13.

[101] Kuhn to the KWS, 12 November 1942, MPG-Archiv, Abt. I, Rep. 29, Nr. 102, fol. 55; and Kuhn to the KWS, 12 December 1942, MPG-Archiv, Abt. I, Rep. 1 A, 540, fol. 262; Quadbeck to Kuhn, 1 April 1943, MPG-Archiv, Abt. II, Rep. 23 B, Nr. 51 and telegram (L

TABLE 13.3. *Scientific Staff of the Chemical Weapons Department at the KWI for Medical Research (Status: around March 1943)*[a]

Name	Year of Birth	Party Membership	Areas of Research
Richard Kuhn	1900	nonmember	vitamins, pharmaceuticals, (protection against) chemical weapons[b]
Helmut Beinert	1913	NSDAP NSD Student League 1936–1939 SA 1937–1938	phase theory, organic compounds, chemical weapons
Otto Dann	1914	SA 1934	organic sulfur compounds, chemical weapons
Dietrich Jerchel	1913	SA 1935–1937 NSDAP 1940	enzymatic poisons, chemical weapons
Konrad Henkel	1915	nonmember	synthetic organic chemistry, chemical weapons
Günther Quadbeck	1915	Hitler Youth (1932–1934) NSDAP (from 1/5/1933)[c] SS candidate[d]	skin injuries caused by *Lost*, nerve gas weapons
Friedrich Weygand	1911	NSDAP (candidate) NSD Lecturer's Corps SA 1933–1934	lactoflavin, oxyquinone, pyrimidine, trilone,[e] protection against chemical weapons

[a] Unless otherwise specified, the data were compiled from the notes Richard Kuhn made in the research catalog of the RFR, MPG-Archiv, Abt. I, Rep. 29, Nr. 103, fol. 52.
[b] Catalog card RFR, Richard Kuhn, MPG-Archiv, Abt. I, Rep. 29, Nr. 103, fol. 72. The entry "Protection against Chemical Weapons" was erased but still can be recognized in the original document.
[c] Questionnaire for executing the Law for the Restoration of the Professional Civil Service of 7 April 1933, signed by Günter Quadbeck, 8 November 1942, MPG-Archiv, II. Abt., Rep. 23, Nr. 51.
[d] Since 9 November 1934 Quadbeck, an SS candidate, had been a member of the SS Motor Brigade 1/, Archiv der Bundesbeauftragen für die Unterlagen der ehemaligen Staatssicherheit der DDR (Berlin), AV 15/78, fols. 33–34; see also BArch, ZA I 7384 A.1.
[e] Trilone was a code name for the nerve gases Tabun and Sarin; see the articles "Trilon" and "Trilons" in *Römpps Chemie-Lexikon*, 8th ed. (Stuttgart: Franckh, 1988), 4352.

studies on the possibilities for treating mustard gas injuries to the skin. He was able to demonstrate a certain therapeutic effectiveness of cyclical carbohydrates for mustard gas injuries.[102] However, the emphasis of the research in the Chemical Weapons Department in Heidelberg was on decrypting the still unclear modes of action of the new nerve gases Tabun and Sarin.

These novel nerve gases were discovered before the war, independent of the KWI for Medical Research, by Gerhard Schrader of IG Farben in Leverkusen and Wuppertal-Elberfeld; Schrader had been researching organic phosphoric acid esters as potential pesticides.[103] He synthesized Tabun for the first time on 23 December 1936[104] and Sarin two years later on 10 December 1938.[105] The toxic effect of these two nerve gases surpassed that of all chemical agents of warfare known at the time. Within two years after the discovery of Tabun, IG Farben, in close collaboration with the HWA, developed a large-scale technical production method.[106] After the German attack on Poland, the board of directors of IG Farbenindustrie and the Supreme Command of the Armed Forces agreed to erect the first factory for Tabun production in Dyhernfurth near Breslau (today's Wrocław).[107] In late 1940, one year after construction began in Dyhernfurth, Kuhn became involved in the research collaboration on nerve gases. Until this time, the HWA and IG Farben had been able to determine the dose of the two nerve gases for various mammals and, approximately, for humans as well. However, the decisive problem – which biochemical and physiological reactions were responsible for the deadly effect of the new nerve gas – was still unclear.[108] In addition to determining

Wehr 2 IA 1 Nr. 36 203/43) to the KWI for Medical Research, 15 May 1943, MPG-Archiv, Abt. II, Rep. 23 B, Nr. 51.

[102] Quadbeck, Versuche mit Cyclodecapentaen. Der blaue Kohlenwasserstoff $C_{10}H_{10}$, 30 July 1943, BArch, BMA, RH 12–23/1299.

[103] Gerhard Schrader, *Die Entwicklung neuer insektizider Phosphorsäure-Ester*, 3rd revised ed. (Weinheim an die Bergstrasse: Verlag Chemie, 1963), 2.

[104] Gerhard Schrader, Nr. 13 – Arbeiten aus der Tabun-, Sarin- und Somanreihe, Dustbin, den 8 October 1945, fol. 7, PRO London, FO 1031/239; further S. A. Mumford and E. A. Perren, "The Development of New Insecticides by Gerhard Schrader," *BIOS Final Report 714* (London: H. M. Stationery, 1945), 24; Robert Harris and Jeremy Paxman, *Eine höhere Form des Tötens. Die geheime Geschichte der B- und C-Waffen* (Düsseldorf: Econ, 1983), 73–74; and (SIPRI) Stockholm International Peace Research Institute (ed.), *The Rise of Chemical and Biological Warfare. A Study of the Historical, Technical, Military, Legal and Political Aspects of CBW, and Possible Disarmament Measures* (Stockholm: Stockholm International Peace Research Institute, 1971), vol. 1, 71.

[105] Gerhard Schrader, Nr. 8 – Arbeiten aus der Tabun-, Sarin- und Somanreihe, Dustbin, 13 October 1945, fol. 8, PRO London, FO 1031/239.

[106] Schmaltz, *Kampfstoff-Forschung*, 438–446

[107] Schmaltz, *Kampfstoff-Forschung*, 449 ff.

[108] Wolfgang Wirth, Betr.: Interrogation of 27 November 1945 (Dr. Merewether/Dr. Williams), 29 November 1945, fol. 1, PRO London, FO 1031/104; and Wolfgang Wirth, Beantwortung von Fragen zur Interrogation durch eine englische Kommission am 26.8.1945, 28 August 1945, fol. 7, NA, RG 319, Entry 85, Box 1352, MIS No. ID 206481.

the mechanism of action, the working group headed by Kuhn in Heidelberg was also searching for potential antidotes and for even more poisonous nerve gases as an integral component of their research program.[109]

The KWIMR was one of the world's leading institutes in the area of vitamin research. Proceeding from the established models and methods from vitamin research, in 1943 Kuhn's working group succeeded in explicitly determining the biochemical mechanism of action of the nerve gas. They identified the main effect to be the strong inhibition of acetylcholinesterase, which is of vital importance to the function of the neurotransmitter acetylcholine for transmitting stimuli in the brain. The hypothesis advanced by scientists of the Military Academy of Surgeons, that further enzyme systems were involved in the effect of nerve gas, was thus refuted.[110] On the basis of the cholinesterase inhibition, the working group in Heidelberg developed a specific procedure to verify the degree of toxicity of nerve gases.

Presumably in this context, in April 1943 Kuhn asked the KWS General Administration to assist him in procuring the brains of "young, healthy humans."[111] The fact that the Secretary General of the KWS, Ernst Telschow, subsequently contacted the Reich Ministry of Justice in this regard supports the assumption that the organs of victims executed by the Nazi justice system were to be procured. The Ministry of Justice official contacted by Telschow was Johannes Eichler, who ran the Department of Criminal and Trial Law in the Penal System Division. From Eichler, Telschow received the information "that the Anatomical Research Institute in Heidelberg had a large number of these organs from Stuttgart." Eichler advised Telschow that he, or Kuhn, should "immediately contact the Anatomical Research Institute in Heidelberg," to "request dispensation."[112] Whether and to what extent brains from the departments of anatomy in Heidelberg and Stuttgart were actually delivered to the KWIMR cannot as yet be established with any certainty.

There is no evidence that scientists at the KWIMR participated directly in experiments on human subjects in concentration camps. However, Kuhn, in his capacity as division head of the RFR, along with the Reich Commissioner for Health and Hygiene (*Reichsbevollmächtigter für das Gesundheits- und Sanitätswesen*) Karl Brandt, a key figure of the Nazi "euthanasia" program,[113]

---

[109] Schmaltz, *Kampfstoff-Forschung*, 482–514, and Ebbinghaus and Roth, here 25–26.

[110] Florian Schmaltz, "Neurosciences and Research on Chemical Weapons of Mass Destruction in Nazi Germany," *Journal of the History of the Neurosciences*, 15 (2006), 186–209.

[111] Telschow, file note, 8 April 1943, MPG-Archiv, Abt. I, Rep. 1 A, Nr. 2576, fol. 309.

[112] Telschow to Kuhn (personally!), 22 April 1943, MPG-Archiv, Abt. I, Rep. 29, Nr. 104, fol. 19, and also Bernd Gausemeier, "Rassenhygienische Radikalisierung und kollegialer Konsens," in Carola Sachse (ed.), Die Verbindung nach Auschwitz. Biowissenschaften und Menschenversuche an Kaiser-Wilhelm-Instituten. Dokumentation eines Symposiums (Göttingen: Wallstein, 2003), 178–199, here 191, and Schmaltz, *Kampfstoff-Forschung*, 511–514.

[113] Ulf Schmidt, *Karl Brandt. The Nazi Doctor. Medicine and Power in the Third Reich* (London: Continuum, 2007).

approved funding from the RFR for phosgene experiments on prisoners – experiments that were conducted in the Natzweiler concentration camp by the physician Otto Bickenbach.[114] Even when Bickenbach faced a French Military Court in 1947 on charges of war crimes because of these experiments on humans, during which at least four prisoners died of lung edemas in excruciating pain, Kuhn justified the human experiments as "outstandingly thorough science." They had "pursued a lofty goal for humanity as a whole" and the findings acquired would "be a blessing for many."[115]

In spring 1944, Richard Kuhn and his assistant Konrad Henkel synthesized the nerve gas Soman, whose effect was far stronger than that of even Tabun and Sarin.[116] Although Soman did not go into large-scale production before the end of the war, the discovery was momentous; after the end of the war most of the Soman was transferred to the arsenal of the Allies' chemical weapons and remains one of the most effective chemical weapons even today, just behind the VX nerve gas discovered in the 1950s.

THE KWS AND CHEMICAL WEAPONS RESEARCH IN NATIONAL SOCIALISM

How can the specific contribution of the KWS to gas protection and chemical weapons research in National Socialism be assessed? Organizationally, chemical weapons research within the KWS during National Socialism was structurally distinct from the tight, military organization of research during World War I; in National Socialism no such strong centralization by the KWS can be established. Coordinating functions in the area of gas protection and chemical weapons research were exercised above all by the Gas Protection Department of the HWA, reorganized in 1934, and the agencies under its command, particularly the Army Gas Protection Laboratory in Spandau and the Institute for Pharmacology and Military Toxicology of the Military Academy of Surgeons. These agencies coordinated the allocation of contracts to the KWS.

---

[114] Biologische und physikalisch-chemische Untersuchungen an Plasma-Eiweiss-Körpern zur Frage der Wirkungsweise von Kampfstoffen und Bakteriengiften, BArch, R 26 III/271, fol. 52. The application was extended on 15 November 1944; see BArch, RFR catalog, Bi 3/12, Bickenbach, Otto. For comprehensive information on Bickenbach's research, see Schmaltz, *Kampfstoff-Forschung*, 521–562, and Florian Schmaltz, "Otto Bickenbach's Human Experiments with Chemical Warfare Agents at the Concentration Camp Natzweiler in the Context of the SS-Ahnenerbe and the Reichsforschungsrat," in Wolfgang U. Eckart (ed.), *Man, Medicine and the State. The Human Body as an Object of Government Sponsored Research in the 20th Century* (Stuttgart: Steiner, 2006), 139–156.

[115] Kuhn to Rechtsanwalt Eber, 5 August 1947, MPG-Archiv, Abt. III, Rep. 25, Nr. 54.

[116] Kuhn to Baumann, 5 September 1945, NA, RG 319, Entry 85, Box 1352, MIS No. ID 206481; and E. F. Edson, D. C. Evans, R. E. F. Edelstein and L. D. T. Williams, "Interrogation of Certain German Personalities Connected with Chemical Warfare," BIOS Final Report 542 (London: H. M. Stationery Office, 1946), 5.

The sponsorship policy of the RFR in the field of chemical weapons research was controlled almost exclusively by two KWI directors. Aside from a few individual research contracts granted to the Division of Medical Research under Ferdinand Sauerbruch and to the Division of Military Medicine under Wilhelm Richter, Thiessen and Kuhn coordinated the entire spectrum of research sponsored by the RFR on gas protection and chemical weapons research at the universities and technical colleges. The only other body of the KWS so heavily involved in the RFR was the KWI for Metals Research (Stuttgart); Werner Köster had been appointed director of the Division of Non-Ferrous Metals in 1937. Analogous to the principle of self-administration so characteristic of Nazi economic policy, the directors of specialized sections of the RFR enjoyed a great degree of latitude for the armaments research they initiated and controlled at institutes inside and outside the universities. The approval of research applications depended on their decisions alone. They themselves were subject to no further expert scrutiny by other scientists, as the DFG's mechanisms of self-control still existing in the Weimar Republic had been eliminated in accordance with an RFR organized according to the "*Führer* [leader] principle."

Collaborating with the military secured the KWIs significant resources for research and protected the scientists working on projects essential to the war from dangerous deployment on the front. Because of their exposed position as science managers, Thiessen and Kuhn came into indirect and direct contact with Nazi officials involved in the crimes of the National Socialist regime. Above all, as directors of Divisions of the RFR, whose management was dominated by the SS in the final phase of the war, they had connections to the concentration camps. Thus they were active within a scientific network organized according to a division of labor, which encouraged human experiments on concentration camp inmates and the exploitation of inmates as construction workers and qualified laborers on German weapons research. Science, too, participated in the increasingly brutal mobilization of the last resources for the war in the final months before defeat.

The KWS served as an outstanding research institution for the military, making available scientific resources oriented to the military's needs whenever the military had short-term requirements for expert knowledge and experimental systems that were not at its disposal. The strong support for chemical weapons research can also serve as a further example of how National Socialism was anything but antagonistic to science per se. Anti-Semitism and the sponsorship of research on Weapons of Mass Destruction were indeed elements that complemented Nazi science policy. The weapons research conducted in the laboratories of IG Farben and the KWS during National Socialism led to the discovery of the nerve gases Tabun, Sarin, and Soman, which are still available today as weapons of mass destruction and, as a legacy of Nazi research, still have the capacity to harm future generations of humanity.

14

Nuclear Weapons and Reactor Research at the Kaiser Wilhelm Institute for Physics

Mark Walker

BACKGROUND

The story of the Kaiser Wilhelm Institute for Physics (*KWI für Physik*, KWIP)[1] begins with Albert Einstein. In 1914, Max Planck lured his young colleague to Berlin with an attractive package of positions and benefits that allowed Einstein to work without any teaching obligations.[2] Two years later, Einstein published his work on general relativity and quickly became famous. In 1917, Einstein was given a "paper" Kaiser Wilhelm Institute

---

[1] In 2004, copies of documents from the Kaiser Wilhelm Institute for Physics were returned to the Max Planck Society (*Max-Planck-Gesellschaft*) from the Atomic Archives of the Russian Federation. These documents had been seized by Soviet forces at the very end of the war and transferred to the Soviet Union, where they were evaluated in the context of the Soviet atomic bomb project. Together with the Heisenberg Papers at the Max Planck Institute for Physics and Astrophysics in Munich – which were evacuated from Berlin along with the institute in the last years of the war to Hechingen and Haigerloch in southwestern Germany – these papers provide a fairly complete documentation of the research of this institute during the Second World War and significantly change our historical understanding of the work done at the KWIP on nuclear reactors and nuclear weapons during the Second World War. The most sensational and hitherto unavailable documents include (1) a patent application by Carl Friedrich von Weizsäcker in 1941 on a nuclear reactor and how the transuranic elements it produces could be used as a nuclear explosive, and (2) a popular lecture on nuclear fission and its applications by Werner Heisenberg before Armaments Minister Albert Speer and others in June of 1942. Many duplicates of the so-called G-Reports (German-Reports on Atomic Energy) now located at the Deutsches Museum in Munich are included, but there are also some technical reports and scientific papers that have not been available previously. There is also a wealth of information on the day-to-day operation of the institute, which sheds light on the atmosphere and environment in which these scientists were working.

[2] See Horst Kant, "Albert Einstein, Max von Laue, Peter Debye und das Kaiser-Wilhelm-Institut für Physik in Berlin (1917–1939)," in Bernhard vom Brocke and Hubert Laitko (eds.), *Die Kaiser-Wilhelm-/Max-Planck-Gesellschaft und ihre Institute; Studien zu ihrer Geschichte: Das Harnack-Prinzip* (Berlin: De Gruyter, 1996), 227–243.

I would like to thank Cathryn Carson, Birgit Kolboske, Helmut Maier, and Rüdiger Hachtmann for their helpful comments on this essay.

(KWI) including a salary, an office, and grant money he could dispense. Four years later, Einstein received the Nobel Prize. Max von Laue, also a Nobel laureate, became the second director of the institute and handled most of the administration. Einstein was one of the few German scientists who had real political significance in Germany because of his fame, outspoken internationalism during the First World War and Weimar Republic, public advocacy of Zionism, and public criticism of anti-Semitism.[3] When the National Socialists came to power in Germany in 1933, Einstein was in the United States, where he stayed.

Max Planck, another Nobel laureate for physics who became president of the Kaiser Wilhelm Society (*Kaiser-Wilhelm Gesellschaft*, KWS) in 1930, wanted very much to establish a "real" KWIP.[4] He managed to do this with money from the American Rockefeller Foundation, despite the Foundation's misgivings about the policies of the National Socialist (NS) government. After all, this came after the purge of the German civil service in 1933 and passage of the infamous Nuremberg Race Laws in 1935.

Although Rockefeller was concerned about what the NS regime might subsequently do with the institute, in the end it was unwilling to renege on past promises and reluctant to recognize that its support had been or indeed could be politicized. The new KWIP opened in 1936 with the respected Dutch physicist and Nobel laureate Peter Debye as its director. Debye built a world-class laboratory for investigating low-temperature physics. The KWIP staff included Laue and two young physicists who would play an important role in the German "uranium project," Carl Friedrich von Weizsäcker and Karl Wirtz.[5]

During 1939, the KWIP was rocked by two different shocks: (1) publication of the discovery of nuclear fission, the result of a collaboration between the experimental chemists Otto Hahn and Fritz Strassmann at the KWI for Chemistry (KWIC) and their former colleague and theoretical physicist Lise Meitner;[6] and (2) the start of the Second World War. Just two weeks

[3] See David Rowe and Robert Schulman (eds.), *Einstein on Politics: His Private Thoughts and Public Stands on Nationalism, Zionism, War, Peace, and the Bomb* (Princeton: Princeton University Press, 2007).

[4] John Heilbron, *The Dilemmas of an Upright Man: Max Planck as Spokesman for German Science* (Berkeley: University of California Press, 1986), 175–179; Kristie Macrakis, "Wissenschaftsförderung durch die Rockefeller Stiftung im 'Dritten Reich.' Die Entscheidung, das Kaiser-Wilhelm-Institut für Physik finanziell zu unterstützen, 1934–1939," *Geschichte und Gesellschaft*, 12 (1986), 348–379.

[5] For Debye and the KWIP, see Horst Kant, "Peter Debye und das Kaiser-Wilhelm-Institut für Physik in Berlin," in Helmut Albrecht (ed.), *Naturwissenschaft und Technik in der Geschichte (25 Jahre Lehrstuhl für Geschichte der Naturwissenschaft und Technik am Historischen Institut der Universität Stuttgart)* (Stuttgart: GNT-Verlag, 1993), 161–177.

[6] For fission and the relationship between Hahn and Meitner, see Ruth Lewin Sime, *Lise Meitner: A Life in Physics* (Berkeley: University of California Press, 1996); also see Elisabeth Crawford, Ruth Lewin Sime, and Mark Walker, "A Nobel Tale of Wartime Injustice," *Nature*,

after war broke out, KWS Secretary General Ernst Telschow informed the KWIP:[7]

In the short term the main emphasis of the research should be on work important for military technology and the war economy ... [including] cooperation with firms that are working on war contracts or other tasks important for the war.

LIGHTNING WAR

German Army Ordnance (*Heereswaffenamt*, HWA) had been contacted about the potential use of nuclear fission as a weapon before the invasion of Poland, and immediately after the outbreak of war it moved quickly to secure a monopoly on this research.[8] One of the most important steps the HWA made was to take over the KWIP to devote it to military research. Debye could have stayed as director but would have had to become a German citizen. Instead, he accepted an offer of a visiting professorship in the United States and never returned.[9] Kurt Diebner, a physicist in the research section of HWA, moved into the KWIP as the acting director. This angered the KWS administration, not because the KWIP would now be involved with military research but rather because the KWS was forced to accept a scientist who did not measure up to their standards for KWI directors. The same thing had

382 (1996), 393–95, and Elisabeth Crawford, Ruth Lewin Sime, and Mark Walker, "A Nobel Tale of Postwar Injustice," *Physics Today*, 50, no. 9 (September 1997), 26–32.

[7] Telschow to Debye (16 September 1939), Archives of the Max Planck Society, Berlin (*Archiv zur Geschichte der Max-Planck-Gesellschaft*, MPG-Archiv), KWIP 9 45–48.

[8] I have written two books on this subject, *German National Socialism and the Quest for Nuclear Power, 1939–1949* (Cambridge: Cambridge University Press, 1989), and after the publication of the Farm Hall transcripts (see below) *Nazi Science: Myth, Truth, and the German Atom Bomb* (New York: Perseus, 1995), which includes a chapter on Farm Hall and an updated chapter on the German nuclear weapons work. The first serious history of the German atomic bomb, although one without a scholarly apparatus, was David Irving, *The German Atomic Bomb: The History of Nuclear Research in Nazi Germany* (New York: Simon and Schuster, 1968). After my first book was published, two alternative histories were published: Thomas Powers, *Heisenberg's War* (New York: Knopf, 1993), which argues that Heisenberg resisted Hitler by trying to deny him nuclear weapons, and Paul Lawrence Rose, *Heisenberg and the Nazi Atomic Bomb Project, 1939–1945: A Study in German Culture* (Berkeley: University of California Press, 1998), which argues that Heisenberg was a Nazi sympathizer and failed to make more progress on nuclear weapons because of scientific incompetence. Recently John Cornwell has written a synthesis of our knowledge of science under National Socialism in general and of uranium research in particular; see John Cornwell, *Hitler's Scientists: Science, War and the Devil's Pact* (New York: Viking, 2003). A recent book, Rainer Karlsch, *Hitlers Bombe. Die geheime Geschichte der deutschen Kernwaffenversuche* (Munich: DVA, 2005), reveals new information about nuclear reactor experiments and tests of a nuclear device carried out in the last year of the war.

[9] See Dieter Hoffmann, "Peter Debye (1884–1966): Ein Dossier," *Max Planck Institut für Wissenschaftsgeschichte, Preprint 314* (Berlin: MPIfWG, 2006) [http://www.mpiwg-berlin.mpg.de/Preprints/P314.PDF].

happened at the start of the Third Reich; when KWI for Physical Chemistry director Fritz Haber resigned in protest, the HWA quickly installed a director and turned the institute toward weapons research. The KWS was mollified when the temporary director was replaced by a scientist it could recognize as director material, Peter Adolf Thiessen, who continued to emphasize military research. The KWS administration's attitude toward the KWIP in 1939 was similar: it wanted to be rid of Diebner but had no problem with turning the physics institute toward research into nuclear energy and nuclear weapons.

The German uranium project was much more than the KWIP and should not be equated with it, but the physics institute did play a central role. Along with the existing KWIP staff, Diebner turned to a young nuclear physicist he knew, Erich Bagge, for recommendations. Bagge suggested his mentor, Werner Heisenberg, Nobel laureate, co-founder of quantum mechanics, professor at the University of Leipzig, and perhaps the best theoretical physicist left in Germany.[10] Heisenberg eventually became one of the most important individuals in the uranium project but nevertheless remained only one of several such scientists. In other words, he was not the German equivalent of Robert Oppenheimer, director of the Los Alamos Weapons Laboratory. Although eventually Diebner and Heisenberg became antagonistic rivals in nuclear reactor experiments, Diebner was concerned foremost with developing nuclear fission into a weapon that Germany could use in the war effort and was grateful that a physicist with Heisenberg's ability and stature had joined his project.[11]

Heisenberg began commuting between Leipzig and Berlin, overseeing nuclear reactor experiments in Leipzig carried out by Robert Döpel, and in Berlin directed by Wirtz. In the winter of 1939–1940, Heisenberg worked out the theory of nuclear fission chain reactions in uranium. His two secret reports[12] provided the foundation for all subsequent German work on nuclear reactors, neutron moderators, and isotope separation. Like all subsequent uranium project reports, these were first submitted to Diebner at

[10] For Heisenberg, see David Cassidy, *Uncertainty: The Life and Science of Werner Heisenberg* (New York: Freeman, 1991); a revised and updated edition of this book is forthcoming, *Beyond Uncertainty: Heisenberg, Quantum Physics, and The Bomb* (New York: Bellevue Literary Press, 2009).

[11] For Heisenberg and the KWIP, see Horst Kant, "Werner Heisenberg und das Kaiser-Wilhelm-Institut für Physik in Berlin," in Bodo Geyer, Helge Herwig, and Helmut Rechenberg (eds.), *Werner Heisenberg – Physiker und Philosoph* (Heidelberg: Spektrum Akademischer Verlag, 1993), 152–158, and Horst Kant, "Werner Heisenberg and the German Uranium Project," *Max-Planck-Insitut für Wissenschaftsgeschichte, Preprint 203* (Berlin: MPIfWG, 2002).

[12] Werner Heisenberg, "Die Möglichkeit der technischen Energiegewinnung aus der Uranspaltung" (6 December 1939), G-39, Archives of the German Museum, Munich (*Archiv des Deutschen Museums*, ADM); Werner Heisenberg, "Bericht über die Möglichkeit technischer Energiegewinnung aus der Uranspaltung (II)," G-40 (29 February 1940), ADM.

HWA, who would then distribute copies on a need-to-know basis. A great deal of relevant information had already been published in the year following the discovery of nuclear fission. Although no scientists wrote openly of nuclear weapons in their publications, if one read between the lines this possibility was clear, and many scientists inside and outside of Germany did so.

In his two-part report, Heisenberg drew in particular on the experimental work on fission published by a group of French and another group of American and émigré researchers, as well as the theoretical analysis provided by his Danish colleague and mentor Niels Bohr, both alone and in collaboration with the American John Wheeler. Heisenberg concluded that a nuclear reactor – what the Germans first called a uranium machine then later a uranium burner – could be built that combined uranium and a moderating substance to control the nuclear fission chain reaction and produce energy in the form of heat. The Austrian physical chemist Paul Harteck had suggested that such a reactor would work better if the uranium and moderator were spatially separated. Heisenberg incorporated this in his analysis and concluded that either heavy water (oxygen combined with deuterium, the rare heavy isotope of hydrogen) or carbon in the form of very pure graphite would be an effective moderator. Ordinary water would not suffice unless the percentage of the very rare lighter isotope of uranium – nuclear weight 235 instead of 238 – were enriched in a given amount of uranium via isotope separation. Moreover, Heisenberg continued, if pure or almost pure uranium 235 could be produced, it would be possible to[13] "manufacture an explosive more than ten times as powerful as existing explosives."

Weizsäcker took the next important step according to a July 1940 report.[14] Once again, building on the information available in scientific publications, he concluded that the resonance absorption of neutrons by the common isotope uranium 238 – whereby neutrons traveling at particular velocities were absorbed – would slow down the nuclear fission chain reaction in a nuclear reactor but had a subsequent benefit. The uranium 238 nuclei that absorbed a neutron would transmute in stages to a stable, man-made transuranic element 94, today called plutonium. This new element could be separated out from the uranium relatively easily because its chemistry would be different. Weizsäcker also noted that plutonium, just like uranium 235, would be a powerful new nuclear explosive.

Although Heisenberg remained very interested in and devoted to the uranium project both as a researcher and administrator, once he had finished his two-part report he clearly no longer found the theoretical problem

---

[13] This quotation is from the first report, G-39 ADM.
[14] Carl Friedrich von Weizsäcker, "Die Möglichkeit der Energiegewinnung aus ^{238}U" (17 July 1940), MPG-Archiv, KWIP 7H Pu 1–5.

very interesting. His younger colleague Weizsäcker similarly turned to other theoretical problems once he had discovered the significance of plutonium. Subsequently, most of the continuing theoretical work was done by two of Weizsäcker's students: Paul Müller and Karl-Heinz Höcker. Both were drafted in 1941 – in Höcker's case at least, against his will. Müller died in Russia; Höcker luckily was able to return to Berlin and scientific work. For the rest of the war, Höcker was responsible for analyzing the nuclear reactor experiments, with both Weizsäcker and Heisenberg looking over his shoulder at his work. In the end, Höcker became one of the most important members of the research project.

The first model nuclear reactors – designs that were not expected to sustain a chain reaction but rather to provide experimental data on nuclear constants and the effectiveness of different designs – were located at two separate locations. In Leipzig, Döpel built designs with alternating spherical layers of uranium and moderator; in Berlin, Wirtz worked with horizontal layers.[15] Heisenberg made sure that the model experiments remained under his control. When his colleagues Walther Bothe at the Physics Division of the Kaiser Wilhelm Institute for Medical Research in Heidelberg, and Harteck, respectively, suggested their own model reactor experiments, Heisenberg used his prestige and institutional connections to forestall them.

The Berlin tests were carried out in an external lab dubbed the "Virus House" to discourage curiosity. By design, the geometric symmetry of the Leipzig reactors simplified the calculations while the horizontal design of the Berlin reactors could be more easily varied. Both models were nevertheless difficult to build and manage, and as these scientists were well aware, they were far from the practical design an operating nuclear reactor would need. At the end of the B-I and B-II tests, the KWIP group concluded that water would not work as a moderator, but heavy water was promising.[16]

The HWA had to decide which moderator it would use, heavy water or graphite. After the war, a myth arose in this regard: Bothe supposedly made a "mistake" and judged carbon unsuitable, with the disastrous result that the Germans came to rely on heavy water. In fact, the story is more complicated. Bothe did test graphite and concluded that it would absorb too many neutrons. However, another physicist, Wilhelm Hanle, was not convinced. He carried out his own tests and demonstrated that Bothe had not sufficiently considered the neutron-absorbing effect

[15] Werner Heisenberg, "Bericht über die ersten Versuche an der im Kaiser Wilhelm-Insitut f. Physik aufgebauten Apparatur" (21 December 1940), MPG-Archiv, KWIP 7H E 3.

[16] Werner Heisenberg, "Bericht über Versuche mit Schichtenanordnungen von Präparat 38 und Paraffin am Kaiser Wilhelm-Institut f. Physik in Bln-Dahlem" (March, 1941), MPG-Archiv, KWIP 1H 170–211.

of impurities in the graphite sample. Hanle sent his results directly to HWA. Scientists there concluded that Hanle was probably right: very pure graphite would work, but the purification process required would be prohibitively expensive.[17]

Heavy water, on the other hand, appeared to be relatively inexpensive. The German chemical giant I.G. Farben had taken over the Norwegian Hydro plant, the only producer of heavy water before the war. The heavy water production plant was expanded with the help of German scientists. In the winter of 1939–1940, Heisenberg had calculated that a uranium heavy water reactor would need around five metric tons of heavy water to operate, and at least in theory, the Norwegian Hydro promised to be able to produce more than enough for this first reactor at a modest cost. It was clear to all concerned that once an operating reactor design was found, additional large-scale heavy water production would have to be started in Germany using other methods. In any case, for the early development phase, HWA decided to go with the apparently cheap heavy water instead of the definitely expensive graphite.

The model reactors made steady progress, although the supply of the two most important materials, purified uranium and heavy water, remained frustratingly low. The "B" series at the KWIP had to use uranium oxide and paraffin, rich in hydrogen, as a moderator. The "L" series in Leipzig first used uranium oxide and ordinary water, then switched to heavy water. The scientists knew that pure uranium and heavy water would be much more effective, but they were not available in sufficient amounts. Nevertheless, the results of the L series in particular offered hope that a nuclear reactor could be built that would sustain a chain reaction.

Other uranium research offered mixed results. On one hand, Paul Harteck and Wilhelm Groth, before giving up in the spring of 1941, had spent a year and a half struggling to get the Clusius-Dickel thermo-diffusion isotope separation tube to work with the compound uranium hexafluoride. They now began work with centrifuges. At the KWIP, Erich Bagge began work on a novel separation method for uranium, an "isotope sluice,"[18] while Horst Korsching investigated producing purified metal uranium through both electrolysis and isotope separation by means of thermo-diffusion.[19] Kurt Starke, a physical chemist working at Hahn's KWIC, succeeded in manufacturing and studying very small amounts of element

[17] "Energiegewinnung aus Uran" (February 1942), 87–88, ADM.
[18] Erich Bagge, "Über die Möglichkeit einer Anreicherung der leichten Uranisotope mit der Isotopenschleuse," G-124 (16 March 1942), ADM.
[19] Horst Korsching, "Über die Herstellung von metallischem Uran durch Elektrolyse" (29 September 1941), MPG-Archiv, KWIP 1H 44–46; Horst Korsching, "Trennung von schwerem und leichtem Benzol durch Thermo-Diffusion in flüssiger Phase," G-102 (5 September 1942), ADM.

93, now called neptunium.[20] This element had a 2.3 day half-life, and as American researchers had argued in a 1940 publication, probably decayed into plutonium.

THE END OF INNOCENCE

In an interview published in 1993, Carl Friedrich von Weizsäcker described his motivation for participating in the German uranium project as follows:[21]

> Actually I was not at all interested in the bomb in a technical sense, nor the reactor. … That was work I had to do. My interests were purely political. It was the dreamy wish, that if I was one of the few people who understand how to make a bomb, then the highest authorities would have to speak with me, including Adolf Hitler.

In a different interview published in 1991, he admitted that he had been naive to think that he could have influenced Hitler's policies: "I admit it, I was crazy."[22]

Sometime between the summer of 1940 and the summer of 1941, Weizsäcker took two important steps. First, he submitted a patent application[23] that emphasized the military applications of nuclear reactors and plutonium. Element 94 could be produced in a "uranium machine," whereby the new transuranic element could be separated "chemically" from the uranium. The "explosive production of energy and neutrons" could be used "in a bomb."

Next, he discussed the military applications of the uranium research with Diebner.[24] Uranium could be used to produce energy in two ways: (1) in its natural form; and (2) in a "highly concentrated effective" form, either pure uranium 235 or a transuranic element. In principle, uranium could be used to "power a rocket"; but at the moment there were still practical difficulties, and this remained a "matter for future development." Much more important were two other applications: as (1) "a heat machine," and (2) as an "explosive."

During the spring, summer, and early fall of 1941, Weizsäcker also enthusiastically participated in German cultural propaganda in occupied Europe.

---

[20] Kurt Starke, "Über die Trennung des künstlich radioaktiven Urans und seines Folgeprodukts (Element 93) vom Uran" (20 May 1941), MPG-Archiv, KWIP 1H 52–70.

[21] Dieter Hoffmann (ed.), *Operation Epsilon. Die Farm-Hall-Protokolle oder Die Angst der Alliierten vor der deutschen Atombombe* (Berlin: Rowohlt Berlin, 1993), 337–338.

[22] Carl Friedrich von Weizsäcker, "Ich gebe zu, ich war verrückt," *Der Spiegel*, 17 (1991).

[23] Carl Friedrich von Weizsäcker, "Energieerzeugung aus dem Uranisotop der Masse 238 und anderen schweren Elementen (Herstellung und Verwendung des Elements 94)," MPG-Archiv, KWIP 7H Pu 6–11; it is not clear what happened once this patent was submitted.

[24] Carl Friedrich von Weizsäcker, "Kurzer Bericht über die eventuelle praktische Auswirkung der Uranuntersuchungen auf Grund einer Rücksprache mit Dr. Diebner," MPG-Archiv, KWIP 56 170–172.

This included scientific intelligence gathering. In March, Weizsäcker submitted a report on a trip to occupied Copenhagen.[25] He had been in Denmark to give talks at the Danish Physical and Astronomical Society, at Bohr's Institute for Theoretical Physics and, with the assistance of the German ambassador, at the "German-Danish Society."

I was able to study the experimental and theoretical work at Bohr's institute, investigations of uranium and thorium fission by fast neutrons and deuterons. I have brought back copies and manuscripts of the work that is of great interest for our current investigations.

The technical production of energy from uranium fission is not being worked on in Copenhagen. They know that such investigations are being done in America, especially from Fermi. However, since the beginning of the war, no clear news has come from America. Bohr clearly did not know that we are working on these questions. Of course I encouraged this belief. Bohr himself brought the conversation to this point. ...

The American journal *Physical Review* was available in Copenhagen up until the issue from January 15, 1941. I have made photocopies of the most important publications. Arrangements have been made for the German Embassy to photocopy the journal for us as it arrives.

In early September, before his trip to Copenhagen with Heisenberg, Weizsäcker also passed on to the German Army information from a Swedish newspaper regarding an Allied atomic bomb project and sent a report to the Reich Ministry of Education and Science (*Reichserziehungsministerium*, REM) on the American advantage over Germany in nuclear physics.[26]

The Plenipotentiary of the German Reich in Denmark reported that Weizsäcker's performance had been impressive:[27]

The large audience followed the talk delivered in Danish before the Physical and Astronomical Society, "Is the World Infinite in Time and Space," with great, approving interest.

For his second public lecture at the Danish-German Society Dr. Weizsäcker spoke on the same subject before a selected group of Danes and Germans. He was able to make this difficult subject so interesting that most of the audience, including the commander of the German troops in Denmark, could easily follow him. At the end the speaker was rewarded with generous applause for his calm and scholarly remarks.

Finally the Institute for Theoretical Physics invited Dr. von Weizsäcker to give a talk before an exclusively scientific audience on the subject: "The Relationship of

[25] Carl Friedrich von Weizsäcker, "Bericht über die Vortragsreise nach Kopenhagen vom 19.-24.3.41" (26 March 1941), MPG-Archiv, KWIP 5–1 352–353.
[26] Only English translations are available for these two documents; Weizsäcker to Oberkommando der Wehrmacht (4 September 1941), National Archives and Records Services, Washington, DC (NAARS), and Weizsäcker to REM (5 September 1941), NAARS.
[27] Der Bevollmächtigte des Deutschen Reiches an das Auswärtige Amt in Berlin (27 March 1941), Federal German Archives (*Bundesarchiv*, BArch), REM 2943, 524–525.

Quantum Mechanics to Kantian Philosophy." The lecture was followed by a lively discussion among the scientists present. ...

In summary, the lectures from Dr. von Weizsäcker were exceptionally effective, both for lay audiences as well as scientific Danish circles. For this reason we are considering inviting Dr. von Weizsäcker, along with Professor Dr. Heisenberg, Leipzig, to a workshop for mathematics, astronomy, and theoretical physics at the newly founded German Cultural Institute this coming fall.

It was possible for an intelligent and politically astute individual like Weizsäcker to appear "crazy" because of the contexts of the uranium work and the war. The scientists had worked out a clear path to nuclear energy and nuclear weapons and had made good progress – enough progress to make their goals appear promising, if still far-off. At this time, the war was going very well for Germany. Most of Europe was conquered, the Third Reich had signed a nonaggression pact with the Soviet Union, Britain was under siege, and the United States was staying out of the war.

Very few members of the German uranium project were enthusiastic National Socialists; rather, many more were opportunistic National Socialists or fellow travelers. Typically, the senior scientists were not members of a National Socialist organization whereas with few exceptions the younger scientists were either members of the NSDAP or one of its ancillary organizations. Whether or not these scientists liked Hitler, at this point he had apparently done what the German Empire had failed to do in the First World War: conquer Europe for Germany. The scientists working on uranium at the KWIP were able to serve their country as scientists instead of frontline soldiers but had no reason to expect that their work would be relevant for the war Germany was fighting.

In contrast to his friend, former student, and colleague Weizsäcker, Heisenberg appears to have been more ambivalent about the consequences of the model nuclear reactors and isotope separation methods he and his colleagues were working on. Here it is worthwhile to remember the definition of ambivalence: contradictory emotional or psychological attitudes toward a particular person or object, often with one attitude inhibiting the expression of another.[28]

In April of 1941, when Germany was expanding the war by invading Yugoslavia and Greece, in America the émigré physicist Rudolf Ladenburg passed on a striking message to his colleague Lyman Briggs:[29]

---

[28] Online version of *Webster's Third New International Dictionary, Unabridged*, accessed 15 August 2005.

[29] Rudolf Ladenburg to Lyman Briggs (14 April 1941), National Archives, Washington, DC (NA), Record Group 227, S-I Briggs, Box 5, Ladenburg Folder; this document, along with other sources, is used by Powers to argue that Heisenberg deliberately resisted Hitler by denying him nuclear weapons.

It may interest you that a colleague of mine who arrived from Berlin via Lisbon a few days ago, brought the following message: a reliable colleague who is working at a technical research laboratory asked him to let us know that a large number of German physicists are working intensively on the problem of the uranium bomb under the direction of Heisenberg, that Heisenberg himself tries to delay the work as much as possible; fearing the catastrophic results of a success. But he cannot help fulfilling the orders given to him, and if the problem can be solved, it will be solved probably in the near future. So he gave the advice to us to hurry up if the U.S.A. will not come too late.

Two weeks later, another émigré physicist, Leo Szilard, wrote to Isidor Rabi, the 1944 Nobel laureate and one of the leading scientists in the wartime American RADAR project:[30] "Ladenburg says he is pretty sure that a large number of German physicists are working intensively on the problem of the uranium bomb under the direction of Heisenberg."

In the spring of 1941, Heisenberg may have feared the consequences of success for the German uranium project (given the historical sources available, there is no way to know for sure), but that begs the question of what "success" would have meant at this time. From the perspective of most Germans, Germany had won the war in Europe; it was only a matter of time before its enemies would cease their resistance. At this time, Germany's armed forces and the National Socialist leadership did not need nuclear weapons. At best, such weapons would have appeared to be of future importance.

The problematic part of this quotation is the claim that "Heisenberg himself tries to delay the work as much as possible." His work in the uranium project is well documented, including what he did and said, who received this information, and how they responded to it. This all makes clear that Heisenberg had not been delaying the uranium work from September 1939 to April 1941, and he also did not delay it from April 1941 to the end of the war. As will be shown below, however, he did not push the development of nuclear weapons as hard as he could have.

Whatever innocence the KWIP scientists might have had probably began to evaporate in June. Tensions between Germany and the United States escalated. In August, the American and British governments announced the Atlantic Charter, formally allying the two against Germany. Hitler unleashed Operation Barbarossa, the German invasion of the Soviet Union on June 22. Although at first the "lightning war" (*Blitzkrieg*) was successful here as well, the war had now profoundly changed. Germany was fighting an enemy with vast territory and resources.

---

[30] Szilard to Rabi (28 April 1941), Library of Congress, Washington, DC, Box 7, Folder 16 Rabi Papers.

Moreover, this was a different quality of warfare, an ideologically driven war of subjugation and extermination.[31] Heisenberg, like many Germans, was clearly affected by the ideological nature of the war with the Soviet Union; when Heisenberg visited occupied Holland in 1943, in a private conversation he told a colleague:[32]

Only a nation which rules ruthlessly can maintain itself. Democracy cannot develop sufficient energy to rule Europe. There are, therefore, only two possibilities: Germany and Russia. And then perhaps a Europe led by Germany would be the lesser evil.

There is evidence that the KWIP researchers had become ambivalent about their uranium work just before Heisenberg's and Weizsäcker's September trip to Copenhagen. On August 28, Wirtz submitted a patent for a nuclear reactor, including the names of all the KWIP scientists, and, in contrast to Weizsäcker's earlier patent application, with no references to nuclear explosives.[33] Of course, the patent office still had Weizsäcker's submission and would not have forgotten that it had mentioned the possibility of plutonium bombs, and an operating nuclear reactor was still the precondition for further research on nuclear weapons; but the KWIP patent application does suggest that these scientists no longer wanted to emphasize nuclear explosives.

The visit of the two German physicists to Denmark in September 1941 has inspired both historians and playwrights.[34] When they traveled to Copenhagen, German troops were laying siege to Leningrad and in Germany the remaining Jews had just been forced to wear the star of David on the outside of their clothes. After the war, Heisenberg and Weizsäcker themselves insisted that they had gone to Copenhagen to help Bohr and to enlist his assistance in forestalling the creation of all nuclear weapons. For his part, after the war Bohr and other Danish colleagues recalled that his German colleagues had urged him to collaborate with the German occupation authorities and that Heisenberg had expressed pleasure at the German victories in the East. In particular, while Bohr did remember Heisenberg bringing up the

---

[31] See, for example, Omer Bartov, *Hitler's Army: Soldiers, Nazis, and War in the Third Reich* (New York: Oxford University Press, 1941).

[32] Gerard Kuiper to Major Fischer (30 June 1945), University of Arizona, Tucson, Gerard Kuiper Papers.

[33] "Patentanmeldung. Technische Energiegewinnung, Neutronenerzeugung und Herstellung neuer Elemente durch Spaltung von Uran oder verwandten schweren Elementen" (28 August 1941), MPG-Archiv, KWIP 7H 24, 25–1 to 25–14.

[34] Michael Frayn, *Copenhagen* (New York: Anchor Books, 1998). For commentaries on the Bohr letters, along with the recently published Bohr letters, see Matthias Dörries (ed.), *Michael Frayn's Copenhagen in Debate: Historical Essays and Documents on the 1941 Meeting between Niels Bohr and Werner Heisenberg* (Berkeley: Office for History of Science and Technology, University of California, 2005); for the online version of the letters, http://www.nbi.dk/NBA/papers/introduction.htm (accessed 15 August 2005).

question of nuclear weapons, he also insisted that his German colleague had not stated or implied that Germany would not make them. Perhaps the truth lies somewhere between: Heisenberg and Weizsäcker went to Bohr with ambivalent feelings about their uranium work, the war, and their National Socialist government, and returned to Germany more troubled than before.

In contrast to the time before Operation Barbarossa, the Danish scientists were no longer pretending that the German occupiers were welcome guests in Denmark. A letter from Heisenberg to his wife describes his visit:[35]

The conversation quickly turned to questions of humanity and the misfortune of our time; agreement about humanity came as a matter of course; but political questions were difficult, for even a man like Bohr was unable completely to separate thought, emotion, and hate. But they probably should not be separated. ...

We had a few scientific discussions in Bohr's institute; the Copenhagen colleagues do not know much more than we do. Tomorrow the lectures at the German Cultural Institute begin; the first official lecture is mine, tomorrow evening. Unfortunately the members of Bohr's institute will not come for political reasons. It is strange, how the Danes, even though they can live completely undisturbed and are doing very well, can be full of so much hate or fear that an understanding in the area of culture – which earlier was self-evident – has now become almost impossible. I gave a little talk in Danish at Bohr's institute, which was naturally just like before (the people at the German Cultural Institute explicitly approved it), but they do not want to go into the German Institute as a matter of principle because at and after the opening there was a series of snappy speeches on the New Order in Europe.

All accounts agree that these discussions of the "purely human problems" were difficult and unsettling. Whatever Heisenberg said to Bohr about uranium, and whatever Bohr said in reply – no one actually knows for sure what was said in this regard – Heisenberg's and Weizsäcker's experiences in Copenhagen must have provided them considerable food for thought. Afterward, Weizsäcker was much more cautious about participating in cultural propaganda.[36] The uranium project must have looked very different once they returned. Thereafter, the mention of nuclear explosives was avoided by the KWIP scientists – with a few important exceptions described below.

SELLING URANIUM RESEARCH

If Operation Barbarossa represented a profound change for the German uranium project, then the events of November and December 1941 transformed

[35] http://werner-heisenberg.unh.edu/kop-letter.htm (accessed 10 August 2005); also see Werner Heisenberg, *Liebe Eltern!: Briefe aus kritischer Zeit 1918 bis 1945. Mit Dokumenten aus dem Familienarchiv*, edited by Anna Maria Hirsch-Heisenberg (Munich: Langen Müller, 2003), especially 301–302 and 321.

[36] For Heisenberg's and Weizsäcker's foreign lectures during the war, see Walker, *Nazi*, 123–181.

it. First, the German lightning war ground to a halt in the Russian winter. As Adolf Hitler's generals told him, the lightning war was finished. The Japanese attack on Pearl Harbor and Hitler's subsequent decision to declare war on the United States made it a true world war. Now Germany, its allies Italy and Japan, and the territories it occupied or dominated were fighting the Soviet Union, the British Empire, and the United States. It was a war of attrition with Germany holding far fewer resources and much less manpower.

Two days before the attack on Pearl Harbor, the HWA summoned the institute directors involved in the uranium project to a meeting and for the first time asked for a timetable: when would these new weapons be ready? Would they be able to influence the outcome of the war, from either side? Just a few weeks before, Heisenberg had drafted an important status report:[37]

At the moment, the work on producing energy in the uranium machine has reached a relatively clear stage as far as physics is concerned. There is no longer any doubt that a self-sustaining reactor can be built in principle. Undoubtedly this main goal must be reached as soon as possible. ...

Today the only necessary work is that which contributes immediately to reaching the goal of a self-sustaining reactor in the shortest possible time; among these, the most important are those that determine the pace of the work. ...

The prerequisites for the construction of a machine with heavy water and metal uranium are:

(1) Acquiring 5–10 tons of heavy water
(2) Acquiring 5–10 tons of metal uranium in suitably cast forms
(3) Carrying-out intermediate experiments
(4) The construction of a technical reactor

A certain critical mass of capable scientists is necessary [for this work]. ... Even if the work is cut back severely, the two nuclear physics institutes that have been most important for the development up until now (KWI for Medical Research, Physics Section in Heidelberg; and KWI for Physics in Berlin-Dahlem) must remain capable of work.

When Heisenberg mentioned deadlines, he was a little evasive. Since they could not expect the Norwegian Hydro to provide enough heavy water for a large-scale project, heavy water production would have to begin in Germany. However, "the production [of heavy water] on a large scale will only be possible in Germany during 1942 if the number of workers is increased considerably." The timetable Heisenberg gave for the large-scale

[37] Werner Heisenberg, "Zur Durchführung der Arbeiten an der Uranmaschine" (27 November 1941), MPG-Archiv, KWIP 56 84–91.

nuclear reactor experiment was also imprecise. "The experiment can be carried out approximately two months after the delivery of the uranium metal pieces." Perhaps most important, nowhere in this report does Heisenberg mention nuclear explosives or indeed any military application of nuclear fission.

In February 1942, Diebner and other staff scientists at the HWA prepared a long overview report on the uranium project entitled "Energy Production from Uranium."[38] This report is notable for its explicit discussion of nuclear explosives, but nevertheless with a cautious tone:[39]

If this "chain reaction" develops slowly, the uranium represents a heat-producing machine; if it develops quickly, [then it is] an explosive of the greatest effect. ...

Besides the complete separation of [uranium] isotopes, which is certainly possible in principle, but is technically very difficult, today we know in theory another way to the manufacture of explosives, but one that can only be tested when a heat-producing machine is running. When neutrons are absorbed by uranium 238, a substance ("element 94") is formed that is even easier to fission than uranium 235. Since this substance is chemically different from uranium, it must be easy to separate out from a [uranium] machine that has been shut down. However, today we know neither the amount which will be produced, nor its properties exactly enough for a certain prediction. ... The explosive could be detonated by bring together a sufficient amount (presumably around 10–100 kg). ...

The pace of materials acquisition today determines the further development of the experimental work. When the necessary amounts of metal uranium and heavy water are available, then the construction of a self-sustaining machine will be attempted.

If it is successful – as one must expect after the laboratory experiments – then the further development includes three tasks:

(1) The development of the machine into a technically usable apparatus.
(2) The technical, and especially military applications of the machine [propulsion of ships; submarines; airplanes and ground vehicles; fixed energy sources; source of penetrating radiation; and the medical-biological area].
(3) The manufacture of a uranium explosive.

The HWA concluded that uranium would not decide the outcome of the war from either side and that the research project should be transferred to a civilian authority. The new priorities in the war economy had an immediate effect on the uranium project. Harteck and Weizsäcker – both by now senior scientists – were called up for regular military duty. Heisenberg and the Leipzig physical chemist Karl-Dietrich Bonhoeffer used the excellent

---

[38] "Energiegewinnung aus Uran" (February 1942), ADM.
[39] "Energiegewinnung aus Uran" (February 1942), 9, 12–13, 15–17, ADM.

personal connections they had with high-ranking military officers to reverse these orders. Heisenberg and his colleagues were now faced with the necessity of convincing the military authorities of the importance and relevance of their work or losing their exemptions from direct military service. As a result, over the next two years Heisenberg gave several remarkable popular lectures on nuclear energy and weapons.

Beginning in 1941 and in the shadow of the looming war between Germany and the United States, German scientists began mentioning the American competition in nuclear physics and uranium research when they lectured before and prepared memoranda for military, political, and industrial leaders. Perhaps the best example of this is the January 1942 memorandum sent by German Physical Society president and industrial physicist Carl Ramsauer to REM on the dangerous decline of theoretical physics in Germany.[40] Surprisingly, there was never any similar mention of Soviet science and engineering, even though this eventually played an important role in defeating Germany.

In February 1942, a series of popular lectures was held before the Reich Research Council (*Reichsforschungsrat*, RFR) and leading political, industrial, and military figures in the National Socialist state in order to sell the project. Heisenberg gave a provocative talk[41] carefully designed to attract interest without promising what he could not deliver and, as he put it after the war, "tailored to the level of understanding of a Reich minister of the time:"[42]

The behavior of neutrons in uranium can be compared to the behavior of a population, whereby the fission process is analogous to marriage [with children] and the capture process analogous to death. In ordinary uranium, the number of deaths far outweighs the number of births, so that a population will die out after a short time.

Obviously an improvement is only possible if (1) the number of births per marriage increases; (2) the number of marriages rises; or (3) the probability of death is reduced.

Option (1) is not possible. ... An increase in the number of fissions (2) can be achieved if one enriches the uranium isotope 235, which can be fissioned at low

---

[40] Dieter Hoffmann, "Carl Ramsauer, die Deutsche Physikalische Gesellschaft und die Selbstmobilisierung der Physikerschaft im 'Dritten Reich,'" in Helmut Maier (ed.), *Rüstungsforschung im Nationalsozialismus. Organisation, Mobilisierung und Entgrenzung der Technikwissenschaften* (Göttingen: Wallstein, 2002), 273–304.

[41] Werner Heisenberg, "Die theoretischen Grundlagen für die Energiegewinnung aus der Uranspaltung" (26 February 1942), Samuel Goudsmit Papers, American Institute of Physics, Center for the History of Physics, College Park, Maryland (SGP); this has been published as Walter Blum, Hans-Peter Dürr, and Helmut Rechenberg (eds.), *Werner Heisenberg: Gesammelte Werke / Collected Works. Series A / Part II* (Berlin: Springer Verlag, 1989), 517–525.

[42] Heisenberg to Goudsmit (5 January 1948) SGP.

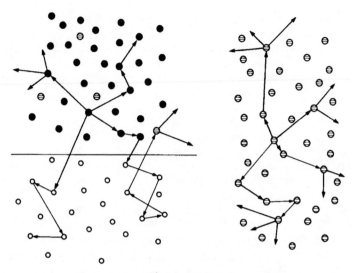

FIGURE 14.1: Chain reactions in uranium

Source: Originally published in Mark Walker, *German National Socialism and the Quest for Nuclear Power, 1939–1949* (Cambridge: Cambridge University Press, 1989), 56.

energies, but is rare. Indeed if it would be possible to produce pure uranium 235, then the situation on the right side of [Figure 14.1] takes place.

After one or several collisions, every neutron that had not exited through the outer layer would cause a further fission. Here the probability of death through capture is vanishingly small when compared to the probability of increase. Thus if a large enough amount of uranium 235 is piled up, then the neutron loss to the outside remains small compared to the increase inside. The number of neutrons increases enormously and the entire fission energy of 15 billion calories per ton is released in a small fraction of a second. Pure isotope uranium 235 thus undoubtedly represents an explosive of utterly unimaginable effect. However, this explosive is very difficult to produce.

A large part of the Army Ordnance research groups is working on enrichment or pure production of the isotope uranium 235. American researchers also appear to be pursuing this goal with great effort. ...

A [uranium] machine ... [would be] suitable for heating a steam turbine and over time can transfer all of its great energy to such a heat machine. Such machines can be practically applied in transportation vehicles, for example, in ships, which would have a huge radius of movement from the great amounts of energy in a relatively small amount of uranium. Since the machine does not burn oxygen, it would be especially advantageous in submarines.

Thanks to an idea from Weizsäcker, as soon as such a machine is in operation, the question of creating explosives takes on new meaning. When uranium is transformed in the machine a new substance (element number 94) is created, which very probably is an explosive of the same unimaginable effect as pure uranium 235. This substance can be separated much more easily out of uranium than uranium isotope 235, since it can be separated chemically. ...

The results achieved up until now can be summarized in the following way: (1) creating energy from uranium fission is undoubtedly possible, if isotope uranium 235 can be enriched. The *pure production* of uranium 235 would lead to an explosive of unimaginable effect.

(2) Ordinary uranium can also be used in a layer arrangement with heavy water to create energy. A layer arrangement of these materials can transfer its great energy over time to a heat engine. Thus this is a means to store very large amounts of technically usable energy in a relatively small amount of substance. The operating machine can also be used to produce an enormously strong explosive; it also promises many other scientifically and technically important applications.

By summer 1942, the uranium project was once again on firm footing. The RFR had taken over the project, which ensured continuing financial support. Both Kaiser Wilhelm president and industrialist Albert Vögler and Reich Armaments Minister Albert Speer took a keen interest in the work. In June of that year, Heisenberg gave a second talk before Speer and another group of dignitaries.[43] This lecture is notable for how it differed from the February talk. The analogy to deaths and births was not used, but there was even more emphasis on the American threat:

The interest in these newest developments [nuclear fission] was exceptionally great in America. A few days after the discovery American radio broadcast extensive reports and within half a year a large number of scientific publications on this subject had appeared in America.

The German uranium project had just recently had promising experimental results:

After a series of important preliminary work ... we have finally succeeded in building a small experimental device, with around 150 liters heavy water and 600 kilograms metal uranium that actually increased the number of neutrons inserted into it and produced energy. According to the results we have now, an expansion of the diameter of this device ... by three-to-six times would lead to a uranium burner, that is, a device that can spontaneously deliver large amounts of energy without external neutrons being added.

When Heisenberg mentioned nuclear explosives, he did so in a diffident way:

After the uranium burner has been built, it does not appear impossible that one day the path shown by Weizsäcker could be taken to an explosive substance more than a million times more powerful than those available today.

---

[43] Werner Heisenberg, "Die Arbeiten am Uranproblem" (4 June 1942), MPG-Archiv, KWIP 56 174–178.

Heisenberg closed his talk cautiously:

At the moment, the time needed for the technical development of such a burner is being determined by the availability of materials, especially the production of heavy water. But even aside from the question of materials, a great deal of scientific developmental work has to be done.

Even when one takes into account the difficulty of such developmental work, one has to recognize that in the next few years new land of the greatest significance for technology can be discovered. Since we know that many of the best laboratories in America are working on this problem, we can hardly afford not to pursue these questions in Germany. Even if one considers that such developments usually take a long time, one has to reckon with the possibility that if the war with America lasts several years more, then the technical exploitation of nuclear energy can one day suddenly play a decisive role.

Finally, in 1943, after Speer's support and goodwill had been secured, Heisenberg gave a final popular talk before the Reich Aviation Academy,[44] which was very interested in weapons development. Indeed, this was the part of the war when the search for "wonder weapons" that could help Germany turn the tide had begun in earnest. Here he did not mention nuclear explosives at all – although some people in his audience probably could remember that he had in the past. Indeed, Heisenberg told his audience that scientists were working to produce pure uranium 235 but never said what it would be good for. His conclusion was much milder than in his previous two talks:

If such a [uranium] burner can be built, then it could be used to power steam engines and in ships and other forms of transportation for which it is important to store the largest possible amount of energy in a small space. It goes without saying that before this goal is achieved, many other purely technical problems need to be solved with regard to the transfer of heat, the corrosion of the metals used, and so on.

In summary, the first step toward a very important technical development has been taken and, according to the experimental results available today, there is no doubt that nuclear energy can be liberated for technical goals on a large scale. On the other hand, the practical continuation of this development will naturally encounter great difficulties because of the strained war economy.

Heisenberg has gone from graphic portrayals, where he dangled the possibility of powerful new weapons before leading soldiers, industrialists, and National Socialist leaders, to an apparent desire to downplay bombs in favor of nuclear energy for the war effort, something that also impressed and interested political, industrial, and military leaders. Of course, the cat was already out of the bag. The KWIP scientists could not make people forget about nuclear explosives. But they clearly had become more and more

---

[44] Werner Heisenberg, "Die Energiegewinnung aus der Atomkernspaltung," G-217 (6 May 1943), ADM; this has been published as Blum, Dürr, and Rechenberg, 570–575.

ambivalent about the military consequences of their work and did not push as hard as they could have to make atomic bombs.

HEISENBERG VERSUS DIEBNER

Now that the HWA was giving up control of the uranium project, the KWS moved quickly to push Diebner out and replace Debye with a new director. Although Heisenberg was perhaps the obvious choice because he had been attached to the KWIP as an advisor, Bothe, who arguably would have been more qualified to oversee experimental work, was also considered. However, Harteck insisted that Heisenberg was the best choice while Hahn and Laue explained that Bothe was not appropriate "because of the difficulty of working with [him]."[45]

Heisenberg's recent political rehabilitation also played an important role. In 1937, Heisenberg had been attacked in the SS weekly *Das Schwarze Korps*[46] as a "White Jew" and "The Ossietzky of Physics." Indeed, according to this article, "Heisenberg is only one example among others. Together they are the place holders of Judaism in German spiritual life, who must disappear just like the Jews themselves." Heisenberg appealed directly to SS Reichsführer Heinrich Himmler.

A year later, after an "especially correct and especially tough" investigation, Himmler replied to Heisenberg:[47]

I am pleased to be able to inform you that I do not support the attack in *Das Schwarze Korps* through his [Johannes Stark's] article and that I have forbidden any further attack against you. ...

P.S. However, I do consider it right that, in the future you clearly separate for your audience the recognition of scientific research results from the human and political conduct of the researchers.

Heisenberg had already heard this advice from Ludwig Prandtl, the aeronautical researcher who had spoken with Himmler. In a letter to Prandtl,[48] Heisenberg reassured his colleague:

Actually I have always followed Himmler's advice in private conversations ... even before he gave it to me, because I never was sympathetic toward Einstein's public conduct. However, in lectures I have always spoken on purely scientific topics and therefore have had no opportunity to say something about Einstein the person (or Stark). But I will gladly follow Himmler's advice and, when I speak about the theory of relativity, simultaneously emphasize that I do not share Einstein's politics and

[45] Aktennotiz (22 January 1942), MPG-Archiv.
[46] "'Weisse Juden' in der Wissenschaft," *Das Schwarze Korps* (15 July 1937), 6.
[47] Himmler to Heisenberg (21 July 1938), SGP.
[48] Heisenberg to Prandtl (8 March 1938), MPG-Archiv, IX 4 1935–1939.

worldview – which by the way Mr. Himmler can see from the fact that I did not and do not have the intention of leaving Germany.

The SS report was positive, although the last sentence (see below) does not ring true:[49]

Heisenberg is a man of exceptional scientific reputation. His strength lies in the good school of physicists he has trained, including von Weizsäcker, Flügge, and others.

Heisenberg's character and conduct are decent. Heisenberg is the apolitical scholar type. If he is also ready at any time to stand up for Germany, that is because he believes that one is either "born a good German, or not."

... Over the course of the years Heisenberg has become more and more convinced by the successes of National Socialism and today is positive toward it. However, he believes that, aside from the occasional participation in a [political indoctrination] camp and similar things, an active political role is not appropriate for a university teacher. Today Heisenberg also fundamentally rejects the alienation[50] of German living space by Jews.

Heisenberg clearly deserved this appointment, but merit was not the only reason he got it. For his part, Heisenberg knew very well whom he had to thank for the KWIP post. In a 1943 letter to Himmler,[51] Heisenberg wrote:

A few years ago you let me ... know through your staff that you desired ... a public rehabilitation of my honor. ... In May of last year I was appointed director of the Kaiser Wilhelm Institute for Physics in Berlin-Dahlem, and I thank you for the rehabilitation of my honor connected to this appointment.

Heisenberg also followed Himmler's advice. In an article entitled "The Assessment of 'Modern Theoretical Physics,'" published in the *Journal for the Entire Science*,[52] the house journal for the "Aryan Physics"[53] movement, Heisenberg said this about Einstein and relativity:

America would have been discovered if Columbus had never lived; the theory of electric phenomena would also have been found without Maxwell, electric waves without Herz; for the discoverers cannot change the facts. In the same way the theory of relativity would undoubtedly have been created without Einstein. ... As far as the *correctness* of a theory is concerned, it is best to completely ignore the history of the discovery.

Heisenberg's increased prestige and influence at the KWIP inevitably meant a loss of the same for Diebner, who responded to his exile by gathering together a group of younger scientists and whatever materials were

---

[49] Himmler to Mentzel (REM) (26 May 1939), BArch REM 2943, 370–372.
[50] *Überfremdung.*
[51] Heisenberg to Himmler (4 February 1943), SGP.
[52] *Zeitschrift für die gesamte Naturwissenschaft.*
[53] *Deutsche Physik.*

available at the HWA experimental center in Gottow in order to carry out his own model nuclear reactor experiments. Essentially, there was now a division of labor in the uranium project, whereby Diebner's group tried to achieve the greatest neutron multiplication while Heisenberg's group was working to refine and correct the theory.[54]

Diebner challenged the KWIP layer design by using a three-dimensional lattice of cubes. Although his group was also hampered by a shortage of materials, they improvised: model experiment G-I used paraffin disks with cube-shaped holes into which uranium oxide powder was added, spoonful by spoonful;[55] G-II used metal uranium cubes made out of plates frozen in heavy ice;[56] G-III used cast uranium cubes – with some made out of plates as well – suspended in heavy water.[57]

The experimental outcome in Gottow was clearly better than anything the experiments in Leipzig or Berlin-Dahlem had achieved. Höcker was asked to interpret the Gottow experiments and concluded that the lattice design was inherently superior to layers. But Höcker went on to argue that cylinders represented a much more effective solution than the impractical cube lattice.[58] Abraham Esau, the Plenipotentiary for Nuclear Physics in RFR, accepted this argument.[59] Höcker also cautiously suggested to Heisenberg that a design using cylinders would be best.[60]

The Leipzig model reactor experiments stopped when Heisenberg became director of the KWIP. The B-series of horizontal layer designs were slowed down by the steadily deteriorating war. The Norwegian production of heavy water never reached the levels the Germans expected. Heavy water was not the highest priority for the Norwegian Hydro, which had to produce synthetic nitrogen for both fertilizer and explosives manufacture. Allied sabotage and bombings also interrupted heavy water production. The large metal uranium plates Heisenberg had ordered for the KWIP experiments were difficult for the Auergesellschaft to produce. As a result, while Diebner's group was enjoying one success after another with improvised experiments using the materials at hand, the reactor

---

[54] I want to thank Cathryn Carson for this point.

[55] Friedrich Berkei, Kurt Diebner, et al., Bericht über einen Würfelversuch mit Uranoxyd und Paraffin, November 1942," ADM.

[56] K. Diebner, G. Hartwig, W. Herrmann, H. Westmeyer, W. Czulius, F. Berkei, and K. H. Höcker, "Bericht über einen Versuch mit Würfeln aus Uran-Metall und Schwerem Eis," G-212 ADM.

[57] Kurt Diebner, "Über die Neutronenvermehrung einer Anordnung aus Uranwürfeln und Schwerem Wasser (G III)," ADM

[58] Karl-Heinz Höcker, "Über die Anordnung von Uran und Streusubstanz in der U-Maschine" (25 January 1943), MPG-Archiv, KWIP 1H 84–97.

[59] Abraham Esau, "Bericht über den Stand der Arbeiten auf dem Gebiet der Kernphysik" (1 July 1943), MPG-Archiv, KWIP 56 63–71.

[60] Höcker to Heisenberg (14 August 1943), MPG-Archiv, KWIP 7H Die Erfahrung mit den Reaktoren, 29.

experiments under Heisenberg languished because they had to wait for the large cast metal plates and sufficient amounts of heavy water.[61]

The work at the KWIP was also hampered by tensions between Heisenberg and Esau. For a while this worked to Diebner's benefit – for example, when Esau transferred the KWIP's heavy water to him – but eventually Heisenberg and KWS president Vögler were able to persuade their patron Armaments Minister Speer to force Esau out. His replacement was Walther Gerlach, professor for Experimental Physics at the University of Munich. Gerlach balanced support for both Diebner and Heisenberg. The KWIP group's goal of achieving a self-sustaining chain reaction was doomed to failure as long as they stayed with the horizontal layer design, but Heisenberg was determined to carry it out.

TWILIGHT OF THE GODS

At the start of 1944, most of the KWIP was involved in "work important for the war."[62] The "Production of Energy from Nuclear Fission" work enjoyed the highest priority. The low temperature physics section of the institute was developing cold-resistant devices for use by frontline troops under a contract with the SS. The KWIP optical laboratory was working on a spectroscopic process needed by industry. Finally, in 1944, Wirtz was able to carry out experiments B-VI and B-VII using metal uranium plates and heavy water in the new state-of-the-art bunker laboratory at the KWIP. The results were inferior to the Gottow experiments with regard to neutron multiplication. The ever-deteriorating war now made work in Berlin almost impossible. However, Heisenberg nevertheless reported these results in positive terms to Vögler:[63]

The results of the first large-scale experiment in the bunker laboratory are quite good. The results correspond in all essential points to expectations. The neutron increase is higher than all previous experiments. The Gottow experiments also show that changing the geometric arrangement of the metal [uranium] can increase this still further.

Vögler was a consistently strong supporter of Heisenberg and the uranium work at the KWIP[64]:

If I can help in any way to accelerate the acquisition of the necessary material, then please give me the corresponding papers. I am also happy to meet again with

[61] Werner Heisenberg, Fritz Bopp, Erich Fischer, Carl Friedrich von Weizsäcker, and Karl Wirtz, "Messungen an Schichtenanordnungen aus 38-Metall und Paraffin" (30 October 1942), MPG-Archiv, KWIP 56 121–140.

[62] "Bericht über die laufenden kriegswichtigen Arbeiten des Kaiser Wihelm-Instituts für Physik" (6 January 1944), MPG-Archiv, KWIP 56 97.

[63] Heisenberg to Vögler (3 April 1944), MPG-Archiv, KWIP 29 357–358.

[64] Vögler to Heisenberg (31 October 1944), MPG-Archiv, KWIP 5-2 314.

Minister Speer, who as you know is exceptionally interested in these questions and asks me about it at every opportunity.

A few months earlier, in April 1944, Vögler had explicitly asked about nuclear explosives:[65] "Have the experiments brought us closer to the manufacture of so-called energy bombs?" No response to this question from Heisenberg has been found.

Thanks to the support of Speer, most KWIs were able to evacuate Berlin and seek quieter locations. The KWIP settled in Hechingen in southwest Germany, with a nuclear reactor experiment set up in neighboring Haigerloch. In fact, Heisenberg and Wirtz had embraced Höcker's suggestion and intended to bypass Diebner's effective but impractical cube lattice design and use an arrangement of cast metal uranium cylinders immersed in heavy water. Unfortunately, the ever-deteriorating war made this impossible. Instead, Wirtz was forced to copy Diebner's design and use a lattice of uranium cubes suspended in heavy water.

Gerlach had pressured the KWIP group to carry out a large-scale reactor experiment:[66]

I am very anxious to hear what you think of the suggestion, as soon as possible, to use all the cubes to make a large-scale experiment. I consider it urgently necessary that we do not wait until the cylinders are finished. Again and again the officials overseeing research and development have pressured us to do this, and I have to admit that they are right in the sense that many people have been exempted from frontline service in order to carry out such experiments. I have now begun to halt work, both in physics in general and in nuclear physics, which is less important than the main problem [uranium]. In this way physicists and technicians are being freed up for the most important work.

Neither at the time nor afterward did Heisenberg or Wirtz give Diebner the credit he deserved for developing the lattice reactor design. The final KWIP model reactor experiment urged by Gerlach had almost but not quite enough heavy water and uranium to go critical – but in the end that was fortunate. Because of their determination to achieve a self-sustaining chain reaction and constraints caused by the war, this experiment did not include much in the way of safety equipment. If it had gone critical, the scientists might have been subjected to strong radiation.

With Gerlach's support, Diebner's group continued their work. A final reactor experiment, G-IV, used a lattice of uranium cubes in the shape of a sphere.[67] Rainer Karlsch argues that this may even have gone critical for a short time and apparently ended in an accident. Evidence suggests that

[65] Vögler to Heisenberg (12 April 1944), MPG-Archiv, KWIP 56 79.
[66] Gerlach to Heisenberg (30 October 1944), MPG-Archiv, KWIP 7H P 33.
[67] Diebner to Heisenberg (10 November 1944), MPG-Archiv, KWIP 5–1 26.

some of the scientists working for Diebner took a significant further step by building and testing a nuclear weapon design in the last desperate months of the war.[68] This weapon was nothing like the atomic bombs dropped on Japan the following August; rather, it sought to use hollow-point explosive charges to provoke nuclear fission in small samples of significantly enriched uranium, and nuclear fusion in a small amount of lithium-deuteride. It is not clear that this design worked in the sense that it succeeded in provoking nuclear reactions. It is clear that a group of German scientists designed and tested what they thought would be a nuclear weapon. Diebner and Gerlach kept this weapon and its test a closely guarded secret. None of the other uranium project scientists, including Heisenberg and Weizsäcker, found out about it.

By 1944, the KWIP personnel had grown to fifty, including fifteen women. The breakdown is as follows:[69]

19 physicists (18 men, 1 woman)
9 lab technicians (1 man, 8 women)
7 mechanics (men)
3 cleaners (women)
2 pipe fitters (men)
2 secretaries (women)
1 carpenter (man)
1 chemical technician (man)
1 concierge (man)
1 electrician (man)
1 engineer (man)
1 glass blower (man)
1 helper (woman)
1 laborer (man)
also
4 (men) in military service, not counting those who were deceased

By this time, Heisenberg was looking toward the postwar period. In May of that year, he told his older colleague Laue about his plans for the KWIP:[70]

I have reminded ... a few institute members that the contracts for scientists who started during the war run out at the end of the war. I have justified this by arguing that, especially for scientists, it is easier now than it will be at the end of the war to

[68] For the G-IV experiment and the nuclear weapon test, see Rainer Karlsch, *Hitlers Bombe. Die geheime Geschichte der deutschen Kernwaffenversuche* (Munich: DVA, 2005), 115–161, 209–237; also see Rainer Karlsch and Mark Walker, "New Light on Hitler's Bomb," *Physics World* (June 2005), 15–18.
[69] "Personalliste" (20 March 1944), MPG-Archiv, KWIP 6cn 1–15.
[70] Heisenberg to Laue (5 June 1944), MPG-Archiv, KWIP 5–1 158.

find another position. Thus I have given these members the possibility of leaving the institute, of course after first consulting me. I consider this step necessary because I am convinced that the institute's work will have to be restricted after the war and because I would like to avoid the sudden appearance of great hardship. On the other hand, I did not send this letter to all members who started during the war, rather only to those whom I believe would have to leave if I am forced to shrink the institute.

Several months later, Heisenberg was more explicit:[71]

... because I feel that all such changes should wait until after the war. After the war is ended the institute will need a completely new research program, and none of us can now foresee which work the institute will be able to do, or even in which form the institute will continue.

REHABILITATION

As the Allied armies advanced into Germany from all sides, a special scientific intelligence-gathering unit, the Alsos Mission, followed behind the American armies with the specific task of finding and neutralizing any "German atomic bomb."[72] When the scientific head of this mission, the Dutch-born and now naturalized American physicist Samuel Goudsmit came to Hechingen, the uranium, heavy water, and scientific reports were hidden. Wirtz and Weizsäcker told Goudsmit that he would have to wait and talk to Heisenberg, who had gone to Bavaria to be with his family. However, when the Alsos Mission found the buried materials and the reports hidden in a cesspool, Wirtz and Weizsäcker changed their minds and cooperated.

When Goudsmit found Heisenberg, he made an ambivalent impression by appearing both anti-Nazi and nationalistic. Ironically, Heisenberg and the rest of his colleagues believed that they were ahead of the Americans in the race to harness nuclear fission. Heisenberg told Goudsmit he would be very interested in the work they had been doing. Eventually, ten German scientists were interned in Farm Hall, a country estate in England.[73] More than half of the captive scientists – Bagge, Heisenberg, Korsching, Laue, Weizsäcker, and Wirtz – had worked at the KWIP. They enjoyed the good food and hospitality at Farm Hall until their tranquility was shattered by the news of Hiroshima.

Each of the interned scientists reacted differently to the news. The other scientists at Farm Hall had already maneuvered Diebner into the position of

[71] Heisenberg to Laue (14 November 1944), MPG-Archiv, KWIP 5–1 162.
[72] For the Alsos Mission, see Walker, *German*, 153–160.
[73] For Farm Hall, see Walker, *Nazi*, 207–241; Charles Frank (ed.), *Operation Epsilon: The Farm Hall Transcripts* (London: IOP, 1993), and Jeremy Bernstein (ed.), *Hitler's Uranium Club: The Secret Recordings at Farm Hall*, 2nd ed. (New York: Copernicus Books, 2001).

a scapegoat as the "Nazi" in the group. Gerlach acted like a defeated general and his colleagues feared that he would commit suicide – behavior that makes much more sense after the revelations that he had helped Diebner build and test a nuclear weapon. Hahn was self-righteous, insisting that he had had nothing to do with the military applications of his discovery. Heisenberg was concerned with his scientific reputation. Finally, Weizsäcker worked hard to develop arguments and explanations that would help them in the future – for example, that they had not really wanted to make atomic bombs.

When the Farm Hall scientists returned to Germany in 1946, the KWIP and the KWS were reestablished in Göttingen, within the British zone of occupation.[74] When the KWS was refounded as the Max Planck Society, the KWIP was renamed the Max Planck Institute for Physics. Its members played very important roles in the postwar development of science in West Germany.[75] Laue became the first president of the German Physical Society in the British Zone.[76] Heisenberg gained a great deal of influence as an informal advisor to West German chancellor Konrad Adenauer, although the physicist's initiatives were not always successful.[77] He helped found the

---

[74] See Klaus Hentschel and Gerhard Rammer, "Nachkriegsphysik an der Leine. Eine Göttinger Vogelperspektive," in Dieter Hoffmann (ed.), *Physik in Nachkriegsdeutschland* (Frankfurt am Main: Verlag Harri Deutsch, 2003), 27–56, and Mark Walker, "Otto Hahn: Responsibility and Repression," in *Physics in Perspective*, 8, no. 2 (2006), 116–163.

[75] See Michael Eckert, "Neutrons and Politics: Maier-Leibnitz and the Emergence of Pile Neutron Research in the FRG," *Historical Studies in the Physical and Biological Sciences*, 19, no. 1 (1988), 81–113; Michael Eckert, "Die Anfänge der Atompolitik in der Bundesrepublik Deutschland," *Vierteljahrshefte für Zeitgeschichte*, 37, no. 1 (1989), 115–143; Michael Eckert, "Das 'Atomei': Der erste bundesdeutsche Forschungsreaktor als Katalysator nuklearer Interessen in Wissenschaft und Politik," in Michael Eckert and Maria Osietzki (eds.), *Wissenschaft für Macht und Markt. Kernforschung und Mikroelektronik in der Bundesrepublik Deutschland* (Munich: Beck Verlag, 1989), 74–95; and Michael Eckert, "Kernenergie und Westintegration. Die Zähmung des westdeutschen Nuklearnationalismus," in Ludolf Herbst, Werner Bührer, and Hanno Sowade (eds.), *Vom Marshallplan zur EWG. Die Eingliederung der Bundesrepublik Deutschland in die westliche Welt* (Munich: R. Oldenbourg Verlag, 1990), 313–334.

[76] See Gerhard Rammer, "'Sauberkeit im Kreise der Kollegen': Die Vergangenheitspolitik der DPG," in Dieter Hoffmann and Mark Walker (eds.), *Physiker zwischen Autonomie und Anpassung. Die Deutsche Physikalische Gesellschaft im Dritten Reich* (Weinheim: VCH-Verlag Chemie, 2006).

[77] See Cathryn Carson, "New Models for Science in Politics: Heisenberg in West Germany," *Historical Studies in the Physical and Biological Sciences*, 30, no. 1 (1999), 115–171; Cathryn Carson, "A Scientist in Public: Werner Heisenberg after 1945," *Endeavour*, 23, no. 1, (1999), 31–34; Cathryn Carson, "Old Programs, New Policies? Nuclear Reactor Studies after 1945 in the Max-Planck-Institut für Physik," in Doris Kaufmann (ed.), *Geschichte der Kaiser-Wilhelm-Gesellschaft im Nationalsozialismus. Bestandsaufnahme und Perspektiven der Forschung*, 2 vols. (Göttingen: Wallstein, 2000), vol. 2, 726–749; Cathryn Carson, "Nuclear Energy Development in Postwar West Germany: Struggles over Cooperation in the Federal Republic's First Reactor Station," *History and Technology*, 18, no. 3 (2002), 233–270;

short-lived German Research Council (*Deutscher Forschungsrat*), which
was eventually absorbed into the German Research Foundation (*Deutsche
Forschungsgemeinschaft*), was instrumental in arranging the West German
participation in CERN and other international projects, and served on the
German Atomic Commission.

Weizsäcker spoke with and thereby influenced the writer Robert Jungk,
whose 1956 book *Brighter than a Thousand Suns* popularized the myth that
Heisenberg, Weizsäcker, and their colleagues had resisted Hitler by denying
him nuclear weapons.[78] When Heisenberg failed to get the first West German
nuclear reactor station to come to Munich, Wirtz became the director of the
new Institute for Neutron Physics and Reactor Technology at the Karlsruhe
Nuclear Research Center. Finally, all of these scientists participated in the
1957 Göttingen Manifesto, where they called for strong support of nuclear
research but refused to have anything to do with West German development of nuclear weapons. This public statement was a consistent continuation of their ambivalent attitude toward nuclear reactors and their military
consequences that began during the war and continued during the postwar
period.

HISTORIANS AND "HITLER'S BOMB"

Most historians who have examined the history of the German efforts during World War II to harness nuclear fission for nuclear energy and nuclear
weapons have focused on Werner Heisenberg: what he did or did not do,
what he wanted or intended to do. In fact, the history of the German "uranium project" is far greater than Heisenberg or even the KWIP. Heisenberg
was one of the most important scientists working on nuclear fission during
World War II, but he was also only one of several such scientists.

Three historians have published interpretations of Heisenberg that differ among themselves, and differ from this author's interpretation. In 1993,
Thomas Powers argued that Heisenberg had resisted Hitler by leading a
conspiracy to deny the German "Führer" nuclear weapons.[79] Two years
later, Paul Lawrence Rose portrayed Heisenberg as a Nazi sympathizer who

Cathryn Carson, "Heisenberg and the Framework of Science Policy," *Fortschritte der Physik*,
50, nos. 5–7 (2002), 432–436; Cathryn Carson and Michael Gubser, "Science Advising and
Science Policy in Post-War West Germany: The Example of the Deutscher Forschungsrat,"
Minerva, 40 (2002), 147–179; Cathryn Carson, "Objectivity and the Scientist: Heisenberg
Rethinks," *Science in Context*, 16 (2003), 243–269.

[78] Robert Jungk, *Brighter than a Thousand Suns: A Personal History of the Atomic Scientists*
(New York: Harcourt Brace, 1958); also see Jungk's foreword to Mark Walker, *Die
Uranmaschine. Mythos und Wirklichkeit der deutschen Atombombe* (Berlin: Siedler Verlag,
1990), and his memoirs, Robert Jungk, *Trotzdem: mein Leben für die Zukunft* (Munich:
Hanser, 1993).

[79] Powers.

failed to make nuclear weapons for Hitler only because of his arrogance and incompetence.[80] Cathryn Carson has published several sophisticated and subtle papers analyzing Heisenberg's postwar career as scientist, science policy maker, and intellectual, arguing that Heisenberg's statements were more differentiated after the war than many were willing or able to see: whereas after the war others – including in particular the author Robert Jungk – portrayed Heisenberg as a resistance fighter, Heisenberg himself did not.[81]

Thomas Powers was right in his 1993 book[82] to emphasize the April 1941 letter from Ladenburg as an important historical source for Heisenberg's mixed feelings about the uranium research, but he was wrong to take it as proof that Heisenberg resisted Hitler by denying him nuclear weapons. Heisenberg neither denied Hitler nuclear weapons nor resisted him. The recently returned KWIP papers, together with the "G-Reports" and the Heisenberg Papers in Munich, clearly document that Heisenberg did not slow down, divert, stop, camouflage, or hide the progress he and his colleagues were making toward nuclear reactors, nuclear explosives, and nuclear weapons. Paul Lawrence Rose was right in his 1998 book[83] to reject the postwar claims that Heisenberg and Weizsäcker had diverted, slowed down, or stopped research in order to resist Hitler, but he was wrong to follow Goudsmit's postwar analysis[84] and claim that German scientific incompetence had been the cause. Once again, now that the KWIP papers are available, we have a fairly complete documentation of what these scientists did or did not do.[85] Heisenberg's assumption that a nuclear reactor would regulate itself was dangerous but not incompetent. He and his colleagues clearly understood well how nuclear explosives could be created and how nuclear weapons in principle would work. The German scientists made some mistakes – their counterparts in the United States sometimes did as well – but these were not the reason Germany did not attempt the industrial-scale development of nuclear weapons.

Cathryn Carson was right to argue that Heisenberg's postwar statements need to be examined more carefully. It is clear that during the postwar period Heisenberg was being portrayed as a resistance fighter who led a conspiracy to deny nuclear weapons to Hitler, but Carson argues that Heisenberg was not responsible for this portrayal; rather, his sometimes suggestive and

---

[80] Rose.
[81] Cathryn Carson, "Reflections on Copenhagen," in Dörries, 7–17; Carson, "New," especially 134–135.
[82] Powers.
[83] Rose.
[84] Samuel Goudsmit, *Alsos,* 2nd ed. (Los Angeles: Tomash, 1983).
[85] The one frustrating exception is the actual calculation of critical mass that clearly was done at least once but has not yet been found.

vague statements on what he did during the war reflected his reluctance to participate in this discussion and his ambivalence about the work on uranium done during the National Socialist period. An unexpected type of continuity is now clear: a continuity of ambiguous ambivalence. During the war, Heisenberg was ambivalent about nuclear reactors and their consequences; after the war, Heisenberg was ambivalent about what he had done with nuclear reactors. During the war, Heisenberg gave evasive but suggestive answers when asked about nuclear weapons; after the war, he gave evasive but suggestive answers when asked about his wartime work on nuclear weapons. In fact, Heisenberg was quite consistent.

Finally, Rainer Karlsch was right to question whether the research carried out at the KWIP, or indeed the entire known uranium project, was the whole story of nuclear reactors and nuclear weapons under Hitler. His revelations of an additional model reactor experiment, G-IV, as well as a subsequent nuclear weapon test carried out by HWA scientists have placed the KWIP work in the proper context. Compared with Diebner, Gerlach, and the other scientists involved in the nuclear test, Heisenberg and Weizsäcker clearly did not try as hard as they could have done to create nuclear weapons for the National Socialists to use. Weizsäcker tried quite hard for a while, then fell into line with his more ambivalent senior colleague Heisenberg.

CONCLUSION

Now we have come to a question that has often been asked: did German scientists try to make nuclear weapons for Hitler? New documents reinforce this author's original interpretation[86] of "Hitler's Bomb": the project scientists were neither resistance fighters nor incompetent; rather, they produced good scientific work that appears modest only when compared to the Manhattan Project. The administrators were neither stupid nor short-sighted; rather, they made reasonable science policy decisions even though they decided not to boost uranium research up to the industrial level and make a realistic effort to achieve nuclear weapons during the war. Paradoxically, these new sources also reveal that these scientists were both more and less enthusiastic about creating nuclear weapons for Hitler's government and military than has previously been assumed. Moreover, the key to understanding this paradox is, again as this author has previously argued, chronology – recognizing and appreciating change over time.

During the period from the September 1939 German invasion of Poland to the spring of 1941, before the invasion of the Soviet Union, Heisenberg worked out the basic theory of nuclear reactors, including the possibility of using pure or nearly pure U-235 as a nuclear explosive, and von Weizsäcker

---

[86] See footnote 1 above; Walker, *German.*

recognized that an operating nuclear reactor would produce a transuranic element 94 (plutonium) that would be just as good a nuclear explosive as U-235. Weizsäcker did not stop there; he submitted a patent that explicitly explained how nuclear reactors could be used to manufacture nuclear explosives and discussed with an official from Army Ordnance the possible military applications of nuclear fission. Heisenberg did not keep quiet about plutonium – as suggested in Michael Frayn's drama *Copenhagen;* rather, he told Hitler's Armaments Minister Albert Speer that the nuclear reactors they were working on could be used to make nuclear explosives for atomic bombs.

However, while the many reports and lectures do make clear that the researchers at the KWIP and other members of the uranium project were making good progress toward nuclear weapons – even though by the end of the war in Europe they had unknowingly fallen far behind their competition in the United States – these documents also demonstrate a growing ambivalence toward the future military applications of their work. Heisenberg's popular lectures before audiences of prominent political, military, and industrial leaders show this very clearly. In February 1942, Heisenberg speaks of nuclear explosives many times more powerful than any then available; in June of the same year he mentions nuclear explosives in a very reserved and diffident way; in the spring of the next year he does not mention nuclear explosives at all in a lecture on the applications of nuclear fission. Heisenberg – like the rest of his colleagues in the German uranium project – did not stop working on the nuclear reactors or isotope separation that everyone knew eventually would lead to nuclear explosives and atomic bombs, but he did stop publicizing these weapons.

When the Second World War began, German scientists at the KWIP took up research on nuclear fission, chain reactions, isotope separation, transuranic elements, and nuclear reactors with enthusiasm and with few misgivings. As long as the war was going well for Germany and its National Socialist leadership, so that nuclear weapons were not needed, these scientists retained their enthusiasm and worked hard to advance their research. When the war began to turn sour, they were confronted with the reality of both what a National Socialist victory would mean for Europe and what a defeat would mean for Germany. They did not stop working, divert, or slow down their progress, or resist National Socialism. However, as the revelations about Diebner's last reactor experiment and nuclear weapon test demonstrate, Heisenberg, von Weizsäcker, and Wirtz also clearly did not push as hard as they could to create nuclear weapons. The history of the Kaiser Wilhelm Institute for Physics during World War II demonstrates that scientists did not have to be enthusiastic about National Socialism or the war to work on weapons of mass destruction for the Third Reich.

THE POSTWAR "POLITICS OF THE PAST"

15

"Whitewash Culture": How the Kaiser Wilhelm/Max Planck Society Dealt with the Nazi Past

Carola Sachse

CONSTRUCTED CONTINUITY – MANUFACTURED SUPPRESSION

Contemporary discussion of the "zero hour" (*Stunde Null*) – sometime between the end of war and monetary reform – was replaced long ago by historiographic discussion of a dominating continuity, especially with regard to West German economic and science elites. On the other hand, in a 1995 article, Mitchell Ash concluded that personal continuity in the scientific community did not happen of its own accord. In fact, it was constructed with persistence and finesse in the course of the denazification of "incriminated" individuals and networks.[1] This chapter will use this thesis to demonstrate that the associated mental procedure – in popular psychology referred to as the "repression" ("*Verdrängung*") of participation in National Socialist rule, violence, and crime – was more than just an unconscious psychological process. At the same time, it was a communicative process used by the scientific elites while reconstituting their disciplines and institutions in postwar Germany. As such, it was bound to a manner of discourse that first had to be established, tested, and agreed upon; its message, however, had to be adjusted repeatedly to accommodate the changing political constellations and social contexts of the postwar era. But "repression" was not only a

[1] Mitchell G. Ash, "Verordnete Umbrüche – Konstruierte Kontinuitäten: Zur Entnazifizierung von Wissenschaftlern und Wissenschaften nach 1945," *Zeitschrift für Geschichtswissenschaft*, 43 (1995), 903–923. See also Bernd Weisbrod (ed.), *Akademische Vergangenheitspolitik. Beiträge zur Wissenschaftskultur der Nachkriegszeit* (Göttingen: Wallstein, 2002); Jonathan Wiesen, *West German Industry and the Challenge of the Nazi Past* (Chapel Hill: University of North Carolina Press, 2001).

I would like to thank Gerhard Baader, Reinhard Rürup, and Wolfgang Schieder for critical reading of the first draft; for thorough discussions and pointing out numerous sources to me. I thank my colleagues from the Research Program "History of the Kaiser Wilhelm Society in the National Socialist Era" and Achim Trunk in particular. Nele Lehmann has supported my archive and literature research with competence and efficiency for which I thank her.

mental but also an active process, when scientific communities unburdened themselves of overly "incriminated" colleagues and tried to drive them out of their circles.[2] That is, "repression" was multifaceted, a carefully and elaborately manufactured product of individuals, institutions, and networks. It was a constitutive element of the construct "continuity."

Among the numerous examples of repression within the West German scientific community, the "Verschuer Case" stands out as a prominent and well-documented case study. Peter Kröner has already scrutinized the postwar career of hereditary pathologist Otmar von Verschuer (1896–1969), who from 1935 to 1942 was professor at the University of Frankfurt am Main, when he left to become the last director of the Kaiser Wilhelm Institute for Anthropology, Human Heredity and Eugenics (KWIA), serving until the end of the war.[3] In the meantime, the public debate over how the Max Planck Society (*Max-Planck-Gesellschaft*, MPS) has dealt with its Nazi past has expanded the "Verschuer Case" to include its long-standing president and honorary chairman, Adolf Butenandt (1903–1995).[4]

Before this "politics of the past" (*Vergangenheitspolitik*) is investigated, the following facts, which have been known for a long time, should be recapitulated. Josef Mengele (1911–1979) was one of Verschuer's most ambitious

[2] On "*Täterkreisverengung*," see Michael Schüring, "Ein 'unerfreulicher Vorgang.' Das Max-Planck-Institut für Züchtungsforschung in Voldagsen und die gescheiterte Rückkehr von Max Ufer," in Susanne Heim (ed.), *Autarkie und Ostexpansion. Pflanzenzucht und Agrarforschung im Nationalsozialismus* (Göttingen: Wallstein, 2002), 280–299, here 289. For a general reference for postwar West Germany, see Norbert Frei, *Vergangheitspolitik. Die Anfänge der Bundesrepublik und die NS-Vergangenheit* (Munich: Beck, 1996).

[3] Peter Kröner, *Von der Rassenhygiene zur Humangenetik. Das Kaiser-Wilhelm-Institut für Anthropologie, menschliche Erblehre und Eugenik nach dem Kriege* (Stuttgart: G. Fischer, 1998).

[4] Ernst Klee, "Augen aus Auschwitz," *Die Zeit* (27 January 2000); Benno Müller-Hill, "The Blood from Auschwitz," *History and Philosophy of the Life Sciences*, 21 (1999), 331–365; Benno Müller-Hill, "Das Blut von Auschwitz und das Schweigen der Gelehrten," in Doris Kaufmann (ed.), *Geschichte der Kaiser-Wilhelm-Gesellschaft im Nationalsozialismus. Bestandsaufnahme und Perspektiven der Forschung*, 2 vols. (Göttingen: Wallstein, 2000), vol. 1, 189–227; Robert Proctor, "Adolf Butenandt (1903–195). Nobelpreisträger, Nationalsozialist und MPG-Präsident. Ein erster Blick in den Nachlass," *Ergebnisse. Vorabdrucke aus dem Forschungsprogramm "Geschichte der Kaiser-Wilhelm-Gesellschaft im Nationalsozialismus*," No. 2 (Berlin: Forschungsprogramm, 2000; further quoted as *Ergebnisse*, No., and year); Ernst Klee, *Deutsche Medizin im Dritten Reich. Karrieren vor und nach 1945* (Frankfurt am Main: Fischer, 2001), 348–394; see Achim Trunk's chapter in this volume; Carola Sachse (ed.), *Die Verbindung nach Auschwitz. Biowissenschaften und Menschenversuche an Kaiser-Wilhelm-Instituten* (Göttingen: Wallstein, 2003); for a more recent, comprehensive source, see Hans-Walter Schmuhl, *Grenzüberschreitungen. Das Kaiser-Wilhelm-Institut für Anthropologie, menschliche Erblehre und Eugenik 1927–1945* (Göttingen: Wallstein, 2005), English translation Hans-Walter Schmuhl, *The Kaiser Wilhelm Institute for Anthropology, Human Heredity and Eugenics, 1927–1945: Crossing Boundaries* (Dordrecht: Springer, 2008).

students from his days at the University of Frankfurt, with doctorates in both medicine and anthropology, and until late 1942 he was a medical doctor in the *Waffen-SS*. During the first months of 1943, Mengele spent some time at the KWIA where he caught up on the current research of his former Ph.D. supervisor, in particular, Verschuer's concept of the heredity of "specific proteins." The assumption at that time was that if these proteins could be verified, they might facilitate a serological determination of racial affiliation. Furthermore, he was interested in institute assistant Karin Magnussen's (1908 – 1997) project on the heredity of "iris heterochromia," an ocular pigment anomaly. Mengele assumed his post as camp physician in Auschwitz-Birkenau in May 1943. During the following months, he sent blood samples of people from different ethnic origins and the heterochromous eye pairs of the murdered members of a so-called gypsy clan to Dahlem.[5]

On May 3, 1946, Robert Havemann (1910–1982), a physical chemist and communist who had been persecuted by the Nazis and appointed president of the Kaiser Wilhelm Society (*Kaiser-Wilhelm-Gesellschaft*, KWS) in Berlin by the Soviets, published these facts in the Berlin *Neue Zeitung* newspaper. Verschuer, who had taken his equipment and defected to Hesse during the last months of war, at once initiated his *Spruchkammer* (denazification trial court) procedure in Frankfurt am Main in the hope of rehabilitation. His hearing ended in November 1946 with his categorization as a *Mitläufer* (fellow traveler, someone who neither resisted nor enthusiastically supported National Socialism but rather went along with it) and a fine. Havemann, who regarded this judgment as too mild, turned to the Hessian authorities. Thereupon the Hessian minister of education banned Verschuer in February 1947 from teaching and researching. Two and half years later, a commission consisting of three directors of Kaiser Wilhelm Institutes and a Berlin university professor convened in Stuttgart to write a memorandum explaining why Verschuer was nonetheless suitable as a university professor. Immediately afterward, the Hessian minister of education lifted the professional ban. Beginning in November 1949, Verschuer was once again on the payroll of the KWS/MPS where he remained until he was awarded a professorship for human genetics at the University of Münster in 1951.[6]

---

[5] The extensive research on these subjects is summarized in Carola Sachse and Benoit Massin, "Biowissenschaftliche Forschung an Kaiser-Wilhelm-Instituten und die Verbrechen des NS-Regimes. Informationen über den gegenwärtigen Wissensstand," *Ergebnisse*, 3 (2000). On Magnussen, also see Hans Hesse, *Augen aus Auschwitz. Ein Lehrstück über nationalsozialistischen Rassenwahn und medizinische Forschung – Der Fall Dr. Karin Magnussen* (Essen: Klartext, 2001); Benoit Massin, "Mengele, die Zwillingsforschung und die 'Auschwitz-Dahlem Connection,'" in Sachse, *Verbindung*, 201–254; Schmuhl, *Grenzüberschreitungen*, 482–502. Also see Achim Trunk's chapter in this volume and Michael Zimmermann (ed.), *Zwischen Erziehung und Vernichtung. Zigeunerpolitik und Zigeunerforschung im Europa des 20. Jahrhunderts* (Stuttgart: Franz Steiner, 2007).

[6] In detail, Kröner, *Rassenhygiene*.

The "Memorandum Concerning Prof. Dr. med. Otmar Frhr. v. Verschuer," composed in Stuttgart, is at the heart of this chapter.[7] This well-known and often quoted source demonstrates the nature and process of this "suppression" and "displacement" within the MPS. Four contextualizing lines of reasoning make this result comprehensible: first, the time this memorandum was written will be examined more closely; second, the interests and motives of the authors will be elaborated; third, the memorandum will be compared to similar sources from that time; and fourth, the sustainability of the memorandum in a past that does not want to pass will be tested.

ONE MONDAY IN SEPTEMBER 1949

On a Monday in September 1949, a few days after the first West German parliament (*Bundestag*) had convened, four professors who referred to each other as "eminently respectable scientists and undisputed personalities" came together in Stuttgart to reexamine the case of the disputed racial researcher Verschuer, who, as the accused, was present as well. They intended to put their findings in a report and give it to the founding president of the MPS, Otto Hahn (1879–1968), for further use.[8] One member of the panel was the pharmacologist and Berlin university professor Wolfgang Heubner. The remaining three members were directors of Kaiser Wilhelm Institutes (KWI):

- Boris Rajewski (1893–1974) from the KWI for Biophysics in Frankfurt am Main (after the end of the war in the U.S. zone of occupation), chair of the Medical-Biological Section and senator of the MPS
- Max Hartmann (1876–1962) from the KWI for Biology (transferred from Berlin-Dahlem to Hechingen, later in the French zone of occupation)
- Adolf Butenandt (1903–1995) from the KWI for Biochemistry (transferred from Berlin-Dahlem to Tübingen, later in the French zone of occupation), 1939 Nobel laureate for chemistry, since 1960 president and later honorary chairman of the MPS

Those three bioscientists and acting KWI directors shared an acute problem. The Western occupying powers had just acknowledged the re-founding of the Max Planck Society as the successor to the Kaiser Wilhelm Society.

---

[7] Copies of the "Denkschrift" are located in several different places in the Archives of the Max Planck Society, Berlin (*Archiv zur Geschichte der Max-Planck-Gesellschaft*, MPG-Archiv), for example, in these files: II. Abt. Rep. 1A (Personalia Verschuer), No. 6; Abt. III, Rep. 84/2 [former folder 357]; III. Abt. Rep. 47 (Hartmann papers), No. 1505; henceforth quoted as Denkschrift, 1949.

[8] MPG-Archiv, Abt. III, Rep. 84/2 (former folder 357): letter from Verschuer to Butenandt, 5 August 1949.

The return of the biosciences institutes located in the French zone (which only reluctantly gave up their blessed seclusion) to the mother ship – and hence the institutional reunion of the renowned KWS bioscientists with their compromised former colleague from the old Dahlem days, Otmar von Verschuer – was imminent.[9] For the MPS General Administration, the problem had likewise grown more acute. In the years leading up to the foundation of the West German state, KWS committees in the different occupation zones had been able to pass around the Verschuer case almost without any consequences.

During the last months of the war, Verschuer had moved essential parts of his institute and scientific equipment to his family's estate in the Hessian city of Solz in the U.S. zone without having previously arranged the matter with the secretary general of the KWS, Ernst Telschow (1889–1988). Years later, Telschow was still fuming about that. Since July 1945, Verschuer had no longer drawn a salary from the KWS General Administration, which had by now been transferred to the British zone in Göttingen.[10] However, in early 1949 Verschuer hired a lawyer to push through his salary claims with the General Administration. He had a notably stronger hand now, since the Königstein Agreement from March 1949 had put the financing of the future nationwide MPS on a sustainable federal basis. The resumption of paying salaries could no longer be denied for technical reasons.[11] The Verschuer case threatened to carry over to the newly founded MPS and be a burden to the return of first-rate bioscientific research in the Federal German Republic.

The fourth party of the Stuttgart round, pharmacologist Wolfgang Heubner (1877–1957), had been given emeritus status in 1948 by the Berlin Friedrich Wilhelm University and had been building up the Pharmacological Institute at the Berlin Free University since 1949.[12] He had to make amends for a past absence (see below). Heubner had been the former superior of Robert Havemann, who had set the investigation of Verschuer in motion in early 1946 with his intervention with the U.S. oversight authorities in Hesse

[9] On the "Opposition der 'Tübinger Herren,'" see Manfred Heinemann, "Der Wiederaufbau der Kaiser-Wilhelm-Gesellschaft und die Neugründung der Max-Planck-Gesellschaft (1945–1949)," in Rudolf Vierhaus and Bernhard vom Brocke (eds.), *Forschung im Spannungsfeld von Politik und Gesellschaft. Geschichte und Struktur der Kaiser-Wilhelm/Max-Planck-Gesellschaft* (Stuttgart: Deutsche Verlags-Anstalt, 1990), 407–470, here 450 f.; Jeffrey Lewis, "Kalter Krieg in der Max-Planck-Gesellschaft. Göttingen und Tübingen – eine Vereinigung mit Hindernissen, 1948–1949," in Wolfgang Schieder and Achim Trunk (eds.), *Adolf Butenandt und die Kaiser-Wilhelm-Gesellschaft. Wissenschaft, Industrie und Politik im "Dritten Reich"* (Göttingen: Wallstein, 2004), 403–443.

[10] MPG-Archiv, Abt. III, Rep. 84/2 (former folder 357): letter from Verschuer to Butenandt, 30 September 1946.

[11] MPG-Archiv, II. Abt. Rep. 1A, Personalia Verschuer, No. 7, note 4 January 1950.

[12] Johanna Therese Kneer, "Wolfgang Heubner (1877–1957). Leben und Werk," Ph.D. diss, University of Tübingen (1989).

and a newspaper article on the "racial fanatic" Verschuer and his connection to the concentration camp physician Josef Mengele in Auschwitz.[13] Verschuer then asked Heubner for support, and Heubner in turn asked Havemann to form a fact-finding committee. The Dahlem commission consisted of nine men. However, when it convened for its only meeting in August 1946, four of them – including Heubner – were unable to attend.[14] The verdict that the commission reached, following a contentious vote and in December 1946 finally recorded in a letter to Heubner, was damaging to Verschuer and could not be diminished by the exoneration Heubner subsequently submitted.

From that time on, Verschuer's connection to Mengele in Auschwitz and its gruesome details were documented and made public. Verschuer had confirmed the basic facts in a written statement to Otto Hahn – that is, that Verschuer had received blood sera from multiethnic inmates for his research on alleged race-specific proteins, and that his assistant Karin Magnussen had taken delivery of heterochromous eye pairs from the members of a so-called gypsy clan murdered in Auschwitz.[15] Moreover, the most notorious racist-political quotes from Verschuer's public talks and publications during National Socialism were readily accessible. In November 1946, the Frankfurt denazification court (*Spruchkammer*) had declared Verschuer a Nazi *Mitläufer* (fellow traveler).[16] Following a renewed intervention from Havemann, the Hessian ministry of education banned him in late February 1947 from "managing or researching at the Kaiser Wilhelm Institute for Anthropology."[17]

[13] Kröner, *Rassenhygiene*, 93 ff. On Havemann's part in the Berlin postwar era, see Dieter Hoffmann, "Der Physikochemiker Robert Havemann (1910–1982) – eine deutsche Biographie," in Dieter Hoffmann and Kristie Macrakis (eds.), *Naturwissenschaft und Technik in der DDR* (Berlin: Akademie, 1997), 319–336.

[14] Present were Karl von Lewinski (KWI for Comparative and International Private Law) as secretary, Kurt Gottschaldt (1902–1991, KWI for Anthropology), Robert Havemann, Hans Nachtsheim (1890–1979, KWI for Anthropology), and Otto Heinrich Warburg (1887–1970, KWI for Cell Physiology). Missing were Wolfgang Heubner, Prof. Dr. Nitsche, and Robert Rompe (1905–1993, physicist at the biomedical research center Berlin-Buch in the process of organization at that time). Hermann Muckermann (1877–1962, KWI for Anthropology) had refused to participate; MPG-Archiv, III. Abt. Rep. 47 (Hartmann papers), No. 1505: letter from Lewinski to Heubner, 23 December 1946.

[15] MPG-Archiv, II. Abt. Rep 1A, Personalia Verschuer, No. 5: letter from Verschuer to Hahn, 23 May 1946 (including four annexes).

[16] MPG-Archiv, Abt. III, Rep. 84/2 (former folder 357): Spruchkammerbescheid, 16 July 1946.

[17] MPG-Archiv, II. Abt. Rep 1A, Personalia Verschuer, No. 5: Erlass des Hessischen Staatsministeriums (Minister für Kultus und Unterricht) to Verschuer, 28 February 1947 (Tgb.No.IX/10850/47 Dr.K./P.). The Hessian Ministry of State (Minister for Economy and Traffic) authorized specific research work (family and twin pathological research, research on the heredity of tuberculosis disposition, paternity proofs) at Verschuer's privately operated "Institute for Anthropology" in Solz with a letter dated 5 April 1947 (signed by ministry official Dr. Frowein). During that time expert work was a major source of income for Verschuer. Yet at the time of the Stuttgart meeting the professional ban was still valid,

A NONE TOO ALTRUISTIC AND RATHER BELATED ACT
OF FRIENDSHIP

As an act of friendship, the Stuttgart commission's report countering the Dahlem verdict was rather belated. In fact, the disputed colleague's professional rehabilitation was only a secondary consideration at the meeting in September 1949. First, the four scientists wanted to stave off major damages to their own scientific discipline and the MPS.

Butenandt certainly was the most reliable of Verschuer's friends in the KWS/MPS, whose very ambivalent support of their compromised colleague was driven throughout by self-serving motives. Since 1945, Butenandt had already been pursuing the idea of appointing Verschuer to the professorship of anthropology at Tübingen, which Wilhelm Gieseler (1900–1976) had to vacate due to his Nazi activities.[18] Yet, when Verschuer told him about Havemann's "torpedo" in March 1946, Butenandt played it safe by taking six weeks to answer Verschuer's urgent letters, some sent by messenger.[19] When in September 1946 Verschuer asked Butenandt for a "whitewash certificate" for denazification (*Persilschein*) to aid his stagnating appointment to Frankfurt University, Butenandt evaded the request by passing it on to their colleague Alfred Kühn (1885–1968) from the KWI for Biology in Hechingen. Kühn had at the time been involved in Verschuer's appointment as director of the KWIA.[20]

But Kühn was similarly at best willing to declare that Verschuer's appointment had not been "influenced by Nazi party politics" (*Parteirücksichten*), an honor he also claimed for himself. Politely but firmly, he refused any further interventions in favor of Verschuer that would have required prior authorization from higher French authorities.[21] Kühn had warned Butenandt already in late 1945 that "under given circumstances" it would be "very imprudent" to propose a man like Verschuer, who had been a party member, for an appointment in Tübingen. Kühn quoted the head of the Scientific Mission of the French military government who had indicated that "the problem of cleansing will naturally come up again."

though modified; working as a professor in particular would have required a special permit by the Ministry for Verschuer, according to a letter of the Hessian State Ministry (Minister of Culture and Education), 8 July 1949.

[18] MPG-Archiv, Abt. III, Rep. 84/2 (former folder 357): letter from Verschuer to Butenandt, 7 January 1946; letters from Butenandt to Verschuer, 31 January, 22 February 1946.

[19] MPG-Archiv, Abt. III, Rep. 84/2 (former folder 357): letters from Verschuer to Butenandt, 4, 18, and 28 March, 2 April 1946; letter from Butenandt to Verschuer, 16 April 1946.

[20] MPG-Archiv, Abt. III, Rep. 84/2 (former folder 357): letter from Verschuer to Butenandt, 30 September 1946; letter from Butenandt to Verschuer, 19 October 1946.

[21] Archives of the Institute for History of Medicine of Heidelberg University, Kuhn Papers (*Archiv des Instituts für Geschichte der Medizin der Universität Heidelberg, NL Kühn*): letter from Kühn to Verschuer, 22 October 1946. I thank Hans-Jörg Rheinberger for indicating this source to me.

Considering that sooner or later the KWS would become again "an inter-allied affair," Kühn pleaded early for a strategy of limited self-purification. The elitist research organization should on its own make sure "that the seriously incriminated had to resign," since otherwise "the situation would deteriorate for everybody, no doubt," Kühn wrote.[22] After Havemann had provoked Verschuer's professional ban in Hesse, Butenandt's enthusiasm for placing Verschuer in Tübingen was waning as well.[23] Yet, he assured Verschuer in a letter that he would continue to work "in silence ... on all projects of our interest and the realization of our goals."[24] But after these plans failed with the appointment of Günther Just (1892–1950) to the Tübingen professorship in the summer of 1948, Butenandt did not contact Verschuer for a whole year.[25]

Rajewski played a doubly false game in Frankfurt am Main. He and Verschuer had been acquaintances since the days of Verschuer's professorship in Frankfurt. Yet, in November 1945, Verschuer himself considered a "close personal and scientific connection" with him "impossible": "My acquaintance with his personality is sufficient to know that I will not be able to maintain and establish a mutual KWS spirit with him."[26] But in the hour of need, ranks were closed. Rajewski did not mind at all when Verschuer transferred the Berlin-evacuated institute equipment from Solz to his own KWI for Biophysics in Frankfurt. He was even interested in offering it to the town or university of Frankfurt as the basis for a yet to be founded Institute for Anthropology at Frankfurt University.[27]

But Rajewski was by no means interested in Verschuer as an institute director. Rajeweski was involved in committees at the KWS as well as for higher education policy at Frankfurt University. In 1948, he was rumored to be the coming dean of his faculty and was appointed chancellor in 1949. But until 1949, he took no steps to advance the plans (pursued by Verschuer's old friends from the medical faculty since the end of war, which had been put on ice by Havemann's intervention) for Verschuer's reappointment to

---

[22] MPG-Archiv, Abt. III, Rep. 84/1, No. 596: letter from Kühn to Butenandt, 30 November 1945; on Kühn's also see Schüring, "Vorgang," 288 f.

[23] MPG-Archiv, Abt. III, Rep. 84/2 (former folder 357): letters from Butenandt to Verschuer, 27 June and 12 August 1946, 12 February 1947

[24] MPG-Archiv, Abt. III, Rep. 84/2 (former folder 357): letter from Butenandt to Verschuer, 19 June 1947.

[25] MPG-Archiv, Abt. III, Rep. 84/2 (former folder 357): letter from Butenandt to Verschuer, 27 August 1948 and 1 August 1949. On the history of the Tübingen chair for anthropology, see Kröner, *Rassenhygiene*, 150–173.

[26] MPG-Archiv, Abt. III, Rep. 84/1, No. 601: letter from Verschuer to Butenandt, 16 November 1945.

[27] For the developing conflicts about the institute equipment until the mid-1950s between the former heads of department at the KWI for Anthropology, especially Gottschaldt, Nachtsheim, and Muckermann, see Kröner, *Rassenhygiene*, 222–235.

the chair he had held from 1936 to 1942.[28] Instead, in the summer of 1948, Rajewski, in his position as chair of the Biological-Medical Section of the MPS, agreed with his colleague Hartmann that a resurrection of the KWIA was out of question for the time being, in particular due to the "question of the institute's director."[29] As late as 1950, Rajeweski told a representative of the General Administration that his own position toward Verschuer was "more negative than benevolent."[30]

For his part, Hartmann made a distinction between his science policy intentions and his humanitarian collegial attitude when he approached the MPS president after Verschuer had asked him for assistance in April 1949:[31]

Although I objected right from the beginning to the establishment of a Kaiser Wilhelm Institute for Human Heredity and Anthropology, and also regard a reestablishment of such within the scope of the Max Planck Society as inopportune, I nevertheless consider the whole position taken and the accusations against Verschuer to be extremely unfair. Of all the investigations into human heredity, Professor von Verschuer's twin research is by far the most significant. ... Given that he now cannot work freely, rather instead, as I was told by someone else, has to struggle to make ends meet, I consider it an obligation of honor for the Max Planck Society to take care of him.[32]

Verschuer knew he had enemies in the General Administration of the KWS/MPS. During his visits to Göttingen he felt as though he was looking into "abysses."[33] In 1946, interim president Max Planck had refused to intervene with the allies in favor of Verschuer.[34] His successor Otto Hahn would have preferred to have been ignorant of Verschuer and his science. If anthropological or human genetic research was to be continued at all in the newly founded MPS, it would have to be as far away as possible, hidden behind the "Iron Curtain" in Berlin and directed by the Jesuit Hermann Muckermann (1877–1962); Muckermann, whose reappointment was supported by the Allies, had been dismissed as head of department at the KWIA in 1933. Another possible choice was former department head Hans Nachtsheim,

---

[28] MPG-Archiv, II. Abt. Rep 1A: Personalia Verschuer, No. 5: note Telschow, 4 October 1948.

[29] MPG-Archiv, III. Abt. Rep 47: Hartmann papers, No. 1172, letters from Rajewski to Hartmann, 21 June (quote) and 13 July 1948; letter from Hartmann to Rajewski, 3 August 1948.

[30] MPG-Archiv, II. Abt. Rep 1A, Personalia Verschuer, No. 7: memo Pollay, 20 March 1950.

[31] MPG-Archiv, III. Abt. Rep 47, Hartmann papers, No. 1505: letter from Verschuer to Hartmann, 12 April 1949.

[32] MPG-Archiv, II. Abt. Rep 1A, Personalia Verschuer, No. 6: letter from Hartmann to Hahn, 29 June 1949.

[33] MPG-Archiv, Abt. III, Rep. 84/2 (former folder 357): letter from Verschuer to Butenandt, 16 May 1946.

[34] MPG-Archiv, II. Abt. Rep 1A, Personalia Verschuer, No. 5: letter from Verschuer to Planck, 7 October 1946 and draft of Planck's answer, undated.

who had remained in Berlin, kept distance between himself and the NSDAP, and participated as a member of the Havemann Commission in demolishing his former director.[35]

Without a doubt, however, Verschuer's worst enemy was Ernst Telschow, who – in spite of his own active participation as a party and state official during the Third Reich – had been Secretary General of the KWS/MPS since 1937 and was still powerful. Telschow clearly did not take *moral* offense at Verschuer's racist political statements or his scientific cooperation with Mengele in Auschwitz. He remained, for example, quite well disposed toward Verschuer's former assistant Karin Magnussen, the ex-Nazi activist and iris heterochromia researcher, who had initially remained in Berlin. Instead, Telschow took *personal* offense at Verschuer's "desertion" from Dahlem to Solz in February 1945.[36] However, after the collapse of the Third Reich, Telschow regarded Verschuer as an incalculable liability for the future of the MPS.

Verschuer in turn coincided in his characterization of the "gray eminence" of the KWS/MPS with Butenandt and paradoxically also largely with the Jewish scientist Otto Meyerhoff (1884–1953), who had been displaced in 1938:

Just like Telschow pushed through the National Socialist revolution within the KWS ... , and removed Jews and Jewish half-breeds from the KWS, he now is not only keen to make "reparations" but also anxious to deny everything he considers possibly damaging to him in the eyes of the new powers. Obviously the "advancement of the General Administration" is given priority over the "advancement of sciences," a distressing experience we frequently had during the last years in Dahlem![37]

---

[35] MPG-Archiv, Abt. III, Rep. 84/2 (former folder 357): letter from Verschuer to Butenandt, 16 May 1946; II. Abt. Rep 1A, Personalia Verschuer, No. 6: letter from Hahn to Muckermann, 21 April 1949. See also Kröner Rassenhygiene, 199, and Dagmar Grosch-Obenauer, "Hermann Muckermann und die Eugenik," Ph.D. diss., University of Mainz (1986).

[36] See Kröner, *Rassenhygiene*, 100–102. As late as 1960 Telschow still expressed his personal reservations against Verschuer, who in 1945 had "defected from Berlin and abandoned his employees," MPG-Archiv, Abt. II, Rep 1A (Personalia Verschuer), March 1955–July 1986: excerpt from the minutes (draft) of the meeting of the Besprechungskreis "Wissenschaftspolitik" in Hamburg on 30 September 1960. On the occasion of Telschow's obituary in 1988, Karin Magnussen expressed once more with warm words her gratitude and regard toward the deceased secretary general in a letter to Butenandt, 27 October 1988, MPG-Archiv, Abt. III, Rep. 84/2, No. 3705.

[37] MPG-Archiv, Abt. III, Rep. 84/2 (former folder 357): letter from Verschuer to Butenandt, 23 July 1946 and Butenandt's answers, 12 August 1946 and 17 December 1946. On Meyerhoff, see Michael Schüring, "Ein Dilemma der Kontinuität. Das Selbstverständnis der Max-Planck-Gesellschaft und der Umgang mit Emigrantinnen und Emigranten in den 1950er Jahren," in Rüdiger vom Bruch and Brigitte Kaderas (eds.), *Wissenschaft und Wissenschaftspolitik. Bestandsaufnahmen zu Formationen, Brüchen und Kontinuitäten im Deutschland des 20. Jahrhundert* (Stuttgart: Steiner, 2002), 453–463; also see Schüring's chapter in this volume.

Yet neither Hahn nor Telschow possessed an effective strategy to get rid of Verschuer's legacy discreetly. Their critical comments about Verschuer to the Hessian ministries confirmed them in maintaining their professional ban and not appointing Verschuer to Frankfurt University.[38] Thus, Rajewski, Hahn, and Telschow themselves had obstructed the elegant solution of getting rid of him by facilitating his appointment elsewhere.

Verschuer for his part was not willing to accept a subordinate position, mediocre research contracts, and a meager income; instead, he was adamant about restitution of his contract with the Kaiser Wilhelm Society for permanent, lifelong tenure.[39] The attempt to push him away silently was thwarted, not only by Verschuer's self-confident obstinacy but also by his scientific reputation, which Hartmann, Butenandt, and Rajewski acknowledged, both among themselves as well as to him. Verschuer's research work with twins was indisputable.[40] Butenandt valued in particular the research on heredity of tuberculosis resistance or disposition that Karl Diehl had performed during the last war years in an outpost of the KWIA. Butenandt was in favor of resuming cooperation with Diehl after his move to the Taunus.[41] In spite of all the public attacks, Verschuer was acknowledged beyond the realm of the KWS/MPS – for instance, as a member of the Prussian Academy of Sciences (*Preussische Akademie der Wissenschaften*) and co-founder of the Academy of Sciences (*Akademie für Wissenschaften*) in Mainz.[42] Perhaps these were the reasons the MPS had never considered the direct solution of giving him notice. So, like it or not, the obstacles standing in the way of another appointment had to be removed, unless one was willing to welcome Verschuer and his former institute back into the reconstituting circle of the

---

[38] MPG-Archiv, II. Abt. Rep. 1A, Personalia Verschuer, No. 5: letter from Hahn to Hessisches Staatsministerium (Ministry of the Interior), 18 March 1947 and 11 February 1948; note Telschow, 4 October 1948.

[39] MPG-Archiv, III. Abt. Rep 47, Hartmann papers, No. 1505: letter from Verschuer to Hartmann, 12 April 1949.

[40] MPG-Archiv, Abt. II, Rep. 1A, Personalia Verschuer, No. 6: letter from Hartmann to Hahn, 29 June 1949.

[41] MPG-Archiv, Abt. III, Rep. 84/2 (former folder 357): letter from Butenandt to Verschuer, 19 June 1947 and 17 December 1949; Abt. II, Rep. 1A, Personalia Verschuer, No. 7: letter from Diehl to Muckermann, 18 December 1949 and letter from Muckermann to Rajewski, 29 December 1949, where he made clear that Verschuer did not understand anything about Diehl's research and praised himself highly regarding the tuberculosis research. See also Sachse and Massin, 37.

[42] Dean's Archive of the Department of Medicine, Frankfurt University (Frankfurt am Main), Human Genetics, Institute for Heredity (*Dekanatsarchiv des Fachbereichs Medizin der Universität Frankfurt am Main, Humangenetik, Institut für Vererbungswissenschaften, DA-FB*), Human Genetics, Institute for Heredity, vol. I, 1933–1986: memo regarding a visit Verschuer paid to the Surgical Clinic on 11 January 1950. I thank Florian Schmaltz for indicating this collection of documents to me, which will be consulted in more detail in the last section.

MPS bioscientists that Butenandt and his colleagues wanted to keep as small and elite as possible.

That was the problem to be solved in the MPS Scientific Council and Senate on July 21 and 22, 1949, and why Hartmann and Butenandt were asked to attend as well. Butenandt emphasized Verschuer's difficult financial situation. President Hahn stressed that the General Administration could act at best according to the "legal regulations for supplanted officials" but was by no means willing to recognize Verschuer's claims to support from the new MPS. Instead, he hoped to move the Hessian minister of education to lift the professional ban with a vote by the Scientific Council. Though Rajewski expressed doubts in the Senate's meeting on July 22,[43] he was nevertheless willing to set up a new commission and refute the negative report from the Havemann commission in 1946.[44] He communicated as much to Verschuer, who took responsibility for scheduling the meeting "with the other gentlemen."[45] First, he asked Hartmann and Heubner, who promptly agreed. Verschuer obviously hesitated in Butenandt's case, as Butenandt had not responded to Verschuer's letter from April 1949 and his description of his financial misery.

But Butenandt by no means wanted to be left out of this commission, and without being asked imposed himself as a "friend":

I hope you are not overly cross with me or even came to the conclusion that you have to count me out as a friend. The duties of the whole term have been so demanding, that only now after its completion can I slowly get around to dealing with an immense correspondence. But among friends actions speak louder than words. I hope that in the meantime Mr. Rajewski has had the chance to tell you about the last Senate meeting of the Max Planck Society. I participated as a guest and had expected that following your request transmitted by Prof. Hartmann, your matter would be somehow open to debate. But that was not the case and I had to bring this issue up under the topic Miscellanea. Though no resolution has yet been adopted ... I nevertheless believe I have achieved that in Göttingen they will no longer hide behind those legal formulations; first of all there is the president's promise for immediate economic support. ... I myself give you my word that I will keep an eye on the affair and will not rest until it is entirely clarified. I ask you to keep me up to date. I rarely see Hartmann and thus had no chance to discuss the matter with him.[46]

[43] MPG-Archiv, II. Abt. Rep. 1A, Personalia Verschuer, No. 6: letter from Hahn to Hartmann, 4 July 1949; Auszug aus der Niederschrift über die Sitzung des Senats, 22 July 1949

[44] From Verschuer's letters to Hartmann, 29 June 1949 (MPG-Archiv, III. Abt. Rep. 47, Hartmann papers, No. 1505) and to Butenandt, 5 August 1949 (MPG-Archiv, Abt. III, Rep. 84/2 [former folder 357]), it follows that Rajewski first suggested the creation of said commission to Verschuer, who then suggested Butenandt, Heubner, and Hartmann.

[45] MPG-Archiv, III. Abt., Rep. 47, Hartmann papers, No. 1505: letter from Verschuer to Hartmann, 26 July 1949.

[46] MPG-Archiv, Abt. III, Rep. 84/2 (former folder 357): letter from Butenandt to Verschuer, 1 August 1949. According to the record, it was Rajewski who, several months later,

Verschuer got the message and immediately asked Butenandt to attend the scheduled meeting of the commission in September 1949.[47]

A MEMORANDUM IS (NOT) A "WHITEWASH CERTIFICATE"

In the attempt to cut their losses according to a kind of "not in my backyard" principle, the Stuttgart commission was conducted with much more effort than was usual for the "whitewash certificates" widely used in the scientific community. Such denazification certificates were required everywhere for presentation at denazification trial courts, reemployment procedures, or job applications during the first postwar years. Well-known scientists like Werner Heisenberg or Arnold Sommerfeld, but also displaced colleagues like James Franck or Lise Meitner, were overwhelmed with requests for denazification certificates.

In particular, the type of "whitewash certificate" that the scientists who had remained in Germany issued each other mostly followed a similar pattern and seldom contained more than one page. First came a brief explanation of how one was acquainted with the person in question. Next came the declaration that he or she had always behaved decently and had more or less openly expressed (or at least confidentially disclosed) opposition to National Socialism. If necessary and possible, individual courses of action or behavior patterns that seemed to prove the first statement were accentuated. In this regard, support of persecuted Jewish acquaintances or colleagues was best. Alternatively, the authors liked to mention the upstanding fight for or skillful maneuver in support of the continuation of an unsoiled science. Whenever possible, membership to the Confessing Church (*Bekennende Kirche*) was emphasized. That was followed by the appeal to the addressee – that is, the denazification trial court, employment, or regulatory agencies – to rehabilitate the person in question or facilitate his or her reentry into the profession. In conclusion, the author noted that he himself had never been a member of the NSDAP or had been classified "not incriminated" (*unbelastet*), or at least held his present office with Allied authorization.[48]

---

tried again to adjust the minutes in favor of Verschuer and his financial claims, a request thwarted by Telschow (MPG-Archiv, II. Abt. Rep. 1A, Personalia Verschuer, No. 6: 2 November 1949).

[47] MPG-Archiv, Abt. III, Rep. 84/2 (former folder 357): letter from Verschuer to Butenandt, 5 August 1949. See also Carola Sachse, "Adolf Butenandt und Otmar von Verschuer. Eine Freundschaft unter Wissenschaftlern (1942–1969)," in Schieder and Trunk, 286–319.

[48] Mark Walker has collected about 60 "*Persilscheine*" predominantly produced by Arnold Sommerfeld and Werner Heisenberg, which he kindly made available to me. Also see Mark Walker, *German National Socialism and the Quest for Nuclear Power, 1939–1949* (Cambridge: Cambridge University Press, 1989), 192–204, and David C. Cassidy, *Uncertainty: The Life and Science of Werner Heisenberg* (New York: Freeman, 1991), 529–530.

The most palpable difference between the Stuttgart memorandum and the source genre "whitewash certificate" is length.[49] The memorandum is thirteen carefully composed pages: introductory protocol, statement of the existing evidence, an argument subdivided into five sections, conclusion, and verdict. The document written down by Heubner and signed by every one of the "four gentlemen involved" signaled in both form and style the significance of the venture. The authors introduced themselves in the first sentence by name and stated that "upon the request" of Verschuer they had convened at that particular place and date. The purpose of this event was, in their words, to comment on the charges made against Verschuer and "to come to decide whether or not the person in question had forfeited the qualification to exercise a public and official function."[50]

That is, they regarded themselves as neither advocates nor experts but as a board of judges. They intended to give neither individual references for their colleague's character nor a collective scientific report on his research practice. Instead, they planned to announce an intersubjective judgment on the professional reusability of the racial scientist and medical geneticist Verschuer. It was a matter of revising the first report, which Huebner had received in December 1946. This report had been written as a letter and also in the form of a legal protocol by the secretary of the Havemann Commission and newly appointed director of the KWI for Foreign and International Private Law, Karl von Lewinski. The second purpose of the self-proclaimed board of judges was to address the Frankfurt Denazification Court ruling and the professional ban of Verschuer by the Hessian minister of culture. The four gentlemen gathered in Stuttgart pronounced themselves the final authority that was willing and authorized to render a definitive judgment.

Yet they used the well-proven whiteners of the prevalent "whitewash certificate" culture for their explanations. On the path to acquittal, the four bioscientists developed these phrases into true argumentative cornerstones, with which they marked out the terrain they claimed in their own interest for defining the politics of the past.

First, they explained the difference between an "experienced scholar" (*erfahrenen Gelehrten*) and a "committed Nazi" (*überzeugten Nationalsozialisten*). This included regularly saying grace at meals, a relatively late entry into the NSDAP, not wearing the party insignia at the institute, restricting the "Nazi salute" to only official events as well as being eventually judged a "fellow traveler" by the Denazification Court. Statements of NSDAP officials, criticizing the accused for an insufficient "inner commitment," were as credible as those made by pastors confirming his visits to

---

[49] Kröner, *Rassenhygiene*, 132–136, and Proctor, 26–3, offer detailed paraphrases of the memorandum.

[50] Denkschrift 1949, 1.

church. A medical geneticist like Verschuer distinguished himself through his conduct not as a "Nazi" but rather "in the spirit of Christian charity," acting – in the affirmative words of the head nurse at Verschuer's institutes in Frankfurt and Dahlem – by putting special emphasis "on taking humane affectionate care of our patients ... given that these were people, who came to us, not seeking the cure of a disease, but rather for a determination whether or not they would be allowed to marry and have children."[51]

Second, the four bioscientists defined the difference between a "racial fanatic" and a scientist who practiced "hereditary biology and eugenics according to scientific and objective principles." They made no positive statement, however, regarding what "scientific" hereditary biology or "objective" eugenics would be. They contented themselves with arguing from the contrary (*argumentum a contrario*): the subject of attacks by the "real racial fanatics" was negative proof (*ex negativo*) that the science was "pure" – for instance, the talk Verschuer gave at the Academy in 1944 on "Hereditary Disposition as Fate and Task" (*Erbanlage als Schicksal und Aufgabe*), which the head of the Racial Policy Office (*Rassenpolitisches Amt*) of the NSDAP, Walter Gross (1904–1945), criticized as "renunciation of National Socialism."[52]

In a second example, the fact that Heinrich Wilhelm Kranz (1897–1945), Verschuer's successor to the Frankfurt professorship and "racial fanatic," preferred hereditary statistics and racial anthropology supposedly proved that the hereditary pathology practiced by Verschuer, first in Frankfurt and later in Dahlem, was science beyond "any political ideology." This was quite a remarkable argumentative turn because the postwar self-reflection and justification debates declared the inner science discourse as rather apolitical and ideology free. Yet, here a dispute over methodology in science was belatedly, but likewise with an exonerating intention, reinterpreted politically. As a scientist, Verschuer had "always maintained a strict objective line" and had strived "to set limits to the race-biased doctrines ... or at least soften their effects," the four scientists argued. This was manifested, it continued, by the fact that Verschuer had "carried out the expert function imposed upon him with utmost human understanding and benevolence toward Jews and Jewish kin."[53]

Third, the self-proclaimed judges stated that a scientist was not responsible for the political opinions and conclusions about race of those who regarded themselves as students of his doctrine. They distinguished Verschuer's followers into his "true pupils," who like their teacher applied "scientific and moral purity,"[54] and the "many younger people" whose growing belief in the

---

[51] Denkschrift 1949, 2–4.
[52] Otmar von Verschuer, "Erbanlage als Schicksal und Aufgabe," *Preussische Akademie der Wissenschaften. Vorträge und Schriften*, 18 (1944).
[53] Denkschrift 1949, 4–6.
[54] Denkschrift 1949, 4.

Nazi ideology strengthened their interest in heredity, hereditary pathology, and eugenics. If Verschuer had granted them a chance as well, this was even better proof of his "good democratic tradition." He had only acknowledged scientific "competence" while regarding "political attitude and conduct outside the institute as a private matter." [55]

The commission invested its greatest argumentative effort on its fourth topic, addressing Verschuer's "Connections to Auschwitz." He had received human specimens from Auschwitz inmates; this was undisputed as its account in the memorandum essentially matches our contemporary knowledge. However, in fierce words that differed distinctly from the tone of the rest of the text, the members of the commission rejected the suggestion that Verschuer had been aware of the mass extermination in Auschwitz at the time the specimens were received. The assumption that Mengele had ever informed Verschuer about the proceedings in Auschwitz was "a captious, unfounded and downright incredible construction." [56] Further on the text called it "not only an unproved, but psychologically rather unlikely deduction" and – this was repeated once more – "a rather arbitrary construction." [57] It was presented as a "fact" that in 1943/44 Verschuer had no other choice than to regard Mengele as an "army doctor" (*Lazarettarzt*) in one of the usual concentration camps. They even dared to question – absurdly so in view of the Nuremberg Medical trial and years of press coverage – whether Mengele himself had been aware of the "*atrocities and killings at Auschwitz*" [58] when he delivered the blood samples to Dahlem in 1943. In doing so, Butenandt, Hartmann, Rajewski, and their secretary Heubner defended their own right to ignorance with a linguistic vehemence that has to be interpreted as an expression of their own consternation.

This question had already divided the Havemann Commission in 1946, which otherwise had agreed on their essential conviction of Verschuer. In a conversation with Havemann in 1946, following his newspaper article, the hereditary biologist Hans Nachtsheim, who after 1946 repeatedly attacked his former institute director Verschuer in public, had already rejected the notion that "the use of material from a concentration camp" had to be regarded "per se as a crime." After all, it was common practice to use "material as well in rather large quantities from jails, and so on," he stated.

One could only reproach Verschuer if he had been aware of the fact that the individuals, from whom the eyes originated, did not die of natural causes or even had been killed to get those eyes. One must not doubt Verschuer's good faith. [59]

---

[55] Denkschrift 1949, 6–7.
[56] Denkschrift 1949, 8.
[57] Denkschrift 1949, 9.
[58] Denkschrift 1949, 8.
[59] MPG-Archiv, III. Abt. Rep 20 B, Nachtsheim papers, No. 13: record Nachtsheim made of a conversation with Havemann on 9 May 1946.

Nachtsheim himself had conducted (in fact, in cooperation with one of Butenandt's staff members, Gerhard Ruhenstroth-Bauer, 1913–2004) low-pressure experiments with six epileptic children from the "euthanasia" institution Brandenburg-Görden – although this was hardly well known at this time.[60] Being a member of the Havemann Commission, he insisted on his minority vote regarding the question of whether Verschuer was aware of the reality of Auschwitz.[61] Similarly, commission member Heubner, who had been unable to attend the meeting of the Havemann commission, had immediately protested against Verschuer's alleged awareness of Auschwitz in early 1947: no evidence existed, he stated, and it was "a false assumption to believe, that in those days everybody had to be aware of what was going on in Auschwitz":

As for myself, I have to say that I had by no means any idea of the many things that I learned during the past year and half, and that I have to concede the possibility of the same condition to anybody else. [62]

In fact, in 1943 Heubner had attended a meeting where one of the topics was the sulphonamide experiments conducted at the women's concentration camp at Ravensbrück, whereby the victims were deliberately wounded, infected with bacteria, and then treated with these drugs in order to test their efficacy. Moreover, he was involved in the seawater experiments conducted on inmates from the Dachau concentration camp. Here the victims were starved and given only sea water to drink.[63] Butenandt, on the other hand, had commissioned his employee Günther Hillmann to assist Verschuer in the experimental evaluation of the blood samples from Auschwitz from October 1944 to February 1945.[64]

---

[60] See Sachse and Massin, 36 f. For a detailed history, see Alexander von Schwerin, *Experimentalisierung des Menschen. Der Genetiker Hans Nachtsheim und die vergleichende Erbpathologie 1920–1945* (Göttingen: Wallstein, 2004), 281–328. On further involvement of Nachtsheim in medical crimes, see Paul Weindling, "Genetik und Menschenversuche in Deutschland, 1940–1950. Hans Nachtsheim, die Kaninchen von Dahlem und die Kinder vom Bullenhuser Damm," in Hans-Walter Schmuhl (ed.), *Rassenforschung Kaiser-Wilhelm-Instituten vor und nach 1933* (Göttingen: Wallstein, 2003), 245–274.

[61] MPG-Archiv, III. Abt. Rep 20 B, Nachtsheim papers, No. 13: letter from Nachtsheim to Lewinski, 17 September 1946.

[62] MPG-Archiv, II. Abt. Rep. 1 A, Personalia Verschuer, No. 5: letter from Heubner to Lewinski, 11 January 1947.

[63] Kneer, *Heubner*, 78–86; both experiments are well known and in 1946/1947 were presented as evidence at the Nuremberg Physicians Trial. See Angelika Ebbinghaus and Karl Heinz Roth, "Kriegswunden. Die kriegschirurgischen Experimente in den Konzentrationslagern und ihre Hintergründe," in Angelika Ebbinghaus and Klaus Dörner (eds.), *Vernichten und Heilen. Der Nürnberger Ärzteprozeß und seine Folgen* (Berlin: Aufbau Verlag, 2002), 177–218; Wolfgang Eckart (ed.), *Man, Medicine, and the State. The Human Body as an Object of Government Sponsored Medical Research in the 20th Century* (Stuttgart: Steiner Verlag, 2006).

[64] See Sachse and Massin, 37 f., and Achim Trunk's chapter in this volume.

Despite the sternly postulated denial that it had been possible to know about Auschwitz, the four colleagues then proceeded to allow for this possibility in Verschuer's case. Evidently, they interrogated him empathically regarding the heterochromatic eye-pairs delivered to his research assistant Karin Magnussen. In any event, he now admitted, in addition to his written statements from 1946 and 1947, that in case of the first delivery of eye-pairs he had read the autopsy report provided.[65] After that, the commission obviously was no longer convinced that Verschuer really did not know more than what they deemed possible for themselves. Hence, they withdrew to the position that at least there was no proof "that Frhr. v. Verschuer would have been compelled to assume that something about the extraction of this eye material might have been unethical."[66]

Following this linguistic somersault in triple subjunctive (in the original German), the commission dealt in the fifth and final section with Verschuer's racist political publications. They could not deny or justify these without losing their own credibility. The commission members were not willing to follow Verschuer when he tried to reinterpret his 1936 eulogy on Hitler's "seizure of power" into a patriotic testimony of hope for reformation.[67] They similarly insisted on rejecting his sentence that the "*Solution to the Jewish Question*" was scientifically grounded in the concept of race. [68] Yet, they were inclined to interpret favorably his jubilation over the racist political implementation of his scientific findings as the "expression of satisfaction by a representative of science that the results of his area of expertise received public attention and acknowledgment," the more so as he had emphasized "'how tremendously' the responsibility of the expert scholar 'had grown'" and had repeatedly called for special welfare state assistance for the victims of forced sterilization. [69]

They conceded that he had been in an awkward position, his science being politically harassed "more from the inside than from the outside." He had to "welcome" racist political measures "out of scientific conviction," "the degree of which then ran contrary to his Christian beliefs." [70] He had been no longer able to distinguish between politics and science and had parroted many things that "buzzed around him daily." Moreover, he had given in to indulgence, misjudgment, and opportunism. Although the commission had

[65] MPG-Archiv, II. Abt., Rep. 1A, Personalia Verschuer, No. 5: statement under oath by Verschuer, 10 May 1946; letter from Verschuer to Hahn, 23 May 1946 (with annexes); III. Abt., Rep. 47, Hartmann papers, No. 1505: statement by Verschuer, 20 February 1947.
[66] Denkschrift 1949, 10.
[67] Otmar von Verschuer, *Rassenhygiene als Wissenschaft und Staatsaufgabe* (*Frankfurter Akademische Reden*, No. 7) (Frankfurt am Main: Bechhold, 1936).
[68] Denkschrift 1949, 11.
[69] Denkschrift 1949, 12.
[70] Denkschrift 1949, 13.

implicitly denied Verschuer's ability to be an independently thinking scientist, they nevertheless did not intend to disqualify him as "researcher, teacher, and expert." Despite "some blotches," he stood out "brightly" when compared to the other representatives of the "heredity- and race-research" (*Erb- und Rassenforschung*). There could be no doubt regarding the scientific need to continue this specific field, and this field still needed Verschuer. [71]

Not one sentence of the four bioscientists' extensive memorandum examined Verschuer's research direction, his scientific paradigms, or his experimental practices. For the sake of their own credibility they were obliged to disassociate themselves from some of his racist political comments. But in view of his "humane and noble attitude," manifested above all in his activities as a church member, they judged his past words and actions as venial sins that did not conflict with his future value at a West German university. Verschuer possessed "all the qualities," they claimed, "that predestined him to be a researcher and teacher for academic youth." [72] The verdict was this:

We consider his reappointment in particular to be highly desirable, since we still consider scientific work in this field valuable and indispensable, in spite of the abuse committed in the name of heritage and race. Therefore we would not want a scientist as experienced as Prof. Frh. v. Verschuer to be sidelined. [73]

SUSTAINABLE SUPPRESSION?

After Heubner had put the memorandum into writing and the other three authors had signed it during a meeting in Tübingen in mid-October 1949, Rajewski received it "for further use." [74] Back in Frankfurt, he immediately saw to it that the dean of the Medical Faculty agreed with the vote and informed the Hessian ministry of education accordingly. Minister Stein was persuaded by the expertise of professional excellence assembled in the Stuttgart commission along with the faculty vote and lifted the professional ban against Verschuer in the beginning of November. Thereupon the Medical Faculty submitted its appointment proposal with Verschuer ranked first. [75]

[71] Denkschrift 1949, 13.
[72] Denkschrift 1949, 13.
[73] Denkschrift 1949, 13.
[74] MPG-Archiv, Abt. III, Rep. 84/2 (former folder 357): letter from Heubner to Butenandt et al., 29 September 1949; Butenandt's response, 17 October 1949 (quotation).
[75] MPG-Archiv, Abt. III, Rep. 84/2 (former folder 357): letter from Stein (Hessian education minister) to Verschuer, 7 November 1949; MPG-Archiv, Abt. II, Rep. 1A, Personalia Verschuer, No. 6: note, 2 November 1949; letter from Rajewski to Hahn, 3 November 1949; memo Seeliger, 9 November 1949; MPG-Archiv, Abt. II, Rep. 1A, Personalia Verschuer, No. 7: file note, 20 March 1950. DA-FB, vol. II, letter from the dean to Rajewski (Rektor of University of Frankfurt), 23 May 1950, withdrawing the list from 9 November 1949.

However, by now the mood in Frankfurt had changed. In the end nobody wanted him there any longer. Since the Frankfurt University was a foundation under public law, along with the Hessian ministry of education, the Frankfurt City Council, which had great influence in the university's board of trustees, also had a say in the appointments.[76] Local political representatives and sensitized university policy committees impeded the reappointment of the incriminated racial researcher to Frankfurt University in opposition to the votes of his renowned colleagues, faculty members, and departmental ministerial supervisors.

At the request of Rajewski, who had taken the office of university chancellor in 1949, a committee was set up in January 1950 including five university deans and three city councilors. This extended "Fellow Traveler Committee" (*Mitläuferausschuss*) summoned Verschuer, and during four sessions examined his racist political and hereditary biological publications, considered his "political behavior in general," and finally came to the conclusion that Verschuer lacked "an indispensable prerequisite for the appointment to a chair," namely, "the integrity of a teacher."[77]

Yet another important voice took the floor – that of the "former, meanwhile reappointed member" of the Medical Faculty, dermatologist Oscar Gans (1888–1983), who in 1946 had returned from exile. He threatened that if Verschuer was appointed, he would "have to draw his necessary conclusions." In view of the "newly created situation," the faculty withdrew its appointment proposal to Verschuer in May 1950.[78] In doing so the university was well advised, since Gans, who in the same year assumed office as dean of the Medical Faculty, found out from Walter Hallstein (1901–1982), state secretary at the Foreign Office, that Verschuer's appointment would have caused "decidedly sharp protest in the United States ... and severe consequences for the relationship between our university and the universities in America."[79]

Rajewski, as head of the MPS's medical-biological section, wanted nothing better than to hand over Verschuer to the university; but as the university's chancellor, Rajewski had to avert political damage to this very university, so he found himself in an awkward conflict of loyalties. As he complained in a letter to MPS president Hahn:

[76] DA-FB, vol. II: letter from the Dean to the Counterpart of Münster University, Rohrschneider, 20 June 1950.
[77] DA-FB, Human Genetics, Institute for Heredity, vol. II: file note regarding Verschuer's visit on 11 January 1950; invitation of the Mitläuferausschuss zum 14 January 1950; record by Verschuer, 13 February 1950; Resolution of the Kuratoriumsausschuss, 15 February 1950 (quotes).
[78] DA-FB, Human Genetics, Institute for Heredity, vol. II: letter from the Dean of the Medical Faculty to the Ministry for Culture and National Education, 19 May 1950.
[79] DA-FB, Human Genetics, Institute for Heredity, vol. II: notation Gans, 2 November 1950.

You will understand the delicate situation I am in. On the one hand, I would like to help Herrn v. Verschuer for I am convinced that he is not as politically incriminated as it appears. On the other hand, the objections and oppositions to his activation are so great that it will be hardly possible to find a satisfactory solution for him. Naturally the Max Planck Society is immediately affected by this whole affair. [80]

The case of Verschuer remained on the MPS agenda. In 1949, the Senate had already taken Butenandt's warning not to "burden" the Society with a new Institute for Anthropology and continued playing for time.[81] This was an enervating but in the end easy game to play. The former department directors of the KWIA who had remained in Berlin, Hans Nachtsheim and Hermann Muckermann, blocked each other with their requests for a new institute, and their claims could also be used to stall Verschuer. Though he was back on the payroll, nobody apart from himself considered establishing a Max Planck Institute under his direction.[82]

More than a year later, in the spring of 1951, Verschuer finally received – thanks to his old teacher, good friend, and predecessor as director of the former KWIA Eugen Fischer – the appointment to the "chair for human hereditary research and anthropology" at the University of Münster, which he renamed right away as a professorship for "Human Genetics."[83] Immediately afterward, Rajeweski wrote MPS Hahn that this news had brought a sense of "release," continuing that at last the "many difficulties hovering above us are solved."[84]

But the aftershocks continued and recurred at longer intervals. Verschuer kept on acting like the "master of the house" at his old Kaiser Wilhelm Institute and demanded in a long-lasting dispute the restitution of the equipment he had evacuated from Berlin.[85] More than anyone else, Butenandt acted as his advocate in the committees of the MPS and finally accomplished the transfer to Münster of the boxes still in storage with Rajewski. But if Butenandt had hoped to get the "skeletons out of the closets" of the elite organization and to keep the unloved friend at a distance, he was mistaken about Verschuer's obstinacy. Hardly established in Münster, Verschuer

[80] MPG-Archiv, Abt. II, Rep. 1A Personalia Verschuer, No. 8: letter from Rajewski to Hahn, 4 April 1950.
[81] MPG-Archiv, II. Abt. Rep. 1A, Personalia Verschuer, No. 6: excerpt from the report of MPS Senate meeting on 18 November 1949; excerpt from the minutes of the Executive Committee meeting on 14 January 1950.
[82] In detail Kröner, *Rassenhygiene*, chap. IV.
[83] DA-FB, vol. II: letter from Rohrschneider to the Dean of the Medical Faculty of Frankfurt University, 1 June 1950; MPG-Archiv, III. Abt., Rep. 84/2: letter from Verschuer to Butenandt, 12 March 1951.
[84] MPG-Archiv, II. Abt. Rep. 1A, Personalia Verschuer, No. 9: letter from Rajewski to Hahn, 31 March 1951.
[85] MPG-Archiv, II. Abt., Rep. 1A, Personalia Verschuer, No. 8: letter from Verschuer to Hahn, 25 May 1950.

decided in the summer of 1954 that time had come for "reparation" for the "injustice" done to him. The "open wound" caused by his "discontinued" Kaiser Wilhelm Institute had to be healed at long last. Verschuer had already conducted a preliminary conversation with Hahn regarding the foundation of a Max Planck Institute for Human Genetics, but the MPS president had reacted dismissively. As usual, Verschuer counted on the support of his best friend within the MPS. As usual, Butenandt did two kinds of things: first, he assured his friend in a Sibylline letter of thanks, that he, Verschuer, was familiar with Butenandt's basic attitude (in that respect) and that he was going to find out from the General Administration exactly what the situation was; second, he wrote a more straightforward letter to Hahn in which he admonished "that no kind of decision making should occur before scrutinizing the quite different conceptions of this matter." Again Butenandt was able to delay the issue according to his wishes and to keep a distance between the Max Planck Society and a Verschuer Institute.[86]

As soon as Butenandt assumed the presidency of the MPS in the summer of 1960, a new opportunity arose to prove his friendship. By now Verschuer had built a small empire in Münster. The Federal Ministry for Atomic Questions was interested, among other things, in possible damage caused by radiation in humans, in mutation, and in radiation genetics. Since 1957, this ministry had funded with 72,000 DM Verschuer's (in his own words) "long-cherished plan for registering hereditary anomalies in the administrative region of Münster."[87] In 1959, the ministry granted him a 500,000 DM building cost subsidy for the extension of his institute.[88]

When Verschuer entered the international arena with a "*Lehrbuch der Humangenetik*" among other activities, his sworn enemy Nachtsheim intervened. Nachtsheim was worried about the international reputation of German human genetics and thus his own. He not only published critical reviews of Verschuer's textbook in professional journals but also wrote polemic letters to the editors of daily newspapers and to government officials.[89] Atomic minister and Verschuer financier Siegfried Balke was alarmed.

[86] MPG-Archiv, III. Abt. Rep. 84/2: letter from Verschuer to Butenandt, 27 November 1954, Butenandt's response, 7 December 1954, letter from Verschuer to Butenandt, 6 August 1955, Butenandt's response, 25 September 1955; II. Abt. Rep. 1A, Personalia Verschuer, No. 10: excerpt from a letter from Butenandt to Hahn, 9 December 1954, letter from Hahn to the North Rhine Westphalian Minister of Education, 24 May 1955.
[87] Verschuer to Fischer, 3 November 1956, quoted from Peter Kröner, "Förderung der Genetik und Humangenetik in der Bundesrepublik durch das Ministerium für Atomfragen in den fünfziger Jahren," in Karin Weisemann, Peter Kröner, and Richard Toellner (eds.), *Wissenschaft und Politik – Genetik und Humangenetik in der DDR (1949–1989)* (Münster: Lit, 1997), 69–82, here 77.
[88] Kröner, "Förderung."
[89] Otmar von Verschuer, *Genetik des Menschen. Lehrbuch der Humangenetik* (Munich: Urban and Schwarzenberg, 1959); reviews from Hans Nachtsheim in *Berichte über die*

At a meeting in September 1960, Balke asked the "Science Policy Discussion Group" (*Besprechungskreis Wissenschaftspolitik*) for a vote. Newly installed MPS president Butenandt deplored Nachtsheim's actions:

The issue v. Verschuer has been scrutinized years ago by a commission on which Herr Heubner also sat. It was unanimously decided at that time that Herr v. Verschuer should regain the unrestricted opportunity to work. This was done very conscientiously at that time and things should have been left alone. [90]

Telschow, just retired but still acting as an advisor, was bound to disagree with Butenandt and pointed out once again the "problematic" character of Verschuer, who had in "1945 defected and abandoned his colleagues." Nevertheless, in response to Balke's inquiry, both the MPS president and former secretary general agreed with the Discussion Group that it would be "inexpedient" to discontinue supporting Verschuer's work.[91] During the last decade of his life, Verschuer was no longer reliant on the friendship of Butenandt. They contented themselves with exchanging offprints and greeting cards expressing mutual devotion on the occasion of significant birthdays.[92] When Verschuer died in August 1969, MPS president Butenandt assured Verschuer's widow in his letter of condolence that "the name Otmar von Verschuer will be inseparably linked to the history of human genetics."[93]

The reconstituting biosciences in the MPS, worried about reconnecting with the international community, tried to repress the memory of Nazi racial research (within the KWS, most of all personified by Verschuer). This process remained incomplete, as repression often is. Verschuer as a person could not be ousted from the MPS community until the early 1950s. Since no one, however, had distanced himself from Verschuer as a person, nor subjected his research approach and methods to (self-)critical reflection,

---

wissenschaftliche Biologie, 141, No. 2 (1960), 133 f.; *Biologisches Zentralblatt*, 79, No. 3 (1960); letter to the editor by Nachtsheim in *Der Tagesspiegel* (17 July 1960). On a controversy in *Die Welt*, see the correspondence between Nachtsheim and Ebbing, 25 and 28 September 1960, MPG-Archiv, II. Abt., Rep. 20 A, Nr. 23.

[90] MPG-Archiv, II. Abt. Rep. 1A, Personalia Verschuer, No. 11: excerpt from the minutes of the Besprechungskreis "Wissenschaftspolitik" meeting on 30 September 1960.

[91] MPG-Archiv, II. Abt. Rep. 1A, Personalia Verschuer, No. 11: excerpt from the minutes of the Besprechungskreis "Wissenschaftspolitik" meeting on 30 September 1960. Unfortunately Kröner, "Förderung," 77, does not specify whether the Ministry of Nuclear Energy granted the 168,000 DM requested by Verschuer in the following year for the basic equipment of his institute's new building. I am grateful to Alexander von Schwerin for this essential source and literature references.

[92] See the Butenandt and Verschuer correspondence in MPG-Archiv, II. Abt. Rep. 1A, Personalia Verschuer, No. 11.

[93] MPG-Archiv, II. Abt. Rep. 1A, Personalia Verschuer, No. 11: letter from Butenandt to Erika von Verschuer, 14 August 1969.

Verschuer could keep on confronting his expert colleagues with claims that
he was entitled to academic prestige, cooperation, and access to international circles of scholarly excellence. This did not change until his death in
1969, when he vanished for almost a decade from the collective memory of
the MPS and its representatives, or at least this is what is documented in the
archives.

When in the early 1980s a younger generation of bioscientists, historians
of science, and journalists reconnected the names of Verschuer, Mengele, and
Butenandt with the crimes in Auschwitz, the MPS honorary president actually
appeared to be quite surprised. When his younger colleague Müller-Hill inter-
viewed him in 1981, the seventy-eight-year-old Butenandt did not remember
the document he had co-authored in 1949, which dealt with the past. Only
after another inquiry by Verschuer's son did he remember "that certainly
important memorandum." When he tracked it down in the "old Tübingen
files," he read it "with the greatest interest." Afterward he still considered
it appropriate to rebut Müller-Hill for "reproaching" the MPS for "lacking
responsibility" and even sent him a copy with regard to their interview:[94]

It would have facilitated our conversation very much if I had remembered the memorandum and the many details mentioned there. I believe that a great deal was done
during the immediate postwar years in the Kaiser Wilhelm/Max Planck Society at
Göttingen to clarify the situation and what had taken place at the institute dedicated
to heredity and eugenics in the Kaiser Wilhelm Society. By the way, the constel-
lation of the aforementioned commission – obviously suggested by Professor von
Verschuer himself – is remarkable, since one could hardly have found more critical
people than Wolfgang Heubner and Max Hartmann.[95]

When Müller-Hill sent him the manuscript he intended to publish, which
offered a different reading of this source, Butenandt was "exceedingly surprised" and eventually tried, with legal help, to prevent its publication.[96]

---

[94] MPG-Archiv, Abt. III, Rep. 84/2 (former folder 357): letter from Helmut v. Verschuer to
Butenandt, 3 April 1981; letter from Butenandt to H. v. Verschuer, 12 May 1981 and Müller-
Hill, 13 May 1981 (quotes). The Butenandt biography written by his former student Karlson
during Butenandt's lifetime does not mention Verschuer: Peter Karlson, *Adolf Butenandt.
Biochemiker, Hormonforscher, Wissenschaftspolitiker* (Stuttgart: Wissenschaftliche
Verlagsgesellschaft, 1990).

[95] MPG-Archiv, Abt. III, Rep. 84/2 (former folder 357): letter from Butenandt to Müller-Hill,
13 May 1981.

[96] The arguments between Müller-Hill on the one hand, and Butenandt, his former colleague
Ruhenstroth-Bauer, and his lawyers on the other, wore on until 1984; the correspondence
can be located in MPG-Archiv, Abt. III, Rep. 84/2 (former folder 357). The quote is from
Butenandt's letter to Müller-Hill, 19 August 1983. The startling book was published
shortly afterward: Benno Müller-Hill, *Tödliche Wissenschaft. Die Aussonderung von Juden,
Zigeunern und Geisteskranken*, (Reinbek: Rowohlt, 1984); the revised edition of the English
translation is Benno Müller-Hill, *Murderous Science: Elimination by Scientific Selection
of Jews, Gypsies, and Others in Germany, 1933–1945* (Woodbury: Cold Spring Harbor

Historical analysis of the Verschuer memorandum and the correspondence between the participants reveals no further involvement of the authors, and Butenandt in particular, in the medical crimes in Auschwitz that was not already known. Butenandt, as a good colleague, did support Verschuer's research on "specific proteins" by asking his staff member Hillmann to assist Verschuer in the experimental handling of the blood samples from Auschwitz. After researching the papers of Karin Magnussen, Ernst Klee has recently made the claim that Butenandt had been the "center" of the Dahlem "interconnected research on genetic agents" (*Verbundforschung über Genwirkstoffe*) and the "biochemical building-block in the Auschwitz research," while Mengele, on the other hand, was the executor of the "Kühn-Butenandt-Verschuer-research."[97]

It is correct, however, that during the 1930s and 1940s several bioscientific Kaiser Wilhelm Institutes, including Butenandt's KWI for Biochemistry, researched interdisciplinary genetic agents (*Genwirkstoffe*), just like other German and international institutions – in fact, mostly based on the expressivity of pigmentation.[98] It is rather likely that Butenandt had been informed about Magnussen's research on eye pigmentation at the adjacent KWIA of his friend and colleague Verschuer. It is not so likely, however, that he had already known about the delivery of the heterochromous eyes of the murdered "gypsy" children from Auschwitz. In his correspondence with Verschuer in 1944/45 during the last months of war, Verschuer's protein project as well as Diehl's work on tuberculosis was mentioned frequently; yet neither Magnussen's pigment research nor her and Mengele's names were ever mentioned.

It could have been misunderstood politeness, intolerable tastelessness, and most likely an expression of successful repression when in 1982 the aged Nobel laureate thanked the retired biology teacher Karin Magnussen for sending him an unsolicited offprint by expressing enthusiasm for her unbowed academic drive.[99] But this by no means proves that in 1943

Laboratory Press, 1998). The interview with Butenandt was not reproduced but only mentioned in a footnote.

[97] Klee, *Deutsche Medizin*, 370 f.

[98] See Karlson, 111, 132–135.

[99] MPG-Archiv, III. Abt., Rep. 84/2, No. 3705 (Korr. Magnussen 1982–1993): letter from Magnussen to Butenandt, 17 January 1982 and Butenandt's response, 20 August 1982. In his talk "Erinnerung und Ausblendung. Ein kritischer Blick in den Briefwechsel Adolf Butenandts (MPG-Präsident 1960–1972)" within the scope of the research programme "History of the Kaiser Wilhelm Society in the National Socialist era," Benno Müller-Hill presented those letters on 17 May 2001 in Berlin. See Benno Müller-Hill, "Selective Perception. The Letters of Adolf Butenandt, Nobel Prize Winner and President of the Max Planck Society," in Giorgio Semenza and Anthony J. Turner (eds.), *Comprehensive Biochemistry*, Vol. 42, *Selected Topics in the History of Biochemistry. Personal Recollections VII* (Amsterdam: Elsevier, 2003), 548–580; Klee, *Deutsche Medizin*, 371.

Butenandt had been the driving force (*spiritus rector*) of one of the most evil criminal collaborations known so far between science and politics within the framework of the KWS.

What does this analysis of the genesis of the Verschuer memorandum and the history of its impacts and influences show us? First, it nourishes the suspicion that the authors did not completely exclude their colleague Verschuer because of their own dubious activities, which were known within their academic surroundings. This has been demonstrated for both Verschuer's advocate Heubner as well as Verschuer's accuser Nachtsheim. They thereby integrated Verschuer as a permanent member into a repression cartel for mastering the politics of the past.

The criminological term "collusion" has recently been suggested in public debate for this activity.[100] At the end of his account of the Verschuer memorandum, Peter Kröner suspects its authors had an "unspoken fear of blackmail."[101] Yet as long as a punishable act does not go beyond an obvious yet in the end unprovable cognizance, the term "self-exculpation," likewise suggested by Kröner,[102] seems more apt. The authors wanted to get rid of the complicity that grew out of their proximity to the core race political areas of Nazi rule that they had gotten themselves into, or possibly even pushed themselves into, but which, in any event, they had not avoided.

The authors of the Verschuer memorandum never dealt critically with the immediate past of their research discipline – neither while composing the memorandum nor later. Instead of dealing with the ethical limits of their experimental work, they used the political ignorance of the scientific actors as an excuse for the indisputable amoral demarcation of scientific practice. They similarly reinterpreted indisputable political complicity as pardonable lapses of an otherwise "decent" colleague. For the sake of their scientific guild's cohesion, they thwarted the enlightenment of historical facts and pursued for decades a policy of obscuration, extenuation, and reinterpretation.

Even after years of public debates on the medical crimes during the Third Reich in general and Verschuer's role in particular, Butenandt claimed the right to pass historical judgment on right and justice for himself and his long deceased comrade-in-arms. As late as 1988, he refuted, without as much as a hint of self-doubt, the excruciatingly embarrassing questions historian of science Christoph Cobet asked him about the interpretation of the 1949 memorandum:

[100] For example, during the science symposium "Biowissenschaften und Menschenversuche an Kaiser-Wilhelm-Instituten. Die Verbindung nach Auschwitz," taking place within the scope of the research program "History of the Kaiser Wilhelm Society in the National Socialist Era" on 7–8 June 2001 in Berlin, see Carola Sachse, "Menschenversuche in Auschwitz überleben, erinnern, verantworten," in Sachse, *Verbindung*, 7–34.
[101] Kröner, *Rassenhygiene*, 138.
[102] Kröner, *Rassenhygiene*, 140.

After studying the documents still available to me once more, I can declare that I still stand behind every word of the memorandum I signed in September 1949 and have no reason to change my view in any way. I am convinced that the three cosignatories (Wolfgang Heubner, Max Hartmann, and Boris Rajewski) who because of their strength of character and bearing enjoyed general admiration and unrestricted confidence, would say the same thing were they still alive and could have experienced and evaluated the events and insights of the years from 1949 to 1988 the way I have. [103]

By composing the *Verschuer* memorandum in September 1949, the MPS as an institution made a well-calibrated effort to purge personnel and straighten the organizational and political front. The bioscientists involved agreed on how to deal with known and possibly still emerging contaminations of their network with Nazi crimes and to harmonize exculpating assessments. They established a discourse with which they wanted to claim, and for a long time maintain, their contemporary power to define what was right and wrong in their own scientific work.

[103] MPG-Archiv, Abt. III, Rep. 84/2 (former folder 357): letter from Butenandt to Cobet, 12 October 1988.

16

The Predecessor: The Uneasy Rapprochement between Carl Neuberg and Adolf Butenandt after 1945

Michael Schüring

I always countered the "gossip" … that there was something improper about your takeover of the KWI for Biochemistry. If a vacant post is offered to someone, they should take it without misgivings. That goes without saying. You will have noticed that also in the United States nobody harbors any resentment against you. You have won favor everywhere – not least among the women.[1]

In this passage in a letter written to Adolf Butenandt in April 1954, Carl Neuberg was alluding to a dark chapter in the relationship between the two scientists. The National Socialists' ouster of his predecessor and Neuberg's subsequent exile from Germany played a significant part in Butenandt's achieving his distinguished career in the Kaiser Wilhelm Society (*Kaiser-Wilhelm-Gesellschaft*, KWS) and Max Planck Society (*Max-Planck-Gesellschaft*, MPS). Yet, the manner in which Neuberg himself exonerated Butenandt for taking over the Kaiser Wilhelm Institute for Biochemistry (*KWI für Biochemie*, KWIBC) illustrates the remarkable nature of postwar relations between German scientists and their exiled colleagues. The facts of the case require careful interpretation, looking beyond the conciliatory façade of mutual esteem.

At the time of his expulsion, Neuberg was certainly bitter. Yet two decades later he seems to have raised the issue out of the blue while writing this letter. Up until then, Butenandt had neither directly enquired about the attitude of his American colleagues toward him nor had he mentioned the existence of what Neuberg describes as "gossip." In this context, Neuberg's remarks seem very ambiguous; he tells Butenandt that his conduct was controversial and pacifies him in the same paragraph. This was surely an indirect

---

[1] Neuberg to Butenandt, 24 April 1954, American Philosophical Society (APS), Carl Neuberg Papers.

I would like to to thank Charlotte Kreutzmueller for the excellent translation as well as Mark Walker and Ruth Lewin Sime for their support.

challenge to Butenandt to comment on the events surrounding Neuberg's ousting. In his reply, however, Butenandt expressed only vague thanks for Neuberg's "appreciative words."[2] Neither of them ever broached the subject again. The relationship between Carl Neuberg and Adolf Butenandt has been the subject of previous critical research.[3] Clearly, it cannot have been a professional, unproblematic "friendship."[4] Nor was it a teacher-student relationship, at least not in a narrow sense. What linked the two scientists were the institute that one had taken over from the other and, above all, the political context in which this had happened.

Thus much remained to be clarified after years of silence. What expectations motivated them to resume relations after the war? On what level were they able to communicate and where did difficulties arise? What does Butenandt's attitude toward his persecuted and exiled predecessor say about his perception of himself, in a professional and political sense? The two scientists never came closer than in the letter quoted above to talking openly about the circumstances surrounding Butenandt's taking over the institute. What were the reasons for this? These questions will be addressed in three stages. First, the events surrounding Neuberg's expulsion will be described. Then the issue of Neuberg's possible "return" as promoted by the MPS's hiring policy will be considered. The last section will consist of a short analytical interpretation of the correspondence between Neuberg and Butenandt, commenting on the fragile relationship, founded on written contact, between two colleagues trying to win mutual recognition.

EXPULSION

Carl Neuberg, born in 1877, studied under Emil Fischer and Alfred Wohl and made his reputation as a scientist in 1911 with the discovery of carboxylase, an enzyme active in fermentation. Today he is regarded as the father of modern biochemistry. In 1913, he was appointed head of the chemistry

---

[2] Butenandt to Neuberg, 5 June 1954, Archives of the Max Planck Society, Berlin (*Archiv zur Geschichte der Max-Planck-Gesellschaft*, MPG-Archiv), III. Abt., Rep. 84, no. 140.

[3] Ute Deichmann, *Flüchten, Mitmachen, Vergessen. Chemiker und Biochemiker in der NS-Zeit* (Weinheim: Wiley-VCH, 2001); Benno Müller-Hill, "Selective Perception. The Letters of Adolf Butenandt, Nobel Prize Winner and President of the Max Planck Society," *Comprehensive Biochemistry*, 24, (2003), 548–578. Müller-Hill's claim that the correspondence between Butenandt and Neuberg in Butenandt's estate begins in November 1949 is not correct. Both the records in the archive of APS and the actual correspondence begin in early 1947. Thus Müller-Hill's assumption that the letters were missing from Butenandt's estate because they were "painful to read" (574) is unfounded. As things stand, the form and content of their correspondence gives no cause to believe that Butenandt removed individual letters.

[4] There is a suggestion of this possibility in the article by Arnold Nordwig, "Vor fünfzig Jahren: Der Fall Neuberg, Aus der Geschichte des Kaiser-Wilhelm-Instituts für Biochemie zur Zeit des Nationalsozialismus," *MPG-Spiegel*, 6 (1983), 49–53, esp. 53.

department of the Kaiser Wilhelm Institute for Experimental Therapy, run by August von Wassermann. Following Wassermann's death in 1925, Neuberg assumed management of the whole institute, which now bore the title Kaiser Wilhelm Institute for Biochemistry.

Carl Neuberg came under § 3 of the "Law for the Restoration of a Professional Civil Service," passed on 7 April 1933 – that is, he was a Jew according to National Socialist doctrine (as were about 90 percent of the KWS employees who were later exiled). Neuberg had never concealed his origins and did not give in to non-Jewish social pressure to conform by being baptized. His rather conservative and patriotic outlook corresponded to the general political orientation predominant in German academic circles during the empire and the Weimar Republic. The National Socialist dogma, which declared that his affiliation with Judaism and his affinity for Germany were incompatible, came as a blow. Still, even after the war he held to a self-image that followed the maxims of national economist Franz Oppenheimer: "German national feeling, Jewish tribal spirit, and West-Elbian native pride."[5] Neuberg wrote to Heinrich Wieland in 1948 that his family had been resident "in the state of Hanover ... – it can be proven ... for three hundred years."[6] Since Neuberg had gained a high civil service rank (*Beamte*) before 1914 and had been decorated several times for his services in the First World War, he initially came under the exemption clauses of the civil service law. He later regretted staying at his post in Germany. "On the bad advice of [Max] Planck and against the better advice of [Walther] Nernst," he did not emigrate in 1933 and therefore arrived too late in the United States to gain a proper footing in the academic world.[7]

Neuberg's comment on the advice of his colleagues gives us a clue as to the conduct of the KWS after 1933. Wherever possible, the General Administration and the president (Max Planck until 1937, then Carl Bosch) tried to keep prominent members of staff, especially directors, on board. Lesser known scientists, whose careers were just beginning, were dismissed – with a few exceptions – immediately after the civil service law was passed.

---

[5] Neuberg to Heinrich Wieland, 3 February 1948; APS, Carl Neuberg Papers.

[6] Neuberg to Heinrich Wieland, 3 February 1948; APS, Carl Neuberg Papers. In his obituary, written in 1956, David Nachmansohn recalled Neuberg's outlook: "He loved Germany as he had known her in his younger days. He felt deeply rooted in German culture and civilization. Nazi persecution and personal tragedy did not change his deep attachment. His strong character did not permit him to burn today what he adored yesterday. Strength of character is also reflected in his attitude toward the Jewish issue. Although completely unorthodox he was a straight and proud Jew. He was full of scorn and contempt for Jews who tried to hide their origin. He did not approve of baptism for purely opportunistic reasons, for promoting a career. This was for him incompatible with the dignity of man, like giving up one's personality." In *Proceedings of the Rudolf Virchow Medical Society in the City of New York*, XV (1956), Separatum, Leo Beck Institute, New York, Neuberg Collection.

[7] Neuberg to Butenandt, 7 March 1947, MPG-Archiv, Abt. III, Rep. 84/ZZ, no. 140.

That amounted to two thirds of the just over one hundred employees of the KWS who were dismissed.[8]

The meritocratic consensus enabling famous scientists to hold on to their posts was disturbed by a group of Nazi activists who created considerable unrest in a part of Berlin (Dahlem, the location of most of the Kaiser Wilhelm Institutes in Berlin) that was usually spared political conflict.[9] A mechanic, Kurt Delatrée-Wegener, whom Neuberg had dismissed on 11 July 1933 for assaulting institute employees, gained the support of some local active Nazi Party members who, ten days later, organized a meeting of the so-called Brandenburg district committee for Labor Peace (*Bezirksleitung Brandenburg für den Arbeitsfrieden*) – a body that apparently did not fall under any official authority.

At this meeting, Neuberg, who attended with a colleague from the General Administration, received serious threats from a member of the SA, among others.[10] The following night, Neuberg again received threatening calls. Friedrich Glum, then head of the KWS General Administration, thereupon called on the support of the Prussian Ministry of Education and the Arts, which declared that the General Administration and the institute directors should "not put up with anything from subordinate party authorities."[11] This official support from the ministry, which insisted on going through the proper channels, was, however, thwarted by a denunciation that Delatrée had already made on July 18.

In a letter to the chair of the works committee of the Dahlem Kaiser Wilhelm Institutes, Delatrée claimed that Neuberg had made disparaging remarks about the Reich Chancellor in a personal conversation in early May.[12] More than ten months later, this finally led to the Prussian Ministry of Culture questioning institute employees about Neuberg's political orientation.[13] Neuberg found out that the ministry was now considering taking disciplinary action against him and in February 1934 appealed to Max Planck for help. The administrative committee consequently submitted a

---

[8] See also Michael Schüring, *Minervas verstossene Kinder: vertriebene Wissenschaftler und die Vergangenheitspolitik der Max-Planck-Gesellschaft* (Göttingen: Wallstein Verlag, 2006).

[9] See also Nordwig, passim, and Richard Beyler, "'Reine' Wissenschaft und personelle 'Säuberungen.'" *Ergebnisse. Vorabdrucke aus dem Forschungsprogramm "Geschichte der Kaiser-Wilhelm-Gesellschaft im Nationalsozialismus,"* no. 16 (Berlin: Forschungsprogramm, 2004).

[10] This can be inferred from a record of Neuberg's of 21 July 1933; MPG-Archiv, Abt. I, Rep. 1A, no. 2035/5.

[11] Memo from Glum to Ernst Telschow, 28 July 1933, MPG-Archiv, Abt. I, Rep. 1A, no. 2035/5.

[12] Minutes of a meeting between Neuberg, Glum, and Telschow on 26 July 1933, MPG-Archiv, Abt. I, Rep. 1A, no. 2035/5.

[13] This information is from a letter, Neuberg to Max Planck, 16 February 1934, MPG-Archiv, Abt. I, Rep. 1A, no. 2035/7.

statement of defense by Neuberg to the ministry but the decision had apparently already been made at that level.[14]

The second managing director of the KWS, Ernst Telschow, recalled that the ministerial official Max Donnevert informed him on April 17, 1934, that even if the outcome of the proceedings were positive, Neuberg's application to become director emeritus would be welcomed. His "honorable retirement" would be easier now than at a later date.[15] Neuberg officially lost his position on October 1 but continued to head the institute temporarily. In a conversation with Telschow in April, Neuberg still expressed his hope that the employees of the institute would be able to keep their jobs should he be forced to retire. Telschow explained that his successor would be able to choose his staff according to his requirements.[16] And that is what happened. In June 1936, Butenandt informed Friedrich Glum that seven members of staff who had been employed by his predecessor could not be retained.[17]

How did Neuberg view the behavior of his colleagues overall? On February 1, 1935, Neuberg wrote to George Barger, a chemist in Edinburgh, asking for a letter of recommendation to enclose with an application for funding from the Rockefeller Foundation. At this point, Neuberg still hoped to be able to continue working in a more modest capacity for the institute that he had run for years. The letter is remarkable, particularly for the following passage:

I would like to emphasize that none of these measures were taken by the Kaiser Wilhelm Society but by the Reich authorities. In fact the president of the Kaiser Wilhelm Society, Professor Planck, has endeavored to have these penalties mitigated, hitherto without any success.

And elsewhere he writes:

All my outstanding professional German colleagues, such as Wieland, Windaus, Hans Fischer, Otto Hahn, Laue, Warburg, Meyerhof, Hartmann and others, have made petitions to the president of the Kaiser Wilhelm Society to the effect that I should be made an emeritus professor, not dismissed. As apart from the pecuniary aspect, the pension amounts to only a fragment of my salary, becoming an emeritus professor would secure my right to a place of work and it is only this that I am still fighting for now.[18]

[14] Max Planck in a communication to the Prussian Minister for Science, Art and National Education of 7 March 1934, MPG-Archiv, Abt. I, 1A, no. 2035/9.
[15] Memo by Telschow, 20 April 1934, MPG-Archiv, Abt. I, Rep. 1A, no. 2035/12.
[16] Memo by Telschow, 20 April 1934, MPG-Archiv, Abt. I, Rep. 1A, no. 2035/12.
[17] On 6 June 1936, Friedrich Glum wrote to Adolf Butenandt: "I have been informed that you do not see any possibility of keeping on the ladies and gentlemen who are currently working in the institute (Dr. Collatz, Gaffron, Hofmann, Schuchardt, Kobel, Fräulein Kühl und Bullmann). The employees in question will then be dismissed by the Kaiser Wilhelm Society." MPG-Archiv, Abt. I, Rep. 1A, no. 2033/3, 203.
[18] Bodleian Library Oxford, Society for the Protection of Science and Learning, MS.SPSL, 370/1, 13.

The colleagues whom Neuberg names in this letter were part of a group of scientists who took a skeptical attitude toward the Nazi regime and disagreed with its policy of dismissal. The letter was apparently not only written to ask Barger for help. Neuberg also managed to convey who among German scientists (apart from his colleagues Otto Meyerhof and Otto Warburg who were themselves under threat) could still be trusted in his view. This was also an attempt to protect those whom he hoped would continue to support him.

However, this letter also makes clear that Neuberg and his colleagues had already accepted "the inevitable" and were now only fighting for his status after dismissal from the director's post. In May 1934, Max Planck and Friedrich Glum still pleaded Neuberg's cause at a meeting of the administrative committee. In the presence of representatives of the Reich Ministry of the Interior and the Reich Ministry for Education and Science (*Reichserziehungsministerium*, REM), represented by the physicist and keen National Socialist Johannes Stark, Planck argued that the higher interests of the state should be considered. The minutes of the meeting record the following:

In his [Planck's] opinion one has to differentiate between the role of teaching and the task of research. Pure research has no other aim than to discover the truth. He therefore regards it as his prerogative not to apply all the individual provisions of the civil service law directly to those scientists engaged in research. This is, according to him, in the interest of the state, which benefits from the results of research.[19]

Stark did not endorse this opinion but the representatives of the KWS played for time by announcing that the case would be reconsidered, apparently hoping to take a dilatory approach to the matter.

A significant aspect of Planck's argument is the manner in which he distinguishes between instruction and research. There was indeed a difference between Nazi bureaucracy's involvement in the universities and Nazi policy on the KWS. For the Nazi regime, it was more important to have control over educational institutions because of their influence on future generations of academics. The National Socialists swiftly achieved a fait accompli by agitating a highly politicized student body and introducing the "*Führer*" principle. The directors of the KWS, which did not receive a charter conforming to National Socialist ideas until 1937, were certainly aware of the difference between the two spheres.[20]

In this context, the loyalty toward the KWS that Neuberg demonstrates in his letter to Barger is understandable; its directors were still trying to

---

[19] MPG-Archiv, Abt. I, Rep. 1A, no. 93.

[20] After his transfer from Göttingen University to Dahlem, Alfred Kühn, for example, thought that a "healthier academic environment" could be found there. This statement was recorded by an employee of the Rockefeller Foundation, in the Rockefeller Archive Center, RG 12.1, Diary W.E. Tisdale, 29.

mitigate the consequences of Neuberg's dismissal by seeking other financial sources and keeping the opportunities for research open to him. This commitment waned when Adolf Butenandt was declared his successor in May 1936. Neuberg's use of the institute gatehouse for modest research activities could only be approved by his successor if the KWS agreed to pay and these activities did not burden his own budget, Butenandt told the General Administration in late July 1936.[21]

Meanwhile, Neuberg had been waiting for months to be given the gatehouse. In February of that year he had written to Planck five times on the matter but did not receive one reply.[22] Just one year previously, Planck had written to George Barger that Neuberg "will be able to continue to work at the institute and that the Kaiser Wilhelm Society will support him in that respect to the best of its ability."[23] His replacement in the post of director finally put an end to Neuberg's work at the institute, which had been made possible by 9,200 Reichsmarks from the Rockefeller Foundation.[24] Neuberg was "secretly" put up in a bakery in Steglitz with a few of his belongings, as Butenandt recalled in an obituary of his predecessor. "His old institute could only afford him this small token of its gratitude," said Butenandt in 1956.[25]

Neuberg judged these events after the war with a characteristic combination of disappointment and mildness. In a letter to Heinrich Wieland he reported:

According to the KWS, Butenandt regarded my staying in two small rooms in the gatehouse of my former institute, where Planck wanted to accommodate me, as "unacceptable" and made his assumption of office conditional upon my complete removal. Well, that would have been in keeping with the times and I think back without bitterness whenever I am reminded of it now.[26]

According to a file note by the General Administration of May 12, 1936, Butenandt allegedly wanted his predecessor to be "in future in no way linked

---

[21] Memo from Telschow, 27 July 1936, MPG-Archiv, Abt. I, Rep. 1A, no. 2033/3, 218.

[22] It is remarkable and probably also typical for Neuberg that he did not mention this disappointment in any letter to friends or former colleagues. He complained about Max Planck's silence only in a conversation with an employee of the Rockefeller Foundation on 26 February 1936, presumably without knowing that notes would be taken; in Rockefeller Archive Center, RG 1.1, Series 717, Germany, Box 13, Folder 108.

[23] Planck to Barger, 20 March 1935, Bodleian Library Oxford, Society for the Protection of Science and Learning, MS.SPSL, 370/1, p. 17.

[24] Note of 2 March 1934, Rockefeller Archive Center, RG 1.1, 717 Germany, Box 13, Folder 108.

[25] Adolf Butenandt, "Nachruf auf Carl Neuberg," *Mitteilungen der Max-Planck-Gesellschaft*, No. 5 (1956), reprinted in Adolf Butenandt, *Das Werk eines Lebens*, Vol. II (Munich: Max Planck Gesellschaft, 1981), 726.

[26] Neuberg to Wieland, 16 December 1948, APS, Carl Neuberg Papers.

to the institute."²⁷ Ute Deichmann has proposed that "the Kaiser Wilhelm Society put [Butenandt] forward as a henchman in order to finally get rid of Neuberg."²⁸ Who exactly acted thus in the name of the KWS, however, is not clear. In any case, it seems strange that Planck did not respond to Neuberg's repeated inquiries, while Neuberg obviously did not find out the whole truth about Butenandt's opinion.

According to a file note by Ernst Telschow of July 27, 1936, Butenandt left the decision of whether to employ his predecessor solely up to the policy (and budget) of the KWS, although Telschow notes that Butenandt had suggested "that the Kaiser Wilhelm Society provide a few thousand marks for Mr. Neuberg as an annual subsidy for his work" and had not spoken out in definite terms against Neuberg's use of part of the institute's premises. There was in any case no mention of "complete removal" here. It is possible that Neuberg's contact with Planck and Butenandt ran via the desks of the General Administration, which coordinated its activities with REM, and that this caused inconsistencies. Ernst Telschow informed Neuberg in person of the results of negotiations with Butenandt and, presumably, tailored them to suit the interests of the KWS. Telschow found that "[Neuberg's] disgruntlement at the Kaiser Wilhelm Society was clearly noticeable."²⁹

Heinrich Wieland, however, was not prepared to believe the version put forward by Neuberg:

What you wrote to me about [Butenandt's] conduct in connection with your retirement has irritated me intensely. I just cannot accept that events took that course: your source may not have been entirely reliable.³⁰

However, Neuberg reaffirmed his version and wrote back that Planck and "the other authorities of the KWS as well as ... other parties" had informed him of the facts. Neuberg said that he could not know whether this had really been the case and it was all the same to him anyway. When questioned about Butenandt by a "Swiss party," Neuberg had said only "laudable" things. Here he is referring to a Swiss education authority that after the war had approached Butenandt's colleagues with inquiries concerning his political conduct during the Nazi era in connection with his planned appointment in Basel.³¹ Neuberg endorsed the predominantly positive statements

²⁷ Quoted from Hans-Jörg Rheinberger, "Virusforschung an den Kaiser-Wilhelm-Instituten," in Doris Kaufmann (ed.), *Geschichte der Kaiser-Wilhelm-Gesellschaft im Nationalsozialismus* (Göttingen: Wallstein Verlag, 2000), 667–698, here 668.

²⁸ Deichmann, 472.

²⁹ File note by Telschow, 27 July 1936, MPG-Archiv, Abt. I, Rep. 1A, no. 2033/3, 218.

³⁰ Wieland to Neuberg, 14 January 1949, APS, Carl Neuberg Papers.

³¹ Those questioned included Max Hartman, whose positive statement was made on 22 July 1948 (MPG-Archiv, Abt. III, Rep. 47, no. 275), and Georg Melchers, who wrote his rather critical statement on 3 June 1938 (MPG-Archiv, Abt. III, Rep. 75, Korrespondenz

made by his German colleagues. He reacted to Wieland's objections with a combination of irony and conciliation:

But I laughed about their euphemistic expression of my "resignation." I always saw it as a metathesis, as a kick in the back; Butenandt certainly did not deal it.[32]

Carl Neuberg left Europe rather late, under adventurous circumstances. His flight meant the end of his career. His decline from being one of the most eminent scientists on the German academic scene to a poorly paid industrial advisor was irreversible. In May 1948, he wrote a long letter to Ernst Telschow describing his experiences and current situation:

As I came to the United States ten years too late, I was no longer able to find a proper position. I am a Research Professor at New York University, which is about the same as our Honorarprofessor, also insofar as it is unpaid. I am forced to earn my living as a consultant for industry, which does not really suit me and at my advanced age is not all pleasure but rather strenuous. I can work on something theoretical on the side though and will soon send you a selection of offprints. I have not properly learned English and am in some respects isolated because of my pro-German attitude, which Americans cannot understand. At least I enjoy a good academic reputation, for example, have recently been made Fellow of the New York Academy of Sciences and received the first examplar of the Carl Neuberg Medal that was established in my honor. (I saw to it that the second award went to an old Dahlem man, Fritz Lipmann. He is a former colleague of Meyerhof and has gained some standing here.) My personal fortunes have been checkered. Exactly fourteen days before the outbreak of war, I was able to leave Germany thanks to old military connections, with a small suitcase and ten Dutch guilders. For three fourths of a year I was a guest of the University of Amsterdam, traveled through France during the war with my German passport (!), took a French transport ship – where the majority of the passengers were Alsatian soldiers, meaning that almost exclusively German was spoken – to Syria. From there I went to the University of Jerusalem for eight months. An adventurous journey, which lasted nearly three months: I traveled by mule, wheelbarrow, car, and finally ship via Trans-Jordan, Iraq, Iran, India, Ceylon, Dutch India, New Guinea and Hawaii to California, where I was received on the last day of January 1941 by my daughter who lives in Los Angeles, and finally dispatched to New York. I could talk to you for days about all the experiences I had and I very much hope that I will still live to see our reunion.[33]

Carl Neuberg never felt at home in the United States. His correspondence with Emil Abderhalden, the still-controversial biochemist whose position at the University of Halle was significantly supported by the KWS, dem-

K-M- 1948 – March 1950). Melchers asserted that Butenandt could have been politically more "restrained" in his position during the National Socialist period.
[32] Neuberg to Wieland, 21 February 1949, APS, Carl Neuberg Papers.
[33] Neuberg to Telschow, 30 March 1948, MPG-Archiv, Abt. II, Rep. 1A, PA Neuberg.

onstrates this.[34] In these later years, Abderhalden became a close friend of Neuberg, allying himself with him in an attitude of defiant self-assertion. When Abderhalden complained about a critical review by an American colleague, Neuberg answered in May 1947:

Nothing is more despised by the Americans than a European outlook. The manner in which German textbooks in particular treat the historical development of a subject goes completely against the grain for people here. Here anything that was not created in America and in the last ten years is regarded as outlawed and has to be discovered again. Have you never noticed how, with the exception of some great American researchers of course, people here live off plagiarism?[35]

In other letters, Neuberg complained to Abderhalden about the Americans' "professional jealousy," and the "fear that by buying a foreign book they may lose a profit, which is what they are all praying for in the temple of their god, the dollar."[36] Furthermore, he found that the daily press "blows up" American works while various German articles on comparable scientific problems went by the board. Younger researchers excused themselves by saying that they "could not study these several hundred European works." In another letter, Neuberg again took up an old commonplace of anti-Americanism, saying, "[It was] not without reason that we in Europe inwardly fought against Americanism, which ends up in the crassest materialism."[37] Over the course of his correspondence with Abderhalden, Neuberg's attacks became ever more biting:

Today's generation consists partly of charlatans who live off pretense. It is astonishing how quickly some emigrants adapt to this obviously lucrative mentality. Many of them know that they are really just thieves but the guild sticks together. Rascals' honor. So it is understandable that people like Max Bergmann and O. Loewi quickly got acclimatized here.[38]

By mentioning Max Bergmann, former director of the KWI for Leather Research, Neuberg was also attacking a former colleague with whom he was directly associated. The validity of his accusations cannot be verified here. It is, however, interesting that in this attack on American priorities, the focus shifts to the oft-cited benefit that American academia gained from

[34] Emil Abderhalden remains the subject of scientific research primarily because of his mistakenly postulated "defense enzymes." On this, see Benno Müller-Hill and Ute Deichmann, "The Fraud of Abderhalden's Enzymes," *Nature*, 393 (1998), 109–111; Michael Kaasch, "Sensation, Irrtum, Betrug? Emil Abderhalden und die Geschichte der Abwehrfermente," *Vorträge und Abhandlungen zur Wissenschaftsgeschichte*, (1999/2000), 145–210.

[35] Neuberg to Abderhalden, 15 May 1947, APS, Carl Neuberg Papers.

[36] Neuberg to Abderhalden, 28 July 1947, APS, Carl Neuberg Papers.

[37] Neuberg to Abderhalden, 27 January 1948; APS, Carl Neuberg Papers.

[38] Neuberg to Abderhalden, 27 January 1948; APS, Carl Neuberg Papers.

migration.[39] Neuberg, aware of his fears for his own reputation, bemoans the losses incurred in the transatlantic transfer of knowledge, exacerbated by a cultural gap in communication, which he puts down to the unwillingness of young Americans to consult German or European publications. But Neuberg's view that his American colleagues were ignorant of history was another expression of his tendency to dwell on the past, combined with the bitter experience that he would not be able to live out his old age in his new home without material worries, as the title of emeritus professor – a public appreciation of his life's work – had promised back in Germany. In his complaint about American plagiarism, Neuberg was venting his anger at the fact that he had to draw the scientific world's attention to himself before he could pass on the scepter of eminence.

The two elderly gentlemen's shared criticisms of the practices of their professional colleagues in America are indicative of the renewed understanding between scientists who stayed in Germany and their exiled colleagues. Neuberg's perception of cultural differences was colored by the dynamics of scientific economy, generational conflicts, and competitive relations, yet such attacks by exiled scientists on their host country were rare. After the war, when the scale of the genocide became apparent and exiles began to see themselves also as survivors, gratitude predominated. Still, Neuberg's underlying discontent with an "American" modern age in science was not only a product of his personal idiosyncrasies. It was also a basic feature of a resentment that was rife among the educated classes in Central Europe and went deeper than the problems that Neuberg mentioned.[40]

THE QUESTION OF RETURN

Neuberg's relationship with Adolf Butenandt should be interpreted against the background of this historical and mental framework. Ute Deichmann has already commented on the ambiguity in the affable manner with which the two scientists communicated.[41] On closer examination, their correspondence shows a carefully balanced relationship characterized by their mutual claims to prestige. Ascertaining the possibility of his rehabilitation obviously

---

[39] People spoke (and to a certain extent still speak) of "Hitler's gift." See Jean Medawar and David Pyke, *Hitler's Gift. Scientists Who Fled Nazi Germany* (London: Richard Cohen Books, 2000). See also Mitchell Ash and Alfons Söllner (eds.), *Forced Migration and Scientific Change. Emigré German-speaking Scientists and Scholars after 1933* (Cambridge: Cambridge University Press, 1996), 3.

[40] See also Alexander Schmidt-Gernig, *Reisen in die Moderne. Der Amerika-Diskurs des deutschen Bürgertums vor dem Ersten Weltkrieg im europäischen Vergleich* (Berlin: Akademie-Verlag, 1997).

[41] Deichmann, 471 ff.

took priority for Neuberg. In 1947, he tried to do this with the following words:

As I have heard from various parties, the Biochemical Journal [*Biochemische Zeitschrift*] is being revived. I do not wish to raise the question of whether I have a right to occupy the editor's office again, but I would be interested to know whether at least the contractual obligation is being fulfilled that, as long as the journal exists, it must say on the front cover "Established by Carl Neuberg." Grassmann adhered to this until 1938. In volume 280 he pays tribute to my contributions over thirty years of managing the editorial office in a nice obituary. ... I am curious to see how the front cover will look.[42]

Although Butenandt made no reference to this in his reply written five months later, he still seemed to appreciate the situation that Neuberg was in. He promised to settle the question of Neuberg's pension from the KWS, which was resolved in 1950.[43] And he even went a considerable step further. In his reply he wrote:

Should you wish to return to Germany at a later date and work in your old institute, I would of course do everything I can to make this possible for you even under these limited and difficult circumstances.[44]

Previous research on Butenandt's conduct in the postwar period has obviously disregarded this crucial passage. In view of the embarrassed silence of a fair number of other German scholars, Butenandt's offer was not standard procedure. Neither was this the only instance of his offering to assist the return of a scholar with whom he was personally acquainted. In April 1947, Butenandt had written to Otto Hahn, president of the MPS at the time, inquiring

whether it would be a good solution for the future of the Kaiser Wilhelm Institute for Physics in Hechingen if one would attempt to call James Franck back to Germany and give him a position in Hechingen. [45]

Butenandt stressed that this was entirely his idea and had not been discussed with anyone else.

---

[42] Neuberg to Butenandt, 7 March 1947, MPG-Archiv, Abt. III, Rep. 84/ZZ, no. 140.
[43] The Max Planck Society paid Neuberg an advance from April 1950 until his reparations claim against the state was settled. In May 1954, Neuberg received a decision from the Federal Ministry of the Interior that awarded him the salary of a university teacher released from performance of any duties. The decision ran: "The applicant is entitled, from 1 April 1951, as a university teacher released from duties, to the salary from the final level H 1 b under the Reich remuneration order, in the amount of 11,600 DM. This includes the sum of rent allowance applicable to pensions." Federal German Archives, in Koblenz, Berlin, and Dahlwitz-Hoppegarten (*Bundesarchiv*, BArch), B 106, no. 67729.
[44] Butenandt to Neuberg, 5 August 1947, MPG-Archiv, Abt. III, Rep. 84/ZZ, no. 140.
[45] Butenandt to Hahn, MPG-Archiv, Abt. III, Rep. 14A, no. 529.

When a replacement was being sought for the chair in physics at Tübingen, it became known that Franck would be prepared to return, the only problem being that he was already past retirement age. The university was determined to get Franck back but could not offer him any other position apart from the chair. Thus the best solution seemed to be to make him an associate of the university but let him work in the institute in Hechingen. It was certain that public funds could be provided for this. Butenandt continued:

Well, I have not been informed in detail about the development of the Hechingen institute over recent months, but have heard that the plan to provide the nuclear physics department with a new head is once again being considered, and that they want to enter into negotiations with [Wolfgang] Gentner on this matter. If this is so, the idea of getting James Franck instead seems to me a good and sensible solution, as by doing so one would serve the interests of both the Hechingen institute and the university and also have a wonderful opportunity to compensate for an injustice done to Franck which weighs heavily on all of us.[46]

Thus, Butenandt managed to combine the interests of the institute with historical and political arguments. The likelihood of personal guilt feelings coming into play seems somewhat far-fetched but cannot be completely ruled out.[47]

The arguments against Butenandt's suggestion were, in Hahn's view, of a purely private nature. He knew Franck intimately, he told Butenandt, and would also be very glad to see his return. But the fact that Franck had already turned down an invitation from Göttingen rendered Hahn pessimistic:

Personally I believe we can assume that he will stay in the United States 1) because his two children and eight grandchildren live in the United States and are American citizens and he values his family very highly, 2) because he married his former colleague Herta Sponer who is also taking a professorship in the United States.[48]

No doubt Hahn was right, and his friend's personal circumstances decided the matter, although Hahn did not mention Butenandt's suggestion to Franck. He wrote to Franck a few weeks later saying that he "sees a very slight, cautious improvement in relations between scientists in different countries," but insisted that "we in Germany should under no circumstances take the first steps."[49]

Hahn was not the only one to exercise such modest, or perhaps simply convenient, restraint. Although the MPS had appointed some of its most

---

[46] Butenandt to Hahn, MPG-Archiv, Abt. III, Rep. 14A, no. 529.
[47] See Ute Deichmann's interpretation of this in Deichmann, 473.
[48] Hahn to Butenandt, 23 April 1947, MPG-Archiv, Abt. III, Rep 14A, no. 529.
[49] Hahn to Franck, 4 June 1947, MPG-Archiv, Abt. III, Rep. 14A, no. 992.

prominent former scientists "foreign scientific members,"[50] its representatives were nevertheless cautious about making offers, especially as it emerged that many former colleagues had little interest in returning to a morally and politically ravaged Germany. Strictly speaking, it would not even have constituted a return. "Re-emigration" may have meant return in a geographical sense, but a seamless continuation from the point when they were forced to leave their positions was no longer possible. The institutes had changed, as had those who had suffered persecution – and even their German colleagues – and therefore the whole structure of the academic world. The time that had passed could not be bridged in a linear manner; it was marked by a series of historical twists and turns that prevented a direct view of the past from being taken. Günter Anders described this in the following way:

> It is characteristic for us not that our lives were interrupted by an interlude (that cannot be remembered), but that the fragmenting of our lives into several lives has become definite; and that means that the second life stands away at an angle from the first, and the third again from the second; that each time there was a "turn in the road," a "bend," that makes looking back – I almost wrote physically – impossible.[51]

This impression was shared by many scientists, who often expressed their political misgivings in no uncertain terms. Lise Meitner (the former director of the physics department of the KWI for Chemistry) spoke of a lack of "mutual understanding" between herself and her potential colleagues abroad after Fritz Strassmann had invited her to join the newly founded Max Planck Institute for Chemistry in Mainz.[52] Otto Meyerhof (former director of the KWI for Medical Research) also declined an invitation from Richard Kuhn, expressing clear criticism of Kuhn's political past.[53] And Albert Einstein turned down foreign membership of the MPS in the famous letter in which he spoke ironically of his "need for personal hygiene."[54] Alfred Kühn, a biologist from Tübingen and one of the more liberal and

---

[50] Besides Carl Neuberg, those appointed were Richard Goldschmidt (former director of the Kaiser Wilhelm Institute for Biology), Rudolf Ladenburg (former employee of the Kaiser Wilhelm Institute for Physical Chemistry), Lise Meitner (former section head of the Kaiser Wilhelm Institute for Chemistry), Otto Meyerhof (former director of the Kaiser Wilhelm Institute for Medical Research), and Michael Polanyi (former employee of the Kaiser Wilhelm Institute for Physical Chemistry).

[51] Quoted from Axel Schildt, "Reise zurück aus der Zukunft. Beiträge von intellektuellen USA-Remigranten zur atlantischen Allianz, zum westdeutschen Amerikabild und zur 'Amerikanisierung' in den fünfziger Jahren," *Exilforschung. Ein internationales Jahrbuch*, 9 (1992), 25–46, here 27.

[52] Meitner to Strassmann, 21 December 1947, quoted from Fritz Krafft, *Im Schatten der Sensation. Leben und Wirken von Fritz Strassmann* (Weinheim: Verlag Chemie, 1981) 184.

[53] Meyerhof to Kuhn, 1 November 1945; copy in MPG-Archiv, Abt. III, Rep. 84/ZZ, Ordner Peter Karlson (Sammlung).

[54] Einstein to Hahn, 28 January 1949, MPG-Archiv, Abt. III, Rep. 14A, no. 814, 5.

politically understanding directors of the MPS, drew the obvious conclusion from experiences such as these. In October 1956, he wrote to Butenandt:

It always touches me when a Jew approaches me, a German, with friendliness and loyalty at conferences abroad or when an emigrant visits me. I never offer my hand first because I want to spare the other man some uneasiness and myself a rejection that I feel is not undeserved.[55]

However, there were other schools of thought within the MPS that disagreed with the restraint shown by Hahn and Kühn. Joachim Hämmerling wrote to his colleague Georg Melchers, with regard to the possible return of biologist Friedrich Brieger, exiled in Brazil:

I regard it as our duty to express our wish to the emigrants to see them here with us again. Whether they want to come or not is irrelevant.[56]

Here, the symbolic value of an invitation to return is emphasized and thus the necessity of demonstrating one's good intentions even at the cost of possibly losing face. It remains debatable whether Butenandt really thought Neuberg would agree to his offer. Neuberg's reply was polite and pragmatic:

I am much obliged to you for your offer of possibly being able to work in the institute again, but what should I do in Germany now that I have reached retirement age and recently celebrated my seventieth birthday? ... Curiously, by their many personal congratulations and commemorative publications, professional colleagues have documented that I am not as forgotten as I thought; but it is in every respect time to hand over the care of the development of our science to the younger generation under the direction of great leaders such as yourself.[57]

There were several reasons that Neuberg was reluctant to return to Germany. Butenandt's mention of the difficult situation regarding funding and supplies for his institute was one of them. Neuberg had disingenuously enclosed a short newspaper article with his letter, reporting on the rise in crime in Tübingen, and asked: "Should I add to the increase in criminality reported by the German New York state newspaper, which brings news from the old homeland that I always read?"[58] Butenandt was in no mood for joking. He asked Neuberg to see things from the perspective of "terrible poverty." Every day people there were "fighting for their lives" and were therefore forced to set "other standards regarding law and order."

Butenandt thought it would be better "to speak of the intellectual efforts which are a feature of life at the university, or of the idealism which the

---

[55] MPG-Archiv, Abt. III, Rep 05, no. 5/2.
[56] Hämmerling to Melchers, 25 September 1947, MPG-Archiv, Abt. III, Rep. 84/ZZ, no. 140.
[57] Neuberg to Butenandt, 25 September 1947, MPG-Archiv, Abt. III, Rep. 84/ZZ, no. 140.
[58] Neuberg to Butenandt, 25 September 1947, MPG-Archiv, Abt. III, Rep. 84/ZZ, no. 140.

students find in their hard struggle for survival when, undeterred, they still make their way to college despite inadequate food and clothing, without suitable accommodation, without heating or textbooks, and can still produce examination results which were probably rarely achieved in earlier times."[59] This complaint, with its rallying cry overtones, surprised Neuberg and perhaps also confirmed him in his decision not to return. But he did not allow himself to be accused of being insufficiently understanding of the conditions in Germany and felt called upon to offer the following clarification of his attitude to Germany:

I was astonished at the fact that you, whom I know to be not only an outstanding researcher but also a man of the world, did not view the newspaper clipping from Tuebingen with humor. It comes from a German newspaper and is anything but hostile to Germany (as proof of this I now enclose an article about Tuebingen and Butenandt). It is manifestly German-friendly and therefore regarded by some with suspicion. I read it every day to stay informed about the old homeland. When they printed the article about the rise in crime they were only trying to make people aware of the seriousness of the situation. The intention is then just about the opposite of what you perhaps assumed.[60]

Butenandt noted this explanation with relief and asked Neuberg to understand that "sometimes, with all that we go through, [we] run the risk of losing our sense of humor."[61] When the situation in Germany had improved again, Neuberg completed a one-year guest research visit at the faculty of agriculture of the technological university in Munich.[62] The MPS awarded him a research grant of 3,600 DM for this purpose in September 1952.[63] Despite their repeated appointments to meet in Germany and the United States, Butenandt and Neuberg always missed each other. They never met in person again.

THE STRUGGLE FOR RECOGNITION

In the meantime, Butenandt had come to appreciate that in Neuberg he had found a mediator between himself and his American counterparts. Neuberg, who like many other former employees of the KWS, sent CARE parcels to Germany; he had also negotiated contact between Germany and representatives of the American chemicals industry, thus making it easier for Butenandt

---

[59] Butenandt to Neuberg, 6 November 1947, MPG-Archiv, Abt. III, Rep. 84/ZZ, no. 140.
[60] Neuberg to Butenandt, 4 December 1947, MPG-Archiv, Abt. III, Rep. 84/ZZ, no. 140.
[61] Butenandt to Neuberg, 18 December 1947, MPG-Archiv, Abt. III, Rep. 84/ZZ, no. 140.
[62] The Bavarian ministry for arts and education granted authorization for this on 11 June 1952; MPG-Archiv, Abt. III, Rep. 1A, PA Neuberg.
[63] This is clear from a letter of the State Central Bank of Lower Saxony of 24 September 1952; MPG-Archiv, Abt. III, Rep. 1A, PA Neuberg.

to establish international scientific relations.[64] This mutual support and rapprochement was accompanied by both open and veiled references to the increasingly one-sidedness of their struggle for recognition. Over time, Butenandt proved to be in the superior position while Neuberg's inquiries became ever more defensive and imploring. In a letter of 12 November 1953 he told his successor:

> You speak endearingly of "my old institute." I was always reasonable enough to stress that the Kaiser Wilhelm Society had got an excellent deal when they handed over the biochemistry institute to you. Since you have been the spiritus rector, the old institute has become infinitely more versatile. Hardly anyone remembers that I coined the term "biochemistry" in 1906, but I am glad that it is firmly established in your workplace and has risen to be held in the highest esteem. Under normal circumstances I would be Director Emeritus and not simply retired, as I was a respectable official who had completed thirty-nine-and-a-half years of service, taking into account the official calculation for wartime service, which brought me – perhaps the only German – three Iron Crosses (1st and 2nd class for services at the front, 2nd class on ribbon for my work with glycerine at home). The Emeritus title has a nonmaterial as well as a material significance. Like my contemporaries who were also forced to emigrate, I would certainly have received the Great Merit Cross of the Federal Republic. An obvious occasion for this, in the view of my German friends (who are not very influential or not prepared to take steps), would be provided by my seventy-fifth birthday, the fortieth anniversary of the discovery of carboxylase, which probably develops all the CO_2 generated in the natural world, and my imminent fiftieth anniversary as an academic teacher. Such outward things count for a lot in the United States. ... You won't think I am so stupid that it is a matter of mere vanity, particularly at my age.[65]

Butenandt followed Neuberg's suggestions. On his initiative, or perhaps that of the MPS, Neuberg was awarded the Federal Republic of Germany's highest decoration for services to the nation in 1954. Butenandt had written to Hahn with reference to this on November 26:

> [I] would like for my part to add that I would be very glad if Neuberg were awarded the Merit Cross. He has certainly deserved it for his scientific achievements and from the letter [quoted above] I get the impression that by giving him this award one could not only put something right for him but also really help him.[66]

The insistence with which Neuberg informed his younger colleague of his achievements was not written in the same tone of detached superiority with which he had rejected the offer to return to Tübingen. The laconic

[64] Neuberg intended to recommend a visit by Butenandt to the United States to Alfred E. Gessler, the vice-president of Interchemical Cooperation. Neuberg to Butenandt, 25 September 1947; MPG-Archiv, Abt. III, Rep. 1A, PA Neuberg. See also Deichmann, 474.
[65] Neuberg to Butenandt, 12 November 1952, MPG-Archiv, Abt. II, Rep. 1A, PA Neuberg.
[66] Butenandt to Hahn, 26 November 1953, MPG-Archiv, Abt. II, Rep. 1A, PA Neuberg.

(and ironic) comments which Neuberg had made about the younger generation of "*Führer*," or leaders, gave way to a rhetoric of quiet desperation, an oppressive anxiety about his own legacy. Neuberg wrote what he actually wanted to hear from others. The list of his own merits reads like a melancholic eulogy, written in honor of himself. The seventy-six-year-old scientist wanted to set the record straight with Butenandt and his German colleagues.

<h2 style="text-align:center">CONCLUSION</h2>

Neuberg's approach to Adolf Butenandt was conciliatory. Their correspondence only touched on political subjects superficially or avoided them completely. Butenandt's party membership was no more the subject of discussion than German scientists' cooperation with the Nazi regime in general. A silent agreement between the two apparently prevailed here. Neuberg's extraordinary respect for Butenandt's scientific achievements and his material and nonmaterial dependence on his former place of work were his key motives. Later, the MPS saw in Neuberg something of an ally, probably less by convenient disregard of the facts than in grateful appreciation of his forbearing attitude. In him, they possessed a reminder of former times that they could refer to on special occasions without greatly distorting the truth. Thus, Butenandt explained in a speech at the opening of a new institute building for the Max Planck Institute for Biochemistry in Munich in 1957:

The fact that Carl Neuberg, despite having been forced to leave his place of work in 1935 and soon after that his fatherland by the legislation of the time, maintained his friendship with and interest in our institute, is an honor for us; we understand his decision not to accept my offer to return in 1945 [actually it was 1947]. Carl Neuberg had promised to come to today's celebration, but death took him from us last year. How gladly we would have thanked him again today for all that he achieved to the glory of our institute and the good of Germany![67]

Things had come full circle. The key historical features of the MPS's self-image remained unifying factors, above and beyond the political changes: scientific glory and national interests. The spirit of Adolf von Harnack had come to life at this moment of solemn self-confirmation. Neuberg's legacy was confirmed at a time of new establishment and geographical reorientation (Munich became the most important center for the MPS). Neuberg himself had wanted it that way and paid the price of a past in soft focus for it. It is important to note that there were very different ways of dealing

<hr>

[67] Adolf Butenandt's address at the opening of the university's new physiology and biochemistry institute and the new institute building of the Max Planck Institute for Biochemistry in Munich in Goethe Strasse, 1957, Adolf Butenandt, *Das Werk eines Lebens*, Volume II, 458–466, here 460.

with experiences of loss among the exiled. There were those who brutally exposed themselves and their former colleagues to the hard facts of injury and discontinuity and there were those who tried to overcome the past in their own way, with melancholy, exhausted mildness. Neuberg was one of the latter. By doing so, however, he was primarily protecting himself from the loss of his biographical identity and possible rejection by his German colleagues.

Butenandt had a feeling for historical continuity, entirely in the interests of the MPS, which placed itself proudly in the tradition of the KWS.[68] His attempt to involve Neuberg in its fortunes again could also be put down to institutional interests. While their shared national feeling remained a strong bond between the two scientists, Butenandt was also aware of the moral dimensions of his relationship with Neuberg and avoided any open discussion of his own past. The fact that Neuberg, with his attachment to the place of his past achievements and his struggle for recognition, accommodated him to a great extent is not to Butenandt's credit.

---

[68] These constructs of continuity and uncompromised institutional identity can also be found at universities; see Stephen Remy, *The Heidelberg Myth. The Nazification and Denazification of a German University* (Cambridge, MA.: Harvard University Press, 2002). German industrialists also participated in political-historical reconstructions of the past, as Jonathan Wiesen has expounded in his highly regarded study, *West German Industry and the Challenge of the Nazi Past, 1945–1955* (Chapel Hill: University of North Carolina, 2001).

Bibliography

German Versions of the Chapters in This Book

These versions include the original German quotations and in many cases are longer and contain more detailed references to sources and literature.

Bernd Gausemeier, "Mit Netzwerk und doppeltem Boden. Die botanische Forschung am Kaiser-Wilhelm-Institut für Biologie und die nationalsozialistische Wissenschaftspolitik," in Susanne Heim (ed.), *Autarkie und Ostexpansion. Pflanzenzucht und Agrarforschung im Nationalsozialismus* (Göttingen: Wallstein, 2002), 180–205.

Moritz Epple, "Rechnen, Messen, Führen. Kriegsforschung am Kaiser-Wilhelm-Institut für Strömungsforschung 1937–1945," in Helmut Maier (ed.), *Rüstungsforschung im Nationalsozialismus. Organisation, Mobilisierung und Entgrenzung der Technikwissenschaften* (Göttingen: Wallstein, 2002), 305–356.

Rüdiger Hachtmann, "Eine Erfolgsgeschichte? Schlaglichter auf die Geschichte der Generalverwaltung der Kaiser-Wilhelm-Gesellschaft im 'Dritten Reich,'" in *Ergebnisse. Vorabdrucke aus dem Forschungsprogramm "Geschichte der Kaiser-Wilhelm-Gesellschaft im Nationalsozialismus,"* No. 19 (Berlin: Forschungsprogramm, 2004) [http://www.mpiwg-berlin.mpg.de/KWG/Ergebnisse/Ergebnisse19.pdf].

Susanne Heim, *Kalorien, Kautschuk, Karrieren. Pflanzenzüchtung und landwirtschaftliche Forschung in Kaiser-Wilhelm-Instituten 1933–1945* (Göttingen: Wallstein, 2003) [excerpt].

Günther Luxbacher, "Roh- und Werkstoffe für die Autarkie. Textilforschung in der Kaiser-Wilhelm-Gesellschaft," *Ergebnisse. Vorabdrucke aus dem Forschungsprogramm "Geschichte der Kaiser-Wilhelm-Gesellschaft im Nationalsozialismus,"* No. 18 (Berlin: Forschungsprogramm, 2004) [http://www.mpiwg-berlin.mpg.de/KWG/Ergebnisse/Ergebnisse18.pdf].

Helmut Maier, "Ideologie, Rüstung und Ressourcen. Das Kaiser-Wilhelm-Institit für Metallforschung und die 'Deutsche Metalle' 1933–1945," in Helmut Maier (ed.), *Rüstungsforschung im Nationalsozialismus. Organisation, Mobilisierung und Entgrenzung der Technikwissenschaften* (Göttingen: Wallstein, 2002), 357–388.

Carola Sachse, "'Persilscheinkultur.' Zum Umgang mit der NS-Vergangenheit in der Kaiser-Wilhelm/Max-Planck-Gesellschaft," in Bernd Weisbrod (ed.), *Akademische Vergangenheitspolitik. Beiträge zur Wissenschaftskultur der Nachkriegszeit* (Göttingen: Wallstein, 2002), 217–246.

Helga Satzinger, "Rasse, Gene und Geschlecht. Zur Konstituierung zentraler biologischer Begriffe bei Richard Goldschmidt und Fritz Lenz, 1916–1936," *Ergebnisse. Vorabdrucke aus dem Forschungsprogramm "Geschichte der Kaiser-Wilhelm-Gesellschaft im Nationalsozialismus*, No. 15 (Berlin: Forschungsprogramm, 2004) [http://www.mpiwg-berlin.mpg.de/KWG/Ergebnisse/Ergebnisse15.pdf].

Wolfgang Schieder, "Spitzenforschung und Politik. Adolf Butenandt in der Weimarer Republik und im 'Dritten Reich,'" in Wolfgang Schieder and Achim Trunk (eds.), *Adolf Butenandt und die Kaiser-Wilhelm-Gesellschaft. Wissenschaft, Industrie und Politik im "Dritten Reich"* (Göttingen: Wallstein, 2004), 23–77.

Florian Schmaltz, *Kampfstoff-Forschung im Nationalsozialismus. Zur Kooperation von Kaiser-Wilhelm-Instituten, Militär und Industrie* (Göttingen: Wallstein Verlag, 2005) [excerpt].

Michael Schüring, "Der Vorgänger. Carl Neubergs Verhältnis zu Adolf Butenandt," in Wolfgang Schieder and Achim Trunk (eds.), *Adolf Butenandt und die Kaiser-Wilhelm-Gesellschaft. Wissenschaft, Industrie und Politik im "Dritten Reich"* (Göttingen: Wallstein, 2004), 346–368.

Hans-Walter Schmuhl, "Hirnforschung und Krankenmord. Das Kaiser-Wilhelm-Institut für Hirnforschung 1937–1945," *Vierteljahrshefte für Zeitgeschichte*, 50 (2002), 559–609.

Bernhard Strebel and Jens-Christian Wagner, "Zwangsarbeit für Forschungseinrichtungen der Kaiser-Wilhelm-Gesellschaft. Ein Überblick," in *Ergebnisse. Vorabdrucke aus dem Forschungsprogramm "Geschichte der Kaiser-Wilhelm-Gesellschaft im Nationalsozialismus*," No. 11 (Berlin: Forschungsprogramm, 2003) [http://www.mpiwg-berlin.mpg.de/KWG/Ergebnisse/Ergebnisse11.pdf].

Achim Trunk, "Zweihundert Blutproben aus Auschwitz. Ein Forschungsvorhaben zwischen Anthropologie und Biochemie (1943–45)," *Ergebnisse. Vorabdrucke aus dem Forschungsprogramm "Geschichte der Kaiser-Wilhelm-Gesellschaft im Nationalsozialismus*, No. 12 (Berlin: Forschungsprogramm, 2003) [http://www.mpiwg-berlin.mpg.de/KWG/Ergebnisse/Ergebnisse12.pdf].

Mark Walker, "Eine Waffenschmided? Kernwaffen- und Reaktorforschung am Kaiser-Wilhelm-Institut für Physik," in Helmut Maier (ed.), *Gemeinschaftsforschung, Bevollmächtigte und der Wissentransfer. Die Rolle der Kaiser-Wilhelm-Gesellschaft im System kriegsrelevanter Forschung des Nationalsozialismus* (Göttingen: Wallstein Verlag, 2007), 352–394.

Primary Sources

Emil Abderhalden, *Abwehrfermente (Die Abderhaldensche Reaktion)*, 6th ed. (Dresden: Steinkopff, 1941).

"Rasse und Vererbung vom Standpunkt der Feinstruktur von blut- und zelleigenen Eiweissstoffen aus betrachtet," *Nova Acta Leopoldina. Neue Folge*, 7 (1939), 59–79.

"Serologische Verwandtschaftsforschung am Menschen und anderen Primaten," in *Tagungsberichte der Deutschen Anthropologischen Gesellschaft. Bericht über die allgemeine Versammlung der Deutschen Anthropologischen Gesellschaft* (Augsburg: Filser, 1926), 88–92.

Emil Abderhalden and Severian Buadze, "Vereinfachter Nachweis von Abwehrproteinasen im Harn," *Fermentforschung*, 14 (1933/1935), 502–521.

"Die Verwendung von Harn an Stelle von Serum zum Nachweis der Abderhaldenschen Reaktion," *Fermentforschung*, 11 (1930), 305–344.

Emil Abderhalden and Ludwig Pincussohn, "Über den Gehalt des Kaninchen- und Hundeplasmas an peptolytischen Fermenten unter verschiedenen Bedingungen. 1. Mitteilung," *Hoppe-Seyler's Zeitschrift für physiologische Chemie*, 61 (1909), 200–204.

Hubert Altwicker, "Schmieden von Aluminium- und Magnesiumlegierungen," in Max Hansen (ed.), *Metallkunde der Nichteisenmetalle (Naturforschung und Medizin in Deutschland 1939–1946, FIAT Review of German Science, 32*, no. 1) (Wiesbaden: Verlag Chemie, 1948), 166–170.

"Anbau von Kautschukpflanzen in der UdSSR. Ein Versager des Sowjet-Systems," *Die chemische Industrie*, 27/28 (1941), 374–378.

W.E. Ankel, "Gerichtete und willkürliche Geschlechtsbestimmung," *Natur und Museum, Senckenbergische Naturforschende Gesellschaft*, 6 (1929), 273–374.

Auergesellschaft, "Ein neuer Hochleistungsfilter," *Gasschutz und Luftschutz*, 1 (1931), 92.

Adolf Beck (ed.), *Magnesium und seine Legierungen* (Berlin: Springer, 1939).

Bekenntnis der Professoren an den deutschen Universitäten und Hochschulen zu Adolf Hitler und dem nationalsozialistischen Staat. Überreicht vom Nationalsozialistischen Lehrerbund Deutschland/Sachsen (Dresden: NSLB, 1933).

Albert Betz, "Die Aerodynamische Versuchsanstalt Göttingen. Ein Beitrag zu ihrer Geschichte," in Walter Boje and Karl Stuchtey (eds.), *Beiträge zur Geschichte der Deutschen Luftfahrtwissenschaft und Technik* (Berlin: Deutsche Akademie der Luftfahrtforschung, 1941), 3–166.

Hans J. Born and Karl G. Zimmer, "Anwendung radioaktiver Isotope bei Untersuchungen über die Filtration von Aerosolen," *Naturwissenschaften*, 28 (1940), 447.

"Untersuchungen an Schwebstoff-Filtern mittels radioaktiver Stoffe," *Die Gasmaske*, 12 (1940), 25–29.

Joachim Brämer, "Aus der Geschichte der Deutschen Versuchsanstalt für Luftfahrt," *Metall*, 16 (1937), 382 f.

Günther Brandt, *Vorschriften zur Metallbewirtschaftung. Eine Zusammenfassung mit Erläuterungen*, 2nd ed., vol. 2 (Berlin: Lüttke, 1936).

Adolf Butenandt, "Die biologische Chemie im Dienste der Volksgesundheit. Festrede am Friedrichstag der Preussischen Akademie der Wissenschaften am 23.1.1941," *Preussische Akademie der Wissenschaften, Vorträge und Schriften*, no. 8 (1941).

"Neuere Beiträge der biologischen Chemie zum Krebsproblem," *Angewandte Chemie*, 53 (1940), 345–352.

Chemische Berichte. Arbeitsgemeinschaft Textilfasern (Berlin: Reichsamt für Wirtschaftsausbau, 1940).

Chemische Berichte. Arbeitsgemeinschaft Zellstoff (Berlin: Reichsamt für Wirtschaftsausbau, November 1941).

Carl Correns, "Geschlechterverteilung und Geschlechtsbestimmung (bei Pflanzen)," *Handwörterbuch der Naturwissenschaften,* vol. 4 (Jena: Fischer, 1913), 975–989.

Carl Correns and Richard Goldschmidt, *Die Vererbung und Bestimmung des Geschlechts. Zwei Vorträge gehalten in der Gesamtsitzung der naturwissenschaftlichen und der medizinischen Hauptgruppe der 84. Versammlung deutscher Naturforscher und Ärzte in Münster am 19.9.1912* (Berlin: Bornträger, 1913).

Werner Daitz, "Völkische Wirtschaft ist wehrhafte Wirtschaft," *Deutsche Technik,* 4 (1936), 255–257.

"Deutsche Technik und Rohstoffwirtschaft," *Zeitschrift des Vereins Deutscher Ingenieure,* 78 (1934), 1285–1290.

"Dr. phil. Theodor Menzen 60 Jahre alt," *Aluminium,* 21 (1939), 86.

Heinz Eisenbarth, "Atemfilter gegen Schwebstoffe," *Die Gasmaske,* 8 (1936), 72–77.

"Atemfilter gegen Schwebstoffe," *Kolloid-Zeitschrift,* 75, no. 2 (1936), 253–256.

Otto Eisentraut, "Zur künftigen Entwicklung der deutschen Metallgewinnung," *Deutsche Technik* (1933/34), 316 f.

"Ernennungen und Beauftragungen," *Aluminium,* 20 (1938), 287.

Lothar Frantzke, *Vom Kautschuk zum Buna* (Berlin: Limpert, 1939).

Georg Garbotz, "Der Verein deutscher Ingenieure im Jahre 1935. Geschäftsbericht, erstattet vom Direktor des VDI," *Zeitschrift des Vereins Deutscher Ingenieure,* 80 (1936), 317–331.

"Glückwunsch und Abschied," *Metallwirtschaft,* 13 (1934), 223.

Friedrich Glum, *Das geheime Deutschland* (Gräfenhainichen: Stilke, 1930).

Henry Görtler, "Weiterentwicklung eines Grenzschichtprofils bei gegebenem Druckverlauf," *Zeitschrift für angewandte Mathematik und Mechanik,* 19 (1939), 129–140.

Richard Goldschmidt, "30 Jahre Vererbungswissenschaft des schwedischen Getreidebaues," *Wissenschaftliches Korrespondenzbüro "Akademia"* 2 [special issue] *Lebendige Wissenschaft* (1929), 4–5.

"Analysis of Intersexuality in the Gypsy Moth," *Quarterly Review of Biology,* 4 (1931), 125–142.

"Die biologischen Grundlagen der konträren Sexualität und des Hermaphroditismus beim Menschen," *Archiv für Rassen- und Gesellschaftsbiologie,* 12 (1916), 1–14.

Einführung in die Vererbungswissenschaft, 2nd ed. (Leipzig: Engelmann, 1913).

"Geschlechtsbestimmung im Tier- und Pflanzenreich," *Biologisches Zentralblatt,* 49 (1929), 641–648.

"Intersexualität und menschliches Zwittertum," *Deutsche Medizinische Wochenschrift,* 57 (1931), 1–12.

The Material Basis of Evolution (New Haven: Yale University Press, 1940).

The Material Basis of Evolution, 2nd ed. (New Haven: Yale University Press, 1982).

Mechanismus und Physiologie der Geschlechtsbestimmung (Berlin: Bornträger, 1920).

Der Mendelismus (Berlin: Parey, 1920).

"Die Nachkommen der alten Siedler der Bonininseln," *Die Naturwissenschaften*, 15 (1927), 449–453.

Physiological Genetics (New York: McGraw-Hill, 1939).

Physiologische Theorie der Vererbung (Berlin: Springer, 1927).

"Das Problem der Geschlechtsbestimmung," *Die Umschau. Übersicht über die Fortschritte und Bewegungen auf dem Gesamtgebiet der Wissenschaft und Technik, sowie ihrer Beziehungen zu Wissenschaft und Kunst*, 14 (1910), 201–205.

Die quantitative Grundlage von Vererbung und Artbildung. Vorträge und Aufsätze über Entwicklungsmechanik der Organismen (Berlin: Springer, 1920).

Die Sexuellen Zwischenstufen (Berlin: Springer, 1931).

Theoretical Genetics (Berkeley: University of California Press, 1955).

Max Haas, "Alfred Wilm, der Erfinder des Duralumins," *Aluminium*, 17 (1935), 502–509.

"Alfed Wilm und die Duralumin-Erfindung," *Aluminium*, 19 (1937), 511–522.

"Aluminium und seine Legierungen im Wiederaufbauplan," *Deutsche Technik*, 2 (1934), 533 f.

"Austauscherfolge durch Aluminium an Stelle von Schwermetallen in Deutschland," *Aluminium*, 21 (1939), 643–649.

"Die europäische Rolle des Aluminiums," *Berichte der Gesellschaft von Freunden der Technischen Hochschule Berlin zu Charlottenburg e. V.*, 1, no. 2 (1942), 67–76.

"Neue Anwendungsgebiete für Leichtmetalle in Deutschland," *Schweizer Archiv für angewandte Wissenschaft und Technik*, 1 (1935), 71.

"Unser Alfred Wilm," *Aluminium*, 22 (1940), 497–501.

"Wie Hans Christian Oersted dem Aluminium den Weg bahnte," *Aluminium*, 21 (1939), 681–687, 811–823.

"Wie das Duralumin erfunden wurde," *Aluminium*, 18 (1936), 366 f.

Joachim Hackbarth, "Versuche über Photoperiodismus bei südamerikanischen Kartoffelklonen," *Der Züchter*, 7 (1935), 95–104.

Max Hansen, *Aufbau der Zwei-Stoff-Legierungen. Eine kritische Zusammenfassung* (Berlin: Springer, 1936).

Max Hartmann, *Die Sexualität* (Jena: Fischer, 1943).

Helmut Heiber (ed.), *Reichsführer! ... Briefe an und von Himmler* (Stuttgart: Deutsche Verlagsanstalt, 1968).

Susanne Heim and Gotz Aly (eds.), *Bevölkerungsstruktur und Massenmord: Neue Dokumente zur deutschen Politik der Jahre 1938–1945* (Berlin: Rotbuch Verlag, 1991).

Klaus Hentschel, *Physics and National Socialism: An Anthology of Primary Sources* (Basel: Birkhäuser, 1996).

Ludwik Hirszfeld and Hanna Hirszfeld, "Serological Differences between the Blood of Different Races," *Lancet*, 180 (1919), 675–679.

Robert Hofstätter, "Unser Wissen über die sekundären Geschlechtscharaktere," *Zentralblatt Grenzgebiete der Medizin und Chirurgie*, 16 (1912/13), 37–420.

Karl Horneck, "Über den Nachweis serologischer Verschiedenheiten der menschlichen Rassen," *Zeitschrift für menschliche Vererbungs- und Konstitutionslehre*, 26, no. 3 (1942), 309–319.

Otto Johannsen, "Verarbeitung des Flockenbastes," *Mitteilungen des Deutschen Forschungsinstitutes für Textilindustrie in Reuttlingen-Stuttgart* (July 1940), 1–34.

Wolfgang Jünger, *Kampf um Kautschuk* (Leipzig: Goldmann, 1942).

Wilhelm Jungermann and Herbert Krafft, *Rohstoffreichtum aus deutscher Erde. Eine Darstellung unserer Rohstoffwirtschaft* (Berlin: Verlag für Sozialpolitik, Wirtschaft u. Statistik, 1939).

Paul Kammerer, *Geschlecht. Fortpflanzung. Fruchtbarkeit. Eine Biologie der Zeugung (Genebiotik)* (Munich: Drei Masken-Verlag, 1927).

Arthur Kessner, *Ausnutzung und Veredlung deutscher Rohstoffe, 3. Aufl. des Buches "Rohstoffersatz"* (Berlin: Verlag des Vereines Deutscher Ingenieure, 1921).

"Umstellung der metallverarbeitenden Industrie auf heimische Rohstoffe," *Deutsche Technik*, 3 (1935), 217–220.

Ernst Klee, *Dokumente zur "Euthanasie"* (Frankfurt am Main: Fischer Taschenbuch, 1985).

Edgar Knapp, "Züchtung durch Mutationsauslösung," in Theodor Roemer and Wilhelm Rudorf (eds.), *Handbuch der Pflanzenzüchtung, Vol. I.: Grundlagen der Pflanzenzüchtung* (Berlin: Parey, 1941), 541–562.

Werner Köster, "Die Bedeutung der physikalischen Chemie für die Metallindustrie," *Zeitschrift für Elektrochemie*, 41, no. 7a (1935), 386–393.

Werner Köster and Walther Dullenkopf, "Das Dreistoffsystem Aluminium-Magnesium-Zink," *Zeitschrift für Metallkunde*, 28 (1936), 309–312, 364–367.

Werner Köster and Kurt Kam, "Über die Aushärtung von Aluminium-Magnesium-Zink-Legierungen und die Rückbildung der Kaltaushärtung," *Zeitschrift für Metallkunde*, 30 (1938), 320–322.

Werner Köster and W. Wolf, "Das Dreistoffsystem Aluminium-Magnesium-Zink," *Zeitschrift für Metallkunde*, 28 (1936), 155–158.

Richard Kuhn and Gerhard Wendt, "Über das aus Reiskleie und Hefe isolierte Adermin (Vitamin B6)," *Berichte der Deutschen Chemischen Gesellschaft*, 71 (1938), 1118.

Richard Kuhn, Gerhard Wendt, Kurt Westphal, and Otto Westphal, "Synthese des Adermins," *Die Naturwissenschaften*, 27 (1939), 469–470.

"Entwicklungsphysiologie," *Fortschritte der Botanik*, 12 (1942–48), 340–441.

"Über die Bedeutung von Licht und Dunkelheit in der photoperiodischen Reaktion von Langtagspflanzen," *Biologisches Zentralblatt*, 61 (1941), 427–432.

Hermann Langbein, *Der Auschwitz-Prozess. Eine Dokumentation* (Frankfurt am Main: Verlag Neue Kritik, 1965).

Gustav A. Langen, "Die Bedeutung der Heimstoffe für das Exportgeschäft," *Deutsche Technik*, 3 (1935), 284 f.

H. Lennartz, "Der Flugzeugbaustoff Duralumin," *Junkers Nachrichten*, 8 (1934), 85–118.

Fritz Lenz, "Erfahrungen über Erblichkeit und Entartung bei Schmetterlingen," *Archiv für Rassen- und Gesellschaftsbiologie*, 14 (1922), 249–301.

Über die krankhaften Erbanlagen des Mannes und die Bestimmung des Geschlechts beim Menschen. Untersuchungen über somatische und idioplasmatische Korrelation zwischen Geschlecht und pathologischer Anlage mit besonderer Berücksichtigung der Hämophilie (Jena: Fischer, 1912).

Artur Mahraun, *Das Jungdeutsche Manifest* (Berlin: Jungdeutscher Verlag, 1927).

Alfred Marcus, *Die grossen Eisen- und Metallkonzerne* (Leipzig: S. Hirzel, 1929), 55–64.

Paul Mathes, "Die Konstitutionstypen des Weibes, insbesondere der intersexuelle Typus," in Josef Halban and Ludwig Seitz (eds.), *Biologie und Pathologie des Weibes*, Vol. III (Berlin: Urban and Schwarzenberg, 1924), 1–112.

Georg Melchers, "Die Wirkung von Genen, tiefen Temperaturen und blühenden Pfropfpartnern auf die Blühreife von *Hyoscamus niger* L.," *Biologisches Zentralblatt*, 57 (1937), 568–614.

Georg Melchers, and Anton Lang, "Weitere Untersuchungen zur Frage der Blühhormone," *Biologisches Zentralblatt*, 61 (1941), 16–39.

Josef Mengele, "Rassenmorphologische Untersuchung des vorderen Unterkieferabschnitts bei vier rassischen Gruppen," *Morphologisches Jahrbuch*, 79 (1937), 60–117.

"Sippenuntersuchungen bei Lippen-Kiefer-Gaumenspalte," *Zeitschrift für menschliche Vererbungs- und Konstitutionslehre*, 23 (1939), 17–43.

"Zur Vererbung der Ohrfistel," *Der Erbarzt*, 8 (1940), 59–60.

Max Mengeringhausen, "Werkstoffumstellung im Armaturenbau," in Verein Deutscher Ingenieure (ed.), *Konstruieren in neuen Werkstoffen. Erfahrungen und Beispiele der Werkstoffumstellung im Maschinen- und Apparatebau* (Berlin: VDI-Verlag, 1942), 81–86.

Christian Mergenthaler, "Staat und Partei sind eins geworden. Unsere Grundsätze verwirklicht," *Vier Jahre Aufbau in Württemberg, Stuttgarter NS-Kurier*, special edition (30 January 1937), 21–23.

"Metallwirtschaft und Weltwirtschaft im Jahre 1933," *Metallwirtschaft*, 13 (1934), 13.

Meyers Konversationslexikon, 7th ed. (Leipzig: Verag des Bibliographischen Institut, 1927).

Alexander Mitscherlich and Fred Mielke, *The Death Doctors* (London: Elek, 1962).

Theodor Mollison, "Serodiagnostik als Methode der Tiersystematik und Anthropologie," in Emil Abderhalden (ed.), *Handbuch der biologischen Arbeitsmethoden*, 9/1 (Munich: Urban & Schwarzenberg, 1923).

Paul J. Möbius, *Der physiologische Schwachsinn des Weibes* (Munich: Matthes and Seitz, 1977), facsimile of the 1905 8th ed.

Thomas H. Morgan, *The Physical Basis of Heredity* (Philadelphia: Lippincott, 1919).

The Theory of the Gene (New Haven: Yale University Press, 1926).

Thomas H. Morgan et al., *The Mechanism of Mendelian Heredity* (New York: Holt, 1915).

Georg Nonnenmacher, "Technik – rassisch gesehen," *Deutsche Technik*, 4 (1936), 534 f.

NSD-Dozentenbund (ed.), *"Wissenschaft und Vierjahresplan." Reden anlässlich der Kundgebung des NSD-Dozentenbundes Gau Gross-Berlin, am Montag, dem 18. Januar 1937, in der Neuen Aula der Universität Berlin* (Berlin: NSD-Dozentenbunde, 1937).

Henry Picker, *Hitlers Tischgespräche im Führerhauptquartier 1941–42* (Bonn: Athenäum-Verlag, 1951).

Karl Pirschle, "Ist der 'd-Stoff' von Petunia artspezifisch?" *Biologisches Zentralblatt*, 60 (1940), 318–326.

Ludwig Prandtl, *Gesammelte Abhandlungen*, ed. Walter Tollmien, Hermann Schlichting, and Henry Görtler, 3 vols. (Berlin: Springer, 1961).

"Geschichtliche Vorbemerkungen," in Ludwig Prandtl (ed.), *Ergebnisse der Aerodynamischen Versuchsanstalt zu Göttingen, 1. Lieferung* (Munich: Oldenbourg, 1921), 1–7.

Ludwig Prandtl and Hermann Schlichting, "Das Widerstandsgesetz rauher Platten," *Werft, Reederei, Hafen*, 15 (1934), 1–4.

Augustin M. Prentiss, *Chemicals in War. A Treatise on Chemical Warfare* (New York: McGraw-Hill, 1937).

Reichshandbuch der Deutschen Gesellschaft (Berlin: Deutsche Wirtschaftsverlag, 1930).

Stefan Reiner, *Kautschuk-Fibel. Einführung in die Chemie und Technologie der natürlichen und synthetischen Kautschukarten*, 2nd ed. (Berlin: Union, 1942).

Hans Röhrig and Lothar Lux, "Ein neues Heim für die Forschungs- und Entwicklungsarbeit der Vereinigte Aluminium-Werke Aktiengesellschaft," *Aluminium*, 19 (1937), 658–664.

David Rowe and Robert Schulman (eds.), *Einstein on Politics: His Private Thoughts and Public Stands on Nationalism, Zionism, War, Peace, and the Bomb* (Princeton: Princeton University Press, 2007).

Wilhelm Rudorf, "Pflanzenphysiologische Untersuchungen (Keimstimmung, Photoperiodismus usw.)," *Der Forschungsdienst, Sonderheft* 8 (1938), 192–197.

Julius Schaxel, *Das Geschlecht, seine Erscheinungen, seine Bestimmung, sein Wesen bei Mensch und Tier* (Jena: Urania-Verlag-Gesellschaft, 1926).

Ernst Schilling, *Die Faserstoffe des Pflanzenreiches* (Leipzig: Hirzel, 1924).

"Weissblühender Flachs in den Niederlanden," *Die Bastfaser* (1941), 58–61.

Paul C. W. Schmidt (ed.), *Wer leitet? Die Männer der Wirtschaft und der einschlägigen Verwaltung 1941/42* (Berlin: Hoppenstedt, 1942).

Franz Schrader, *Die Geschlechtschromosomen* (Berlin: Bornträger, 1928).

Karl Schraivogel, "Heimwerkstoffe im Flugzeug- und Flugmotorenbau," *Luftfahrt-Forschung*, 14 (1937), 224–227.

Franz Schwanitz, "Experimentelle Erzeugung polyploider Pflanzenrassen," *Der Forschungsdienst*, 4 (1937), 455–463.

Albert Speer, Foreword, in "Hans von Schulz," *Jahrbuch der Metalle*, (1943), 9.

Carl Heinrich Stratz, *Die Rassenschönheit des Weibes* (Stuttgart: Enke, 1901).

Joseph Straub, "Quantitative und qualitative Verschiedenheiten polyploider Pflanzenreihen," *Biologisches Zentralblatt*, 60 (1940), 659–669.

Wege zur Polyploidie. Eine Anleitung zur Herstellung von Pflanzen mit Riesenwuchs (Berlin: Borntraeger, 1941).

Hans Stubbe, "Der Einfluss der Ernährung auf die Entstehung erblicher Veränderungen," *Angewandte Chemie*, 52 (1939), 599–602.

"Entwicklung und Stand der Mutationsforschung in der Gattung Antirrhinum," *Die Natuwissenschaften*, 22 (1934), 260–264.

Spontane und strahleninduzierte Mutabilität (Leipzig: Thieme, 1937).

"Untersuchungen über experimentelle Auslösung von Mutationen bei Antirrhinum majus IV. (Über die Beziehung zwischen Dosis und Genmutationsrate nach Röntgenbestrahlung männlicher Gonen)," *ZIAV*, 64 (1933), 181–204.

"Über den Einfluss artfemden Plasmas auf die Konstanz der Gene," *ZIAV*, 70 (1935), 161–169.

"Weitere Untersuchungen über Samenalter und Genmutabilität bei *Antirrhinum majus*," *ZIAV*, 70 (1935), 533–537.

Alfred H. Sturtevant and George W. Beadle, *An Introduction to Genetics* (Philadelphia: W. B. Saunders, 1939).

Hermann Teschemacher (ed.), *Handbuch des Aufbaus der gewerblichen Wirtschaft*, 3 vols., *Vol. 1: Reichsgruppe Industrie, Reichsgruppe Energiewirtschaft, Reichsgruppe Banken, Reichsgruppe Versicherungen* (Leipzig: Lühe, 1936).

Peter Adolf Thiessen, "Georg Grube zum 60. Geburtstag," *Zeitschrift für Elektrochemie*, 49 (1943), 193–198.

Georg Thomas, "Wehrkraft und Wirtschaft," in Richard Donnevert (ed.), *Wehrmacht und Partei*, 2nd ed. (Leipzig: J. A. Barth, 1939), 152–166.

Nikolai Timoféeff-Ressovsky, Karl G. Zimmer, and Max Delbrück, "Über die Natur der Genmutation und der Genstruktur," *Nachrichten von der Gesellschaft der Wissenschaften zu Göttingen, Math.-Nat. Klasse, Fachgruppe VI, N.F.*, 1 (1935), No. 13.

Friedrich Tobler, *Deutsche Faserpflanzen und Pflanzenfasern* (Munich: Lehmann, 1938).

Textilersatzstoffe (Dresden: Globus, 1917).

"Vernünftige Werbung für Austausch-Werkstoffe!" *Metall*, 13 (1934), 876.

50 Jahre Preussische Höhere Fachschule für Textilindustrie (Sorau: Forschungsinstitut Sorau, 1936).

Adolf von Harnack (ed.), *Handbuch der Kaiser-Wilhelm-Gesellschaft zur Förderung der Wissenschaften* (Berlin: Hobbing, 1928).

Nikolaj I. Vavilov, "Geographische Genzentren unserer Kulturpflanzen," *ZIAV Suppl.* 1 (1928), 342–369.

Otmar von Verschuer, "Emil Abderhalden, Rasse und Vererbung vom Standpunkt der Feinstruktur von blut- und zelleigenen Eiweissstoffen aus betrachtet," *Nova Acta Leopoldina. Neue Folge*, 7, no. 46 (1939).

"Erbanlage als Schicksal und Aufgabe," *Preussische Akademie der Wissenschaften. Vorträge und Schriften*, 18 (1944).

Genetik des Menschen. Lehrbuch der Humangenetik (Munich: Urban and Schwarzenberg, 1959).

Leitfaden der Rassenhygiene (Leipzig: Thieme, 1941).

Rassenhygiene als Wissenschaft und Staatsaufgabe (Frankfurter Akademische Reden, No. 7) (Frankfurt am Main: Bechhold, 1936).

"Die Wirkung von Genen und Parasiten," *Ärztliche Forschung*, 2 (1948), 378–388.

[Fritz von Wettstein], "Erbwunder der Pflanze. Ein Gespräch mit Prof. Wettstein, dem neuen Leiter des Kaiser-Wilhelm-Instituts für Biologie," *Deutsche Allgemeine Zeitung* (1 November 1934).

Fritz von Wettstein, "Die natürliche Formenmannigfaltigkeit," in Theodor Roemer and Wilhelm Rudorf (eds.), *Handbuch der Pflanzenzüchtung, Vol. I: Grundlagen der Pflanzenzüchtung* (Berlin: Parey, 1941), 8–45.

"Über deutsches und amerikanisches Forschen," in *Das Jahrzehnt 1930–1940 im Spiegel der Arbeit des Stifterverbandes der Deutschen Forschungsgemeinschaft (Notgemeinschaft der Deutschen Wissenschaft)* (Berlin: Deutsche Forschungsgemeinschaft, 1940), 171–179.

"Über plasmatische Vererbung und über das Zusammenwirken von Genen und Plasma," *Berichte der Deutschen Botanischen Gesellschaft*, 46 (1928), 32–49.

"Was ist aus der neueren Vererbungsforschung für die Pflanzenzüchtung zu verwerten?" *Der Forschungsdienst, Sonderheft*, 14 (1941), 116–130.

Fritz von Wettstein and Karl Pirschle, "Über die Wirkung heteroplastischer Pfropfungen und die Übertragung eines genbedingten Stoffes durch Pfropfung bei *Petunia*," *Biologisches Zentralblatt*, 58 (1938), 123–142.

Fritz von Wettstein and Joseph Straub, "Experimentelle Untrsuchungen zum Artbildungsproblem III. Weitere Beobachtungen an polyploiden *Bryum*-Sippen," *ZIAV*, 80 (1942), 271–280.

Walczyk and Werzmirzowsky, "Das Kaiser-Wilhelm-Institut für Bastfaserforschung," *Deutsche Textilwirtschaft*, No. 1 (1941), 6.

Otto Walchner, "Profilmessungen bei Kavitation," in Günther Kempf and Ernst Foerster (eds.), *Hydromechanische Probleme des Schiffsantriebs*, vol. 1 (Munich: Oldenbourg, 1932), 256–267.

Otto Walchner and Adolf Busemann, "Profileigenschaften bei Überschallgeschwindigkeit," *Forschungen aus dem Gebiet des Ingenieurwesens*, 4 (1933), 87–92.

"'Weisse Juden' in der Wissenschaft," *Das Schwarze Korps* (15 July 1937), 6.

E. Wieprecht, "Die Bewirtschaftungsmassnahmen der Überwachungsstelle für Metalle," *Metallwirtschaft*, 17 (1938), 1175–1180.

Wirtschaftsgruppe Nichteisenmetall-Industrie (ed.), *Bericht der Wirtschaftsgruppe Nichteisenmetall-Industrie über die Jahre 1936/37 und 1937/38* (Berlin: Wirtschaftsgruppe Nichteisenmetall-Industrie, 1938).

Paul Zimmermann, *Metallwirtschaft*, 17 (1938), 785.

"Zinklegierungen bei Giesche," *Metallwirtschaft*, 21 (1942), 143.

Secondary Sources

Mark Adams, Garland Allen, and Sheila F. Weiss, "Human Heredity and Politics: A Comparative International Study of the Eugenics Record Office at Cold Springs Harbor (United States), the Kaiser Wilhelm Institute for Anthropology, Human Heredity, and Eugenics (Germany), and the Maxim Gorky Medical Genetics Institute (USSR)," in Carola Sachse and Mark Walker (eds.), *Politics and Science in Wartime: Comparative International Perspectives on the Kaiser Wilhelm Institutes, Osiris 20* (Chicago: University of Chicago Press, 2005), 232–262.

Helmuth Albrecht and Armin Hermann, "Die Kaiser-Wilhelm-Gesellschaft im Dritten Reich (1933–1945)," in Rudolf Vierhaus and Bernhard vom Brocke (eds.), *Forschung im Spannungsfeld von Politik und Gesellschaft. Geschichte und Struktur der Kaiser-Wilhelm-/Max-Planck-Gesellschaft aus Anlass ihres 75jährigen Bestehens* (Stuttgart: DVA, 1990), 356–406.

Garland Allen, "Opposition to the Mendelian-Chromosome Theory: The Physiological and Developmental Genetics of Richard Goldschmidt," *Journal of the History of Biology*, 7 (1974), 49–92.

Thomas Hunt Morgan: The Man and His Science (Princeton: Princeton University Press, 1978).

Michael Thad Allen, *The Business of Genocide: The SS, Slave Labor, and the Concentration Camps* (Chapel Hill: University of North Carolina Press, 2002).

Götz Aly, "Die "Aktion T4" und die Stadt Berlin," in Arbeitsgruppe zur Erforschung der Geschichte der Karl-Bonhoeffer-Nervenklinik (ed.), *Totgeschwiegen 1933–1945. Zur Geschichte der Wittenauer Heilstätten, seit 1957 Karl-Bonhoeffer-Nervenklinik*, 2nd ed. (Berlin: Hentrich, 1989), 137–150.

"Forschen an Opfern. Das Kaiser-Wilhelm-Institut für Hirnforschung und die 'T4'," in Götz Aly (ed.), *Aktion T4, 1939–1945* (Berlin: Hentrich, 1987), 153–160.

"Der saubere und der schmutzige Fortschritt," *Beiträge zur nationalsozialistischen Gesundheits- und Sozialpolitik*, 2 (1985), 9–78.

Götz Aly, and Susanne Heim, *Architects of Annihilation: Auschwitz and the Logic of Destruction* (Princeton: Princeton University Press, 2003).

John D. Anderson Jr., *A History of Aerodynamics and its Impact on Flying Machines* (Cambridge: Cambridge University Press, 1997).

Arbeitsgruppe zur Erforschung der Geschichte der Karl-Bonhoeffer-Nervenklinik (ed.), *Totgeschwiegen 1933–1945. Zur Geschichte der Wittenauer Heilstätten, seit 1957 Karl-Bonhoeffer-Nervenklinik*, 2nd ed. (Berlin: Hentrich, 1989).

Mitchell Ash, "Denazifying Scientists and Science," in Matthias Judt and Burghard Ciesla (eds.), *Technology Transfer Out of Germany* (Amsterdam: Harwood, 1996), 61–80.

"Emigration und Wissenschaftswandel als Folgen der nationalsozialistischen Wissenschaftspolitik," in Doris Kaufmann (ed.), *Geschichte der Kaiser-Wilhelm-Gesellschaft im Nationalsozialismus. Bestandsaufnahme und Perspektiven der Forschung*, 2 vols. (Göttingen: Wallstein Verlag, 2000), vol. 2, 610–631.

Gestalt Psychology in German Culture 1890–1967: Holism and the Quest for Objectivity (Cambridge: Cambridge University Press, 1995).

"Kurt Gottschaldt (1902–1991) – und die psychologische Forschung vom Nationalsozialismus zur DDR – konstruierte Kontinuitäten," in Dieter Hoffmann and Kristie Macrakis (eds.), *Naturwissenschaft und Technik in der DDR* (Berlin: Akademie, 1997), 337–359.

"Scientific Changes in Germany 1933, 1945, 1990: Towards a Comparison," *Minerva* 37 (1999), 329–354.

"Verordnete Umbrüche – Konstruierte Kontinuitäten: Zur Entnazifizierung von Wissenschaftlern und Wissenschaften nach 1945," *Zeitschrift für Geschichtswissenschaft*, 43 (1995), 903–925.

"Wissenschaft und Politik als Ressourcen für einander," in Rüdiger vom Bruch and Brigitte Kaderas (eds.), *Wissenschaften und Wissenschaftspolitik: Bestandsaufnahmen zu Formationen, Brüchen und Kontinuitäten im Deutschland des 20. Jahrhunderts* (Stuttgart: Franz Steiner Verlag, 2002), 32–51.

"Wissenschaftswandlungen und politische Umbrüche im 20. Jahrhundert – was hatten sie miteinander zu tun?" in Rüdiger vom Bruch, Uta Gerhardt, and Aleksandra Pawliczek (eds.), *Kontinuitäten und Diskontinuitäten in der Wissenschaftsgeschichte des 20. Jahrhunderts* (Stuttgart: Franz Steiner, 2006), 19–37.

Mitchell Ash and Alfons Söllner (eds.), *Forced Migration and Scientific Change. Emigré German-speaking Scientists and Scholars after 1933* (Cambridge: Cambridge University Press, 1996).

Gerhard Baader, "Auf dem Weg zum Menschenversuch im Nationalsozialismus. Historische Vorbedingungen und der Beitrag der Kaiser-Wilhelm-Institute,"

Carola Sachse (ed.), *Die Verbindung nach Auschwitz. Biowissenschaften und Menschenversuche am Kaiser-Wilhelm-Institute* (Göttingen: Wallstein, 2003), 105–157.

Gerhard Baader, Susan Lederer, Morris Low, Florian Schmaltz, and Alexander von Schwerin, "Pathways to Human Experimentation, 1933–1945: Germany, Japan, and the United States," in Carola Sachse and Mark Walker (eds.), *Politics and Science in Wartime: Comparative International Perspectives on the Kaiser Wilhelm Institutes, Osiris 20* (Chicago: University of Chicago Press, 2005), 205–231.

Gerhard Baader and Ulrich Schultz (eds.), *Medizin und Nationalsozialismus: Tabuisierte Vergangenheit – ungebrochene Tradition?* (Berlin [West]: Verlagsgesellschaft Gesundheit, 1980).

David Bankier and Arnold Harttung (eds.), *Die öffentliche Meinung im Hitler-Staat. Die "Endlösung" und die Deutschen – eine Berichtigung* (Berlin: Verlag Spitz, 1995).

Omer Bartov, *Hitler's Army: Soldiers, Nazis, and War in the Third Reich* (New York: Oxford University Press, 1991).

Zygmunt Bauman, *Modernity and the Holocaust* (Ithaca: Cornell University Press, 1989).

Heinrich Becker, Hans-Joachim Dahms, and Cornelia Wegeler (eds.), *Die Universität Göttingen unter dem Nationalsozialismus*, 2nd ed. (Munich: Saur, 1998).

Heike Bernhardt, *Anstaltspsychiatrie und "Euthanasie" in Pommern 1933 bis 1945. Die Krankenmorde an Kindern und Erwachsenen am Beispiel der Landesheilanstalt Ueckermünde* (Frankfurt am Main: Mabuse-Verlag, 1994).

Jeremy Bernstein (ed.), *Hitler's Uranium Club: The Secret Recordings at Farm Hall*, 2nd ed. (New York: Copernicus Books, 2001).

Holger Berschel, *Bürokratie und Terror. Das Judenreferat der Gestapo Düsseldorf 1935 bis 1945* (Essen: Klartext-Verlag, 2001).

Alan Beyerchen, "German Scientists and Research Institutions in Allied Occupation Policy," *History of Education Quarterly*, 22, no. 3 (1982), 289–299.

Scientists under Hitler: Politics and the Physics Community in the Third Reich (New Haven: Yale University Press, 1977).

"What We Now Know about Nazism and Science," *Social Research*, 59 (1992), 615–641.

Richard Beyler, "Maintaining Discipline in the Kaiser Wilhelm Society during the National Socialist Regime," *Minerva*, 44, no. 3 (2006), 251–266.

"Rahmenbedingungen und Autoritäten der Physikergemeinschaft im Dritten Reich," in Dieter Hoffmann and Mark Walker (eds.), *Physiker zwischen Autonomie und Anpassung – Die DPG im Dritte Reich* (Weinheim: VCH, 2006), 59–90.

"'Reine' Wissenschaft und personelle 'Säuberungen.' Die Kaiser-Wilhelm/ Max-Planck-Gesellschaft 1933 und 1945," *Ergebnisse. Vorabdrucke aus dem Forschungsprogramm "Geschichte der Kaiser-Wilhelm-Gesellschaft im Nationalsozialismus,"* No. 16 (Berlin: Forschungsprogramm, 2004) [http:// www.mpiwg-berlin.mpg.de/KWG/Ergebnisse/Ergebnisse16.pdf].

Richard Beyler, Alexei Kojevnikov, and Jessica Wang, "Purges in Comparative Perspective: Rules for Exclusion and Inclusion in the Scientific Community under Political Pressure," in Carola Sachse and Mark Walker (eds.), *Politics and Science in Wartime: Comparative International Perspectives on the Kaiser Wilhelm Institutes, Osiris 20* (Chicago: University of Chicago Press, 2005), 23–48.

Heinz Bielka, *Die Medizinisch-Biologischen Institute Berlin-Buch. Beiträge zur Geschichte* (Berlin: Springer, 1997).

Gisela Bock, *Zwangssterilisation im Nationalsozialismus. Studien zur Rassenpolitik und Frauenpolitik* (Opladen: Westdeutscher Verlag, 1986).

Willi A. Boelcke, *Die deutsche Wirtschaft 1930–1945. Interna des Reichswirtschaftsministeriums* (Düsseldorf: Droste, 1983).

Willi A. Boelcke (ed.), *Deutschlands Rüstung im Zweiten Weltkrieg. Hitlers Konferenzen mit Albert Speer 1942–1945* (Frankfurt am Main: Athenaion, 1969).

Horst Boog, *Die deutsche Luftwaffenführung 1935–1946. Führungsprobleme, Spitzengliederung, Generalstabausbildung* (Stuttgart: Deutsche Verlags-Anstalt, 1982).

Joseph Borkin, *Die unheilige Allianz der I.G. Farben. Eine Interessengemeinschaft im Dritten Reich* (Frankfurt/Main: Campus, 1981).

Karl Brandt, Otto Schiller, and Franz Ahlgrimm, *Management of Agriculture and Food in the German-Occupied and Other Areas of Fortress Europe: A Study in Military Government* (Stanford: Stanford University Press, 1953).

Martin Broszat (ed.), *Kommandant in Auschwitz. Autobiographische Aufzeichnungen des Rudolf Höss* (Munich: DTV, 1989).

Frederic J. Brown, *Chemical Warfare. A Study in Restraints* (Princeton: Princeton University Press, 1981).

Stephen G. Brush, "Nettie M. Stevens and the Discovery of Sex Determination by Chromosomes," *Isis*, 69 (1978), 163–172.

Lutz Budrass, *Flugzeugindustrie und Luftrüstung in Deutschland 1918–1945* (Düsseldorf: Droste, 1998).

"Zwischen Unternehmen und Luftwaffe. Die Luftfahrtforschung im 'Dritten Reich,'" in Helmut Maier (ed.), *Rüstungsforschung im Nationalsozialismus. Organisation, Mobilisierung und Entgrenzung der Technikwissenschaften* (Göttingen: Wallstein, 2002), 142–182.

Michael Burleigh, *Germany Turns Eastwards. A Study of Ostforschung in the Third Reich* (Cambridge: Cambridge University Press, 1988).

Adolf Butenandt, *Das Werk eines Lebens*, vols. 1 and 2 (Göttingen: Vandenhoeck und Ruprecht, 1981).

David Cahan, *An Institute for an Empire: The Physikalisch-Technische Reichsanstalt 1871–1918* (Cambridge: Cambridge University Press, 1989).

Cathryn Carson, "Heisenberg and the Framework of Science Policy," *Fortschritte der Physik*, 50, nos. 5–7 (2002), 432–436.

"New Models for Science in Politics: Heisenberg in West Germany," *Historical Studies in the Physical and Biological Sciences*, 30, no. 1 (1999), 115–171.

"Nuclear Energy Development in Postwar West Germany: Struggles over Cooperation in the Federal Republic's First Reactor Station," *History and Technology*, 18, no. 3 (2002), 233–270.

"Objectivity and the Scientist: Heisenberg Rethinks," *Science in Context*, 16 (2003), 243–269.

Cathryn Carson, "Old Programs, New Policies? Nuclear Reactor Studies after 1945 in the Max-Planck-Institut für Physik," in Doris Kaufmann (ed.), *Geschichte der Kaiser-Wilhelm-Gesellschaft im Nationalsozialismus. Bestandsaufnahme und Perspektiven der Forschung*, 2 vols. (Göttingen: Wallstein, 2000), vol. 2, 726–749.

"Reflections on Copenhagen," in Matthias Dörries (ed.), *Michael Frayn's Copenhagen in Debate: Historical Essays and Documents on the 1941 Meeting between Niels Bohr and Werner Heisenberg* (Berkeley: Office for History of Science and Technology, University of California, 2005), 7–17.

"A Scientist in Public: Werner Heisenberg after 1945," *Endeavour*, 23, no. 1, (1999), 31–34.

Cathryn Carson and Michael Gubser, "Science Advising and Science Policy in Post-War West Germany: The Example of the Deutscher Forschungsrat," *Minerva*, 40 (2002), 147–179.

Gradon Carter, *Porton Down. 75 Years of Chemical and Biological Research* (London: Stationery Office Books, 1992).

Gradon Carter and Brain Balmer, "Chemical and Biological Warfare and Defence, 1945–50," in Robert Bud and Philip Gummett (eds.), *Cold War, Hot Science: Applied Research in Britain's Defence Laboratories, 1945–1990* (Amsterdam: Harwood, 1999), 295–338.

Beyond Uncertainty: Heisenberg, Quantum Physics, and the Bomb (New York: Bellevue Literary Press, 2009).

"Controlling German Science I: U.S. and Allied Forces in Germany, 1945–1947," *Historical Studies in the Physical and Biological Sciences*, 24 (1994), 197–235.

David Cassidy, "Controlling German Science II: Bizonal Occupation and the Struggle over West German Science Policy, 1946–1949," *Historical Studies in the Physical and Biological Sciences*, 26 (1996), 197–239.

David Cassidy, *Uncertainty: The Life and Science of Werner Heisenberg* (New York: Freeman, 1991).

Burghard Ciesla, "Abschied von der 'reinen' Wissenschaft. 'Wehrtechnik' und Anwendungsforschung in der Preussischen Akademie nach 1933," in Wolfram Fischer (ed.), *Die Preussische Akademie der Wissenschaften zu Berlin 1914–1945* (Berlin: Akademie Verlag, 2000), 483–513.

"Das Heereswaffenamt und die Kaiser-Wilhelm-Gesellschaft im 'Dritten Reich.' Die militärischen Forschungsbeziehungen zwischen 1918 und 1945," in Helmut Maier (ed.), *Gemeinschaftsforschung, Bevollmächtigte und der Wissenstransfer. Die Rolle der Kaiser-Wilhelm-Gesellschaft im System kriegsrelevanter Forschung des Nationalsozialismus* (Göttingen: Wallstein Verlag, 2007), 32–76.

John Connelly and Michael Grüttner (eds.), *Zwischen Autonomie und Anpassung: Universitäten in den Diktaturen des 20. Jahrhunderts* (Paderborn: Schöningh, 2003).

Gustavo Corni and Horst Gies, *Butter-Brot-Kanonen: Die Ernährungswirtschaft in Deutschland unter der Diktatur Hitlers* (Berlin: Akademie Verlag, 1997).

John Cornwell, *Hitler's Scientists: Science, War and the Devil's Pact* (New York: Viking, 2003).

Elisabeth Crawford, Ruth Lewin Sime, and Mark Walker, "A Nobel Tale of Postwar Injustice," *Physics Today*, 50, no. 9 (September 1997), 26–32.

Elisabeth Crawford, Ruth Lewin Sime, and Mark Walker, "A Nobel Tale of Wartime Injustice," *Nature*, 382 (1996), 393–95.

Gabriele Czarnowski, *Das kontrollierte Paar. Ehe- und Sexualpolitik im Nationalsozialismus* (Weinheim: Deutscher Studienverlag, 1991).

Danuta Czech, *Kalendarium der Ereignisse im Konzentrationslager Auschwitz-Birkenau 1939–1945* (Reinbek: Rohwolt, 1989).

Herwig Czech, "Dr. Heinrich Gross, Die wissenschaftliche Verwertung der NS-Euthanasie in Österreich," *Dokumentationsarchiv des österreichischen Widerstandes, Jahrbuch* (1999), 53–70.

Ute Deichmann, *Biologists under Hitler* (Cambridge, MA: Harvard University Press, 1996).

"'Dem Duce, dem Tenno und userem Führer ein dreifaches Sieg Heil!'" in Dieter Hoffmann and Mark Walker (eds.), *Physiker zwischen Autonomie und Anpassung – Die DPG im Dritte Reich* (Weinheim: VCH, 2006), 459–498.

Flüchten, Mitmachen, Vergessen. Chemiker und Biochemiker in der NS-Zeit (Weinheim: VCH, 2001).

"Kriegsbezogene biologische, biochemische und chemische Forschung an den Kaiser Wilhelm-Instituten für Züchtungsforschung, für Physikalische Chemie und Elektrochemie und für Medizinische Forschung," in Doris Kaufmann (ed.), *Geschichte der Kaiser-Wilhelm-Gesellschaft im Nationalsozialismus. Bestandsaufnahme und Perspektiven der Forschung*, 2 vols. (Göttingen: Wallstein, 2000), vol. 1, 231–257.

"Proteinforschung an Kaiser-Wilhelm-Instituten von 1930 bis 1950 im internationalen Vergleich," in *Ergebnisse. Vorabdrucke aus dem Forschungsprogramm "Geschichte der Kaiser-Wilhelm-Gesellschaft im Nationalsozialismus,"* No. 21 (Berlin: Forschungsprogramm, 2004) [http://www.mpiwg-berlin.mpg.de/KWG/Ergebnisse/Ergebnisse21.pdf].

"An Unholy Alliance," *Nature*, 405 (2000), 739.

Wilhelm Deist, "Rüstungsforschung und Wehrmacht. Ein Kommentar," in Doris Kaufmann (ed.), *Geschichte der Kaiser-Wilhelm-Gesellschaft im Nationalsozialismus. Bestandsaufnahme und Perspektiven der Forschung*, 2 vols. (Göttingen: Wallstein, 2000), vol. 1, 363–370.

Charlotte Delbo, *Auschwitz and After* (New Haven: Yale University Press, 1995).

Deutsche Gesellschaft für Metallkunde (ed.), *50 Jahre Deutsche Gesellschaft für Metallkunde e. V. im Spiegel der Zeitschrift für Metallkunde* (Stuttgart: Riederer-Verlag, 1969).

Michael R. Dietrich, "From Gene to Genetic Hierarchy: Richard Goldschmidt and the Problem of the Gene," in Peter J. Beurton, Raphael Falk, and Hans-Jörg Rheinberger (eds.), *The Concept of the Gene in Development and Evolution. Historical and Epistemological Perspectives* (Cambridge: Cambridge University Press, 2000), 91–114.

"Of Moths and Men: Theo Lang and the Persistence of Richard Goldschmidt's Theory of Homosexuality, 1916–1960," *History and Philosophy of the Life Sciences*, 22 (2000), 219–247.

"On the Mutability of Genes and Geneticists: The "Americanization" of Richard Goldschmidt and Victor Yollos," *Perspectives on Science*, 4 (1996), 321–346.

"Richard Goldschmidt: Hopeful Monsters and Other 'Heresies,'" *Nature Reviews Genetics*, 4 (2003), 68–74.

"Richard Goldschmidt's 'Heresies' and the Evolutionary Synthesis," *Journal of the History of Biology*, 28 (1995), 431–461.

Burkhard Dietz, Michael Fessner, and Helmut Maier (eds.), *Technische Intelligenz und "Kulturfaktor Technik". Kulturvorstellungen von Technikern und Ingenieuren zwischen Kaiserreich und Bundesrepublik Deutschland* (Münster: Waxmann, 1996).

Ronald Doel, Dieter Hoffmann, and Nikolai Krementsov, "National States and International Science: A Comparative History of International Science Congresses in Hitler's Germany, Stalin's Russia, and Cold War United States," in Carola Sachse and Mark Walker (eds.), *Politics and Science in Wartime: Comparative International Perspectives on the Kaiser Wilhelm Institutes, Osiris 20* (Chicago: University of Chicago Press, 2005), 49–76.

Klaus Dörner, Angelika Ebbinghaus, Karsten Linne, Karl Heinz Roth, and Paul Weindling (eds.), *Der Nürnberger Ärzteprozess 1946/47. Wortprotokolle, Anklage- und Verteidigungsmaterial, Quellen zum Umfeld* (Munich: Saur, 2000).

Matthias Dörries (ed.), *Michael Frayn's Copenhagen in Debate: Historical Essays and Documents on the 1941 Meeting between Niels Bohr and Werner Heisenberg* (Berkeley: Office for History of Science and Technology, University of California, 2005).

Arthur Douglass Merriman, *A Dictionary of Metallurgy* (London: MacDonald and Evans, 1958).

Angelika Ebbinghaus, "Chemische Kampfstoffe in der deutschen Rüstungs- und Kriegswirtschaft, in Dietrich Eichholtz (ed.), *Krieg und Wirtschaft. Studien zur deutschen Wirtschaftsgeschichte 1939–1945* (Berlin: Metropol, 1999), 171–194.

Angelika Ebbinghaus and Klaus Dörner (eds.), *Vernichten und Heilen. Der Nürnberger Ärzteprozess und seine Folgen* (Berlin: Aufbau-Verlag, 2001).

"Kriegswunden. Die kriegschirurgischen Experimente in den Konzentrationslagern und ihre Hintergründe," in Angelika Ebbinghaus and Klaus Dörner (ed.), *Vernichten und Heilen. Der Nürnberger Ärzteprozeß und seine Folgen* (Berlin: Aufbau-Verlag, 2001), 177–218.

"Vernichtungsforschung: Der Nobelpreisträger Richard Kuhn, die Kaiser Wilhelm-Gesellschaft und die Entwicklung von Nervenkampfstoffen während des 'Dritten Reichs,'" 1999. *Zeitschrift für Sozialgeschichte des 20. und 21. Jahrhunderts,* 17, no. 1 (2002), 15–50, 21.

"Von der Rockefeller Foundation zur Kaiser Wilhelm/Max-Planck-Gesellschaft: Adolf Butenandt als Biochemiker und Wissenschaftspolitiker des 20. Jahrhunderts," *Zeitschrift für Geschichtswissenschaft,* 50 (2002), 389–418.

Hans Ebert and Hermann J. Rupieper, "Technische Wissenschaft und national-sozialistische Rüstungspolitik. Die Wehrtechnische Fakultät der TH Berlin 1933–1945," in Reinhard Rürup (ed.), *Wissenschaft und Gesellschaft. Beiträge zur Geschichte der TH/TU Berlin 1879–1979* (Berlin: Springer, 1979), 469–491.

Wolfgang Eckart (ed.), *Man, Medicine, and the State. The Human Body as an Object of Government Sponsored Medical Research in the 20th Century* (Stuttgart: Steiner Verlag, 2006).

Michael Eckert, "Die Anfänge der Atompolitik in der Bundesrepublik Deutschland," *Vierteljahrshefte für Zeitgeschichte,* 37, no. 1 (1989), 115–143.

"Das 'Atomei': Der erste bundesdeutsche Forschungsreaktor als Katalysator nuklearer Interessen in Wissenschaft und Politik," in Michael Eckert and Maria Osietzki (eds.), *Wissenschaft für Macht und Markt. Kernforschung und Mikroelektronik in der Bundesrepublik Deutschland* (Munich: Verlag C. H. Beck, 1989), 74–95.

"Die Deutsche Physikalische Gesellschaft und die 'Deutsche Physik,'" in Dieter Hoffmann and Mark Walker (eds.), *Physiker zwischen Autonomie und Anpassung – Die DPG im Dritte Reich* (Weinheim: VCH, 2006), 139–172

"Kernenergie und Westintegration. Die Zähmung des westdeutschen Nuklearnationalismus," in Ludolf Herbst, Werner Bührer, and Hanno Sowade (eds.), *Vom Marshallplan zur EWG. Die Eingliederung der Bundesrepublik Deutschland in die westliche Welt* (Munich: R. Oldenbourg Verlag, 1990), 313–334.

Michael Eckert, "Neutrons and Politics: Maier-Leibnitz and the Emergence of Pile Neutron Research in the FRG," *Historical Studies in the Physical and Biological Sciences*, **19**, no. 1 (1988), 81–113.

"Strategic Internationalism and the Transfer of Technical Knowledge: The United States, Germany, and Aerodynamics after World War I," *Technology and Culture*, **46** (2005), 104–131.

Michael Eckert, "Theoretische Physiker in Kriegsprojekten. Zur Problematik einer internationalen vergleichenden Analyse," in Doris Kaufmann (ed.), *Geschichte der Kaiser-Wilhelm-Gesellschaft im Nationalsozialismus. Bestandsaufnahme und Perspektiven der Forschung*, 2 vols. (Göttingen: Wallstein, 2000), vol. 1, 296–308.

Dietrich Eichholtz, *Geschichte der deutschen Kriegswirtschaft 1939–1945. Vol. III: 1943–1945* (Berlin: Akademie-Verlag, 1996), 205–208.

Dietrich Eichholtz (ed.), *Krieg und Wirtschaft. Studien zur deutschen Wirtschaftsgeschichte* (Berlin: Metropol, 1999).

Christiane Eifert, "Die neue Frau. Bewegung und Alltag," in Manfred Görtemaker (ed.), *Weimar in Berlin: Porträt einer Epoche* (Berlin: be.bar-Verlag, 2002), 82–103.

Olga Elina, Susanne Heim, and Nils Roll-Hansen, "Plant Breeding on the Front: Imperialism, War, and Exploitation," in Carola Sachse and Mark Walker (eds.), *Politics and Science in Wartime: Comparative International Perspectives on the Kaiser Wilhelm Institutes, Osiris 20* (Chicago: University of Chicago Press, 2005), 161–179.

John Ellis Van Courtland Moon, "Project Sphinx: The Question of the Use of Gas in the Planned Invasion of Japan," *Journal of Strategic Studies*, **12**, no. 3 (1989), 303–323.

"United States Chemical Warfare Policy in World War II: A Captive of Coalition Policy?" *Journal of Military History*, **60**, no. 3 (1996), 495–511.

Gerda Engelbracht, *Der tödliche Schatten der Psychiatrie. Die Bremer Nervenklinik 1933–1945* (Bremen: Donat, 1997).

Moritz Epple, *Die Entstehung der Knotentheorie. Kontexte und Konstruktionen einer modernen mathematischen Theorie* (Wiesbaden: Vieweg, 1999).

"Rechnen, Messen, Führen. Kriegsforschung am Kaiser-Wilhelm-Institut für Strömungsforschung 1937–1945," in Helmut Maier (ed.), *Rüstungsforschung im Nationalsozialismus. Organisation, Mobilisierung und Entgrenzung der Technikwissenschaften* (Göttingen: Wallstein, 2002), 305–356.

"Knot Invariants in Vienna and Princeton during the 1920s. Epistemic Configurations of Mathematical Research," *Science in Context*, **17** (2004), 131–164.

Moritz Epple, Andreas Karachalios, and Volker Remmert, "Aerodynamics and Mathematics in National Socialist Germany and Fascist Italy: A Comparison of Research Institutes," in Carola Sachse and Mark Walker (eds.), *Politics and Science in Wartime: Comparative International Perspectives on the Kaiser Wilhelm Institutes, Osiris 20* (Chicago: University of Chicago Press, 2005), 131–158.

Moritz Epple and Volker Remmert, "'Eine ungeahnte Synthese zwischen reiner und angewandter Mathematik.' Kriegsrelevante mathematische Forschung in Deutschland während des II. Weltkrieges," in Doris Kaufmann (ed.), *Geschichte der Kaiser-Wilhelm-Gesellschaft im Nationalsozialismus. Bestandsaufnahme und Perspektiven der Forschung*, 2 vols. (Göttingen: Wallstein, 2000), vol. 1, 258–295.

René Erbe, *Die nationalsozialistische Wirtschaftspolitik 1933–1939 im Lichte der modernen Theorie* (Zurich: Polygraphischer Verlag, 1958).

Paul Erker, "Die Rolle der Forschung bei der Ersatzstoff-Produktion. Das Beispiel Continental AG/Reifenindustrie," in Doris Kaufmann (ed.), *Geschichte der Kaiser-Wilhelm-Gesellschaft im Nationalsozialismus. Bestandsaufnahme und Perspektiven der Forschung*, 2 vols. (Göttingen: Wallstein Verlag, 2000), vol. 1, 411–425.

Michael G. Esch (ed.), *Die Medizinische Akademie Düsseldorf im Nationalsozialismus* (Essen: Klartext-Verlag, 1997).

Rob Evans, *Gassed: British Chemical Warfare Experiments on Humans* (London: House of Stratus, 2000).

Lothar Evers, "Entschädigungsregelungen und -verfahrensweisen in der Nachkriegszeit – Offene Rechnungen," in Carola Sachse (ed.), *Die Verbindung nach Auschwitz. Biowissenschaften und Menschenversuche am Kaiser-Wilhelm-Institute* (Göttingen: Wallstein, 2003), 306–315.

Sabine Fahrenbach and Achim Thom (eds.), *Der Arzt als "Gesundheitsführer". Ärztliches Wirken zwischen Ressourcenerschliessung und humanitärer Hilfe im Zweiten Weltkrieg* (Frankfurt am Main: Mabuse-Verlag, 1991).

Heiner Fangerau, "Der 'Baur-Fischer-Lenz' in der Buchkritik 1921–1940: Eine quantifizierende Untersuchung zur zeitgenössischen Rezeption rassenhygienischer Theorien," *Medizinhistorisches Journal*, 38 (2003), 57–81.

John Farquharson, *The Plough and the Swastika: The NSDAP and Agriculture in Germany 1928–45* (London: Sage, 1976).

"Die faschistischen Wehrwirtschaftsführer in der westdeutschen Wirtschaft," *Berichte des deutschen Wirtschaftsinstituts*, 5, no. 9/10 (1954), 1–64.

Ruth Federspiel, "Mobilisierung der Rüstungsforschung? Werner Osenberg und das Planungsamt im Reichsforschungsrat 1943–1945," in Helmut Maier (ed.), *Rüstungsforschung im Nationalsozialismus. Organisation, Mobilisierung und Entgrenzung der Technikwissenschaften* (Göttingen: Wallstein, 2002), 72–105.

Gerald Feldman, *Allianz and the German Insurance Business, 1933–1945* (Cambridge: Cambridge University Press, 2001).

"Historische Vergangenheitsbearbeitung. Wirtschaft und Wissenschaft im Vergleich," *Ergebnisse. Vorabdrucke aus dem Forschungsprogramm "Geschichte der Kaiser-Wilhelm-Gesellschaft im Nationalsozialismus,"* no. 13 (Berlin: Forschungsprogramm, 2003) [http://www.mpiwg-berlin.mpg.de/KWG/Ergebnisse/Ergebnisse13.pdf].

Martin Fiedler and Bernhard Lorentz, "Kontinuitäten in den Netzwerkbeziehungen der deutschen Wirtschaftselite zwischen Weltwirtschaftskrise und 1950. Eine quantitative und qualitative Analyse," in Volker R. Berghahn, Stefan Unger, and Dieter Ziegler (eds.), *Die deutsche Wirtschaftselite im 20. Jahrhundert. Kontinuität und Modernität* (Essen: Klartext-Verlag, 2003), 51–74.

Kurt Finker, *Jungdeutscher Orden (Jungdo) 1920–1933, in Lexikon zur Parteigeschichte*, vol. 3 (Leipzig: Bibliographisches Institut, 1985), 138–148.

Wolfram Fischer (ed.), *Die Preussische Akademie der Wissenschaften zu Berlin 1914–1945* (Berlin: Akademie Verlag, 2000).

Sören Flachowsky, "'Alle Arbeit des Instituts dient mit leidenschaftlicher Hingabe der deutschen Rüstung.' Das Kaiser-Wilhelm-Institut für Eisenforschung als inter-institutionelle Schnittstelle kriegsrelevanter Wissensproduktion 1917–1945," in Helmut Maier (ed.), *Gemeinschaftsforschung, Bevollmächtigte und der Wissenstransfer. Die Rolle der Kaiser-Wilhelm-Gesellschaft im System kriegsrelevanter Forschung des Nationalsozialismus* (Göttingen: Wallstein Verlag, 2007), 153–214.

Von der Notgemeinschaft zum Reichsforschungsrat: Wissenschaftspolitik im Kontext von Autarkie, Aufrüstung und Krieg (Stuttgart: Steiner, 2008).

Ludwik Fleck, *Entstehung und Entwicklung einer wissenschaftlichen Tatsache. Einführung in die Lehre vom Denkstil und Denkkollektiv* (Frankfurt am Main: Suhrkamp, 1994).

Michael Flitner, "Agrarische Modernisierung im genetischen Diskurs. Ansatzpunkte zu einem internationalen Vergleich 1925–1939," in Susanne Heim (ed.), *Autarkie und Ostexpansion. Pflanzenzucht und Agrarforschung im Nationalsozialismus* (Göttingen: Wallstein, 2002), 91–117.

Sammler, Räuber und Gelehrte. Die politischen Interessen an pflanzengenetischen Ressourcen 1895–1995 (Frankfurt am Main: Campus Verlag, 1995).

Paul Forman, "Behind Quantum Electronics: National Security as Basis for Physical Research in the United States, 1940–1960." *Historical Studies in the Physical and Biological Sciences*, 18 (1987): 149–229.

"Eine Einführung in das Wissenschaftsleben der Weimarer Republik," in Dieter Hoffmann and Mark Walker (eds.), *Physiker zwischen Autonomie und Anpassung – Die DPG im Dritte Reich* (Weinheim: VCH, 2006), 29–58.

"The Financial Support and Political Alignment of Physicists in Weimar Germany," *Minerva*, 12 (1974), 39–66.

"Scientific Internationalism and the Weimar Physicists: The Ideology and Its Manipulation in Germany after World War I," *Isis*, 64, no. 2 (1973), 150–180.

"Weimar Culture, Causality, and Quantum Theory, 1918–1927: Adaptation by German Physicists to a Hostile Intellectual Environment," *Historical Studies in the Physical Sciences*, 3 (1971), 1–115.

Charles Frank (ed.), *Operation Epsilon: The Farm Hall Transcripts* (London: IOP, 1993).

Michael Frayn, *Copenhagen* (New York: Anchor Books, 1998).

Norbert Frei, *Vergangheitspolitik. Die Anfänge der Bundesrepublik und die NS-Vergangenheit* (Munich: Beck, 1996).

Carl Freytag, "'Bürogenerale' und 'Frontsoldaten' der Wissenschaft. Atmosphärenforschung in der Kaiser-Wilhelm-Gesellschaft während des Nationalsozialismus," in Helmut Maier (ed.), *Gemeinschaftsforschung, Bevollmächtigte und der Wissenstransfer. Die Rolle der Kaiser-Wilhelm-Gesellschaft im System kriegsrelevanter Forschung des Nationalsozialismus* (Göttingen: Wallstein Verlag, 2007), 215–267.

Peter Fritsche, *A Nation of Fliers: German Aviation and the Popular Imagination* (Cambridge, MA: Harvard University Press, 1992).

Rainer Froebe, "Bauen und Vernichten. Die Zentralbauleitung Auschwitz und die 'Endlösung.' " *Beiträge zur Geschichte des Nationalsozialismus*, 16 (2000), 155–209.

Jean-Paul Gaudillière, "Biochemie und Industrie. Der "Arbeitskreis Butenandt-Schering" im Nationalsozialismus," in Wolfgang Schieder and Achim Trunk (eds.), *Adolf Butenandt und die Kaiser-Wilhelm-Gesellschaft. Wissenschaft, Industrie und Politik im "Dritten Reich"* (Göttingen: Wallstein Verlag, 2004), 198–246.

Jean-Paul Gaudillière and Bernd Gausemeier, "Molding National Research Systems: The Introduction of Penicillin to Germany and France," in Carola Sachse and Mark Walker (eds.), *Politics and Science in Wartime: Comparative International Perspectives on the Kaiser Wilhelm Institutes, Osiris 20* (Chicago: University of Chicago Press, 2005), 180–202.

Bernd Gausemeier, "An der Heimatfront. 'Kriegswichtige' Forschungen am Kaiser-Wilhelm-Institut für Biochemie," in Wolfgang Schieder and Achim Trunk (eds.), *Adolf Butenandt und die Kaiser-Wilhelm-Gesellschaft. Wissenschaft, Industrie und Politik im "Dritten Reich"* (Göttingen: Wallstein, 2004), 134–168.

"Mit Netzwerk und doppeltem Boden. Die botanischen Forschung am Kaiser-Wilhelm-Institut für Biologie und die nationalsozialistische Wissenschaftspolitik," in Susanne Heim (ed.), *Autarkie und Ostexpansion. Pfanzenzucht und Agrarforschung im Nationalsozialismus* (Göttingen: Wallstein Verlag, 2002), 180–205.

Natürliche Ordnungen und politische Allianzen. Biologische und biochemische Forschung an Kaiser-Wilhelm-Instituten 1933–1945 (Göttingen: Wallstein, 2005).

"Rassenhygienische Radikalisierung und kollegialer Konsens. Verschuer, Butenandt und die Blutproben aus Auschwitz," in Carola Sachse (ed.), *Die Verbindung nach Auschwitz. Biowissenschaften und Menschenversuche am Kaiser-Wilhelm-Institute* (Göttingen: Wallstein, 2003), 178–199.

Günther W. Gellermann, *Der Krieg, der nicht stattfand. Möglichkeiten, Überlegungen und Entscheidungen der deutschen Obersten Führung zur Verwendung chemischer Kampfstoffe im zweiten Weltkrieg* (Koblenz: Bernard und Graefe, 1986).

Generalverwaltung der Max-Planck-Gesellschaft (ed.), *50 Jahre Kaiser-Wilhelm-Gesellschaft und Max-Planck-Gesellschaft zur Förderung der Wissenschaften 1911/1961. Beiträge und Dokumente* (Göttingen: Max-Planck-Gesellschaft, 1961).

Ute Gerhard and Jürgen Link, "Zum Anteil der Kollektivsymbolik an den Nationalstereotypen," in Jürgen Link and Wulf Wülfing (eds.), *Nationale Mythen und Symbole in der zweiten Hälfte des 19. Jahrhunderts. Strukturen und Funktionen von Konzepten nationaler Identität* (Stuttgart: Klett-Cotta, 1991), 16–52.

Ulfried Geuter, *The Professionalization of Psychology in Nazi Germany* (Cambridge: Cambridge University Press, 1992).

Reinhard Giersch, "Deutsche Stiftung (DStg), 1920–1940," in *Lexikon zur Parteiengeschichte. Die bürgerliche und kleinbürgerlichen Parteien und Verbände in Deutschland*, vol. II (Leipzig: Pahl-Rugenstein, 1984), 359–366.

Ulrich Giersch and Ulrich Kubisch, *Gummi – Die elastische Faszination* (Berlin: Nicolai, 1995).

Scott F. Gilbert, "Cellular Politics: Ernest Everett Just, Richard B. Goldschmidt, and the Attempt to Reconcile Embryology and Genetics," in Ronald Rainger, Keith Benson, and Jane Maienschein (eds.), *The American Development of Biology* (Philadelphia: University of Pennsylvania Press, 1988), 311 – 346.

Franz Gilles, "Der Reichsrechnungshof zwischen obrigkeitsstaatlicher Tradition und geforderter Demokratisierung," in Theo Pirker (ed.), *Rechnungshöfe als Gegenstand zeitgeschichtlicher Forschung* (Berlin: Duncker and Humblot, 1987), 19–34.

John Gimbel, *Science, Technology, and Reparations. Exploitation and Plunder in Post-war Germany* (Palo Alto: Stanford University Press, 1990).

Richard Goldschmidt, *In and Out of the Ivory Tower. The Autobiography of Richard B. Goldschmidt* (Seattle: University of Washington Press, 1960).

Michael Gordin, Walter Grunden, Mark Walker, and Zuoyue Wang, "'Ideologically Correct' Science," in Mark Walker (ed.), *Science and Ideology: A Comparative History* (London: Routledge, 2003), 35–65.

Samuel Goudsmit, *Alsos*, 3rd ed. (New York: Springer, 1996).

Steven J. Gould, "Introduction," in Richard Goldschmidt, *The Material Basis of Evolution*, 2nd ed. (New Haven: Yale University Press, 1982), xiii–xlii

Rolf Grabow, "Zu einigen wissenschaftshistorischen Aspekten der Entwicklung aushärtbarer Aluminiumlegierungen," *NTM*, 17 (1980), 69–79.

Margaret B.W.Graham and Bettye H. Pruitt, *R & D for Industry. A Century of Technical Innovation at Alcoa* (Cambridge: Cambridge University Press, 1990).

Ursula Grell, "Gesundheit ist Pflicht. Das öffentliche Gesundheitswesen Berlins 1933–1939," in Arbeitsgruppe zur Erforschung der Geschichte der Karl-Bonhoeffer-Nervenklinik (ed.), *Totgeschwiegen 1933–1945. Zur Geschichte der Wittenauer Heilstätten, seit 1957 Karl-Bonhoeffer-Nervenklinik*, 2nd ed. (Berlin: Hentrich, 1989), 49–76.

Olaf Groehler, *Der lautlose Tod. Einsatz und Entwicklung deutscher Giftgase von 1914 bis 1945* (Reinbek bei Hamburg: Rowohlt, 1989).

Michael Grüttner, *Biographisches Lexikon zur nationalsozialistischen Wissenschaftspolitik* (Heidelberg: Synchron, 2004).

"Die deutschen Universitäten unter dem Hakenkreuz," in John Connelly and Michael Grüttner (eds.), *Zwischen Autonomie und Anpassung: Universitäten in den Diktaturen des 20. Jahrhunderts* (Paderborn: Schöningh, 2003), 67–100.

"Wissenschaftspolitik im Nationalsozialismus," in Doris Kaufmann (ed.), *Geschichte der Kaiser-Wilhelm-Gesellschaft im Nationalsozialismus. Bestandsaufnahme und Perspektiven der Forschung*, 2 vols. (Göttingen: Wallstein Verlag, 2000), vol. 2, 557–585.

Walter Grunden, Yutaka Kawamura, Eduard Kolchinsky, Helmut Maier, and Masakatsu Yamazaki, "Laying the Foundation for Wartime Research: A Comparative Overview of Science Mobilization in National Socialist Germany, Japan, and the Soviet Union," in Carola Sachse and Mark Walker (eds.), *Politics and Science in Wartime: Comparative International Perspectives on the Kaiser Wilhelm Institutes, Osiris 20* (Chicago: University of Chicago Press, 2005), 79–106.

Walter Grunden, Mark Walker, and Masakatsu Yamazaki, "Wartime Nuclear Weapons Research in Germany and Japan," in Carola Sachse and Mark Walker (eds.), *Politics and Science in Wartime: Comparative International Perspectives on the Kaiser Wilhelm Institutes, Osiris 20* (Chicago: University of Chicago Press, 2005), 107–130.

Ludwig F. Haber, *The Poisonous Cloud. Chemical Warfare in the First World War* (Oxford: Oxford University Press, 1986).

Rüdiger Hachtmann, "Eine Erfolgsgeschichte? Schlaglichter auf die Geschichte der Generalverwaltung der Kaiser-Wilhelm-Gesellschaft im 'Dritten Reich,'" in *Ergebnisse. Vorabdrucke aus dem Forschungsprogramm "Geschichte der Kaiser-Wilhelm-Gesellschaft im Nationalsozialismus,"* No. 19 (Berlin: Forschungsprogramm, 2004) [http://www.mpiwg-berlin.mpg.de/KWG/Ergebnisse/Ergebnisse19.pdf].

"Der Ertrag eines erfolgreichen Wissenschaftsmanagements: Die Etatentwicklung wichtiger Kaiser-Wilhelm-Institute 1929 bis 1944," in Helmut Maier (ed.), *Gemeinschaftsforschung, Bevollmächtigte und der Wissenstransfer. Die Rolle der Kaiser-Wilhelm-Gesellschaft im System kriegsrelevanter Forschung des Nationalsozialismus* (Göttingen: Wallstein Verlag, 2007), 561–598.

"Die Kaiser-Wilhelm-Gesellschaft 1933 bis 1945: Politik und Selbstverständnis einer Grossforschungseinrichtung," *Vierteljahrshefte für Zeitgeschichte,* 56 (2008), 19–52.

"Vernetzung um jeden Preis. Zum politischen Alltagshandeln der Generalverwaltung der Kaiser-Wilhelm-Gesellschaft im 'Dritten Reich,'" in Helmut Maier (ed.), *Gemeinschaftsforschung, Bevollmächtigte und der Wissenstransfer. Die Rolle der Kaiser-Wilhelm-Gesellschaft im System kriegsrelevanter Forschung des Nationalsozialismus* (Göttingen: Wallstein Verlag, 2007), 77–152.

Wissenschaftsmanagement im Dritten Reich. Die Geschichte der Kaiser-Wilhelm-Gesellschaft 1930/33 bis 1945/48 (Göttingen: Wallstein, 2008).

Michael Hagner, *Geniale Gehirne. Zur Geschichte der Elitegehirnforschung,* 2nd ed. (Göttingen: Wallstein Verlag, 2005), 235–287.

"Im Pantheon der Gehirne. Die Elite- und Rassengehirnforschung von Oskar und Cécile Vogt," in Hans-Walter Schmuhl (ed.), *Rassenforschung an Kaiser-Wilhelm-Instituten vor und nach 1933* (Göttingen: Wallstein Verlag, 2003), 99–144.

Notker Hammerstein, *Die deutsche Forschungsgemeinschaft in der Weimarer Republik und im Dritten Reich. Wissenschaftspolitik in Republik und Diktatur* (Munich: Beck, 1999).

Kai Handel, "Die Arbeitsgemeinschaft Rotterdam und die Entwicklung von Halbleiterdetektoren. Hochfrequenzforschung in der militärischen Krise 1943–1945," in Helmut Maier (ed.), *Rüstungsforschung im Nationalsozialismus. Organisation, Mobilisierung und Entgrenzung der Technikwissenschaften* (Göttingen: Wallstein, 2002), 250–270.

Sabine Hanrath, *Zwischen "Euthanasie" und Psychiatriereform. Anstaltspsychiatrie in Westfalen und Brandenburg: Ein deutsch-deutscher Vergleich (1945–1964)* (Paderborn: Schöningh, 2002).

Anne Harrington, *Reenchanted Science: Holism and German Culture from Wilhelm II to Hitler* (Princeton: Princeton University Press, 1996).

Robert Harris and Jeremy Paxman, *Eine höhere Form des Tötens. Die geheime Geschichte der B- und C-Waffen* (Düsseldorf: Econ, 1983).

Jonathan Harwood, "German Science and Technology under National Socialism," in *Perspectives on Science*, 5, no. 1, (1997), 128–151.

"Politische Ökonomie der Pflanzenzucht in Deutschland ca. 1870 bis 1933," in Susanne Heim (ed.), *Autarkie und Ostexpansion. Pflanzenzucht und Agrarforschung im Nationalsozialismus* (Göttingen: Wallstein, 2002), 14–33.

"Eine vergleichende Analyse zweier genetischer Forschungsinstitute: die Kaiser-Wilhelm-Institute für Biologie und für Züchtungsforschung," in Bernhard vom Brocke and Hubert Laitko (eds.), *Die Kaiser-Wilhelm-/Max-Planck- Gesellschaft und ihre Institute. Studien zu ihrer Geschichte: Das Harnack-Prinzip* (Berlin: de Gruyter, 1996), 331–348.

"The Rise of the Party-Political Professor? Changing Self-Understandings among German Academics, 1890–1933," in Doris Kaufmann (ed.), *Geschichte der Kaiser-Wilhelm-Gesellschaft im Nationalsozialismus. Bestandsaufnahme und Perspektiven der Forschung*, 2 vols. (Göttingen: Wallstein Verlag, 2000), vol. 1, 21–45.

Styles of Scientific Thought: The German Genetics Community 1900–1933 (Chicago: University of Chicago Press, 1993).

Karin Hausen, "Mütter, Söhne und der Markt der Symbole und Waren: Der deutsche Muttertag 1923–1933," in Hans Medick and David Sabean (eds.), *Emotionen und materielle Interessen. Sozialanthropologische und historische Beiträge zur Familienforschung* (Göttingen: Vandenhoeck and Ruprecht, 1984), 473–523.

Peter Hayes, "Die 'Arisierungen' der Degussa AG. Geschichte und Bilanz," in Irmtrud Wojak and Peter Hayes (eds.), *"Arisierung" im Nationalsozialismus. Volksgemeinschaft, Raub, Gedächtnis* (Frankfurt am Main: Campus, 2000), 85–123, 92–93.

From Cooperation to Complicity. Degussa in the Third Reich (Cambridge: Cambridge University Press, 2005).

Industry and Ideology. IG Farben in the Nazi Era (Cambridge: Cambridge University Press, 2001).

Helmut Heiber, *Universität unterm Hakenkreuz, Teil II: Die Kapitulation der Hohen Schulen, Vol. 2: Das Jahr 1933 und seine Themen* (Munich: Saur, 1994).

John Heilbron, *The Dilemmas of an Upright Man: Max Planck as Spokesman for German Science* (Berkeley: University of California Press, 1986), 175–179.

Susanne Heim (ed.), *Autarkie und Ostexpansion. Pflanzenzucht und Agrarforschung im Nationalsozialismus* (Göttingen: Wallstein, 2002).

Susanne Heim, "Expansion Policy and the Role of Agricultural Research in Nazi Germany," *Minerva*, 44, no. 3 (2006), 267–284.

"Forschung für die Autarkie," in Susanne Heim (ed.), *Autarkie und Ostexpansion. Pflanzenzucht und Agrarforschung im Nationalsozialismus* (Göttingen: Wallstein, 2002), 145–177.

Kalorien, Kautschuk, Karrieren. Pflanzenzüchtung und landwirtschaftliche Forschung in Kaiser-Wilhelm-Instituten 1933–1945 (Göttingen: Wallstein, 2003).

Plant Breeding and Agrarian Research in Kaiser-Wilhelm-Institutes 1933–1945 (Boston: Springer 2008).

"Die reine Luft der wissenschaftlichen Forschung." Zum Selbstverständnis der Wissenschaftler der Kaiser-Wilhelm-Gesellschaft," in *Ergebnisse. Vorabdrucke aus dem Forschungsprogramm "Geschichte der Kaiser-Wilhelm-Gesellschaft im*

Nationalsozialismus," No. 7 (Berlin: Forschungsprogramm, 2002) [http://www. mpiwg-berlin.mpg.de/KWG/Ergebnisse/Ergebnisse7.pdf].

"Research for Autarky. The Contribution of Scientists to Nazi Rule in Germany," in *Ergebnisse. Vorabdrucke aus dem Forschungsprogramm "Geschichte der Kaiser-Wilhelm-GesellschaftimNationalsozialismus,"* No.4 (Berlin:Forschungsprogramm, 2001) [http://www.mpiwg-berlin.mpg.de/KWG/Ergebnisse/Ergebnisse4.pdf].

Susanne Heim, "'Vordenker der Vernichtung.' Wissenschaftliche Experten als Berater der nationalsozialistischen Politik," Doris Kaufmann (ed.), *Geschichte der Kaiser-Wilhelm-Gesellschaft im Nationalsozialismus. Bestandsaufnahme und Perspektiven der Forschung*, 2 vols. (Göttingen: Wallstein Verlag, 2000), vol. 1, 77–91.

Manfred Heinemann, "Der Wiederaufbau der Kaiser-Wilhelm-Gesellschaft und die Neugründung der Max-Planck-Gesellschaft (1945–1949)," in Rudolf Vierhaus and Bernhard vom Brocke (eds.), *Forschung im Spannungsfeld von Politik und Gesellschaft. Geschichte und Struktur der Kaiser-Wilhelm/Max-Planck-Gesellschaft* (Stuttgart: Deutsche Verlags-Anstalt, 1990), 407–470.

Klaus Hentschel, *The Mental Aftermath: The Mentality of German Physicists 1945–1949* (Oxford: Oxford University Press, 2007).

Klaus Hentschel and Gerhard Rammer, "Kein Neuanfang: Physiker an der Universität Göttingen 1945–1955," *Zeitschrift für Geschichtswissenschaft*, 48 (2000), 718–741.

Klaus Hentschel and Gerhard Rammer, "Nachkriegsphysik an der Leine. Eine Göttinger Vogelperspektive," in Dieter Hoffmann (ed.), *Physik in Nachkriegsdeutschland* (Frankfurt am Main: Verlag Harri Deutsch, 2003), 27–56.

"Physicists at the University of Göttingen, 1945–1955," *Physics in Perspective*, 3, no. 1 (2001), 189–209.

Ulrich Herbert (ed.), *Europa und der "Reichseinsatz." Ausländische Zivilarbeiter, Kriegsgefangene und KZ-Häftlinge in Deutschland 1938–1945* (Essen: Klartext-Verlag, 1991).

Fremdarbeiter. Politik und Praxis des "Ausländer-Einsatzes" in der Kriegswirtschaft des Dritten Reiches, 2nd ed. (Berlin: Dietz, 1999).

Ulrich Herbert, Karin Orth, and Christoph Dieckmann (eds.), *Die nationalsozialistischen Konzentrationslager. Entwicklung und Struktur*, vol. 2 (Göttingen: Wallstein, 1998).

Jeffrey Herf, *Reactionary Modernism: Technology, Culture, and Politics in Weimar and the Third Reich* (Cambridge: Cambridge University Press, 1984).

"'Reactionary Modernism' and After: Modernity and Nazi Germany Reconsidered," Doris Kaufmann (ed.), *Geschichte der Kaiser-Wilhelm-Gesellschaft im Nationalsozialismus. Bestandsaufnahme und Perspektiven der Forschung*, 2 vols. (Göttingen: Wallstein Verlag, 2000), vol. 1, 65–76.

Hans Hesse, *Augen aus Auschwitz. Ein Lehrstück über nationalsozialistischen Rassenwahn und medizinische Forschung – Der Fall Dr. Karin Magnussen* (Essen: Klartext, 2001).

Uwe Heyll, "Friedrich Panse und die psychiatrische Erbforschung," in Michael G. Esch (ed.), *Die Medizinische Akademie Düsseldorf im Nationalsozialismus* (Essen: Klartext-Verlag, 1997), 318–340.

Andrew Hodges, *Alan Turing: The Enigma* (New York: Simon and Schuster, 1989).

Ekkehard Höxtermann, "Zur Geschichte des Hormonbegriffes in der Botanik und zur Entdeckungsgeschichte der 'Wuchsstoffe,'" *History and Philosophy of the Life Sciences*, 16 (1994), 311–337.

Dieter Hoffmann, "Die Ramsauer-Ära und die Selbstmobilisierung der Deutschen Physikalischen Gesellschaft," in Dieter Hoffmann and Mark Walker (eds.), *Physiker zwischen Autonomie und Anpassung – Die DPG im Dritte Reich* (Weinheim: VCH, 2006), 173–215.

"Carl Ramsauer, die Deutsche Physikalische Gesellschaft und die Selbstmobilisierung der Physikerschaft im 'Dritten Reich,'" in Helmut Maier (ed.), *Rüstungsforschung im Nationalsozialismus. Organisation, Mobilisierung und Entgrenzung der Technikwissenschaften* (Göttingen: Wallstein, 2002), 273–304.

Dieter Hoffmann (ed.), *Operation Epsilon. Die Farm-Hall-Protokolle oder Die Angst der Alliierten vor der deutschen Atombombe* (Berlin: Rowohlt Berlin, 1993).

"Der Physikochemiker Robert Havemann (1910–1982) – eine deutsche Biographie," in Dieter Hoffmann and Kristie Macrakis (eds.), *Naturwissenschaft und Technik in der DDR* (Berlin: Akademie, 1997), 319–336.

"Das Verhältnis der Akademie zu Republik und Diktatur. Max Planck als Sekretar," in Wolfram Fischer (ed.), *Preussische Akademie der Wissenschaften zu Berlin 1914–1945* (Berlin: Akademie Verlag, 2000), 53–85.

Dieter Hoffmann and Mark Walker (eds.), *Physiker zwischen Autonomie und Anpassung – Die DPG im Dritte Reich* (Weinheim: VCH, 2006).

Kathrin Hoffmann-Curtius, "Geschlechterspiel im Dadaismus," *Kunstforum*, 128 (October–December 1994), 166–169.

Joachim S. Hohmann and Günther Wieland, *MfS-Operativvorgang "Teufel." "Euthanasie"-Arzt Otto Hebold vor Gericht* (Berlin: Metropol, 1996).

Barbara Hopmann, *Von der Montan zur Industrieverwaltungsgesellschaft (IVG) 1916–1951* (Stuttgart: Steiner, 1996).

Klaus Hornung, *Der Jungdeutsche Orden* (Düsseldorf: Droste, 1958).

Uwe Hossfeld and Carl-Gustaf Thornström, "'Rasches Zupacken.' Heinz Brücher und das botanische Sammelkommando der SS nach Russland 1943," in Susanne Heim (ed.), *Autarkie und Ostexpansion. Pflanzenzucht und Agrarforschung im Nationalsozialismus* (Göttingen: Wallstein, 2002), 119–144.

H. Hug, "Aluminium-Zink-Magnesium-Legierungen," in Dietrich Altenpohl (ed.), *Aluminium und Aluminiumlegierungen* (Berlin: Springer, 1965), 770–785.

David Irving, *The German Atomic Bomb: The History of Nuclear Research in Nazi Germany* (New York: Simon and Schuster, 1968).

Walther Jaenicke, *100 Jahre Bunsen-Gesellschaft 1894–1994* (Darmstadt: Steinkopff, 1994).

Christan Jansen, Lutz Niethammer, and Bernd Weisbrod (eds.), *Von der Aufgabe der Freiheit. Politische Verantwortung und bürgerliche Gesellschaft im 19. und 20. Jahrhundert. Festschrift für Hans Mommsen* (Berlin: Akademie Verlag, 1995).

Hinrich Jasper, *Maximinian de Crinis (1889–1945). Eine Studie zur Psychiatrie im Nationalsozialismus* (Husum: Matthiesen, 1991).

Gottfried Jayme (ed.), *50 Jahre Cellulosechemie an der Technischen Hochschule Darmstadt 1908–1958* (Darmstadt: Institut für Cellulosechemie, 1958).

Jeffrey Johnson, *The Kaiser's Chemists: Science and Modernization in Imperial Germany* (Chapel Hill: University of North Carolina Press, 1990).

Daniel P. Jones, "Chemical Warfare Research during World War I: A Model of Cooperative Research," in John Parascondola and James C. Whorton (eds.), *Chemistry and Modern Society. Historical Essays in Honor of Aaron J. Ihde* (Washington, DC: American Chemical Society, 1983), 165–185.

Paul R. Josephson, *Totalitarian Science and Technology,* 2nd ed. (Atlantic Highlands: Humanity Books, 2005).

Robert Jungk, *Brighter than a Thousand Suns: A Personal History of the Atomic Scientists* (New York: Harcourt Brace, 1958).

Trotzdem: mein Leben für die Zukunft (Munich: Hanser, 1993).

Michael Kaasch, "Sensation, Irrtum, Betrug? Emil Abderhalden und die Geschichte der Abwehrfermente," *Vorträge und Abhandlungen zur Wissenschaftsgeschichte* (1999/2000), 145–210.

Edda Käding, *Engagement und Verantwortung. Hans Stubbe, Genetiker und Züchtungsforscher. Eine Biographie* (Müncheberg: ZALF, 1999).

Walter Kaiser and Norbert Gilson, *Heraeus – Pioniere der Werkstofftechnologie. Von der Hanauer Platinschmelze zum internationalen Technologieunternehmen* (Munich: Piper, 2001).

Horst Kant, "Albert Einstein, Max von Laue, Peter Debye und das Kaiser-Wilhelm-Institut für Physik in Berlin (1917–1939)," in Bernhard vom Brocke and Hubert Laitko (eds.), *Die Kaiser-Wilhelm-/Max-Planck-Gesellschaft und ihre Institute; Studien zu ihrer Geschichte: Das Harnack-Prinzip* (Berlin: De Gruyter, 1996), 227–243.

"Peter Debye und das Kaiser-Wilhelm-Institut für Physik in Berlin," in Helmut Albrecht (ed.), *Naturwissenschaft und Technik in der Geschichte (25 Jahre Lehrstuhl für Geschichte der Naturwissenschaft und Technik am Historischen Institut der Universität Stuttgart)* (Stuttgart: GNT-Verlag, 1993), 161–177.

"Peter Debye und die Deutsche Physikalische Gesellschaft," in Dieter Hoffmann, Fabio Bevilacqua, and Roger Stuewer (eds.), *The Emergence of Modern Physics* (Pavia: Universita degli Studi die Pavia, 1996), 505–520.

"Werner Heisenberg and the German Uranium Project," *Max-Planck-Insitut für Wissenschaftsgeschichte, Preprint 203* (Berlin: MPIfWG, 2002).

"Werner Heisenberg und das Kaiser-Wilhelm-Institut für Physik in Berlin," in Bodo Geyer, Helge Herwig, and Helmut Rechenberg (eds.), *Werner Heisenberg – Physiker und Philosoph* (Heidelberg: Spektrum Akademischer Verlag, 1993), 152–158.

Rainer Karlsch, "Boris Rajewsky und das Kaiser-Wilhelm-Institut für Biophysik in der Zeit des Nationalsozialismus," in Helmut Maier (ed.), *Gemeinschaftsforschung, Bevollmächtigte und der Wissenstransfer. Die Rolle der Kaiser-Wilhelm-Gesellschaft im System kriegsrelevanter Forschung des Nationalsozialismus* (Göttingen: Wallstein Verlag, 2007), 395–452.

Hitler's Bombe. Die geheime Geschichte der deutschen Kernwaffenversuche (Munich: DVA, 2005).

Rainer Karlsch and Mark Walker, "New Light on Hitler's Bomb," *Physics World* (June, 2005), 15–18.

Peter Karlson, *Adolf Butenandt. Biochemiker, Hormonforscher, Wissenschaftspolitiker* (Stuttgart: Wissenschaftliche Verlagsgesellschaft, 1990).

Michael H. Kater, *Das "Ahnenerbe" der SS, 1935–1945. Ein Beitrag zur Kulturpolitik des Dritten Reiches,* 2nd ed. (Munich: Oldenbourg, 1997).

Doris Kaufmann, "Eugenik – Rassenhygiene – Humangenetik. Zur lebenswissenschaftlichen Neuordnung der Wirklichkeit in der ersten Hälfte des 20. Jahrhunderts," in Richard van Dülmen (ed.), *Erfindung des Menschen. Schöpfungsträume und Körperbilder 1500–2000* (Wien: Böhlau, 1998), 347–365.

Doris Kaufmann (ed.), *Geschichte der Kaiser-Wilhelm-Gesellschaft im Nationalsozialismus. Bestandsaufnahme und Perspektiven der Forschung*, 2 vols. (Göttingen: Wallstein, 2000).

Doris Kaufmann, "'Rasse und Kultur.' Die amerikanische Kulturanthropologie um Franz Boas (1858–1942) in der ersten Hälfte des 20. Jahrhunderts – ein Gegenentwurf zur Rassenforschung in Deutschland," in Hans-Walter Schmuhl (ed.), *Rassenforschung an Kaiser-Wilhelm-Instituten vor und nach 1933* (Göttingen: Wallstein, 2003), 309–327.

"Wissenschaft im Nationalsozialismus," in Max-Planck-Gesellschaft zur Förderung der Wissenschaften e.V. (ed.), *Ethos der Forschung. Ethics of Research. Ringberg-Symposium October 1999* (Munich: Generalverwaltung der Max-Planck-Gesellschaft, 2000), 11–23.

Lily E. Kay, *The Molecular Vision of Life. Caltech, the Rockefeller Foundation, and the Rise of the New Biology* (Oxford: Oxford University Press, 1993).

Sven Keller, *Günzburg und der Fall Josef Mengele. Die Heimatstadt und die Jagd auf den NS-Verbrecher* (Munich: Oldenbourg, 2003).

Franz-Werner Kersting, *Anstaltsärzte zwischen Kaiserreich und Bundesrepublik. Das Beispiel Westfalen* (Paderborn: Schöningh, 1996).

Franz-Werner Kersting and Hans-Walter Schmuhl, "Einleitung," in Franz-Werner Kersting and Hans-Walter Schmuhl (eds.), *Quellen zur Geschichte der Anstaltspsychiatrie in Westfalen, Vol. 2: 1914 – 1955* (Paderborn: Schöningh, 2004), 1–64.

Mieczylaw Kieta, "Das Hygiene-Institut der Waffen-SS und Polizei in Auschwitz," *Die Auschwitz-Hefte*, 1 (1987), 213–217.

Hermann Klare, *Geschichte der Chemiefaserforschung* (Berlin: Akademie-Verlag, 1985).

Ernst Klee, "Augen aus Auschwitz," *Die Zeit* (27 January 2000).

Auschwitz, die NS-Medizin und ihre Opfer (Frankfurt am Main: Fischer, 1997).

Deutsche Medizin im Dritten Reich. Karrieren vor und nach 1945 (Frankfurt am Main; Fischer, 2001).

Otto Klein, "Wir fürchteten jeden Tag um unser Leben," in Carola Sachse (ed.), *Die Verbindung nach Auschwitz. Biowissenschaften und Menschenversuche am Kaiser-Wilhelm-Institute* (Göttingen: Wallstein, 2003), 89–93.

Gerhard Koch, *Humangenetik und Neuropsychiatrie in meiner Zeit (1932–1978). Jahre der Entscheidung* (Erlangen: Palm and Enke, 1993).

Werner Köster, "50 Jahre Deutsche Gesellschaft für Metallkunde. Festvortrag am 27. Mai 1969," *Metall*, 23 (1969), 661–666.

Ulrike Kohl, *Die Präsidenten der Kaiser-Wilhelm-Gesellschaft im Nationalsozialismus. Max Planck, Carl Bosch und Albert Vögler zwischen Wissenschaft und Macht* (Stuttgart: Steiner, 2002).

Robert E. Kohler, *Lords of the Fly. Drosophila Genetics and the Experimental Life* (Chicago: University of Chicago, 1994).

Christoph Kopke (ed.), *Medizin und Verbrechen: Festschrift zum 60. Geburtstag von Walter Wuttke* (Ulm: Klemm und Oelschläger, 2001).

Eva Mozes Kor, "Heilung von Auschwitz und Mengeles Experimenten," in Carola Sachse (ed.), *Die Verbindung nach Auschwitz. Biowissenschaften und Menschenversuche an Kaiser-Wilhelm-Instituten – Dokumentation eines Symposiums* (Göttingen: Wallstein Verlag, 2003), 59–70.

Eva Mozes Kor and Mary Wright, *Echoes from Auschwitz. Dr. Mengele's Twins – The Story of Eva and Miriam Mozes* (Terre Haute: Candles, 1996).

Fritz Krafft, *Im Schatten der Sensation. Leben und Wirken von Fritz Strassmann* (Weinheim: Verlag Chemie, 1981).

Christoph Kreutzmüller, "Zum Umgang der Kaiser-Wilhelm-Gesellschaft mit Geld und Gut. Immobilientransfers und jüdische Stiftungen 1933–1945," in *Ergebnisse. Vorabdrucke aus dem Forschungsprogramm "Geschichte der Kaiser-Wilhelm-Gesellschaft im Nationalsozialismus,"* No. 27 (Berlin: Forschungsprogramm, 2005) [http://www.mpiwg-berlin.mpg.de/KWG/Ergebnisse/Ergebnisse27.pdf].

Vera Kriegel, "... endlich den höchsten Berg gefunden," in Carola Sachse (ed.), *Die Verbindung nach Auschwitz. Biowissenschaften und Menschenversuche am Kaiser-Wilhelm-Institute* (Göttingen: Wallstein, 2003), 76–82.

Hans-Peter Kröner, "Das Kaiser-Wilhelm-Institut für Anthropologie, menschliche Erblehre und Eugenik und die Humangenetik in der Bundesrepublik Deutschland," in Doris Kaufmann (ed.), *Geschichte der Kaiser-Wilhelm-Gesellschaft im Nationalsozialismus. Bestandsaufnahme und Perspektiven der Forschung*, 2 vols. (Göttingen: Wallstein Verlag, 2000), vol. 2, 653–666.

Von der Rassenhygiene zur Humangenetik. Das Kaiser-Wilhelm-Institut für Anthropologie, menschliche Erblehre und Eugenik nach dem Kriege (Stuttgart: Fischer, 1998).

Martina Krüger, "Kinderfachabteilung Wiesengrund. Die Tötung behinderter Kinder in Wittenau," in Arbeitsgruppe zur erforschung der Geschichte Der Karl-Bonhoeffer-Nervenklinik (ed.), *Totgeschwiegen 1933–1945. Zur Geschichte der Wittenauer Heilstätten, seit 1957 Karl-Bonhoeffer-Nervenklinik*, 2nd ed. (Berlin: Hentrich, 1989), 151–176.

Helena Kubica, "Dr. Mengele und seine Verbrechen im Konzentrationslager Auschwitz-Birkenau," *Hefte von Auschwitz*, 20 (1997), 369–455.

Stefan Kühl, *Die Internationale der Rassisten. Aufstieg und Niedergang der internationalen Bewegung für Eugenik und Rassenhygiene im 20. Jahrhundert* (Frankfurt am Main: Campus, 1997).

The Nazi Connection: Eugenics, American Racism, and German National Socialism (New York: Oxford University Press, 1994).

Alfred Kühn, *Grundriss der Vererbungslehre*, 6th ed. (Heidelberg: Quelle and Meyer, 1973).

Rolf-Ulrich Kunze, *Ernst Rabel und das Kaiser-Wilhelm-Institut für ausländisches und internationales Privatrecht 1926–1945* (Göttingen: Wallstein Verlag, 2004).

Martin Kutz, "Kriegserfahrung und Kriegsvorbereitung. Die agrarwirtschaftliche Vorbereitung des Zweiten Weltkrieges in Deutschland vor dem Hintergrund der Weltkrieg I-Erfahrung," *Zeitschrift für Agrargeschichte und Agrarsoziologie*, 32 (1984), 59–82, 135–164.

Jona Laks, "Erinnerung gegen das Vergessen," in Carola Sachse (ed.), *Die Verbindung nach Auschwitz. Biowissenschaften und Menschenversuche am Kaiser-Wilhelm-Institute* (Göttingen: Wallstein, 2003), 52–58.

"Jeder Mensch hat einen Namen," in Carola Sachse (ed.), *Die Verbindung nach Auschwitz. Biowissenschaften und Menschenversuche am Kaiser-Wilhelm-Institute* (Göttingen: Wallstein, 2003), 328.

Anton Lang, "Some Recollections and Reflections," *Annual Review of Plant Physiology*, 31 (1980), 1–28.

Bruno Latour and Steve Woolgar, *Laboratory Life. The Social Construction of Scientific Facts* (Beverly Hills: Sage, 1979).

Joachim Lehmann, "Faschistische Agrarpolitik im zweiten Weltkrieg: zur Konzeption von Herbert Backe," *Zeitschrift für Geschichtswissenschaft*, 28 (1980), 948–956.

Jeffrey Lewis, "Kalter Krieg in der Max-Planck-Gesellschaft. Göttingen und Tübingen – eine Vereinigung mit Hindernissen, 1948–1949," in Wolfgang Schieder and Achim Trunk (eds.), *Adolf Butenandt und die Kaiser-Wilhelm-Gesellschaft. Wissenschaft, Industrie und Politik im "Dritten Reich"* (Göttingen: Wallstein, 2004), 403–443.

Robert J. Lifton, *The Nazi Doctors: Medical Killing and the Psychology of Genocide* (New York: Basic, 1986).

Joachim Lilla, *Statisten in Uniform. Die Mitglieder des Reichstags 1933–1945* (Düsseldorf: Droste, 2004).

Freddy Litten, *Der Rücktritt Richard Willstätters 1924/25 und seine Hintergründe* (Munich: Institut für Geschichte der Naturwissenschaften, 1999).

Bernhard Lorentz, *Industrieelite und Wirtschaftspolitik 1928–1950: Heinrich Dräger und das Drägerwerk* (Paderborn: Schöningh, 2001), 148–157, 273–283.

Niels C. Lösch, *Rasse als Konstrukt. Leben und Werk Eugen Fischers* (Frankfurt am Main: Lang, 1997).

Bettina Löser, "Der Beitrag des Kaiser Wilhelm-Institutes für Faserstoffchemie in Berlin-Dahlem," *Mitteilungen der Fachgruppe Geschichte der Chemie*, 7 (1992), 50–61.

"Zur Gründungsgeschichte des Kaiser Wilhelm-Institutes für Faserstoffchemie in Berlin-Dahlem," *NTM-Schriftenreihe Geschichte der Naturwissenschaft, Technik und Medizin*, 28, no. 1 (1991), 73–93.

"Zur Gründungsgeschichte und Entwicklung des Kaiser-Wilhelm-Institutes für Faserstoffchemie in Berlin-Dahlem (1914/19–1934)," in Bernhard vom Brocke and Hubert Laitko (eds.), *Die Kaiser-Wilhelm-, Max-Planck-Gesellschaft und ihre Institute. Studien zu ihrer Geschichte: Das Harnack-Prinzip* (Berlin: de Gruyter, 1996).

Herbert Loos, "Die Heil- und Pflegeanstalt Berlin-Herzberge während der Jahre des Zweiten Weltkrieges," in Sabine Fahrenbach and Achim Thom (eds.), *Der Arzt als "Gesundheitsführer." Ärztliches Wirken zwischen Ressourcenerschliessung und humanitärer Hilfe im Zweiten Weltkrieg* (Frankfurt am Main: Mabuse-Verlag, 1991).

Gabriele Lotfi, *KZ der Gestapo. Arbeitserziehungslager im Dritten Reich* (Stuttgart: DVA, 2000).

Karl-Heinz Ludwig, *Technik und Ingenieure im Dritten Reich* (Düsseldorf: Droste Verlag, 1974).

Valdis Lumans, *Himmler's Auxiliaries. The Volksdeutsche Mittelstelle and the German National Minorities of Europe 1933–44* (Chapel Hill: University of North Carolina Press, 1993).

Günter Luxbacher, "Kohle-Öl-Benzin. Die Fischer-Tropsch-Synthese in der interinstitutionellen Kooperation 1933–1944," in Helmut Maier (ed.), *Gemeinschaftsforschung, Bevollmächtigte und der Wissenstransfer. Die Rolle der Kaiser-Wilhelm-Gesellschaft im System kriegsrelevanter Forschung des Nationalsozialismus* (Göttingen: Wallstein Verlag, 2007), 453–502.

"Massenproduktion wider Willen: der Rohstoff Baumwolle und die Maschinisierung der österreichischen Spinnerei," in *200 Jahre erste Baumwollmaschinen-Spinnerei in Sachsen* (Chemnitz: Selbstverlag des Chemnitzer Geschichtsvereins, 1999), 102–111.

"Roh- und Werkstoffe für die Autarkie. Textilforschung in der Kaiser-Wilhelm-Gesellschaft," *Ergebnisse. Vorabdrucke aus dem Forschungsprogramm "Geschichte der Kaiser-Wilhelm-Gesellschaft im Nationalsozialismus*, No. 18 (Berlin: Forschungsprogramm, 2004) [http://www.mpiwg-berlin.mpg.de/KWG/Ergebnisse/Ergebnisse18.pdf].

"Die technologische Mobilisierung der Botanik. Konzept und Wirkung der Technischen Rohstofflehre und Warenkunde im 19. Jahrhundert," *Technikgeschichte*, 68, no. 4 (2001), 307–333.

"Wertarbeit mit Ersatzstoffen? Ausstellungen als Bühne deutscher Werkstoffpolitik 1916 bis 1942," *Dresdner Beiträge zur Geschichte der Technikwissenschaften* (2006), 3–24.

Roy Macleod, "The Chemists Go to War: The Mobilisation of Civilian Chemists and the British War Effort, 1914–1918," *Annals of Science*, 50 (1993), 455–481.

Kristie Macrakis, *Surviving the Swastika: Scientific Research in Nazi Germany* (New York: Oxford University Press, 1993).

"'Surviving the Swastika' Revisited: The Kaiser-Wilhelm-Gesellschaft and Science Policy in Nazi Germany," in Doris Kaufmann (ed.), *Geschichte der Kaiser-Wilhelm-Gesellschaft im Nationalsozialismus. Bestandsaufnahme und Perspektiven der Forschung*, 2 vols. (Göttingen: Wallstein Verlag, 2000), vol. 2, 586–599.

"Wissenschaftsförderung durch die Rockefeller Stiftung im 'Dritten Reich.' Die Entscheidung, das Kaiser-Wilhelm-Institut für Physik finanziell zu unterstützen, 1934-1939," *Geschichte und Gesellschaft*, 12 (1986), 348–379.

Kristie Macrakis and Dieter Hoffmann (eds.), *Science under Socialism : East Germany in Comparative Perspective* (Cambridge, MA: Harvard University Press, 1999).

Jane Maienschein, "What Determines Sex? A Study of Convergent Research Approaches, 1880–1916," *Isis*, 75 (1984), 457–480.

Helmut Maier, "Einleitung," in Helmut Maier (ed.), *Rüstungsforschung im Nationalsozialismus. Organisation, Mobilisierung und Entgrenzung der Technikwissenschaften* (Göttingen: Wallstein Verlag, 2002), 7–29.

Erwin Marx (1893–1980), Ingenieurwissenschaftler in Braunschweig, und die Forschung und Entwicklung auf dem Gebiet der elektrischen Energieübertragung auf weite Entfernungen zwischen 1918 und 1950 (Stuttgart: GNT, 1993).

"Flugzeugschrott und Suppentöpfe: Aluminiumrecycling in Deutschland vor und nach 1945," in Roland Ladwig (ed.), *Recycling in Geschichte und Gegenwart* (Georg-Agricola-Gesellschaft: Freiberg, 2003), 75–94.

Forschung als Waffe. Rüstungsforschung in der Kaiser-Wilhelm-Gesellschaft und das Kaiser-Wilhelm-Institut für Metallforschung 1900–1945/48, 2 vols. (Göttingen: Wallstein Verlag, 2007).

Helmut Maier (ed.), *Gemeinschaftsforschung, Bevollmächtigte und der Wissenstransfer. Die Rolle der Kaiser-Wilhelm-Gesellschaft im System kriegsrelevanter Forschung des Nationalsozialismus* (Göttingen: Wallstein Verlag, 2007).

Helmut Maier, "Ideologie, Rüstung und Ressourcen. Das Kaiser-Wilhelm-Institit für Metallforschung und die 'Deutsche Metalle' 1933–1945," in Helmut Maier (ed.), *Rüstungsforschung im Nationalsozialismus. Organisation, Mobilisierung und Entgrenzung der Technikwissenschaften* (Göttingen: Wallstein, 2002), 357–388.

"Nationalsozialistische Technikideologie und die Politisierung des 'Technikerstandes.' Fritz Todt und die *Deutsche Technik*," in Burkhard Dietz, Michael Fessner, and Helmut Maier (eds.), *Technische Intelligenz und "Kulturfaktor Technik." Kulturvorstellungen von Technikern und Ingenieuren zwischen Kaiserreich und Bundesrepublik Deutschland* (Münster: Waxmann, 1996), 253–268.

"'New Age Metal' or 'Ersatz'? Technological Uncertainties and Ideological Implications of Aluminium Up to the 1930s," *ICON*, 3 (1997), 181–201.

Helmut Maier (ed.), *Rüstungsforschung im Nationalsozialismus. Organisation, Mobilisierung und Entgrenzung der Technikwissenschaften* (Göttingen: Wallstein, 2002).

Helmet Maier, "'Unideologische Normalwissenschaft' oder Rüstungsforschung? Wandlungen naturwissenschaftlich-technologischer Forschung und Entwicklung im 'Dritten Reich,'" in Rüdiger Vom Bruch and Brigitte Kaderas (eds.), *Wissenschaften und Wissenschaftspolitik: Bestandsaufnahmen zu Formationen, Brüchen und Kontinuitäten im Deutschland des 20. Jahrhunderts* (Stuttgart: Franz Steiner Verlag, 2002), 253–262.

"'Wehrhaftmachung' und 'Kriegswichtigkeit.' Zur rüstungstechnologischen Relevanz des Kaiser-Wilhelm-Instituts für Metallforschung in Stuttgart vor und nach 1945," *Ergebnisse. Vorabdrucke aus dem Forschungsprogramm "Geschichte der Kaiser-Wilhelm-Gesellschaft im Nationalsozialismus,"* No. 5 (Berlin: Forschungsprogramm, 2002) [http://www.mpiwg-berlin.mpg.de/KWG/Ergebnisse/Ergebnisse5.pdf].

Ulrich Majer, "Vom Weltruhm der zwanziger Jahre zur Normalität der Nachkriegszeit. Die Geschichte der Chemie in Göttingen von 1930–1950," in Heinrich Becker, Hans-Joachim Dahms, and Cornelia Wegeler (eds.), *Die Universität Göttingen unter dem Nationalsozialismus*, 2nd ed. (Munich: Saur, 1998), 589–629.

Karl-Heinz Manegold, *Universität, Technische Hochschule und Industrie. Ein Beitrag zur Emanzipation der Technik im 19. Jahrhundert unter besonderer Berücksichtigung der Bestrebungen von Felix Klein* (Berlin: Duncker and Humblot, 1970).

Hubert Markl, "Die ehrlichste Art der Entschuldigung ist die Offenlegung der Schuld," in Carola Sachse (ed.), *Die Verbindung nach Auschwitz. Biowissenschaften und Menschenversuche am Kaiser-Wilhelm-Institute* (Göttingen: Wallstein, 2003), 41–51.

Ulrich Marsch, *Notgemeinschaft der Deutschen Wissenschaft. Gründung und frühe Geschichte 1920–1925* (Frankfurt am Main: Peter Lang, 1994).

"Von der Syntheseindustrie zur Kriegswirtschaft. Brüche und Kontinuitäten in Wissenschaft und Politik," in Helmut Maier (ed.), *Rüstungsforschung im Nationalsozialismus. Organisation, Mobilisierung und Entgrenzung der Technikwissenschaften* (Göttingen: Wallstein, 2002), 33–51.

Zwischen Wissenschaft und Wirtschaft. Industrieforschung in Deutschland und Grossbritannien 1880–1936 (Paderborn: Schöningh, 2000).

Dieter Martinetz, *Der Gaskrieg 1914–1918. Entwicklung, Herstellung und Einsatz chemischer Kampfstoffe* (Bonn: Bernard und Graefe, 1996).

Vom Giftpfeil zum Chemiewaffenverbot. Zur Geschichte der chemischen Kampfmittel (Frankfurt am Main: Thun, 1996).

Benoit Massin, "Mengele, die Zwillingsforschung und die 'Auschwitz-Dahlem Connection,'" in Carola Sachse (ed.), *Die Verbindung nach Auschwitz. Biowissenschaften und Menschenversuche am Kaiser-Wilhelm-Institute* (Göttingen: Wallstein, 2003), 201–254.

"Rasse und Vererbung als Beruf. Die Hauptforschungsrichtungen am Kaiser-Wilhelm-Institut für Anthropologie, menschliche Erblehre und Eugenik im Nationalsozialismus," in Hans-Walter Schmuhl (ed.), *Rassenforschung an Kaiser-Wilhelm-Instituten vor und nach 1933* (Göttingen: Wallstein Verlag, 2003), 190–244.

Teresa Meade and Mark Walker (eds.), *Science, Medicine, and Cultural Imperialism* (New York: St. Martin's Press, 1991).

Jean Medawar and David Pyke, *Hitler's Gift. Scientists Who Fled Nazi Germany* (London: Richard Cohen Books, 2000).

Stanislaw Meducki, "Agrarwissenschaftliche Forschungen in Polen während der deutschen Okkupation. Die landwirtschaftliche Forschungsanstalt in Pulawy," in Susanne Heim (ed.), *Autarkie und Ostexpansion. Pflanzenzucht und Agrarforschung im Nationalsozialismus* (Göttingen: Wallstein, 2002), 233–249.

Herbert Mehrtens, "Angewandte Mathematik und Anwendungen der Mathematik im nationalsozialistischen Deutschland," *Geschichte und Gesellschaft*, 12 (1986), 317–347.

"Die 'Gleichschaltung' der mathematischen Gesellschaften im nationalsozialistischen Deutschland," *Jahrbuch Überblicke Mathematik*, 18 (1985), 83–103.

"Irresponsible Purity: The Political and Moral Structure of Mathematical Sciences in the National Socialist State," in Monika Renneberg and Mark Walker (eds.), *Science, Technology, and National Socialism* (Cambridge: Cambridge University Press, 1993), 324–338, 411–413.

"Kollaborationsverhältnisse: Natur- und Technikwissenschaften im NS-Staat und ihre Histoire," in Christoph Meinel and Peter Voswinckel (eds.), *Medizin, Naturwissenschaft, Technik und Nationalsozialismus. Kontinuitäten und Diskontinuitäten* (Stuttgart: GNT, 1994), 13–32.

"Mathematics and War: Germany 1900–1945," in Jose M. Sanchez-Ron and Paul Forman (eds.), *National Military Establishments and the Advancement of Science and Technology: Studies in Twentieth Century History* (Dordrecht: Kluwer Academic, 1996), 87–134.

Moderne – Sprache – Mathematik. Eine Geschichte des Streits um die Grundlagen der Disziplin und des Subjekts formaler Systeme (Frankfurt am Main: Suhrkamp, 1990).

"Wissenschaftspolitik im NS-Staat- Strukturen und regionalgeschichtliche Aspekte," in Wolfram Fischer, (ed.), *Exodus von Wissenschaften aus Berlin. Fragestellungen-Ergebniss-Desiderate. Entwicklungen vor und nach 1933*

(Akademie der Wissenschaften zu Berlin, Forschungsbericht 7), (Berlin: de Gruyter, 1994), 245–266.

Herbert Mehrtens and Steffen Richter (eds.), *Naturwissenschaft, Technik, und NS-Ideologie: Beiträge zur Wissenschaftsgeschichte des Dritten Reichs* (Frankfurt am Main: Suhrkamp, 1980).

Christoph Meinel and Peter Voswinckel (eds.), *Medizin, Naturwissenschaft, Technik und Nationalsozialismus. Kontinuitäten und Diskontinuitäten* (Stuttgart: GNT, 1994).

Georg Melchers, "Fritz von Wettstein 1895–1945," *Berichte der Deutschen Botanischen Gesellschaft,* 100 (1987), 396–405.

"Max-Planck-Institut für Biologie in Tübingen/Abteilung von Wettstein," *Jahrbuch der Max-Planck-Gesellschaft* (1961/II), 111–134.

Lothar Mertens, *DFG-Forschungsförderung 1933–1937* (Berlin: Akademie Verlag, 2004).

"Nur 'zweite Wahl' oder Die Berufung Adolf Butenandts zum Direktor des KWI für Biochemie," *Berichte zur Wissenschaftsgeschichte,* 26 (2003), 213–22.

Torsten Meyer, "Zwischen Ideologie und Wissenschaft: "Technik und Kultur" im Werk Werner Sombarts," in Burkhard Dietz, Michael Fessner, and Helmut Maier (eds.), *Technische Intelligenz und "Kulturfaktor Technik." Kulturvorstellungen von Technikern und Ingenieuren zwischen Kaiserreich und Bundesrepublik Deutschland* (Münster: Waxmann, 1996), 67–86.

Florian Mildenberger, "Ein Zoologe auf Abwegen. Richard B. Goldschmidt (1878–1958) als Sexualforscher und seine Rezeption im Dritten Reich," *Sudhoffs Archiv,* 85 (2001), 64–81.

A.D. Merriman, *A Dictionary of Metallurgy* (London: MacDonald and Evans, 1958).

Hans Mommsen, *Das Volkswagenwerk und seine Arbeiter im Dritten Reich* (Düsseldorf: Econ, 1996).

Rolf-Dieter Müller (ed.), *Die deutsche Wirtschaftspolitik in den besetzten sowjetischen Gebieten 1941–1943. Der Abschlussbericht des Wirtschaftsstabes Ost und Aufzeichnungen eines Angehörigen des Wirtschaftskommandos Kiew* (Boppard am Rhein: Boldt, 1991).

Rolf-Dieter Müller, "Kriegsführung, Rüstung und Wissenschaft. Zur Rolle des Militärs bei der Steuerung der Kriegstechnik unter besonderer Berücksichtigung des Heereswaffenamtes 1935–1945," in Helmut Maier (ed.), *Rüstungsforschung im Nationalsozialismus. Organisation, Mobilisierung und Entgrenzung der Technikwissenschaften* (Göttingen: Wallstein, 2002), 52–71.

Der Manager der Kriegswirtschaft. Hans Kehrl. Ein Unternehmer in der Politik des Dritten Reiches (Essen: Klartext-Verlag, 1999).

Benno Müller-Hill, "The Blood from Auschwitz and the Silence of the Scholars," *History and Philosophy of the Life Sciences,* 21 (1999), 331–365.

"Genetics after Auschwitz," *Holocaust and Genocide Studies,* 2 (1987), 3–20.

"Genetics of Susceptibility to Tuberculosis. Mengele's Experiments in Auschwitz," *Nature Reviews Genetics,* 2 (2001), 631–634.

Murderous Science: Elimination by Scientific Selection of Jews, Gypsies, and Others in Germany, 1933–1945 (New York: Oxford University Press, 1988).

"Selective Perception. The Letters of Adolf Butenandt Nobel Prize Winner and President of the Max-Planck-Society," in Giorgio Semenza and Anthony J. Turner (eds.), *Comprehensive Biochemistry, Vol. 42, Selected Topics in the History of*

Biochemistry. Personal Recollections, VII (Amsterdam: Elsevier Science, 2003), 548–580.

Benno Müller-Hill and Ute Deichmann, "The Fraud of Abderhalden's Enzymes," *Nature*, 393 (1998), 109–111.

Dorothee Mussgnug, *Die vertriebenen Heidelberger Dozenten. Zur Geschichte der Ruprecht-Karl-Universität nach 1933* (Heidelberg: Winter, 1988).

David Nachmansohn, *German-Jewish Pioneers in Science, 1900–1933* (New York: Springer, 1979).

"Carl Neuberg," *Proceedings of the Rudolf Virchow Medical Society in the City of New York*, XV (1956), Separatum.

Hans Nachtsheim, review of Verschuer, *Genetik des Menschen in Berichte über die wissenschaftliche Biologie*, 141, no. 2 (1960), 133 f.

Michael Neufeld, *The Rocket and the Reich: Peenemünde and the Coming of the Ballistic Missile* (New York: Free Press, 1995).

Von Braun: Dreamer of Space, Engineer of War (New York: Knopf, 2007).

Arnold Nordwig, "Vor fünfzig Jahren: Der Fall Neuberg, Aus der Geschichte des Kaiser-Wilhelm-Instituts für Biochemie zur Zeit des Nationalsozialismus," *MPG-Spiegel*, 6 (1983), 49–53.

David E. Nye, *Electrifying America: Social Meanings of a New Technology, 1880–1940* (Cambridge, MA: MIT Press, 1990).

Miklós Nyiszli, *Auschwitz. A Doctor's Eyewitness Account* (New York: Fell, 1960).

Gerhard Oberkofler and Peter Goller, *Richard Kuhn. Skizzen zur Karriere eines österreichischen Nobelpreisträgers* (Innsbruck: Archiv der Leopold-Franzens-Universität, 1992).

Otto Gerhard Oexle, "Hahn, Heisenberg und die anderen. Anmerkungen zu 'Kopenhagen,' 'Farm Hall' und 'Göttingen,'" *Ergebnisse. Vorabdrucke aus dem Forschungsprogramm "Geschichte der Kaiser-Wilhelm-Gesellschaft im Nationalsozialismus,"* No. 9 (Berlin: Forschungsprogramm, 2003) [http://www.mpiwg-berlin.mpg.de/KWG/Ergebnisse/Ergebnisse9.pdf].

Moshe Offer, "Dafür bin ich am Leben geblieben," in Carola Sachse (ed.), *Die Verbindung nach Auschwitz. Biowissenschaften und Menschenversuche am Kaiser-Wilhelm-Institute* (Göttingen: Wallstein, 2003), 83–88.

Marilyn Bailey Ogilvie, "Nettie Marie Stevens (1861–1912)," in Louise S. Grinstein, Carol A. Biermann, and Rose K. Rose (eds.), *Women in the Biological Sciences. A Bibliographical Sourcebook* (Westport: Greenwood Press, 1997), 517–523.

Josiane Olff-Nathan (ed.), *La science sous le Troisième Reich* (Paris: Seuil, 1993).

Saul Oren-Hornfeld, "Die '11' von Sachsenhausen," in Carola Sachse (ed.), *Die Verbindung nach Auschwitz. Biowissenschaften und Menschenversuche am Kaiser-Wilhelm-Institute* (Göttingen: Wallstein, 2003), 94–100.

Henry Orenstein, *I Shall Live. Surviving the Holocaust 1939–1945* (Oxford: Beaufort Books, 1988).

Karin Orth, *Das System der nationalsozialistischen Konzentrationslager. Eine politische Organisationsgeschichte* (Hamburg: Hamburger Ed., 1999), 113–221.

Maria Osietzki, "The Ideology of Early Particle Accelerators. An Association between Knowledge and Power," in Monika Renneberg and Mark Walker (eds.), *Science, Technology and National Socialism* (Cambridge: Cambridge University Press, 1994), 255–270.

Diane Paul, "Die bemerkenswerte Karriere von Nikolai Wladimorivich Timoféeff-Ressovsky," in Heinz Bielka and Ganten Detlev (eds.), *Festschrift anlässlich der Gründung des Max-Delbrück-Centrums für Molekulare Medizin 1992 in Berlin-Buch* (Bernau: Blankenburg, 1993), 30–34.

Diane B. Paul and Costas B. Krimbas, "Nikolai W. Timoféeff-Ressovsky," *Scientific American*, 2 (1992), 64–70.

Jürgen Peiffer, "Assessing Neuropathological Research Carried Out on Victims of the 'Euthanasia' Programme," *Medizinhistorisches Journal*, 34 (1999), 339–356.

Hirnforschung in Deutschland 1849 bis 1974. Briefe zur Entwicklung von Psychiatrie und Neurowissenschaften sowie zum Einfluss des politischen Umfeldes auf Wissenschaftler (Berlin: Springer, 2004).

Hirnforschung im Zwielicht: Beispiele verführbarer Wissenschaft aus der Zeit des Nationalsozialismus (Husum: Matthiesen, 1997).

"Neuropathologische Forschung an "Euthanasie"-Opfern in zwei Kaiser-Wilhelm-Instituten," in Doris Kaufmann (ed.), *Geschichte der Kaiser-Wilhelm-Gesellschaft im Nationalsozialismus. Bestandsaufnahme und Perspektiven der Forschung*, 2 vols. (Göttingen: Wallstein Verlag, 2000), vol. 1, 151–173.

"Wissenschaftliches Erkenntnisstreben als Tötungsmotiv? Zur Kennzeichnung von Opfern auf deren Krankenakten und zur Organisation und Unterscheidung von Kinder-"Euthanasie" und T4-Aktion," *Ergebnisse. Vorabdrucke aus dem Forschungsprogramm "Geschichte der Kaiser-Wilhelm-Gesellschaft im Nationalsozialismus,"* No. 23 (Berlin: Forschungsprogramm, 2005) [http://www.mpiwg-berlin.mpg.de/KWG/Ergebnisse/Ergebnisse23.pdf].

Dieter Petzina, *Autarkiepolitik im Dritten Reich. Der nationalsozialistische Vierjahresplan* (Stuttgart: Deutsche Verlagsanstalt, 1968).

Hartmut Petzold, *Moderne Rechenkünstler. Die Industrialisierung der Rechentechnik in Deutschland* (Munich: Beck Verlag, 1992).

Franciszek Piper, "Die Ausbeutung der Arbeit der Häftlinge," in Waclaw Długoborski and Franciszek Piper (eds.), *Auschwitz 1940–1945. Studien zur Geschichte des Konzentrations- und Vernichtungslagers Auschwitz*, vol. II: *Die Häftlinge. Existenzbedingungen, Arbeit und Tod* (Oswiecim: Verlag des Staatlichen Museums Auschwitz-Birkenau, 1999), 83–167.

Ute Planert, *Antifeminismus im Kaiserreich. Diskurs, soziale Formation und politische Mentalität* (Göttingen: Vandenhoeck and Ruprecht, 1998).

"ReaktionäreModernisten.ZumVerhältnisvonAntisemitismusundAntifeminismus in der völkischen Bewegung," *Jahrbuch für Antisemitismusforschung*, 11 (2002), 31–51.

Gottfried Plumpe, *Die IG-Farbenindustrie-AG: Wirtschaft, Technik und Politik 1904–1945* (Berlin: Duncker and Humblot, 1990).

Wanda Poltawska, "Die 'Kinder von Auschwitz.' Das Syndrom der paroxysmalen Hypermnesie," in Carola Sachse (ed.), *Die Verbindung nach Auschwitz. Biowissenschaften und Menschenversuche am Kaiser-Wilhelm-Institute* (Göttingen: Wallstein, 2003), 285–305.

Reiner Pommerin, *Sterilisierung der Rheinlandbastarde. Das Schicksal einer farbigen deutschen Minderheit 1918–1937* (Düsseldorf: Droste, 1979).

Gerald L. Posner and John Ware, *Mengele. The Complete Story* (New York: McGraw-Hill, 1986).

Thomas Potthast, "'Rassenkreise' und die Bedeutung des 'Lebensraums.' Zur Tier-Rassenforschung in der Evolutionsbiologie," in Hans-Walter Schmuhl (ed.), *Rassenforschung an Kaiser-Wilhelm-Instituten vor und nach 1933* (Göttingen: Wallstein, 2003), 275–308.

Thomas Powers, *Heisenberg's War* (New York: Knopf, 1993).

Claus Priesner, "Georg Masing," in *Neue Deutsche Biographie*, vol. 16 (Berlin: Duncker and Humblot, 1990), 354 f.

Robert Proctor, "Adolf Butenandt (1903–1995). Nobelpreisträger, Nationalsozialist und MPG-Präsident. Ein erster Blick in den Nachlass," *Ergebnisse. Vorabdrucke aus dem Forschungsprogramm "Geschichte der Kaiser-Wilhelm-Gesellschaft im Nationalsozialismus,"* No. 2 (Berlin: Forschungsprogramm, 2000) [http://www.mpiwg-berlin.mpg.de/KWG/Ergebnisse/Ergebnisse2.pdf].

The Nazi War on Cancer (Princeton: Princeton University Press, 1999).

Racial Hygiene: Medicine under the Nazis (Cambridge, MA: Harvard University Press, 1988).

Alexandra Przyrembel, "Friedrich Glum und Ernst Telschow. Die Generalsekretäre der Kaiser-Wilhelm-Gesellschaft: Handlungsfelder und Handlungsoptionen der 'Verwaltenden' von Wissen während des Nationalsozialismus," *Ergebnisse. Vorabdrucke aus dem Forschungsprogramm "Geschichte der Kaiser-Wilhelm-Gesellschaft im Nationalsozialismus,"* No. 20 (Berlin: Forschungsprogramm, 2004) [http://www.mpiwg-berlin.mpg.de/KWG/Ergebnisse/Ergebnisse20.pdf].

"Rassenschande." Reinheitsmythos und Vernichtungslegitimation im Nationalsozialismus (Göttingen: Wallstein Verlag, 2003).

Gerhard Rammer, "Göttinger Physiker nach 1945. Über die Wirkung kollegialer Netze," *Göttinger Jahrbuch* (2003), 83–104.

"Nachkriegsphysik an der Leine: Eine Göttinger Vogelperspektive," in Dieter Hoffmann (ed.), *Physik im Nachkriegsdeutschland* (Frankfurt am Main: Verlag Harri Deutsch, 2003), 27–56.

"'Sauberkeit im Kreise der Kollegen': Die Vergangenheitspolitik der DPG," in Dieter Hoffmann and Mark Walker (eds.), *Physiker zwischen Autonomie und Anpassung. Die Deutsche Physikalische Gesellschaft im Dritten Reich* (Weinheim: VCH-Verlag Chemie, 2006), 359–420.

Manfred Rasch, "Forschung zwischen Staat und Industrie. Überlegungen zu einer Forschungsgeschichte der Kaiser-Wilhelm-Gesellschaft im 'Dritten Reich,'" in Doris Kaufmann (ed.), *Geschichte der Kaiser-Wilhelm-Gesellschaft im Nationalsozialismus. Bestandsaufnahme und Perspektiven der Forschung*, 2 vols. (Göttingen: Wallstein Verlag, 2000), vol. 1, 373–397.

"Über Albert Vögler und sein Verhältnis zur Politik," *Mitteilungsblatt des Instituts für soziale Bewegungen*, 28 (2003), 127–156.

Ephraim Reichenbach, "Meine wahre Familie," in Carola Sachse (ed.), *Die Verbindung nach Auschwitz. Biowissenschaften und Menschenversuche am Kaiser-Wilhelm-Institute* (Göttingen: Wallstein, 2003), 73–74.

Volker Remmert, "Die Deutsche Mathematiker-Vereinigung im Dritten Reich," in Dieter Hoffmann and Mark Walker (eds.), *Physiker zwischen Autonomie und Anpassung – Die DPG im Dritte Reich* (Weinheim: VCH, 2006), 421–458.

Stephen Remy, *The Heidelberg Myth. The Nazification and Denazification of a German University* (Cambridge, MA.: Harvard University Press, 2002).

Jürgen Renn, Giuseppe Castagnetti, and Peter Damerow, "Albert Einstein. Alte und neue Kontexte in Berlin," in Jürgen Kocha (ed.), *Die Königlich Preussische Akademie der Wissenschaften zu Berlin im Kaiserreich* (Berlin: Akademie, 1999), 333–354.

Monika Renneberg and Mark Walker (eds.), *Science, Technology, and National Socialism* (Cambridge: Cambridge University Press, 1993).

"Scientists, Engineers, and National Socialism," in Monika Renneberg and Mark Walker (eds.), *Science, Technology, and National Socialism* (Cambridge: Cambridge University Press, 1993), 1–17.

Hans-Jörg Rheinberger, "Ephestia: The Experimental Design of Alfred Kühn's Physiological Developmental Genetics," *Journal of the History of Biology*, 33 (2000), 535–576.

Experiment – Differenz – Schrift. Zur Geschichte epistemischer Dinge (Marburg: Basilisken-Presse, 1992).

Toward a History of Epistemic Things. Synthesizing Proteins in the Test Tube (Stanford: Stanford University Press, 1997).

"Virusforschung an den Kaiser-Wilhelm-Instituten für Biochemie und für Biologie," in Doris Kaufmann, (ed.), *Geschichte der Kaiser-Wilhelm-Gesellschaft im Nationalsozialismus. Bestandsaufnahme und Perspektiven der Forschung*, 2 vols. (Göttingen: Wallstein Verlag, 2000), vol. 2, 667–698.

"Die Zusammenarbeit zwischen Adolf Butenandt und Alfred Kühn," Wolfgang Schieder, and Achim Trunk (eds.), *Adolf Butenandt und die Kaiser-Wilhelm-Gesellschaft. Wissenschaft, Industrie und Politik im "Dritten Reich"* (Göttingen: Wallstein, 2004), 169–197.

Gotthold Rhode, "Die Freie Stadt Danzig," in Theodor Schieder (ed.), *Handbuch der europäischen Geschichte*, vol. 7 (Stuttgart: Klett-Cotta, 1979).

Donald Richter, *Chemical Soldiers. British Gas Warfare in World War I* (Lawrence: University Press of Kansas, 1992).

Jochen Richter, "Das Kaiser-Wilhelm-Institut für Hirnforschung und die Topographie der Grosshirnhemisphären. Ein Beitrag zur Institutsgeschichte der Kaiser-Wilhelm-Gesellschaft und zur Geschichte der architektonischen Hirnforschung," in Bernhard vom Brocke and Hubert Laitko (eds.), *Die Kaiser-Wilhelm-Gesellschaft/Max-Planck-Gesellschaft und ihre Institute* (Berlin: de Gruyter, 1996), 349–408.

Steffen Richter, *Forschungsförderung in Deutschland 1920–1936. Dargestellt am Beispiel der Notgemeinschaft der Deutschen Wissenschaft und ihrem Wirken für das Fach Physik* (Düsseldorf: VDI, 1972).

Katrin Rieder, "XX gleich Frau, XY gleich Mann? Die Kategorie Geschlecht in der Entwicklung der Genetik," *Ariadne, Forum für Frauen- und Geschlechtergeschichte*, 41 (2003), 8–18.

Renate Rissom, *Fritz Lenz und die Rassenhygiene* (Husum: Matthiesen, 1983).

Hans-Jakob Ritter and Volker Roelcke, "Psychiatric Genetics in Munich and Basel between 1925 and 1945: Program – Practices – Cooperative Arrangements," in Carola Sachse and Mark Walker (eds.), *Politics and Science in Wartime: Comparative International Perspectives on the Kaiser Wilhelm Institutes, Osiris* 20 (Chicago: University of Chicago Press, 2005), 263–288.

Volker Roelcke, "Programm und Praxis der psychiatrischen Genetik an der Deutschen Forschungsanstalt für Psychiatrie unter Ernst Rüdin. Zum Verhältnis von

Wissenschaft, Politik und Rasse-Begriff vor und nach 1933," in Hans-Walter Schmuhl (ed.), *Rassenforschung an Kaiser-Wilhelm-Instituten vor und nach 1933* (Göttingen: Wallstein Verlag, 2003), 38–67.

Volker Roelcke, "Psychiatrische Wissenschaft im Kontext nationalsozialistischer Politik und 'Euthanasie.' Zur Rolle von Ernst Rüdin und der Deutschen Forschungsanstalt für Psychiatrie/Kaiser-Wilhelm-Institut," in Doris Kaufmann (ed.), *Geschichte der Kaiser-Wilhelm-Gesellschaft im Nationalsozialismus. Bestandsaufnahme und Perspektiven der Forschung*, 2 vols. (Göttingen: Wallstein, 2000), vol. 1, 112–150.

Mechtild Rössler, "*Wissenschaft und Lebensraum*": Geographische Ostforschung im Nationalsozialismus (Berlin: Reimer Verlag, 1990).

Mechtild Rössler and Sabine Schleiermacher (eds.), *Der "Generalplan Ost": Hauptlinien der nationalsozialistischen Planungs- und Vernichtungspolitik* (Berlin: Akademie Verlag, 1993).

Nils Roll-Hansen, "A New Perspective on Lysenko?" *Annals of Science*, 42 (1985), 261–278.

Paul Lawrence Rose, *Heisenberg and the Nazi Atomic Bomb Project, 1939–1945: A Study in German Culture* (Berkeley: University of California Press, 1998).

Karl-Heinz Roth, "Schöner neuer Mensch. Der Paradigmenwechsel der klassischen Genetik und seine Auswirkungen auf die Bevölkerungsbiologie des 'Dritten Reiches,'" in Heidrun Kaupen-Haas (ed.), *Der Griff nach der Bevölkerung. Aktualität und Kontinuität nazistischer Bevölkerungspoltik* (Nördlingen: Greno, 1986), 11–63.

"Tödliche Höhen. Die Unterdruckkammer-Experimente im Konzentrationslager Dachau und ihre Bedeutung für die luftfahrtmedizinische Forschung des 'Dritten Reiches,'" in Angelika Ebbinghaus and Klaus Dörner (eds.), *Vernichten und Heilen. Der Nürnberger Ärzteprozess und seine Folgen* (Berlin: Aufbau-Verlag, 2001), 110–151.

Julius C. Rotta, *Die Aerodynamische Versuchsanstalt in Göttingen, ein Werk Ludwig Prandtls. Ihre Geschichte von den Anfängen bis 1925* (Göttingen: Vandenhoeck and Ruprecht, 1990).

David E. Rowe, "Klein, Hilbert, and the Göttingen Mathematical Tradition," *Osiris*, 5 (1989), 186–213.

Wilhelm Rudorf, "Max-Planck-Institut für Züchtungsforschung," *Jahrbuch der Max-Planck-Gesellschaft* (1961), 848.

Reinhard Rürup, *Schicksale und Karrieren. Gedenkbuch für die von den Nationalsozialisten aus der Kaiser-Wilhelm-Gesellschaft vertriebenen Forscherinnen und Forscher* (Göttingen: Wallstein Verlag, 2008).

"Schlussbemerkungen," in Carola Sachse (ed.), *Die Verbindung nach Auschwitz. Biowissenschaften und Menschenversuche am Kaiser-Wilhelm-Institute* (Göttingen: Wallstein, 2003), 319–324.

Walter Ruske, *100 Jahre Deutsche Chemische Gesellschaft* (Weinheim: Verlag Chemie, 1967).

Carola Sachse, "Adolf Butenandt und Otmar von Verschuer. Eine Freundschaft unter Wissenschaftlern (1942–1969)," in Wolfgang Schieder and Achim Trunk (eds.), *Adolf Butenandt und die Kaiser-Wilhelm-Gesellschaft. Wissenschaft, Industrie und Politik im "Dritten Reich"* (Göttingen: Wallstein, 2004), 286–319.

"Menschenversuche in Auschwitz überleben, erinnern, verantworten," in Carola Sachse (ed.), *Die Verbindung nach Auschwitz. Biowissenschaften und Menschenversuche am Kaiser-Wilhelm-Institute* (Göttingen: Wallstein, 2003), 7–34.

"'Persilscheinkultur.' Zum Umgang mit der NS-Vergangenheit in der Kaiser-Wilhelm/Max-Planck-Gesellschaft," in Bernd Weisbrod (ed.), *Akademische Vergangenheitspolitik. Beiträge zur Wissenschaftskultur der Nachkriegszeit* (Göttingen: Wallstein, 2002), 217–246.

Carola Sachse (ed.), *Die Verbindung nach Auschwitz. Biowissenschaften und Menschenversuche am Kaiser-Wilhelm-Institute* (Göttingen: Wallstein, 2003).

Carola Sachse and Benoit Massin, "Biowissenschaftliche Forschung in Kaiser-Wilhelm-Instituten und die Verbrechen des NS-Regimes. Informationen über den gegenwärtigen Wissensstand," *Ergebnisse. Vorabdrucke aus dem Forschungsprogramm "Geschichte der Kaiser-Wilhelm-Gesellschaft im Nationalsozialismus,"* No. 3 (Berlin: Forschungsprogramm, 2000) [http://www.mpiwg-berlin.mpg.de/KWG/Ergebnisse/Ergebnisse3.pdf].

Carola Sachse and Mark Walker, "Introduction," in Carola Sachse and Mark Walker (eds.), *Politics and Science in Wartime: Comparative International Perspectives on the Kaiser Wilhelm Institutes, Osiris 20* (Chicago: University of Chicago Press, 2005), 1–20.

Carola Sachse and Mark Walker (eds.), *Politics and Science in Wartime: Comparative International Perspectives on the Kaiser Wilhelm Institutes, Osiris 20* (Chicago: University of Chicago Press, 2005).

Jose M. Sanchez-Ron and Paul Forman (eds.), *National Military Establishments and the Advancement of Science and Technology: Studies in Twentieth Century History* (Dordrecht: Kluwer Academic, 1996).

Jan Sapp, *Beyond the Gene. Cytoplasmatic Inheritance and the Struggle for Authority in Genetics* (New York: Oxford University Press, 1987).

Helga Satzinger, "Adolf Butenandt, Hormone und Geschlecht. Ingredienzien einer wissenschaftlichen Karriere," in Wolfgang Schieder and Achim Trunk (eds.), *Adolf Butenandt und die Kaiser-Wilhelm-Gesellschaft. Wissenschaft, Industrie und Politik im "Dritten Reich"* (Göttingen: Wallstein, 2004), 78–133.

Die Geschichte der genetisch orientierten Hirnforschung von Cécile und Oskar Vogt (1875–1962, 1870–1959) in der Zeit von 1895 bis ca. 1927 (Stuttgart: Deutscher Apotheker-Verlag, 1998).

"Krankheiten als Rassen. Politische und wissenschaftliche Dimensionen eines internationalen Forschungsprogramms am Kaiser-Wilhelm-Institut für Hirnforschung (1919–1939)," in Hans-Walter Schmuhl (ed.), *Rassenforschung an Kaiser-Wilhelm-Instituten vor und nach 1933* (Göttingen: Wallstein, 2003), 145–189.

"Rasse, Gene und Geschlecht. Zur Konstituierung zentraler biologischer Begriffe bei Richard Goldschmidt und Fritz Lenz, 1916–1936," *Ergebnisse. Vorabdrucke aus dem Forschungsprogramm "Geschichte der Kaiser-Wilhelm-Gesellschaft im Nationalsozialismus,* No. 15 (Berlin: Forschungsprogramm, 2004) [http://www.mpiwg-berlin.mpg.de/KWG/Ergebnisse/Ergebnisse15.pdf].

Helga Satzinger and Annette Vogt, "Elena Aleksandrovna Timoféeff-Ressovsky (1898–1973) und Nikolaj Vladimirovich Timoféeff-Ressovsky (1900–1981)," in Ilse Jahn, and Michael Schmitt (eds.), *Darwin & Co. Eine Geschichte der Biologie in Portraits*, vol. 2 (Munich: Beck, 2001), 442–470.

Elvira Scheich, "Elisabeth Schiemann (1881–1972), Patriotin im Zwiespalt," in Susanne Heim (ed.), *Autarkie und Ostexpansion. Pflanzenzucht und Agrarforschung im Nationalsozialismus* (Göttingen: Wallstein, 2002), 250–279.

Rudolf Schick and Hans Stubbe, "Die Gene von *Antirrhinum majus III.*," *ZIAV*, 66 (1934), 425–462.

Wolfgang Schieder, "Die extremen Erfahrungen der Opfer übertreffen das Vorstellungsvermögen der Historiker," in Carola Sachse (ed.), *Die Verbindung nach Auschwitz. Biowissenschaften und Menschenversuche am Kaiser-Wilhelm-Institute* (Göttingen: Wallstein, 2003), 37–38.

"Das italienische Experiment. Der Faschismus als Vorbild in der Weimarer Republik," *Historische Zeitschrift*, 262 (1996), 73–125.

"Die extreme Erfahrungen der Opfer übertreffen das Vorstellungsvermögen der Historiker," in Carola Sachse (ed.), *Die Verbindung nach Auschwitz. Biowissenschaften und Menschenversuche am Kaiser-Wilhelm-Institute* (Göttingen: Wallstein, 2003), 37–38.

"Spitzenforschung und Politik. Adolf Butenandt in der Weimarer Republik und im 'Dritten Reich,'" in Wolfgang Schieder and Achim Trunk (eds.), *Adolf Butenandt und die Kaiser-Wilhelm-Gesellschaft. Wissenschaft, Industrie und Politik im "Dritten Reich"* (Göttingen: Wallstein, 2004), 23–77.

Wolfgang Schieder and Achim Trunk (eds.), *Adolf Butenandt und die Kaiser-Wilhelm-Gesellschaft. Wissenschaft, Industrie und Politik im "Dritten Reich"* (Göttingen: Wallstein, 2004).

Axel Schildt, "Reise zurück aus der Zukunft. Beiträge von intellektuellen USA-Remigranten zur atlantischen Allianz, zum westdeutschen Amerikabild und zur 'Amerikanisierung' in den fünfziger Jahren," *Exilforschung. Ein internationales Jahrbuch*, 9 (1992), 25–46.

Florian Schmaltz, *Kampfstoff-Forschung im Nationalsozialismus. Zur Kooperation von Kaiser Wilhelm Instituten, Militär und Industrie* (Göttingen: Wallstein Verlag, 2005).

"Neurosciences and Research on Chemical Weapons of Mass Destruction in Nazi Germany," *Journal of the History of the Neurosciences*, 15 (2006), 186–209.

"Otto Bickenbach's Human Experiments with Chemical Warfare Agents at the Concentration Camp Natzweiler in the Context of the SS-Ahnenerbe and the Reichsforschungsrat," in Wolfgang U. Eckart (ed.), *Man, Medicine and the State. The Human Body as an Object of Government Sponsored Research in the 20th Century* (Stuttgart: Steiner, 2006), 139–156.

"Peter Adolf Thiessen und Richard Kuhn und die Chemiewaffenforschung im NS-Regime," in Helmut Maier (ed.), *Gemeinschaftsforschung, Bevollmächtigte und der Wissenstransfer. Die Rolle der Kaiser-Wilhelm-Gesellschaft im System kriegsrelevanter Forschung des Nationalsozialismus* (Göttingen: Wallstein Verlag, 2007), 305–351.

"Richard Kuhn," in Noretta Koertge (ed.), *New Dictionary of Scientific Biography. Ibn Al-Haytham-Luria* (Detroit: Thomson Gale, 2008), vol. 4, 167–170.

Florian Schmaltz and Karl-Heinz Roth, "Neue Dokumente zur Vorgeschichte des I.G. Farben-Werks Auschwitz-Monowitz. Zugleich eine Stellungnahme zur

Kontroverse zwischen Hans Deichmann und Peter Hayes," *1999. Zeitschrift für Sozialgeschichte des 20. und 21. Jahrhunderts*, 13, no. 2 (1998), 100–116.

Ulf Schmidt, *Karl Brandt. The Nazi Doctor. Medicine and Power in the Third Reich* (London: Continuum, 2007).

Alexander Schmidt-Gernig, *Reisen in die Moderne. Der Amerika-Diskurs des deutschen Bürgertums vor dem Ersten Weltkrieg im europäischen Vergleich* (Berlin: Akademie-Verlag, 1997).

Stéphane Schmitt, "L'oeuvre de Richard Goldschmidt: un tentative de synthèse de la génétique, de la biologie du développement et de la théorie de l'évolution autour du concept d'homéose," *Revue d'histoire des sciences*, 53 (2000), 381–401.

Gerhard Schrader, *Die Entwicklung neuer insektizider Phosphorsäure-Ester*. 3rd Ed. Aufl. (Weinheim an die Bergstrasse: Verlag Chemie, 1963).

Hans-Walther Schmuhl, *Grenzüberschreitungen. Das Kaiser-Wilhlem-Institut für Anthropologie, menschliche Erblehre und Eugenik 1927–1945* (Göttingen: Wallstein Verlag, 2005).

"Hirnforschung und Krankenmord. Das Kaiser-Wilhelm-Institut für Hirnforschung 1937–1945," *Vierteljahrshefte für Zeitgeschichte*, 50 (2002), 559–609.

The Kaiser Wilhelm Institute for Anthropology, Human Heredity and Eugenics, 1927–1945: Crossing Boundaries (Heidelberg: Springer, 2008).

Hans-Walter Schmuhl (ed.), *Rassenforschung an Kaiser-Wilhelm-Instituten vor und nach 1933* (Göttingen: Wallstein, 2003).

Brigitte Schröder-Gudehus, "The Argument for the Self-Government and Public Support of Science in Weimar Germany," *Minerva*, 10, no. 4 (1972), 537–70.

"Challenge to Transnational Loyalties: International Scientific Organizations after World War I," *Science Studies*, 3 (1973), 93–118.

Michael Schüring, "Ein Dilemma der Kontinuität. Das Selbstverständnis der Max-Planck-Gesellschaft und der Umgang mit Emigrantinnen und Emigranten in den 1950er Jahren," in Rüdiger vom Bruch and Brigitte Kaderas (eds.), *Wissenschaft und Wissenschaftspolitik. Bestandsaufnahmen zu Formationen, Brüchen und Kontinuitäten im Deutschland des 20. Jahrhundert* (Stuttgart: Steiner, 2002), 453–463.

"Expulsion, Compensation, and the Legacy of the Kaiser Wilhelm Society," *Minerva*, 44, no. 3 (2006), 307–324.

Minervas verstossene Kinder. Vertriebene Wissenschaftler und die Vergangenheitspolitik der Max-Planck-Gesellschaft (Göttingen: Wallstein, 2006).

"Ein 'unerfreulicher Vorgang.' Das Max-Planck-Institut für Züchtungsforschung in Voldagsen und die gescheiterte Rückkehr von Max Ufer," in Susanne Heim (ed.), *Autarkie und Ostexpansion. Pflanzenzucht und Agrarforschung im Nationalsozialismus* (Göttingen: Wallstein, 2002), 280–299.

"Der Vorgänger. Carl Neubergs Verhältnis zu Adolf Butenandt," in Wolfgang Schieder, and Achim Trunk (eds.), *Adolf Butenandt und die Kaiser-Wilhelm-Gesellschaft. Wissenschaft, Industrie und Politik im "Dritten Reich"* (Göttingen: Wallstein, 2004), 346–368.

Arthur Schulenburg, *Giesserei Lexikon* (Berlin: Schiele and Schön, 1958).

Dietmar Schulze, *"Euthanasie" in Bernburg. Die Landes-Heil- und Pflegeanstalt Bernburg/Anhaltische Nervenklinik in der Zeit des Nationalsozialismus* (Essen: Verlag die Blaue Eule, 1999).

Lore Shelley, *Auschwitz–The Nazi Civilization* (Lanham, MD: University Press of America, 1992).

Lore Shelley (ed.), *Criminal Experiments on Human Beings in Auschwitz and War Research Laboratories. Twenty Women Prisoners' Accounts* (San Francisco: Mellen University Press, 1991).

(ed.), *Secretaries of Death. Accounts by Former Prisoners Who Worked in the Gestapo of Auschwitz* (New York: Shengold, 1986).

Gustav Siebel, "Die technischen Magnesiumlegierungen und die magnesiumhaltigen Aluminiumlegierungen. Zusammenfassender Bericht über die Forschungs- und Entwicklungsarbeiten der I.G.-Farbenindustrie AG, Bitterfeld von 1920 bis 1945," *Zeitschrift für Metallkunde*, 43 (1952), 238–244.

Reinhard Siegmund-Schultze, *Mathematiker auf der Flucht vor Hitler. Quellen und Studien zur Emigration einer Wissenschaft* (Wiesbaden: Vieweg, 1998).

Ruth Lewin Sime, "From Exceptional Prominence to Prominent Exception. Lise Meitner at the Kaiser Wilhelm Institute for Chemistry," *Ergebnisse. Vorabdrucke aus dem Forschungsprogramm "Geschichte der Kaiser-Wilhelm-Gesellschaft im Nationalsozialismus,"* No. 24 (Berlin: Forschungsprogramm, 2005) [http://www.mpiwg-berlin.mpg.de/KWG/Ergebnisse/Ergebnisse24.pdf].

Lise Meitner: A Life in Physics (Berkeley: University of California Press, 1996).

"Otto Hahn und die Max-Planck-Gesellschaft. Zwischen Vergangenheit und Erinnerung," *Ergebnisse. Vorabdrucke aus dem Forschungsprogramm "Geschichte der Kaiser-Wilhelm-Gesellschaft im Nationalsozialismus,"* No. 14 (Berlin: Forschungsprogramm, 2004) [http://www.mpiwg-berlin.mpg.de/KWG/Ergebnisse/Ergebnisse14.pdf].

"The Politics of memory: Otto Hahn and the Third Reich," *Physics in Perspective*, 8, no. 1 (2006), 3–51.

"'Die "Uranspaltung" hat da die ganze Situation gerettet.' Otto Hahn und das Kaiser-Wilhelm-Institut für Chemie im Zweiten Weltkrieg," in Helmut Maier (ed.), *Gemeinschaftsforschung, Bevollmächtigte und der Wissenstransfer. Die Rolle der Kaiser-Wilhelm-Gesellschaft im System kriegsrelevanter Forschung des Nationalsozialismus* (Göttingen: Wallstein Verlag, 2007), 268–305.

(SIPRI) Stockholm International Peace Research Institute (ed.), *The Rise of Chemical and Biological Warfare. A Study of the Historical, Technical, Military, Legal and Political Aspects of CBW, and Possible Disarmament Measures*, vol. 1 (Stockholm: Stockholm International Peace Research Institute, 1971).

Hugh R. Slotten, "Humane Chemistry or Scientific Barbarism," *Journal of American History*, 77 (1990), 476–498.

Werner Sörgel, *Metallindustrie und Nationalsozialismus. Eine Untersuchung über Struktur und Funktion industrieller Organisationen in Deutschland 1929 bis 1939* (Frankfurt am Main: Europäische Verlag-Anstalt, 1965).

Rolf Sonnemann et al., *Geschichte der Technischen Universität Dresden 1928–1988*, 2nd ed. (Berlin: Deutsche Verlag der Wissenschaften, 1988).

Edward M. Spiers, "Gas and the North-West Frontier (Chemical Warfare in World War I)," *Journal of Strategic Studies*, 6, no. 4 (1983), 94–112.

Mark Spoerer, *Zwangsarbeit unter dem Hakenkreuz. Ausländische Zivilarbeiter, Kriegsgefangene und Häftlinge im Deutschen Reich und im besetzten Europa* (Stuttgart: DVA, 2001).

Heinz A. Staab, "50 Jahre Kaiser-Wilhelm-/ Max-Planck-Institut für Medizinische Forschung Heidelberg," *Heidelberger Jahrbücher*, 24 (1980), 47–70.

Sybille Steinbacher, *"Musterstadt Auschwitz." Germanisierungspolitik und Judenmord in Ostoberschlesien* (Munich: Saur, 2000).

Curt Stern, "Richard Benedikt Goldschmidt (1878–1958): A Biographical Memoir," in Leonie K. Piternick (ed.), *Richard Goldschmidt. Controversial Geneticist and Creative Biologist. A Critical Review of His Contributions with an Introduction by Karl von Frisch, Experienta Supplementum*, vol. 35 (Basel: Birkhäuser, 1980), 68–99.

Irene Stoehr, "Von Max Sering zu Konrad Meyer- ein "machtergreifender" Generationenwechsel in der Agrar- und Siedlungswissenschaft," in Susanne Heim (ed.), *Autarkie und Ostexpansion. Pflanzenzucht und Agrarforschung im Nationalsozialismus* (Göttingen: Wallstein Verlag, 2002), 57–90.

Heiko Stoff, "Adolf Butenandt in der Nachkriegszeit, 1945–1956. Reinigung und Assoziierung," in Wolfgang Schieder and Achim Trunk (eds.), *Adolf Butenandt und die Kaiser-Wilhelm-Gesellschaft. Wissenschaft, Industrie und Politik im "Dritten Reich"* (Göttingen: Wallstein, 2004), 369–402.

"'Eine zentrale Arbeitsstätte mit nationalen Zielen.' Wilhelm Eitel und das KWI für Silikatforschung 1926–1945," in Helmut Maier (ed.), *Gemeinschaftsforschung, Bevollmächtigte und der Wissenstransfer. Die Rolle der Kaiser-Wilhelm-Gesellschaft im System kriegsrelevanter Forschung des Nationalsozialismus* (Göttingen: Wallstein Verlag, 2007), 503–560.

Raymond Stokes, "Privileged Applications: Research and Development at I.G. Farben during the National Socialist Period," in Doris Kaufmann (ed.), *Geschichte der Kaiser-Wilhelm-Gesellschaft im Nationalsozialismus. Bestandsaufnahme und Perspektiven der Forschung*, 2 vols. (Göttingen: Wallstein Verlag, 2000), vol. 1, 398–410.

Dietrich Stoltzenberg, *Fritz Haber. Chemiker, Nobelpreisträger, Deutscher, Jude* (Weinheim: VCH, 1994).

Daniel Stone, "The Giesche Company: Anaconda Copper's Subsidiary in Interwar Poland," *Slavic Review*, 56 (1997), 679–697.

Jochen Streb, "Technologiepolitik im Zweiten Weltkrieg. Die staatliche Förderung der Synthesekautschukproduktion im deutsch-amerikanischen Vergleich," *Vierteljahrshefte für Zeitgeschichte*, 50 (2002), 367–397.

Bernhard Strebel and Jens-Christian Wagner, "Zwangsarbeit für Forschungseinrichtungen der Kaiser-Wilhelm-Gesellschaft 1939–1945. Ein Überblick," *Ergebnisse. Vorabdrucke aus dem Forschungsprogramm "Geschichte der Kaiser-Wilhelm-Gesellschaft im Nationalsozialismus, No. 11* (Berlin: Forschungsprogramm, 2003) [http://www.mpiwg-berlin.mpg.de/KWG/Ergebnisse/Ergebnisse11.pdf].

Christian Streit, *Keine Kameraden. Die Wehrmacht und die sowjetischen Kriegsgefangenen 1941–1945* (Stuttgart: Deutsche Verlagsanstalt, 1978).

Anne Sudrow, "Vom Leder zum Kunststoff. Werkstoff-Forschung auf der 'Schuhprüfstrecke' im Konzentrationslager Sachsenhausen 1940–1945," in Helmut Maier (ed.), *Rüstungsforschung im Nationalsozialismus. Organisation, Mobilisierung und Entgrenzung der Technikwissenschaften* (Göttingen: Wallstein, 2002), 214–249.

Margit Szöllosi-Janze, *Fritz Haber 1868–1934. Eine Biographie* (Munich: Beck, 1998).

"National Socialism and the Sciences: Reflections, Conclusions and Historical Perspectives," in Margit Szöllösi-Janze (ed.), *Science in the Third Reich* (Oxford: Berg, 2001), 1–35.

(ed.), *Science in the Third Reich* (Oxford: Berg, 2001).

Margit Szöllösi-Janze, "Der Wissenschaftler als Experte. Kooperationsverhältnisse von Staat, Militär, Wirtschaft und Wissenschaft, 1914–1933," in Doris Kaufmann (ed.), *Geschichte der Kaiser-Wilhelm-Gesellschaft im Nationalsozialismus. Bestandsaufnahme und Perspektiven der Forschung*, 2 vols. (Göttingen: Wallstein Verlag, 2000), vol. 1, 46–64.

Margit Szöllösi-Janze and Helmuth Trischler (eds.), *Grossforschung in Deutschland* (Frankfurt am Main: Campus Verlag, 1990).

Henryk Świebocki, "Die lagernahe Widerstandsbewegung," *Hefte von Auschwitz*, 19 (1995), 5–187.

Eckart Teichert, *Autarkie und Grossraumwirschaft in Deutschland 1930–1939: aussenwirtschaftspolitische Konzeptionen zwischen Wirtschaftskrise und Zweitem Weltkrieg* (Munich: Oldenbourg, 1984).

Georg Thomas, *Geschichte der deutschen Wehr- und Rüstungswirtschaft (1918–1943/45)*, ed. Wolfgang Birkenfeld (Boppard: Boldt, 1966).

Eva Tichauer, *I Was No. 20832 at Auschwitz* (London: Mitchell Vallentine, 2000).

Cordula Tollmien, "Das Kaiser-Wilhelm-Institut für Strömungsforschung verbunden mit der Aerodynamischen Versuchsanstalt," in Heinrich Becker, Hans-Joachim Dahms, and Cornelia Wegeler (eds.), *Die Universität Göttingen unter dem Nationalsozialismus*, 2nd ed. (Munich: Saur, 1998) 684–708.

George Topas, *The Iron Furnace. A Holocaust Survivor's Story* (Lexington: University Press of Kentucky, 1990).

Wilhelm Treue, "Gummi in Deutschland zwischen 1933 und 1945," *Wehrwissenschaftliche Rundschau*, 5 (1955), 169–185.

"Trilon" and "Trilons" in *Römpps Chemie-Lexikon*, 8th ed. (Stuttgart: Franckh, 1988), 4352.

Helmuth Trischler, "'Big Science' or 'Small Science'? Die Luftfahrtforschung im Nationalsozialismus," in Doris Kaufmann (ed.), *Geschichte der Kaiser-Wilhelm-Gesellschaft im Nationalsozialismus. Bestandsaufnahme und Perspektiven der Forschung*, 2 vols. (Göttingen: Wallstein, 2000), vol. 1, 328–362.

Luft- und Raumfahrtforschung in Deutschland 1900–1970. Politische Geschichte einer Wissenschaft (Frankfurt am Main: Campus, 1992).

"Wachstum – Systemnähe – Ausdifferenzierung. Grossforschung im Nationalsozialismus," in Rüdiger vom Bruch, and Brigitte Kaderas (eds.), *Wissenschaften und Wissenschaftspolitik: Bestandsaufnahmen zu Formationen, Brüchen und Kontinuitäten im Deutschland des 20. Jahrhunderts* (Stuttgart: Franz Steiner Verlag, 2002), 241–252.

Ulrich Trumpener, "The Road to Ypres: The Beginning of Gas Warfare in World War I," *Journal of Modern History*, **47**, no. 3 (1975), 460–480.

Achim Trunk, "Biochemistry in Wartime: The Life and Lessons of Adolf Butenandt," *Minerva*, **44**, no. 3 (2006), 285–306.

"Rassenforschung und Biochemie. Ein Projekt – und die Frage nach dem Beitrag Butenandts," in Wolfgang Schieder and Achim Trunk (eds.), *Adolf Butenandt und die Kaiser-Wilhelm-Gesellschaft. Wissenschaft, Industrie und Politik im "Dritten Reich"* (Göttingen: Wallstein, 2004), 247–285.

"Zweihundert Blutproben aus Auschwitz. Ein Forschungsvorhaben zwischen Anthropologie und Biochemie (1943–45)," *Ergebnisse. Vorabdrucke aus dem Forschungsprogramm "Geschichte der Kaiser-Wilhelm-Gesellschaft im Nationalsozialismus,"* No. 12 (Berlin: Forschungsprogramm, 2003) [http://www.mpiwg-berlin.mpg.de/KWG/Ergebnisse/Ergebnisse12.pdf].

Marianne Ufer, "Dreifaches Exil. Rumänien, Afghanistan, Brasilien," in *Ergebnisse. Vorabdrucke aus dem Forschungsprogramm "Geschichte der Kaiser-Wilhelm-Gesellschaft im Nationalsozialismus,"* No. 8 (Berlin: Forschungsprogramm, 2003) [http://www.mpiwg-berlin.mpg.de/KWG/Ergebnisse/Ergebnisse8.pdf].

United States Department of Commerce, Business and Defense Services Administration, Materials Survey, Aluminum (Washington: U.S. Department of Commerce, November 1956).

Robert-Jan Van Pelt and Debórah Dwork, *Auschwitz. Von 1279 bis heute* (Munich: Pendo, 2000).

"Verzeichnis der Veröffentlichungen des Kaiser Wilhelm-Instituts für Metallforschung 1921–1949," in Werner Köster and Hans von Schulz (eds.), *25 Jahre Kaiser Wilhelm-Institut für Metallforschung 1921–1946* (Stuttgart: Riederer, 1949), 121–166.

Rudolf Vierhaus and Bernhard vom Brocke (eds.), *Forschung im Spannungsfeld von Politik und Gesellschaft. Geschichte und Struktur der Kaiser-Wilhelm-/Max-Planck-Gesellschaft aus Anlass ihres 75jährigen Bestehens* (Stuttgart: DVA, 1990).

Ulrich Völklein, *Josef Mengele. Der Arzt von Auschwitz* (Göttingen: Steidl, 2002).

Bernhard vom Brocke, "Die Kaiser-Wilhelm-Gesellschaft in der Weimarer Republik," in Rudolf Vierhaus and Bernhard Vom Brocke (eds.), *Forschung im Spannungsfeld von Politik und Gesellschaft. Geschichte und Struktur der Kaiser-Wilhelm-/Max-Planck-Gesellschaft* (Stuttgart: Deutsche Verlags-Anstalt, 1990), 251–271.

Bernhard vom Brocke and Hubert Laitko (eds.), *Die Kaiser-Wilhelm-/Max-Planck-Gesellschaft und ihre Institute. Studien zu ihrer Geschichte: Das Harnack-Prinzip* (Berlin/New York: de Gruyter, 1996).

Rüdiger vom Bruch and Brigitte Kaderas (eds.), *Wissenschaften und Wissenschaftspolitik: Bestandsaufnahmen zu Formationen, Brüchen und Kontinuitäten im Deutschland des 20. Jahrhunderts* (Stuttgart: Franz Steiner Verlag, 2002).

Michael von Cranach and Hans-Ludwig Siemen (eds.), *Psychiatrie im Nationalsozialismus. Die bayerischen Heil- und Pflegeanstalten zwischen 1933 und 1945* (Munich: Oldenbourg, 1999).

Alexander von Schwerin, *Experimentalisierung des Menschen. Der Genetiker Hans Nachtsheim und die vergleichende Erbpathologie 1920–1945* (Göttingen: Wallstein, 2004).

Carl Friedrich von Weizsäcker, "Ich gebe zu, ich war verrückt," *Der Spiegel,* 17 (1991).

Theodor Wagner-Jauregg, *Mein Lebensweg als bioorganischer Chemiker* (Stuttgart: Wissenschaftliche Verlagsgesellschaft, 1985).

Mark Walker, "A Comparative History of Nuclear Weapons," in Doris Kaufmann (ed.), *Geschichte der Kaiser-Wilhelm-Gesellschaft im Nationalsozialismus.*

Bestandsaufnahme und Perspektiven der Forschung, 2 vols. (Göttingen: Wallstein Verlag, 2000), vol. 1, 309–327.

"Die deutsche Physikalische Gesellschaft im Kontext des Nationalsozialismus," in Dieter Hoffmann and Mark Walker (eds.), *Physiker zwischen Autonomie und Anpassung – Die DPG im Dritte Reich* (Weinheim: VCH, 2007), 1–27.

"Eine Waffenschmided? Kernwaffen- und Reaktorforschung am Kaiser-Wilhelm-Institut für Physik," in Helmut Maier (ed.), *Gemeinschaftsforschung, Bevollmächtigte und der Wissentransfer. Die Rolle der Kaiser-Wilhelm-Gesellschaft im System kriegsrelevanter Forschung des Nationalsozialismus* (Göttingen: Wallstein Verlag, 2007), 352–394.

German National Socialism and the Quest for Nuclear Power, 1939–1949 (Cambridge: Cambridge University Press, 1989).

"Göttingen as a Scientific Borderland," in Nicolaas Rupke (ed.), *Göttingen and the Development of the Natural Sciences* (Göttingen: Wallstein Verlag, 2002), 170–177.

"Introduction," to "Science in the Nazi Regime: The Kaiser Wilhelm Society under Hitler," *Minerva*, 44, no. 3 (2006), 241–250.

"Legends Surrounding the German Atomic Bomb," in Teresa Meade, and Mark Walker (eds.), *Science, Medicine, and Cultural Imperialism* (New York: St. Martin's Press, 1991), 178–204.

Nazi Science: Myth, Truth, and the German Atom Bomb (New York: Perseus, 1995).

"The Nazification and Denazification of Physics," in Matthias Judt, and Burghard Ciesla (eds.), *Technology Transfer Out of Germany* (Amsterdam: Harwood, 1996), 49–59.

"Otto Hahn: Responsibility and Repression," *Physics in Perspective*, 8, no. 2 (2006), 116–163.

"Otto Hahn: Verantwortung und Verdrängung," in *Ergebnisse. Vorabdrucke aus dem Forschungsprogramm "Geschichte der Kaiser-Wilhelm-Gesellschaft im Nationalsozialismus,"* No. 10 (Berlin: Forschungsprogramm, 2003) [http://www.mpiwg-berlin.mpg.de/KWG/Ergebnisse/Ergebnisse10.pdf].

Mark Walker (ed.), *Science and Ideology: A Comparative History* (London: Routledge, 2003).

Mark Walker, *Die Uranmaschine. Mythos und Wirklichkeit der deutschen Atombombe* (Berlin: Siedler Verlag, 1990).

Mark Walker, "Von Kopenhagen bis Göttingen, und zurück: Verdeckte Vergangenheitspolitik in den Naturwissenschaften," in Bernd Weisbrod (ed.), *Akademische Vergangenheitspolitik. Beiträge zur Wissenschaftskultur der Nachkriegszeit* (Göttingen: Wallstein Verlag, 2002), 247–259.

Bernd Walter, *Psychiatrie und Gesellschaft in der Moderne. Geisteskrankenfürsorge in der Provinz Westfalen zwischen Kaiserreich und NS-Regime* (Paderborn: Schöningh, 1996).

Günter Wassermann and Peter Wincierz (eds.), *Das Metall-Laboratorium der Metallgesellschaft AG 1918–1981* (Frankfurt am Main: Metallgesellschaft, 1981).

Matthias Weber, "Rassenhygienische und genetische Forschungen an der Deutschen Forschungsanstalt für Psychiatrie/Kaiser-Wilhelm-Institut in München vor und nach 1933," in Doris Kaufmann (ed.), *Geschichte der Kaiser-Wilhelm-*

Gesellschaft im Nationalsozialismus. Bestandsaufnahme und Perspektiven der Forschung, 2 vols. (Göttingen: Wallstein, 2000), vol. 1, 95–111.

Paul Weindling, "Akteure in eigene Sache. Die Aussagen der Überlebenden und die Verfolgung der medizinischen Kriegsverbrechen nach 1945," in Carola Sachse (ed.), *Die Verbindung nach Auschwitz. Biowissenschaften und Menschenversuche an Kaiser-Wilhelm-Instituten* (Göttingen: Wallstein Verlag, 2003), 255–282.

"Genetik und Menschenversuche in Deutschland, 1940–1950. Hans Nachtsheim, die Kaninchen von Dahlem und die Kinder vom Bulenhuser Damm," in Hans-Walter Schmuhl (ed.), *Rassenforschung an Kaiser-Wilhelm-Instituten vor und nach 1933* (Göttingen: Wallstein Verlag, 2003), 245–274.

Health, Race, and German Politics between National Unification and Nazism, 1870–1945 (Cambridge: Cambridge University Press, 1989).

"'Tales from Nuremberg': The Kaiser Wilhelm Institute for Anthropology and Allied Medical War Crimes Policy," in Doris Kaufmann (ed.), *Geschichte der Kaiser-Wilhelm-Gesellschaft im Nationalsozialismus. Bestandsaufnahme und Perspektiven der Forschung*, 2 vols. (Göttingen: Wallstein Verlag, 2000), vol. 2, 635–652.

"Verdacht, Kontrolle, Aussöhnung. Adolf Butenandts Platz in der Wissenschaftspolitik der Westalliierten (1945–1955)," in Wolfgang Schieder and Achim Trunk (eds.), *Adolf Butenandt und die Kaiser-Wilhelm-Gesellschaft. Wissenschaft, Industrie und Politik im "Dritten Reich"* (Göttingen: Wallstein, 2004), 320–345.

Rainer Weinert, *"Die Sauberkeit der Verwaltung im Kriege." Der Rechnungshof des Deutschen Reiches 1938–1946* (Opladen: Westdeutscher Verlag, 1993).

Peter Weingart, Jürgen Kroll, and Kurt Bayertz, *Rasse, Blut und Gene. Geschichte der Eugenik und Rassenhygiene in Deutschland* (Frankfurt am Main: Suhrkamp, 1988).

Max Weinreich, *Hitler's Professors: The Part of Scholarship in Germany's Crimes against the Jewish People*, reprint ed. (New Haven: Yale University Press, 1999).

Bernd Weisbrod (ed.), *Akademische Vergangenheitspolitik. Beiträge zur Wissenschaftskultur der Nachkriegszeit* (Göttingen: Wallstein, 2002).

Bernd Weisbrod, "Das 'Geheime Deutschland' und das 'Geistige Bad Harzburg': Friedrich Glum und das Dilemma des demokratischen Konservativismus am Ende der Weimarer Republik," in Christan Jansen, Lutz Niethammer, and Bernd Weisbrod (eds.), *Von der Aufgabe der Freiheit. Politische Verantwortung und bürgerliche Gesellschaft im 19. und 20. Jahrhundert. Festschrift für Hans Mommsen* (Berlin: Akademie Verlag, 1995), 285–308.

Reiner Weisenseel, "Heil- und Pflegeanstalt Ansbach," in Michael von Cranach, and Hans-Ludwig Siemen (eds.), *Psychiatrie im Nationalsozialismus. Die bayerischen Heil- und Pflegeanstalten zwischen 1933 und 1945* (Munich: Oldenbourg, 1999), 143–157.

Burghard Weiss, "Gross, teuer und gefährlich? Kernphysikalische Forschungstechnologien an Instituten der Kaiser-Wilhelm-Gesellschaft vor, während und nach Ende des "Dritten Reiches,'" in Doris Kaufmann (ed.), *Geschichte der Kaiser-Wilhelm-Gesellschaft im Nationalsozialismus. Bestandsaufnahme und Perspektiven der Forschung*, 2 vols. (Göttingen: Wallstein Verlag, 2000), vol. 2, 699–725.

"Harnack-Prinzip und Wissenschaftswandel. Die Einführung kernphysikalischer Grossgeräte (Beschleuniger) an den Instituten der KWS," in Bernhard vom

Brocke and Hubert Laitko (eds.), *Die Kaiser-Wilhelm/Max-Planck-Gesellschaft und ihre Institute* (Berlin: de Gruyter, 1996), 541–560.

"The 'Minerva' Project: The Accelerator Laboratory at the Kaiser Wilhelm Institute/ Max Planck Institute of Chemistry: Continuity in Fundamental Research," in Monika Renneberg and Mark Walker (eds.), *Science, Technology, and National Socialism* (Cambridge: Cambridge University Press, 1993), 271–290, 400–408.

"Rüstungsforschung am Forschungsinstitut der Allgemeinen Elektricitäts-Gesellschaft bis 1945," in Helmut Maier (ed.), *Rüstungsforschung im Nationalsozialismus. Organisation, Mobilisierung und Entgrenzung der Technikwissenschaften* (Göttingen: Wallstein, 2002), 109–141.

Sheila Faith Weiss, "German Eugenics, 1890–1933," in Dieter Kuntz and Susan Bachrach (eds.), *Deadly Medicine: Creating the Master Race* (Washington: U.S. Holocaust Museum, 2004), 15–39 and 206–207.

"Humangenetik und Politik als wechselseitige Ressourcen Das Kaiser-Wilhelm-Institut für Anthropologie, menschliche Erblehre und Eugenik im 'Dritten Reich,'" in *Ergebnisse. Vorabdrucke aus dem Forschungsprogramm "Geschichte der Kaiser-Wilhelm-Gesellschaft im Nationalsozialismus,"* No. 17 (Berlin: Forschungsprogramm, 2004) [http://www.mpiwg-berlin.mpg.de/KWG/Ergebnisse/Ergebnisse17.pdf].

"Race and Class in Fritz Lenz's Eugenics," *Medizinhistorisches Journal*, 27 (1992), 5–25.

"'The Sword of our Science' as a Foreign Policy Weapon. The Political Function of German Geneticists in the International Arena during the Third Reich," in *Ergebnisse. Vorabdrucke aus dem Forschungsprogramm "Geschichte der Kaiser-Wilhelm-Gesellschaft im Nationalsozialismus,"* No. 22 (Berlin: Forschungsprogramm, 2005) [http://www.mpiwg-berlin.mpg.de/KWG/Ergebnisse/Ergebnisse22.pdf].

Petra Werner (ed.), *Vitamine als Mythos. Dokumente zur Geschichte der Vitaminforschung* (Berlin: Akademie-Verlag, 1998).

Otto Westphal, "Richard Kuhn zum Gedächtnis," *Angewandte Chemie*, 80, no. 13 (1968), 501–519.

Richard Wetzell, "Kriminalbiologische Forschung an der Deutschen Forschungsanstalt für Psychiatrie in der Weimarer Republik und im Nationalsozialismus," in Hans-Walter Schmuhl (ed.), *Rassenforschung an Kaiser-Wilhelm-Instituten vor und nach 1933* (Göttingen: Wallstein, 2003), 68–98.

Thomas Wieland, "Die politischen Aufgaben der deutschen Pflanzenzüchtung," in Susanne Heim (ed.), *Autarkie und Ostexpansion. Pflanzenzucht und Agrarforschung im Nationalsozialismus* (Göttingen: Wallstein Verlag, 2002), 35–56.

Jonathan Wiesen, *West German Industry and the Challenge of the Nazi Past* (Chapel Hill: University of North Carolina Press, 2001).

Richard Willstätter, *Aus meinem Leben* (Weinheim: Verlag Chemie, 1949), 342–346.

Rolf Winau, "Versuche mit Menschen. Historische Entwicklung und ethischer Diskurs," in Carola Sachse (ed.), *Die Verbindung nach Auschwitz. Biowissenschaften und Menschenversuche am Kaiser-Wilhelm-Institute* (Göttingen: Wallstein, 2003), 158–177.

Ulrike Winkler (ed.), *Stiften gehen. NS-Zwangsarbeit und Entschädigungsdebatte* (Cologne: PapyRossa-Verlag, 2000).

Peter-Christian Witt, "Wirtschaftsfinanzierung zwischen Inflation und Deflation: die Kaiser-Wilhelm-Gesellschaft 1918/19 bis 1934/35. Forschung im Spannungsfeld von Politik und Gesellschaft," in Rudolf Vierhaus, and Bernhard vom Brocke (eds.), *Forschung im Spannungsfeld von Politik und Gesellschaft. Geschichte und Struktur der Kaiser-Wilhelm-/Max-Planck-Gesellschaft aus Anlass ihres 75jährigen Bestehens* (Stuttgart: DVA, 1990), 579–656.

Stefan L. Wolff, Die Ausgrenzung und Vertreibung der Physiker im Nationalsozialismus – welche Rolle spielte die Deutsche Physikalische Gesellschaft? in Dieter Hoffmann, and Mark Walker (eds.), *Physiker zwischen Autonomie und Anpassung – Die DPG im Dritte Reich* (Weinheim: VCH, 2006), 91–138.

Gilbert F. Wittemore Jr., "World War I, Poison Gas Research and the Ideals of American Chemists," *Social Studies of Science*, 5 (1975), 135–163.

Maria Zarifi, "Das deutsch-griechische Forschungsinstitut für Biologie in Piräus 1942–1944," in Susanne Heim (ed.), *Autarkie und Ostexpansion. Pflanzenzucht und Agrarforschung im Nationalsozialismus* (Göttingen: Wallstein, 2002), 206–232.

Wolfgang Zecha, *"Unter die Masken." Giftgas auf den Kriegsschauplätzen Österreich-Ungarns im Ersten Weltkrieg* (Vienna: öbv und hpt, 2000).

Anna Zięba, "Die Geflügelfarm Harmense," *Hefte von Auschwitz*, 11 (1970), 39–72.

"Nebenlager Rajsko," *Hefte von Auschwitz*, 9 (1966), 75–108.

Kurt Zierold, *Forschungsförderung in drei Epochen. Deutsche Forschungsgemeinschaft Geschichte-Arbeitsweise-Kommentar* (Wiesbaden: Franz Steiner, 1968).

Andreas Zilt, "Rüstungsforschung in der westdeutschen Stahlindustrie. Das Beispiel der Vereinigte Stahlwerke AG und Kohle- und Eisenforschung GmbH," in Helmut Maier (ed.), *Rüstungsforschung im Nationalsozialismus. Organisation, Mobilisierung und Entgrenzung der Technikwissenschaften* (Göttingen: Wallstein, 2002), 183–213.

Michael Zimmermann (ed.), *Zwischen Erziehung und Vernichtung. Zigeunerpolitik und Zigeunerforschung im Europa des 20. Jahrhunderts* (Stuttgart: Franz Steiner, 2007).

Zdenek Zofka, "Der KZ-Arzt Josef Mengele. Zur Typologie eines NS-Verbrechers," *Vierteljahrshefte für Zeitgeschichte*, 34 (1986), 245–267.

Lotte Zumpe (ed.), *Wirtschaft und Staat in Deutschland 1933 bis 1945* (Vaduz: Topos-Verlag, 1980).

Susanne zur Nieden, "Erbbiologische Forschungen zur Homosexualität an der Deutschen Forschungsanstalt für Psychiatrie während der Jahre des Nationalsozialismus. Zur Geschichte von Theo Lang," *Ergebnisse. Vorabdrucke aus dem Forschungsprogramm "Geschichte der Kaiser-Wilhelm-Gesellschaft im Nationalsozialismus,"* No. 25 (Berlin: Forschungsprogramm, 2005) [http://www.mpiwg-berlin.mpg.de/KWG/Ergebnisse/Ergebnisse25.pdf].

Index

LaVergne, TN USA
15 January 2011
212556LV00003B/6/P